Cloud-Native Observability with OpenTelemetry

Learn to gain visibility into systems by combining tracing, metrics, and logging with OpenTelemetry

Alex Boten

BIRMINGHAM—MUMBAI

Cloud-Native Observability with OpenTelemetry

Copyright © 2022 Packt Publishing

All rights reserved. No part of this book may be reproduced, stored in a retrieval system, or transmitted in any form or by any means, without the prior written permission of the publisher, except in the case of brief quotations embedded in critical articles or reviews.

Every effort has been made in the preparation of this book to ensure the accuracy of the information presented. However, the information contained in this book is sold without warranty, either express or implied. Neither the author, nor Packt Publishing or its dealers and distributors, will be held liable for any damages caused or alleged to have been caused directly or indirectly by this book.

Packt Publishing has endeavored to provide trademark information about all of the companies and products mentioned in this book by the appropriate use of capitals. However, Packt Publishing cannot guarantee the accuracy of this information.

Group Product Manager: Rahul Nair
Publishing Product Manager: Shrilekha Malpani
Senior Editor: Arun Nadar
Content Development Editor: Sujata Tripathi
Technical Editor: Rajat Sharma
Copy Editor: Safis Editing
Project Coordinator: Shagun Saini
Proofreader: Safis Editing
Indexer: Pratik Shirodkar
Production Designer: Ponraj Dhandapani
Marketing Coordinator: Nimisha Dua

First published: April 2022

Production reference: 1140422

Published by Packt Publishing Ltd.
Livery Place
35 Livery Street
Birmingham
B3 2PB, UK.

ISBN 978-1-80107-770-5

www.packt.com

To my mother, sister, and father. Thank you for teaching me to persevere in the face of adversity, always be curious, and work hard.

Foreword

It has never been a better time to be a software engineer.

As engineers, we are motivated by impact and efficiency—and who can argue that both are not skyrocketing, particularly in comparison with time spent and energy invested?

These days, you can build out a scalable, elastic, distributed system to serve your code to millions of users per day with a few clicks—without ever having to personally understand much about operations or architecture. You can write lambda functions or serverless code, hit save, and begin serving them to users immediately.

It feels like having superpowers, especially for those of us who remember the laborious times before. Every year brings more powerful APIs and higher-level abstractions – many, many infinitely complex systems that "just work" at the click of a button or the press of a key.

But when it *doesn't* "just work," it has gotten harder than ever to untangle the reasons and understand why.

Superpowers don't come for free it turns out. The winds of change may be sweeping us all briskly out toward a sea of ever-expanding options, infinite flexibility, automated resiliency, and even cost-effectiveness, but these glories have come at the price of complexity—skyrocketing, relentlessly compounding complexity and the cognitive overload that comes with it.

Systems no longer fail in predictable ways. Static dashboards are no longer a viable tool for understanding your systems. And though better tools will help, digging ourselves out of this hole is not merely an issue of switching from one tool to another. We need to rethink the way software gets built, shipped, and maintained, to be *production-focused* from day 1.

For far too long now, we have been building and shipping software in the dark. Software engineers act like all they need to do is write tests and make sure their code passes. While tests are important, all they can really do is validate the logic of your code and increase your confidence that you have not introduced any serious regressions. Operations engineers, meanwhile, rely on monitoring checks, but those are a blunt tool at best. Most bugs will never rise to the criticality of a paging alert, which means that as a system gets more mature and sophisticated, most issues will have to be found and reported by your users.

And this isn't just a problem of bugs, firefighting, or outages. This is about understanding your software in the wild—as *your users* run *your code* on *your infrastructure*, at a given time. Production remains far too much of a black box for too many people, who are then forced to try and reason about it by reading lines of code and using elaborate mental models.

Because we've all been shipping code blindly, all this time, we ship changes we don't fully understand to a production system that is a hairball of changes we've never truly understood. We've been shipping blindly for years and years now, leaving SRE teams and ops teams to poke at the black boxes and try to clean up the mess—all the while still blindfolded. The fact that anything has *ever* worked is a testament to the creativity and dedication of these teams.

A funny thing starts happening when people begin instrumenting their code for observability and inspecting it in production—regularly, after every deployment, as a habit. You find bugs *everywhere,* bugs you never knew existed. It's like picking up a rock and watching all the little nasties lurking underneath scuttle away from the light.

With monitoring tools and aggregates, we were always able to see that errors existed, but we had no way of correlating them to an event or figuring out what was different about the erroring requests. Now, all of a sudden, we are able to look at an error spike and say, "Ah! All of these errors are for requests coming from clients running app version 1.63, calling the `/export` endpoint, querying the primaries for mysql-shard3, shard5, and shard7, with a payload of over 10 KB, and timing out after 15 seconds." Or we can pull up a trace and see that one of the erroring requests was issuing thousands of serial database queries in a row. *So* many gnarly bugs and opaque behaviors become shallow once you can visualize them. It's the most satisfying experience in the world.

But yes, you do have to instrument your code. (Auto-instrumentation is about as effective as automated code commenting.) So let's talk about that.

I can hear you now—"Ugh, instrumentation!" Most people would rather get bitten by a rattlesnake than refactor their logging and instrumentation code. I know this, and so does every vendor under the sun. This is why even legacy logging companies are practically printing money. Once they get your data flowing in, it takes an act of God to move it or turn it off.

This is a big part of the reason we, as an industry, are so behind when it comes to public, reusable standards and tooling for instrumentation and observability, which is why I am so delighted to participate in the push for OpenTelemetry. Yes, it's in the clumsy toddler years of technological advancement. But it will get better. It *has gotten* better. I was cynical about OTel in the early days, but the community excitement and uptake have exceeded my expectations at every step. As well it should. Because the promise of OpenTelemetry is that you may need to instrument your code once, but only once. And then you can move from vendor to vendor *without re-instrumenting.*

This means vendors will have to compete for your business on features, usability, and cost-effectiveness, instead of vendor lock-in. OTel has the potential to finally break this stranglehold—to make it so you only instrument once, and you can move from vendor to vendor with just a few lines of configuration changes. This is brilliant—this changes everything. This is one battle you should absolutely join and fight.

Software systems aren't going to get simpler anytime soon. Yet the job of developing and maintaining software may paradoxically be poised to get faster and easier, by forcing us to finally adopt better real-time instrumentation and telemetry. Going from monitoring to observability is like the difference between **visual flight rating (VFR)** and **instrument flight rating (IFR)** for pilots. Yeah, learning to fly (or code) by instrumentation feels a little strange at first, but once you master it, you can fly so much faster, farther, and more safely than ever before.

It's not *just* about observability. There are lots of dovetailing trends in tech right now—feature flags, chaos engineering, progressive deployment, and so on—all of which center production, and focus on shrinking the distance and tightening the feedback loops between dev and prod. Together they deliver compounding benefits that help teams move swiftly and safely, devoting more of their time to solving new and interesting puzzles that move the business forward, and less time to toil and yak shaving.

It's not just about observability... but it starts with observability. The ability to see what is happening is the most important feedback loop of all.

And observability starts with instrumentation.

So, here we go.

Charity Majors

CTO, Honeycomb

Contributors

About the author

Alex Boten is a senior staff software engineer at Lightstep and has spent the last 10 years helping organizations adapt to a cloud-native landscape. From building core network infrastructure to mobile client applications and everything in between, Alex has first-hand knowledge of how complex troubleshooting distributed applications is.

This led him to the domain of observability and contributing to open source projects in the space. A contributor, approver, and maintainer in several aspects of OpenTelemetry, Alex has helped evolve the project from its early days in 2019 into the massive community effort that it is today.

More than anything, Alex loves making sense of the technology around us and sharing his learnings with others.

About the reviewer

Yuri Grinshteyn strongly believes that reliability is a key feature of any service and works to advocate for site reliability engineering principles and practices. He graduated from Tufts University with a degree in computer engineering and has worked in monitoring, diagnostics, observability, and reliability throughout his career. Currently, he is a site reliability engineer at Google Cloud, where he works with customers to help them achieve appropriate reliability for their services; previously, he worked at Oracle, Compuware, Hitachi Consulting, and Empirix. You can find his work on YouTube, Medium, and GitHub. He and his family live just outside of San Francisco and love taking advantage of everything California has to offer.

Table of Contents

Preface

Section 1: The Basics

1
The History and Concepts of Observability

Understanding cloud-native applications	4	OpenTracing	11
		OpenCensus	13
Looking at the shift to DevOps	6	Observability for cloud-native software	15
Reviewing the history of observability	7	Understanding the concepts of OpenTelemetry	16
Centralized logging	8	Signals	16
Using metrics and dashboards	8	Pipelines	20
Applying tracing and analysis	9	Resources	22
		Context propagation	23
Understanding the history of OpenTelemetry	10	Summary	25

2
OpenTelemetry Signals – Traces, Metrics, and Logs

Technical requirements	28	Metrics	39
Traces	33	Anatomy of a metric	40
Anatomy of a trace	34	Data point types	42
Details of a span	37	Exemplars	47
Additional considerations	38	Additional considerations	47

Logs	48	Additional considerations	52
Anatomy of a log	48	Semantic conventions	52
Correlating logs	50	**Summary**	**55**

3
Auto-Instrumentation

Technical requirements	58	**Runtime hooks and monkey**	
What is auto-instrumentation?	60	**patching**	**66**
Challenges of manual instrumentation	60	Instrumenting libraries	66
Components of auto-instrumentation	61	The Instrumentor interface	67
Limits of auto-instrumentation	62	Wrapper script	68
Bytecode manipulation	**63**	**Summary**	**71**
OpenTelemetry Java agent	64		

Section 2: Instrumenting an Application

4
Distributed Tracing – Tracing Code Execution

Technical requirements	76	**Propagating context**	**106**
Configuring the tracing pipeline	77	Additional propagator formats	109
Getting a tracer	79	Composite propagator	110
Generating tracing data	80	**Recording events, exceptions,**	
The Context API	82	**and status**	**116**
Span processors	90	Events	117
Enriching the data	92	Exceptions	118
ResourceDetector	94	Status	122
Span attributes	96	**Summary**	**125**
SpanKind	100		

5

Metrics – Recording Measurements

Technical requirements	128	Customizing metric outputs with views	149
Configuring the metrics pipeline	129	Filtering	149
Obtaining a meter	132	Dimensions	152
Push-based and pull-based exporting	134	Aggregation	155
Choosing the right OpenTelemetry instrument	137	The grocery store	157
Counter	138	Number of requests	158
Asynchronous counter	140	Request duration	162
An up/down counter	142	Concurrent requests	167
Asynchronous up/down counter	143	Resource consumption	169
Histogram	145	Summary	171
Asynchronous gauge	147		
Duplicate instruments	148		

6

Logging – Capturing Events

Technical requirements	174	A logging signal in practice	185
Configuring OpenTelemetry logging	175	Distributed tracing and logs	187
		OpenTelemetry logging with Flask	189
Producing logs	177	Logging with WSGI middleware	191
Using LogEmitter	177	Resource correlation	192
The standard logging library	180	Summary	193

7

Instrumentation Libraries

Technical requirements	196	Command-line options	204
Auto-instrumentation configuration	198	Requests library instrumentor	205
		Additional configuration options	206
OpenTelemetry distribution	201	Manual invocation	206
OpenTelemetry configurator	202	Double instrumentation	210
Environment variables	203		

Automatic configuration	211	Shopper	221
Configuring resource attributes	211	**Flask library instrumentor**	**225**
Configuring traces	213	Additional configuration options	225
Configuring metrics	215		
Configuring logs	216	**Finding instrumentation**	
Configuring propagation	217	**libraries**	**226**
Revisiting the grocery store	**218**	OpenTelemetry registry	226
Legacy inventory	218	opentelemetry-bootstrap	227
Grocery store	219	**Summary**	**227**

Section 3: Using Telemetry Data

8
OpenTelemetry Collector

Technical requirements	**232**	**Transporting telemetry**	
The purpose of OpenTelemetry		**via OTLP**	**249**
Collector	**234**	Encodings and protocols	251
Understanding the components		Additional design considerations	251
of OpenTelemetry Collector	**235**	**Using OpenTelemetry Collector**	**252**
Receivers	236	Configuring the exporter	253
Processors	239	Configuring the collector	254
Exporters	247	Modifying spans	258
Extensions	248	Filtering metrics	259
Additional components	249	**Summary**	**262**

9
Deploying the Collector

Technical requirements	**264**	**System-level telemetry**	**272**
Collecting application		Deploying the agent	272
telemetry	**267**	Connecting the sidecar and the agent	274
Deploying the sidecar	269	Adding resource attributes	277

| Collector as a gateway | 279 | OpenTelemetry Operator | 282 |
| Autoscaling | 282 | Summary | 282 |

10
Configuring Backends

Technical requirements	286	Running in production	306
Backend options for analyzing telemetry data	288	High availability	306
		Scalability	306
Tracing	289	Data retention	307
Metrics	299	Privacy regulations	308
Logging	302	Summary	308

11
Diagnosing Problems

Technical requirements	310	Experiment #3 – unexpected shutdown	323
Introducing a little chaos	311	Using telemetry first to answer questions	326
Experiment #1 – increased latency	313		
Experiment #2 – resource pressure	318	Summary	328

12
Sampling

Technical requirements	330	Sampling at the application level via the SDK	338
Concepts of sampling across signals	331	Using the OpenTelemetry Collector to sample data	340
Traces	332		
Metrics	333	Tail sampling processor	340
Logs	333	Summary	345
Sampling strategies	334		
Samplers available	337		

Index

Other Books You May Enjoy

Preface

Cloud-Native Observability with OpenTelemetry is a guide to helping you look for answers to questions about your applications. This book teaches you how to produce telemetry from your applications using an open standard to retain control of data. OpenTelemetry provides the tools necessary for you to gain visibility into the performance of your services. It allows you to instrument your application code through vendor-neutral APIs, libraries and tools.

By reading *Cloud-Native Observability with OpenTelemetry*, you'll learn about the concepts and signals of OpenTelemetry - traces, metrics, and logs. You'll practice producing telemetry for these signals by configuring and instrumenting a distributed cloud-native application using the OpenTelemetry API. The book also guides you through deploying the collector, as well as telemetry backends necessary to help you understand what to do with the data once it's emitted. You'll look at various examples of how to identify application performance issues through telemetry. By analyzing telemetry, you'll also be able to better understand how an observable application can improve the software development life cycle.

By the end of this book, you'll be well-versed with OpenTelemetry, be able to instrument services using the OpenTelemetry API to produce distributed traces, metrics and logs, and more.

Who this book is for

This book is for software engineers and systems operators looking to better understand their infrastructure, services, and applications by using telemetry data like never before. Working knowledge of Python programming is assumed for the example applications you'll build and instrument using the OpenTelemetry API and SDK. Some familiarity with Go programming, Linux, Docker, and Kubernetes is preferable to help you set up additional components in various examples throughout the book.

What this book covers

Chapter 1, The History and Concepts of Observability, provides an overview of the evolution of observability. It describes the challenges and fragmentation that ultimately created the need for an open standard. It provides an overview of both OpenTracing and OpenCensus. The last section of this chapter dives into OpenTelemetry, how it started, and how it got to where it is today. This concepts chapter will provide you with an overview of different concepts vital in understanding OpenTelemetry. This chapter introduces signals before going over the pipeline for generating, processing, and exporting telemetry. The resources section will describe the purpose of resources.

Chapter 2, OpenTelemetry Signals – Traces, Metrics, and Logs, describes the different signals that comprise OpenTelemetry: traces, metrics, and logs. It begins by giving you an understanding of the concepts of distributed tracing by defining spans, traces, and context propagation. The following section explores metrics by looking at the different measurements and the instruments OpenTelemetry offers to capture this information. The section on logging describes how logging fits in with the other signals in OpenTelemetry. Semantic conventions are also covered in this chapter to understand their significance and role in each signal.

Chapter 3, Auto-Instrumentation, explains the challenges of manual instrumentation and how the OpenTelemetry project sets out to solve those challenges. After that, you will dive into the mechanics of auto instrumentation in different languages.

Chapter 4, Distributed Tracing – Tracing Code Execution, begins by introducing the grocery store application we will instrument throughout the book. You will then start using the OpenTelemetry APIs to configure a tracing pipeline and its various components: the tracer provider, span processor, and exporter. After obtaining a tracer, you will instrument code to generate traces. The remainder of the chapter will discuss augmenting that tracing data with attributes, events, links, statuses, and exceptions.

Chapter 5, Metrics – Recording Measurements, teaches you how to capture application metrics. You will begin by configuring the components of a metrics pipeline: the meter provider, meter, and exporter. The chapter then describes the instruments available in OpenTelemetry to collect metrics before using each one in the context of the grocery store application.

Chapter 6, Logging – Capturing Events, covers logging, the last of the core signals of OpenTelemetry discussed in this book. The chapter walks you through configuring the components of the logging pipeline to emit telemetry. You will then use existing logging libraries to enhance logged events through correlation with OpenTelemetry.

Chapter 7, *Instrumentation Libraries*, teaches you how to use instrumentation libraries to instrument the grocery store application automatically after learning how to do so manually. Using auto instrumentation and environment variables supported by OpenTelemetry, this chapter shows you how to obtain telemetry from your code quickly.

Chapter 8, *OpenTelemetry Collector*, explores another core component that OpenTelemetry provides: the OpenTelemetry Collector. The Collector allows users to collect and aggregate data before transmitting it to various backends. This chapter describes the concepts present in the Collector, presents its use cases, and explains the challenges it solves. After learning about the **OpenTelemetry Protocol** (**OTLP**), you will modify the grocery store application to emit telemetry to the collector via OTLP.

Chapter 9, *Deploying the Collector*, puts the OpenTelemetry Collector to work in a Kubernetes environment in various deployment scenarios. You will use Kubernetes to deploy the Collector as a sidecar, agent, and gateway to collect application-level and system-level telemetry.

Chapter 10, *Configuring Backends*, teaches you about various open source telemetry backend options to store and visualize data. This chapter explores using OpenTelemetry with Zipkin, Jaeger, Prometheus, and Loki utilizing a local environment. You will configure exporters in application code and the OpenTelemetry Collector to emit data to these backends. After instrumenting and collecting all the telemetry from applications, it's finally time to start using this information to identify issues in a system.

Chapter 11, *Diagnosing Problems*, dives into techniques used to correlate data across the different OpenTelemetry signals to identify the root cause of common problems in production effectively. This chapter introduces you to chaos engineering and tools to generate synthetic loads and service interruptions to produce different scenarios.

Chapter 12, Sampling, explains the concept of sampling and how it applies to distributed tracing. Head, tail, and probability sampling strategies are introduced in this chapter. You will configure sampling using the OpenTelemetry APIs and the OpenTelemetry Collector, comparing the results of different sampling configurations.

To get the most out of this book

The examples in this book were developed on macOS x86-64 using versions of Python ranging from 3.6 to 3.9. The latest version of OpenTelemetry for Python tested is version 1.10.0, which includes experimental support for both metrics and logging. It's likely that the API will change in subsequent releases, so be aware of the version installed as you go through the examples. Consult the changelog of the OpenTelemetry Python repository (https://github.com/open-telemetry/opentelemetry-python/blob/main/CHANGELOG.md) for the latest updates.

Software/hardware covered in the book	Operating system requirements
OpenTelemetry for Python 1.9.0+	Any modern operating system capable of running Python 3.6+ and Docker. Examples developed on macOS x86-64. Testing of many examples has also been performed on Ubuntu Linux and macOS arm64.
OpenTelemetry Collector v0.42.0+	Any modern operating system capable of running Python 3.6+ and Docker. Examples developed on macOS x86-64. Testing of many examples has also been performed on Ubuntu Linux and macOS arm64.

Many examples in the book rely on Docker and Docker Compose to deploy environments locally. As of January 2022, the license for Docker Desktop still allows users to install it for free for personal use, education, and non-commercial open source projects. If the licensing prevents you from using Docker Desktop, there are alternatives available.

If you are using the digital version of this book, we advise you to type the code yourself or access the code from the book's GitHub repository (a link is available in the next section). Doing so will help you avoid any potential errors related to the copying and pasting of code.

Download the example code files

You can download the example code files for this book from GitHub at https://github.com/PacktPublishing/Cloud-Native-Observability. If there's an update to the code, it will be updated in the GitHub repository.

We also have other code bundles from our rich catalog of books and videos available at https://github.com/PacktPublishing/. Check them out!

Download the color images

We also provide a PDF file that has color images of the screenshots and diagrams used in this book. You can download it here: `https://static.packt-cdn.com/downloads/9781801077705_ColorImages.pdf`.

Conventions used

There are a number of text conventions used throughout this book.

`Code in text`: Indicates code words in text, database table names, folder names, filenames, file extensions, pathnames, dummy URLs, user input, and Twitter handles. Here is an example: "The code then calls the global `set_meter_provider` method to set the meter provider for the entire application."

A block of code is set as follows:

```
from opentelemetry._metrics import set_meter_provider
from opentelemetry.sdk._metrics import MeterProvider
from opentelemetry.sdk.resources import Resource

def configure_meter_provider():
    provider = MeterProvider(resource=Resource.create())
    set_meter_provider(provider)

if __name__ == "__main__":
    configure_meter_provider()
```

When we wish to draw your attention to a particular part of a code block, the relevant lines or items are set in bold:

```
from opentelemetry._metrics import get_meter_provider, set_meter_provider
...
if __name__ == "__main__":
    configure_meter_provider()
    meter = get_meter_provider().get_meter(
        name="metric-example",
        version="0.1.2",
        schema_url=" https://opentelemetry.io/schemas/1.9.0",
    )
```

Any command-line input or output is written as follows:

```
$ git clone https://github.com/PacktPublishing/Cloud-Native-Observability
$ cd Cloud-Native-Observability/chapter7
```

Bold: Indicates a new term, an important word, or words that you see onscreen. For instance, words in menus or dialog boxes appear in **bold**. Here is an example: "Search for traces by clicking the **Run Query** button."

> Tips or Important Notes
> Appear like this.

Get in touch

Feedback from our readers is always welcome.

General feedback: If you have questions about any aspect of this book, email us at customercare@packtpub.com and mention the book title in the subject of your message.

Errata: Although we have taken every care to ensure the accuracy of our content, mistakes do happen. If you have found a mistake in this book, we would be grateful if you would report this to us. Please visit www.packtpub.com/support/errata and fill in the form.

Piracy: If you come across any illegal copies of our works in any form on the internet, we would be grateful if you would provide us with the location address or website name. Please contact us at copyright@packt.com with a link to the material.

If you are interested in becoming an author: If there is a topic that you have expertise in and you are interested in either writing or contributing to a book, please visit authors.packtpub.com.

Share Your Thoughts

Once you've read *Cloud-Native Observability with OpenTelemetry*, we'd love to hear your thoughts! Scan the QR code below to go straight to the Amazon review page for this book and share your feedback.

https://packt.link/r/1801077703

Your review is important to us and the tech community and will help us make sure we're delivering excellent quality content.

Section 1: The Basics

In this part, you will learn about the origin of OpenTelemetry and why it was needed. We will then dive into the various components and concepts of OpenTelemetry.

This part of the book comprises the following chapters:

- *Chapter 1, The History and Concepts of Observability*
- *Chapter 2, OpenTelemetry Signals: Traces, Metrics, and Logs*
- *Chapter 3, Auto-Instrumentation*

1
The History and Concepts of Observability

The term **observability** has only been around in the software industry for a short time, but the concepts and goals it represents have been around for much longer. Indeed, ever since the earliest days of computing, programmers have been trying to answer the question: is the system doing what I think it should be?

For some, observability consists of buying a one-size-fits-all solution that includes logs, metrics, and traces, then configuring some off-the-shelf integrations and calling it a day. These tools *can* be used to increase visibility into a piece of software's behavior by providing mechanisms to produce and collect telemetry. The following are some examples of telemetry that can be added to a system:

- Keeping a count of the number of requests received
- Adding a log entry when an event occurs
- Recording a value for current memory consumption on a machine
- Tracing a request from a client all the way to a backend service

However, producing high-quality telemetry is only one part of the observability challenge. The other part is ensuring that events occurring across the different types of telemetry can be correlated in meaningful ways during analysis. The goal of observability is to answer questions that you may have about the system:

- If a problem occurred in production, what evidence would you have to be able to identify it?
- Why is this service suddenly overwhelmed when it was fine just a minute ago?
- If a specific condition from a client triggers an anomaly in some underlying service, would you know it without customers or support calling you?

These are some of the questions that the domain of observability can help answer. Observability is about empowering the people who build and operate distributed applications to understand their code's behavior while running in production. In this chapter, we will explore the following:

- Understanding cloud-native applications
- Looking at the shift to DevOps
- Reviewing the history of observability
- Understanding the history of OpenTelemetry
- Understanding the concepts of OpenTelemetry

Before we begin looking at the history of observability, it's important to understand the changes in the software industry that have led to the need for observability in the first place. Let's start with the shift to the cloud.

Understanding cloud-native applications

The way applications are built and deployed has drastically changed in the past few years with the increased adoption of the internet. An unprecedented increase in demand for services (for example, streaming media, social networks, and online shopping) powered by software has raised expectations for those services to be readily available. In addition, this increase in demand has fueled the need for developers to be able to scale their applications quickly. Cloud providers, such as Microsoft, Google, and Amazon, offer infrastructure to run applications at the click of a button and at a fraction of the cost, and reduce the risk of deploying servers in traditional data centers. This enables developers to experiment more freely and reach a wider audience. Alongside this infrastructure, these cloud providers also offer managed services for databases, networking infrastructure, message queues, and many other services that, in the past, organizations would control internally.

One of the advantages these cloud-based providers offer is freeing up organizations to focus on the code that matters to their businesses. This replaces costly and time-consuming hardware implementations, or operating services they lack expertise in. To take full advantage of cloud platforms, developers started looking at how applications that were originally developed as monoliths could be re-architected to take advantage of cloud platforms. The following are challenges that could be encountered when deploying monoliths to a cloud provider:

- Scaling a monolith is traditionally done by increasing the number of resources available to the monolith, also known as vertical scaling. Vertically scaling applications can only go as far as the largest available resource offered by a cloud provider.
- Improving the reliability of a monolith means deploying multiple instances to handle multiple failures, thus avoiding downtime. This is also known as horizontal scaling. Depending on the size of the monolith, this could quickly ramp up costs. This can also be wasteful if not all components of the monolith need to be replicated.

The specific challenges of building applications on cloud platforms have led developers to increasingly adopt a service-oriented architecture, or microservice architecture, that organizes applications as loosely coupled services, each with limited scope. The following figure shows a monolith architecture on the left, where all the services in the application are tightly coupled and operate within the same boundary. In contrast, the microservices architecture on the right shows us that the services are loosely coupled, and each service operates independently:

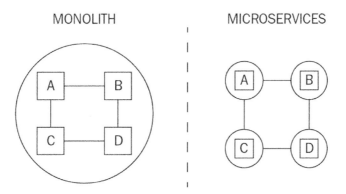

Figure 1.1 – Monolith versus microservices architecture

Applications built using microservices architecture provide developers with the ability to scale only the components needed to handle the additional load, meaning horizontal scaling becomes a much more attractive option. As it often does, a new architecture comes with its own set of trade-offs and challenges. The following are some of the new challenges cloud-native architecture presents that did not exist in traditional monolithic systems:

- Latency introduced where none existed before, causing applications to fail in unexpected ways.
- Dependencies can and will fail, so applications must be built defensively to minimize cascading failures.
- Managing configuration and secrets across services is difficult.
- Service orchestration becomes complex.

With this change in architecture, the scope of each application is reduced significantly, making it easier to understand the needs of scaling each component. However, the increased number of independent services and added complexity also creates challenges for **traditional operations** (**ops**) teams, meaning organizations would also need to adapt.

Looking at the shift to DevOps

The shift to microservices has, in turn, led to a shift in how development teams are organized. Instead of a single large team managing a monolithic application, many teams each manage their own microservices. In traditional software development, a software development team would normally hand off the software once it was deemed complete. The handoff would be to an operations team, who would deploy the software and operate it in a production environment. As the number of services and teams grew, organizations found themselves growing their operations teams to unmanageable sizes, and quite often, those teams were still unable to keep up with the demands of the changing software.

This, in turn, led to an explosion of development teams that began the transition from the traditional development and operations organization toward the use of new hybrid DevOps teams. Using the DevOps approach, development teams write, test, build, package, deploy, and operate the code they develop. This ownership of the code through all stages of its life cycle empowers many developers and organizations to accelerate their feature development. This approach, of course, comes with different challenges:

- Increased dependencies across development teams mean it's possible that no one has a full picture of the entire application.
- Keeping track of changes across an organization can be difficult. This makes the answer to the "what caused this outage?" question more challenging to find.

Individual teams must become familiar with many more tools. This can lead to too much focus on the tools themselves, rather than on their purpose. The quick adoption of DevOps creates a new problem. Without the right amount of visibility across the systems managed by an organization, teams are struggling to identify the root causes of issues encountered. This can lead to longer and more frequent outages, severely impacting the health and happiness of people across organizations. Let's look at how the methods of observing systems have evolved to adapt to this changing landscape.

Reviewing the history of observability

In many ways, being able to understand what a computer is doing is both fun and challenging when working with software. The ability to understand how systems are behaving has gone through quite a few iterations since the early 2000s. Many different markets have been created to solve this need, such as systems monitoring, log management, and application performance monitoring. As is often the case, when new challenges come knocking, the doors of opportunity open to those willing to tackle those challenges. Over the same period, countless vendors and open source projects have sprung up to help people who are building and operating services in managing their systems. The term observability, however, is a recent addition to the software industry and comes from control theory.

Wikipedia (`https://en.wikipedia.org/wiki/Observability`) defines observability as:

> *"In control theory, observability is a measure of how well internal states of a system can be inferred from knowledge of its external outputs."*

Observability is an evolution of its predecessors, built on lessons learned through years of experience and trial and error. To better understand where observability is today, it's important to understand where some of the methods used today by cloud-native application developers come from, and how they have changed over time. We'll start by looking at the following:

- Centralized logging
- Metrics and dashboards
- Tracing and analysis

Centralized logging

One of the first pieces of software a programmer writes when learning a new language is a form of observability: "Hello, World!". Printing some text to the terminal is usually one of the quickest ways to provide users with feedback that things are working, and that's why "Hello, World" has been a tradition in computing since the late 1960s.

One of my favorite methods for debugging is still to add print statements across the code when things aren't working. I've even used this method to troubleshoot an application distributed across multiple servers before, although I can't say it was my proudest moment, as it caused one of our services to go down temporarily because of a typo in an unfamiliar editor. Print statements are great for simple debugging, but unfortunately, this only scales so far.

Once an application is large enough or distributed across enough systems, searching through the logs on individual machines is not practical. Applications can also run on ephemeral machines that may no longer be present when we need those logs. Combined, all of this created a need to make the logs available in a central location for persistent storage and searchability, and thus centralized logging was born.

There are many available vendors that provide a destination for logs, as well as features around searching, and alerting based on those logs. There are also many open source projects that have tried to tackle the challenges of standardizing log formats, providing mechanisms for transport, and storing the logs. The following are some of these projects:

- **Fluentd** – `https://www.fluentd.org`
- **Logstash** – `https://github.com/elastic/logstash`
- **Apache Flume** – `https://flume.apache.org`

Centralized logging additionally provides the opportunity to produce metrics about the data across the entire system.

Using metrics and dashboards

Metrics are possibly the most well-known of the tools available in the observability space. Think of the temperature in a thermometer, the speed on the odometer of a car, or the time on a watch. We humans love measuring and quantifying things. From the early days of computing, being able to keep track of how resources were utilized was critical in ensuring that multi-user environments provided a good user experience for all users of the system.

Nowadays, measuring application and system performance via the collection of metrics is common practice in software development. This data is converted into graphs to generate meaningful visualizations for those in charge of monitoring the health of a system.

These metrics can also be used to configure alerting when certain thresholds have been reached, such as when an error rate becomes greater than an acceptable percentage. In certain environments, metrics are used to automate workflows as a reaction to changes in the system, such as increasing the number of application instances or rolling back a bad deployment. As with logging, over time, many vendors and projects provided their own solutions to metrics, dashboards, monitoring, and alerting. Some of the open source projects that focus on metrics are as follows:

- **Prometheus** – `https://prometheus.io`
- **StatsD** – `https://github.com/statsd/statsd`
- **Graphite** – `https://graphiteapp.org`
- **Grafana** – `https://github.com/grafana/grafana`

Let's now look at tracing and analysis.

Applying tracing and analysis

Tracing applications means having the ability to run through the application code and ensure it's doing what is expected. This can often, but not always, be achieved in development using a debugger such as GDB (`https://www.gnu.org/software/gdb/`) or PDB (`https://docs.python.org/3/library/pdb.html`) in Python. This becomes impossible when debugging an application that is spread across multiple services on different hosts across a network. Researchers at Google published a white paper on a large-scale distributed tracing system built internally: Dapper (`https://research.google/pubs/pub36356/`). In this paper, they describe the challenges of distributed systems, as well as the approach that was taken to address the problem. This research is the basis of distributed tracing as it exists today. After the paper was published, several open source projects sprung up to provide users with the tools to trace and visualize applications using distributed tracing:

- **OpenTracing** – `https://opentracing.io`
- **OpenCensus** – `https://opencensus.io`
- **Zipkin** – `https://zipkin.io`
- **Jaeger** – `https://www.jaegertracing.io`

As you can imagine, with so many tools, it can be daunting to even know where to begin on the journey to making a system observable. Users and organizations must spend time and effort upfront to even get started. This can be challenging when other deadlines are looming. Not only that, but the time investment needed to instrument an application can be significant depending on the complexity of the application, and the return on that investment sometimes isn't made clear until much later. The time and money invested, as well as the expertise required, can make it difficult to change from one tool to another if the initial implementation no longer fits your needs as the system evolves.

Such a wide array of methods, tools, libraries, and standards has also caused fragmentation in the industry and the open source community. This has led to libraries supporting one format or another. This leaves it up to the user to fix any gaps within the environments themselves. This also means there is effort required to maintain feature parity across different projects. All of this could be addressed by bringing the people working in these communities together.

With a better understanding of different tools at the disposal of application developers, their evolution, and their role, we can start to better appreciate the scope of what OpenTelemetry is trying to solve.

Understanding the history of OpenTelemetry

In early 2019, the **OpenTelemetry** project was announced as a merger of two existing open source projects: **OpenTracing** and **OpenCensus**. Although initially, the goal of this endeavor was to bring these two projects together, its ambition to provide an observability framework for cloud-native software goes much further than that. Since OpenTelemetry combines concepts of both OpenTracing and OpenCensus, let's first look at each of these projects individually. Please refer to the following Twitter link, which announced OpenTelemetry by combining both concepts:

```
https://twitter.com/opencensusio/status/1111388599994318848.
```

Figure 1.2 - Screenshot of the aforementioned tweet

OpenTracing

The OpenTracing (`https://opentracing.io`) project, started in 2016, was focused on solving the problem of increasing the adoption of distributed tracing as a means for users to better understand their systems. One of the challenges identified by the project was that adoption was difficult because of cost instrumentation and the lack of consistent quality instrumentation in third-party libraries. OpenTracing provided a specification for **Application Programming Interface** (**APIs**) to address this problem. This API could be leveraged independently of the implementation that generated distributed traces, therefore allowing application developers and library authors to embed calls to this API in their code. By default, the API would act as a no-op operation, meaning those calls wouldn't do anything unless an implementation was configured.

Let's see what this looks like in code. The call to an API to trace a specific piece of code resembles the following example. You'll notice the code is accessing a global variable to obtain a *Tracer* via the `global_tracer` method. A **Tracer** in OpenTracing, and in OpenTelemetry (as we'll discuss later in *Chapter 2, OpenTelemetry Signals – Tracing, Metrics, and Logging*, and *Chapter 4, Distributed Tracing – Tracing Code Execution*), is a mechanism used to generate trace data. Using a globally configured tracer means that there's no configuration required in this instrumentation code – it can be done completely separately. The next line starts aprimary building block, `span`. We'll discuss this further in *Chapter 2, OpenTelemetry Signals – Tracing, Metrics, and Logging*, but it is shown here to give you an idea of how a Tracer is used in practice:

```
import opentracing
tracer = opentracing.global_tracer()
with tracer.start_active_span('doWork'):
    # do work
```

The default no-op implementation meant that code could be instrumented without the authors having to make decisions about how the data would be generated or collected at instrumentation time. It also meant that users of instrumented libraries, who didn't want to use distributed tracing in their applications, could still use the library without incurring a performance penalty by not configuring it. On the other hand, users who wanted to configure distributed tracing could choose how this information would be generated. The users of these libraries and applications would choose a Tracer implementation and configure it. To comply with the specification, a Tracer implementation only needed to adhere to the API defined (https://github.com/opentracing/opentracing-python/blob/master/opentracing/tracer.py), which includes the following methods:

- Start a new span.
- Inject an existing span's context into a carrier.
- Extract an existing span from a carrier.

Along with the specification for this API, OpenTracing also provides semantic conventions. These conventions describe guidelines to improve the quality of the telemetry emitted by instrumenting. We'll discuss semantic conventions further when exploring the concepts of OpenTelemetry.

OpenCensus

OpenCensus (https://opencensus.io) started as an internal project at Google, called Census, but was open sourced and gained popularity with a wider community in 2017. The project provided libraries to make the generation and collection of both traces and metrics simpler for application developers. It also provided the OpenCensus Collector, an agent run independently that acted as a destination for telemetry from applications and could be configured to process the data before sending it along to backends for storage and analysis. Telemetry being sent to the collector was transmitted using a wire format specified by OpenCensus. The collector was an especially powerful component of OpenCensus. As shown in *Figure 1.3*, many applications could be configured to send data to a single destination. That destination could then control the flow of the data without having to modify the application code any further:

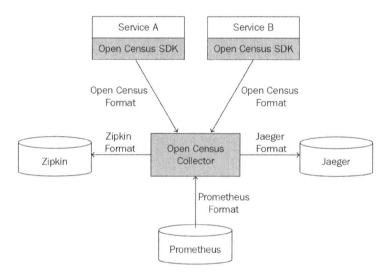

Figure 1.3 – OpenCensus Collector data flow

The concepts of the API to support distributed tracing in OpenCensus were like those of OpenTracing's API. In contrast to OpenTracing, however, the project provided a tightly coupled API and **Software Development Kit (SDK)**, meaning users could use OpenCensus without having to install and configure a separate implementation. Although this simplified the user experience for application developers, it also meant that in certain languages, the authors of third-party libraries wanting to instrument their code would depend on the SDK and all its dependencies. As mentioned before, OpenCensus also provided an API to generate application metrics. It introduced several concepts that would become influential in OpenTelemetry:

- **Measurement**: This is the recorded output of a measure, or a generated metric point.
- **Measure**: This is a defined metric to be recoded.

- **Aggregation**: This describes how the measurements are aggregated.
- **Views**: These combine measures and aggregations to determine how the data should be exported.

To collect metrics from their applications, developers defined a *measure* instrument to record *measurements*, and then configured a *view* with an *aggregation* to emit the data to a backend. The supported aggregations were *count*, *distribution*, *sum*, and *last value*.

As the two projects gained popularity, the pain for users only grew. The existence of both projects meant that it was unclear for users what project they should rely on. Using both together was not easy. One of the core components of distributed tracing is the ability to propagate context between the different applications in a distributed system, and this didn't work out of the box between the two projects. If a user wanted to collect traces and metrics, they would have to use OpenCensus, but if they wanted to use libraries that only supported OpenTracing, then they would have to use both – OpenTracing for distributed traces, and OpenCensus for metrics. It was a mess, and when there are too many standards, the way to solve all the problems is to invent a new standard!

It was a mess, and when there are too many standards, the way to solve all the problems is to invent a new standard! The following XKCD comic captures the sentiment very aptly:

Figure 1.4 – How standards proliferate comic (credit: XKCD, https://xkcd.com/927/)

Sometimes a new standard is a correct solution, especially when that solution:

- Is built using the lessons learned from its predecessors
- Brings together the communities behind other standards
- Supersedes two existing competing standards

The OpenCensus and OpenTracing organizers worked together to ensure the new standard would support a migration path for existing users of both communities, allowing the projects to eventually become deprecated. This would also make the lives of users easier by offering a single standard to use when instrumenting applications. There was no longer any need to guess what project to use!

Observability for cloud-native software

OpenTelemetry aims to standardize how applications are instrumented and how telemetry data is generated, collected, and transmitted. It also aims to give users the tools necessary to correlate that telemetry across systems, languages, and applications, to allow them to better understand their software. One of the initial goals of the project involved ensuring all the functionality that was key to both OpenCensus and OpenTracing users would become part of the new project. The focus on pre-existing users also leads to the project organizers establishing a migration path to ease the transition from OpenTracing and OpenCensus to OpenTelemetry. To accomplish its lofty goals, OpenTelemetry provides the following:

- An open specification
- Language-specific APIs and SDKs
- Instrumentation libraries
- Semantic conventions
- An agent to collect telemetry
- A protocol to organize, transmit, and receive the data

The project kicked off with the initial commit on May 1, 2019, and brought together the leaders from OpenCensus and OpenTracing. The project is governed by a governance committee that holds elections annually, with elected representatives serving on the committee for two-year terms. The project also has a technical committee that oversees the specification, drives project-wide discussion, and reviews language-specific implementations. In addition, there are various **special interest groups** (**SIGs**) in the project, focused on features or technologies supported by the project. Each language implementation has its own SIG with independent maintainers and approvers managing separate repositories with tools and processes tailored to the language. The initial work for the project was heavily focused on the open specification. This provides guidance for the language-specific implementations. Since its first commit, the project has received contributions from over 200 organizations, including observability leaders and cloud providers, as well as end users of OpenTelemetry. At the time of writing, OpenTelemetry has implementations in 11 languages and 18 special interest or working groups.

Since the initial merger of OpenCensus and OpenTracing, communities from additional open source projects have participated in OpenTelemetry efforts, including members of the Prometheus and OpenMetrics projects. Now that we have a better understanding of how OpenTelemetry was brought to life, let's take a deeper look at the concepts of the project.

Understanding the concepts of OpenTelemetry

OpenTelemetry is a large ecosystem. Before diving into the code, having a general understanding of the concepts and terminology used in the project will help us. The project is composed of the following:

- Signals
- Pipelines
- Resources
- Context propagation

Let's look at each of these aspects.

Signals

With its goal of providing an open specification for encompassing such a wide variety of telemetry data, the OpenTelemetry project needed to agree on a term to organize the categories of concern. Eventually, it was decided to call these **signals**. A signal can be thought of as a standalone component that can be configured, providing value on its own. The community decided to align its work into deliverables around these signals to deliver value to its users as soon as possible. The alignment of the work and separation of concerns in terms of signals has allowed the community to focus its efforts. The tracing and baggage signals were released in early 2021, soon followed by the metrics signal. Each signal in OpenTelemetry comes with the following:

- A set of specification documents providing guidance to implementors of the signal
- A data model expressing how the signal is to be represented in implementations
- An API that can be used by application and library developers to instrument their code
- The SDK needed to allow users to produce telemetry using the APIs
- Semantic conventions that can be used to get consistent, high-quality data
- Instrumentation libraries to simplify usage and adoption

The initial signals defined by OpenTelemetry were tracing, metrics, logging, and baggage. Signals are a core concept of OpenTelemetry and, as such, we will become quite familiar with them.

Specification

One of the most important aspects of OpenTelemetry is ensuring that users can expect a similar experience regardless of the language they're using. This is accomplished by defining the standards for what is expected of OpenTelemetry-compliant implementations in an open specification. The process used for writing the specification is flexible, but large new features or sections of functionality are often proposed by writing an **OpenTelemetry Enhancement Proposal** (**OTEP**). The OTEP is submitted for review and is usually provided along with prototype code in multiple languages, to ensure the proposal isn't too language-specific. Once an OTEP is approved and merged, the writing of the specification begins. The entire specification lives in a repository on GitHub (https://github.com/open-telemetry/opentelemetry-specification) and is open for anyone to contribute or review.

Data model

The data model defines the representation of the components that form a specific signal. It provides the specifics of what fields each component must have and describes how all the components interact with one another. This piece of the signal definition is particularly important to give clarity as to what use cases the APIs and SDKs will support. The data model also explains to developers implementing the standard how the data should behave.

API

Instrumenting applications can be quite expensive, depending on the size of your code base. Providing users with an API allows them to go through the process of instrumenting their code in a way that is vendor-agnostic. The API is decoupled from the code that generates the telemetry, allowing users the flexibility to swap out the underlying implementations as they see fit. This interface can also be relied upon by library and frameworks authors, and only configured to emit telemetry data by end users who wish to do so. A user who instruments their code by using the API and does not configure the SDK will not see any telemetry produced by design.

SDK

The SDK does the bulk of the heavy lifting in OpenTelemetry. It implements the underlying system that generates, aggregates, and transmits telemetry data. The SDK provides the controls to configure how telemetry should be collected, where it should be transmitted, and how. Configuration of the SDK is supported via in-code configuration, as well as via environment variables defined in the specification. As it is decoupled from the API, using the SDK provided by OpenTelemetry is an option for users, but it is not required. Users and vendors are free to implement their own SDKs if doing so will better fit their needs.

Semantic conventions

Producing telemetry can be a daunting task, since you can call anything whatever you wish, but doing so would make analyzing this data difficult. For example, if server A labels the duration of an `http.server.duration` request and server B labels it `http.server.request_length`, calculating the total duration of a request across both servers requires additional knowledge of this difference, and likely additional operations. One way in which OpenTelemetry tries to make this a bit easier is by offering semantic conventions, or definitions for different types of applications and workloads to improve the consistency of telemetry. Some of the types of applications or protocols that are covered by semantic conventions include the following:

- HTTP
- Database
- Message queues
- **Function-as-a-Service (FaaS)**
- **Remote procedure calls (RPC)**
- Process metrics

The full list of semantic conventions is quite extensive and can be found in the specification repository. The following figure shows a sample of the semantic convention for tracing database queries:

Attribute	Type	Description	Examples	Required
db.system	string	An identifier for the database management system (DBMS) product being used. See below for a list of well-known identifiers.	other_sql	Yes
db.connection_string	string	The connection string used to connect to the database. It is recommended to remove embedded credentials.	Server=(localdb)\v11.0;Integrated Security=true;	No
db.user	string	Username for accessing the database.	readonly_user ; reporting_user	No
net.peer.ip	string	Remote address of the peer (dotted decimal for IPv4 or RFC5952 for IPv6).	127.0.0.1	See below.
net.peer.name	string	Remote hostname or similar, see note below.	example.com	See below.
net.peer.port	int	Remote port number.	80 ; 8080 ; 443	Conditional [1]
net.transport	string	Transport protocol used. See note below.	IP.TCP	Conditional [2]

Table 1.1 – Database semantic conventions as defined in the OpenTelemetry specification (https://github.com/open-telemetry/opentelemetry-specification/blob/main/specification/trace/semantic_conventions/database.md#connection-level-attributes)

The consistency of telemetry data reported will ultimately impact the user of that data's ability to use this information. Semantic conventions provide both the guidelines of what telemetry should be reported, as well as how to identify this data. They provide a powerful tool for developers to learn their way around observability.

Instrumentation libraries

To ensure users can get up and running quickly, instrumentation libraries are made available by OpenTelemetry SIGs in various languages. These libraries provide instrumentation for popular open source projects and frameworks. For example, in Python, the instrumentation libraries include Flask, Requests, Django, and others. The mechanisms used to implement these libraries are language-specific and may be used in combination with auto-instrumentation to provide users with telemetry with close to zero code changes required. The instrumentation libraries are supported by the OpenTelemetry organization and adhere to semantic conventions.

Signals represent the core of the telemetry data that is generated by instrumenting cloud-native applications. They can be used independently, but the real power of OpenTelemetry is to allow its users to correlate data across signals to get a better understanding of their systems. Now that we have a general understanding of what they are, let's look at the other concepts of OpenTelemetry.

Pipelines

To be useful, the telemetry data captured by each signal must eventually be exported to a data store, where storage and analysis can occur. To accomplish this, each signal implementation offers a series of mechanisms to generate, process, and transmit telemetry. We can think of this as a pipeline, as represented in the following figure:

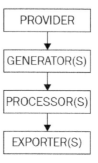

Figure 1.5 – Telemetry pipeline

The components in the telemetry pipeline are typically initialized early in the application code to ensure no meaningful telemetry is missed.

> **Important note**
> In many languages, the pipeline is configurable via environment variables. This will be explored further in *Chapter 7, Instrumentation Libraries*.

Once configured, the application generally only needs to interact with the generator to record telemetry, and the pipeline will take care of collecting and sending the data. Let's look at each component of the pipeline now.

Providers

The starting point of the telemetry pipeline is the provider. A provider is a configurable factory that is used to give application code access to an entity used to generate telemetry data. Although multiple providers may be configured within an application, a default global provider may also be made available via the SDK. Providers should be configured early in the application code, prior to any telemetry data being generated.

Telemetry generators

To generate telemetry at different points in the code, the telemetry generator instantiated by a provider is made available in the SDK. This generator is what most users will interact with through the instrumentation of their application and the use of the API. Generators are named differently depending on the signal: the tracing signal calls this a tracer, the metrics signal a meter. Their purpose is generally the same – to generate telemetry data. When instantiating a generator, applications and instrumenting libraries must pass a name to the provider. Optionally, users can specify a version identifier to the provider as well. This information will be used to provide additional information in the telemetry data generated.

Processors

Once the telemetry data has been generated, processors provide the ability to further modify the contents of the data. Processors may determine the frequency at which data should be processed or how the data should be exported. When instantiating a generator, applications and instrumenting libraries must pass a name to the provider. Optionally, users can specify a version identifier to the provider as well.

Exporters

The last step before telemetry leaves the context of an application is to go through the exporter. The job of the exporter is to translate the internal data model of OpenTelemetry into the format that best matches the configured exporter's understanding. Multiple export formats and protocols are supported by the OpenTelemetry project:

- OpenTelemetry protocol
- Console
- Jaeger
- Zipkin
- Prometheus
- OpenCensus

The pipeline allows telemetry data to be produced and emitted. We'll configure pipelines many times over the following chapters, and we'll see how the flexibility provided by the pipeline accommodates many use cases.

Resources

At their most basic, resources can be thought of as a set of attributes that are applied to different signals. Conceptually, a resource is used to identify the source of the telemetry data, whether a machine, container, or function. This information can be used at the time of analysis to correlate different events occurring in the same resource. Resource attributes are added to the telemetry data from signals at the export time before the data is emitted to a backend. Resources are typically configured at the start of an application and are associated with the providers. They tend to not change throughout the lifetime of the application. Some typical resource attributes would include the following:

- A unique name for the service: `service.name`
- The version identifier for a service: `service.version`
- The name of the host where the service is running: `host.name`

Additionally, the specification defines resource detectors to further enrich the data. Although resources can be set manually, resource detectors provide convenient mechanisms to automatically populate environment-specific data. For example, the **Google Cloud Platform (GCP)** resource detector (https://www.npmjs.com/package/@opentelemetry/resource-detector-gcp) interacts with the Google API to fill in the following data:

Google Cloud Platform resource detector attributes	
`cloud.provider`	`k8s.cluster.name`
`cloud.account.id`	`k8s.namespace.name`
`cloud.availability_zone`	`k8s.pod.name`
`host.id`	`container.name`

Table 1.2 – GCP resource detector attributes

Resources and resource detectors adhere to semantic conventions. Resources are a key component in making telemetry data-rich, meaningful, and consistent across an application. Another important aspect of ensuring the data is meaningful is context propagation.

Context propagation

One area of observability that is particularly powerful and challenging is context propagation. A core concept of distributed tracing, context propagation provides the ability to pass valuable contextual information between services that are separated by a logical boundary. Context propagation is what allows distributed tracing to tie requests together across multiple systems. OpenTelemetry, as OpenTracing did before it, has made this a core component of the project. In addition to tracing, context propagation allows for user-defined values (known as baggage) to be propagated. Baggage can be used to annotate telemetry across signals.

Context propagation defines a context API as part of the OpenTelemetry specification. This is independent of the signals that may use it. Some languages already have built-in context mechanisms, such as the `ContextVar` module in **Python 3.7+** and the `context` package in Go. The specification recommends that the context API implementations leverage these existing mechanisms. OpenTelemetry also provides for the interface and implementation of mechanisms required to propagate context across boundaries. The following abbreviated code shows how two services, A and B, would use the context API to share context:

```
from opentelemetry.propagate import extract, inject

class ServiceA:
    def client_request():
        inject(headers, context=current_context)
        # make a request to ServiceB and pass in headers

class ServiceB:
    def handle_request():
        # receive a request from ServiceA
        context = extract(headers)
```

In *Figure 1.6*, we can see a comparison between two requests from service A to service B. The top request is made without propagating the context, with the result that service B has neither the trace information nor the baggage that service A does. In the bottom request, this contextual data is injected when service A makes a request to service B, and extracted by service B from the incoming request, ensuring service B now has access to the propagated data:

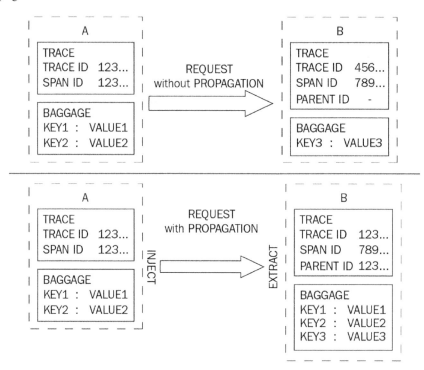

Figure 1.6 – Request between service A and B with and without context propagation

The propagation of context we have demonstrated allows backends to tie the two sides of the request together, but it also allows service B to make use of the dataset in service A. The challenge with context propagation is that when it isn't working, it's hard to know why. The issue could be that the context isn't being propagated correctly due to configuration issues or possibly a networking problem. This is a concept we'll revisit many times throughout the book.

Summary

In this chapter, we've looked at what observability is, and the challenges it can solve as regards the use of cloud-native applications. By exploring the different mechanisms available to generate telemetry and improve the observability of applications, we were also able to gain an understanding of how the observability landscape has evolved, as well as where some challenges remain.

Exploring the history behind the OpenTelemetry project gave us an understanding of the origin of the project and its goals. We then familiarized ourselves with the components forming tracing, metrics, logging signals, and pipelines to give us the terminology and building blocks needed to start producing telemetry using OpenTelemetry. This learning will allow us to tackle the first challenge of observability – producing high-quality telemetry. Understanding resources and context propagation will help us correlate events across services and signals to allow us to tackle the second challenge – connecting the data to better understand systems.

Let's now take a closer look at how this all works together in practice. In the next chapter, we will dive deeper into the concepts of distributed tracing, metrics, logs, and semantic conventions by launching a grocery store application instrumented with OpenTelemetry. We will then explore the telemetry generated by this distributed system.

2
OpenTelemetry Signals – Traces, Metrics, and Logs

Learning how first to instrument an application can be a daunting task. There's a fair amount of terminology to understand before jumping into the code. I always find that seeing the finish line helps me get motivated and stay on track. This chapter's goal is to see what telemetry generated by OpenTelemetry looks like in practice while learning about the theory. In this chapter, we will dive into the specifics of the following:

- Distributed tracing
- Metrics
- Logs
- Producing consistent quality data with semantic conventions

To help us get a more practical sense of the terminology and get comfortable with telemetry, we will look at the data using various open source tools that can help us to query and visualize telemetry.

Technical requirements

This chapter will use an application that is already instrumented with OpenTelemetry, a grocery store, and several backends to walk through the different concepts of the signals. The environment we will be launching relies on Docker Compose. The first step is to install Docker by following the installation instructions at `https://docs.docker.com/get-docker/`. Ensure Docker is running on your local system by using the following command:

```
$ docker version
Client:
 Cloud integration: 1.0.14
 Version:           20.10.6
 API version:       1.41
 Go version:        go1.16.3 ...
```

Next, let's ensure Compose is also installed by running the following command:

```
$ docker compose version
Docker Compose version 2.0.0-beta.1
```

> **Important Note**
>
> Compose was added to the Docker client in more recent client versions. If the previous command returns an error, follow the instructions on the Docker website (`https://docs.docker.com/compose/install/`) to install Compose. Alternatively, you may want to try the `docker-compose` command to see if you already have an older version installed.

The following diagram shows an overview of the containers we are launching in the Docker environment to give you an idea of the components involved. The applications on the left are emitting telemetry processed by the Collector and forwarded to the telemetry backends. The diagram also shows the port number exposed by each container for future reference.

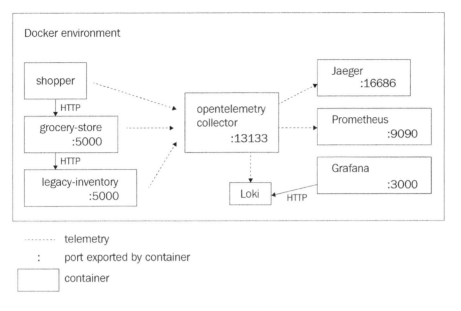

Figure 2.1 – Containers within Docker environment

This chapter briefly introduces the following open source projects that support the storage and visualization of OpenTelemetry data:

- Jaeger (https://www.jaegertracing.io)
- Prometheus (https://prometheus.io)
- Loki (https://github.com/grafana/loki)
- Grafana (https://grafana.com/oss/grafana/)

I strongly recommend visiting the website for each project to gain familiarity with the tools as we will use them throughout the chapter. Each of these tools will be revisited in *Chapter 10, Configuring Backends*. No prior knowledge of them is required to go through the examples, but they are pretty helpful to have in your toolbelt. The configuration files necessary to launch the applications in this chapter are available in the companion repository (https://github.com/PacktPublishing/Cloud-Native-Observability) in the chapter2 directory. The following downloads the repository using the git command:

```
$ git clone https://github.com/PacktPublishing/Cloud-Native-Observability
$ cd Cloud-Native-Observability/chapter02
```

To bring up the applications and telemetry backends, run the following command:

```
$ docker compose up
```

We will test the various tools to ensure each one is working as expected and is accessible from your browser. Let's start with **Jaeger** by accessing the following URL: `http://localhost:16686`. The following screenshot shows the interface you should see:

Figure 2.2 – The Jaeger web interface

The next backend this chapter will use for metrics is **Prometheus**; let's test the application by visiting `http://localhost:9090`. The following screenshot is a preview of the Prometheus web interface:

Figure 2.3 – The Prometheus web interface

The last tool we need to ensure is working in our backend for logs is **Loki**. We will use **Grafana** as a dashboard to visualize the logs being emitted. Begin by visiting `http://localhost:3000/explore` to ensure Grafana is up; you should be greeted by an interface like the one in *Figure 2.4*:

Figure 2.4 – The Grafana web interface

The next application we will check is the OpenTelemetry Collector, which acts as the routing layer for all the telemetry produced by the example application. The Collector exposes a health check endpoint discussed in *Chapter 8, OpenTelemetry Collector*. For now, it's enough to know that accessing the endpoint will give us information about the health of the Collector, using the following `curl` command:

```
$ curl localhost:13133
{"status":"Server available","upSince":"2021-10-03T15:42:02.734
5149Z","uptime":"9.3414709s"}
```

Lastly, let's ensure the containers forming the grocery store demo application are running. To do this, we use `curl` again in the following commands to access an endpoint in the applications that returns a status showing the application's health. It's possible to use any other tool capable of making HTTP requests, including the browser, to accomplish this. The following checks the status of the grocery store:

```
$ curl localhost:5000/healthcheck
{
    "service": "grocery-store",
    "status": "ok"
}
```

The same command can be used to check the status of the inventory application by specifying port `5001`:

```
$ curl localhost:5001/healthcheck
{
    "service": "inventory",
    "status": "ok"
}
```

The shopper application represents a client application and does not provide any endpoint to expose its health status. Instead, we can look at the logs emitted by the application to get a sense of whether it's doing the right thing or not. The following uses the `docker logs` command to look at the output from the application. Although it may vary slightly, the output should contain information about the shopper connecting to the grocery store:

```
$ docker logs -n 2 shopper
DEBUG:urllib3.connectionpool:http://grocery-store:5000 "GET /
products HTTP/1.1" 200 107
INFO:shopper:message="add orange to cart"
```

The same `docker logs` command can be used on any of the other containers if you're interested in seeing more information about them. Once you're done with the chapter, you can clean up all the containers by running `stop` to terminate the running containers, and `rm` to delete the containers themselves:

```
$ docker compose stop
$ docker compose rm
```

All the examples in this chapter will expect that the Docker Compose environment is already up and running. When in doubt, come back to this technical requirement section to ensure your environment is still running as expected. Now, let's see what these OpenTelemetry signals are all about, starting with traces.

Traces

Distributed tracing is the foundation behind the tracing signal of OpenTelemetry. A distributed trace is a series of event data generated at various points throughout a system tied together via a unique identifier. This identifier is propagated across all components responsible for any operation required to complete the request, allowing each operation to associate the event data to the originating request. The following diagram gives us a simplified example of what a single request may look like when ordering groceries through an app:

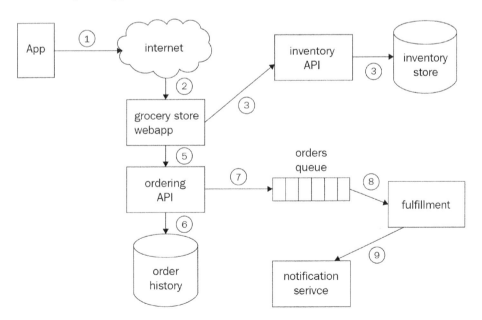

Figure 2.5 – Example request through a simplified ordering system

Each **trace** represents a unique request through a system that can be either synchronous or asynchronous. Synchronous requests occur in sequence with each unit of work completed before continuing. An example of a synchronous request may be of a client application making a call to a server and waiting or blocking until a response is returned before proceeding. In contrast, asynchronous requests can initiate a series of operations that can occur simultaneously and independently. An example of an asynchronous request is a server application submitting messages to a queue or a process that batches operations. Each operation recorded in a trace is represented by a **span**, a single unit of work done in the system. Let's see what the specifics of the data captured in the trace look like.

Anatomy of a trace

The definition of what constitutes a trace has evolved as various systems have been developed to support distributed tracing. The **World Wide Web Consortium (W3C)**, an international group that collaborates to move the web forward, assembled a working group in 2017 to produce a definition for tracing. In February 2020, the first version of the **Trace Context** specification was completed, with its details available on the W3C's website (https://www.w3.org/TR/trace-context-1/). OpenTelemetry follows the recommendation from the W3C in its definition of the **SpanContext**, which contains information about the trace and must be propagated throughout the system. The elements of a trace available within a span context include the following:

- A unique identifier, referred to as a **trace ID**, identifies the request through the system.
- A second identifier, the **span ID**, is associated with the span that last interacted with the context. This may also be referred to as the **parent identifier**.
- **Trace flags** include additional information about the trace, such as the sampling decision and trace level.
- Vendor-specific information is carried forward using a **Trace state** field. This allows individual vendors to propagate information necessary for their systems to interpret the tracing data. For example, if a vendor needs an additional identifier to be present in the trace information, this identifier could be inserted as `vendorA=123456` in the trace state field. Other vendors would add their own as needed, allowing traces to be shared across vendors.

A span can represent a method call or a subset of the code being called within a method. Multiple spans within a trace are linked together in a parent-child relationship, with each child span containing information about its parent. The first span in a trace is called the **root** span and is identified because it does not have a parent span identifier. The following shows a typical visualization of a trace and the spans associated with it. The horizontal axis indicates the duration of the entire trace operation. The vertical axis shows the order in which the operations captured by spans took place, starting with the first operation at the top:

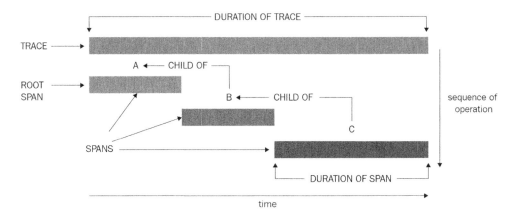

Figure 2.6 – Visual representation of a trace

Let's look closer at a trace by bringing up a sample generated from the telemetry produced by the grocery store application. Access the Jaeger web interface by opening a browser to the following URL: `http://localhost:16686/`.

Search for a trace by selecting a service from the drop-down and clicking the **Find Traces** button. The following screenshot shows the traces found for the shopper service:

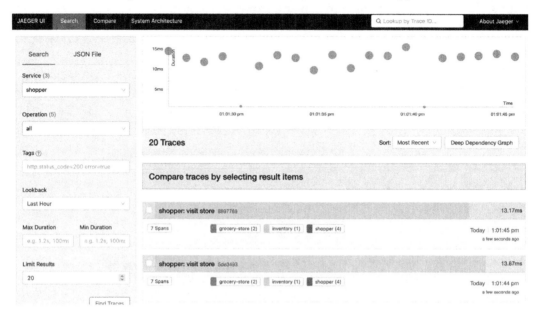

Figure 2.7 – Traces search result

To obtain details about a specific trace, select one of the search results by clicking on the row. The following screenshot, *Figure 2.8*, shows the details of the trace generated by a request through the grocery store applications. It includes the following:

1. The unique trace ID for this request. In OpenTelemetry, this is represented by a 128-bit integer. It's worth noting that other systems may represent this as a 64-bit integer. The integer is encoded into a string containing hexadecimal characters in many systems.
2. The start time for the request.
3. The total duration of the request through the system is calculated by subtracting the time the root span is finished from its start time.
4. A count of the number of services included in this request.
5. A count of spans recorded in this request is shown in Total Spans.

6. A hierarchical view of the spans in the trace.

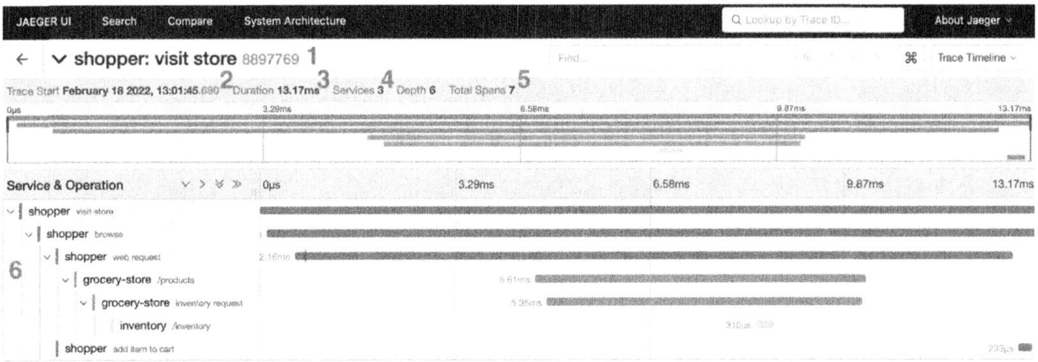

Figure 2.8 – A trace in Jaeger

The preceding screenshot gives us an immediate sense of where time may be spent as the system processes the request. It also provides us with a glimpse into what the underlying code may look like without ever opening an editor. Additional details are captured in spans; let's look at those now.

Details of a span

As mentioned previously, the work captured in a trace is broken into separate units or operations, each represented by a span. The span is a data structure containing the following information:

- A unique identifier
- A parent span identifier
- A name describing the work being recorded
- A start and end time

In OpenTelemetry, a span identifier is represented by a 64-bit integer. The start and end times are used to calculate the operation's duration. Additionally, spans can contain metadata in the form of key-value pairs. In the case of Jaeger and Zipkin, these pairs are referred to as **tags**, whereas OpenTelemetry calls them **attributes**. The goal is to enrich the data provided with the additional context in both cases.

Look for the following details in *Figure 2.9*, which shows the detailed view of a specific span as shown in Jaeger:

1. The name identifies the operation represented by this span. In this case, **/inventory** is the operation's name.
2. **SpanID** is the unique 64-bit identifier represented in hex-encoded formatting.
3. **Start Time** is when the operation recorded its start time relative to the start of the request. In the case shown here, the operation started 8.36 milliseconds after the beginning of the request.
4. **Duration** is the time it took for the operation to complete and is calculated using the start and end times recorded in the span.
5. **The Service name** identifies the application that triggered the operation and recorded the telemetry.
6. **Tags** represent additional information about the operation being recorded.
7. **Process** shows information about the application or process fulfilling the requested operation.

Figure 2.9 – Span details

Many of the tags captured in the span shown previously rely on semantic conventions, which will be discussed further in this chapter.

Additional considerations

When producing distributed traces in a system, it's worth considering the additional visibility's tradeoffs. Generating tracing information can potentially incur performance overhead at the application level. It can result in added latency if tracing information is gathered and transmitted inline. There is also memory overhead to consider, as collecting information inevitably allocates resources. These concerns can be largely mitigated using configuration available in OpenTelemetry, as we'll see in *Chapter 4, Distributed Tracing – Tracing Code Execution*.

Depending on where the data is sent, additional costs, such as bandwidth or storage, can also become a factor. One of the ways to mitigate these costs is to reduce the amount of data produced by sampling only a certain amount of the data. We will dive deeper into sampling in *Chapter 12, Sampling*.

Another challenging aspect of producing distributed tracing data is ensuring that all the services correctly propagate the context. Failing to propagate the trace ID across the system means that requests will be broken into multiple traces, making them difficult to use or not helpful at all.

The last thing to consider is the effort required to instrument an application correctly. This is a non-trivial amount of effort, but as we'll see in future chapters, OpenTelemetry provides instrumentation libraries to make this easier.

Now that we have a deeper understanding of traces, let's look at metrics.

Metrics

Just as distributed traces do, metrics provide information about the state of a running system to developers and operators. The data collected via metrics can be aggregated over time to identify trends and patterns in applications graphed through various tools and visualizations. The term *metrics* has a broad range of applications as they can capture low-level system metrics such as CPU cycles, or higher-level details such as the number of blue sweaters sold today. These examples would be helpful to different groups in an organization.

Additionally, metrics are critical to monitoring the health of an application and deciding when an on-call engineer should be alerted. They form the basis of **service level indicators** (**SLIs**) (https://en.wikipedia.org/wiki/Service_level_indicator) that measure the performance of an application. These indicators are then used to set **service level objectives** (**SLOs**) (https://en.wikipedia.org/wiki/Service-level_objective) that organizations use to calculate error budgets.

> **Important Note**
> SLIs, SLOs, and **service level agreements** (**SLAs**) are essential topics in production environments where third-party dependencies can impact the availability of your service. There are entire books dedicated to the issue that we will not cover here. The Google **site reliability engineering** (**SRE**) book is a great resource for this: https://sre.google/sre-book/service-level-objectives/.

The metrics signal of OpenTelemetry combines various existing open source formats into a unified data model. Primarily, it looks to *OpenMetrics*, *StatsD*, and *Prometheus* for existing definitions, requirements, and usage, wanting to ensure the use-cases of each of those communities are understood and addressed by the new standard.

Anatomy of a metric

Just about anything can be a metric; record a value at a given time, and you have yourself a metric. The common fields a metric contains include the following:

- A **name** identifies the metric being recorded.
- A **data point value** may be an integer or a floating-point value. Note that in the case of a histogram or a summary, there is more than one value associated with the metric.
- Additional **dimension** information about the metric. The representation of these dimensions varies depending on the metrics backend. In Prometheus, these dimensions are represented by labels, whereas in StatsD, it is common to add a prefix in the metric's name. In OpenTelemetry, dimensions are added to metrics via attributes.

Let's look at data produced by metrics sent from the demo application. Access the Prometheus interface via a browser and the following URL: `http://localhost:9090`. The user interface for Prometheus allows us to query the time-series database by using the metric's name. The following screenshot contains a table showing the value of the `request_counter` metric. Look for the following details in the resulting table:

1. The name of the metric, in this case, `request_counter`.
2. The dimensions recorded for this metric are displayed in curly braces as key-value pairs with the key emboldened. In the example shown, the `service_name` label caused two different metrics to be recorded, one for the `shopper` service and another for the `store` service.

3. A reported value, in this example, is an integer. This value may be the last received or a calculated current value depending on the metric type.

Figure 2.10 – Table view of metric in Prometheus

The table view shows the current value as cumulative. An alternative representation of the recorded metric is shown in the following figure. As the data received by Prometheus is stored over time, a line graph can be generated. Click the **Graph** tab of the interface to see what the data in a chart looks like:

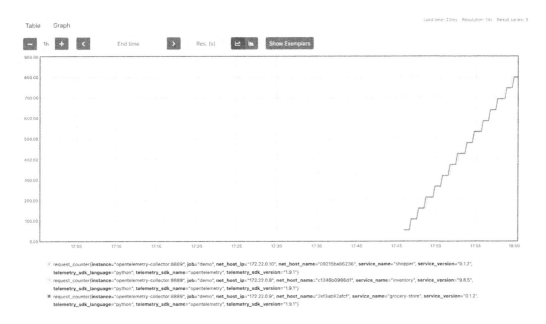

Figure 2.11 – Graph view of the same metric in Prometheus

By looking at the values for the metric over time, we can deduce additional information about the service, for example, its start time or trends in its usage. Visualizing metrics also provides opportunities to identify anomalies.

Data point types

A metric is a more generic term that encapsulates different measurements that can be used to represent a wide array of information. As such, the data is captured using various data point types. The following diagram compares different kinds of data points that can be captured within a metric:

Histogram	Values
Min	0
Max	100
Count	20
Interval	10
Distribution	
0-10	1
10-20	1
20-30	1
30-40	2
40-50	4
50-60	4
60-70	3
70-80	2
80-90	1
90-100	1

Summary	Values
Count	10
Min	0.99ms
Max	3.44ms
Sum	8.56ms
Quantiles	
p50	1.37ms
p75	2.82ms
p99	3.44ms

Gauge	Value
Last value	37.5

Counter	Value
Last increment	19

Figure 2.12 – Comparison of counter, gauge, histogram, and summary data points

Each data point type can be used in different scenarios and has slightly different meanings. It's worth noting that even though competing standards provide support for types using the same name, their definition may vary. For example, a counter in StatsD (https://github.com/statsd/statsd/blob/master/docs/metric_types.md#counting) resets every time the value has been flushed, whereas, in Prometheus (https://prometheus.io/docs/concepts/metric_types/#counter), it keeps its cumulative value until the process recording the counter is restarted. The following definitions describe how data point types are represented in the OpenTelemetry specification:

- A **sum** measures incremental changes to a recorded value. This incremental change is either monotonic or non-monotonic and must be associated with an aggregation temporality. The temporality can be either of the following:

    A. **Delta** aggregation: The reported values contain the change in value from its previous recording.

    B. **Cumulative** aggregation: The value reported includes the previously reported sum in addition to the delta being reported.

> **Important Note**
> A cumulative sum will reset when an application restarts. This is useful to identify an event in the application but may be surprising if it's not accounted for.

The following diagram shows an example of a sum counter reporting the number of visits over a period of time. The table on the right-hand side shows what values are to be expected depending on the type of temporal aggregation chosen:

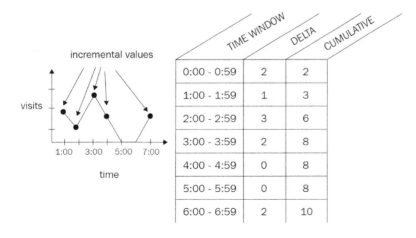

Figure 2.13 – Sum showing delta and cumulative aggregation values

A sum data point also includes the time window for calculating the sum.

- A **gauge** represents non-monotonic values that only measure the last or current known value at observation. This likely means some information is missing, but it may not be relevant. For example, the following diagram represents temperatures recorded at an hourly interval. More specific data points could provide greater granularity as to the rise and fall of the temperature. These incremental changes in the temperature may not be required if the goal is to observe trends over weeks or months.

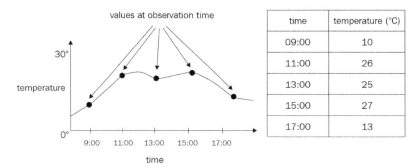

Figure 2.14 – Gauge values recorded

Unlike gauge definitions in other specifications, a gauge in OpenTelemetry is never incremented or decremented; it is only ever set to the value being recorded. A timestamp of the observation time must be included with the data point.

- A **histogram** data point provides a compressed view into a more significant number of data points by grouping the data into a distribution and summarizing the data, rather than reporting individual measurements for every detail represented. The following diagram shows sample histogram data points representing a distribution of response durations.

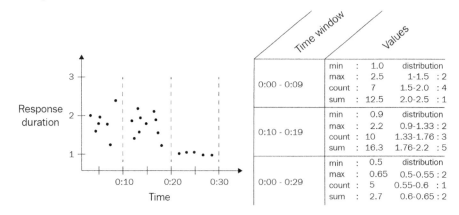

Figure 2.15 – Histogram data points

Like sums, histograms also support a delta or a cumulative aggregation and must contain a time window for the recorded observation. Note that in the case of cumulative aggregation, the data points captured in the distribution will continue to accumulate with each recording.

- The **summary** data type provides a similar capability to histograms, but it's specifically tailored around providing quantiles of a distribution. A **quantile**, sometimes also referred to as **percentile**, is a fraction between zero and one, representing a percentage of the total number of values recorded that falls under a certain threshold. For example, consider the following 10 response times in milliseconds: 1.1, 2.9, 7.5, 8.3, 9, 10, 10, 10, 10, 25. The 0.9-quantile, or the 90th percentile, equals 10 milliseconds.

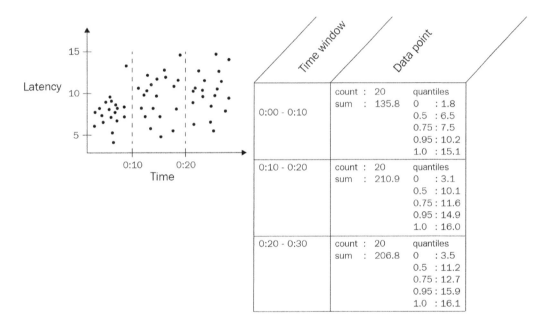

Figure 2.16 – Summary data points

A summary is somewhat similar to a histogram, where the histogram contains a maximum and a minimum value; the summary includes a 1.0-quantile and 0.0-quantile to represent the same information. The 0.5-quantile, also known as median, is often expressed in the summary. For a summary data point, the quantile calculations happen in the producer of the telemetry, which can become expensive for applications. OpenTelemetry supports summaries to provide interoperability with OpenMetrics (https://openmetrics.io) and Prometheus and prefers the usage of a histogram, which moves the calculation of quantiles to the receiver of the telemetry. The following screenshot shows histogram values recorded by the inventory service for the http_request_duration_milliseconds_bucket metric stored in Prometheus. The data shown represents requests grouped into buckets. Each bucket represents the request duration in milliseconds:

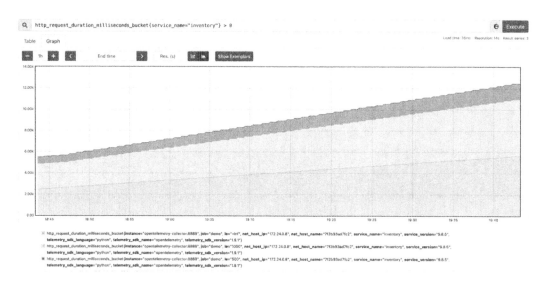

Figure 2.17 – Histogram value in Prometheus

The count of requests per bucket can then calculate quantiles for further analysis. Now that we're familiar with the different types of metric data points, let's see how metrics can be combined with tracing to provide additional insights.

Exemplars

Metrics are often helpful on their own, but when correlated with tracing information, they provide much more context and depth on the events occurring in a system. **Exemplars** offer a tool to accomplish this in OpenTelemetry by enabling a metric to contain information about an active span. Data points defined in OpenTelemetry include an `exemplar` field as part of their definition. This field contains the following:

- A trace ID of the current span in progress
- The span ID of the current span in progress
- A timestamp of the event measured
- A set of attributes associated with the exemplar
- The value being recorded

The direct correlation that exemplars provide replaces the guesswork that involves cobbling metrics and traces with timestamps today. Although exemplars are already defined in the stable metrics section of the OpenTelemetry protocol, the implementation of exemplars is still under active development at the time of writing.

Additional considerations

A concern that often arises with any telemetry is the importance of managing cardinality. **Cardinality** refers to the uniqueness of a value in a set. While counting cars in a parking lot, the number of wheels will likely offer a meager value and low cardinality result as most cars have four wheels. The color, make, and model of cars produces higher cardinality. The license plate, or vehicle identification number, results in the highest cardinality, providing the most valuable data to know in an event concerning a specific vehicle. For example, if the lights have been left on and the owners should be notified, calling out for the person with a four-wheeled car won't work nearly as well as calling for a specific license plate. However, the count of cars with specific license plates will always be one, making the counter itself somewhat useless.

One of the challenges with high-cardinality data is the increased storage cost. Specifically, in the case of metrics, it's possible to significantly increase the number of metrics being produced and stored by adding a single attribute or label. Suppose an application creating a counter for each request processed uses a unique identifier as the metric's name. In that case, the producer or receiver may translate this into a unique time series for each request. This results in a sudden and unexpected increase in load in the system. This is sometimes referred to as **cardinality explosion**.

When choosing attributes associated with produced metrics, it's essential to consider the scale of the services and infrastructure producing the telemetry. Some questions to keep in mind are as follows:

- Will scaling components of the system increase the number of metrics in a way that is understood? When a system scales, the last thing anyone wants is for an unexpected spike in metrics to cause outages.
- Are any attributes specific to instances of an application? This could cause problems in the case of a crashing application.

Using labels with finite and knowable values (for example, countries rather than street names) may be preferable depending on how the data is stored. When choosing a solution, understanding the storage model and limits of the telemetry backend must also be considered.

Logs

Although logs have evolved, what constitutes a **log** is quite broad. Also known as log files, a log is a record of events written to output. Traditionally, logs would be written to a file on disk, searching through as needed. A more recent practice is to emit logs to remote services using the network. This provides long-term storage for the data in a location and improves searchability and aggregation.

Anatomy of a log

Many applications define their formats for what constitutes a log. There are several existing standard formats. An example includes the Common Log Format often used by web servers. It's challenging to identify commonalities across formats, but at the very least, a log should consist of the following:

- A **timestamp** recording the time of the event
- The **message** or payload representing the event

This message can take many forms and include various application-specific information. In the case of structured logging, the log is formatted as a series of key-value pairs to simplify identifying the different fields contained within the log. Other formats record logs in a specific order with a separating character instead. The following shows an example log emitted by the standard formatter in **Flask**, a Python web framework that shows the following:

- A timestamp is enclosed in square brackets.
- A space-delimited set of elements forms the message logged, including the client IP, the HTTP method used to make a request, the request's path, the protocol version, and the response code:

```
172.20.0.9 - - [11/Oct/2021 18:50:25] "GET /inventory HTTP/1.1" 200 -
```

The previous sample is an example of the Common Log Format mentioned earlier. The same log may look something like this as a structured log encoded as JSON:

```
{
    "host": "172.20.0.9",
    "date": "11/Oct/2021 18:50:25",
    "method": "GET",
    "path": "/inventory",
    "protocol": "HTTP/1.1",
    "status": 200
}
```

As you can see with structured logs, identifying the information is more intuitive if you're not already familiar with the type of logs produced. Let's see what logs our demo application produces by looking at the Grafana interface, at http://localhost:3000/explore.

This brings us to the explore view, which allows us to search through telemetry generated by the demo application. Ensure that **Loki** is selected from the data source drop-down in the top left corner. Filter the logs using the {job="shopper"} query to retrieve all the logs generated by the shopper application. The following screenshot shows a log emitted to the Loki backend, which contains the following:

1. The name of the application is under the job label.
2. A timestamp of the log is shown both as a timestamp and as a nanosecond value.

3. The body of the logged event.
4. Additional labels and values associated with the event.

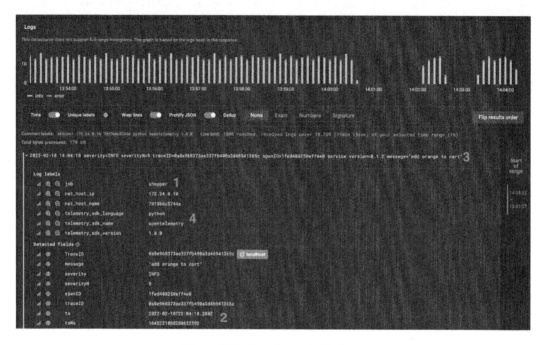

Figure 2.18 – Log shown in Grafana

Now that we can search for logs, let's see how we can combine the information provided by logs with other signals via correlation to give us more context.

Correlating logs

In the same way that information provided by metrics can be augmented by combining them with other signals, logs too can provide more context by embedding tracing information. As we'll see in *Chapter 6, Logging - Capturing Events*, one of the goals of the logging signal in OpenTelemetry is to provide correlation capability to already existing logging libraries. Logs recorded via OpenTelemetry contain the trace ID and span ID for any span active at the time of the event. The following screenshot shows the details of a log record containing the `traceID` and `spanID` attributes:

Logs 51

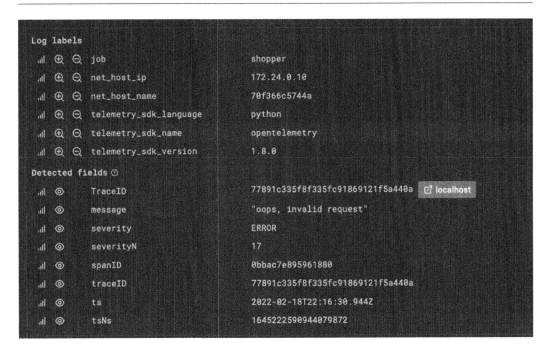

Figure 2.19 – Log containing trace ID

Using these attributes can then reveal the specific request that triggered this event. The following screenshot demonstrates what the corresponding trace looks like in Jaeger. If you'd like to try for yourself, copy the `traceID` attribute into the **Lookup by Trace ID** field to search for the trace:

Figure 2.20 – Corresponding trace in Jaeger

The correlation demonstrated in the previous example makes exploring events faster and less error-prone. As we will see in *Chapter 6, Logging - Capturing Events*, the OpenTelemetry specification provides recommendations for what information should be included in logs being emitted. It also provides guidelines for how existing formats can map their values with OpenTelemetry.

Additional considerations

The free form of traditional logs makes them incredibly convenient to use without considering their structure. If you want to add any data to the logs, just call a function and print anything you'd like; it'll be great. However, this can pose some challenges. One of these challenges is the opportunity for leaking potentially private information into the logs and transmitting it to a centralized logging platform. This problem applies to all telemetry, but it's particularly easy to do with logs. This is especially true when logs contain debugging information, which may include data structures with passwords fields or private keys. It's good to review any logging calls in the code to ensure the logged data does not contain information that should not be logged.

Logs can also be overly verbose, which can cause unexpected volumes to be generated. This may make sifting through the logs for useful information difficult, if not impossible, depending on the size of the environment. It can also lead to unanticipated costs when using centralized logging platforms. Specific libraries or frameworks generate much debugging information. Ensuring the correct severity level is configured goes a long towards addressing this concern. However, it's hard to predict just how much data will be needed upfront. On more than one occasion, I've responded to alerts in the middle of the night, wishing for a more verbose log level to be configured.

Semantic conventions

High-quality telemetry allows the data consumer to find answers to questions when needed. Sometimes critical operations can lack instrumentation causing blind spots in the observability of a system. Other times, the processes are instrumented, but the data is not rich enough to be helpful. The OpenTelemetry project attempts to solve this through semantic conventions defined in the specification. These conventions cover the following:

- Attributes that should be present for traces, metrics, and logs.
- Resource attribute definitions for various types of workloads, including hosts, containers, and functions. The resource attributes described by the specification also include characteristics specific to multiple popular cloud platforms.

- Recommendations for what telemetry should be emitted by components participating in various scenarios such as messaging systems, client-server applications, and database interactions.

These semantic conventions help ensure that the data generated when following the OpenTelemetry specification is consistent. This simplifies the work of folks instrumenting applications or libraries by providing guidelines for what should be instrumented and how. It also means that anyone analyzing telemetry produced by standard-compliant code can understand the meaning of the data by referencing the specification for additional information.

Following semantic conventions recommendations from a specification in a Markdown document can be challenging when writing code. Thankfully, OpenTelemetry also provides some tools to help.

Adopting semantic conventions

Semantic conventions are great, but it makes sense to turn the recommendations into code to make it practical for developers to use them. The OpenTelemetry specification repository provides a folder that contains the semantic conventions described as YAML for this specific reason (`https://github.com/open-telemetry/opentelemetry-specification/tree/main/semantic_conventions`). These are combined with the semantic conventions generator (`https://github.com/open-telemetry/build-tools/blob/v0.7.0/semantic-conventions/`) to produce code in various languages. This code is shipped as independent libraries in some languages, helping guide developers. We will repeatedly rely upon the semantic conventions package in Python in further chapters as we instrument application code.

Schema URL

A challenge of semantic conventions is that as telemetry and observability evolve, so will the terminology used to describe events that we want to observe. An example of this happened when the `db.hbase.namespace` and `db.cassandra.keyspace` keys were renamed to use `db.name` instead. Such a change would cause problems for anyone already using this field as part of their analysis, or even alerting. To ensure the semantic conventions can evolve as needed while remaining backward-compatible with existing instrumentation, the OpenTelemetry community introduced the **schema URL**.

> **Important Note**
>
> The OpenTelemetry community understands the importance of backward compatibility in instrumentation code. Going back and re-instrumenting an application because of a new version of a telemetry library is a pain. As such, a significant amount of effort has gone into ensuring that components defined in OpenTelemetry remain interoperable with previous versions. The project defines its versioning and stability guarantees as part of the specification (https://github.com/open-telemetry/opentelemetry-specification/blob/main/specification/versioning-and-stability.md).

The schema URL is a field added to the telemetry generated for logs, metrics, resources, and traces tying the emitted telemetry to a version of the semantic conventions. This field allows the producers and consumers of telemetry to understand how to interpret the data. The schema also provides instructions for converting data from one version to another, as per the following example:

1.8.0 schema

```
file_format: 1.0.0
schema_url: https://opentelemetry.io/schemas/1.8.0
versions:
  1.8.0:
    spans:
      changes:
        - rename_attributes:
            attribute_map:
              db.cassandra.keyspace: db.name
              db.hbase.namespace: db.name
  1.7.0:
  1.6.1:
```

Continuing with the previous example, imagine a producer of Cassandra telemetry is emitting `db.cassandra.keyspace` as the name for a Cassandra database and specifying the schema as `1.7.0`. It sends the data to a backend that implements schema `1.8.0`. By reading the schema URL and implementing the appropriate translation, the backend can produce telemetry in its expected version, which is powerful! Schemas decouple systems involved in telemetry, providing them with the flexibility to evolve independently.

Summary

This chapter allowed us to learn or review some concepts that will assist us when instrumenting applications using OpenTelemetry. We looked at the building blocks of distributed tracing, which will come in handy when we go through instrumenting our first application with OpenTelemetry in *Chapter 4, Distributed Tracing – Tracing Code Execution*. We also started analyzing tracing data using tools that developers and operators make use of every day.

We then switched to the metrics signal; first, looking at the minimal contents of a metric, then comparing different data types commonly used to produce metrics and their structures. Discussing exemplars gave us a brief introduction to how correlating metrics with traces can create a more complete picture of what is happening within a system by combining telemetry across signals.

Looking at log formats and searching through logs to find information about the demo application allowed us to get familiar with yet another tool available in the observability practitioner's toolbelt.

Lastly, by leveraging semantic conventions defined in OpenTelemetry, we can begin to produce consistent, high-quality data. Following these conventions removes the painful task of naming things, which everyone in the software industry agrees is hard for producers of telemetry. Additionally, these conventions remove the guesswork when interpreting the data.

Knowing the theory and concepts behind instrumentation and telemetry is excellent to provide us with the tools to do all the instrumentation work ourselves. Still, what if I were to tell you it may not be necessary to instrument every call in every library manually? The next chapter will cover how auto-instrumentation looks to help developers in their quest for better visibility into their systems.

3
Auto-Instrumentation

The purpose of telemetry is to give people information about systems. This data is used to make informed decisions about ways to improve software and prevent disasters from occurring. In the case of an outage, analytics tools can help us investigate the root cause of the interruption by interpreting telemetry. Once the event has been resolved, the recorded traces, metrics, and logs can be correlated retroactively to gain a complete picture of what happened. In all these cases, the knowledge that's gained from telemetry assists in solving problems, be it future, present, or past, in applications within an organization. Being able to see the code is very rarely the bread and butter of an organization, which sometimes makes conversations about investing in observability difficult. Decision-makers must constantly make tradeoffs regarding where to invest. The upfront cost of instrumenting code can be a deterrent to even getting started, especially if a solution is complicated to implement and will fail to deliver any value for a long time. Auto-instrumentation looks to alleviate some of the burdens of instrumenting code manually.

In this chapter, we will cover the following topics:

- What is auto-instrumentation?
- Bytecode manipulation
- Runtime hooks and monkey patching

We will look at some example code in Java and Python, as well as the emitted telemetry, to understand the power of auto-instrumentation. Let's get started!

Technical requirements

The application in this chapter simulates the broken telephone game. If you're not familiar with this game, it is played by having one person think of a phrase and whisper it to the second player. The second player listens to the best of their ability and whispers it to the third player; this continues until the last player shares the message they received with the rest of the group.

Each application represents a player, with the first one printing out the message it is sending, then placing the message in a request object that's sent to the next application. The last application in the game will print out the message it receives. The following diagram shows the data flow of requests and responses through the system:

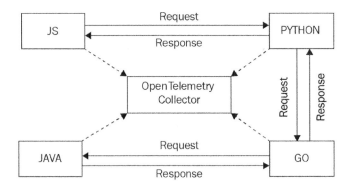

Figure 3.1 – Architectural diagram of the example application

The communication between each service is done via gRPC (https://grpc.io), a remote procedure call system developed by Google. For the sake of this chapter, it is enough to know that the applications do the following:

- Share a common understanding of the data structure of a service and a message via the protocol buffer's definition file.
- Send data to each other using the protocol.

The telemetry that's emitted by each application is sent to the OpenTelemetry Collector via the OpenTelemetry exporter that's configured in each service. The collector then forwards it to Jaeger, which we'll use to visualize tracing information collected.

The examples in this chapter are provided within Docker containers to make launching them easier; this also means you don't need to install separate runtime languages and libraries on your system. If you went through the Docker setup steps in the previous chapter, you can skip ahead to *Step 3*:

1. Ensure Docker is installed on your system by following the instructions on the Docker website (https://docs.docker.com/get-docker/). The following command shows the version of Docker that's running on your local system:

    ```
    $ docker version
    Client:
      Cloud integration: 1.0.14
      Version:           20.10.6
      API version:       1.41
      Go version:        go1.16.3 ...
    ```

2. Verify that docker compose is installed on your system using the following command. If it is not installed, follow the directions on the Docker website (https://docs.docker.com/compose/install/) to install it:

    ```
    $ docker compose version
    Docker Compose version 2.0.0-beta.1
    ```

3. Download a copy of the companion repository from GitHub and launch the Docker environment that's available in the chapter3 directory:

    ```
    $ git clone https://github.com/PacktPublishing/Cloud-Native-Observability
    $ cd Cloud-Native-Observability/chapter03
    $ docker compose up
    ```

The applications that form the demo system for this chapter are written in JavaScript, Python, Go, and Java. The code for the application in each language that will be shown in this chapter is also available in this book's GitHub repository, in the chapter3 directory; each language is in a separate folder. We will look through some of the code in this chapter, but not all of it.

Lastly, although it is not a requirement for this chapter, if you're interested in exploring the trace information that's emitted from the demo application, the best way to see it is through the Jaeger web interface. The **Docker compose** environment launches Jaeger along with the demo app, so you can verify that it is up and running by launching a web browser and visiting http://localhost:16686.

What is auto-instrumentation?

In the very early days of the OpenTelemetry project, a proposal was created to support producing telemetry without manual instrumentation. As we mentioned earlier in this book, OpenTelemetry uses **OpenTelemetry Enhancement Proposals** or **OTEPs** to propose significant changes or new work before producing a specification. One of the very first OTEPs to be produced by the project (`https://github.com/open-telemetry/oteps/blob/main/text/0001-telemetry-without-manual-instrumentation.md`) described the need to support users that wanted to produce telemetry without having to modify the code to do so:

> *Cross-language requirements for automated approaches to extracting portable telemetry data with zero source code modification. – OpenTelemetry Enhancement Proposal #0001*

Being able to get started with OpenTelemetry with very little effort for new users was very much a goal from the start of the project. The hope was to address one of the pain points of producing telemetry: the cost of manual instrumentation.

Challenges of manual instrumentation

Instrumenting an application can be a difficult task. This is especially true for someone who hasn't done so before. Instrumenting applications is a skill that takes time and practice to perfect. Some of the things that can be challenging when instrumenting code are as follows:

- The libraries and APIs that are provided by telemetry frameworks can be hard to learn how to use. With auto-instrumentation, users do not have to learn how to use the libraries and APIs directly; instead, they rely on a simplified user experience that can be tuned via configuration.

- Instrumenting applications can be tricky. This can be especially true for legacy applications where the original author of the code is no longer around. By reducing the amount of code that needs to be modified, auto-instrumentation reduces the surface of the changes that need to be made and minimizes the risks involved.

- Knowing what to instrument and how it should be done takes practice. The authors of auto-instrumentation tooling and libraries ensure that the telemetry that's produced by auto-instrumentation follows the semantic conventions defined by OpenTelemetry.

Additionally, it's not uncommon for systems to contain applications written in different languages. This adds to the complexity of manually instrumenting code as it requires developers to learn how to instrument in multiple languages. Auto-instrumentation provides the necessary tooling to minimize the effort here, as the goal of the OpenTelemetry project is to support the same configuration across languages. This means that, in theory, the auto-instrumentation experience will be *fairly consistent*. I say *fairly* here because the libraries and tools are still changing, so some inconsistencies are being worked through in the project.

Components of auto-instrumentation

In terms of OpenTelemetry, auto-instrumentation is made up of two parts. The first part is composed of instrumentation libraries. These libraries are provided and supported by members of the OpenTelemetry community, who use the OpenTelemetry API to instrument popular third-party libraries and frameworks in each language. The following table lists some of the instrumentation libraries that are provided by OpenTelemetry in various languages at the time of writing:

Language	Libraries
Go	gin, gomemcache, gorilla/mux, net/http
Erlang	Cowboy, Ecto, Phoenix
Java	Akka, gRPC, Hibernate, JDBC, Kafka, Spring, Tomcat
JavaScript	fetch, grpc-js, http, xml-http-request
.NET	AspNetCore, GrpcNetClient, SqlClient, StackExchangeRedis
Python	Boto, Celery, Django, Flask, gRPC, Redis Requests, SQLAlchemy
Ruby	ActiveJob, Faraday, Mongo, Rack, Rails

Figure 3.2 – Some of the available instrumentation libraries in OpenTelemetry

Most of these instrumentation libraries are specific to a particular third-party library of a language. For example, the `Boto` instrumentation library instruments method calls that are specific to the Boto library. However, there are cases where multiple instrumentation libraries could be used to instrument the same thing. An example of this is the `Requests` and `urllib3` instrumentation libraries, which would, in theory, instrument the same thing since `Requests` is built on top of `urllib3`. When choosing instrumentation libraries, a good rule of thumb is to find the library that is the most specific to your use case. If more than one fits, inspect the data that's emitted by each library to find the one that fits your needs.

The details of how exactly instrumentation libraries are implemented vary from language to language and sometimes even from library to library. Some of these details will become clearer as we progress through this chapter and look at some of the mechanisms that are used in Java and Python libraries.

As we mentioned at the beginning of this section, two components form auto-instrumentation. The second component is a mechanism that's provided by OpenTelemetry to allow users to automatically invoke the instrumentation libraries without additional work on the part of the user. This mechanism is sometimes called an **agent** or a **runner**. In practice, the purpose of this tool is to configure OpenTelemetry and load the instrumentation libraries that can be used to then generate telemetry.

> **Important Note**
> Auto-instrumentation is still being actively developed and the OpenTelemetry specification around auto-instrumentation, its implementation, and how configuration should be specified is still in development. The adoption in different languages is, at the time of writing, in various stages. For the examples in this chapter, the Python and Java examples use full auto-instrumentation with both instrumentation libraries and an agent. The JavaScript and Go code only leverage instrumentation libraries.

Limits of auto-instrumentation

Auto-instrumentation is a good place to start the journey of instrumenting an application and gaining more visibility into its inner workings. However, there are some limitations as to what can be achieved with automatic instrumentation, all of which we should take into consideration.

The first limitation may seem obvious, but it is that auto-instrumentation cannot instrument application-specific code. As such, the instrumentation that's produced via auto-instrumentation is always going to be missing some critical information about your application. For example, consider the following simplified code example of a client application making a web request via the instrumented `requests` HTTP library:

```
def do_something_important():
    # doing many important things

def client_request():
    do_something_important()
    requests.get("https://webserver")
```

If auto-instrumentation were exclusively used to instrument the previous example, telemetry would be generated for the call that was made via the library, but no information would be captured about what happened when the `do_something_important` function was called. This would likely be undesirable as it could leave many questions unanswered.

Another limitation of auto-instrumentation is that it may instrument things you're not interested in. This may result in the same network call being recorded multiple times, or generated data that you're not interested in using. An effort is being made in OpenTelemetry to support configuration to give users fine-grained control over how telemetry is generated via instrumentation libraries.

With this in mind, let's learn how auto-instrumentation is implemented in Java.

Bytecode manipulation

The Java implementation of auto-instrumentation for OpenTelemetry leverages the **Java Instrumentation API** to instrument code (https://docs.oracle.com/javase/8/docs/api/java/lang/instrument/Instrumentation.html). This API is defined as part of the Java language and can be used by anyone interested in collecting information about an application.

OpenTelemetry Java agent

The OpenTelemetry Java agent is distributed to users via a single **Java archive** (**JAR**) file, which can be downloaded from the `opentelemetry-java-instrumentation` repository (https://github.com/open-telemetry/opentelemetry-java-instrumentation/releases). The JAR contains the following components:

- The `javaagent` module. This is called by the Java Instrumentation API.
- Instrumenting libraries for various frameworks and third-party libraries.
- The tooling to initialize and configure the OpenTelemetry components. These will be used to produce telemetry and deliver it to its destination.

The JAR is invoked by passing it to the Java runtime via the `-javaagent` command-line option. The Java OpenTelemetry agent supports configuration via command-line arguments, also known in Java as **system properties**. The following command is an example of how the agent can be used in practice:

```
java -javaagent:/app/opentelemetry-javaagent.jar \
     -Dotel.resource.attributes=service.name=broken-telephone-java\
     -Dotel.traces.exporter=otlp \
     -jar broken-telephone.jar
```

Note that the preceding command is also how the demo application is launched inside the container. Using the Java agent to load the OpenTelemetry agent gives the library a chance to modify the bytecode before any other code is executed. The following diagram shows some of the components that are involved in the initialization process when the OpenTelemetry agent is used. `OpenTelemetryAgent` starts the process, while `OpenTelemetryInstaller` uses the configuration provided at invocation time to configure the emitters of telemetry. Meanwhile, `AgentInstaller` loads Byte Buddy, an open source library for modifying Java code at runtime, which is used to instrument the code via bytecode injection:

Bytecode manipulation 65

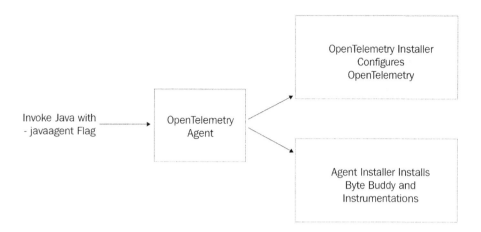

Figure 3.3 – OpenTelemetry Java agent loading order

`AgentInstaller` also loads all the third-party instrumentation libraries that are available in the OpenTelemetry agent.

> **Important Note**
> The mechanics of bytecode injection are outside the scope of this book. For the sake of this chapter, it's enough to know that the Java agent injects the instrumentation code at runtime. If you're interested in learning more, I recommend spending some time browsing the Byte Buddy site: https://bytebuddy.net/#/.

The following code shows the Java code that handles gRPC requests for the broken telephone server. The specifics of the code are not overly important here, but pay attention to any instrumentation code you can see:

BrokenTelephoneServer.java

```
    static class BrokenTelephoneImpl extends
BrokenTelephoneGrpc.BrokenTelephoneImplBase {

        @Override
        public void saySomething(Brokentelephone.
BrokenTelephoneRequest req,
                StreamObserver<Brokentelephone.
BrokenTelephoneResponse> responseObserver) {
            Brokentelephone.BrokenTelephoneResponse reply =
```

```
Brokentelephone.BrokenTelephoneResponse.newBuilder()
                .setMessage("Hello " + req.getMessage()).
build();
        responseObserver.onNext(reply);
        responseObserver.onCompleted();
    }
}
```

As you can see, there is no mention of OpenTelemetry anywhere in the code. The real magic happens when the agent is called at runtime and instruments the application via bytecode injection, as we'll see shortly. With this, we now have an idea of how auto-instrumentation works in Java. Now, let's compare this to the Python implementation.

Runtime hooks and monkey patching

In Python, unlike in Java, where a single archive contains everything that's needed to support auto-instrumentation, the implementation relies on several separate components that must be discussed to help us fully understand how auto-instrumentation works.

Instrumenting libraries

Instrumentation libraries in Python rely on one of two mechanisms to instrument third-party libraries:

- Event hooks are exposed by the libraries being instrumented, allowing the instrumenting libraries to register and produce telemetry as events occur.
- Any intercepting calls to libraries are instrumented and are replaced at runtime via a technique known as **monkey patching** (https://en.wikipedia.org/wiki/Monkey_patch). The instrumenting library receives the original call, produces telemetry data, and then calls the underlying library.

Monkey patching is like bytecode injection in that the applications make calls to libraries without suspecting that those calls have been replaced along the way. The following diagram shows how the `opentelemetry-instrumentation-redis` monkey patch calls `redis.Redis.execute_command` to produce telemetry data before calling the underlying library:

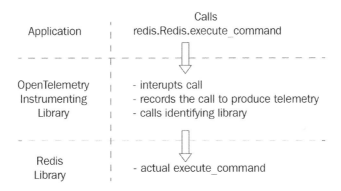

Figure 3.4 – Monkey-catched call to the Redis library

Each instrumentation library adheres to an interface to register and deregister itself. At the time of writing, in Python, unlike in Java, the different instrumentation libraries are packaged independently. This has the advantage of reducing the number of dependencies that are required to install the instrumentation libraries. However, it does have the disadvantage of requiring users to know what packages they will need to install. There are a few ways to work around this, which we'll explore in *Chapter 7*, *Instrumentation Libraries*.

The Instrumentor interface

To ensure a consistent experience for the users of instrumentation libraries, as well as ensuring the developers of those libraries know what needs to be implemented, the OpenTelemetry Python community has defined the `Instrumentor` (https://opentelemetry-python-contrib.readthedocs.io/en/latest/instrumentation/base/instrumentor.html) interface. This interface requires library authors to provide implementations for the following methods:

- `_instrument`: This method contains any initialization logic for the instrumenting library. This is where monkey patching or registering for event hooks takes place.

- `_uninstrument`: This method provides the logic to deregister the library from event hooks or remove any monkey patching. This may also contain any additional cleanup operations.

- `instrumentation_dependencies`: This method returns a list of the library and the versions that the instrumentation library supports.

In addition to fulfilling the Instrumentor interface, if an instrumentation library wishes to be available for auto-instrumentation, it must register itself via an entry point. An entry point is a Python mechanism that allows modules to make themselves discoverable by registering a class or method via a string at installation time.

> **Important Note**
> Additional information on entry points is available in the official Python documentation: `https://packaging.python.org/specifications/entry-points/`.

Other Python code can then load this code by doing a lookup for an entry point by name and executing it.

Wrapper script

For those mechanisms to be triggered, the Python implementation ships a script that can be called to wrap any Python application. The `opentelemetry-instrument` script finds all the instrumentations that have been installed in an environment by loading the entry points registered under the `opentelemetry_instrumentor` name.

The following diagram shows two different instrumentation library packages, `opentelemetry-instrumentation-foo` and `opentelemetry-instrumentation-bar`, registering a separate Python class in the `opentelemetry_instrumentor` entry point's catalog. This catalog is globally available within the Python environment and when `opentelemetry-instrument` is invoked, it searches that catalog and loads any instrumentation that's been registered by calling the `instrument` method:

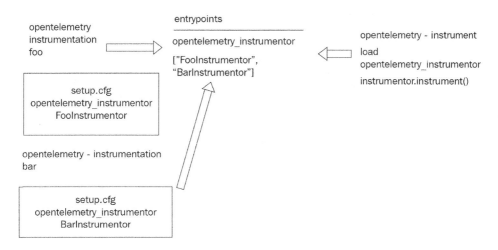

Figure 3.5 – Package registration

The `opentelemetry-instrument` script is made available via the `opentelemetry-instrumentation` Python package. The following code shows the gRPC server implemented in Python. As you can see, as with the previous example, it does not mention OpenTelemetry:

brokentelephone.py

```
#!/usr/bin/env python3

from concurrent import futures

import grpc
import brokentelephone_pb2
import brokentelephone_pb2_grpc

class Player(brokentelephone_pb2_grpc.BrokenTelephoneServicer):
    def SaySomething(self, request, context):
        return brokentelephone_pb2.BrokenTelephoneResponse(
            message="Hello, %s!" % request.message
        )

def serve():
    server = grpc.server(futures.ThreadPoolExecutor(max_workers=10))
```

```
    brokentelephone_pb2_grpc.add_BrokenTelephoneServicer_to_
server(Player(), server)
    server.add_insecure_port("[::]:50051")
    server.start()
    server.wait_for_termination()

if __name__ == "__main__":
    serve()
```

As we saw in the Java code example, the preceding code is strictly application code – there's no instrumentation in sight. The following command shows an example of how auto-instrumentation is invoked in Python:

```
opentelemetry-instrument ./broken_telephone.py
```

The following screenshot shows a trace that's been generated by our sample application. As we can see, the originating request was made by the brokentelephone-js service to Python, Go, and finally the Java application. The trace information was generated by the gRPC instrumentation library in each of those languages:

Figure 3.6 – Sample trace generated automatically across all broken telephone services

If you'd like to see a trace for yourself, the demo application should allow you to do so. Just browse to the Jaeger interface at `http://localhost:16686` and search for a trace, as we did in *Chapter 2, OpenTelemetry Signals – Traces, Metrics, and Logs*. The generated trace can give us a glimpse into the data flow through our entire sample application. Although the broken telephone is somewhat trivial, you can imagine how this information would be useful for mapping information across a distributed system. With very little effort, we're able to see where time is spent in our system.

Summary

With auto-instrumentation, it's possible to reduce the time that's required to instrument an existing application. Reducing the friction to get started with telemetry gives users a chance to try it before investing significant amounts of time in manual instrumentation. And although the data that's generated via auto-instrumentation is likely not enough to get to the bottom of issues in complex systems, it's a solid starting point. Auto-instrumentation can also be quite useful when you're instrumenting an unfamiliar system.

The use of instrumentation libraries allows users to gain insight into what the libraries they're using are doing, without having to learn the ins and outs of them. The OpenTelemetry libraries that are available at the time of writing can be used to instrument existing code by following the online documentation that's been made available by each language. As we'll learn in *Chapter 7, Instrumentation Libraries*, using these libraries can be tremendously useful in reducing the code that's needed to instrument applications.

In this chapter, we compared two different implementations of auto-instrumentation by looking at the Java implementation, which utilizes bytecode injection, and the Python implementation, which uses runtime hooks and monkey patching. In each case, the implementation leverages features of the language that allows the implementation to inject telemetry at appropriate times in the code's execution. Before diving into auto-instrumentation, however, it is useful to understand how each signal can be leveraged independently, starting with distributed tracing. We will do this in the next chapter.

Section 2: Instrumenting an Application

In this part, you will walk through instrumenting an application by using the signals offered by OpenTelemetry: distributed tracing, metrics, and logging.

This part of the book comprises the following chapters:

- *Chapter 4, Distributed Tracing – Tracing Code Execution*
- *Chapter 5, Metrics – Recording Measurements*
- *Chapter 6, Logging – Capturing Events*
- *Chapter 7, Instrumentation Libraries*

4
Distributed Tracing – Tracing Code Execution

So, now that we have an understanding of the concepts of OpenTelemetry and are familiar with the different signals it covers, it's time to start instrumenting application code. In *Chapter 2, OpenTelemetry Signals – Tracing, Metrics, and Logging*, we covered the terminology and concepts of those signals by looking at a system that was instrumented with OpenTelemetry. Now, it's time to get hands-on with some code to start generating telemetry ourselves, and to do this, we're going to first look at implementing a tracing signal.

In this chapter, we will cover the following topics:

- Configuring OpenTelemetry
- Generating tracing data
- Enriching the data with attributes, events, and links
- Adding error handling information

By the end of this chapter, you'll have instrumented several applications with OpenTelemetry and be able to trace how those applications are connected via distributed tracing. This will start giving you a sense of how distributed tracing can be used in your own applications going forward.

Technical requirements

At the time of writing, OpenTelemetry for Python supports Python 3.6+. All Python examples in this book will use Python 3.8, which can be downloaded and installed by following the instructions at https://docs.python.org/3/using/index.html. The following command can verify which version of Python is installed. It's possible for multiple versions to be installed simultaneously on a single system, which is why both python and python3 are shown here:

```
$ python --version
$ python3 --version
```

It is recommended to use a virtual environment to run the examples in this book (https://docs.python.org/3/library/venv.html). A virtual environment in Python allows you to install packages in isolation from the rest of the system, meaning that if anything goes wrong, you can always delete the virtual environment and start a fresh one. The following commands will create a new virtual environment in a folder called cloud_native_observability:

```
$ mkdir cloud_native_observability
$ python3 -m venv cloud_native_observability
$ source cloud_native_observability/bin/activate
```

The example code in this chapter will rely on a few different third-party libraries – Flask and Request. The following command will install all the required packages for this chapter using the package installation for Python, pip:

```
$ pip install flask requests
```

Now that we have a virtual environment configured and the libraries needed, we will install the necessary Python packages to use OpenTelemetry. The main libraries we'll need for this section are the API and SDK packages:

```
$ pip install opentelemetry-api opentelemetry-sdk
```

The `pip freeze` command lists all the installed packages in this Python environment; we can use it to confirm whether the correct packages are installed:

```
$ pip freeze | grep opentelemetry
opentelemetry-api==1.3.0
opentelemetry-sdk==1.3.0
opentelemetry-semantic-conventions==0.22b0
```

The version of the packages installed in your environment may differ, as the OpenTelemetry project is still very much under active development, and releases are pretty frequent. It's important to remember this as we work through the examples, as some methods may be slightly different, or the output may vary.

> **Important Note**
> The OpenTelemetry APIs should not change unless a major version is released.

Configuring the tracing pipeline

With the packages now installed, we're ready to take our first step to generate distributed traces with OpenTelemetry – configuring the tracing pipeline. The tracing pipeline is what allows the tracing data we explored in *Chapter 2, OpenTelemetry Signals – Traces, Metrics, and Logs*, to be generated when the OpenTelemetry API calls are made. The pipeline also defines where and how the data will be emitted. Without a tracing pipeline, a no-op implementation is used by the API, meaning the code will not generate distributed traces. The tracing pipeline configures the following:

- `TracerProvider` to determine how spans should be generated
- A `Resource` object, which identifies the source of the spans
- `SpanProcessor` to describe how spans will be exported
- `SpanExporter` to describe where the spans will be exported

The following code imports the `TracerProvider`, `ConsoleSpanExporter`, and `SimpleSpanProcessor` classes from the SDK to configure a tracer provider. In this example, `ConsoleSpanExporter` will be used to output traces from the application to the console. The last step to configure the tracer provider is to call the `set_tracer_provider` method, which will set the global tracer provider to the provider we instantiated. The code will be placed in the `configure_tracer` method, which will be called before we do anything else in the code:

shopper.py

```
#!/usr/bin/env python3
from opentelemetry import trace
from opentelemetry.sdk.trace import TracerProvider
from opentelemetry.sdk.trace.export import import ConsoleSpanExporter, SimpleSpanProcessor


def configure_tracer():
    exporter = ConsoleSpanExporter()
    span_processor = SimpleSpanProcessor(exporter)
    provider = TracerProvider()
    provider.add_span_processor(span_processor)
    trace.set_tracer_provider(provider)


if __name__ == "__main__":
    configure_tracer()
```

Throughout this chapter, as we iterate over the application and add more code, each time we do so, we will test the code and inspect its output using the following command, unless specified otherwise:

```
$ python ./shopper.py
```

Running this command for the initial code will not output anything. This allows us to confirm that the modules have been found and imported correctly, and that the code doesn't have any errors in it.

> **Important Note**
> A common mistake when first configuring `TracerProvider` is to forget to set the global `TracerProvider`, causing the API to use a default no-op implementation of `TracerProvider`. This default is configured intentionally for the use case where a user does not wish to enable tracing within their application.

Although it may not seem like much, configuring `TracerProvider` for an application is a critical first step before we can start collecting distributed traces. It's a bit like gathering all the ingredients before baking a cake, so let's get baking!

Getting a tracer

With the tracing pipeline configured, we can now obtain the generator for our tracing data, `Tracer`. The `TracerProvider` interface defines a single method to allow us to obtain a tracer, `get_tracer`. This method requires a name argument and, optionally, a version argument, which should reflect the name and version of the instrumenting module. This information is valuable for users to quickly identify what the source of the tracing data is. An example shown in *Figure 4.1* shows how the values passed into `get_tracer` will vary, depending on where the call is made. Inside the library calls to requests and Flask, the name and version will reflect those libraries, whereas in the `shopper` and `grocery_store` modules, the name and version will reflect those modules.

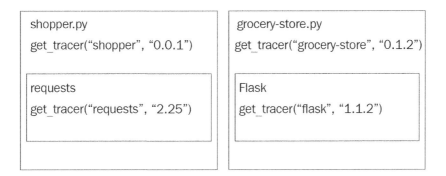

Figure 4.1 – The tracer name and version configuration at different stages of an application

To get the first tracer, the following code will be added to `shopper.py` immediately at the end of `configure_tracer` to return a tracer from the method:

shopper.py

```python
def configure_tracer():
    exporter = ConsoleSpanExporter()
    span_processor = SimpleSpanProcessor(exporter)
    provider = TracerProvider()
    provider.add_span_processor(span_processor)
    trace.set_tracer_provider(provider)
    return trace.get_tracer("shopper.py", "0.0.1")

if __name__ == "__main__":
    tracer = configure_tracer()
```

It's important to remember to make the name and version meaningful; the name should be unique within the scope of the application it instruments. The instrumentation scope could be a package, module, or even a class. It's finally time to start using this tracer and trace the application! There are several ways to create a span in OpenTelemetry; let's explore them now.

Generating tracing data

It's finally time to start generating telemetry from the application! There are several ways to create a span in OpenTelemetry; the first one we'll use is to call `start_span` on the `tracer` instance we obtained previously. This will create a `span` object, using the only required string argument as the name of the span. The `span` object is the building block of distributed tracing and is intended to represent a unique unit of work in our application. In the following example, we will create a new Span object before calling a method that will do some work. Since our application is a *shopper*, the first thing the shopper will do is browse the store. In order for the tracing data to be useful, it's important to use a meaningful name in the creation of the span. Once `browse` has returned, we will call `end` on the `span` object to signal that the work is complete:

shopper.py

```python
def browse():
    print("visiting the grocery store")
```

```
if __name__ == "__main__":
    tracer = configure_tracer()
    span = tracer.start_span("visit store")
    browse()
    span.end()
```

Running the code will output our first trace to the console. The `ConsoleSpanExporter` automatically outputs the data as formatted JSON to make it easier to read:

shopper.py output

```
visiting the grocery store
{
    "name": "visit store",
    "context": {
        "trace_id": "0x4c6fd97f286439b1a4bb109f12bf2095",
        "span_id": "0x6ea2219c865f6c4b",
        "trace_state": "[]"
    },
    "kind": "SpanKind.INTERNAL",
    "parent_id": null,
    "start_time": "2021-06-26T20:26:47.176169Z",
    "end_time": "2021-06-26T20:26:47.176194Z",
    "status": {
        "status_code": "UNSET"
    },
    "attributes": {},
    "events": [],
    "links": [],
    "resource": {
        "telemetry.sdk.language": "python",
        "telemetry.sdk.name": "opentelemetry",
        "telemetry.sdk.version": "1.3.0",
        "service.name": "unknown_service"
    }
}
```

Some of the data worth noting in the preceding output is as follows:

- The `name` field of the span we provided.
- The automatically generated trace and span identifiers – `trace_id` and `span_id`.
- The `start_time` and `end_time` timestamps, which can be used to calculate the duration of an operation being traced.
- The `parent_id` identifier is not set. This identifies the span created as the beginning of a trace, otherwise known as `root span`.
- The `status_code` field of the span is set to `UNSET` by default.

With the preceding span information from the JSON output, we now have the first piece of data about the work that our application is doing. One of the most critical pieces of information generated in this data is `trace_id`. This trace identifier is a 128-bit integer that allows operations to be tied together in a distributed trace and represents the single request through the entire system. `span_id` is a 64-bit integer used to identify the specific unit of work in the request and also relationships between different operations. In this next code example, we'll add another operation to our trace to see how this identifier works, but we'll need to take a brief detour to look at the Context API before continuing too far.

> **Important Note**
> The examples in this chapter will only use `ConsoleSpanExporter`.
> We will explore additional exporters in *Chapter 8, The OpenTelemetry Collector*, and *Chapter 10, Configuring a Backend*, when we look at the OpenTelemetry Collector and different backends.

The Context API

In order to tie spans together, we'll need to activate our spans before starting new ones. Activating a span in OpenTelemetry is synonymous with setting the span in the current context object. The `Context` object is a mechanism used across signals to share data about the application either in-process or across API boundaries via propagation. No matter where you are in the application code, it's possible to get the current span by using the `Context` API. The `Context` object can be thought of as an immutable data store with a consistent API across implementations. In Python, the implementation relies on `ContextVars`, as previously discussed in *Chapter 1, The History and Concepts of Observability*, but not all languages have the notion of a context built into the language itself. The Context API ensures that users will have a consistent experience when using OpenTelemetry. The API definition for interacting with the context is fairly minimal:

- `get_value`: Retrieves a value for a given key from the context. The only required argument is a key and, optionally, a `context` argument. If no context is passed in, the value returned will be pulled from the global context.
- `set_value`: Stores a value for a certain key in the context. The method receives a key, value, and optionally, a context argument to set the value into. As mentioned before, the context is immutable, so the return value is a new `Context` object with the new value set.
- `attach`: Calling `attach` associates the current execution with a specified context. In other words, it sets the current context to the context passed in as an argument. The return value is a unique token, which is used by the `detach` method described next.
- `detach`: To return the context to its previous state, this method receives a token that was obtained by attaching to another context. Upon calling it, the context that was current at the time `attach` was called is restored.

Don't worry if the description doesn't quite make sense yet; the next example will help clarify things. In the following code, we activate the span by setting it in the context via the `set_span_in_context` method, which, under the hood, calls the current context's `set_value` method. The return value of this call is a new immutable `context` object, which we can then attach to before starting the second span:

shopper.py

```python
from opentelemetry import context, trace
if __name__ == "__main__":
    tracer = configure_tracer()
    span = tracer.start_span("visit store")
    ctx = trace.set_span_in_context(span)
    token = context.attach(ctx)
    span2 = tracer.start_span("browse")
    browse()
    span2.end()
    context.detach(token)
    span.end()
```

Running the application and looking at the output once again, we can now see that the `trace_id` value for both spans is the same. We can also see that the `browse` span has a `parent_id` field that matches `span_id` of the `visit store` span:

shopper.py output

```
visiting the grocery store
{
    "name": "browse",
    "context": {
        "trace_id": "0x03c197ae7424cc492ab1c92112490be1",
        "span_id": "0xb7396b0e6ccab2fd",
        "trace_state": "[]"
    },
    "kind": "SpanKind.INTERNAL",
    "parent_id": "0x8dd8c60c67518a8d",
}
{
    "name": "visit store",
    "context": {
        "trace_id": "0x03c197ae7424cc492ab1c92112490be1",
        "span_id": "0x8dd8c60c67518a8d",
        "trace_state": "[]"
    },
    "kind": "SpanKind.INTERNAL",
    "parent_id": null,
}
```

Starting and ending spans manually can be useful in many cases, but as demonstrated by the previous code, managing the context manually can be somewhat cumbersome. More often than not, it is easier in Python to use a context manager to wrap the work we want to trace. The `start_as_current_span` convenience method allows us to do exactly this by creating a new Span object, setting it as the current span in a context, and calling the `attach` method. Additionally, it will automatically end the span once the context has been exited. The following code shows us how we can simplify the previous code we wrote:

shopper.py

```python
if __name__ == "__main__":
    tracer = configure_tracer()
    with tracer.start_as_current_span("visit store"):
        with tracer.start_as_current_span("browse"):
            browse()
```

This method simplifies the code quite a bit. The automatic management of the context can be used to quickly create hierarchies of spans. In the following code, we will add one new method and one more span. We'll then run the code to observe how each span will use the previous span in the context as the new span's parent:

shopper.py

```python
def add_item_to_cart(item):
    print("add {} to cart".format(item))


if __name__ == "__main__":
    tracer = configure_tracer()
    with tracer.start_as_current_span("visit store"):
        with tracer.start_as_current_span("browse"):
            browse()
            with tracer.start_as_current_span("add item to cart"):
                add_item_to_cart("orange")
```

Running the shopper application, we're starting to see what is appearing to be more and more like a real trace. Looking at the output from the new code, we can see three different operations captured. The order in which output appears in your terminal may vary; we will review operations in the same order in which they appear in the code. The first operation to look at is `visit store`, as mentioned previously; the root span can be identified by the `parent_id` field being `null`:

shopper.py output

```
{
    "name": "visit store",
    "context": {
        "trace_id": "0x9251fa73b421a143a7654afb048a4fc7",
        "span_id": "0x08c9bf4cccd7ba5d",
        "trace_state": "[]"
    },
    "kind": "SpanKind.INTERNAL",
    "parent_id": null,
    "start_time": "2021-06-26T21:43:20.441933Z",
    "end_time": "2021-06-26T21:43:20.442222Z",
    "status": {
        "status_code": "UNSET"
    },
    "attributes": {},
    "events": [],
    "links": [],
    "resource": {
        "telemetry.sdk.language": "python",
        "telemetry.sdk.name": "opentelemetry",
        "telemetry.sdk.version": "1.3.0",
        "service.name": "unknown_service"
    }
}
```

The next operation to review in the output is the browse span. Note that the span's parent_id identifier is equal to the span_id identifier of the visit store span. trace_id also matches, which indicates that the spans are connected in the same trace:

shopper.py output

```
{
    "name": "browse",
    "context": {
        "trace_id": "0x9251fa73b421a143a7654afb048a4fc7",
        "span_id": "0xa77587668be46030",
        "trace_state": "[]"
    },
    "kind": "SpanKind.INTERNAL",
    "parent_id": "0x08c9bf4cccd7ba5d",
    "start_time": "2021-06-26T21:43:20.442091Z",
    "end_time": "2021-06-26T21:43:20.442212Z",
    "status": {
        "status_code": "UNSET"
    },
    "attributes": {},
    "events": [],
    "links": [],
    "resource": {
        "telemetry.sdk.language": "python",
        "telemetry.sdk.name": "opentelemetry",
        "telemetry.sdk.version": "1.3.0",
        "service.name": "unknown_service"
    }
}
```

The last span to review is the add item to cart span. As with the previous span, its trace_id identifier will also match the previous spans. In this case, the parent_id identifier of the add item to cart span now matches the span_id identifier of the browse span:

shopper.py output

```
{
    "name": "add item to cart",
    "context": {
        "trace_id": "0x9251fa73b421a143a7654afb048a4fc7",
        "span_id": "0x6470521265d80512",
        "trace_state": "[]"
    },
    "kind": "SpanKind.INTERNAL",
    "parent_id": "0xa77587668be46030",
    "start_time": "2021-06-26T21:43:20.442169Z",
    "end_time": "2021-06-26T21:43:20.442191Z",
    "status": {
        "status_code": "UNSET"
    },
    "attributes": {},
    "events": [],
    "links": [],
    "resource": {
        "telemetry.sdk.language": "python",
        "telemetry.sdk.name": "opentelemetry",
        "telemetry.sdk.version": "1.3.0",
        "service.name": "unknown_service"
    }
}
```

Not too bad – the code looks much simpler than the previous example, and we can already see how easy it is to trace code in applications. The last method we can use to start a span is by using a **decorator**. A decorator is a convenient way to instrument code without having to add any tracing specific information to the code itself. This makes the code a bit cleaner.

> **Important Note**
> Using the decorator means you will need to keep an instance of a tracer initialized and available globally for the decorators to be able to use it.

Refactoring the shopper.py code, we will move the instantiation of the tracer out of the main method and add decorators to each of the methods we've defined previously. Note that the code in main is simplified significantly:

shopper.py

```python
tracer = configure_tracer()

@tracer.start_as_current_span("browse")
def browse():
    print("visiting the grocery store")
    add_item_to_cart("orange")

@tracer.start_as_current_span("add item to cart")
def add_item_to_cart(item):
    print("add {} to cart".format(item))

@tracer.start_as_current_span("visit store")
def visit_store():
    browse()

if __name__ == "__main__":
    visit_store()
```

Run the program once again; the spans will be printed as they were before. The output will not have changed with this refactor, but the code looks much cleaner. As with the previous example, context management is handled for us, so we don't need to worry about interacting with the Context API. Reading the code is much simpler with decorators, and it's also easy for someone new to the code to implement new methods with the same pattern when adding code to the application.

Span processors

A quick note about the span processor used in the code so far – the initial configuration of the tracing pipeline used `SimpleSpanProcessor`. This does all of its processing in line with the export happening as soon as the span ends. This means that every span added to the code will add latency in the application, which is generally not what we want. This may be the right choice in some cases – for example, if it's impossible to guarantee that threads other than the main thread will finish before a program is interrupted. However, it's generally recommended that span processing happens out of band from the main thread. An alternative to `SimpleSpanProcessor` is `BatchSpanProcessor`. *Figure 4.2* shows how the execution of the program is interrupted by `SimpleSpanProcessor` to export a span, whereas with `BatchSpanProcessor`, another thread handles the export operation:

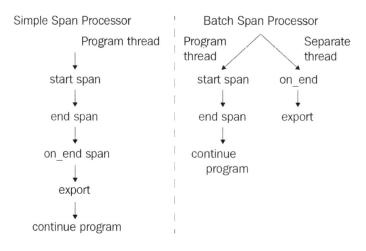

Figure 4.2 – SimpleSpanProcessor versus BatchSpanProcessor

As the name suggests, `BatchSpanProcessor` groups the export of spans. It does this by launching a separate thread that exports spans on a schedule or when there's a certain number of items in the queue. This prevents adding unnecessary latency to the normal application code paths. Configuring `BatchSpanProcessor` is done much like `SimpleSpanProcessor`. For the remainder of the examples in this chapter, we will use this new processor. The following refactor updates the imports and code in the tracer configuration to use `BatchSpanProcessor`:

shopper.py

```python
from opentelemetry.sdk.trace.export import BatchSpanProcessor, ConsoleSpanExporter


def configure_tracer():
    exporter = ConsoleSpanExporter()
    span_processor = BatchSpanProcessor(exporter)
    provider = TracerProvider()
    provider.add_span_processor(span_processor)
    trace.set_tracer_provider(provider)
    return trace.get_tracer("shopper.py", "0.0.1")
```

Run the application now to confirm that the program still works and that the output is the same with the new span processor in place. Although it may not look like much has changed, if you look closely at the `start_time` and `end_time` fields of each span produced, the duration of each span has changed. *Figure 4.3* shows a chart comparing output from running the program with each type of span processor. The duration of the `visit store` span is significantly shorter using `BatchSpanProcessor` because the processing of each span is happening asynchronously:

	start_time	end_time	duration
SimpleSpanProcessor			
visit store	2021-07-02T16:57:56.075531Z	2021-07-02T16:57:56.076188Z	657μs
browse	2021-07-02T16:57:56.075598Z	2021-07-02T16:57:56.076079Z	481μs
add item to cart	2021-07-02T16:57:56.075644Z	2021-07-02T16:57:56.075663Z	19μs
BatchSpanProcessor			
visit store	2021-07-02T17:12:41.748660Z	2021-07-02T17:12:41.748892Z	232μs
browse	2021-07-02T17:12:41.748734Z	2021-07-02T17:12:41.748879Z	145μs
add item to cart	2021-07-02T17:12:41.748828Z	2021-07-02T17:12:41.748855Z	27μs

Figure 4.3 – Span durations using SimpleSpanProcessor and BatchSpanProcessor

Even though microseconds may not seem like much in our example, this type of performance impact is critical to systems in production. `BatchSpanProcessor` is a much better choice for running real-world applications. Now, we have a better sense of how to generate tracing data via the API, but the data we've produced so far could be improved. It doesn't have nearly enough details to make it truly useful, so let's tackle that next.

Enriching the data

You may have noticed in output from the previous examples that each span emitted contains a `resource` attribute. The `resource` attribute provides an immutable set of attributes, representing the entity producing the telemetry. `resource` attributes are not specific to tracing. Any signal that emits telemetry leverages resource attributes by adding them to the data produced at export time. As covered in *Chapter 1*, *The History and Concepts of Observability*, the resource in an application is associated with the telemetry generator, which, in the case of tracing, is `TracerProvider`. The resource attribute on the span output we've seen so far is automatically provided by the SDK with some information about the SDK itself, as well as a default `service.name`. The service name is used by many backends to identify the services sending traces to them; however, as you can see, the default value of `unknown_service` is not a super useful name. Let's fix this. The following code will create a new `Resource` object with a service name and version number, and then pass it in as an argument to the `TracerProvider` constructor:

shopper.py

```python
from opentelemetry.sdk.resources import Resource
from opentelemetry.sdk.trace import TracerProvider
from opentelemetry.sdk.trace.export import BatchSpanProcessor, ConsoleSpanExporter

def configure_tracer():
    exporter = ConsoleSpanExporter()
    span_processor = BatchSpanProcessor(exporter)
    resource = Resource.create(
        {
            "service.name": "shopper",
            "service.version": "0.1.2",
        }
    )
    provider = TracerProvider(resource=resource)
```

```
    provider.add_span_processor(span_processor)
    trace.set_tracer_provider(provider)
    return trace.get_tracer("shopper.py", "0.0.1")
```

The output from the application will now include the information added in the resource attribute along with the automatically populated data, as shown here:

```
"resource": {
    "telemetry.sdk.language": "python",
    "telemetry.sdk.name": "opentelemetry",
    "telemetry.sdk.version": "1.3.0",
    "service.name": "shopper",
    "service.version": "0.1.2"
}
```

This is much more useful than `unknown_service`; however, we now have the name and version hardcoded in two places. Even worse, the names and versions don't match. Let's fix this before going further by refactoring the `configure_tracer` method to expect the `name` and `version` arguments, as follows:

shopper.py

```
def configure_tracer(name, version):
    exporter = ConsoleSpanExporter()
    span_processor = BatchSpanProcessor(exporter)
    resource = Resource.create(
        {
            "service.name": name,
            "service.version": version,
        }
    )
    provider = TracerProvider(resource=resource)
    provider.add_span_processor(span_processor)
    trace.set_tracer_provider(provider)
    return trace.get_tracer(name, version)
tracer = configure_tracer("shopper", "0.1.2")
```

After running the application, the output should remain the same as it was before the change. The code is now less error-prone, as we only have one place to set the service name and version information, and `configure_tracer` can be reused to configure OpenTelemetry for different applications, which will come in handy shortly.

Some additional information you may want to populate in the resource includes things such as the hostname or, in the case of a dynamic runtime environment, an instance identifier of some sort. The OpenTelemetry SDK provides an interface to provide some of the details about a resource automatically; this is known as the `ResourceDetector` interface.

ResourceDetector

As its name suggests, the purpose of the `ResourceDetector` attribute is to detect information that will automatically be populated into a resource. A resource detector is a great way to extract information about a platform running an application, and there are already existing detectors for some popular cloud providers. This information can be a useful way to group applications by region or host when trying to pinpoint application performance issues. The interface for `ResourceDetector` specifies a single method to implement, `detect`, which returns a resource. Let's implement a `ResourceDetector` interface that we can reuse in all the services of the grocery store. This detector will automatically fill in the hostname and IP address of the machine running the code; to accomplish this, Python's `socket` library will come in handy. Place the following code in a new file in the same directory as `shopper.py`:

local_machine_resource_detector.py

```python
import socket
from opentelemetry.sdk.resources import Resource, ResourceDetector


class LocalMachineResourceDetector(ResourceDetector):
    def detect(self):
        hostname = socket.gethostname()
        ip_address = socket.gethostbyname(hostname)
        return Resource.create(
            {
                "net.host.name": hostname,
                "net.host.ip": ip_address,
            }
        )
```

To make use of this new module, let's import it into the shopper application. The code in `configure_tracer` will also be updated to call this new `ResourceDetector` first, before adding the service name and version information. As mentioned earlier, a resource is immutable, meaning that there's no method to call to update a specific resource. Adding new attributes to the resource generated by our resource detector is done via a call to a resource's `merge` method. `merge` creates a new resource from the caller's attributes and then updates that new resource to include all the attributes of the resource passed in as an argument. The following update to the code imports the module we just created, and creates a new resource by calling `LocalMachineResourceDetector` and calls `merge` to ensure that our previous resource information is not lost:

shopper.py

```python
from opentelemetry.sdk.resources import Resource
from opentelemetry.sdk.trace import TracerProvider
from opentelemetry.sdk.trace.export import ConsoleSpanExporter, SimpleSpanProcessor
from local_machine_resource_detector import LocalMachineResourceDetector
def configure_tracer(name, version):
    exporter = ConsoleSpanExporter()
    span_processor = SimpleSpanProcessor(exporter)
    local_resource = LocalMachineResourceDetector().detect()
    resource = local_resource.merge(
        Resource.create(
            {
                "service.name": name,
                "service.version": version,
            }
        )
    )
    provider = TracerProvider(resource=resource)
    return trace.get_tracer(name, version)
```

The output from running the code will now contain all the resources seen in the previous example, but it will also include the information generated by `LocalMachineResourceDetector`:

```
"resource": {
    "telemetry.sdk.language": "python",
    "telemetry.sdk.name": "opentelemetry",
    "telemetry.sdk.version": "1.3.0",
    "net.host.name": "myhost.local",
    "net.host.ip": "192.168.128.47",
    "service.name": "shopper",
    "service.version": "0.1.2"
}
```

> **Important Note**
>
> If the same resource attribute is included in both the caller and the resource passed into `merge`, the attributes of the argument resource will override the caller. For example, if `resource_one` has an attribute of `foo=one` and `resource_two` has an attribute of `foo=two`, the resulting resource from calling `resource_one.merge(resource_two)` will have an attribute of `foo=two`.

Feel free to play around with `ResourceDetector` and see what other useful information you can add about your machine. Try adding some environment variables or the version of Python running on your system; this can be valuable when troubleshooting applications!

Span attributes

Looking through the tracing data being emitted, we can start to get an idea of what is happening in the code we're writing. Now, let's figure out what data we should add about our shopper to make this trace even more useful. As the shopper application will be used as an HTTP client, we can take a look at the semantic conventions available in the specification to inspire us; *Figure 4.4* (https://github.com/open-telemetry/opentelemetry-specification/blob/main/specification/trace/semantic_conventions/http.md#http-client-server-example) shows us the `span` attributes to add if we want to adhere to OpenTelemetry's semantic conventions, as well as some sample values:

Attribute name	Value
http.method	"GET"
http.flavor	"1.1"
http.url	"https://example.com:8080/webshop/articles/4?s=1"
net.peer.ip	"192.0.2.5"
http.status_code	200

Figure 4.4 – The HTTP client span attributes semantic conventions

A valid attribute must be either a string, a 64-bit integer, a float, or a Boolean. An attribute can also be an array of any of those values, but it must be a homogenous array, meaning the elements of the array must be a single type.

> **Important Note**
> `Null` or `None` values are not encouraged in attributes, as the handling of null values in backends may differ and thus create unexpected behavior.

In the next example, we will update the `browse` method to include the recommended attributes for a client application. Since we're using decorators here, we'll need to get the current span by calling the `get_current_span` method. Once we have the span, we can call the `set_attribute` method, which requires two arguments – the key to set and the value. Since we have not yet started the server, we'll set a placeholder value for `http.url` and `net.peer.ip`:

shopper.py

```
@tracer.start_as_current_span("browse")
def browse():
    print("visiting the grocery store")
    span = trace.get_current_span()
    span.set_attribute("http.method", "GET")
    span.set_attribute("http.flavor", "1.1")
    span.set_attribute("http.url", "http://localhost:5000")
    span.set_attribute("net.peer.ip", "127.0.0.1")
```

Looking at the output from running the program, we will expect to see the attributes added to the browse span; let's take a look:

```
"name": "browse",
"attributes": {
    "http.method": "GET",
    "http.flavor": "1.1",
    "http.url": "http://localhost:5000",
    "net.peer.ip": "127.0.0.1"
},
```

Excellent! The data is there. It's a bit inconvenient to make independent calls to a method when wanting to set multiple attributes; thankfully, there's a convenient method to address this. The code can be simplified by making a single call to set_attributes and passing in a dictionary with the same values:

shopper.py

```
span.set_attributes(
    {
        "http.method": "GET",
        "http.flavor": "1.1",
        "http.url": "http://localhost:5000",
        "net.peer.ip": "127.0.0.1",
    }
)
```

Setting so many attributes, it can be easy for a typo to sneak in. This would, at best, be caught during a review but, at worst, could mean missing some critical data. Imagine a scenario where some alerting is configured to rely on the url and flavor attributes, but somewhere along the way, *flavor* is spelled as *flavour*. The correctness of the tracing data is critical, and to make setting these attributes more easy, a semantic conventions package provides constants that can be used instead of hardcoding common keys and values. The following is a refactor of the code to make use of the opentelemetry-semantic-conventions package:

shopper.py

```
from opentelemetry.semconv.trace import HttpFlavorValues, SpanAttributes
```

```python
@tracer.start_as_current_span("browse")
def browse():
    print("visiting the grocery store")
    span = trace.get_current_span()
    span.set_attributes(
        {
            SpanAttributes.HTTP_METHOD: "GET",
            SpanAttributes.HTTP_FLAVOR: HttpFlavorValues.HTTP_1_1.value,
            SpanAttributes.HTTP_URL: "http://localhost:5000",
            SpanAttributes.NET_PEER_IP: "127.0.0.1",
        }
    )
```

Of course, using semantic conventions alone may not give us enough information about the specifics of the application. One of the powers of attributes is to add meaningful data about the transaction being traced to allow us to understand what happened. One aspect of the shopper application that will likely be unique once we start processing real data is information about the items and quantities added to the cart. The following code adds attributes to the span to record that information:

shopper.py

```python
@tracer.start_as_current_span("browse")
def browse():
    print("visiting the grocery store")
    span = trace.get_current_span()
    span.set_attributes(
        {
            SpanAttributes.HTTP_METHOD: "GET",
            SpanAttributes.HTTP_FLAVOR: str(HttpFlavorValues.HTTP_1_1),
            SpanAttributes.HTTP_URL: "http://localhost:5000",
            SpanAttributes.NET_PEER_IP: "127.0.0.1",
        }
    )
    add_item_to_cart("orange", 5)
```

```python
@tracer.start_as_current_span("add item to cart")
def add_item_to_cart(item, quantity):
    span = trace.get_current_span()
    span.set_attributes({
        "item": item,
        "quantity": quantity,
    })
    print("add {} to cart".format(item))
```

The topic of span attributes will be revisited when we introduce the server later in this chapter. Attributes are also a key component of other signals, so we'll come back to them throughout the book. One last thing to be aware of when thinking of attributes, and really any data being recorded in traces, is to be cognizant of **Personally Identifiable Information (PII)**. Whenever possible, save yourself the trouble and remove all PII from the telemetry. We'll cover more on this topic in *Chapter 8, OpenTelemetry Collector*.

SpanKind

Another piece of information that is useful about a span is SpanKind. SpanKind is a qualifier that categorizes the span and provides additional information about the relationship between spans in a trace. The following categories for span kinds are defined in OpenTelemetry:

- INTERNAL: This indicates that the span represents an operation that is internal to an application, meaning that this specific operation has no external dependencies or relationships. This is the default value for a span when not set.

- CLIENT: This identifies the span as an operation making a request to a remote service, which should be identified as a *server* span. The request made by this operation is synchronous, and the client should wait for a response from the server.

- SERVER: This indicates that the span is an operation responding to a synchronous request from a *client* span. In a client/server, the *client* is identified as the parent span to the *server*, as it is the originator of the request.

- PRODUCER: This identifies the operation as an originator of an asynchronous request. Unlike in the case of the *client* span, the *producer* is not expecting a response from the *consumer* of the asynchronous request.

- CONSUMER: This identifies the operation as a *consumer* of an asynchronous request from a *producer*.

As you may have noticed so far, all the spans that we've created have been identified as *internal*. The following information can be found throughout the output we've generated until now:

```
"kind": "SpanKind.INTERNAL"
```

Now is a good time to start making the shopper application a bit more realistic by adding some calls to a grocery store server. Knowing that this will be a client using HTTP requests to retrieve data from the server, we will set SpanKind to CLIENT on the operation that makes a call to the server. On the receiving side, we will set SpanKind on the operation that is responding to the request to SERVER. The way to set kind is by passing the kind argument when creating the span. The following code adds a web request from the client to the server in the browse method. The HTTP request will be facilitated by using the requests (https://docs.python-requests.org/) library. The request to the server will be wrapped by a context manager, which starts a new span named web request with the kind set to CLIENT:

shopper.py

```python
import requests
from common import configure_tracer


@tracer.start_as_current_span("browse")
def browse():
    print("visiting the grocery store")
    with tracer.start_as_current_span(
        "web request", kind=trace.SpanKind.CLIENT
    ) as span:
        url = "http://localhost:5000"
        span.set_attributes(
            {
                SpanAttributes.HTTP_METHOD: "GET",
                SpanAttributes.HTTP_FLAVOR: str(HttpFlavorValues.HTTP_1_1),
                SpanAttributes.HTTP_URL: url,
                SpanAttributes.NET_PEER_IP: "127.0.0.1",
            }
```

```
            )
            resp = requests.get(url)
            span.set_attribute(SpanAttributes.HTTP_STATUS_CODE,
 resp.status_code)
```

So far, all the code written was done on the client side; let's talk about the server side. Before starting on the server, in order to reduce the duplication of code, `configure_tracer` has been moved into a separate `common.py` module and placed in the same directory as the rest of the code. In this refactor, we've also updated the previously hardcoded `service.name` and `service.version` attribute keys to use values from the semantic conventions package:

common.py

```
from opentelemetry import trace
from opentelemetry.sdk.resources import Resource
from opentelemetry.sdk.trace import TracerProvider
from opentelemetry.sdk.trace.export import import BatchSpanProcessor, ConsoleSpanExporter
from opentelemetry.semconv.resource import ResourceAttributes
from local_machine_resource_detector import LocalMachineResourceDetector

def configure_tracer(name, version):
    exporter = ConsoleSpanExporter()
    span_processor = BatchSpanProcessor(exporter)
    local_resource = LocalMachineResourceDetector().detect()
    resource = local_resource.merge(
        Resource.create(
            {
                ResourceAttributes.SERVICE_NAME: name,
                ResourceAttributes.SERVICE_VERSION: version,
            }
        )
    )
    provider = TracerProvider(resource=resource)
```

```
        provider.add_span_processor(span_processor)
        trace.set_tracer_provider(provider)
        return trace.get_tracer(name, version)
```

This code can now be used in both `shopper.py` and the new server code in `grocery_store.py` to instantiate a tracer. The server code uses Flask (https://flask.palletsprojects.com/en/1.1.x/) to provide an API, and the initial code for the application will implement a single route handler. We won't dive too deeply into the nuts and bolts of how Flask works in this book. For the purpose of our application, it's enough to know that the response handler can be configured with a path via the route decorator and that the `run` method launches a web server. An additional decorator to create a span on the handler sets the kind to SERVER, as it is the operation that is responding to the CLIENT span instrumented previously. Note that in the code, there are also several attributes being set following the semantic conventions; the Flask library conveniently makes most of the information available quite easily:

grocery_store.py

```
from flask import Flask, request
from opentelemetry import trace
from opentelemetry.semconv.trace import HttpFlavorValues, SpanAttributes
from opentelemetry.trace import SpanKind
from common import configure_tracer

tracer = configure_tracer("0.1.2", "grocery-store")
app = Flask(__name__)

@app.route("/")
@tracer.start_as_current_span("welcome", kind=SpanKind.SERVER)
def welcome():
    span = trace.get_current_span()
    span.set_attributes(
        {
            SpanAttributes.HTTP_FLAVOR: request.environ.get("SERVER_PROTOCOL"),
            SpanAttributes.HTTP_METHOD: request.method,
            SpanAttributes.HTTP_USER_AGENT: str(request.user_agent),
```

```
                SpanAttributes.HTTP_HOST: request.host,
                SpanAttributes.HTTP_SCHEME: request.scheme,
                SpanAttributes.HTTP_TARGET: request.path,
                SpanAttributes.HTTP_CLIENT_IP: request.remote_addr,
            }
        )
    return "Welcome to the grocery store!"

if __name__ == "__main__":
    app.run()
```

Of course, to see the traces we must first run the application; to get the server running, use the following command:

```
python grocery_store.py
```

If another application is already running on the default port that Flask uses, `5000`, you may encounter the `Address already in use` error. Ensure only one instance of the server is running at any given time.

> **Important Note**
>
> It's possible to run the server with `debug` mode enabled to have it automatically updated every time the code changes. This is convenient when doing rapid development but should never be left enabled outside of development. Debug mode also causes problems with auto-instrumentation, as we discussed in *Chapter 3, Auto-Instrumentation*. Enabling debug mode is accomplished by calling the `run` method as follows: `run(debug=True)`.

In any future examples, the server will always need to be run before the shopper; otherwise, the client application will throw HTTP connection exceptions. I find it particularly helpful to use a terminal that supports split screens to have both the client and the server running side by side. Let's run both applications now and inspect the output data emitted. The server operation named / will be identified as a SERVER span:

grocery_store.py output

```
{
    "name": "/",
    "context": {
        "trace_id": "0xe7f562a98f81a36ba81aaf1e239dd718",
        "span_id": "0x51daed87f12f5bc0",
        "trace_state": "[]"
    },
    "kind": "SpanKind.SERVER",
    "parent_id": null,
}
```

On the client side, the operation named `web request` will be identified as a CLIENT span:

shopper.py output

```
{
    "name": "web request",
    "context": {
        "trace_id": "0xc2747c6a8c7f7e12618bf69d7d71a1c8",
        "span_id": "0x88b7afb56d248244",
        "trace_state": "[]"
    },
    "kind": "SpanKind.CLIENT",
    "parent_id": "0xe756587bc381338c",
}
```

This new data is starting to help define the ties between different services and describe the relationships between the components of the system, which is great. By exploring the tracing data alone, we can start getting a clearer idea of the role that each application plays. Oddly enough though, the data we're currently generating doesn't appear to be fully connected yet. The `trace_id` identifier between the client and the server doesn't match, and moreover, the SERVER span doesn't contain `parent_id`; it seems we forgot about propagation!

Propagating context

Getting the information from one service to another across the network boundary requires some additional work, namely, propagating the context. Without this context propagation, each service will generate a new trace independently, which means that the backend will not be able to tie the services together at analysis time. As shown in *Figure 4.5*, a trace without propagation between services is missing the link between services, which means the traces will be more difficult to correlate:

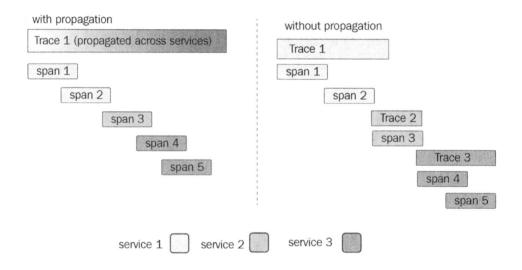

Figure 4.5 – Traces with and without propagation

Specifically, the data needed to propagate the context between services is `span_context`. This includes four key pieces of information:

- `span_id`: The identifier of the current span
- `trace_id`: The identifier of the current trace
- `trace_flags`: The additional configuration flags available to control tracing levels and sampling, as per the W3C Trace Context specification (https://www.w3.org/TR/trace-context/#trace-flags)
- `trace_state`: A set of vendor-specific identification data as per the W3C Trace Context specification (https://www.w3.org/TR/trace-context/#tracestate-header)

The `span_context` information is used anytime a new span is started. `trace_id` is set as the current new span's trace ID, and `span_id` will be used as the new span's parent ID. When a new span is started in a different service, if the context isn't propagated correctly, the new span has no information from which to pull the data it needs. Context must be serialized and injected across boundaries into a carrier for propagation to occur. On the receiving end, the context must be extracted from the carrier and deserialized. The carrier medium used to transport the context, in the case of our application, is HTTP headers. OpenTelemetry's **Propagators API** provides the methods we'll use in the next example. On the client side, we'll call the `inject` method to set `span_context` in a dictionary that will be passed into the HTTP request as headers:

shopper.py

```python
from opentelemetry.propagate import inject
@tracer.start_as_current_span("browse")
def browse():
    print("visiting the grocery store")
    with tracer.start_as_current_span(
        "web request", kind=trace.SpanKind.CLIENT
    ) as span:
        headers = {}
        inject(headers)
        resp = requests.get(url, headers=headers)
```

On the server side, it is a little more complicated, as we need to ensure the context is extracted before the decorator instantiates the span in the request handler. Conveniently, Flask has a mechanism available via decorators to call methods before and after a request is handled. This allows us to extract the `context` from the request headers and attach to the `context` before the request handler is called. The call to attach will return a token that will be stored in the `context` of the request. Once the request has been processed, the call to detach restores the previous `context`:

grocery_store.py

```python
from opentelemetry import context
from opentelemetry.propagate import extract

@app.before_request
def before_request_func():
```

```
        token = context.attach(extract(request.headers))
        request.environ["context_token"] = token

@app.teardown_request
def teardown_request_func(err):
    token = request.environ.get("context_token", None)
    if token:
        context.detach(token)
```

Testing the new code will show that the context is now propagated; remember to restart the server as well as run the client. Take a look at the following output, paying special attention to `trace_id` and `span_id`:

shopper.py output

```
{
    "name": "web request",
    "context": {
        "trace_id": "0x1fe2dc4e2e750e4598463749300277ed",
        "span_id": "0x5771b0a074e00a5b",
        "trace_state": "[]"
    },
    "kind": "SpanKind.CLIENT",
}
```

If everything went according to plan, the client and the server should be part of the same trace. The output on the server side shows the span containing a `parent_id` field which matches the client's `span_id` field. As well, note the `trace_id` field which matches on both sides of the request:

grocery_store.py output

```
{
    "name": "/",
    "context": {
        "trace_id": "0x1fe2dc4e2e750e4598463749300277ed",
        "span_id": "0x26f143d0f8a9c0bd",
        "trace_state": "[]"
    },
```

```
        "kind": "SpanKind.SERVER",
        "parent_id": "0x5771b0a074e00a5b",
}
```

Now that the services are connected, let's explore propagation a bit further!

Additional propagator formats

The propagation we've used so far in the example is the **W3C Trace Context** propagation format. The Trace Context format is fairly recent and is by no means the only propagation format out there. There are additional propagators available to use with OpenTelemetry to support interoperability with other tracing standards. Additional propagators supported by OpenTelemetry and available at the time of writing include B3, Jaeger, and ot-trace. Currently supported propagators implement a `TextMapPropagator` interface with an `inject` method and an `extract` method. A propagator is configured globally using the `set_global_textmap` method. The following code shows an example of configuring a `B3MultiFormat` propagator for an application. This propagator can be found by installing the `opentelemetry-propagator-b3` package:

```
from opentelemetry.propagators.b3 import B3MultiFormat
from opentelemetry.propagate import set_global_textmap

set_global_textmap(B3MultiFormat())
```

> **Important Note**
> Troubleshooting propagation issues can be difficult and time-consuming. Services can easily be misconfigured to propagate data using different formats and doing so will result in propagation not working at all.

If you decided to use the previous code in either the shopper or the grocery store applications but not both, you may have noticed propagation breaking. It's not uncommon for applications in the wild to have different propagation formats configured. Thankfully, it's possible to configure multiple propagators simultaneously in OpenTelemetry by using a composite propagator.

Composite propagator

A composite propagator allows users to configure multiple propagators from different cross-cutting concerns. In its current implementation in many languages, the composite propagator can support multiple propagators for the same signal. This functionality provides backward compatibility with older systems while being future-proof. `CompositePropagator` has the same interface as any propagator but supports passing in a list of propagators at initialization. This list is then iterated through at injection and extraction time. This next example introduces one additional service, a legacy inventory system that is configured to use B3 propagation. *Figure 4.6* shows the flow of the request from the shopper, through the store, and to the inventory system that we will be adding in the next example:

Figure 4.6 – A request to the legacy inventory system

Since the grocery store needs to propagate requests using both W3C Trace Context and B3, we'll need to update the code to configure `CompositePropagator` to support this. The first thing to do before diving into the code is to ensure that the B3 propagator package is installed:

```
pip install opentelemetry-propagator-b3
```

For the sake of simplifying the server code, the following code shows a new method being added to `common.py` to set span attributes in a server handler. This new method, `set_span_attributes_from_flask`, can be used both in `legacy_inventory.py` (as we'll see shortly) and in `grocery_store.py`:

common.py

```
from flask import request
from opentelemetry.semconv.trace import SpanAttributes

def set_span_attributes_from_flask():
```

```
    span = trace.get_current_span()
    span.set_attributes(
        {
            SpanAttributes.HTTP_FLAVOR: request.environ.
get("SERVER_PROTOCOL"),
            SpanAttributes.HTTP_METHOD: request.method,
            SpanAttributes.HTTP_USER_AGENT: str(request.user_
agent),
            SpanAttributes.HTTP_HOST: request.host,
            SpanAttributes.HTTP_SCHEME: request.scheme,
            SpanAttributes.HTTP_TARGET: request.path,
            SpanAttributes.HTTP_CLIENT_IP: request.remote_addr,
        }
    )
```

The `legacy_inventory.py` service code is another Flask server application with a single handler that, for now, returns a hardcoded list of items and quantities encoded using JSON. The following code is very similar to the grocery store code. The configuration for both the Flask app and OpenTelemetry should be familiar, the significant difference being how we configure OpenTelemetry in this new service is the propagator, by calling `set_global_textmap`. It's also important to remember to set the `port` number to a different value than the default Flask port by passing an argument to `app.run`; otherwise, we will run into a socket error when trying to run both `grocery_store.py` and `legacy_inventory.py`:

legacy_inventory.py

```
from flask import Flask, jsonify, request
from opentelemetry import context
from opentelemetry.propagate import extract, set_global_textmap
from opentelemetry.propagators.b3 import B3MultiFormat
from opentelemetry.trace import SpanKind
from common import configure_tracer, set_span_attributes_from_
flask

tracer = configure_tracer("legacy-inventory", "0.9.1")
app = Flask(__name__)
set_global_textmap(B3MultiFormat())
```

```python
@app.before_request
def before_request_func():
    token = context.attach(extract(request.headers))
    request.environ["context_token"] = token

@app.teardown_request
def teardown_request_func(err):
    token = request.environ.get("context_token", None)
    if token:
        context.detach(token)

@app.route("/inventory")
@tracer.start_as_current_span("/inventory", kind=SpanKind.SERVER)
def inventory():
    set_span_attributes_from_flask()
    products = [
        {"name": "oranges", "quantity": "10"},
        {"name": "apples", "quantity": "20"},
    ]
    return jsonify(products)

if __name__ == "__main__":
    app.run(debug=True, port=5001)
```

In the grocery store application, we will configure `CompositePropagator` to support both the W3C Trace Context and B3 formats. Add the following code to `grocery_store.py`:

grocery_store.py

```python
from opentelemetry.propagate import extract, inject, set_global_textmap
from opentelemetry.propagators.b3 import B3MultiFormat
from opentelemetry.propagators.composite import CompositePropagator
from opentelemetry.trace.propagation import tracecontext
```

```
set_global_textmap(CompositePropagator([tracecontext.
TraceContextTextMapPropagator(), B3MultiFormat()]))
```

Additionally, the following handler will be added to the store, which will make a request to the legacy inventory service. The key thing to remember here is to ensure the context is present in the headers by calling `inject` and that the headers are passed into the request:

grocery_store.py

```python
import requests
from common import set_span_attributes_from_flask
...
@app.route("/")
@tracer.start_as_current_span("welcome", kind=SpanKind.SERVER)
def welcome():
    set_span_attributes_from_flask()
    return "Welcome to the grocery store!"


@app.route("/products")
@tracer.start_as_current_span("/products", kind=SpanKind.SERVER)
def products():
    set_span_attributes_from_flask()
    with tracer.start_as_current_span("inventory request") as span:
        url = "http://localhost:5001/inventory"
        span.set_attributes(
            {
                SpanAttributes.HTTP_METHOD: "GET",
                SpanAttributes.HTTP_FLAVOR: str(HttpFlavorValues.HTTP_1_1),
                SpanAttributes.HTTP_URL: url,
                SpanAttributes.NET_PEER_IP: "127.0.0.1",
            }
        )
        headers = {}
        inject(headers)
        resp = requests.get(url, headers=headers)
        return resp.text
```

The last change we need before trying this out is an update to the shopper application's `browse` method to send a request to the new endpoint:

shopper.py

```
def browse():
    print("visiting the grocery store")
    with tracer.start_as_current_span(
        "web request", kind=trace.SpanKind.CLIENT
    ) as span:
        url = "http://localhost:5000/products"
```

Now, we have a third application to launch; the following commands need to be run from separate terminal windows, and remember to ensure no other applications are running on ports `5000` and `5001` to avoid socket errors:

```
$ python ./legacy_inventory.py
$ python ./grocery_store.py
$ python ./shopper.py
```

Once the legacy inventory server is up and running, making a request from the shopper should yield some exciting results. In the output, we'll be looking for `trace_id` to be consistent across all three services, and, as in the previous example of propagation, `parent_id` of the server span should match `span_id` of the corresponding client request span:

shopper.py output

```
    "name": "web request",
    "context": {
        "trace_id": "0xb2a655bfd008007711903d8a72130813",
        "span_id": "0x3c183afa2640a2bb",
    },
```

The following output from the grocery store includes two spans. The span named /products represents the request received from the client, and if the context is successfully extracted, `trace_id` will match the previous output. The second span is the request to the inventory service:

grocery_store.py output

```
    "name": "/products",
    "context": {
        "trace_id": "0xb2a655bfd008007711903d8a72130813",
        "span_id": "0x77883e3459f83fb6",
    },
    "parent_id": "0x3c183afa2640a2bb",
----
    "name": "inventory request",
    "context": {
        "trace_id": "0xb2a655bfd008007711903d8a72130813",
        "span_id": "0x8137dbaaa3f40062",
    },
    "parent_id": "0x77883e3459f83fb6",
```

The last output is from the inventory service. Remember that this service is using a different propagator format. If the propagation was configured correctly, `trace_id` should remain consistent with the other two services, and `parent_id` should reflect that the parent operation is the `inventory request` span:

legacy_inventory.py output

```
    "name": "/inventory",
    "context": {
        "trace_id": "0xb2a655bfd008007711903d8a72130813",
        "span_id": "0x3306b21b8000912b",
    },
    "parent_id": "0x8137dbaaa3f40062",
```

This was a lot of work, but once you get propagation configured and working across a system, it's rare that you'll need to go back and make changes to it. It's a set-it-and-forget-it type of operation. If you happen to be working with a brand-new code base, choose a single propagation format and stick to it; it will save you a lot of headaches. We've now grasped one of the most important concepts in distributed tracing, the propagation of span context across systems. Let's take a look at where else propagation can help us.

> **Important Note**
> A possible alternative when working with large code bases and multiple propagator formats is to always configure all available propagation formats. This may seem like overkill, but sometimes, it makes sense to prioritize interoperability over saving a few bytes.

Recording events, exceptions, and status

Quickly identifying when an issue arises is a key aspect of distributed tracing. As demonstrated in *Figure 4.7* with the Jaeger interface, in many backends, traces that contain errors are highlighted to make them easy to find for users of data:

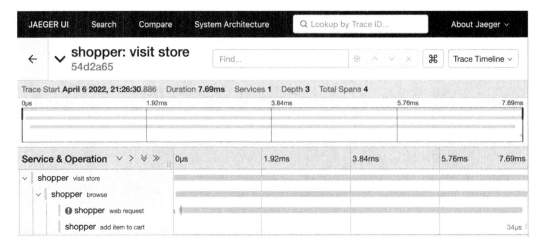

Figure 4.7 – The trace view in Jaeger

In the following sections, we will explore the facilities that OpenTelemetry provides to capture events, record exceptions, and set the status of a span.

Events

In addition to attributes, an **event** provides the facility to record data about a span that occurs at a specific time. Events are similar to logs in OpenTracing in that they contain a timestamp and can contain a list of attributes or key/value pairs. An event is added via an `add_event` method on the span, which accepts a name argument and, optionally, a timestamp and a list of attributes, as shown in the following code:

shopper.py

```
span.add_event("about to send a request")
resp = requests.get(url, headers=headers)
span.add_event("request sent", attributes={"url": url},
timestamp=0)
```

As you'll see in the following output, the list of events is kept in the order in which they are added; they are not ordered by the timestamps they are recorded with:

shopper.py output

```
"events": [
    {
        "name": "about to send a request",
        "timestamp": "2021-07-12T06:38:49.793903Z",
        "attributes": {}
    },
    {
        "name": "request sent",
        "timestamp": "1970-01-01T00:00:00.000000Z",
        "attributes": {
            "url": "http://localhost:5000/products"
        }
    }
],
```

Events differ from attributes in that they have a time dimension to them, which can be helpful to better understand the sequence of things inside a span. There are also events that have a special meaning, as we'll see with exceptions.

Exceptions

In OpenTelemetry, the concepts of exceptions and the status of a span are intentionally kept separate. A span may contain many exceptions, but these exceptions don't necessarily mean that the status of the span should be set as an error. For example, a user may want to record exceptions when a request is made to a specific service, but there may be retry logic that will cause the operation to eventually succeed anyway. Recording those exceptions may be useful to identify areas of the code that can be improved. The initial definition of an **exception** in the OpenTelemetry specification is that an exception is as follows:

- Recorded as an event
- The specific name exception
- Contains the minimum of either `exception.type` or an `exception.message` attribute

The following code records an exception if a request to the grocery store fails by creating one such event. Let's add a `try/except` block in the `browse` method to capture the exception and change `url` to make the request intentionally fail:

shopper.py

```python
    try:
        url = "invalid_url"
        resp = requests.get(url, headers=headers)
        span.add_event(
            "request sent",
            attributes={"url": url},
            timestamp=0,
        )
        span.set_attribute(
            SpanAttributes.HTTP_STATUS_CODE,
            resp.status_code
        )
    except Exception as err:
        attributes = {
            SpanAttributes.EXCEPTION_MESSAGE: str(err),
        }
        span.add_event("exception", attributes=attributes)
```

Running the code will produce an exception that will be caught. This exception will then be recoded as an event and added to the tracing data emitted at the console:

shopper.py output

```
    "events": [
        {
            "name": "exception",
            "timestamp": "2021-07-10T04:13:05.287376Z",
            "attributes": {
                "exception.message": "Invalid URL 'invalid_url': No schema supplied. Perhaps you meant http://invalid_url?"
            }
        }
    ]
```

Although this provides us with more information, it's not practical to have to write so many lines of code every time we want to record an exception. Thankfully, the OpenTelemetry specification has defined a span method in the API to address this. The following code replaces the code in the except block of the previous example to use the record_exception method on the span, instead of manually creating an event. Semantically, these are equivalent, but the method is much more convenient. The method accepts an exception as its first argument and supports optional parameters to pass in additional event attributes, as well as a timestamp:

shopper.py

```
        try:
            url = "invalid_url"
            resp = requests.get(url, headers=headers)
            ...
        except Exception as err:
            span.record_exception(err)
```

Next time the code is run, the exception event is automatically generated for us. Taking a closer look at the output, it's even more useful than before, as we now see the following:

- The message populated as we did before
- The exception type
- A stack trace capturing exactly where in the code the exception was raised

This allows us to immediately find the problematic code and resolve the issue:

shopper.py output

```
        "events": [
            {
                "name": "exception",
                "timestamp": "2021-07-10T04:17:07.328665Z",
                "attributes": {
                    "exception.type": "MissingSchema",
                    "exception.message": "Invalid URL 'invalid_url': No schema supplied. Perhaps you meant http://invalid_url?",
                    "exception.stacktrace": "Traceback (most recent call last):\n  File \"/Users/alex/dev/cloud_native_observability/lib/python3.8/site-packages/opentelemetry/trace/__init__.py\", line 522, in use_span\n    yield span\n  File \"/Users/alex/dev/cloud_native_observability/lib/python3.8/site-packages/opentelemetry/sdk/trace/__init__.py\", line 879, in start_as_current_span\n    yield span_context\n  File \"/Users/alex/dev/cloud-native-observability/chapter4/./shopper.py\", line 110, in browse\n    resp = requests.get(\"invalid_url\", headers=headers)\n  File \"/Users/alex/dev/cloud_native_observability/lib/python3.8/site-packages/requests/api.py\", line 76, in get\n    return request('get', url, params=params, **kwargs)\n  File \"/Users/alex/dev/cloud_native_observability/lib/python3.8/site-packages/requests/api.py\", line 61, in request\n    return session.request(method=method, url=url, **kwargs)\n  File \"/Users/alex/dev/cloud_native_observability/lib/python3.8/site-
```

```
packages/requests/sessions.py\", line 528, in request\n       prep
= self.prepare_request(req)\n  File \"/Users/alex/dev/cloud_
native_observability/lib/python3.8/site-packages/requests/
sessions.py\", line 456, in prepare_request\n       p.prepare(\n
File \"/Users/alex/dev/cloud_native_observability/lib/
python3.8/site-packages/requests/models.py\", line 316, in
prepare\n    self.prepare_url(url, params)\n  File \"/Users/
alex/dev/cloud_native_observability/lib/python3.8/site-
packages/requests/models.py\", line 390, in prepare_url\n
raise MissingSchema(error)\nrequests.exceptions.MissingSchema:
Invalid URL 'invalid_url': No schema supplied. Perhaps you
meant http://invalid_url?\n",
                "exception.escaped": "False"
            }
        }
    ],
```

This type of detail about exceptions in a system is incredibly valuable when debugging, especially when the events may have occurred minutes, hours, or even days ago. It's worth noting that the format of the stack trace is language-specific, as described in *Figure 4.8* (https://github.com/open-telemetry/opentelemetry-specification/blob/main/specification/trace/semantic_conventions/exceptions.md#stacktrace-representation):

Language	Format
C#	the return value of Exception.ToString()
Go	the return value of runtime.Stack
Java	the contents of Throwable.printStackTrace()
Javascript	the return value of error.stack as returned by V8
Python	the return value of traceback.format_exc()
Ruby	the return value of Exception.full_message

Figure 4.8 – The stack trace format per language

Additionally, the Python SDK also automatically captures uncaught exceptions and adds an exception event to the span that is active when the exception occurs. We can update the code we just wrote in the previous example to remove the `try/except` block, leaving the invalid URL. The following code has the same effect as calling `record_exception` directly:

shopper.py

```
resp = requests.get("invalid_url", headers=headers)
```

Recording exceptions in spans is valuable, but in the event that it is preferable not to do so, it's possible to set an optional flag when creating a span to disable the functionality. You can try it in the previous example by setting the `record_exception` optional argument, as follows:

shopper.py

```
    with tracer.start_as_current_span(
        "web request", kind=trace.SpanKind.CLIENT, record_exception=False
    ) as span:
```

Now that we understand how exceptions are recorded, let's further investigate how or even if these exceptions connect to the status of a span.

Status

As mentioned previously in this chapter, the span status has significant benefits to users. Quickly being able to filter through traces based on the span status makes things much easier for operators. The *status* is composed of a status code and, optionally, a description. There are currently three supported span status codes:

- UNSET
- OK
- ERROR

The default status code on any new span is UNSET. This default behavior ensures that when a span status code is set to OK, it has been done intentionally. An earlier version of the specification defaulted a span status code to OK, which left room for misinterpretations – was the span really OK or did the code return before an error status code was set? The decision to set the span status is really up to the application developer or operators of the service. The interface to set a status on a span receives a Status object, which is composed of StatusCode and a description string. This next example sets the span status code to OK based on the response from the web request. Note that we're using a feature of the Requests library's Response object to return True if the HTTP status code on the response is between 200 and 400:

shopper.py

```
from opentelemetry.trace import Status, StatusCode
def browse():
    with tracer.start_as_current_span(
        "web request", kind=trace.SpanKind.CLIENT, record_exception=False
    ) as span:
        url = "http://localhost:5000/products"
        resp = requests.get(url, headers=headers)
        if resp:
            span.set_status(Status(StatusCode.OK))
        else:
            span.set_status(
                Status(StatusCode.ERROR, "status code: {}".format(resp.status_code))
            )
```

With the code in place, test the application first with the http://localhost:5000/products URL to see the following output when a valid URL is used:

shopper.py output with valid URL

```
    "status": {
        "status_code": "OK"
    }
```

Now, update the URL to an invalid endpoint such as `http://localhost:5000/invalid` to see the following output when the response contains an error code:

shopper.py output with invalid URL

```
"status": {
    "status_code": "ERROR",
    "description": "status code: 404"
}
```

> **Important Note**
> The `description` field will only be used if the status code is set to ERROR; it is ignored otherwise.

Another thing to note about status codes is that, as per semantic convention, instrumentation libraries should not change the status code to OK unless they are providing a configuration option to do this. This is to prevent having an instrumentation library unexpectedly change the outcome of the span. They are, however, encouraged to set the status code to ERROR when errors defined in the semantic convention for the type of instrumentation library are encountered.

As with recording exceptions, it's also possible to configure spans to automatically set the status when an exception occurs. This is accomplished via a `set_status_on_exception` argument, available when starting a span:

shopper.py

```
with tracer.start_as_current_span(
    "web request",
    kind=trace.SpanKind.CLIENT,
    set_status_on_exception=True,
) as span:
```

Play around with the code and see what the status output is when using this setting. Although it may seem like a lot of work, handling errors and setting the status on spans meaningfully will make a world of difference at analysis time. Not only that, but having to work through the different scenarios in the code at instrumentation time is a forcing function to really ensure a solid understanding of what the code is expected to do. And when things go wrong, as they will, having this data will make a world of difference.

Summary

And just like that, you've explored many important concepts of the tracing signal in OpenTelemetry! There was quite a bit to grasp in this chapter, but hopefully, the concepts we've been exploring so far are starting to make more sense now that there's some code behind them. With this knowledge, you now know how to configure different components of the OpenTelemetry tracing pipeline to obtain a tracer and export data to the console. You also have the ability to start spans in various ways, depending on your application's needs. We then spent some time improving the data emitted by enriching it using attributes, resources, and resource detectors. Last but not least, we took a look at the important topic of events, status, and exceptions to capture some important information about errors when they happen in code.

Our understanding of the Context API will allow us to share information across our application, and knowing how to use the Propagation API will allow us to ensure that information is shared across application boundaries.

Although you probably have many more questions, you now know enough to look through some existing applications or plan ahead for instrumenting new applications through distributed tracing. As some of the components we've explored in this chapter are similar across signals, many of the concepts that may not quite make sense yet will become clearer as we take a look at the next chapter, which looks at metrics. Let's go measure some things!

5
Metrics – Recording Measurements

Tracing code execution throughout a system is one way to capture information about what is happening in an application, but what if we're looking to measure something that would be better served by a more lightweight option than a trace? Now that we've learned how to generate distributed traces using OpenTelemetry, it's time to look at the next signal: **metrics**. As we did in *Chapter 4, Distributed Tracing – Tracing Code Execution*, we will first look at configuring the OpenTelemetry pipeline to produce metrics. Then, we'll continue to improve the telemetry emitted by the grocery store application by using the instruments OpenTelemetry puts at our disposal. In this chapter, we will do the following:

- Configure OpenTelemetry to collect, aggregate, and export metrics to the terminal.
- Generate metrics using the different instruments available.
- Use metrics to gain a better understanding of the grocery store application.

Augmenting the grocery store application will allow us to put the different instruments into practice to grasp better how each instrument can be used to record measurements. As we explore other metrics that are useful to produce for cloud-native applications, we will seek to understand some of the questions we may answer using each instrument.

Technical requirements

As with the examples in the previous chapter, the code is written using **Python 3.8**, but OpenTelemetry Python supports **Python 3.6+** at the time of writing. Ensure you have a compatible version installed on your system following the instructions at https://docs.python.org/3/using/index.html. To verify that a compatible version is installed on your system, run the following commands:

```
$ python --version
$ python3 --version
```

On many systems, both `python` and `python3` point to the same installation, but this is not always the case, so it's good to be aware of this if one points to an unsupported version. In all examples, running applications in Python will call the `python` command, but they can also be run via the `python3` command, depending on your system.

The first few examples in this chapter will show a standalone example exploring how to configure OpenTelemetry to produce metrics. The code will require the OpenTelemetry API and SDK packages, which we'll install via the following `pip` command:

```
$ pip install opentelemetry-api==1.10.0 \
              opentelemetry-sdk==1.10.0 \
              opentelemetry-propagator-b3==1.10.0
```

Additionally, we will use the **Prometheus** exporter to demonstrate a pull-based exporter to emit metrics. This exporter can be installed via `pip` as well:

```
$ pip install opentelemetry-exporter-prometheus==0.29b0
```

For the later examples involving the grocery store application, you can download the sample from *Chapter 4, Distributed Tracing – Tracing Code Execution,* and add the code along with the examples. The following `git` command will clone the companion repository:

```
$ git clone https://github.com/PacktPublishing/Cloud-Native-Observability
```

The `chapter04` directory in the repository contains the code for the grocery store. The complete example, including all the code in the examples from this chapter, is available in the `chapter05` directory. I recommend adding the code following the examples and using the complete example code as a reference if you get into trouble. Also, if you haven't read *Chapter 4, Distributed Tracing – Tracing Code Execution*, it may be helpful to skim through the details of how the grocery store application is built in that chapter to get your bearings.

The grocery store depends on the **Requests** library (`https://docs.python-requests.org/`) to make web requests at various points and the **Flask** library (`https://flask.palletsprojects.com`) to provide a lightweight web server for some of the services. Both libraries can be installed via the following `pip` command:

```
$ pip install flask requests
```

Additionally, the chapter will utilize a third-party open source tool (`https://github.com/rakyll/hey`) to generate some load on the web application. The tool can be downloaded from the repository. The following commands download the macOS binary and rename it to `hey` using `curl` with the `-o` flag, then ensure the binary is executable using `chmod`:

```
$ curl -o hey https://hey-release.s3.us-east-2.amazonaws.com/hey_darwin_amd64
$ chmod +x ./hey
```

If you have a different load generation tool you're familiar with, and there are many, feel free to use that instead if you prefer. This should be everything we need to start; let's start measuring!

Configuring the metrics pipeline

The metrics signal was designed to be conceptually similar to the tracing signal. The metrics pipeline consists of the following:

- A **MeterProvider** to determine how metrics should be generated and provide access to a **meter**.
- The meter is used to create **instruments**, which are used to record **measurements**.
- **Views** allow the application developer to filter and process metrics produced by the **software development kit (SDK)**.

- A **MetricReader**, which collects **metrics** being recorded.
- The **MetricExporter** provides a mechanism to translate metrics into an output format for various protocols.

There are quite a few components, and a picture always helps me grasp concepts more quickly. The following figure shows us the different elements in the pipeline:

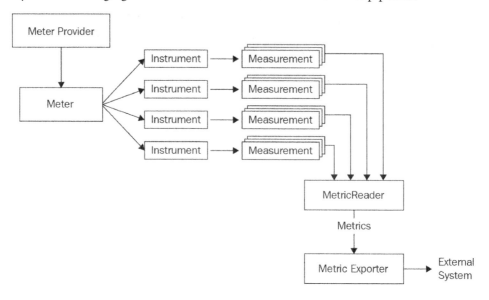

Figure 5.1 – Metrics pipeline

`MeterProvider` can be associated with a resource to identify the source of metrics produced. We'll see shortly how we can reuse the `LocalMachineResourceDetector` we created in *Chapter 4, Distributed Tracing – Tracing Code Execution*, with metrics. For now, the first example instantiates `MeterProvider` with an empty resource. The code then calls the `set_meter_provider` global method to set the `MeterProvider` for the entire application.

Add the following code to a new file named `metrics.py`. Later in the chapter, we will refactor the code to add a `MeterProvider` to the grocery store, but to get started, the simpler, the better.

metrics.py

```
from opentelemetry._metrics import set_meter_provider
from opentelemetry.sdk._metrics import MeterProvider
from opentelemetry.sdk.resources import Resource
```

```
def configure_meter_provider():
    provider = MeterProvider(resource=Resource.create())
    set_meter_provider(provider)

if __name__ == "__main__":
    configure_meter_provider()
```

Run the code with the following command to ensure it runs without any errors:

`python ./metrics.py`

No errors and no output? Well done, you're on the right track!

> **Important Note**
> The previous code shows that the metric modules are located at `_metrics`. This will change to `metrics` once the packages have been marked stable. Depending on when you're reading this, it may have already happened.

Next, we'll need to configure an exporter to tell our application what to do with metrics once they're generated. The OpenTelemetry SDK contains `ConsoleMetricExporter` that emits metrics to the console, useful when getting started and debugging. `PeriodicExportingMetricReader` can be configured to periodically export metrics. The following code configures both components and adds the reader to the `MeterProvider`. The code sets the export interval to `5000` milliseconds, or 5 seconds, overriding the default of `60` seconds:

metrics.py

```
from opentelemetry._metrics import set_meter_provider
from opentelemetry.sdk._metrics import MeterProvider
from opentelemetry.sdk.resources import Resource
from opentelemetry.sdk._metrics.export import (
    ConsoleMetricExporter,
    PeriodicExportingMetricReader,
)


def configure_meter_provider():
    exporter = ConsoleMetricExporter()
```

```
    reader = PeriodicExportingMetricReader(exporter, export_
interval_millis=5000)
    provider = MeterProvider(metric_readers=[reader],
resource=Resource.create())
    set_meter_provider(provider)

if __name__ == "__main__":
    configure_meter_provider()
```

Run the code once more. The expectation is that the output from running the code will still not show anything. The only reason to run the code is to ensure our dependencies are fulfilled, and there are no typos.

> **Important Note**
>
> Like `TracerProvider`, `MeterProvider` uses a default no-op implementation in the API. This allows developers to instrument code without worrying about the details of how metrics will be generated. It does mean that unless we remember to set the global `MeterProvider` to use `MeterProvider` from the SDK package, any calls made to the API to generate metrics will result in no metrics being generated. This is one of the most common gotchas for folks working with OpenTelemetry.

We're almost ready to start producing metrics with an exporter, a metric reader, and a `MeterProvider` configured. The next step is getting a meter.

Obtaining a meter

With `MeterProvider` globally configured, we can use a global method to obtain a meter. As mentioned earlier, the meter will be used to create instruments, which will be used throughout the application code to record measurements. The meter receives the following arguments at creation time:

- The `name` of the application or library generating metrics
- An optional `version` identifies the version of the application or library producing the telemetry

- An optional `schema_url` to describe the data generated

> **Important Note**
> The schema URL was introduced in OpenTelemetry as part of the *OpenTelemetry Enhancement Proposal 152* (https://github.com/open-telemetry/oteps/blob/main/text/0152-telemetry-schemas.md). The goal of schemas is to provide OpenTelemetry instrumented applications a way to signal to external systems consuming the telemetry what the semantic versioning of the data produced will look like. Schema URL parameters are optional but recommended for all producers of telemetry: meters, tracers, and log emitters.

This information is used to identify the application or library producing the metrics. For example, application *A* making a web request via the `requests` library may contain more than one meter:

- The first meter is created by application *A* with a name identifying it with the version number matching the application.

- A second meter is created by the `requests` instrumentation library with the name `opentelemetry-instrumentation-requests` and the instrumentation library version.

- The `urllib` instrumentation library creates the third meter with the name `opentelemetry-instrumentation-urllib`, a library utilized by the `requests` library.

Having a name and a version identifier is critical in differentiating the source of the metrics. As we'll see later in the chapter, when we look at the *Views* section, this identifying information can also be used to filter out the telemetry we're not interested in. The following code uses the `get_meter_provider` global API method to access the global `MeterProvider` we configured earlier, and then calls `get_meter` with a name, version, and `schema_url` parameter:

metrics.py

```
from opentelemetry._metrics import get_meter_provider, set_meter_provider
...
```

```
if __name__ == "__main__":
    configure_meter_provider()
    meter = get_meter_provider().get_meter(
        name="metric-example",
        version="0.1.2",
        schema_url=" https://opentelemetry.io/schemas/1.9.0",
    )
```

In OpenTelemetry, instruments used to record measurements are associated with a single meter and must have unique names within the context of that meter.

Push-based and pull-based exporting

OpenTelemetry supports two methods for exporting metrics data to external systems: push-based and pull-based. A push-based exporter sends measurements from the application to a destination at a regular interval on a trigger. This trigger could be a maximum number of metrics to transfer or a schedule. The push-based method will be familiar to users of **StatsD** (https://github.com/statsd/statsd), where a network daemon opens a port and listens for metrics to be sent to it. Similarly, the ConsoleSpanExporter for the tracing signal in *Chapter 4, Distributed Tracing – Tracing Code Execution*, is a push-based exporter.

On the other hand, a pull-based exporter exposes an endpoint pulled from or scraped by an external system. Most commonly, a pull-based exporter exposes this information via a web endpoint or a local socket; this is the method popularized by Prometheus (https://prometheus.io). The following diagram shows the data flow comparison between a push and a pull model:

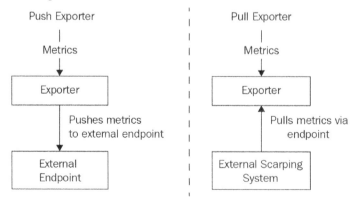

Figure 5.2 – Push versus pull-based reporting

Notice the direction of the arrow showing the interaction between the exporter and an external system. When configuring a pull-based exporter, remember that system permissions may need to be configured to allow an application to open a new port for incoming requests. One such pull-based exporter defined in the OpenTelemetry specification is the Prometheus exporter.

The pipeline configuration for a pull exporter is slightly less complex. The metric reader interface can be used as a single point to collect and expose metrics in the Prometheus format. The following code shows how to expose a Prometheus endpoint on port `8000` using the `start_http_server` method from the Prometheus client library. It then configures `PrometheusMetricReader` with a `prefix` parameter to provide a namespace for all metrics generated by our application. Finally, the code adds a call waiting for input from the user before exiting; this gives us a chance to see the exposed metrics before the application exits:

```
from opentelemetry.exporter.prometheus import PrometheusMetricReader
from prometheus_client import start_http_server

def configure_meter_provider():
    start_http_server(port=8000, addr="localhost")
    reader = PrometheusMetricReader(prefix="MetricExample")
    provider = MeterProvider(metric_readers=[reader], resource=Resource.create())
    set_meter_provider(provider)

if __name__ == "__main__":
    ...
    input("Press any key to exit...")
```

If you run the application now, you can use a browser to see the Prometheus formatted data available by visiting `http://localhost:8000`. Alternatively, you can use the `curl` command to see the output data in the terminal as per the following example:

```
$ curl http://localhost:8000
# HELP python_gc_objects_collected_total Objects collected during gc
# TYPE python_gc_objects_collected_total counter
python_gc_objects_collected_total{generation="0"} 1057.0
```

```
python_gc_objects_collected_total{generation="1"} 49.0
python_gc_objects_collected_total{generation="2"} 0.0
# HELP python_gc_objects_uncollectable_total Uncollectable
object found during GC
# TYPE python_gc_objects_uncollectable_total counter
python_gc_objects_uncollectable_total{generation="0"} 0.0
python_gc_objects_uncollectable_total{generation="1"} 0.0
python_gc_objects_uncollectable_total{generation="2"} 0.0
# HELP python_gc_collections_total Number of times this
generation was collected
# TYPE python_gc_collections_total counter
python_gc_collections_total{generation="0"} 55.0
python_gc_collections_total{generation="1"} 4.0
python_gc_collections_total{generation="2"} 0.0
# HELP python_info Python platform information
# TYPE python_info gauge
python_info{implementation="CPython",major="3",minor="8",
patchlevel="0",version="3.9.0"} 1.0
```

The Prometheus client library generates the previous data; note that there are no OpenTelemetry metrics generated by our application, which makes sense since we haven't generated anything yet! We'll get to that next. We'll see in *Chapter 11*, *Diagnosing Problems*, how to integrate OpenTelemetry with a Prometheus backend. For the sake of simplicity, the remainder of the examples in this chapter will be using the push-based `ConsoleMetricExporter` configured earlier. If you're more familiar with Prometheus, please use this configuration instead.

Choosing the right OpenTelemetry instrument

We're now ready to generate metrics from our application. If you recall, in tracing, the **tracer** produces **spans**, which are used to create distributed traces. By contrast, the meter does not generate metrics; an **instrument** does. The meter's role is to produce instruments. OpenTelemetry offers many different instruments to record measurements. The following figure shows a list of all the instruments available:

Instrument	Synchronicity	Monotonic
Counter	Synchronous	Yes
Asynchronous Counter	Asynchronous	Yes
UpDownCounter	Synchronous	No
Asynchronous UpDownCounter	Asynchronous	No
Histogram	Synchronous	No
Asynchronous Gauge	Asynchronous	No

Figure 5.3 – OpenTelemetry instruments

Each instrument has a specific purpose, and the correct instrument depends on the following:

- The type of measurement being recorded
- Whether the measurement must be done synchronously
- Whether the values being recorded are monotonic or not

For **synchronous** instruments, a method is called on the instrument when it is time for a measurement to be recorded. For **asynchronous** instruments, a callback method is configured at the instrument's creation time.

Each instrument has a `name` and `kind` property. Additionally, a unit and a description may be specified.

Counter

A **counter** is a commonly available instrument across metric ecosystems and implementations over the years, although its definition across systems varies. In OpenTelemetry, a counter is an increasing monotonic instrument, only supporting non-negative value increases. The following diagram shows a sample graph representing a monotonic counter:

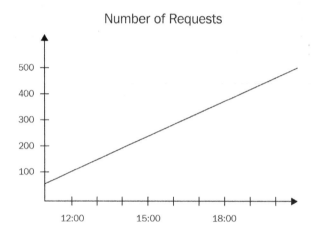

Figure 5.4 – Increasing monotonic counter graph

A counter can be used to represent the following:

- Number of requests received
- Count of orders processed
- CPU time utilization

The following code instantiates a counter to keep a tally of the number of items sold in the grocery store. The code uses the add method to increment the counter and passes the locale of the customer as an attribute:

metrics.py

```
if __name__ == "__main__":
    ...
    counter = meter.create_counter(
        "items_sold",
        unit="items",
        description="Total items sold"
```

```
    )
    counter.add(6, {"locale": "fr-FR", "country": "CA"})
    counter.add(1, {"locale": "es-ES"})
```

Running the code outputs the counter with all its attributes:

output

```
{"attributes": {"locale": "fr-FR", "country": "CA"},
"description": "Total items sold", "instrumentation_info":
"InstrumentationInfo(metric-example, 0.1.2, https://
opentelemetry.io/schemas/1.9.0)", "name": "items_sold",
"resource": "BoundedAttributes({'telemetry.sdk.language':
'python', 'telemetry.sdk.name': 'opentelemetry', 'telemetry.
sdk.version': '1.10.0', 'service.name': 'unknown_service'},
maxlen=None)", "unit": "items", "point": {"start_time_
unix_nano": 1646535699616146000, "time_unix_nano":
1646535699616215000, "value": 7, "aggregation_temporality": 2,
"is_monotonic": true}}
{"attributes": {"locale": "es-ES"}, "description": "Total items
sold", "instrumentation_info": "InstrumentationInfo(metric-
example, 0.1.2, https://opentelemetry.io/
schemas/1.9.0)", "name": "items_sold", "resource":
"BoundedAttributes({'telemetry.sdk.language': 'python',
'telemetry.sdk.name': 'opentelemetry', 'telemetry.sdk.version':
'1.10.0', 'service.name': 'unknown_service'}, maxlen=None)",
"unit": "items", "point": {"start_time_unix_nano":
1646535699616215001, "time_unix_nano": 1646535699616237000,
"value": 0, "aggregation_temporality": 2, "is_monotonic":
true}}
```

Note that the attributes themselves do not influence the value of the counter. They are only augmenting the telemetry with additional dimensions about the transaction. A monotonic instrument like the counter cannot receive a negative value. The following code tries to add a negative value:

```
if __name__ == "__main__":
    ...
    counter.add(6, {"locale": "fr-FR", "country": "CA"})
    counter.add(-1, {"unicorn": 1})
```

This code results in the following warning, which provides the developer with a helpful hint:

output
```
Add amount must be non-negative on Counter items_sold.
```

Knowing to use the right instrument can help avoid generating unexpected data. It's also good to consider adding validation to the data being passed into instruments when unsure of the data source.

Asynchronous counter

The **asynchronous counter** can be used as a counter. Its only difference is that it is used asynchronously. Asynchronous counters can represent data that is only ever-increasing, and that may be too costly to report synchronously or is more appropriate to record on set intervals. Some examples of this would be reporting the following:

- CPU time utilized by a process
- Total network bytes transferred

The following code shows us how to create an asynchronous counter using the `async_counter_callback` callback method, which will be called every time `PeriodExportingMetricReader` executes. To ensure the instrument has a chance to record a few measurements, we've added `sleep` in the code as well to pause the code before exiting:

metrics.py
```
import time
from opentelemetry._metrics.measurement import Measurement

def async_counter_callback():
    yield Measurement(10)

if __name__ == "__main__":
    ...
    # async counter
    meter.create_observable_counter(
        name="major_page_faults",
        callback=async_counter_callback,
```

```
        description="page faults requiring I/O",
        unit="fault",
)
time.sleep(10)
```

If you haven't commented out the output from the instrument, you should see the output from both counters now. The following output omits the previous example's output for brevity:

output

```
{"attributes": "", "description": "page faults requiring
I/O", "instrumentation_info": "InstrumentationInfo(metric-
example, 0.1.2, https://opentelemetry.io/
schemas/1.9.0)", "name": "major_page_faults", "resource":
"BoundedAttributes({'telemetry.sdk.language': 'python',
'telemetry.sdk.name': 'opentelemetry', 'telemetry.sdk.version':
'1.10.0', 'service.name': 'unknown_service'}, maxlen=None)",
"unit": "fault", "point": {"start_time_unix_nano":
1646538230507539000, "time_unix_nano": 1646538230507614000,
"value": 10, "aggregation_temporality": 2, "is_monotonic":
true}}
{"attributes": "", "description": "page faults requiring
I/O", "instrumentation_info": "InstrumentationInfo(metric-
example, 0.1.2, https://opentelemetry.io/
schemas/1.9.0)", "name": "major_page_faults", "resource":
"BoundedAttributes({'telemetry.sdk.language': 'python',
'telemetry.sdk.name': 'opentelemetry', 'telemetry.sdk.version':
'1.10.0', 'service.name': 'unknown_service'}, maxlen=None)",
"unit": "fault", "point": {"start_time_unix_nano":
1646538230507539000, "time_unix_nano": 1646538235507059000,
"value": 20, "aggregation_temporality": 2, "is_monotonic":
true}}
```

These counters are great for ever-increasing values, but measurements go up and down sometimes. Let's see what OpenTelemetry has in store for that.

An up/down counter

The following instrument is very similar to the counter. As you may have guessed from its name, the difference between the counter and the **up/down counter** is that the latter can record values that go up and down; it is non-monotonic. The following diagram shows us what a graph representing a non-monotonic counter may look like:

Figure 5.5 – Non-monotonic counter graph

Creating an `UpDownCounter` instrument is done via the `create_up_down_counter` method. Increment and decrement operations are done via the single `add` method with either positive or negative values:

metrics.py

```
if __name__ == "__main__":
    ...
    inventory_counter = meter.create_up_down_counter(
        name="inventory",
        unit="items",
        description="Number of items in inventory",
    )
    inventory_counter.add(20)
    inventory_counter.add(-5)
```

Choosing the right OpenTelemetry instrument   143

The previous example's output will be as follows:

output

```
{"attributes": "", "description": "Number of
items in inventory", "instrumentation_info":
"InstrumentationInfo(metric-example, 0.1.2, https://
opentelemetry.io/schemas/1.9.0)", "name": "inventory",
"resource": "BoundedAttributes({'telemetry.sdk.language':
'python', 'telemetry.sdk.name': 'opentelemetry', 'telemetry.
sdk.version': '1.10.0', 'service.name': 'unknown_service'},
maxlen=None)", "unit": "items", "point": {"start_time_
unix_nano": 1646538574503018000, "time_unix_nano":
1646538574503083000, "value": 15, "aggregation_temporality": 2,
"is_monotonic": false}}
```

Note the previous example only emits a single metric. This is expected as the two recordings were aggregated into a single value for the period reported.

Asynchronous up/down counter

As you may imagine, as the counter has an asynchronous counterpart, so does `UpDownCounter`. The **asynchronous up/down counter** allows us to increment or decrement a value on a set interval. As you will see shortly, it is pretty similar in nature to the **asynchronous gauge**. The main difference between the two is that the asynchronous up/down counter should be used when the values being recorded are additive in nature, meaning the measurements can be added across dimensions. Some examples of metrics that could be recorded via this instrument are as follows:

- Changes in the number of customers in a store
- Net revenue for an organization across business units

The following creates an asynchronous up/down counter to keep track of the current number of customers in a store. Note that, unlike its synchronous counterpart, the value recorded in the asynchronous up/down counter is an absolute value, not a delta. As per the previous asynchronous example, an `async_updowncounter_callback` callback method does the work of reporting the measure:

metrics.py

```
def async_updowncounter_callback():
    yield Measurement(20, {"locale": "en-US"})
    yield Measurement(10, {"locale": "fr-CA"})
```

```python
if __name__ == "__main__":
    ...
    upcounter_counter = meter.create_observable_up_down_counter(
        name="customer_in_store",
        callback=async_updowncounter_callback,
        unit="persons",
        description="Keeps a count of customers in the store"
    )
```

The output will start to look familiar based on the previous examples we've already run through:

output

```
{"attributes": {"locale": "en-US"}, "description": "Keeps a count of customers in the store", "instrumentation_info": "InstrumentationInfo(metric-example, 0.1.2, https://opentelemetry.io/schemas/1.9.0)", "name": "customer_in_store", "resource": "BoundedAttributes({'telemetry.sdk.language': 'python', 'telemetry.sdk.name': 'opentelemetry', 'telemetry.sdk.version': '1.10.0', 'service.name': 'unknown_service'}, maxlen=None)", "unit": "persons", "point": {"start_time_unix_nano": 1647735390164970000, "time_unix_nano": 1647735390164986000, "value": 20, "aggregation_temporality": 2, "is_monotonic": false}}
{"attributes": {"locale": "fr-CA"}, "description": "Keeps a count of customers in the store", "instrumentation_info": "InstrumentationInfo(metric-example, 0.1.2, https://opentelemetry.io/schemas/1.9.0)", "name": "customer_in_store", "resource": "BoundedAttributes({'telemetry.sdk.language': 'python', 'telemetry.sdk.name': 'opentelemetry', 'telemetry.sdk.version': '1.10.0', 'service.name': 'unknown_service'}, maxlen=None)", "unit": "persons", "point": {"start_time_unix_nano": 1647735390164980000, "time_unix_nano": 1647735390165009000, "value": 10, "aggregation_temporality": 2, "is_monotonic": false}}
```

Counters and up/down counters are suitable for many data types, but not all. Let's see what other instruments allow us to measure.

Histogram

A **histogram** instrument is useful when comparing the frequency distribution of values across large data sets. Histograms use buckets to group the data they represent and effectively identify outliers or anomalies. Some examples of data representable by histograms are as follows:

- Response times for requests to a service
- The height of individuals

Figure 5.6 shows a sample histogram chart representing the response time for requests. It looks like a bar chart, but it differs in that each bar represents a bucket containing a range for the values it contains. The *y* axis represents the count of elements in each bucket:

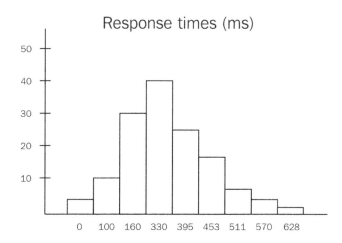

Figure 5.6 – Histogram graph

To capture information in a histogram, the buckets specified must be able to contain all the values it expects to record. For example, take a histogram containing two buckets with explicit upper bounds of `0` ms and `10` ms. Any measurement greater than `10` ms bound would be excluded from the histogram. Both Prometheus and OpenTelemetry address this by capturing any value beyond the maximum upper boundary in an additional bucket. The histograms we'll explore in this chapter all use explicit boundaries, but OpenTelemetry also provides experimental support for exponential histograms (https://github.com/open-telemetry/opentelemetry-specification/blob/main/specification/metrics/datamodel.md#exponentialhistogram).

Histograms can be, and are often, used to calculate percentiles. The following code creates a histogram via the `create_histogram` method. The method used to produce a metric with a histogram is named `record`:

metrics.py

```python
if __name__ == "__main__":
    ...
    histogram = meter.create_histogram(
        "response_times",
        unit="ms",
        description="Response times for all requests",
    )
    histogram.record(96)
    histogram.record(9)
```

In this example, we record two measurements that fall into separate buckets. Notice how they appear in the output:

output

```
{"attributes": "", "description": "Response times for all
requests", "instrumentation_info": "InstrumentationInfo(metric-
example, 0.1.2,  https://opentelemetry.io/
schemas/1.9.0)", "name": "response_times", "resource":
"BoundedAttributes({'telemetry.sdk.language': 'python',
'telemetry.sdk.name': 'opentelemetry', 'telemetry.sdk.
version': '1.10.0', 'service.name': 'unknown_service'},
maxlen=None)", "unit": "ms", "point": {"start_time_unix_nano":
1646539219677439000, "time_unix_nano": 1646539219677522000,
"bucket_counts": [0, 0, 1, 0, 0, 0, 1, 0, 0, 0, 0], "explicit_
bounds": [0.0, 5.0, 10.0, 25.0, 50.0, 75.0, 100.0, 250.0,
500.0, 1000.0], "sum": 105, "aggregation_temporality": 2}}
```

As with the counter and up/down counter, the histogram is synchronous.

Asynchronous gauge

The last instrument defined by OpenTelemetry is the **asynchronous gauge**. This instrument can be used to record measurements that are non-additive in nature; in other words, which wouldn't make sense to sum together. An asynchronous gauge can represent the following:

- The average memory consumption of a system
- The temperature of a data center

The following code uses Python's built-in resource module to measure the maximum resident set size (https://en.wikipedia.org/wiki/Resident_set_size). This value is set in `async_gauge_callback`, which is used as the callback for the gauge we're creating:

metrics.py

```
import resource

def async_gauge_callback():
    rss = resource.getrusage(resource.RUSAGE_SELF).ru_maxrss
    yield Measurement(rss, {})

if __name__ == "__main__":
    ...
    meter.create_observable_gauge(
        name="maxrss",
        unit="bytes",
        callback=async_gauge_callback,
        description="Max resident set size",
    )
    time.sleep(10)
```

Running the code will show us memory consumption information about our application using OpenTelemetry:

output

```
{"attributes": "", "description": "Max resident set size", "instrumentation_info": "InstrumentationInfo(metric-example, 0.1.2, https://opentelemetry.io/schemas/1.9.0)", "name": "maxrss", "resource": "BoundedAttributes({'telemetry.sdk.language': 'python', 'telemetry.sdk.name': 'opentelemetry', 'telemetry.sdk.version': '1.10.0', 'service.name': 'unknown_service'}, maxlen=None)", "unit": "bytes", "point": {"time_unix_nano": 1646539432021601000, "value": 18341888}}
{"attributes": "", "description": "Max resident set size", "instrumentation_info": "InstrumentationInfo(metric-example, 0.1.2, https://opentelemetry.io/schemas/1.9.0)", "name": "maxrss", "resource": "BoundedAttributes({'telemetry.sdk.language': 'python', 'telemetry.sdk.name': 'opentelemetry', 'telemetry.sdk.version': '1.10.0', 'service.name': 'unknown_service'}, maxlen=None)", "unit": "bytes", "point": {"time_unix_nano": 1646539437018742000, "value": 19558400}}
```

Excellent, we now know about the instruments and have started generating a steady metrics stream. The last topic about instruments to be covered is duplicate instruments.

Duplicate instruments

Duplicate instrument registration conflicts arise if more than one instrument is created within a single meter with the same name. This can potentially produce semantic errors in the data, as many telemetry backends uniquely identify metrics via their names. Conflicting instruments may be intentional when two separate code paths need to report the same metric, or, when multiple developers want to record different metrics but accidentally use the same name; naming things is hard. There are a few ways the OpenTelemetry SDK handles conflicting instruments:

- If the conflicting instruments are identical, the values recorded by these instruments are aggregated. The data generated appears as though a single instrument produced them.

- If the instruments are not identical, but the conflict can be resolved via View configuration, the user will not be warned. As we'll see next, views provide a mechanism to produce unique metric streams, differentiating the instruments.

- If the instruments are not identical and their conflicts are not resolved via views, a warning is emitted, and their data is generated without modification.

Individual meters act as a namespace, meaning two meters can separately create identical instruments without any issues. Using a unique namespace for each meter ensures that application developers can create instruments that make sense for their applications without running the risk of interfering with other metrics generated by underlying libraries. This will also make searching for metrics easier once exported outside the application. Let's see how we can shape the metrics stream to fit our needs with views.

Customizing metric outputs with views

Some applications may produce more metrics than an application developer is interested in. You may have noticed this with the example code for instruments; as we added more examples, it became difficult to find the metrics we were interested in. Recall the example mentioned earlier in this chapter: application *A* represents a client library making web requests that could produce metrics via three different meters. If each of those meters keeps a request counter, duplicate data is highly likely to be generated. Duplicated data may not be a problem on a small scale, but when scaling services up to handling thousands and millions of requests, unnecessary metrics can become quite expensive. Thankfully, **views** provide a way for users of OpenTelemetry to configure the SDK only to generate the metrics they want. In addition to providing a mechanism to filter metrics, views can also configure aggregation or be used to add a new dimension to metrics.

Filtering

The first aspect of interest is the ability to customize which metrics will be processed. To select instruments, the following criteria can be applied to a view:

- `instrument_name`: The name of the instrument
- `instrument_type`: The type of the instrument
- `meter_name`: The name of the meter
- `meter_version`: The version of the meter
- `meter_schema`: The schema URL of the meter

The SDK provides a default view as a catch-all for any instruments not matched by configured views.

> **Important note**
> The code in this chapter uses version 1.10.0 which supports the parameter enable_default_view to modify to disable the default view. This has changed in version 1.11.0 with the following change: https://github.com/open-telemetry/opentelemetry-python/pull/2547. If you are using a newer version, you will need to configure a wildcard view with a DropAggregation, refer to the official documentation (https://opentelemetry-python.readthedocs.io/en/latest/sdk/metrics.html) for more information.

The following code selects the inventory instrument we created in an earlier example. Views are added to the MeterProvider as an argument to the constructor.

Another argument is added disabling the default view:

metrics.py

```python
from opentelemetry.sdk._metrics.view import View
def configure_meter_provider():
    exporter = ConsoleMetricExporter()
    reader = PeriodicExportingMetricReader(exporter, export_interval_millis=5000)
    view = View(instrument_name="inventory")
    provider = MeterProvider(
        metric_readers=[reader],
        resource=Resource.create(),
        views=[view],
        enable_default_view=False,
    )
```

The resulting output shows a metric stream limited to a single instrument:

output

```
{"attributes": {"locale": "fr-FR", "country": "CA"},
"description": "total items sold", "instrumentation_info":
"InstrumentationInfo(metric-example, 0.1.2, https://
opentelemetry.io/schemas/1.9.0)", "name": "sold", "resource":
```

```
"BoundedAttributes({'telemetry.sdk.language': 'python',
'telemetry.sdk.name': 'opentelemetry', 'telemetry.sdk.version':
'1.10.0', 'service.name': 'unknown_service'}, maxlen=None)",
"unit": "items", "point": {"start_time_unix_nano":
1647800250023129000, "time_unix_nano": 1647800250023292000,
"value": 6, "aggregation_temporality": 2, "is_monotonic":
true}}
{"attributes": {"locale": "es-ES"}, "description": "total items
sold", "instrumentation_info": "InstrumentationInfo(metric-
example, 0.1.2,  https://opentelemetry.io/schemas/1.9.0)",
"name": "sold", "resource": "BoundedAttributes({'telemetry.
sdk.language': 'python', 'telemetry.sdk.name': 'opentelemetry',
'telemetry.sdk.version': '1.10.0', 'service.name': 'unknown_
service'}, maxlen=None)", "unit": "items", "point": {"start_
time_unix_nano": 1647800250023138000, "time_unix_nano":
1647800250023312000, "value": 1, "aggregation_temporality": 2,
"is_monotonic": true}}
```

The views parameter accepts a list, making adding multiple views trivial. This provides a great deal of flexibility and control for users. An instrument must match all arguments passed into the View constructor. Let's update the previous example and see what happens when we try to create a view by selecting an instrument of the Counter type with the name inventory:

metrics.py

```
from opentelemetry._metrics.instrument import Counter

def configure_meter_provider():
    exporter = ConsoleMetricExporter()
    reader = PeriodicExportingMetricReader(exporter, export_
interval_millis=5000)
    view = View(instrument_name="inventory", instrument_
type=Counter)
    provider = MeterProvider(
        metric_readers=[reader],
        resource=Resource.create(),
        views=[view],
        enable_default_view=False,
    )
```

As you may already suspect, these criteria will not match any instruments, and no data will be produced by running the code.

> **Important Note**
> All criteria specified when selecting instruments are optional. However, if no optional argument is specified, the code will raise an exception as per the OpenTelemetry specification.

Using views to filter instruments based on instrument or meter identification is a great way to reduce the noise and cost of generating too many metrics.

Dimensions

In addition to selecting instruments, it's also possible to configure a view to only report specific dimensions. A dimension in this context is an attribute associated with the metric. For example, a customer counter may record information about customers as per *Figure 5.7*. Each attribute associated with the counter, such as the country the customer is visiting from or the locale their browser is set to, offers another dimension to the metric recorded during their visit:

Customer	Country	Locale
1	Canada	en-US
1	France	fr-FR
1	Canada	fr-FR

Figure 5.7 – Additional dimensions for a counter

Dimensions can be used to aggregate data in meaningful ways; continuing with the previous table, we can obtain the following information:

- Three customers visited our store.
- Two customers visited from Canada and one from France.
- Two had browsers configured to French (fr-FR), and one to English (en-US).

Views allow us to customize the output from our metrics stream. Using the `attributes_keys` argument, we specify the dimensions we want to see in a particular view. The following configures a view to match the `Counter` instruments and to discard any attributes other than `locale`:

metrics.py

```
def configure_meter_provider():
    exporter = ConsoleMetricExporter()
    reader = PeriodicExportingMetricReader(exporter, export_interval_millis=5000)
    view = View(instrument_type=Counter, attribute_keys=["locale"])
    ...
```

You may remember that in the code we wrote earlier when configuring instruments, the `items_sold` counter generated two metrics. The first contained `country` and `locale` attributes; the second contained the `locale` attribute. The configuration in this view will produce a metric stream discarding all attributes not specified via `attribute_keys`:

output

```
{"attributes": {"locale": "fr-FR"}, "description": "Total items sold", ...
{"attributes": {"locale": "es-ES"}, "description": "Total items sold", ...
```

Note that when using `attribute_keys`, all metrics not containing the specified attributes will be aggregated. This is because by removing the attributes, the view effectively transforms the metrics, as per the following table:

Counter operation	Transformed via attribute keys
add(1,{"locale":"fr-FR"})	add(1,{"locale":"fr-FR"})
add(1,{"country":"CA"})	add(1,{})
add(1,{"locale":"en-US", "country":"CA"})	add(1,{"locale":"en-US"})
add(1,{})	add(1,{})

Figure 5.8 – Effect of attribute keys on counter operations

An example of where this may be useful is separating requests containing errors from those that do not, or grouping requests by status code.

In addition to customizing the metric stream attributes, views can also alter their name or description. The following renames the metric generated and updates its description. Additionally, it removes all attributes from the metric stream:

metrics.py

```
def configure_meter_provider():
    exporter = ConsoleMetricExporter()
    reader = PeriodicExportingMetricReader(exporter, export_interval_millis=5000)
    view = View(
        instrument_type=Counter,
        attribute_keys=[],
        name="sold",
        description="total items sold",
    )
    ...
```

The output now shows us a single aggregated metric that is more meaningful to us:

output

```
{"attributes": "", "description": "total items sold",
"instrumentation_info": "InstrumentationInfo(metric-example,
0.1.2, https://opentelemetry.io/schemas/1.9.0)", "name":
"sold", "resource": "BoundedAttributes({'telemetry.sdk.
language': 'python', 'telemetry.sdk.name': 'opentelemetry',
'telemetry.sdk.version': '1.10.0', 'service.name': 'unknown_
service'}, maxlen=None)", "unit": "items", "point": {"start_
time_unix_nano": 1646593079208078000, "time_unix_nano":
1646593079208238000, "value": 7, "aggregation_temporality": 2,
"is_monotonic": true}}
```

Customizing views allow us to focus further on the output of the metrics generated. Let's see how we can combine the metrics with aggregators.

Aggregation

The last configuration of views we will investigate is aggregation. The `aggregation` option gives the view the ability to change the default aggregation used by an instrument to one of the following methods:

- `SumAggregation`: Add the instrument's measurements and set the current value as the sum. The monotonicity and temporality for the sum are derived from the instrument.
- `LastValueAggregation`: Record the last measurement and its timestamp as the current value of this view.
- `ExplicitBucketHistogramAggregation`: Use a histogram where the boundaries can be set via configuration. Additional options for this aggregation are `boundaries` for the buckets of the histogram and `record_min_max` to record the minimum and maximum values.

The following table, *Figure 5.9*, shows us the default aggregation for each instrument:

Instrument	Default aggregation
Counter	SumAggregation
Asynchronous Counter	SumAggregation
UpDownCounter	SumAggregation
Asynchronous UpDownCounter	SumAggregation
Histogram	ExplicitBucketHistogramAggregation
Asynchronous Gauge	LastValueAggregation

Figure 5.9 – Default aggregation per instrument

Aggregating data in the SDK allows us to reduce the number of data points transmitted. However, this means the data available at query time is less granular, limiting the user's ability to query it. Keeping this in mind, let's look at configuring the aggregation for one of our counter instruments to see how this works. The following code updates the view configured earlier to use `LastValueAggregation` instead of the `SumAggregation` default:

metrics.py

```
from opentelemetry.sdk._metrics.aggregation import
LastValueAggregation
```

```
def configure_meter_provider():
    exporter = ConsoleMetricExporter()
    reader = PeriodicExportingMetricReader(exporter, export_interval_millis=5000)
    view = View(
        instrument_type=Counter,
        attribute_keys=[],
        name="sold",
        description="total items sold",
        aggregation=LastValueAggregation(),
    )
```

You'll notice in the output now that instead of reporting the sum of all measurements (7) for the counter, only the last value (1) recorded is produced:

output

```
{"attributes": "", "description": "total items sold",
"instrumentation_info": "InstrumentationInfo(metric-example,
0.1.2, https://opentelemetry.io/schemas/1.9.0)", "name":
"sold", "resource": "BoundedAttributes({'telemetry.sdk.
language': 'python', 'telemetry.sdk.name': 'opentelemetry',
'telemetry.sdk.version': '1.10.0', 'service.name': 'unknown_
service'}, maxlen=None)", "unit": "items", "point": {"time_
unix_nano": 1646594506458381000, "value": 1}}
```

Although it's essential to have the ability to configure aggregation, the default aggregation may well serve your purpose most of the time.

> **Important Note**
>
> As mentioned earlier, sum aggregation derives the temporality of the sum reported from its instrument. This temporality can be either *cumulative* or *delta*. This determines whether the reported metrics are to be interpreted as always starting at the same time, therefore, reporting a cumulative metric, or if the metrics reported represent a moving start time, and the reported values contain the delta from the previous report. For more information about temporality, refer to the OpenTelemetry specification found at `https://github.com/open-telemetry/opentelemetry-specification/blob/main/specification/metrics/datamodel.md#temporality`.

The grocery store

It's time to go back to the example application from *Chapter 4, Distributed Tracing - Tracing Code Execution*, to get some practical experience of all the knowledge we've gained so far. Let's start by adding a method to retrieve a meter that will resemble `configure_tracer` from the previous chapter. This method will be named `configure_meter` and will contain the configuration code from an example earlier in this chapter. One main difference is the addition of a resource that uses `LocalMachineResourceDetector`, as we already defined in this module. Add the following code to the `common.py` module:

common.py

```python
from opentelemetry._metrics import get_meter_provider, set_meter_provider
from opentelemetry.sdk._metrics import MeterProvider
from opentelemetry.sdk._metrics.export import (
    ConsoleMetricExporter,
    PeriodicExportingMetricReader,
)

def configure_meter(name, version):
    exporter = ConsoleMetricExporter()
    reader = PeriodicExportingMetricReader(exporter, export_interval_millis=5000)
    local_resource = LocalMachineResourceDetector().detect()
    resource = local_resource.merge(
        Resource.create(
            {
                ResourceAttributes.SERVICE_NAME: name,
                ResourceAttributes.SERVICE_VERSION: version,
            }
        )
    )
    provider = MeterProvider(metric_readers=[reader], resource=resource)
    set_meter_provider(provider)
    schema_url = "https://opentelemetry.io/schemas/1.9.0"
    return get_meter_provider().get_meter(
        name=name,
```

```
            version=version,
            schema_url=schema_url,
    )
```

Now, update `shopper.py` to call this method and set the return value to a global variable named `meter` that we'll use throughout the application:

shopper.py

```
from common import configure_tracer, configure_meter

tracer = configure_tracer("shopper", "0.1.2")
meter = configure_meter("shopper", "0.1.2")
```

We will be adding this line to `grocery_store.py` and `legacy_inventory.py` in the following examples, but you may choose to do so now. Now, to start the applications and ensure the code works as it should, launch the three applications in separate terminals using the following commands in the order presented:

```
$ python legacy_inventory.py
$ python grocery_store.py
$ python shopper.py
```

The execution of `shopper.py` should return right away. If no errors were printed out because of running those commands, we're off to a good start and are getting closer to adding metrics to our applications!

Number of requests

When considering what metrics are essential to get insights about an application, it can be overwhelming to think of all the things we could measure. A good place is to start is with the *golden signals* as documented in the Google **Site Reliability Engineering (SRE)** book, https://sre.google/sre-book/monitoring-distributed-systems/#xref_monitoring_golden-signals. Measuring the traffic to our application is an easy place to start by counting the number of requests it receives. It can help answer questions such as the following:

- What is the traffic pattern for our application?
- Is the application capable of handling the traffic we expected?

- How successful is the application?

In future chapters, we'll investigate how this metric can be used to determine if the application should be scaled automatically. A metric such as the total number of requests a service can handle is likely a number that would be revealed during benchmarking.

The following code calls `configure_meter` and creates a counter via the `create_counter` method to keep track of the incoming requests to the server application. The `request_counter` value is incremented before the request is processed:

grocery_store.py

```python
from common import configure_meter, configure_tracer, set_span_attributes_from_flask

tracer = configure_tracer("grocery-store", "0.1.2")
meter = configure_meter("grocery-store", "0.1.2")
request_counter = meter.create_counter(
    name="requests",
    unit="request",
    description="Total number of requests",
)

@app.before_request
def before_request_func():
    token = context.attach(extract(request.headers))
    request_counter.add(1)
    request.environ["context_token"] = token
```

The updated grocery store code should reload automatically, but restart the grocery store application if it does not. Once the updated code is running, make the following three requests to the store by using `curl`:

```
$ curl localhost:5000
$ curl localhost:5000/products
$ curl localhost:5000/none-existent-url
```

This should give us output similar to the abbreviated output. Pay attention to the increasing `value` field, which increases by one with each visit:

```
127.0.0.1 - - [06/Mar/2022 11:44:41] "GET / HTTP/1.1" 200 -
{"attributes": "", "description": "Total number of requests",
... "point": {"start_time_unix_nano": 1646595826470792000,
"time_unix_nano": 1646595833190445000, "value": 1,
"aggregation_temporality": 2, "is_monotonic": true}}
127.0.0.1 - - [06/Mar/2022 11:44:46] "GET /products HTTP/1.1"
200 -
{"attributes": "", "description": "Total number of requests",
... "point": {"start_time_unix_nano": 1646595826470792000,
"time_unix_nano": 1646595883232762000, "value": 2,
"aggregation_temporality": 2, "is_monotonic": true}}
127.0.0.1 - - [06/Mar/2022 11:44:47] "GET /none-existent-url
HTTP/1.1" 404 -
{"attributes": "", "description": "Total number of requests",
... "point": {"start_time_unix_nano": 1646595826470792000,
"time_unix_nano": 1646595888236270000, "value": 3,
"aggregation_temporality": 2, "is_monotonic": true}}
```

In addition to counting the total number of requests, it's helpful to have a way to track the different response codes. In the previous example, if you look at the output, you'll notice the last response's status code indicated a `404` error, which would be helpful to identify differently from other responses.

Keeping a separate counter would allow us to calculate an error rate that could infer the service's health. Alternatively, using attributes can accomplish this, as well. The following moves the code to increment the counter where the response status code is available. This code is then recorded as an attribute on the metric:

grocery_store.py

```python
@app.before_request
def before_request_func():
    token = context.attach(extract(request.headers))
    request.environ["context_token"] = token


@app.after_request
def after_request_func(response):
    request_counter.add(1, {"code": response.status_code})
```

```
    return response
```

To trigger the new code, use the following `curl` command:

```
$ curl localhost:5000/none-existent-url
```

The result includes the status code attribute:

output

```
{"attributes": {"code": 404}, "description": "Total
number of requests", "instrumentation_info":
"InstrumentationInfo(grocery-store, 0.1.2, https://
opentelemetry.io/schemas/1.9.0)", "name": "requests",
"resource": "BoundedAttributes({'telemetry.sdk.language':
'python', 'telemetry.sdk.name': 'opentelemetry', 'telemetry.
sdk.version': '1.10.0', 'net.host.name': 'host', 'net.host.
ip': '127.0.0.1', 'service.name': 'grocery-store', 'service.
version': '0.1.2'}, maxlen=None)", "unit": "request", "point":
{"start_time_unix_nano": 1646598200103414000, "time_unix_nano":
1646598203067451000, "value": 1, "aggregation_temporality": 2,
"is_monotonic": true}}
```

Send a few more requests through to obtain different status codes. You can start seeing how this information can calculate error rates. The name given to metrics is significant.

> **Important Note**
> It's not possible to generate telemetry where there is no instrumentation. However, it *is* possible to filter out undesired telemetry using the configuration in the SDK and the OpenTelemetry collector. Remember this when instrumenting code. We'll visit how the collector can filter telemetry in *Chapter 8, OpenTelemetry Collector*, and *Chapter 9, Deploying the Collector*.

The data has shown us how to use a counter to produce meaningful data enriched with attributes. The value of this data will become even more apparent once we look at analysis tools in *Chapter 10, Configuring Backends*.

Request duration

The next metric to produce is request duration. The goal of understanding the request duration across a system is to be able to answer questions such as the following:

- How long did the request take?
- How much time did each service add to the total duration of the request?
- What is the experience for users?

Request duration is an interesting metric to understand the health of a service and can often be the symptom of an underlying issue. Collecting the duration is best done via a histogram, which can provide us with the organization and visualization necessary to understand the distribution across many requests. In the following example, we are interested in measuring the duration of operations within each service. We are also interested in capturing the duration of upstream requests and the network latency costs across each service in our distributed application. *Figure 5.10* shows how this will be measured:

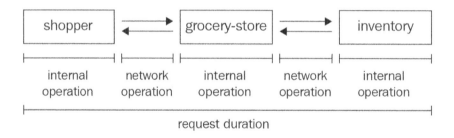

Figure 5.10 – Measuring request duration

We can use the different measurements across the entire request to understand where time is spent. This could help differentiate network issues from application issues. For example, if a request from `shopper.py` to `grocery_store.py` takes 100 ms, but the operation within `grocery_store.py` takes less than 1 ms, we know that the additional 99 ms were spent outside the application code.

> **Important Note**
> When a network is involved, unexpected latency can always exist. This common fallacy of cloud-native applications must be accounted for when designing applications. Investment in network engineering and deploying applications within closer physical proximity significantly reduces latency.

In the following example, the `upstream_duration_histo` histogram is configured to record the duration of requests from `shopper.py` to `grocery_store.py`. An additional histogram, `total_duration_histo`, is created to capture the duration of the entire operation within the shopper application. The period is calculated using the `time_ns` method from the `time` library, which returns the current time in nanoseconds, which we convert to milliseconds:

shopper.py

```
import time

total_duration_histo = meter.create_histogram(
    name="duration",
    description="request duration",
    unit="ms",
)

upstream_duration_histo = meter.create_histogram(
    name="upstream_request_duration",
    description="duration of upstream requests",
    unit="ms",
)

def browse():
    ...
        start = time.time_ns()
        resp = requests.get(url, headers=headers)
        duration = (time.time_ns() - start)/1e6
        upstream_duration_histo.record(duration)
    ...

def visit_store():
    start = time.time_ns()
    browse()
    duration = (time.time_ns() - start)/1e6
    total_duration_histo.record(duration)
```

The next step is to configure a histogram in `grocery_store.py` to record upstream requests and operation durations. For brevity, I will omit the instantiation of the two histograms to the following code, as the code is identical to the previous example. The following uses methods decorated with Flask's `before_request` and `after_request` to calculate the beginning and end of the entire operation. We also need to calculate the upstream request that occurs in the `products` method:

grocery_store.py

```python
@app.before_request
def before_request_func():
    token = context.attach(extract(request.headers))
    request_counter.add(1, {})
    request.environ["context_token"] = token
    request.environ["start_time"] = time.time_ns()


@app.after_request
def after_request_func(response):
    request_counter.add(1, {"code": response.status_code})
    duration = (time.time_ns() - request.environ["start_time"]) / 1e6
    total_duration_histo.record(duration)
    return response


@app.route("/products")
@tracer.start_as_current_span("/products", kind=SpanKind.SERVER)
def products():
    ...
        inject(headers)
        start = time.time_ns()
        resp = requests.get(url, headers=headers)
        duration = (time.time_ns() - start) / 1e6
        upstream_duration_histo.record(duration)
```

Lastly, for this example, let's add duration calculation for `legacy_inventory.py`. The code will be more straightforward since this service has no upstream requests yet, thus, we'll only need to define a single histogram:

legacy_inventory.py

```python
from flask import request
import time

total_duration_histo = meter.create_histogram(
    name="duration",
    description="request duration",
    unit="ms",
)

@app.before_request
def before_request_func():
    token = context.attach(extract(request.headers))
    request.environ["start_time"] = time.time_ns()

@app.after_request
def after_request_func(response):
    duration = (time.time_ns() - request.environ["start_time"]) / 1e6
    total_duration_histo.record(duration)
    return response
```

Now that we have all these histograms in place, we can finally look at the duration of our requests. The following output combines the output from all three applications to give us a complete picture of the time spent across the system. Pay close attention to the sum value recorded for each histogram. As we're only sending one request through, the sum equates the value for that single request:

output

```
{"attributes": "", "description": "duration of
upstream requests", "instrumentation_info":
"InstrumentationInfo(shopper, 0.1.2, https://opentelemetry.io/
schemas/1.9.0)", "name": "upstream_request_duration", "unit":
```

```
"ms", "point": {"start_time_unix_nano": 1646626129420576000,
"time_unix_nano": 1646626129420946000, "bucket_counts": [0, 0,
0, 0, 0, 0, 0, 0, 0, 0, 1], "explicit_bounds": [0.0, 5.0, 10.0,
25.0, 50.0, 75.0, 100.0, 250.0, 500.0, 1000.0], "sum": 18.981,
"aggregation_temporality": 2}}
```

```
{"attributes": "", "description": "request duration",
"instrumentation_info": "InstrumentationInfo(shopper,
0.1.2, https://opentelemetry.io/schemas/1.9.0)", "name":
"duration", "unit": "ms", "point": {"start_time_unix_nano":
1646626129420775000, "time_unix_nano": 1646626129420980000,
"bucket_counts": [0, 0, 0, 1, 0, 0, 0, 0, 0, 0, 0], "explicit_
bounds": [0.0, 5.0, 10.0, 25.0, 50.0, 75.0, 100.0, 250.0,
500.0, 1000.0], "sum": 19.354, "aggregation_temporality": 2}}
```

```
{"attributes": "", "description": "request duration",
"instrumentation_info": "InstrumentationInfo(grocery-store,
0.1.2, https://opentelemetry.io/schemas/1.9.0)", "name":
"duration", "unit": "ms", "point": {"start_time_unix_nano":
1646626129419257000, "time_unix_nano": 1646626133006672000,
"bucket_counts": [0, 0, 0, 1, 0, 0, 0, 0, 0, 0, 0], "explicit_
bounds": [0.0, 5.0, 10.0, 25.0, 50.0, 75.0, 100.0, 250.0,
500.0, 1000.0], "sum": 10.852, "aggregation_temporality": 2}}
```

```
{"attributes": "", "description": "duration of
upstream requests", "instrumentation_info":
"InstrumentationInfo(grocery-store, 0.1.2, https://
opentelemetry.io/schemas/1.9.0)", "name": "upstream_request_
duration", "unit": "ms", "point": {"start_time_unix_nano":
1646626129419136000, "time_unix_nano": 1646626135619575000,
"bucket_counts": [0, 0, 0, 1, 0, 0, 0, 0, 0, 0, 0], "explicit_
bounds": [0.0, 5.0, 10.0, 25.0, 50.0, 75.0, 100.0, 250.0,
500.0, 1000.0], "sum": 10.36, "aggregation_temporality": 2}}
```

```
{"attributes": "", "description": "request duration",
"instrumentation_info": "InstrumentationInfo(legacy-inventory,
0.9.1, https://opentelemetry.io/schemas/1.9.0)", "name":
"duration", "unit": "ms", "point": {"start_time_unix_nano":
1646626129417730000, "time_unix_nano": 1646626134436096000,
"bucket_counts": [0, 1, 0, 0, 0, 0, 0, 0, 0, 0, 0], "explicit_
bounds": [0.0, 5.0, 10.0, 25.0, 50.0, 75.0, 100.0, 250.0,
500.0, 1000.0], "sum": 0.494, "aggregation_temporality": 2}}
```

The difference in upstream_request_duration and duration sums for each application gives us the duration of the operation within each application. Looking closely at the data produced, we can see a significant portion of the request, 93% in this case, is spent communicating between applications.

If you're looking at this and wondering, *Couldn't distributed tracing calculate the duration of the request and latency instead?*, you're right. This type of information is also available via distributed tracing, so long as all the operations along the way are instrumented.

Concurrent requests

Another critical metric is the concurrent number of requests an application is processing at any given time. This helps answer the following:

- Is the application a bottleneck for a system?
- Can the application handle a surge in requests?

Normally, this value is obtained by calculating a rate of the number of requests per second via the counter added earlier. However, since we need practice with instruments and have yet to send our data to a backend that allows for analysis, we'll record it manually.

It's possible to use several instruments to capture this. For the sake of this example, we will use an up/down counter, but we could have also used a gauge as well. We will increment the up/down counter every time a new request begins and decrement it after each request:

grocery_store.py

```python
concurrent_counter = meter.create_up_down_counter(
    name="concurrent_requests",
    unit="request",
    description="Total number of concurrent requests",
)

@app.before_request
def before_request_func():
    ...
    concurrent_counter.add(1)

@app.after_request
def after_request_func(err):
    ...
    concurrent_counter.add(-1)
```

To ensure we can see multiple users connected simultaneously, we will use a different tool than `shopper.py`, which we've used for this far. The `hey` load generation program allows us to generate hundreds of requests in parallel, enabling us to see the up/down counter in action. Run the program now with the following command to generate `300` requests with a maximum concurrency of `10`:

```
$ hey -n 3000 -c 10 http://localhost:5000/products
```

That command should have created enough parallel connections. Let's look at the metrics generated; we should expect to see the recorded value going up as the number of concurrent requests increases, and then going back down:

output

```
{"attributes": "", "description": "Total number
of concurrent requests", "instrumentation_info":
"InstrumentationInfo(grocery-store, 0.1.2, https://
opentelemetry.io/schemas/1.9.0)", "name": "concurrent_
requests", "unit": "request", "point": {"start_time_unix_nano":
1646627738799214000, "time_unix_nano": 1646627769865503000,
"value": 10, "aggregation_temporality": 2, "is_monotonic":
false}}
{"attributes": "", "description": "Total number
of concurrent requests", "instrumentation_info":
"InstrumentationInfo(grocery-store, 0.1.2, https://
opentelemetry.io/schemas/1.9.0)", "name": "concurrent_
requests", "unit": "request", "point": {"start_time_unix_nano":
1646627738799214000, "time_unix_nano": 1646627774867317000,
"value": 0, "aggregation_temporality": 2, "is_monotonic":
false}}
```

We will come back to using this tool later, but it's worth keeping around if you want to test the performance of your applications. We will be looking at some additional tools to generate load in *Chapter 11, Diagnosing Problems*. Try pushing the load higher to see if you can cause the application to fail altogether by increasing the number of requests or concurrency.

Resource consumption

The following metrics we will capture from our applications are runtime performance metrics. Capturing the performance metrics of an application can help us answer questions such as the following:

- How many resources does my application need?
- What budget will I need to run this service for the next 6 months?

This often helps guide decisions of what resources will be needed as the business needs change. Quite often, application performance metrics, such as memory, CPU, and network consumption, indicate where time could be spent reducing the cost of an application.

> **Important Note**
>
> In the following example, we will focus specifically on runtime application metrics. These do not include system-level metrics. There is an essential distinction between the two. Runtime application metrics should be recorded by each application individually. On the other hand, system-level metrics should only be recorded once for the entire system. Reporting system-level metrics from multiple applications running on the same system is problematic. This will cause system performance metrics to be duplicated, which will require de-duplication either at transport or at analysis time. Another problem is that querying the system for metrics is expensive, and doing so multiple times places an unnecessary burden on the system.

When looking for runtime metrics, there are many metrics to choose from. Let's record the memory consumption that we will measure using an asynchronous gauge. One of the tools available to provide a way to measure memory statistics in Python comes with the standard library. The resource package (https://docs.python.org/3/library/resource.html) provides usage information about our process. Additional third-party libraries are available, such as psutil (https://psutil.readthedocs.io/), which provides even more information about the resource utilization of your process. It's an excellent package for collecting information about CPU, disk, and network usage.

As the implementation for capturing this metric will be the same across all the applications in the system, the code for the callback will be placed in common.py. The following creates a record_max_rss_callback method to record the maximum resident set size for the application. It also defines a convenience method called start_recording_memory_metrics, which creates the asynchronous gauge. Add these methods to common.py now:

common.py

```
import resource
from opentelemetry._metrics.measurement import Measurement

def record_max_rss_callback():
    yield Measurement(resource.getrusage(resource.RUSAGE_SELF).ru_maxrss)

def start_recording_memory_metrics(meter):
    meter.create_observable_gauge(
        callback=record_max_rss_callback,
        name="maxrss",
        unit="bytes",
        description="Max resident set size",
    )
```

Next, add a call to start_recording_memory_metrics in each application in our system. Add the following code to shopper.py, legacy_inventory.py, and grocery_store.py:

shopper.py

```
from common import start_recording_memory_metrics

if __name__ == "__main__":
    start_recording_memory_metrics(meter)
```

After adding this code to each application and ensuring they have been reloaded, each should start reporting the following values:

output

```
{"attributes": "", "description": "Max resident set size",
"instrumentation_info": "InstrumentationInfo(legacy-inventory,
0.9.1, https://opentelemetry.io/schemas/1.9.0)", "name":
"maxrss", "resource": "BoundedAttributes({'telemetry.sdk.
language': 'python', 'telemetry.sdk.name': 'opentelemetry',
'telemetry.sdk.version': '1.10.0', 'net.host.name': 'host',
'net.host.ip': '10.0.0.141', 'service.name': 'legacy-
inventory', 'service.version': '0.9.1'}, maxlen=None)", "unit":
"bytes", "point": {"time_unix_nano": 1646637404789912000,
"value": 33083392}}
```

And just like that, we have memory telemetry about our applications. I urge you to add additional usage metrics to the application and look at the `psutil` library mentioned earlier to expand the telemetry of your services. The metrics we added to the grocery store are by no means exhaustive. Instrumenting the code and gaining familiarity with instruments gives us a starting point from which to work.

Summary

We've covered much ground in this chapter about the metrics signal. We started by familiarizing ourselves with the different components and terminology of the metrics pipeline and how to configure them. We then looked at all the ins and outs of the individual instruments available to record measurements and used each one to record sample metrics.

Using views, we learned to aggregate, filter, and customize the metric streams being emitted by our application to fit our specific needs. This will be handy when we start leveraging instrumentation libraries. Finally, we returned to the grocery store to get hands-on experience with instrumenting an existing application and collecting real-world metrics.

Metrics is a deep topic that goes well beyond what has been covered in this chapter, but hopefully, what you've learned thus far is enough to start considering how OpenTelemetry can be used in your code. The next chapter will look at the third and final signal we will cover in this book – logging.

6
Logging – Capturing Events

Metrics and traces go a long way in helping understand the behaviors and intricacies of cloud-native applications. Sometimes though, it's useful to log additional information that can be used at debug time. Logging gives us the ability to record information in a way that is perhaps more flexible and freeform than either tracing or metrics. That flexibility is both wonderful and terrible. It allows logs to be customized to fit whatever need arises using natural language, which often, but not always, makes it easier to interpret by the reader. But the flexibility is often abused, resulting in a mess of logs that are hard to search through and even harder to aggregate in any meaningful way. This chapter will take a look at how **OpenTelemetry** tackles the challenges of logging and how it can be used to improve the telemetry generated by an application. We will cover the following topics:

- Configuring OpenTelemetry to export logs
- Producing logs via the OpenTelemetry API and a standard logging library
- The logging signal in practice within the context of the grocery store application

Along the way, we will learn about standard logging in Python as well as logging with Flask, giving us a chance to use an instrumentation library as well. But first, let's ensure we have everything we need set up.

Technical requirements

If you've already completed *Chapter 4*, *Distributed Tracing*, or *Chapter 5*, *Metrics - Recording Measurements*, the setup here will be quite familiar. Ensure the version of Python in your environment is at least Python 3.6 by running the following commands:

```
$ python --version
$ python3 --version
```

This chapter will rely on the OpenTelemetry API and SDK packages that are installable via `pip` with the following command. The examples in this chapter are using the version 1.9.0 `opentelemetry-api` and `opentelemetry-sdk` packages:

```
$ pip install opentelemetry-api \
              opentelemetry-sdk \
              opentelemetry-propagator-b3
```

> **Important Note**
>
> The OpenTelemetry examples in this chapter rely on an experimental release of the logging signal for OpenTelemetry. This means it's possible that by the time you're reading this, the updated packages have moved methods to different packages. The release notes available for each release should help you identify where the packages have moved to (https://github.com/open-telemetry/opentelemetry-python/releases).

Additionally, in this chapter, we will use an instrumentation package made available by the OpenTelemetry Python community. This instrumentation will assist us when adding logging information to Flask applications that are part of the grocery store. Install the package via `pip` with the following command:

```
$ pip install opentelemetry-instrumentation-wsgi
```

The code for this chapter is available in the `companion` repository. The following uses `git` to copy the repository locally:

```
$ git clone https://github.com/PacktPublishing/Cloud-Native-Observability
```

The completed code for the examples in this chapter is available in the `chapter06` directory. If you're interested in writing the code yourself, I suggest you start by copying the code in the `chapter04` directory and following along.

Lastly, we will need to install the libraries that the grocery store relies on. This can be done via the following `pip` command:

```
$ pip install flask requests
```

We're now ready to start logging!

Configuring OpenTelemetry logging

Unlike with the two signals we covered in *Chapter 4*, *Distributed Tracing*, and *Chapter 5*, *Metrics - Recording Measurements*, the logging signal in OpenTelemetry does not concern itself with standardizing a logging interface. Many languages already have an established logging API, and a decision early on in OpenTelemetry was made to leverage those pre-existing tools. Although OpenTelemetry provides an API capable of producing logging, which we'll use shortly, the signal is intent on hooking into the existing logging facilities. Its focus is to augment the logs produced and provide a mechanism to correlate those logs with other signals. *Figure 6.1* shows us the components of the logging pipeline:

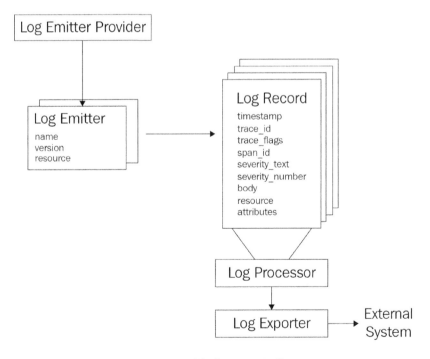

Figure 6.1 – The logging pipeline

These components combine to produce log records and emit them to external systems. The logging pipeline is comprised of the following:

- A `LogEmitterProvider`, which provides a mechanism to instantiate one or more log emitters
- The `LogEmitter`, which produces `LogRecord` data
- The `LogProcessor`, which consumes log records and passes them on to a `LogExporter` for sending the data to a backend

First, as with all the other OpenTelemetry signals, we must configure the provider. The following code instantiates a `LogEmitterProvider` from the SDK, passes in a resource via the `resource` argument, and then sets the global log emitter via the `set_log_emitter_provider` method:

logs.py

```python
from opentelemetry.sdk._logs import LogEmitterProvider, set_log_emitter_provider
from opentelemetry.sdk.resources import Resource

def configure_log_emitter_provider():
    provider = LogEmitterProvider(resource=Resource.create())
    set_log_emitter_provider(provider)
```

Configuring `LogEmitter` alone won't allow us to produce telemetry. We'll need a log processor and an exporter to go a step further. Let's add `BatchLogProcessor`, which, as the name suggests, batches the processing of log records. We will also use a `ConsoleLogExporter` to output logging information to the console:

logs.py

```python
from opentelemetry.sdk._logs.export import ConsoleLogExporter, BatchLogProcessor
from opentelemetry.sdk._logs import LogEmitterProvider, set_log_emitter_provider
from opentelemetry.sdk.resources import Resource

def configure_log_emitter_provider():
    provider = LogEmitterProvider(resource=Resource.create())
    set_log_emitter_provider(provider)
```

```
    exporter = ConsoleLogExporter()
    provider.add_log_processor(BatchLogProcessor(exporter))
```

With OpenTelemetry configured, we're now ready to start instrumenting our logs.

Producing logs

Following the pattern from previous signals, we should be ready to get an instance of a log producer and start logging, right? Well, not quite – let's find out why.

Using LogEmitter

Using the same method that we used for metrics and tracing, we can now obtain `LogEmitter`, which will allow us to use the OpenTelemetry API to start producing logs. The following code shows us how to accomplish this using the `get_log_emitter` method:

logs.py

```
from opentelemetry.sdk._logs import (
    LogEmitterProvider,
    get_log_emitter_provider,
    set_log_emitter_provider,
)

if __name__ == "__main__":
    configure_log_emitter_provider()
    log_emitter = get_log_emitter_provider().get_log_emitter(
        "shopper",
        "0.1.2",
    )
```

With `LogEmitter` in hand, we're now ready to generate `LogRecord`. The `LogRecord` contains the following information:

- `timestamp`: A time associated with the log record in nanoseconds.
- `trace_id`: A hex-encoded identifier of the trace to correlate with the log record. There will be more on this, the span identifier, and trace flags shortly.
- `span_id`: A hex-encoded identifier of the span to correlate with the log record.

- `trace_flags`: Trace flags associated with the trace active when the log record was produced.
- `severity_text`: A string representation of the severity level.
- `severity_number`: A numeric value of the severity level.
- `body`: The contents of the log message being recorded.
- `resource`: The resource associated with the producer of the log record.
- `attributes`: Additional information associated with the log record in the form of key-value pairs.

Each one of those fields can be passed as an argument to the constructor; note that all those fields are optional. The following creates `LogRecord` with some minimal information and calls `emit` to produce a log entry:

logs.py

```
import time
from opentelemetry.sdk._logs import (
    LogEmitterProvider,
    LogRecord,
    get_log_emitter_provider,
    set_log_emitter_provider,
)

if __name__ == "__main__":
    configure_log_emitter_provider()
    log_emitter = get_log_emitter_provider().get_log_emitter(
        "shopper",
        "0.1.2",
    )
    log_emitter.emit(
        LogRecord(
            timestamp=time.time_ns(),
            body="first log line",
        )
    )
```

After all this work, we can finally see a log line! Run the code, and the output should look something like this:

output

```
{"body": "first log line", "name": null, "severity_number":
"None", "severity_text": null, "attributes": null, "timestamp":
1630814115049294000, "trace_id": "", "span_id": "", "trace_
flags": null, "resource": ""}
```

As you can see, there's a lot of information missing to give us a full picture of what was happening. One of the most important pieces of information associated with a log entry is the severity level. The OpenTelemetry specification defines 24 different log levels categorized in 6 severity groups, as shown in the following figure:

SeverityNumber range	Range name	Meaning
1-4	TRACE	A fine-grained debugging event. Typically disabled in default configurations.
5-8	DEBUG	A debugging event.
9-12	INFO	An informational event. Indicates that an event happened.
13-16	WARN	A warning event. Not an error but is likely more important than an informational event.
17-20	ERROR	An error event. Something went wrong.
21-24	FATAL	A fatal error such as an application or system crash.

Figure 6.2 – Log severity levels defined by OpenTelemetry

When defining the severity level, all log levels above that number are reported.

Let's ensure the log record we generate sets a meaningful severity level:

logs.py

```
from opentelemetry.sdk._logs.severity import SeverityNumber

if __name__ == "__main__":
    ...
    log_emitter.emit(
        LogRecord(
            timestamp=time.time_ns(),
            body="first log line",
            severity_number=SeverityNumber.INFO,
```

```
        )
    )
```

There – now at least readers of those logs should be able to know how important those log lines are. Run the code and look for the severity number in the output:

output

```
{"body": "first log line", "name": null, "severity_
number": "<SeverityNumber.INFO: 9>", "severity_text": null,
"attributes": null, "timestamp": 1630814944956950000, "trace_
id": "", "span_id": "", "trace_flags": null, "resource": ""}
```

As mentioned earlier in this chapter, one of the goals of the OpenTelemetry logging signal is to remain interoperable with existing logging APIs. Looking at how much work we just did to get a log line with minimal information, it really seems like there should be a better way, and there is!

The standard logging library

What if we tried using the standard logging library available in Python to interact with OpenTelemetry instead? The logging library has been part of the standard Python library since version 2.3 and is used by many popular frameworks, such as *Django* and *Flask*.

> **Important Note**
>
> The standard logging module in Python is quite powerful and flexible. If you're not familiar with it, it may take some time to get used to it. I recommend reading the Python docs available on python.org here: https://docs.python.org/3/library/logging.html.

The Python implementation of the OpenTelemetry signal provides an additional component to use, `OTLPHandler`. The following figure shows where `OTLPHandler` fits in with the rest of the logging pipeline:

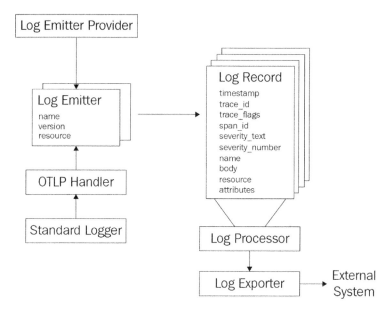

Figure 6.3 – OTLPHandler uses LogEmitter to produce logs

`OTLPHandler` extends the standard logging library's `logging.Handler` class and uses the configured `LogEmitter` to produce log records.

> **Important note:**
> The OTLPHandler was renamed LoggingHandler in releases of the opentelemetry-sdk package newer than 1.10.0. Be sure to update any references to it in the examples if you've installed a newer version.

The following code block first imports the `logging` module. Then, using the `getLogger` method, a standard `Logger` object is obtained. This is the object we will use anytime a log line is needed from the application. Finally, `OTLPHandler` is added to `logger`, and a `warning` message is logged:

logs.py

```
import logging
from opentelemetry.sdk._logs import (
    LogEmitterProvider,
```

```
    LogRecord,
    OTLPHandler,
    get_log_emitter_provider,
    set_log_emitter_provider,
)

if __name__ == "__main__":
    ...
    logger = logging.getLogger(__file__)
    handler = OTLPHandler()
    logger.addHandler(handler)
    logger.warning("second log line")
```

Let's see how the information generated differs from the previous example; many of the fields are automatically filled in for us:

- The timestamp is set to the current time.
- The severity number and text are set based on the method used to record a log – in this case, the `warning` method sets the log severity to WARN.
- Trace and span information is set by pulling information from the current context. As our example does not include starting a trace, we should expect the values in these fields to be invalid.
- Resource data is set via the log emitter provider.

This provides us with a significant improvement in the data generated.

output

```
{"body": "second log line", "name": null, "severity_number":
"<SeverityNumber.WARN: 13>", "severity_text": "WARNING",
"attributes": {}, "timestamp": 1630810960785737984,
"trace_id": "0x00000000000000000000000000000000", "span_
id": "0x0000000000000000", "trace_flags": 0, "resource":
"BoundedAttributes({'telemetry.sdk.language': 'python',
'telemetry.sdk.name': 'opentelemetry', 'telemetry.sdk.version':
'1.9.0', 'service.name': 'unknown_service'}, maxlen=None"}
```

Not only does this output contain richer data, but we also didn't need to work nearly as hard to obtain it, and we used a standard library to generate the logs. The `attributes` field doesn't appear to contain anything useful yet – let's fix that. `OTLPHandler` creates the `attribute` dictionary by looking at any extra attributes defined in the standard `LogRecord`. The following code passes an `extra` argument at logging time:

logs.py

```
if __name__ == "__main__":
    ...
    logger.warning("second log line", extra={"key1": "val1"})
```

As with other attribute dictionaries we may have encountered previously, they should contain information relevant to the specific event being logged. The output should now show us the additional attributes:

output

```
{"body": "second log line", "name": null, "severity_
number": "<SeverityNumber.WARN: 13>", "severity_text":
"WARNING", "attributes": {"key1": "val1"}, "timestamp":
1630946024854904064, "trace_id": "0x00000000000000000000
000000000", "span_id": "0x0000000000000000", "trace_flags":
0, "resource": "BoundedAttributes({'telemetry.sdk.language':
'python', 'telemetry.sdk.name': 'opentelemetry', 'telemetry.
sdk.version': '1.9.0', 'service.name': 'unknown_service'},
maxlen=None"}
```

Let's produce one last example with the standard logger and update the previous code to record a log using the `info` method. This should give us the same severity as the example where we used the log emitter directly:

logs.py

```
import logging
if __name__ == "__main__":
    ...
    logger.info("second log line")
```

Run the code again to see the result. If you're no longer seeing a log with the *second log line* as its body and are perplexed, don't worry – you're not alone. This is due to a feature of the standard logging library. The Python logging module creates a `root` logger, which is used anytime a more specific logger isn't configured. By default, the root logger is configured to only log messages with a severity of a warning or higher. Any logger instantiated via `getLogger` inherits that severity, which explains why our info level messages are not displayed. Our example can be fixed by calling `setLevel` for the logger we are using in our program:

logs.py

```python
if __name__ == "__main__":
    ...
    logger = logging.getLogger(__file__)
    logger.setLevel(logging.DEBUG)
    handler = OTLPHandler()
    logger.addHandler(handler)
    logger.info("second log line")
```

The output should now contain the log line as we expected:

output

```
{"body": "second log line", "name": null, "severity_number": "<SeverityNumber.INFO: 9>", "severity_text": "INFO", "attributes": {}, "timestamp": 1630857128712922112, "trace_id": "0x00000000000000000000000000000000", "span_id": "0x0000000000000000", "trace_flags": 0, "resource": "BoundedAttributes({'telemetry.sdk.language': 'python', 'telemetry.sdk.name': 'opentelemetry', 'telemetry.sdk.version': '1.9.0, 'service.name': 'unknown_service'}, maxlen=None)"}
```

An alternative way to configure the log level of the root logger is to use the `basicConfig` method of the logging module. This allows you to configure the severity level, formatting, and so on (https://docs.python.org/3/library/logging.html#logging.basicConfig). Another benefit of using the existing logging library means that with a little bit of additional configuration, any existing application should be able to leverage OpenTelemetry logging. Speaking of an existing application, let's return to the grocery store.

A logging signal in practice

Getting familiar with the logging signal theory is great; now it's time to put it into practice. Before using OpenTelemetry logging in the grocery store, let's take a minute to move the configuration code into the `common.py` module:

common.py

```
import logging
from opentelemetry.sdk._logs.export import ConsoleLogExporter, BatchLogProcessor
from opentelemetry.sdk._logs import (
    LogEmitterProvider,
    OTLPHandler,
    set_log_emitter_provider,
)

def configure_logger(name, version):
    provider = LogEmitterProvider(resource=Resource.create())
    set_log_emitter_provider(provider)
    exporter = ConsoleLogExporter()
    provider.add_log_processor(BatchLogProcessor(exporter))
    logger = logging.getLogger(name)
    logger.setLevel(logging.DEBUG)
    handler = OTLPHandler()
    logger.addHandler(handler)
    return logger
```

With the code in place, we can now obtain a logger in the same fashion as we obtained a tracer and a meter previously. The following code updates the shopper application to instantiate a logger via `configure_logger`. Additionally, let's update the `add_item_to_cart` method to use `logger.info` rather than `print`:

shopper.py

```
from common import configure_tracer, configure_meter, configure_logger

tracer = configure_tracer("shopper", "0.1.2")
```

```python
meter = configure_meter("shopper", "0.1.2")
logger = configure_logger("shopper", "0.1.2")

@tracer.start_as_current_span("add item to cart")
def add_item_to_cart(item, quantity):
    span = trace.get_current_span()
    span.set_attributes(
        {
            "item": item,
            "quantity": quantity,
        }
    )
    logger.info("add {} to cart".format(item))
```

Use the following commands in separate terminals to launch the grocery store, the legacy inventory, and finally, the shopper applications:

```
$ python legacy_inventory.py
$ python grocery_store.py
$ python shopper.py
```

Pay special attention to output running from the previous command; it should include similar output, confirming that our configuration is correct:

output

```
{"body": "add orange to cart", "name": null, "severity_
number": "<SeverityNumber.INFO: 9>", "severity_text":
"INFO", "attributes": {}, "timestamp": 1630859469283874048,
"trace_id": "0x67a8df13b8d5678912a8101bb5724fa4", "span_
id": "0x0fc5e89573d7f794", "trace_flags": 1, "resource":
"BoundedAttributes({'telemetry.sdk.language': 'python',
'telemetry.sdk.name': 'opentelemetry', 'telemetry.sdk.version':
'1.9.0', 'service.name': 'unknown_service'}, maxlen=None)"}
```

This is a great starting point; let's see how we can correlate the information from this log line with the information from our traces.

Distributed tracing and logs

We saw earlier in this chapter that the `LogRecord` class contains fields for span and trace identifiers as well as trace flags. The intention behind this is to allow logs to be correlated with specific traces and spans, permitting the end user to gain a better understanding of what their application is doing when it's running in production. So often, the process of correlating telemetry involves searching tirelessly through events using a timestamp as a mechanism to match up different sources of information. This is not always practical for the following reasons:

- Many operations happen concurrently on the same system, making it difficult to know which operation caused the event.
- The difficulty caused by operations happening simultaneously is exacerbated in distributed systems as even more operations are occurring.
- The clocks across different systems may, and often do, drift. This drift causes timestamps to not match.

A mechanism developed to address this has been to produce a unique event identifier for each event and add this identifier to all logs recorded. One challenge of this is ensuring that this information is then propagated across the entire system; this is exactly what the trace identifier in OpenTelemetry does. As shown in *Figure 6.4*, the trace and span identifiers can pinpoint the specific operation that triggers a log to be recorded:

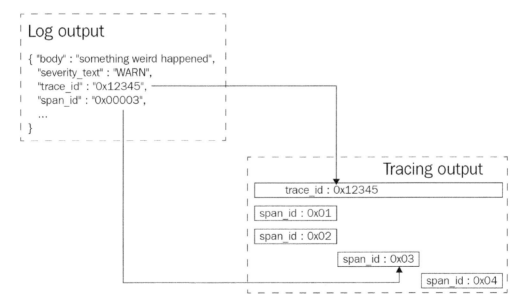

Figure 6.4 – Log and trace correlation

Returning to the output from the previous example, the following shows the logging output as well as a snippet of the tracing output containing the name of the operations and their identifiers. See whether you can determine from the output which operation triggered the log record:

output

```
{"body": "add orange to cart", "name": null, "severity_
number": "<SeverityNumber.INFO: 9>", "severity_text":
"INFO", "attributes": {}, "timestamp": 1630859469283874048,
"trace_id": "0x67a8df13b8d5678912a8101bb5724fa4", "span_
id": "0x0fc5e89573d7f794", "trace_flags": 1, "resource":
"BoundedAttributes({'telemetry.sdk.language': 'python',
'telemetry.sdk.name': 'opentelemetry', 'telemetry.sdk.version':
'1.9.0', 'service.name': 'unknown_service'}, maxlen=None)"}
{
    "name": "web request",
    "context": {
        "trace_id": "0x67a8df13b8d5678912a8101bb5724fa4",
        "span_id": "0x6e4e03cacd3411b5",
    },
}
{
    "name": "add item to cart",
    "context": {
        "trace_id": "0x67a8df13b8d5678912a8101bb5724fa4",
        "span_id": "0x0fc5e89573d7f794",
    },
}
{
    "name": "browse",
    "context": {
        "trace_id": "0x67a8df13b8d5678912a8101bb5724fa4",
        "span_id": "0x5a2262c9dd473b40",
    },
}
{
    "name": "visit store",
```

```
        "context": {
            "trace_id": "0x67a8df13b8d5678912a8101bb5724fa4",
            "span_id": "0x504caee882574a9e",
        },
}
```

If you've guessed that the log line was generated by the *add item to cart* operation, you've guessed correctly. Although this particular example is simple since you're already familiar with the code itself, you can imagine how valuable this information can be to troubleshoot an unfamiliar system. Equipped with the information provided by the distributed trace associated with the log record, you're empowered to jump into the source code and debug an issue faster. Let's see how we can use OpenTelemetry logging with the other applications in our system.

OpenTelemetry logging with Flask

As covered previously in the chapter, many frameworks, including Flask, use the standard logging library in Python. This makes configuring OpenTelemetry for the grocery store similar to how any changes to logging in Flask would be done. The following code imports and uses `configure_logger` to set up the logging pipeline. Next, we use the logging module's `dictConfig` method to add `OTLPHandler` to the `root` logger, and configure the severity level to `DEBUG` to ensure all our logs are output. In a production setting, you will likely want to make this option configurable rather than hardcode it to debug level to save costs:

grocery_store.py

```python
from logging.config import dictConfig
from common import (
    configure_meter,
    configure_tracer,
    configure_logger,
    set_span_attributes_from_flask,
    start_recording_memory_metrics,
)
tracer = configure_tracer("grocery-store", "0.1.2")
meter = configure_meter("grocery-store", "0.1.2")
logger = configure_logger("grocery-store", "0.1.2")
dictConfig(
```

```
    {
        "version": 1,
        "handlers": {
            "otlp": {
                "class": "opentelemetry.sdk._logs.OTLPHandler",
            }
        },
        "root": {"level": "DEBUG", "handlers": ["otlp"]},
    }
)
app = Flask(__name__)
```

Ensure some requests are sent to the grocery store either by running `shopper.py` or via `curl` and see what the output from the server looks like now. The following output shows it before the change on the first line and after the change on the second line:

output

```
127.0.0.1 - - [05/Sep/2021 10:58:28] "GET /products HTTP/1.1" 200 -
{"body": "127.0.0.1 - - [05/Sep/2021 10:58:48] \"GET /products HTTP/1.1\" 200 -", "name": null, "severity_number": "<SeverityNumber.INFO: 9>", "severity_text": "INFO", "attributes": {}, "timestamp": 1630864728996940032, "trace_id": "0x00000000000000000000000000000000", "span_id": "0x0000000000000000", "trace_flags": 0, "resource": "BoundedAttributes({'telemetry.sdk.language': 'python', 'telemetry.sdk.name': 'opentelemetry', 'telemetry.sdk.version': '1.9.0', 'service.name': 'unknown_service'}, maxlen=None)"}
```

We can see the original message is now recorded as the body of the message, and all the additional information is also presented. Although, if we look closely, we can see that the `span_id`, `trace_id`, and `trace_flags` information is missing. It looks like the context for our request is lost somewhere along the way, so let's fix that. What is confusing about this is that we already have hooks defined to handle `before_request` and `teardown_request`, which, in theory, should ensure that the trace information is available. However, the log record we see is generated by Flask's built-in web server (`wsgi`), not the Flask application, and is triggered after the original request has been completed as far as Flask knows. We can address this by creating middleware ourselves, but thankfully, we don't have to.

Logging with WSGI middleware

The OpenTelemetry community publishes a package that provides support for instrumenting an application that uses a `wsgi`-compatible implementation, such as the built-in Flask server. The `opentelemetry-instrumentation-wsgi` package provides the middleware that hooks into the appropriate mechanisms to make trace information for the duration of the request. The following code imports the middleware and updates the Flask app to use it:

grocery_store.py

```python
from opentelemetry.instrumentation.wsgi import
OpenTelemetryMiddleware
...
app = Flask(__name__)
app.wsgi_app = OpenTelemetryMiddleware(app.wsgi_app)
```

With the middleware in place, a new request to our application should allow us to see the `span_id`, `trace_id`, and `trace_flags` components that we expect:

output

```
{"body": "127.0.0.1 - - [05/Sep/2021 11:39:36] \"GET /
products HTTP/1.1\" 200 -", "name": null, "severity_
number": "<SeverityNumber.INFO: 9>", "severity_text":
"INFO", "attributes": {}, "timestamp": 1630867176948227072,
"trace_id": "0xf999a4164ac2f20c20549f19abd4b434", "span_
id": "0xed5d3071ece38633", "trace_flags": 1, "resource":
"BoundedAttributes({'telemetry.sdk.language': 'python',
'telemetry.sdk.name': 'opentelemetry', 'telemetry.sdk.version':
'1.9.0', 'service.name': 'unknown_service'}, maxlen=None)"}
```

We will look at how this works in more detail in *Chapter 7*, *Instrumentation Libraries*, and see how we can simplify the application code using instrumentation libraries. For the purpose of this example, it's enough to know that the middleware enables us to see the tracing information in the log we are recording.

Resource correlation

Another piece of data that OpenTelemetry logging uses when augmenting telemetry is the resource attribute. As you may remember from previous chapters, the resource describes the source of the telemetry. This will allow us to correlate events occurring across separate signals for the same resource. In *Chapter 4, Distributed Tracing*, we defined a `LocalMachineResourceDetector` class that produces an OpenTelemetry resource that includes information about the local machine. Let's update the code in `configure_logger` that instantiates the `LogEmitterProvider` to use this resource, rather than create an empty resource:

common.py

```
def configure_logger(name, version):
    local_resource = LocalMachineResourceDetector().detect()
    resource = local_resource.merge(
        Resource.create(
            {
                ResourceAttributes.SERVICE_NAME: name,
                ResourceAttributes.SERVICE_VERSION: version,
            }
        )
    )
    provider = LogEmitterProvider(resource=resource)
    set_log_emitter_provider(provider)
    ...
```

With the change in place, run `shopper.py` once again to see that the log record now contains more meaningful data about the source of the log entry:

```
{"body": "add orange to cart", "name": null, "severity_
number": "<SeverityNumber.INFO: 9>", "severity_text":
"INFO", "attributes": {}, "timestamp": 1630949852869427968,
"trace_id": "0x2ff0e5c9886f2672c3af4468483d341d", "span_
id": "0x40d72ae565b4c19a", "trace_flags": 1, "resource":
"BoundedAttributes({'telemetry.sdk.language': 'python',
'telemetry.sdk.name': 'opentelemetry', 'telemetry.sdk.version':
'1.9.0', 'net.host.name': 'MacBook-Pro.local', 'net.host.ip':
'127.0.0.1', 'service.name': 'shopper', 'service.version':
'0.1.2'}, maxlen=None)"}
```

Looking at the previous output, we now know the name and version of the service. We also have valuable information about the machine that generated this information. In a distributed system, this information can be used in combination with metrics generated by the same resource to identify problems with a specific system, compute node, environment, or even region.

Summary

With the knowledge of this chapter ingrained in our minds, we have now covered the core signals that OpenTelemetry helps produce. Understanding how to produce telemetry by manually instrumenting code is a building block on the road to improving observability. Without telemetry, the job of understanding what a system is doing is much more difficult.

In this chapter, we learned about the purpose of the logging implementation in OpenTelemetry, as well as how it is intended to co-exist with existing logging implementations. After configuring the logging pipeline, we learned how to use the OpenTelemetry API to produce logs and compared doing so with using a standard logging API. Returning to the grocery store, we explored how logging can be correlated with traces and metrics. This allowed us to understand how we may be able to leverage OpenTelemetry logging within existing applications to improve our ability to use log statements when debugging applications.

Finally, we scratched the surface of how instrumentation libraries can help to make the production of telemetry easier. We will take an in-depth look at this in the next chapter, dedicated to simplifying the grocery store application by leveraging existing instrumentation libraries.

7
Instrumentation Libraries

Understanding the ins and outs of the OpenTelemetry API is quite helpful for manually instrumenting code. But what if we could save ourselves some of that work and still have visibility into what our code is doing? As covered in *Chapter 3*, *Auto-Instrumentation*, one of the initial objectives of OpenTelemetry is providing developers with tools to instrument their applications at a minimal cost. Instrumentation libraries combined with auto-instrumentation enable users to start with OpenTelemetry without learning the APIs, and leverage the community's efforts and expertise.

This chapter will investigate the components of auto-instrumentation, how they can be configured, and how they interact with instrumentation libraries. Diving deeper into the implementation details of instrumentation libraries will allow us to understand precisely how telemetry data is produced. Although telemetry created automatically may seem like magic, we'll seek to unveil the mechanics behind this illusion. The chapter covers the following main topics:

- Auto-instrumentation configuration and its components
- The Requests library instrumentor
- Automatic configuration

- Revisiting the grocery store
- The Flask library instrumentor
- Finding instrumentation libraries

With this information, we will revisit some of our existing code in the grocery store to simplify our code and manage and improve the generated telemetry. Along the way, we will look at the specifics of existing third-party libraries supported by the OpenTelemetry project. Let's start with setting up our environment.

Technical requirements

The examples in this chapter are provided in this book's companion repository, found here: https://github.com/PacktPublishing/Cloud-Native-Observability. The source code can be downloaded via `git` as per the following command:

```
$ git clone https://github.com/PacktPublishing/Cloud-Native-Observability
$ cd Cloud-Native-Observability/chapter07
```

The completed examples from this chapter are in the `chapter7` directory. If you'd prefer the refactor along, copy the code from `chapter6` as a starting point. Next, we'll need to ensure the version of Python on your system is at least 3.6. You can verify it with the following commands:

```
$ python --version
Python 3.8.9
$ python3 --version
Python 3.8.9
```

This chapter will use the same `opentelemetry-api`, `opentelemetry-sdk`, and `opentelemetry-propagator-b3` packages we installed in previous chapters. In addition, we will use the `opentelemetry-instrumentation` and `opentelemetry-distro` packages. Install the packages via `pip` now:

```
$ pip install opentelemetry-api \
              opentelemetry-sdk \
              opentelemetry-instrumentation \
              opentelemetry-propagator-b3 \
              opentelemetry-distro
```

We will need to install additional packages libraries used by our applications: the Flask and Requests libraries. Lastly, we will install the instrumentation libraries that automatically instrument the calls for those libraries. The standard naming convention for instrumentation libraries in OpenTelemetry is to prefix the library's name being instrumented with `opentelemetry-instrumentation-`. Use `pip` to install those packages now:

```
$ pip install flask \
            opentelemetry-instrumentation-flask \
            requests \
            opentelemetry-instrumentation-requests
```

Ensure all the required packages have been installed by looking at the output from `pip freeze`, which lists all the packages installed:

```
$ pip freeze | grep opentelemetry
opentelemetry-api==1.9.0
opentelemetry-distro==0.28b0
opentelemetry-instrumentation==0.28b0
opentelemetry-instrumentation-flask==0.28b0
opentelemetry-instrumentation-requests==0.28b0
opentelemetry-instrumentation-wsgi==0.28b0
opentelemetry-propagator-b3==1.9.0
opentelemetry-proto==1.9.0
opentelemetry-sdk==1.9.0
opentelemetry-semantic-conventions==0.28b0
opentelemetry-util-http==0.28b0
```

Throughout the chapter, we will rely on two scripts made available by the `opentelemetry-instrumentation` package: `opentelemetry-instrument` and `opentelemetry-bootstrap`. Ensure these scripts are available in your path with the following commands:

```
$ opentelemetry-instrument --help
usage: opentelemetry-instrument [-h]...
$ opentelemetry-bootstrap --help
usage: opentelemetry-bootstrap [-h]...
```

Now that we have all the packages installed and the code available, let's see how auto-instrumentation works in practice.

Auto-instrumentation configuration

Since auto-instrumentation aims to get started as quickly as possible, let's see how fast we can generate telemetry with as little code as possible. The following code makes a web request to `https://www.cloudnativeobservability.com` and prints the HTTP response code:

http_request.py

```
import requests

url = "https://www.cloudnativeobservability.com"
resp = requests.get(url)
print(resp.status_code)
```

When running the code, assuming network connectivity is available and the URL we're requesting connects us to a server that is operating normally, we should see 200 printed out:

```
$ python http_request.py
200
```

Great, the program works; now it's time to instrument it. The following command uses the `opentelemetry-instrument` application to wrap the application we created. We will look more closely at the command and its options shortly. For now, run the command:

```
$ opentelemetry-instrument --traces_exporter console \
                           --metrics_exporter console \
                           --logs_exporter console \
                           python http_request.py
```

If everything went according to plan, we should now see the following output, which contains telemetry:

output

```
200
{
    "name": "HTTP GET",
    "context": {
        "trace_id": "0x953ca1322b930819077a921a838df0cd",
        "span_id": "0x5b3b72c9c836178a",
        "trace_state": "[]"
    },
    "kind": "SpanKind.CLIENT",
    "parent_id": null,
    "start_time": "2021-11-25T17:38:21.331540Z",
    "end_time": "2021-11-25T17:38:22.033434Z",
    "status": {
        "status_code": "UNSET"
    },
    "attributes": {
        "http.method": "GET",
        "http.url": "https://www.cloudnativeobservability.com",
        "http.status_code": 200
    },
    "events": [],
    "links": [],
    "resource": {
        "telemetry.sdk.language": "python",
        "telemetry.sdk.name": "opentelemetry",
        "telemetry.sdk.version": "1.9.0",
        "telemetry.auto.version": "0.28b0",
        "service.name": "unknown_service"
    }
}
```

Okay, that's exciting, but what just happened? *Figure 7.1* shows how the `opentelemetry-instrument` command is instrumenting the code for our web request by doing the following:

1. Loading the configuration options defined by the `OpenTelemetryDistro` class, which is part of the `opentelemetry-distro` package.
2. Automatically configuring the telemetry pipelines for traces, metrics, and logs via `OpenTelemetryConfigurator`. The details of how this configuration is set will become clearer shortly.
3. Iterating through instrumentor classes registered via entry points in the Python environment under `opentelemetry_instrumentor` to find available instrumentation libraries. In doing so, it finds and loads the `RequestsInstrumentor` class defined in the `opentelemetry-instrumentation-requests` package.
4. With the instrumentation library loaded, the call to `get` is now processed by the `requests` instrumentation library, which creates a span before calling the original `get` method.

The preceding steps are depicted in the following diagram:

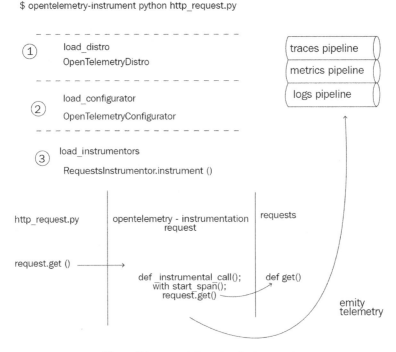

Figure 7.1 – opentelemetry-instrument

The configuration of the telemetry pipeline involves a few different mechanisms loaded via entry points at various times before the application code is executed. Thinking back to *Chapter 3, Auto-Instrumentation*, we introduced entry points (https://packaging.python.org/specifications/entry-points/) as a mechanism that allows Python packages to register classes or methods globally. The combination of entry points, interfaces, and options to choose from can make the configuration process a bit complex to understand.

OpenTelemetry distribution

The first step in the configuration process is loading classes registered under the `opentelemetry_distro` entry point. This entry point is reserved for classes adhering to the **BaseDistro** interface, and its purpose is to allow implementors to set configuration options at the earliest possible time. The term *distro* is short for distribution, a concept that is still being officially defined in OpenTelemetry. Essentially, a distro is a way for users to customize OpenTelemetry to fit their needs, allowing them to reduce the complexity of deploying and using OpenTelemetry. For example, the default configuration for OpenTelemetry Python is to configure an OpenTelemetry protocol exporter for all signals. This is accomplished via the `OpenTelemetryDistro` class mentioned previously. The following code shows us how the `OpenTelemetryDistro` class configures the default exporter by setting environment variables:

OpenTelemetryDistro class

```
class OpenTelemetryDistro(BaseDistro):
    """
    The OpenTelemetry provided Distro configures a default
    configuration out of the box.
    """
    def _configure(self, **kwargs):
        os.environ.setdefault(OTEL_TRACES_EXPORTER, "otlp_proto_grpc")
        os.environ.setdefault(OTEL_METRICS_EXPORTER, "otlp_proto_grpc")
        os.environ.setdefault(OTEL_LOGS_EXPORTER, "otlp_proto_grpc")
```

As a user, you could create your distribution to preconfigure all the specific parameters needed to tailor auto-instrumentation for your environment: for example, protocol, destination, and transport options. A list of open source examples extending the `BaseDistro` interface can be found here: https://github.com/PacktPublishing/Cloud-Native-Observability/tree/main/chapter7#opentelemetry-distro-implementations. With those options configured, you can then provide an entry point to your implementation of the `BaseDistro` interface, package it up, and add this new package as a dependency in your applications. Therefore, the distribution makes deploying a consistent configuration across a distributed system easier.

OpenTelemetry configurator

The next piece of the configuration puzzle is what is currently known in OpenTelemetry Python as the configurator. The purpose of the configurator is to load all the components defined in the configuration specified by the distro. Another way is to think of the distro as the co-pilot, deciding where the car needs to go, and the configurator as the driver. The configurator is an extensible and declarative interface for configuring OpenTelemetry. It is loaded by auto-instrumentation via, and you may have guessed it, an entry point. The `opentelemetry_configurator` entry point is reserved for classes adhering to the `_BaseConfigurator` interface, whose sole purpose is to prepare the logs, metrics, and traces pipelines to produce telemetry.

> **Important Note**
> As you may have noticed, the `_BaseConfigurator` class is preceded by an underscore. This is done intentionally for classes that are not officially part of the supported OpenTelemetry API in Python and warrant extra caution. Methods and classes that are not supported formally can and often do change with new releases.

The implementation of the `_BaseConfigurator` interface loaded in the previous example, the `OpenTelemetryConfigurator` class configures a telemetry pipeline for each signal using components from the standard `opentelemetry-sdk` package. As a user, this configurator is precisely what you want most of the time. However, if a user wishes to provide an alternative SDK, it would be possible to provide their configurator implementation to use this SDK instead.

This covers the two main entry points used by auto-instrumentation. We will continue discussing additional entry points throughout this chapter. As a reference, the following table captures the entry points used by OpenTelemetry Python along with the interface each entry point expects. The table also shows us a brief description of what each entry point is used for:

Entry point identifier	Interface	Purpose
opentelemetry_distro	BaseDistro	Provides configuration to the configurator. The `OpenTelemetryDistro` sets exporters to use OTLP via environment variables.
opentelemetry_instrumentor	Instrumentor	Registers available instrumentation libraries, all of which are loaded by auto-instrumentation by default.
opentelemetry_configurator	Configurator	Applies the available configuration. The OpenTelemetry SDK provides an implementation which loads configuration from environment variables.
opentelemetry_tracer_provider	TracerProvider	Allows users to load a custom implementation of a `TracerProvider`.
opentelemetry_meter_provider	MeterProvider	Allows users to load a custom implementation of a `MeterProvider`.
opentelemetry_log_emitter_provider	LogEmitterProvider	Allows users to load a custom implementation of a `LogEmitterProvider`.
opentelemetry_traces_exporter	SpanExporter	Registers span exporters available for auto-instrumentation.
opentelemetry_metrics_exporter	MetricExporter	Registers metric exporters available for auto-instrumentation.
opentelemetry_logs_exporter	LogExporter	Registers log exporters available for auto-instrumentation.
opentelemetry_id_generator	IdGenerator	Registers ID generators available for auto-instrumentation.

Figure 7.2 – Entry points used in OpenTelemetry Python

Similar to `OpenTelemetryDistro`, the `OpenTelemetryConfigurator` class and its parent use environment variables to achieve its goal of configuring OpenTelemetry for the end use.

Environment variables

To provide additional flexibility to users, OpenTelemetry supports the configuration of many of its components across all languages via environment variables. These variables are defined in the OpenTelemetry specification, ensuring each compliant language implementation understands them. This allows users to re-use the same configuration options across any language they choose. I recommend reading the complete list of options available in the specification repository found here: `https://github.com/open-telemetry/opentelemetry-specification/blob/main/specification/sdk-environment-variables.md`.

We will look more closely at specific variables as we refactor the grocery store further in this chapter. Many, but not all, of the environment variables used by auto-instrumentation are part of the specification linked previously. This is because the implementation details of each language may require additional variables not relevant to others. Language-specific environment variables are supported in the following format:

```
OTEL_{LANGUAGE}_{FEATURE}
```

As we'll see shortly, Python-specific options are prefixed with `OTEL_PYTHON_`. Any option with this prefix will only be found in Python, and the naming convention helps set that expectation with users.

Command-line options

The last tool available to configure OpenTelemetry without editing the application code is the use of command-line arguments, which can be set when invoking `opentelemetry-instrument`. Recall the command we used to call in the earlier example:

```
$ opentelemetry-instrument --traces_exporter console \
                          --metrics_exporter console \
                          --logs_exporter console \
                          python http_request.py
```

This command used command-line arguments to override the traces, metrics, and logs exporters to use the console exporter instead of the configured default. All options available via command line can be listed using the `--help` flag when invoking `opentelemetry-instrument`. These options are the same as those available through environment variables, with a slightly easier name for convenience. The name of the command-line argument is the name of the environment variable in lowercase without the `OTEL_` or `OTEL_PYTHON` prefix. The following table shows a few examples:

Environment variable	Command line argument
OTEL_TRACES_EXPORTER	--traces_exporter
OTEL_PYTHON_METER_PROVIDER	--meter_provider
OTEL_PYTHON_ID_GENERATOR	--id_generator

Figure 7.3 – Environment variable to command-line argument translations

With that, we've covered how auto-instrumentation configures OpenTelemetry to generate the telemetry we saw. But what about the instrumented call? Let's see how the Requests library instrumentation works.

Requests library instrumentor

The Instrumentor interface provides instrumentation libraries with the minimum requirements a library must provide to support auto-instrumentation. Implementors must provide an implementation for `_instrument` and `_uninstrument`, that's all. The instrumentation implementation details vary from one library to another depending on whether the library offers any event or callback mechanisms for instrumentation. In the case of the Requests library, the `opentelemetry-instrumentation-requests` library relies on monkey patching the `Session.request` and `Session.send` methods from the `requests` library. This instrumentation library does the following:

1. Provides a wrapper method for the library calls that it instruments, and intercepts calls through those wrappers
2. Upon invocation, creates a new span by calling the `start_as_current_span` method of the OpenTelemetry API, ensuring the span name follows semantic conventions
3. Injects the context information into the request headers via the context API's `attach` method to ensure the tracing data is propagated to the request's destination
4. Reads the response and sets the status code accordingly via the span's `set_status` method

> **Important Note**
> Instrumentation libraries must check if the span will be recorded before adding additional attributes to avoid potentially costly operations. This is done to minimize the instrumentation's impact on existing applications when it is not in use.

Additional implementation details can be found in the `opentelemetry-python-contrib` repository: https://github.com/open-telemetry/opentelemetry-python-contrib/blob/main/instrumentation/opentelemetry-instrumentation-requests/src/opentelemetry/instrumentation/requests/__init__.py. The code may inspire you to write and contribute an instrumentation library of your own.

Additional configuration options

The Requests instrumentation library supports the following additional configurable options:

- `span_callback`: A callback mechanism to inject additional information into a span is available via this parameter. For example, this allows users to inject additional information from the response into the span.
- `name_callback`: The default name of a span created by the requests instrumentation library is in the `HTTP {method}` format. The `name_callback` parameter allows users to customize the name of the span as needed.
- `excluded_urls`: There are HTTP destinations for which capturing telemetry may not be desirable, a typical case being requests made to a health check endpoint. The `excluded_urls` parameter supports configuring a comma-separated list of URLs exempt from telemetry. This parameter is also configurable via the `OTEL_PYTHON_REQUESTS_EXCLUDED_URLS` environment variable and is available for use with auto-instrumentation.

As you may have noted by reading the description of each configuration option, not all these options are available for configuration via auto-instrumentation. It's possible to use instrumentation libraries without auto-instrumentation. Let's see how.

Manual invocation

The following code updates the previous example to configure a tracer and instrument the `requests.get` call via the instrumentation library:

http_request.py

```python
import requests

from opentelemetry import trace
from opentelemetry.sdk.trace import TracerProvider
from opentelemetry.sdk.trace.export import (
    BatchSpanProcessor,
    ConsoleSpanExporter,
)
from opentelemetry.instrumentation.requests import RequestsInstrumentor

def configure_tracer():
```

```
    exporter = ConsoleSpanExporter()
    span_processor = BatchSpanProcessor(exporter)
    provider = TracerProvider()
    provider.add_span_processor(span_processor)
    trace.set_tracer_provider(provider)

configure_tracer()
RequestsInstrumentor().instrument()

url = "https://www.cloudnativeobservability.com"
resp = requests.get(url)
print(resp.status_code)
```

This is quite a bit of additional code. Since we're no longer relying on auto-instrumentation, we must configure the tracing pipeline manually. Running this code without invoking `opentelemetry-instrument` looks like this:

```
$ python http_request.py
```

This should yield very similar telemetry to what we saw earlier. The following shows an excerpt of that output:

output

```
200
{
    "name": "HTTP GET",
    "context": {
        "trace_id": "0xc2ee1f399911a10d361231a46c6fec1b",
...
```

We can further customize the telemetry produced by configuring additional options we discussed previously. The following code example will customize the name of the span and add other attributes to the data generated. It does so by doing the following:

- Adding a `rename_span` method to replace the HTTP prefix in the name
- Adding the `add_response_attribute` method to append header information from the response object as a span attribute
- Updating the call to `instrument` to utilize the new functionality

http_request.py

```
def rename_span(method, url):
    return f"Web Request {method}"

def add_response_attributes(span, response):
    span.set_attribute("http.response.headers", str(response.headers))

configure_tracer()
RequestsInstrumentor().instrument(
    name_callback=rename_span,
    span_callback=add_response_attributes,
)
```

Running the updated code should give us the slightly updated telemetry as per the following abbreviated sample output:

output

```
200
{
    "name": "Web Request GET",
    "attributes": {
        "http.method": "GET",
        "http.url": "https://www.cloudnativeobservability.com",
        "http.status_code": 200,
        "http.response.headers": "{'Connection': 'keep-alive', 'Content-Length': '1864', 'Server': 'GitHub.com'
...
```

With this, we've now seen how to leverage the Requests instrumentation library without using auto-instrumentation. The added flexibility of the features not available through auto-instrumentation is nice, but configuring pipelines is tedious. Thankfully, it's possible to get the best of both worlds by using auto-instrumentation and configuring the instrumentor manually. Update the example to remove all the configuration code. The following is all that should be left:

http_request.py

```python
import requests

from opentelemetry.instrumentation.requests import RequestsInstrumentor

def rename_span(method, url):
    return f"Web Request {method}"

def add_response_attributes(span, response):
    span.set_attribute("http.response.headers", str(response.headers))

RequestsInstrumentor().instrument(
    name_callback=rename_span,
    span_callback=add_response_attributes,
)

resp = requests.get("https://www.cloudnativeobservability.com")
print(resp.status_code)
```

Run the new code via the following command we used earlier in the chapter:

```
$ opentelemetry-instrument --traces_exporter console \
                          --metrics_exporter console \
                          --logs_exporter console \
                          python http_request.py
```

Looking at the output, it's clear that something didn't go as planned. The following warning appears at the top of the output:

```
Attempting to instrument while already instrumented
```

Additionally, if you look through the telemetry generated, the span name is back to its original value, and the `response headers` attribute is missing. Recall that the `opentelemetry-instrument` script iterates through all the installed instrumentors before calling the application code. This means that by the time our application code is executed, the `Request` instrumentor has already instrumented the Requests library.

Double instrumentation

Many instrumentation libraries have a safeguard in place to prevent double instrumentation. Double instrumentation in most cases would mean that every piece of telemetry generated is recorded twice. This causes all sorts of problems, from potential added performance costs to making telemetry analysis difficult.

We can ensure that the library isn't instrumented first to mitigate this issue. Add the following method call to your code:

http_request.py

```
import requests

from opentelemetry.instrumentation.requests import
RequestsInstrumentor
...
RequestsInstrumentor().uninstrument()
RequestsInstrumentor().instrument(
    name_callback=rename_span,
    span_callback=add_response_attributes,
)
```

Running this code once more shows us that the warning is gone and that the telemetry contains the customization we expected. All this with much simpler code. Great! Let's see now how we can apply this to the grocery store.

Automatic configuration

We added new instrumentation in the past three chapters and watched how we could generate more information each time we instrumented the code. We will now see how we can continue to provide the same level of telemetry but simplify our lives by removing some of the code. The first code we will be removing is the configuration code we extracted into the common.py module. If you recall from previous chapters, the purpose of the configure_tracer, configure_meter, and configure_logger methods, which we will review in detail shortly, is to do the following:

- Configure the emitter of telemetry.
- Configure the destination and mechanism to output the telemetry.
- Add resource information to identify our service.

As we saw earlier in this chapter, the opentelemetry-instrument script enables us to remove the code doing the configuration by interpreting environment variables or command-line arguments that will do the same thing. We will review the configuration code for each signal and look at the flags that can be used to replace the code with environment variables. One of the configurations common to all signals is the resource information; let's start there.

Configuring resource attributes

A resource provides information about the source of the telemetry. If you look through the common.py code, you may recall that each method used to configure a signal also called methods to configure the resource. The code looks something like the following:

common.py

```
    local_resource = LocalMachineResourceDetector().detect()
    resource = local_resource.merge(
        Resource.create(
            {
                ResourceAttributes.SERVICE_NAME: name,
                ResourceAttributes.SERVICE_VERSION: version,
            }
        )
    )
```

The code uses a resource detector to fill in the hostname and IP address automatically. A current limitation of auto-instrumentation in Python is the lack of support for configuring resource detectors. Thankfully, since the functionality of our resource detector is somewhat limited, it's possible to replace it, as we'll see shortly.

The code also adds a service name and version information to our resource. Resource attributes can be configured for auto-instrumentation through one of the following options:

Environment variable	Command line argument
OTEL_RESOURCE_ATTRIBUTES	--resource_attributes

Figure 7.4 – Resource configuration

Note that the command-line arguments are shown here for reference only. For the remainder of the chapter, the commands used to run applications will use environment variables. The format of the parameters used for both methods is interchangeable. However, the OpenTelemetry specification only officially supports environment variables. These are consistent across implementations.

The following shows how using only environment variables to configure resources can produce the same result as the previous code. The example uses the `hostname` system utility to retrieve the name of the current host and `ipconfig` to retrieve the IP address. The invocation for these tools may vary depending on your system:

```
$ OTEL_RESOURCE_ATTRIBUTES="service.name=chap7-Requests-app,
                            service.version=0.1.2,
                            net.host.name='hostname',
                            net.host.ip='ipconfig getifaddr en0'" \
opentelemetry-instrument --traces_exporter console \
                         --metrics_exporter console \
                         --logs_exporter console \
                         python http_request.py
```

The resource information in the output from this command now includes the following details:

output

```
    "resource": {
        "telemetry.sdk.language": "python",
        "telemetry.sdk.name": "opentelemetry",
```

```
        "telemetry.sdk.version": "1.9.0",
        "service.name": "chap7-Requests-app",
        "service.version": "0.1.2",
        "net.host.name": "cloud",
        "net.host.ip": "10.0.0.141",
        "telemetry.auto.version": "0.28b0"
    }
```

We can now start configuring signals with resource attributes out of the way.

Configuring traces

The following code shows the `configure_tracer` method used to configure the tracing pipeline. Note that the code no longer contains resource configuration as we've already taken care of that:

common.py

```
def configure_tracer(name, version):
    exporter = ConsoleSpanExporter()
    span_processor = BatchSpanProcessor(exporter)
    provider = TracerProvider()
    provider.add_span_processor(span_processor)
    trace.set_tracer_provider(provider)
    return trace.get_tracer(name, version)
```

The main components to configure for tracing to emit telemetry are as follows:

- `TracerProvider`
- `SpanProcessor`
- `SpanExporter`

It's possible to set both `TracerProvider` and `SpanExporter` via environment variables. This is not the case for `SpanProcessor`. The OpenTelemetry SDK for Python defaults to using `BatchSpanProcessor` when auto-instrumentation is used in combination with the `opentelemetry-distro` package. Options for configuring `BatchSpanProcessor` are available via environment variables.

> **Important Note**
> `BatchSpanProcessor` will satisfy most use cases. However, if your application requires an alternative `SpanProcessor` implementation, it can be specified via a custom OpenTelemetry distribution package. Custom span processors can filter or enhance data before it is exported.

Another component we haven't talked about much yet is the sampler, which we'll cover in *Chapter 12, Sampling*. For now, it's enough to know that the sampler is also configurable via environment variables.

The following table shows the options for configuring the tracing pipeline. The acronym BSP stands for `BatchSpanProcessor`:

Environment variable	Command line argument
OTEL_PYTHON_TRACER_PROVIDER	--tracer_provider
OTEL_TRACES_EXPORTER	--traces_exporter
OTEL_TRACES_SAMPLER	--traces_sampler
OTEL_TRACES_SAMPLER_ARG	--traces_sampler_arg
OTEL_BSP_EXPORT_TIMEOUT	--bsp_export_timeout
OTEL_BSP_MAX_EXPORT_BATCH_SIZE	--bsp_max_export_batch_size
OTEL_BSP_MAX_QUEUE_SIZE	--bsp_max_queue_size
OTEL_BSP_SCHEDULE_DELAY	--bsp_schedule_delay

Figure 7.5 – Tracing configuration

As we continue adding configuration options, the command used to launch the application can get quite unruly. To alleviate this, I recommend exporting each variable as we go along. The following exports the OTEL_RESOURCE_ATTRIBUTES variable we previously set:

```
$ export OTEL_RESOURCE_ATTRIBUTES="service.name=chap7-Requests-app, service.version=0.1.2, net.host.name='hostname', net.host.ip='ipconfig getifaddr en0'"
```

We've already configured the exporter via command-line arguments in previous examples. The following shows us configuring the exporter and provider via environment variables. The `console` and `sdk` strings correspond to the name of the entry point for the `ConsoleSpanExporter` and the OpenTelemetry SDK `TracerProvider` classes:

```
$ OTEL_TRACES_EXPORTER=console \
  OTEL_PYTHON_TRACER_PROVIDER=sdk \
  opentelemetry-instrument --metrics_exporter console \
                           --logs_exporter console \
                           python http_request.py
```

Reading the output from the previous command is uneventful as it is just setting the same configuration in another way. However, we can now move on to metrics with this configuration in place.

Configuring metrics

The configuration for metrics is similar to the configuration for tracing, as we can see from the following code for the `configure_meter` method:

common.py

```
def configure_meter(name, version):
    exporter = ConsoleMetricExporter()
    provider = MeterProvider()
    set_meter_provider(provider)
    return get_meter_provider().get_meter(
        name=name,
        version=version,
    )
```

At the time of writing, the specification for metrics is reaching stability. As such, the support for auto-instrumentation and configuration will likely solidify over the coming months. For now, this section will focus on the options that are available and not likely to change, which covers the following:

- `MeterProvider`
- `MetricExporter`

The following table shows the options available to configure the metrics pipeline:

Environment variable	Command line argument
OTEL_PYTHON_METER_PROVIDER	--meter_provider
OTEL_METRICS_EXPORTER	--metrics_exporter

Figure 7.6 – Metrics configuration

The following command is provided as a reference for configuring `MeterProvider` and `MetricsExporter` via environment variables:

```
$ OTEL_METRICS_EXPORTER=console \
  OTEL_PYTHON_METER_PROVIDER=sdk \
  opentelemetry-instrument --logs_exporter console \
                           python http_request.py
```

Note that running the previous command as is results in an error as it does not configure the tracing signal. Any signal not explicitly configured defaults to using the **OpenTelemetry Protocol** (**OTLP**) exporter, which we've not installed in this environment. As the application does not currently produce metrics, we wouldn't expect to see any changes in the telemetry emitted.

Configuring logs

The `configure_logger` method configures the following OpenTelemetry components:

- `LogEmitterProvider`
- `LogProcessor`
- `LogExporter`

common.py

```
def configure_logger(name, version):
    provider = LogEmitterProvider()
    set_log_emitter_provider(provider)
    exporter = ConsoleLogExporter()
    provider.add_log_processor(BatchLogProcessor(exporter))
    logger = logging.getLogger(name)
    logger.setLevel(logging.DEBUG)
```

```
handler = OTLPHandler()
logger.addHandler(handler)
return logger
```

As with metrics, the configuration and auto-instrumentation for the logging signal are still currently under development. The following table can be used as a reference for the environment variables and command-line arguments available to configure logging at the time of writing:

Environment variable	Command line argument
OTEL_PYTHON_LOG_EMITTER_PROVIDER	--log_emitter_provider
OTEL_LOGS_EXPORTER	--logs_exporter

Figure 7.7 – Logging configuration

As with the tracing configuration's span processor, there isn't currently a mechanism for configuring the log processor via auto-instrumentation. This can change in the future. Using those options, we know how to configure the last signal for auto-instrumentation:

```
$ OTEL_LOGS_EXPORTER=console \
  OTEL_PYTHON_LOG_EMITTER_PROVIDER=sdk \
  opentelemetry-instrument python http_request.py
```

We're almost ready to revisit the grocery store code with the signals and resources configured. The last thing left to configure is propagation.

Configuring propagation

Context propagation provides the ability to share context information across distributed systems. This can be accomplished via various mechanisms, as we discovered in *Chapter 4, Distributed Tracing – Tracing Code Execution*. To ensure applications can interoperate with any of the propagation formats, OpenTelemetry supports configuring propagators via the following environment variable:

Environment variable	Command line argument
OTEL_PROPAGATORS	--propagators

Figure 7.8 – Propagator configuration

Later in this chapter, an application will need to configure the `B3` and `TraceContext` propagators. OpenTelemetry makes it possible to configure multiple propagators by specifying a comma-separated list. As mentioned earlier, with so many configuration options, using environment variables can become hard to manage. An effort is underway to add support for configuration files to OpenTelemetry, but the timeline on when that will be available is still in flux.

Recall the code we instrumented in the last three chapters. Let's go through it now and leverage configuration and the instrumentation libraries wherever possible.

Revisiting the grocery store

It's finally time to use all this new knowledge about auto-instrumentation to clean up the grocery store application. This section will showcase the simplified code that continues to produce the telemetry we've come to expect over the last few chapters. The custom decorators have been removed, as has the code configuring the tracer provider, meter provider, and log emitter provider. All we're left with now is the application code.

Legacy inventory

The legacy inventory service is a great place to start. It is a small Flask application with a single endpoint. The Flask instrumentor, installed at the beginning of the chapter via the `opentelemetry-instrumentation-flask` package, will replace the manual instrumentation code we previously added. The following code instantiates the Flask app and provides the `/inventory` endpoint:

legacy_inventory.py

```
#!/usr/bin/env python3
from flask import Flask, jsonify

app = Flask(__name__)

@app.route("/inventory")
def inventory():
    products = [
        {"name": "oranges", "quantity": "10"},
        {"name": "apples", "quantity": "20"},
    ]
    return jsonify(products)
```

```
if __name__ == "__main__":
    app.run(port=5001)
```

If you remember from previous chapters, this service was configured to use the B3 format propagator. This will be reflected in the configuration options we pass in when starting the service via auto-instrumentation:

```
$ OTEL_RESOURCE_ATTRIBUTES="service.name=legacy-inventory,
                            service.version=0.9.1,
                            net.host.name='hostname',
                            net.host.ip='ipconfig getifaddr en0'" \
    OTEL_TRACES_EXPORTER=console \
    OTEL_PYTHON_TRACER_PROVIDER=sdk \
    OTEL_METRICS_EXPORTER=console \
    OTEL_PYTHON_METER_PROVIDER=sdk \
    OTEL_LOGS_EXPORTER=console \
    OTEL_PYTHON_LOG_EMITTER_PROVIDER=sdk \
    OTEL_PROPAGATORS=b3 \
    opentelemetry-instrument python legacy_inventory.py
```

With this service running, let's look at the next one.

Grocery store

The next service to revisit is the grocery store. This service is also a Flask application and will leverage the same instrumentation library. In addition, it will use the Requests instrumentor to add telemetry to the calls it makes to the legacy inventory. The code looks like this:

grocery_store.py

```
#!/usr/bin/env python3
from logging.config import dictConfig
import requests
from flask import Flask
from opentelemetry.instrumentation.wsgi import
OpenTelemetryMiddleware
```

```python
dictConfig(
    {
        "version": 1,
        "handlers": {
            "otlp": {
                "class": "opentelemetry.sdk._logs.OTLPHandler",
            }
        },
        "root": {"level": "DEBUG", "handlers": ["otlp"]},
    }
)
app = Flask(__name__)
app.wsgi_app = OpenTelemetryMiddleware(app.wsgi_app)

@app.route("/")
def welcome():
    return "Welcome to the grocery store!"

@app.route("/products")
def products():
    url = "http://localhost:5001/inventory"
    resp = requests.get(url)
    return resp.text

if __name__ == "__main__":
    app.run(port=5000)
```

Running the application will look very similar to running the legacy inventory with only a few different parameters:

- `service.name` and `service.version` will be updated to reflect the different applications.
- The propagators will be configured to use both `B3` and `TraceContext` formats, making it possible for context to be propagated from the shopper through to the legacy inventory.

In a separate terminal window, with the legacy inventory service still running, run the following to start the grocery store:

```
$ OTEL_RESOURCE_ATTRIBUTES="service.name=grocery-store,
                           service.version=0.1.2,
                           net.host.name='hostname',
                           net.host.ip='ipconfig getifaddr en0'" \
OTEL_TRACES_EXPORTER=console \
OTEL_PYTHON_TRACER_PROVIDER=sdk \
OTEL_METRICS_EXPORTER=console \
OTEL_PYTHON_METER_PROVIDER=sdk \
OTEL_LOGS_EXPORTER=console \
OTEL_PYTHON_LOG_EMITTER_PROVIDER=sdk \
OTEL_PROPAGATORS=b3,tracecontext \
   opentelemetry-instrument python grocery_store.py
```

The grocery store is up and running. Now we just need to generate some requests via the shopper service.

Shopper

Finally, the shopper application initiates the request through the system. The `RequestsInstrumentor` instruments web requests to the grocery store. Of course, the backend requests don't tell the whole story about what goes on inside the shopper application.

As discussed in *Chapter 3*, *Auto-Instrumentation*, auto-instrumentation can be pretty valuable. In rare cases, it can even be enough to cover most of the functionality within an application. Applications focused on Create, Read, Update, and Delete operations (https://en.wikipedia.org/wiki/CRUD) may not contain enough business logic to warrant manual instrumentation. Operators of applications relying heavily on instrumented libraries may also gain enough visibility from auto-instrumentation.

However, you'll want to add additional details about your code in most scenarios. For those cases, it's crucial to combine auto-instrumentation with manual instrumentation. Such is the case for the last application in our system. The following code shows us the simplified version of the shopper service. As you can see from the code, there is still manual instrumentation code, but no configuration to be seen, as this is all managed by auto-instrumentation. Additionally, you'll note that the `get` call from the requests module no longer requires manual instrumentation:

shopper.py

```python
#!/usr/bin/env python3
import logging
import requests
from opentelemetry import trace
from opentelemetry.sdk._logs import OTLPHandler

tracer = trace.get_tracer("shopper", "0.1.2")
logger = logging.getLogger("shopper")
logger.setLevel(logging.DEBUG)
logger.addHandler(OTLPHandler())

@tracer.start_as_current_span("add item to cart")
def add_item_to_cart(item, quantity):
    span = trace.get_current_span()
    span.set_attributes(
        {
            "item": item,
            "quantity": quantity,
        }
    )
    logger.info("add {} to cart".format(item))

@tracer.start_as_current_span("browse")
def browse():
    resp = requests.get("http://localhost:5000/products")
    add_item_to_cart("orange", 5)
```

```python
@tracer.start_as_current_span("visit store")
def visit_store():
    browse()

if __name__ == "__main__":
    visit_store()
```

It's time to generate some telemetry! Open a third terminal and launch the shopper application with the following command:

```
$ OTEL_RESOURCE_ATTRIBUTES="service.name=shopper,
                           service.version=0.1.3,
                           net.host.name='hostname',
                           net.host.ip='ipconfig getifaddr en0'" \
OTEL_TRACES_EXPORTER=console \
OTEL_PYTHON_TRACER_PROVIDER=sdk \
OTEL_METRICS_EXPORTER=console \
OTEL_PYTHON_METER_PROVIDER=sdk \
OTEL_LOGS_EXPORTER=console \
OTEL_PYTHON_LOG_EMITTER_PROVIDER=sdk \
  opentelemetry-instrument python shopper.py
```

This command should have generated telemetry from all three applications visible in the individual terminal windows.

> **Important note**
> Since the metrics and logging signals are under active development, the instrumentation libraries we use in this chapter only support tracing. Therefore, we will focus on the tracing data being emitted for the time being. It's possible that by the time you're reading this, those libraries also emit logs and metrics.

224　Instrumentation Libraries

We will not go through it in detail since the tracing data being emitted is similar to the data we've already inspected for the grocery store. Looking through the distributed trace generated, we can see the following:

- Spans generated for each application; the `service.name` and `service.version` resource attributes should reflect this.
- The trace ID has been propagated correctly across application boundaries. Check the `trace_id` field across all three terminals to confirm.
- The `Requests` and `Flask` instrumentation libraries have automatically populated attributes.

The following diagram offers a visualization of the spans generated across the system. Spans are identified as having been automatically generated (*A*) or manually generated (*M*).

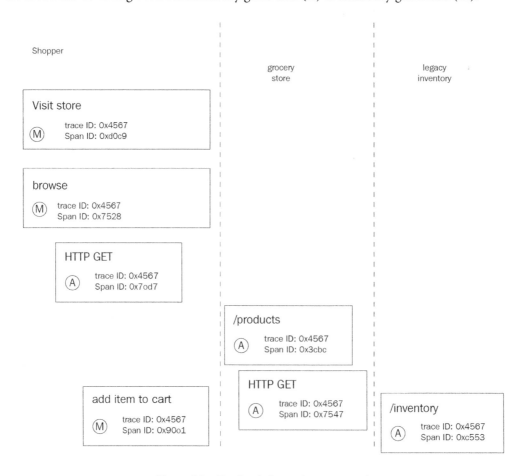

Figure 7.9 – Tracing information generated

This is one of the most exciting aspects of OpenTelemetry. We have telemetry generated by two applications that contain no instrumentation code. The developers of those applications don't need to learn about OpenTelemetry for their applications to produce information about their service, which can be helpful to diagnose issues in the future. Getting started has never been easier. Let's take a quick look at how the Flask instrumentation works.

Flask library instrumentor

Like the Requests library, the Flask instrumentation library contains an implementation of the `BaseInstrumentor` interface. The code is available in the OpenTelemetry Python contrib repository at https://github.com/open-telemetry/opentelemetry-python-contrib/blob/main/instrumentation/opentelemetry-instrumentation-flask/src/opentelemetry/instrumentation/flask/__init__.py. The implementation leverages a few different aspects of the Flask library to achieve instrumentation. It wraps the original Flask app and registers a callback via the `before_request` method. It then provides a middleware to execute instrumentation code at response time. This allows the instrumentation to capture the beginning and the end of requests through the library.

Additional configuration options

The following options are available to configure `FlaskInstrumentor` further:

- `excluded_urls`: Supports a comma-separated list of regular expressions for excluding specific URLs from producing telemetry. This option is also configurable with auto-instrumentation via the `OTEL_PYTHON_FLASK_EXCLUDED_URLS` environment variable.
- `request_hook`: A method to be executed before every Request received by the Flask application.

- response_hook: Similar to the request_hook argument, the response_hook allows a user to configure a method to be performed before a response is returned to the caller.

> **Important Note**
> When using the Flask instrumentation library with auto-instrumentation, it's essential to know that the debug mode may cause issues. By default, the debug mode uses a reloader, which causes the auto-instrumentation to fail. For more information on disabling the reloader, see the OpenTelemetry Python documentation: https://opentelemetry-python.readthedocs.io/en/latest/examples/auto-instrumentation/README.html#instrumentation-while-debugging.

The Requests and Flask instrumentation libraries are just two of many instrumentation libraries available for Python developers.

Finding instrumentation libraries

A challenge with instrumentation libraries is keeping track of which libraries are available across different languages. The libraries available for Python currently live in the opentelemetry-collector-contrib repository (https://github.com/open-telemetry/opentelemetry-python-contrib), but that may not always be the case.

OpenTelemetry registry

The official OpenTelemetry website provides a searchable registry (https://opentelemetry.io/registry/) that includes packages across languages. This information for this registry is stored in a GitHub repository, which can be updated via pull Requests.

opentelemetry-bootstrap

To make getting started even more accessible, the OpenTelemetry Python community maintains the `opentelemetry-bootstrap` tool, installed via the `opentelemetry-instrumentation` package. This tool looks at all installed packages in an environment and lists instrumentation libraries for that environment. It's possible to use the command also to install instrumentation libraries. The following command shows us how to use `opentelemetry-bootstrap` to list packages:

```
$ opentelemetry-bootstrap
opentelemetry-instrumentation-logging==0.28b0
opentelemetry-instrumentation-urllib==0.28b0
opentelemetry-instrumentation-wsgi==0.28b0
opentelemetry-instrumentation-flask==0.28b0
opentelemetry-instrumentation-jinja2==0.28b0
opentelemetry-instrumentation-requests==0.28b0
opentelemetry-instrumentation-urllib3==0.28b0
```

Looking through that list, there are a few additional packages that we may want to install now that we know about them. Conveniently, the `-a install` option installs all the listed packages.

Summary

Instrumentation libraries for third-party libraries are an excellent way for users to use OpenTelemetry with little to no effort. Additionally, instrumentation libraries don't require users to wait for third-party libraries to support OpenTelemetry directly. This helps reduce the burden on the maintainers of those third-party libraries by not asking them to support APIs, which are still evolving.

This chapter allowed us to understand how auto-instrumentation leverages instrumentation libraries to simplify the user experience of adopting OpenTelemetry. By inspecting all the components that combine to make it possible to simplify the code needed to configure telemetry pipelines, we were able to produce telemetry with little to no instrumentation code.

Revisiting the grocery store then allowed us to compare the telemetry generated by auto-instrumented code with manual instrumentation. Along the way, we took a closer look at how different instrumentations are implemented and their configurable options.

Although instrumentation libraries make it possible for users to start using OpenTelemetry today, they require the installation of another library within environments, taking on additional dependencies. As instrumentation libraries have only just started maturing, this may cause users to hesitate to adopt them. Ideally, as OpenTelemetry adoption increases and its API reaches stability across signals, third-party library maintainers will start instrumenting the libraries themselves with OpenTelemetry, removing the need for an additional library. This has already begun with some frameworks, such as Spring in Java and .NET Core libraries.

With the knowledge of OpenTelemetry signals, instrumentation libraries, and auto-instrumentation in our toolbelt, we will now focus on what to do with the telemetry data we're producing. The following few chapters will focus on collecting, transmitting, and analyzing OpenTelemetry data. First, all this data must go somewhere, and the OpenTelemetry Collector is a perfect destination. This will be the topic of the next chapter.

Section 3: Using Telemetry Data

In this part, you will learn how to deploy the OpenTelemetry Collector in conjunction with various backends to visualize the telemetry data as well as identify issues with their cloud-native applications.

This part of the book comprises the following chapters:

- *Chapter 8, OpenTelemetry Collector*
- *Chapter 9, Deploying the Collector*
- *Chapter 10, Configuring Backends*
- *Chapter 11, Diagnosing Problems*
- *Chapter 12, Sampling*

8
OpenTelemetry Collector

So, now that we've learned how to use OpenTelemetry to generate traces, metrics, and logs, we want to do something with all this telemetry data. To make the most of this data, we will need to be able to store and visualize it because, let's be honest – reading telemetry data from the console isn't going to cut it. As we'll discuss in *Chapter 10*, *Configuring Backends*, many destinations can be used for telemetry data. To send telemetry to a backend, the telemetry pipeline for metrics, traces, and logs needs to be configured to use an exporter that's specific to that signal and the backend. For example, if you wanted to send traces to Zipkin, metrics to Prometheus, and logs to Elasticsearch, each would need to be configured in the appropriate application code. Configuring this across dozens of services written in different languages adds to the complexity of managing the code. But now, imagine deciding that one of the backends must be changed because it no longer suits the needs of your business. Although it may not seem like a lot of work on a small scale, in a distributed system with applications that have been produced over many years by various engineers, the amount of effort to update, test, and deploy all that code could be quite significant, not to mention risky.

Wouldn't it be great if there were a way to configure an exporter once, and then use only configuration files to modify the destination of the data? There is – it's called **OpenTelemetry Collector** and this is what we'll be exploring in this chapter.

In this chapter, we will cover the following topics:

- The purpose of OpenTelemetry Collector
- Understanding the components of OpenTelemetry Collector
- Transporting telemetry via OTLP
- Using OpenTelemetry Collector

Let's start by ensuring we have all the tools in place to work with the collector.

Technical requirements

This chapter will introduce OpenTelemetry Collector as a standalone binary, which can be downloaded from https://github.com/open-telemetry/opentelemetry-collector-releases/releases/tag/v0.43.0. It's also possible to build the collector from the source, but this will not be covered in this chapter. The following commands will download the binary that's been compiled for macOS on Intel processors, extract the otelcol file, and ensure the binary can be executed:

```
$ wget -O otelcol.tar.gz https://github.com/open-telemetry/opentelemetry-collector-releases/releases/download/v0.43.0/otelcol_0.43.0_darwin_amd64.tar.gz
$ tar -xzf otelcol.tar.gz otelcol
$ chmod +x ./otelcol
$ ./otelcol --version
otelcol version 0.43.0
```

With the correct binary downloaded, let's ensure that the collector can start by using the following command. It is expected that the process will exit:

```
$ ./otelcol
Error: failed to get config: invalid configuration: no enabled receivers specified in config
2022/02/13 11:52:47 collector server run finished with error: failed to get config: invalid configuration: no enabled receivers specified in config
```

> **Important Note**
> The OpenTelemetry Collector project produces a different binary for various operating systems (Windows, Linux, and macOS) and architectures. You must download the correct one for your environment.

The configuration for the collector is written in YAML format (https://en.wikipedia.org/wiki/YAML), but we'll try to steer clear of most of the traps of YAML by providing complete configuration examples. The collector is written in Go, so this chapter includes code snippets in Go. Each piece of code will be thoroughly explained, but don't worry if the details of the language escape you – the concept of the code is what we'll be focusing on. To send data to OpenTelemetry Collector from Python applications, we'll need to install the **OTLP** exporter, which can be done via pip:

```
$ pip install opentelemetry-exporter-otlp \
               opentelemetry-propagator-b3 \
               opentelemetry-instrumentation-wsgi \
               flask \
               requests
```

> **Important Note**
> The opentelemetry-exporter-otlp package itself does not contain any exporter code. It uses dependencies to pull in a different package for each different encoding and transport option that's supported by **OTLP** We will discuss these later in this chapter.

The completed code and configuration for this chapter is available in this book's GitHub repository in the chapter08 directory:

```
$ git clone https://github.com/PacktPublishing/Cloud-Native-Observability
$ cd Cloud-Native-Observability/chapter08
```

As with the previous chapters, the code in these examples builds on top of the previous chapters. If you'd like to follow along with the code changes, copy the code from the chapter06 folder. Now, let's dive in and figure out what this collector is all about, and why you should care about it.

The purpose of OpenTelemetry Collector

In essence, OpenTelemetry Collector is a process that receives telemetry in various formats, processes it, and then exports it to one or more destinations. The collector acts as a broker between the source of the telemetry, applications, or nodes, for example, and the backend that will ultimately store the data for analysis. The following diagram shows where the collector would be deployed in an environment containing various components:

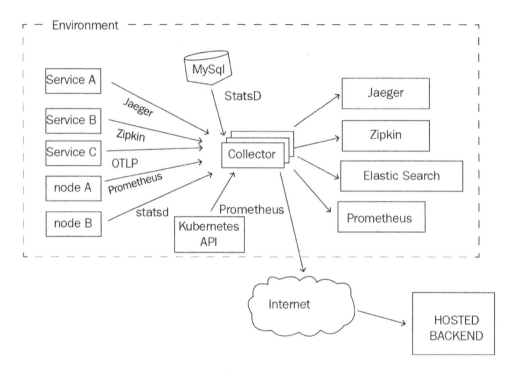

Figure 8.1 – Architecture diagram of an environment with a collector

Deploying a component such as OpenTelemetry Collector is not free as it requires additional resources to be spent on running, operating, and monitoring it. The following are some reasons why deploying a collector may be helpful:

- You can decouple the source of the telemetry data from its destination. This means that developers can configure a single destination for the telemetry data in application code and allow the operators of the collector to determine where that data will go as needed, without having to modify the existing code.

- You can provide a single destination for many data types. The collector can be configured to receive traces, metrics, and logs in many different formats, such as OTLP Jaeger, Zipkin, Prometheus, StatsD, and many more.

- You can reduce latency when sending data to a backend. This mitigates unexpected side effects from occurring when an event causes a backend to be unresponsive. A collector deployment can also be horizontally scaled to increase capacity as required.
- You can modify telemetry data to address compliance and security concerns. Data can be filtered by the collector via processors based on the criteria defined in the configuration. Doing so can stop data leakage and prevent information that shouldn't be included in the telemetry data from ever being stored in a backend.

We will discuss deployment scenarios for the collector in *Chapter 9*, *Deploying the Collector*. For now, let's focus on the architecture and components that provide the functionality of the collector.

Understanding the components of OpenTelemetry Collector

The collector allows users to configure *pipelines* for each signal separately by combining any number of *receivers*, *processors*, and *exporters* as shown in the following diagram. This gives the collector a lot of flexibility in how and where it can be used:

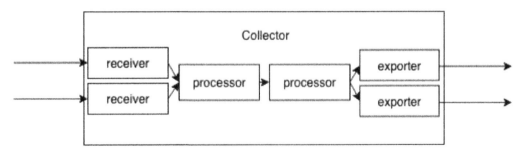

Figure 8.2 – Dataflow through the collector

The initial implementation of the collector was a fork of the OpenCensus Service (https://opencensus.io/service/), which served a similar purpose in the OpenCensus ecosystem. The collector supports many open protocols out of the box for inputs and outputs, which we'll explore in more detail as we take a closer look at each component. Each component in the collector implements the Component interface, which is fairly minimal, as shown in the following code:

```
type Component interface {
    Start(ctx context.Context, host Host) error
```

```
          Shutdown(ctx context.Context) error
}
```

This interface makes it easy for implementors to add additional components to the collector, making it very extensible. Let's look at each component in more detail.

Receivers

The first component in a pipeline is the **receiver**, a component that receives data in various supported formats and converts this data into an internal data format within the collector. Typically, a receiver registers a listener that exposes a port in the collector for the protocols it supports. For example, the Jaeger receiver supports the following protocols:

- Thrift Binary on port `6832`
- Thrift Compact on port `6831`
- Thrift HTTP on port `14268`
- gRPC on port `14250`

> **Important Note**
> Default port values can be overridden via configuration, as we'll see later in this chapter.

It's possible to enable multiple protocols for the same receiver so that each of the protocols listed previously will listen on different ports by default. The following table shows the supported receiver formats for each signal type:

	Traces	Metrics	Logs
Host Metrics		✓	
Jaeger	✓		
Kafka	✓	✓	✓
OpenCensus	✓	✓	
OpenTelemetry (OTLP)	✓	✓	✓
Prometheus		✓	
Zipkin	✓		

Figure 8.3 – Receiver formats per signal

Note that all the receivers shown here are receivers that support data in a specific format. However, an exception is the host metrics receiver, which will be discussed later in this chapter. Receivers can be reused across multiple pipelines and it's possible to configure multiple receivers for the same pipeline. The following configuration example enables the OTLP gRPC receiver and the Jaeger Thrift Binary receiver. Then, it configures three separate pipelines named `traces/otlp`, `traces/jaeger`, and `traces/both`, which use those receivers:

```
receivers:
  otlp:
    protocols:
      grpc:
  jaeger:
    protocols:
      thrift_binary:
service:
  pipelines:
    traces/otlp:
      receivers: [otlp]
    traces/jaeger:
      receivers: [jaeger]
    traces/both:
      receivers: [otlp, jaeger]
```

One scenario where it would be beneficial to create separate pipelines for different receivers is if additional processing needs to occur on the data from one pipeline but not the other. As with the component interface, the interface for receivers is kept minimal, as shown in the following code. The `TracesReceiver`, `MetricsReceiver`, and `LogsReceiver` receivers all embed the same `Receiver` interface, which embeds the `Component` interface we saw previously:

```
type Receiver interface {
  Component
}
type TracesReceiver interface {
  Receiver
}
```

The simplicity of the interface makes it easy to implement additional receivers as needed. As we mentioned previously, the main task of a receiver is to translate data that's being received into various formats, but what about the host metrics receiver?

Host metrics receiver

The **host metrics** receiver can be configured to collect metrics about the host running the collector. It can be configured to scrape metrics for the CPU, disk, memory, and various other system-level details. The following example shows how the `hostmetrics` receiver can be configured to scrape `load`, `memory`, and `network` information from a host every 10 seconds (`10s`):

```
receivers:
  hostmetrics:
    collection_interval: 10s
    scrapers:
      load:
      memory:
      network:
service:
  pipelines:
    metrics:
      receivers: [hostmetrics]
```

The receiver supports additional configuration so that you can include or exclude specific devices or metrics. Configuring this receiver can help you monitor the performance of the host without running additional processes to do so. Once the telemetry data has been received through a receiver, it can be processed further via processors.

Processors

It can be beneficial to perform some additional tasks, such as filtering unwanted telemetry or injecting additional attributes, on the data before passing it to the exporter. This is the job of the processor. Unlike receivers and exporters, the capabilities of processors vary significantly from one processor to another. It's also worth noting that the order of the components in the configuration matters for processors, as the data is passed serially from one processor to another. In addition to embedding the component interface, the processor interface also embeds a consumer interface that matches the signal that's being processed, as shown in the following code snippet. The purpose of the consumer interface is to provide a function that consumes the signal, such as `ConsumeMetrics`. It also provides information about whether the processor will modify the data it processes via the `MutatesData` capability:

```
type Capabilities struct {
  MutatesData bool
}
type baseConsumer interface {
  Capabilities() Capabilities
}
type Metrics interface {
  baseConsumer
  ConsumeMetrics(ctx context.Context, md pdata.Metrics) error
}
type MetricsProcessor interface {
  Processor
  consumer.Metrics
}
```

The following example configures an attributes processor called `attributes/add-key` to insert an attribute with the `example-key` key and sets its value to `first`. The second attributes processor, `attributes/update-key`, updates the value of the `example-key` attribute to the `second` value. The traces pipeline is then configured to add the attribute and update its value:

```
processors:
  attributes/add-key:
    actions:
      - key: example-key
        action: insert
```

```yaml
      value: first
  attributes/update-key:
    actions:
      - key: example-key
        action: update
        value: second
service:
  pipelines:
    traces:
      processors: [attributes/add-key, attributes/update-key]
```

The output that's expected from this configuration is that all the spans that are emitted have an `example-key` attribute set to a value of `second`. Since the order of the processors matters, inverting the processors in the preceding example would set the value to `first`. The previous example is a bit silly since it doesn't make a lot of sense to configure multiple attributes processors in that manner, but it illustrates that ordering the processors matters. Let's see what a more realistic example may look like. The following configuration copies a value from one attribute with the `old-key` key into another one with the `new-key` key before deleting the `old-key` attribute:

```yaml
processors:
  attributes/copy-and-delete:
    actions:
      - key: new-key
        action: upsert
        from_attribute: old-key
      - key: old-key
        action: delete
service:
  pipelines:
    traces:
      processors: [attributes/copy-and-delete]
```

A configuration like the previous one could be used to migrate values or consolidate data coming in from multiple systems, where different names are used to represent the same data. As we mentioned earlier, processors cover a range of functionality. The following table lists the current processors, as well as the signals they process:

	Traces	Metrics	Logs
Attributes	✓		✓
Batch	✓	✓	✓
Filter		✓	
Memory Limiter	✓	✓	✓
Probabilistic Sampling	✓		
Resource	✓	✓	✓
Span	✓		

Figure 8.4 – Processors per signal

Some of these processors will be familiar to you if you've already used an OpenTelemetry SDK. It's worth taking a moment to explore these processors further.

Attributes processor

As we discussed earlier, the **attributes processor** can be used to modify telemetry data attributes. It supports the following operations:

- `delete`: This deletes an attribute for a specified key.
- `extract`: This uses a regular expression to extract values from the specified attribute and `upsert` new attributes resulting from that extraction.
- `hash`: This computes a SHA-1 hash of the value for an existing attribute and updates the value of that attribute to the computed hash.
- `insert`: This inserts an attribute for a specified key when it does not exist. It does nothing if the attribute exists.
- `update`: This updates an existing attribute with a specified value. It does nothing if the attribute does not exist.
- `upsert`: This combines the functionality of `insert` and `update`. If an attribute does not exist, it will insert it with the specified value; otherwise, it will update the attribute with the value.

The attributes processor, along with the span processor, which we'll see shortly, allows you to include or exclude spans based on `match_type`, which can either be an exact match configured as `strict` or a regular expression configured with `regexp`. The matching is applied to one or more of the configured fields: `services`, `span_names`, or `attributes`. The following example includes spans for the `super-secret` and `secret` services:

```
processors:
  attributes/include-secret:
    include:
      match_type: strict
      services: ["super-secret", "secret"]
    actions:
      - key: secret-attr
        action: delete
```

The attributes processor can be quite useful when you're scrubbing **personally identifiable information** (**PII**) or other sensitive information. A common way sensitive information makes its way into telemetry data is via debug logs that capture private variables it shouldn't have, or by user information, passwords, or private keys being recorded in metadata. Data leaks often happen accidentally and are much more frequent than you'd think.

> **Important Note**
> It's possible to configure both an `include` and `exclude` rule at the same time. If that is the case, `include` is checked before `exclude`.

Filter processor

The **filter processor** allows you to include or exclude telemetry data based on the configured criteria. This processor, like the attributes and span processors, can be configured to match names with either `strict` or `regexp` matching. It's also possible to use an expression that matches attributes as well as names. Further scoping on the filter can be achieved by specifying `resource_attributes`. In terms of its implementation, at the time of writing, the filter processor only supports filtering for metrics, though additional signal support has been requested by the community.

Probabilistic sampling processor

Although sampling is a topic that we'll cover in more detail in *Chapter 12, Sampling*, it's important to know that the collector provides a sampling processor for traces known as the **probabilistic sampling processor**. It can be used to reduce the number of traces that are exported from the collector by specifying a sampling percentage, which determines what percentage of traces should be kept. The `hash_seed` parameter is used to determine how the collector should hash the trace IDs to determine which traces to process:

```
processors:
  probabilistic_sampler:
    sampling_percentage: 20
    hash_seed: 12345
```

The `hash_seed` configuration parameter becomes especially important when multiple collectors are connected. For example, imagine that a collector (*A*) has been configured to send its data to another collector (*B*) before sending the data to a backend. With both *A* and *B* configured using the previous example, if 100 traces are sent through the two collectors, a total of 20 of those will be sent through to the backend. If, on the other hand, the two collectors use a different `hash_seed`, collector *A* will send 20 traces to collector *B*, and collector *B* will sample 20% of those, resulting in four traces being sent to the backend. Either case is valid, but it's important to understand the difference.

> **Important Note**
> The probabilistic sampling processor prioritizes the sampling priority attribute before the trace ID hashing if the attribute is present. This attribute is defined in the semantic conventions and was originally defined in OpenTracing. More information on this will be provided in *Chapter 12, Sampling*, but for now, it's just good to be aware of it.

Resource processor

The **resource processor** lets users modify attributes, just like the attributes processor. However, instead of updating attributes on individual spans, metrics, or logs, the resource processor updates the attributes of the resource associated with the telemetry data. The options that are available for configuring the resource processor are the same as for the attributes processor. This can be seen in the following example, which uses `upsert` for the `deployment.environment` attribute and renames the `runtime` attribute to `container.runtime` using the `insert` and `delete` actions:

```
processors:
  resource:
    attributes:
    - key: deployment.environment
      value: staging
      action: upsert
    - key: container.runtime
      from_attribute: runtime
      action: insert
    - key: runtime
      action: delete
```

Now, let's discuss the span processor.

Span processor

It may be useful to manipulate the names of spans or attributes of spans based on their names. This is the job of the **span processor**. It can extract attributes from a span and update its name based on those attributes. Alternatively, it can take the span's name and expand it to individual attributes associated with the span. The following example shows how to rename a span based on the `messaging.system` and `messaging.operation` attributes, which will be separated by the `:` character. The second configuration of the span processor shows how to extract the `storeId` and `orderId` attributes from the span's name:

```
processors:
  span/rename:
    name:
      from_attributes: ["messaging.system", "messaging.operation"]
      separator: ":"
```

```
span/create-attributes:
  name:
    to_attributes:
      rules:
        - ^\/stores\/(?P<storeId>.*)\/.*$
        - ^.*\/orders/(?P<orderId>.*)\/.*$
```

As we mentioned previously, the span processor also supports the `include` and `exclude` configurations to help you filter spans. Not all processors are used to modify the telemetry data; some change the behavior of the collector itself.

Batch processor

The **batch processor** helps you batch data to increase the efficiency of transmitting the data. It can be configured both to send batches based on batch size and a schedule. The following code configures a batch processor to send data every `10s` or every `10000` records and limits the size of the batch to `11000` records:

```
processors:
  batch:
    timeout: 10s # default 200ms
    send_batch_size: 10000 # default 8192
    send_batch_max_size: 11000 # default 0 - no limit
```

It is recommended to configure a batch processor for all the pipelines to optimize the throughput of the collector.

Memory limiter processor

To ensure the collector is conscious of resource consumption, the **memory limiter processor** lets users control the amount of memory the collector consumes. This helps ensure the collector does as much as it can to avoid running out of memory. Limits can be specified either via fixed mebibyte values or percentages that are calculated based on the total available memory. If both are specified, the fixed values take precedence. The memory limiter enforces both soft and hard limits, with the difference defined by a spike limit configuration. It is recommended to use the **ballast extension** alongside the memory limiter. The ballast extension allows the collector to pre-allocate memory to improve the stability of the heap. The recommended size for the ballast is between one-third to one-half of the total memory for the collector. The following code configures the memory limiter to use up to 250 Mib of the memory configured via `limit_mib`, with 50 Mib as the difference between the soft and hard limits, which is configured via `spike_limit_mib`:

```
processors:
  memory_limiter:
    check_interval: 5s
    limit_mib: 250
    spike_limit_mib: 50
extensions:
  memory_ballast:
    size_mib: 125
```

The memory limiter processor, along with the batch processor, are both recommended if you wish to optimize the performance of the collector.

> **Important Note**
> When the processor exceeds soft limits, it returns errors and starts dropping data. If it exceeds hard limits, it will also force garbage collection to free memory.

The memory limiter should be the first processor you configure in the pipeline. This ensures that when the memory threshold is exceeded, the errors that are returned are propagated to the receivers. This allows the receivers to send appropriate error codes back to the client, who can then throttle the requests they are sending. Now that we understand how to process our telemetry data to fit our needs, let's learn how to use the collector to export all this data.

Exporters

The last component of the pipeline is the exporter. The role of the exporter in the collector pipeline is fairly similar to its role in the SDK, as we explored in previous chapters. The exporter takes the data in its internal collector format, marshals it into the output format, and sends it to one or more configured destinations. The interface for the exporter is very similar to the processor interface as it is also a consumer, separated again by a signal. The following code shows us the `LogsExporter` interface, which embeds the interfaces we explored earlier:

```
type LogsExporter interface {
  Exporter
  consumer.Logs
}
```

Multiple exporters of the same type can be configured for different destinations as necessary. It's also possible to configure multiple exporters for the same pipeline to output the data to multiple locations. The following code configures a `jaeger` exporter, which is used for exporting traces, and an `otlp` exporter, which will be used for both traces and metrics:

```
exporters:
  jaeger:
    endpoint: jaeger:14250
  otlp:
    endpoint: otelcol:4317
service:
  pipelines:
    traces:
      exporters: [jaeger, otlp]
    metrics:
      exporters: [otlp]
```

Several other formats are supported by exporters. The following table lists the available exporters, as well as the signals that each supports:

	Traces	Metrics	Logs
File	✓	✓	✓
Jaeger	✓		
Kafka	✓	✓	✓
Logging	✓	✓	✓
OpenCensus	✓	✓	
OpenTelemetry (OTLP)	✓	✓	✓
Prometheus		✓	
Zipkin	✓		

Figure 8.5 – Exporters per signal

Note that in addition to exporting data across different signals to destinations that can be reached over a network, it's also possible to export telemetry data locally to the console via the logs exporter or as JSON to a file via the file exporter. Receivers, processors, and exporters cover the components in the pipeline, but there is yet more to cover about the collector.

Extensions

Although most of the functionality of the collector revolves around the telemetry pipelines, there is additional functionality that is made available via **extensions**. Extensions provide you with another way to extend the collector. The following extensions are currently available:

- ballast: This allows users to configure a memory ballast for the collector to improve the overall stability and performance of the collector.
- health_check: This makes an endpoint available for checking the health of the collector. This can be useful for service discovery or orchestration of the collector.
- pprof: This enables the Go performance profiler, which can be used to identify performance issues within the collector.
- zpages: This enables an endpoint in the collector that provides debugging information about the components in the collector.

Thus far, all the components we've explored are part of the core collector distribution and are built into the binary we'll be using in our examples later in this chapter. However, those are far from the only components that are available.

Additional components

As you can imagine, providing this much functionality in an application can become quite complex. To reduce the complexity of the collector's core functionality without impeding progress and enthusiasm in the community, the main collector repository contains components that are defined as part of the OpenTelemetry specification. With all the flexibility the collector provides, many individuals and organizations are contributing additional receivers, processors, and exporters. These can be found in the `opentelemetry-collector-contrib` repository at `https://github.com/open-telemetry/opentelemetry-collector-contrib`. As the code in this repository is changing rapidly, we won't be going over the components available there, but I strongly suggest browsing through the repository to get an idea of what is available.

Before learning how to use the collector and configuring an application to send data to it, it's important to understand a little bit more about the preferred protocol to receive and export data via the collector. This is known as OTLP.

Transporting telemetry via OTLP

We've mentioned **OTLP** multiple times in this chapter and this book, so let's look at what it is. To ensure that telemetry data is transmitted as efficiently and reliably as possible, OpenTelemetry has defined OTLP. The protocol itself is defined via protocol buffer (`https://developers.google.com/protocol-buffers`) definition files. This means that any client or server that's interested in sending or receiving OTLP only has to implement these definitions to support it. OTLP is the recommended protocol of OpenTelemetry for transmitting telemetry data and is supported as a core component of the collector.

> **Important Note**
> **Protocol buffers** or **protobufs** are a language and platform-agnostic mechanism for serializing data that was originally intended for gRPC. Libraries are provided to generate the code from the protobuf definition files in a variety of languages. This is a much deeper topic than we will have time for in this book, so if you're interested in reading the protocol files, I strongly recommended learning more about protocol buffers – they're pretty cool! The Google developer site that was linked previously is a great resource to get started.

The definition for OTLP (`https://github.com/open-telemetry/opentelemetry-proto`) is divided into multiple sections to cover the different signals. Each component of the protocol provides backward compatibility guaranteed via its maturity level, which allows adopters to get a sense of how often they should expect breaking changes. An alpha level makes no guarantees around breaking changes while a stable level guarantees backward-incompatible changes will be introduced no more frequently than every 12 months. The maturity level of each component is available in the project's `README.md` file and the current state, at the time of writing, can be seen in the following table. It's very likely to change by the time you're reading this as progress is being made quite rapidly!

Component	Maturity
Binary Protobuf Encoding	
collector/metrics/*	Stable
collector/trace/*	Stable
collector/logs/*	Beta
common/*	Stable
metrics/*	Stable
resource/*	Stable
trace/trace.proto	Stable
trace/trace_config.proto	Alpha
logs/*	Beta
JSON encoding	
All messages	Alpha

Figure 8.6 – Maturity level of OTLP components

Taking a closer look at the preceding table (https://github.com/open-telemetry/opentelemetry-proto#maturity-level), note that it includes a different section for protobuf and JSON encoding. Let's talk about why that is.

Encodings and protocols

The specification defines the encodings and protocols that are supported by OTLP. Initially, the following three combinations are supported:

- protobufs over gRPC
- protobufs over HTTP
- JSON over HTTP

Depending on the requirements of your application or the infrastructure that will be used to deploy your code, certain restrictions may guide the decision of which encoding or protocol to choose. For example, users may be deploying applications in an environment that doesn't support gRPC. This was true for a long time with serverless Python environments in various cloud providers. Similarly, gRPC was not supported in the browser, meaning users of OpenTelemetry for JavaScript cannot use gRPC when instrumenting a browser application. Another tradeoff that may cause users to choose one package over another is the impact of serializing and deserializing data using JSON, which can have some serious performance implications in certain languages compared to using protobufs. The different combinations of encodings and protocols exist to provide additional flexibility for users, depending on the requirements of their environments.

One of the requirements for any OpenTelemetry language implementation is to support at least one of these formats before marking a signal as generally available. This ensures that users can use OTLP to export data across their entire system, from application instrumentation to the backend.

Additional design considerations

Backpressure can happen when clients are generating telemetry data faster than the recipients can receive it. To address this, the specification for OTLP also defines how clients should handle responses from servers to manage backpressure when receiving systems become overloaded. Another design goal of the protocol is to ensure it is load balancer-friendly so that you can horizontally scale various components that could be involved in handling telemetry data using OTLP. Equipped with this knowledge of the protocol, let's start sending data to the collector.

Using OpenTelemetry Collector

Now that we're familiar with the core components of OpenTelemetry Collector and OTLP, it's time to start using the collector with the grocery store. The following diagram gives us an idea of how telemetry data is currently configured and where we are trying to go with this chapter:

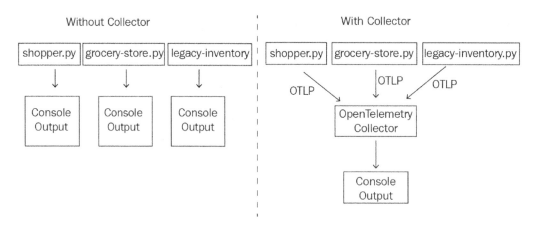

Figure 8.7 – Before and after diagrams of exporting telemetry data

At the beginning of this chapter, we installed the OTLP exporters for Python via the `opentelemetry-exporter-otlp` package. This, in turn, installed the packages that are available for each protocol and encoding:

- `opentelemetry-exporter-otlp-proto-grpc`
- `opentelemetry-exporter-otlp-proto-http`
- `opentelemetry-exporter-otlp-json-http`

The package that includes all the protocols and the encoding is a convenient way to start, but once you're familiar with the requirements for your environment, you'll want to choose a specific encoding and protocol to reduce dependencies.

Configuring the exporter

The following examples will leverage the `otlp-proto-grpc` package, which includes the `exporter` classes we'll use to export telemetry – OTLPSpanExporter, OTLPMetricExporter, and OTLPLogExporter. The code builds on the example applications from *Chapter 6, Logging —Capturing Events*, by updating the `common.py` module to use the OTLP exporters instead of the control exporters, which we've used so far:

common.py

```
from opentelemetry.exporter.otlp.proto.grpc.trace_exporter
  import OTLPSpanExporter
from opentelemetry.exporter.otlp.proto.grpc._metric_exporter
  import OTLPMetricExporter
from opentelemetry.exporter.otlp.proto.grpc._log_exporter
  import OTLPLogExporter

def configure_tracer(name, version):
    ...
    exporter = OTLPSpanExporter()
    ...

def configure_meter(name, version):
    ...
    exporter = OTLPMetricExporter()
    ...

def configure_logger(name, version):
    ...
    exporter = OTLPLogExporter()
    ...
```

By default, as per the specification, the exporters will be configured to send data to a collector running on `localhost:4317`.

Configuring the collector

The following collector configuration sets up the `otlp` receiver, which will be used to receive telemetry data from our application. Additionally, it configures the logging exporter to output useful information to the console:

config/collector/config.yml

```yaml
receivers:
  otlp:
    protocols:
      grpc:
exporters:
  logging:
service:
  pipelines:
    traces:
      receivers: [otlp]
      exporters: [logging]
    metrics:
      receivers: [otlp]
      exporters: [logging]
    logs:
      receivers: [otlp]
      exporters: [logging]
```

> **Important Note**
>
> In the following examples, each time `config.yml` is updated, the collector must be restarted for the changes to take effect.

It's time to see whether the collector and the application can communicate. First, start the collector using the following command from the terminal:

```
./otelcol --config ./config/collector/config.yml
```

If everything is going according to plan, the process should be up and running, and the output from it should list the components that have been loaded. It should also contain a message similar to the following:

collector output

```
2021-05-30T16:19:03.088-0700 info service/application.go:197
Everything is ready. Begin running and processing data.
```

Next, we need to run the application code in a separate terminal. First, launch the legacy inventory, followed by the grocery store, and then the shopper application. Note that `legacy_inventory.py` and `grocery_store.py` will remain running for the remainder of this chapter as we will not make any further changes to them:

```
python legacy_inventory.py
python grocery_store.py
python shopper.py
```

Pay close attention to the output from the terminal running the collector. You should see some output describing the traces, metrics, and logs that have been processed by the collector. The following code gives you an idea of what to look for:

collector output

```
2022-02-13T14:35:47.101-0800    INFO    loggingexporter/
logging_exporter.go:69   LogsExporter      {"#logs": 1}
2022-02-13T14:35:47.110-0800    INFO    loggingexporter/
logging_exporter.go:40   TracesExporter    {"#spans": 4}
2022-02-13T14:35:49.858-0800    INFO    loggingexporter/
logging_exporter.go:40   TracesExporter    {"#spans": 1}
2022-02-13T14:35:50.533-0800    INFO    loggingexporter/
logging_exporter.go:40   TracesExporter    {"#spans": 3}
2022-02-13T14:35:50.535-0800    INFO    loggingexporter/
logging_exporter.go:69   LogsExporter      {"#logs": 2}
```

Excellent – let's do some more fun things with the collector by adding some processors to our configuration! If you look closely at the preceding output, you'll notice that `TracesExporter` is mentioned in three separate instances. Since each of our applications is sending telemetry data, the exporter is called with the new data. The batch processor can improve it's efficiency here by waiting a while and sending a single batch containing all the telemetry data simultaneously. The following code configures the `batch` processor with a `timeout` of 10 seconds (`10s`), so the processor will wait up until that time to send a batch. Then, we can add this processor to each pipeline:

config/collector/config.yml

```yaml
processors:
  batch:
    timeout: 10s
...
  pipelines:
    traces:
      receivers: [otlp]
      processors: [batch]
      exporters: [logging]
    metrics:
      receivers: [otlp]
      processors: [batch]
      exporters: [logging]
    logs:
      receivers: [otlp]
      processors: [batch]
      exporters: [logging]
```

Try running the shopper application once again. This time, the output from the collector should show a single line including the sum of all the spans we saw earlier:

collector output

```
2022-02-13T14:40:07.360-0800    INFO    loggingexporter/
logging_exporter.go:69  LogsExporter    {"#logs": 2}
2022-02-13T14:40:07.360-0800    INFO    loggingexporter/
logging_exporter.go:40  TracesExporter  {"#spans": 8}
```

If you run the shopper application a few times, you'll notice a 10-second delay in the collector outputting information about the telemetry data that's been generated. This is the batch processor at work. Let's make the logging output slightly more useful by updating the logging exporter configuration:

config/collector/config.yml

```
exporters:
  logging:
    loglevel: debug
```

Restarting the collector and running the shopper application again will output the full telemetry data that's been received. What should appear is a verbose list of all the telemetry data the collector is receiving. Look specifically for the span named add item to cart as we'll be modifying it in the next few examples:

collector output

```
Span #0
    Trace ID        : 1592a37b7513b73eaefabde700f4ae9b
    Parent ID       : 2411c263df768eb5
    ID              : 8e6f5cdb56d6448d
    Name            : HTTP GET
    Kind            : SPAN_KIND_SERVER
    Start time      : 2022-02-13 22:41:42.673298 +0000 UTC
    End time        : 2022-02-13 22:41:42.677336 +0000 UTC
    Status code     : STATUS_CODE_UNSET
    Status message  :
Attributes:
     -> http.method: STRING(GET)
     -> http.server_name: STRING(127.0.0.1)
     -> http.scheme: STRING(http)
     -> net.host.port: INT(5000)
     -> http.host: STRING(localhost:5000)
     -> http.target: STRING(/products)
     -> net.peer.ip: STRING(127.0.0.1)
```

So far, our telemetry data is being emitted to a collector from three different applications. Now, we can see all the telemetry data on the terminal running the collector. Let's take this a step further and modify this telemetry data via some processors.

Modifying spans

One of the great features of the collector is its ability to operate on telemetry data from a central location. The following example demonstrates some of the power behind the processors. The following configuration uses two different processors to augment the span we mentioned previously. First, the attributes processor will add an attribute to identify a `location` attribute. Next, the span processor will use the attributes from the span to rename the span so that it includes the `location`, `item`, and `quantity` attributes. The new processors must also be added to the `traces` pipeline's `processors` array:

config/collector/config.yml

```
processors:
  attributes/add-location:
    actions:
      - key: location
        action: insert
        value: europe
  span/rename:
    name:
      from_attributes: [location, item, quantity]
      separator: ":"
...
  pipelines:
    traces:
      processors: [batch, attributes/add-location, span/rename]
```

> **Important Note**
> Remember that the order of the processors matters. In this case, the reverse order wouldn't work as the location attribute would not be populated.

Run the shopper and look at the output from the collector to see the effect of the new processors. The new exported span contains a `location` attribute with the `europe` value, which we configured. Its name has also been updated to `location:item:quantity`:

collector output

```
Span #1
    Trace ID        : 47dac26efa8de0ca1e202b6d64fd319c
    Parent ID       : ee10984575037d4a
    ID              : a4f42124645c4d3b
    Name            : europe:orange:5
    Kind            : SPAN_KIND_INTERNAL
    Start time      : 2022-02-13 22:44:57.072143 +0000 UTC
    End time        : 2022-02-13 22:44:57.07751 +0000 UTC
Status code         : STATUS_CODE_UNSET
    Status message  :
Attributes:
     -> item: STRING(orange)
     -> quantity: INT(5)
     -> location: STRING(europe)
```

This isn't bad for 10 lines of configuration! The final example will explore the `hostmetrics` receiver and how to configure the `filter` processor for metrics.

Filtering metrics

So far, we've looked at how to modify spans, but what about metrics? As we discussed previously, the `hostmetrics` receiver captures metrics about the localhost. Let's see it in action. The following example configures the host metrics receiver to scrape `memory` and `network` information every 10 seconds:

config/collector/config.yml

```
receivers:
  hostmetrics:
    collection_intervals: 10s
    scrapers:
      memory:
```

```
        network:
...
service:
  pipelines:
    metrics:
      receivers: [otlp, hostmetrics]
```

After configuring this receiver, just restart the collector – you should see metrics in the collector output, without running `shopper.py`. The output will include memory and network metrics:

collector output

```
InstrumentationLibraryMetrics #0
InstrumentationLibrary
Metric #0
Descriptor:
     -> Name: system.memory.usage
     -> Description: Bytes of memory in use.
     -> Unit: By
     -> DataType: IntSum
     -> IsMonotonic: false
     -> AggregationTemporality: AGGREGATION_TEMPORALITY_
CUMULATIVE
IntDataPoints #0
Data point labels:
     -> state: used
StartTimestamp: 1970-01-01 00:00:00 +0000 UTC
Timestamp: 2022-02-13 22:48:16.999087 +0000 UTC
Value: 10880851968
Metric #1
Descriptor:
     -> Name: system.network.packets
     -> Description: The number of packets transferred.
     -> Unit: {packets}
     -> DataType: IntSum
     -> IsMonotonic: true
```

```
          -> AggregationTemporality: AGGREGATION_TEMPORALITY_
CUMULATIVE
IntDataPoints #0
Data point labels:
     -> device: lo0
     -> direction: transmit
StartTimestamp: 1970-01-01 00:00:00 +0000 UTC
Timestamp: 2022-02-13 22:48:16.999087 +0000 UTC
Value: 120456
```

Well done – the collector is now generating metrics for you! Depending on the type of system you're running the collector on, you may have many network interfaces available that are generating a lot of metrics. Let's update the configuration to scrape metrics for a single interface to reduce some of the noise. On my host, I will use `lo0` as the interface:

config/collector/config.yml

```
receivers:
  hostmetrics:
    collection_intervals: 10s
    scrapers:
      memory:
      network:
        include:
          match_type: strict
          interfaces: [lo0]
```

> **Important Note**
> Network interface names vary based on the operating system being used. Some common interface names are `lo0`, `eth0`, `en0`, and `wlan0`. If you're unsure, look for the device label in the previous output, which should show you some of the interfaces that are available on your system.

The output will be significantly reduced, but there are still many network metrics to sift through. `system.network.connections` is quite noisy as it collects data points for each `tcp` state. Let's take this one step further and use the `filter` processor to exclude `system.network.connections`:

config/collector/config.yml

```
processors:
  filter/network-connections:
    metrics:
      exclude:
        match_type: strict
        metric_names:
          - system.network.connections
...
  pipelines:
    metrics:
      receivers: [hostmetrics]
      processors: [batch, filter/network-connections]
```

Restarting the collector one last time will yield a much easier-to-read output. Of course, there are many more scenarios to experiment with when it comes to the collector and its components, but this gives you a good idea of how to get started. I recommend spending some time experimenting with different configurations and processors to get comfortable with it. And with that, we now have an understanding of one of the most critical components of OpenTelemetry – the collector.

Summary

In this chapter, you learned about the fundamentals of OpenTelemetry Collector and its components. You now know what role receivers, processors, exporters, and extensions play in the collector and know about the specifics of individual processors.

Additionally, we looked at the definition of the OTLP, its benefits, and the design decisions behind creating the protocol. Equipped with this knowledge, we configured OpenTelemetry Collector for the first time and updated the grocery store to emit data to it. Using a variety of processors, we manipulated the data the collector was receiving to get a working understanding of how to harness the power of the collector.

The next chapter will expand on this knowledge and take the collector from a component that's used in development to a core component of your infrastructure. We'll explore how to deploy the collector in a variety of scenarios to make the most of it.

9
Deploying the Collector

Now that we've learned about the ins and outs of the collector, it's time to look at how we can use it in production. This chapter will explain how the flexibility of the collector can help us to deploy it in a variety of scenarios. Using Docker, Kubernetes, and Helm, we will learn how to use the OpenTelemetry collector in combination with the grocery store application from earlier chapters. This will give us the necessary knowledge to start using the collector in our cloud-native environment.

In this chapter, we will focus on the following main topics:

- Using the collector as a sidecar to collect application telemetry
- Deploying the collector as an agent to collect system-level telemetry
- Configuring the collector as a gateway

Along the way, we'll look at some strategies for scaling the collector. Additionally, we'll spend some more time with the processors that we looked at in *Chapter 8*, *OpenTelemetry Collector*. Unlike the previous chapters, which focused on OpenTelemetry components, this chapter is all about using them. As such, it will introduce a number of tools that you might encounter when working with cloud-native infrastructure.

Technical requirements

This chapter will cover a few different tools that we can use to deploy the collector. We will be using containers to run the sample application and collector; all the examples are available from the public Docker container registry (https://hub.docker.com). Although we won't dive too deeply into what containers are, just know that containers provide a convenient way to build, package, and deploy self-contained applications that are immutable. For us to run containers locally, we will use Docker, just as we did in *Chapter 2, OpenTelemetry Signals - Traces, Metrics and Logs*. The following is a list of the technical requirements for this chapter:

- If you don't already have Docker installed on your machine, follow the instructions available at https://docs.docker.com/get-docker/ to get started on Windows, macOS, and Linux. Once you have it installed, run the following command from a Terminal. If everything is working correctly, there should be no errors reported:

```
$ docker ps
CONTAINER ID    IMAGE      COMMAND     CREATED     STATUS
PORTS           NAMES
```

- Shortly, we will be required to run a command using the `kubectl` Kubernetes command-line tool. This tool interacts with the Kubernetes API, which we'll do continuously throughout the chapter to access our applications once they're running in the cluster. Depending on your environment, you might already have a copy of this tool installed. Check whether that is the case by running the following command:

```
$ kubectl version
Client Version: version.Info{Major:"1", Minor:"17",
GitVersion:"v1.17.0"...
Server Version: version.Info{Major:"1", Minor:"19",
GitVersion:"v1.19.7"...
```

If the output from running the previous command shows `command not found`, go through the installation steps documented on the Kubernetes website at https://kubernetes.io/docs/tasks/tools/.

- In addition to Docker, we will also use Kubernetes (https://kubernetes.io) throughout this chapter. This is because it is one of the leading open source tools used in cloud-native infrastructure. Kubernetes will provide the container orchestration for our examples and the collector. It's worth noting that Kubernetes is not the only container orchestration solution that is available; however, it is one of the more popular ones. There are many different tools available to set up a local Kubernetes cluster. For instance, I'll use **kind** to set up my cluster, which runs a local cluster inside Docker. If you already have access to a cluster, then great! You're good to go. Otherwise, head over to https://kind.sigs.k8s.io/docs/user/quick-start/ and follow the installation instructions for your platform. Once kind is installed, run the following command to start a cluster:

```
$ kind create cluster
Creating cluster "kind" ...
 ✓ Ensuring node image (kindest/node:v1.19.1) 🖼
 ✓ Preparing nodes 📦
 ✓ Writing configuration 📜
 ✓ Starting control-plane 🕹
 ✓ Installing CNI 🔌
 ✓ Installing StorageClass 💾
Set kubectl context to "kind-kind"
You can now use your cluster with:
kubectl cluster-info --context kind-kind
```

The previous command should get the cluster started for you. Getting a cluster up and running is crucial to use the examples in the rest of this chapter. If you're running into issues while setting up a local cluster with kind, you might want to investigate one of the following alternatives:

A. Minikube: https://minikube.sigs.k8s.io/docs/start/

B. K3s: https://k3s.io

C. Docker Desktop: https://docs.docker.com/desktop/kubernetes/

How the cluster is run isn't going to be important; having a cluster is what really matters. Additionally, if running a local cluster isn't feasible, you might want to look at some hosted options:

A. Google Kubernetes Engine: `https://cloud.google.com/kubernetes-engine`

B. Amazon Elastic Kubernetes Service: `https://aws.amazon.com/eks/`

C. Azure Kubernetes Service: `https://azure.microsoft.com/en-us/services/kubernetes-service/`

You should know that there are always costs associated with using a hosted Kubernetes cluster.

- Now, check the state of the cluster using `kubectl`, which we installed earlier. Run the following command to check whether the cluster is ready:

  ```
  $kubectl cluster-info --context kind-kind
  Kubernetes master is running at https://127.0.0.1:62708
  KubeDNS is running at https://127.0.0.1:62708/api/v1/
  namespaces/kube-system/services/kube-dns:dns/proxy
  ```

- Good job at getting this far! I know there are a lot of tools to install, but it'll be worth it! The last tool that we'll use throughout this chapter is *Helm*. This is a package manager for applications running in Kubernetes. Helm will allow us to install applications in our cluster by using the YAML configuration it calls **charts**; these provide the default configuration for many applications that are available to deploy in Kubernetes. The instructions for installing Helm are available from the Helm website at `https://helm.sh/docs/intro/install/`. Once again, to ensure the tool is working and correctly configured in your path, run the following command:

  ```
  helm version
  ```

The full configuration for all the examples in this chapter is available in the companion repository at `https://github.com/PacktPublishing/Cloud-Native-Observability`. Please feel free to look in the `chapter9` folder if any of the examples give you trouble. Great! Now that the hard part is done, let's get to the fun stuff and start deploying OpenTelemetry collectors in our cluster!

Collecting application telemetry

Previously, we looked at how to use the collector running as a local binary. This can be useful for development and testing, but it's not how the collector would be deployed in a production environment. Before going further, here are some Kubernetes concepts that we will be using in this chapter:

- **Pod**: This is a container or a group of containers that form an application.
- **Sidecar**: This is a container that is deployed alongside application containers but isn't tightly coupled with the application in the pod.
- **Node**: This is a representation of a Kubernetes worker; it could be a physical host or a virtual machine.
- **DaemonSet**: This is a pod template specification to ensure a pod is deployed to the configured nodes.

> **Important Note**
> The concepts of Kubernetes form a much deeper topic than we have time for in this book. For our examples, we will only cover the bare minimum that is necessary for this chapter. There is a lot more to cover and, thankfully, many resources are available on the internet regarding this vast topic.

Figure 9.1 shows three different deployment scenarios that can be used to deploy the OpenTelemetry collector in a production environment, which, in this case, is a Kubernetes cluster:

- The first deployment (*1*) is alongside the application containers within the same pod. This deployment is commonly referred to as a **sidecar** deployment.
- The second deployment (*2*) shows the collector running as a container on the same node as the application pod. This **agent** deployment represents a DaemonSet deployment, which means that the collector container will be present in every node in the Kubernetes cluster.
- The third deployment (*3*) is shown running the collector as a gateway. In practice, the containers in the collector service will run on Kubernetes nodes, which may or may not be the same as the ones running the application pod.

Additionally, the following diagram shows the flow for the telemetry data from one collector to another, which we will configure in this chapter:

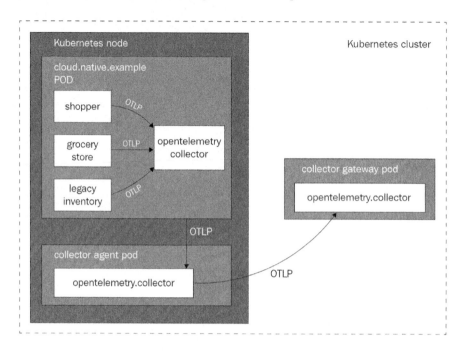

Figure 9.1 – The three deployment options for the collector

In this chapter, we will work through each scenario, starting with collecting application telemetry. We can do this by deploying the collector as close to the application as possible within the same pod. When emitting telemetry from an application, often, it's useful to offload the data as quickly as possible to reduce the resource impact on the application. This allows the application to spend most of its time on what it is meant to do, that is, manage the workloads it was created to manage. To ensure the lowest possible latency while transmitting telemetry, let's look at deploying the collector as close as possible to the application, as a sidecar.

Deploying the sidecar

To reduce that latency and the complexity of collecting telemetry, deploying the collector as a loosely coupled container within the same pod as the application makes the most sense. This ensures the following:

- The application will always have a consistent destination to send its telemetry to since applications within the same pod can communicate with each other via localhost.
- The latency between the application and the collector will not affect the application. This allows the application to offload its telemetry as quickly as possible, preventing unexpected memory loss or CPU pressure for high-throughput applications.

Let's look at how this is done. First, consider the following configuration, which includes the shopper, the grocery store, and the inventory applications. These have been containerized to allow us to deploy them via Kubernetes. In addition to this, the pod configuration contains a collector container. The most important thing to note in the configuration for our use case is the `containers` section, which defines the four containers that make up the application via `name` and `image` containers. Create a YAML file that includes the following configuration:

config/collector/sidecar.yml

```yaml
apiVersion: apps/v1
kind: Deployment
metadata:
  name: cloud-native-example
  labels:
    app: example
spec:
  replicas: 1
  selector:
    matchLabels:
      app: example
  template:
    metadata:
      labels:
        app: example
```

```
      spec:
        containers:
          - name: legacy-inventory
            image: codeboten/legacy-inventory:chapter9
          - name: grocery-store
            image: codeboten/grocery-store:chapter9
          - name: shopper
            image: codeboten/shopper:chapter9
          - name: collector
            image: otel/opentelemetry-collector:0.43.0
```

The default configuration for the collector container configures an OTLP receiver, which you'll remember from *Chapter 8*, *OpenTelemetry Collector*. Additionally, it configures a logging exporter. We will modify this configuration later in this chapter; however, for now, the default is good enough. Let's apply the previous configuration to our cluster by running the following command. This uses the configuration to pull the container images from the Docker repository and creates the deployment and pod running the application:

```
$ kubectl apply -f config/collector/sidecar.yml
deployment.apps/cloud-native-example created
```

We can ensure the pod is up and running with the following command, which gives us details about the pod along with the containers that are running within it:

```
$ kubectl describe pod -l app=example
```

We should be able to view all the details about the pod we configured:

kubectl describe output

```
Name:           cloud-native-example-6bdfd8b6d6-cfhc7
Namespace:      default
Priority:       0 ...
```

With the pod running, we should now be able to look at the logs of the collector sidecar and observe the telemetry flowing. The following command lets us view the logs from any container within the pod. The container can be specified via the -c flag followed by the name of the container in question. The -f flag can be used to tail the logs. You can use the same command to observe the output of the other containers by changing the -c flag to the name of different containers:

```
kubectl logs -l app=example -f -c collector
```

The output of the previous command will contain telemetry from the various applications in the grocery store example. It should look similar to the following:

kubectl logs output

```
Span #6
    Trace ID          : 2ca9779b6ad6d5b1a067dd83ea0942d4
    Parent ID         : 09b499899194ba83
    ID                : c8a1d75232eaf376
    Name              : inventory request
    Kind              : SPAN_KIND_INTERNAL
    Start time        : 2021-06-19 22:38:53.3719469 +0000 UTC
    End time          : 2021-06-19 22:38:53.3759594 +0000 UTC
    Status code       : STATUS_CODE_UNSET
    Status message    :
Attributes:
    -> http.method: STRING(GET)
    -> http.flavor: STRING(HttpFlavorValues.HTTP_1_1)
    -> http.url: STRING(http://localhost:5001/inventory)
    -> net.peer.ip: STRING(127.0.0.1)
```

Now we have a pod with a collector sidecar collecting telemetry! We will come back to make changes to this pod shortly, but first, let's look at the next deployment scenario.

System-level telemetry

As discussed in *Chapter 8*, *OpenTelemetry Collector*, the OpenTelemetry collector can be configured to collect metrics about the system it's running on. Often, this can be helpful when you wish to identify resource constraints on nodes, which is a fairly common problem. Additionally, the collector can be configured to forward data. So, it might be beneficial to deploy a collector on each host or node in your environment to provide an aggregation point for all the applications running on that node. As shown in the following diagram, deploying a collector as an agent can reduce the number of connections needed to send telemetry from each node:

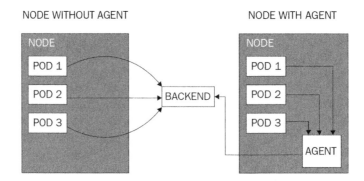

Figure 9.2 – Backend connections from nodes with and without an agent

This can become a significant processing bottleneck if, for example, the backend requires secure connections to be established with some level of frequency and if many applications are running per node.

Deploying the agent

The preferred way to deploy the collector as an agent is by using **Helm Charts**, which is provided by the OpenTelemetry project. You can find this at https://github.com/open-telemetry/opentelemetry-helm-charts. The first step to install a Helm chart is to tell Helm where it should look for the chart using the following command. This adds the open-telemetry repository to Helm:

```
$ helm repo add open-telemetry https://open-telemetry.github.io/opentelemetry-helm-charts
"open-telemetry" has been added to your repositories
```

Then, we can launch the collector service using the following command. This will install the `opentelemetry-collector` Helm chart, using all the default options:

```
$ helm install otel-collector open-telemetry/opentelemetry-collector
```

Let's check to see what happened in our Kubernetes cluster because of the previous command. The collector chart should have deployed the collector using `DaemonSet`. As mentioned earlier in the chapter, a **DaemonSet** is a way to deploy an instance of a pod on all nodes in Kubernetes. The following command lists all deployed `DaemonSet` deployments in our cluster, and you can view the resulting output as follows:

```
$ kubectl get DaemonSet
NAME                                             DESIRED
CURRENT    READY    UP-TO-DATE    AVAILABLE   NODE SELECTOR   AGE
otel-collector-opentelemetry-collector-agent     1                           1
1          1        1             <none>                      3m25s
```

Note that the results might be different depending on how many nodes your cluster has; mine has a single node. Next, let's examine the pods created using the following command:

```
$ kubectl get Pod
NAME                                                         READY
STATUS        RESTARTS     AGE
otel-collector-opentelemetry-collector-agent-hhgkk           1/1
Running       0            4m39s
```

With the collector running as an agent on the node, let's learn about how to forward all the data from the collector sidecar to the agent.

Connecting the sidecar and the agent

It's time to update the sidecar collector configuration to use an OTLP exporter to export data. This can be accomplished using a **ConfigMap**, which gives us the ability to have Kubernetes create a file that will be mounted as a volume inside the container. For brevity, the details of ConfigMap and the volumes in Kubernetes will not be described here. Add the following `ConfigMap` object to the top of the sidecar configuration file:

config/collector/sidecar.yml

```yaml
apiVersion: v1
kind: ConfigMap
metadata:
  name: otel-sidecar-conf
  labels:
    app: opentelemetry
    component: otel-sidecar-conf
data:
  otel-sidecar-config: |
    receivers:
      otlp:
        protocols:
          grpc:
          http:
    exporters:
      otlp:
        endpoint: "$NODE_IP:4317"
        tls:
          insecure: true
    service:
      pipelines:
        traces:
          receivers: [otlp]
          exporters: [otlp]
        metrics:
          receivers: [otlp]
          exporters: [otlp]
        logs:
```

```
      receivers: [otlp]
      exporters: [otlp]
```

The preceding configuration might remind you of the collector-specific configuration we explored in *Chapter 8, OpenTelemetry Collector*. It is worth noting that we will be using the `NODE_IP` environment variable in the configuration of the endpoint for the OTLP exporter.

Following this, we need to update the `containers` section further down. This is so that we can use the `otel-sidecar-conf` ConfigMap and tell the collector container to pass the configuration file at start time via the `command` option. The following configuration also exposes the node's IP address as an environment variable named `NODE_IP`:

config/collector/sidecar.yml

```
apiVersion: apps/v1
kind: Deployment
metadata:
  name: cloud-native-example
  labels:
    app: example
spec:
  replicas: 1
  selector:
    matchLabels:
      app: example
  template:
    metadata:
      labels:
        app: example
    spec:
      containers:
        - name: legacy-inventory
          image: codeboten/legacy-inventory:latest
        - name: grocery-store
          image: codeboten/grocery-store:latest
        - name: shopper
          image: codeboten/shopper:latest
```

```yaml
        - name: collector
          image: otel/opentelemetry-collector:0.27.0
          command:
            - "/otelcol"
            - "--config=/conf/otel-sidecar-config.yaml"
          volumeMounts:
            - name: otel-sidecar-config-vol
              mountPath: /conf
          env:
            - name: NODE_IP
              valueFrom:
                fieldRef:
                  fieldPath: status.hostIP
      volumes:
        - configMap:
            name: otel-sidecar-conf
            items:
              - key: otel-sidecar-config
                path: otel-sidecar-config.yaml
          name: otel-sidecar-config-vol
```

For this new configuration to take effect, we'll go ahead and apply the configuration with the following command:

```
$ kubectl apply -f config/collector/sidecar.yml
```

Looking at the logs for the agent, we can now observe that telemetry is being processed by the collector:

```
kubectl logs -l component=agent-collector -f
2021-06-26T22:57:50.719Z  INFO     loggingexporter/logging_
exporter.go:327       TracesExporter {"#spans": 20}
2021-06-26T22:57:50.919Z INFO loggingexporter/logging_exporter.
go:327      TracesExporter {"#spans": 10}
2021-06-26T22:57:53.726Z INFO loggingexporter/logging_exporter.
go:375      MetricsExporter {"#metrics": 22}
2021-06-26T22:57:54.730Z INFO loggingexporter/logging_exporter.
go:327      TracesExporter {"#spans": 5}
```

While we're here, we might as well take some time to augment the telemetry processed by the collector. We can do this by applying some of the lessons we learned in *Chapter 8, OpenTelemetry Collector*. Let's configure a processor to provide more visibility inside our infrastructure.

Adding resource attributes

One of the great things about the agent collector is being able to ensure information about the node it's running on is present across all the telemetry processed by the agent. Helm allows us to override the default configuration via **YAML**; the following can be used in conjunction with the Helm chart to configure a resource attributes processor to inject information into our telemetry. It does the following:

- It makes an environment variable named NODE_NAME available for use by the resource attributes processor.
- It sets the loglevel parameter of the logging exporter to debug. This allows us to observe the data being emitted by the collector in more detail.
- It configures a resource attributes processor to inject the NODE_NAME environment variable into an attribute with the k8s.node.name key. Additionally, it adds the processor to the pipelines for logs, metrics, and traces.

Create a new config/collector/config.yml configuration file that contains the following configuration. We'll use this to update the Helm chart:

config/collector/config.yml

```
extraEnvs:
  - name: NODE_NAME
    valueFrom:
      fieldRef:
        fieldPath: spec.nodeName
config:
  exporters:
    logging:
      loglevel: debug
agentCollector:
  enabled: true
  configOverride:
    processors:
```

```yaml
      resource:
        attributes:
        - key: k8s.node.name
          value: ${NODE_NAME}
          action: upsert
    service:
      pipelines:
        metrics:
          processors: [batch, memory_limiter, resource]
        traces:
          processors: [batch, memory_limiter, resource]
        logs:
          processors: [batch, memory_limiter, resource]
```

Apply the preceding configuration via Helm using the following command:

```
$ helm upgrade otel-collector open-telemetry/opentelemetry-
collector -f ./config/collector/config.yml
Release "otel-collector" has been upgraded. Happy Helming!
NAME: otel-collector
LAST DEPLOYED: Sun Sep 19 13:22:10 2021
```

Looking at the logs from the agent, we should observe that the telemetry contains the attributes we added earlier:

```
$ kubectl logs -l component=agent-collector -f
```

Now, we have the collector sidecar sending data to the agent, and the agent is adding attributes via a processor:

kubectl logs output

```
2021-09-19T20:30:20.888Z        DEBUG   loggingexporter/
logging_exporter.go:366 ResourceSpans #0
Resource labels:
     -> telemetry.sdk.language: STRING(python)
     -> telemetry.sdk.name: STRING(opentelemetry)
     -> telemetry.sdk.version: STRING(1.3.0)
     -> net.host.name: STRING(cloud-native-example-5d57799766-
w8rjp)
```

```
      -> net.host.ip: STRING(10.244.0.5)
      -> service.name: STRING(grocery-store)
      -> service.version: STRING(0.1.2)
      -> k8s.node.name: STRING(kind-control-plane)
InstrumentationLibrarySpans #0
InstrumentationLibrary 0.1.2 grocery-store
```

> **Important Note**
> You might find it confusing that the previous example is not configuring receivers and exporters for the telemetry pipelines. This is because the values we pass into Helm only override some of the default configurations in the chart. Since we only needed to override the processors, the exporters and receivers continued to use the defaults that had already been configured. If you'd like to look at all the configured defaults, I suggest you refer to the repository at https://github.com/open-telemetry/opentelemetry-helm-charts/blob/main/charts/opentelemetry-collector/values.yaml.

Having this single point to aggregate and add information to telemetry could be used to simplify our application code. If you recall, in *Chapter 4, Distributed Tracing – Tracing Code Execution*, we created a custom `ResourceDetector` parameter to add `net.host.name` and `net.host.ip` attributes to all applications. That code could be removed in favor of injecting the same data via the collector. This means that now, any application could get these attributes without the complexity of utilizing custom code. Next, let's look at standalone service deployment.

Collector as a gateway

The last scenario we'll cover is how to deploy the collector as a standalone service, also known as a gateway. In this mode, the collector can provide a horizontally scalable service to do additional processing on the telemetry before sending it to a backend. Horizontal scaling means that if the service comes under too much pressure, we can launch additional instances of it, which, in this case, is the collector, to manage the increasing load. Additionally, the standalone service can provide a central location for the configuring, sampling, and scrubbing of the telemetry. From a security standpoint, it might also be preferable to have a single service sending traffic outside of your network. This is because it simplifies the rules that need to be configured and reduces the risk and blast radius of vulnerabilities.

> **Important Note**
> If your backend is deployed within your network, it's possible that a standalone service for the collector will be overkill, as you might be happier sending telemetry directly to the backend and saving yourself the trouble of operating an additional service in your infrastructure.

Conveniently, the same Helm chart we used earlier to deploy the collector as an agent can also be used to configure the gateway. This also provides us with an opportunity to configure the agent to export its data to the standalone collector, and therefore, we can feed two birds with one scone by doing both at the same time. Depending on your Kubernetes cluster, the default value of `2Gi` might prevent the service from starting as it did in the case of my `kind` cluster. The following section can be appended to the bottom of the `configuration` file from the previous example to enable `standaloneCollector` and limit its memory consumption to `512Mi`:

config/collector/config.yml

```yaml
standaloneCollector:
  enabled: true
  resources:
    limits:
      cpu: 1
      memory: 512Mi
```

Apply the update to the Helm chart by running the following command again:

```
$ helm upgrade otel-collector open-telemetry/opentelemetry-collector -f ./config/collector/config.yml
```

A nice feature of the OpenTelemetry collector Helm chart is that if both `agentCollector` and `standaloneCollector` are configured, an OTLP exporter is automatically configured on the agent to forward traffic on the standalone collector. The following code depicts a snippet of the Helm chart template to give us an idea of how that will be configured:

config.tpl

```
{{- if .Values.standaloneCollector.enabled }}
exporters:
  otlp:
```

```
      endpoint: {{ include "opentelemetry-collector.fullname" .
}}:4317
      insecure: true
{{- end }}
```

It's time to examine the logs from the new service to check whether the data is reaching the standalone collector. The following command should be familiar now; make sure that you use the `standalone-collector` label when filtering the logs:

```
$ kubectl logs -l component=standalone-collector -f
```

Now the output from the logs shows us the same logs that we observed from the agent collector earlier, being processed by the standalone collector:

kubectl logs output

```
Metric #11
Descriptor:
     -> Name: otelcol_processor_accepted_spans
     -> Description: Number of spans successfully pushed into the next component in the pipeline.
     -> Unit:
     -> DataType: DoubleSum
     -> IsMonotonic: true
     -> AggregationTemporality: AGGREGATION_TEMPORALITY_CUMULATIVE
DoubleDataPoints #0
Data point labels:
     -> processor: memory_limiter
     -> service_instance_id: b208628b-7b0f-4275-9ea8-a5c445582cbc
StartTime: 1632083630725000000
Timestamp: 1632083730725000000
Value: 718.000000
```

If you run `kubectl logs` with the `agent-collector` label, you'll find that because the agent collector is now using the `otlp` exporter instead of the `logging` exporter, it no longer emits logs.

Autoscaling

Unlike the sidecar, which relied on an application pod, or the agent deployment, which relied on individual nodes to scale, the standalone service can be automatically scaled based on CPU and memory constraints. It does this using a Kubernetes feature known as **HorizontalPodAutocaling**, which can be configured via the following:

```
autoscaling:
  enabled: false
  minReplicas: 1
  maxReplicas: 10
  targetCPUUtilizationPercentage: 80
  targetMemoryUtilizationPercentage: 80
```

Depending on the needs of your environment, combining autoscaling with a load balancer might be worth pursuing to provide a high level of reliability and capacity for the service.

OpenTelemetry Operator

Another option for managing the OpenTelemetry collector in a Kubernetes environment is the OpenTelemetry operator (https://github.com/open-telemetry/opentelemetry-operator). If you're already familiar with using operators, they reduce the complexity of deploying and maintaining components in the Kubernetes landscape. In addition to managing the deployment of the collector, the OpenTelemetry operator provides support for auto-instrumenting applications.

Summary

We've only just scratched the surface of how to run the collector in production by looking at very specific use cases. However, you can start thinking about how to apply the lessons you have learned from this chapter to your environments. Whether it be using Kubernetes, bare metal, or another form of hybrid cloud environment, the same principles we explored in this chapter regarding how to best collect telemetry will apply. Collecting telemetry from an application should always be done with minimal impact on the application itself. The sidecar deployment mode provides a collection point as close as possible to the application without adding any dependency to the application itself.

Summary

The deployment of the collector as an agent gives us the ability to collect information about the worker running our applications, which could also allow us to monitor the health of the resources in our cluster. Additionally, this serves as a convenient point to augment the telemetry from applications with resource-specific attributes, which can be leveraged at analysis time. Finally, deploying the collector as a gateway allowed us to start thinking about how to deploy and scale a service to collect telemetry within our networks.

This chapter also gave us a chance to become familiar with some of the tools that OpenTelemetry provides to infrastructure engineers to manage the collector. We experimented with the OpenTelemetry collector container alongside the Helm charts provided by the project. Now that we have our environment deployed and primed to send data to a backend, in the next chapter, we'll take a look at options for open source backends.

10
Configuring Backends

So far, what we've been learning about has focused on the tools that are used to generate telemetry data. Although producing telemetry data is an essential aspect of making a system observable, it would be difficult to argue that the data we've generated in the past few chapters has made our system observable. After all, reading hundreds of lines of output in a console is hardly a practical tool for analysis. Data analysis is an essential aspect of observability that we have only briefly discussed thus far. This chapter is all about the tools we can use to analyze our applications' telemetry.

We are going to cover the following topics:

- Open source telemetry backends to analyze traces, metrics, and logs
- Considerations for running analysis systems in production

Throughout this chapter, we will visualize the data we've generated and start thinking about using it in real life. There is a large selection of analysis tools to choose from, but this chapter will only focus on a select few. It's worth noting that many commercial products (https://opentelemetry.io/vendors/) support OpenTelemetry; this chapter will focus solely on open source projects. This chapter will also skim the surface of the knowledge that you will need to run these telemetry backends in production.

Technical requirements

This chapter will use Python code to directly configure and use backends from a test application. To ensure your environment is set up correctly, run the following commands and ensure Python 3.6 or greater is installed on your system:

```
$ python --version
Python 3.8.9
$ python3 --version
Python 3.8.9
```

If you do not have **Python 3.6+** installed, go to the Python website (https://www.python.org/downloads/) for instructions on installing the latest version.

To test out some of the exporters we'll be using in the chapter, install the following OpenTelemetry packages via pip:

```
$ pip install opentelemetry-distro \
              opentelemetry-exporter-jaeger \
              opentelemetry-exporter-zipkin
```

Additionally, we will use Docker (https://docs.docker.com/get-docker/) to deploy backends. The following code will ensure Docker is up and running in your environment:

```
$ docker version
Client:
 Cloud integration: 1.0.14
 Version:           20.10.6
 API version:       1.41
 Go version:        go1.16.3 ...
```

To launch the backends, we will use Docker Compose once again. Ensure Compose is available by running the following commands:

```
$ docker compose version
Docker Compose version 2.0.0-beta.1
```

Now, download the code and configuration for this chapter from this book's GitHub repository:

```
$ git clone https://github.com/PacktPublishing/Cloud-Native-Observability
$ cd Cloud-Native-Observability/chapter10
```

With the code downloaded, we're ready to launch the backends using Compose:

```
$ docker compose up
```

The following diagram shows the architecture of the environment that we'll be deploying. Initially, the example for this chapter will connect to the backends directly. After that, we will send data to the OpenTelemetry Collector which we'll connect to the telemetry backends. Grafana is connected to Jaeger, Zipkin, Loki, and Prometheus, as we will discuss later in this chapter.

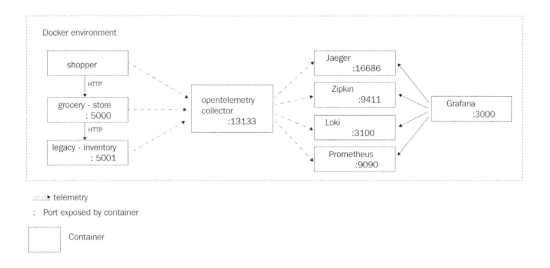

Figure 10.1 – Backend deployment in Docker

The configuration files for all this chapter's examples can be found in the `config` directory. Let's dive in!

Backend options for analyzing telemetry data

The world of observability contains an abundance of tools to provide you with insights into what systems are doing. Within OpenTelemetry, a backend is the destination of the telemetry data and is where it is stored and analyzed. All the telemetry backends that we will explore in this chapter provide the following:

- A destination for the telemetry data. This is usually in the form of a network endpoint, but not always.
- Storage for the telemetry data. The retention period that's supported by the storage is determined by the size of the storage and the amount of data being stored.
- Visualization tooling for the data. All the tools we'll use provide a web interface for displaying and querying telemetry data.

In OpenTelemetry, applications connect to backends via exporters, two of which we've already configured: the *console exporter* and the *OTLP exporter*. Each application can be configured to send data directly via an exporter that's been implemented specifically for that backend. The following table shows a current list of officially supported exporters for the backends by the OpenTelemetry specification, along with their status in the Python implementation:

Exporter	Signal	Status
Jaeger	Tracing	Stable
Zipkin	Tracing	Stable
Prometheus	Metrics	Active development

Figure 10.2 – Status of the exporters in Python for officially supported backends

Each language that implements the OpenTelemetry specification must provide an exporter for these backends. Additional information about the support for each exporter in different languages can be found in the specification repository: https://github.com/open-telemetry/opentelemetry-specification/blob/main/spec-compliance-matrix.md#exporters.

Tracing

Starting with the tracing signal, let's look at some options for visualizing traces. As we work through different backends, we'll see how it's possible to use other methods to configure a backend, starting with auto-instrumentation. The following code makes a series of calls to create a table and insert some data into a local database using SQLite (https://www.sqlite.org/index.html) while logging some information along the way:

sqlite_example.py

```
import logging
import os
import sqlite3

logging.basicConfig(level=logging.DEBUG)
logger = logging.getLogger(__name__)

logger.info("creating database")
con = sqlite3.connect("example.db")
cur = con.cursor()

logger.info("adding table")
cur.execute(
    """CREATE TABLE clouds
            (category text, description text)"""
)

logger.info("inserting values")
cur.execute("INSERT INTO clouds VALUES ('stratus','grey')")
con.commit()
con.close()

logger.info("deleting database")
os.remove("example.db")
```

Run the preceding code to ensure everything is working as expected by running the following command:

```
$ python sqlite_example.py
INFO:__main__:creating database
INFO:__main__:adding table
INFO:__main__:inserting values
INFO:__main__:deleting database
```

Now that we have some working code, let's ensure we can produce telemetry data by utilizing auto-instrumentation. As you may recall from *Chapter 7, Instrumentation Libraries*, Python provides the `opentelemetry-bootstrap` script to detect and install instrumentation libraries for us automatically. The library we're using in our code, `sqlite3`, has a supported instrumentation library that we can install with the following command:

```
$ opentelemetry-bootstrap -a install
Collecting opentelemetry-instrumentation-sqlite3==0.26b1
...
```

The output from the preceding command will produce some logging information that's generated by installing the packages through `pip`. If the output doesn't quite match mine, `opentelemetry-bootstrap` likely found additional packages to install for your environment.

Using `opentelemetry-instrument`, let's ensure that telemetry data is generated by configuring our trusty `console` exporter:

```
$ OTEL_RESOURCE_ATTRIBUTES=service.name=sqlite_example \
  OTEL_TRACES_EXPORTER=console \
  opentelemetry-instrument python sqlite_example.py
```

The output should now contain tracing information that's similar to the following abbreviated output:

output

```
INFO:__main__:creating database
INFO:__main__:adding table
```

```
INFO:__main__:inserting values
INFO:__main__:deleting database
{
    "name": "CREATE",
    "context": {
        "trace_id": "0xf98afa4316b3ac52633270b1e0534ffe",
        "span_id": "0xb52fb818cb0823da",
        "trace_state": "[]"
    },
...
```

Now, we're ready to look at our first telemetry backend by using a working example that utilizes instrumentation to produce telemetry data.

Zipkin

One of the original backends for distributed tracing, Zipkin (https://zipkin.io) was developed and open sourced by Twitter in 2012. The project was made available for anyone to use under the **Apache 2.0** license, and its community is actively maintaining and developing the project. Its core components are as follows:

- A **collector** to receive and index traces.
- A **storage** component, which provides a pluggable interface for storing data in various databases. The three storage options that are supported by Zipkin natively are *Cassandra*, *Elasticsearch*, and *MySQL*.
- A **query service** or API, which can be used to retrieve data from storage.
- As we'll see shortly, there's a **web UI**, which gives users visualization and querying capabilities.

The easiest way to send data from the sample application to Zipkin is by changing the OTEL_TRACES_EXPORTER environment variable, as per the following command:

```
$ OTEL_RESOURCE_ATTRIBUTES=service.name=sqlite_example \
  OTEL_TRACES_EXPORTER=zipkin \
  opentelemetry-instrument python sqlite_example.py
```

292　Configuring Backends

Setting the environment variable to `zipkin` tells auto-instrumentation to load `ZipkinExporter`, which is defined in the `opentelemetry-exporter-zipkin-proto-http` package. This connects to Zipkin via HTTP over port `9411`. Launch a browser and access the Zipkin web UI via `http://localhost:9411/zipkin`.

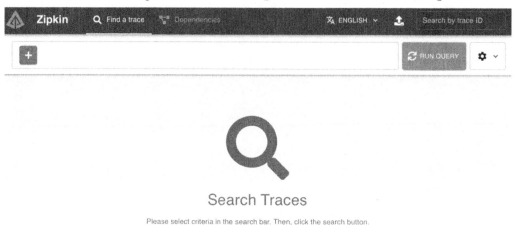

Figure 10.3 – Zipkin UI landing page

Search for traces by clicking the **Run Query** button. The results should show two traces; clicking on the details of one of these will bring up additional span information. This includes the attributes that are automatically populated by the instrumentation library, which are labeled as **Tags** in the Zipkin interface.

Figure 10.4 – Trace details view

The interface for querying lets you search for traces by trace ID, service name, duration, or tag, among other filters. It's also possible to filter traces by specifying a time window for the query. One last feature of Zipkin we will inspect requires multiple services to produce traces. As it happens, we have the grocery store already making telemetry data in our Docker environment; all we need to do is configure it to send data to Zipkin. Since the grocery store has already been configured to send data to the OpenTelemetry Collector, we'll update the collector's configuration to send data to Zipkin. Add the following configuration to enable the Zipkin exporter for the Collector:

config/collector/config.yml

```
receivers:
  otlp:
    protocols:
      grpc:
exporters:
  logging:
    loglevel: debug
  zipkin:
    endpoint: http://zipkin:9411/api/v2/spans
service:
  pipelines:
    traces:
      receivers: [otlp]
      exporters: [logging, zipkin]
    metrics:
      receivers: [otlp]
      exporters: [logging]
    logs:
      receivers: [otlp]
      exporters: [logging]
```

For the configuration changes to take effect, the OpenTelemetry Collector container must be restarted. In terminal, use the following command from the `chapter10` directory:

```
$ docker compose restart opentelemetry-collector
```

An alternative would be to relaunch the entire Docker Compose environment, but restarting just the `opentelemetry-collector` container is more expedient.

> **Important Note**
> Trying to run the `restart` command from other directories will result in an error while trying to find a suitable configuration.

Looking at the Zipkin interface again, searching for traces yields much more interesting results when the traces link spans across services. Try running some queries by searching for specific names or tags and see interesting ways to peruse the data. One more feature worth noting is the dependency graph, as shown in the following screenshot. It provides a service diagram that connects the components of the grocery store.

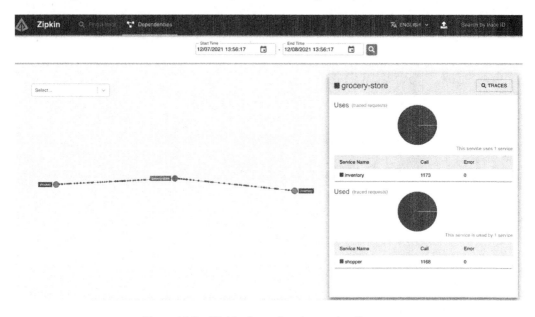

Figure 10.5 – Zipkin dependencies service diagram

The dependencies service diagram can often be helpful if you wish to get a quick overview of a system and understand the flow of information between components. Let's see how this compares with another tracing backend.

Jaeger

Initially developed by engineers at Uber, Jaeger (https://www.jaegertracing.io) was open sourced in 2015. It became a part of the **Cloud Native Computing Foundation** (**CNCF**), the same organization that oversees OpenTelemetry, in 2017. The Jaeger project provides the following:

- An **agent** that runs as close to the application as possible, often on the same host or inside the same pod.

- A **collector** to receive distributed traces that, depending on your deployment, talks directly to a datastore or Kafka for buffering.

- An **ingester** that is (optionally) deployed. Its purpose is to read Kafka data and output it to a datastore.

- A **query** service that fetches data and provides a web UI for users to view it.

Returning to the sample SQLite application for a moment, the following code uses in-code configuration to configure OpenTelemetry with JaegerExporter. It would be easy to update the OTEL_TRACES_EXPORTER variable to jaeger instead of zipkin and run opentelemetry-instrument to accomplish the same thing. Still, auto-instrumentation may not always be possible for an application. Knowing how to configure these exporters manually will surely come in handy someday.

The code in the following example adds the familiar configuration of the tracing pipeline. The following are a couple of things to note:

- JaegerExporter has been configured to use a secure connection by default. We must pass in the insecure argument to change this.

- The code manually invokes SQLite3Instrumentor to trace calls via the sqlite3 library.

Add the following code to the top of the SQLite example code we created previously:

sqlite_example.py

```
...
from opentelemetry import trace
from opentelemetry.exporter.jaeger.proto.grpc import JaegerExporter
from opentelemetry.instrumentation.sqlite3 import SQLite3Instrumentor
from opentelemetry.sdk.trace import TracerProvider
from opentelemetry.sdk.resources import Resource
from opentelemetry.sdk.trace.export import BatchSpanProcessor

def configure_opentelemetry():
    SQLite3Instrumentor().instrument()
    exporter = JaegerExporter(insecure=True)
    provider = TracerProvider(
        resource=Resource.create({"service.name": "sqlite_example"})
    )
    provider.add_span_processor(BatchSpanProcessor(exporter))
    trace.set_tracer_provider(provider)

configure_opentelemetry()
...
```

Running the application with the following command will send data to Jaeger:

```
$ python sqlite_example.py
```

Access the Jaeger interface by browsing to `http://localhost:16686/`. Upon arriving on the landing page, searching for traces should yield results similar to what's shown in the following screenshot. Note that in Jaeger, you'll need to select a service from the dropdown on the left-hand side before you can find traces.

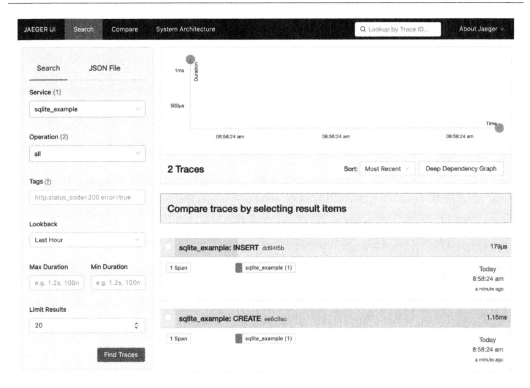

Figure 10.6 – Jaeger search results

Looking through the details for each trace, we can see that the same information we previously found in Zipkin can be seen in Jaeger, although organized slightly differently. Next, let's update the Collector file's configuration to send traces from the grocery store to Jaeger. Add the following `jaeger` section under the `exporters` definition in the Collector configuration file:

config/collector/config.yml

```
...
exporters:
...
  jaeger:
    endpoint: jaeger:14250
    tls:
      insecure: true
service:
  pipelines:
```

```
    traces:
      receivers: [otlp]
      exporters: [logging, zipkin, jaeger]
...
```

Restart the Collector container to reload the updated configuration:

```
$ docker compose restart opentelemetry-collector
```

The Jaeger web UI starts becoming more interesting when more data comes in. For example, note the scatter plot displayed previously in the search results; it's an excellent way to identify outliers. The chart supports clicking on individual traces to bring up additional details.

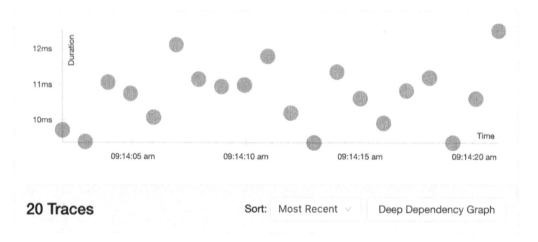

Figure 10.7 – Scatter plot of trace durations

Like Zipkin, Jaeger visualizes the relationship between services via the **System Architecture** diagram. An exciting feature that Jaeger delivers is that you can compare traces by selecting traces of interest from the search results and clicking the **Compare Traces** button. The following screenshot shows a comparison between two traces for the same operation. In one instance, the grocery store failed to connect to the legacy inventory service, resulting in an error and a missing span.

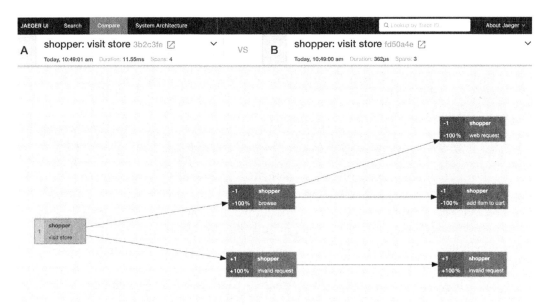

Figure 10.8 – Trace comparison diagram

This visual representation of the trace comparison can help us quickly identify a difference between a typical trace and one where an error occurred, zoning in on where the change was made.

Metrics

As of November 2021, Prometheus is the only officially supported exporter for the metrics signal. Official support for StatsD in the specification was requested some time ago (https://github.com/open-telemetry/opentelemetry-specification/issues/374), but the lack of a specification for StatsD has stopped OpenTelemetry from making it a requirement.

Prometheus

A project initially developed in 2012 by engineers at SoundCloud, Prometheus (https://prometheus.io) is a dominant open source metrics system. Its support for multi-dimensional data and first-class support for alerting quickly made it a favorite of DevOps practitioners. Initially, Prometheus used a pull model only. Applications that wanted to store metrics exposed them via a network endpoint that had been scraped by the Prometheus server. Prometheus now supports the push model via Prometheus Remote Write, allowing producers to send data to a remote server. The components of interest to us currently are as follows:

- The **Prometheus server** collects data from scrape targets and stores it in its **time-series database** (**TSDB**).
- The Prometheus Query Language (**PromQL**) for searching and aggregating metrics.
- Visualization for metrics data via the **Prometheus web UI**.

As the current implementation of the Prometheus exporter for Python is still in development, in this section, we will focus on the data that's produced by the grocery store, which is sent through the Collector. The implementation of the Prometheus exporter in the Collector is also in development at the time of writing, but it is further along. The following configuration can be added to the Collector's configuration to send metrics to Prometheus:

config/collector/config.yml

```
exporters:
  ...
  prometheus:
    endpoint: 0.0.0.0:8889
    resource_to_telemetry_conversion:
      enabled: true
service:
  pipelines:
  ...
    metrics:
      receivers: [otlp]
      exporters: [logging, prometheus]
  ...
```

Reload the Collector with the following command:

```
$ docker compose restart opentelemetry-collector
```

Bring up the Prometheus web interface by pointing your browser to `http://localhost:9090`. Using PromQL, the following query will return all the metrics that have been produced by the OpenTelemetry Collector:

```
{job="opentelemetry-collector"}
```

This can be seen in the following screenshot:

Figure 10.9 – PromQL query results

The pull model makes horizontally scaling Prometheus an easy aspect that makes it a good option for many environments. There are, of course, challenges with running Prometheus at scale, like any other backend. Unfortunately, we don't have the space to dive into data availability across regions and long-term storage, to name just a few challenges. Like Jaeger and OpenTelemetry, Prometheus is also a project under the governance of the CNCF.

Logging

Even with no officially supported backends at the time of writing, it's helpful to have a way to query logs that doesn't require looking at files on disk directly or paying for a service to get started. The tools that we've discussed in this section have exporters available in the OpenTelemetry Collector but may not necessarily have exporters implemented in other languages.

Loki

A project started by Grafana Labs in 2018, Loki is a log aggregation system that's designed to be easy to scale and operate. Its design is inspired by Prometheus and is composed of the following components:

- A **distributor** that validates and pre-processes incoming logging data before sending it off to the ingester
- An **ingester** that writes data to storage and provides a read endpoint for in-memory data
- A **ruler** that interprets configurable rules and triggers actions based on them
- A **querier** that performs queries for both the ingester and storage
- A **query frontend** that acts as a proxy for optimizing requests that are made to the querier

These components can be run in a single deployment or as a separate service to make it easy to deploy them in whichever mode makes the most sense. The OpenTelemetry Collector provides an exporter for Loki, which can be configured as per the following code snippet. The configuration of the Loki exporter supports relabeling attributes and resource attributes before sending the data. In the following example, the `service.name` resource attribute has been relabeled `job`:

config/collector/config.yml

```
exporters:
    ...
```

```
    loki:
        endpoint: http://loki:3100/loki/api/v1/push
        labels:
            resource:
                service.nam": "job"
service:
  pipelines:
...
    logs:
        receivers: [otlp]
        exporters: [logging, loki]
...
```

Once more, restart the Collector to reload the configuration and start sending data to Loki:

```
$ docker compose restart opentelemetry-collector
```

Now, it's time to review this logging data. You may have noticed that the components we mentioned earlier for Loki lack an interface for visualizing the data. That's because the interface of choice for Loki is Grafana, which is a separate project altogether.

Grafana

Grafana (https://grafana.com/grafana/) is an open source tool that's been developed since 2014 by Grafana Labs to allow users to visualize and query telemetry data. Grafana enables users to configure data sources that support various formats for traces, metrics, and logs. This includes Zipkin, Jaeger, Prometheus, and Loki.

Let's see how we can access the logs we sent to our Loki backend. Access the **Explore** section of the Grafana interface via a browser by going to `http://localhost:3000/explore`. In the query field, enter `{job=~"grocery-store|inventory|shopper"}`. This will bring up all the logs for all the grocery store components.

Figure 10.10 – Logs search results

Grafana allows users to create dashboards and alerts for the data that's received via its data sources. Since it's possible to view data from all signals, it's also possible to see data across all signals within a single dashboard. An example of such a dashboard has been preconfigured in the development environment and is accessible via the following URL: `http://localhost:3000/d/otel/opentelemetry`.

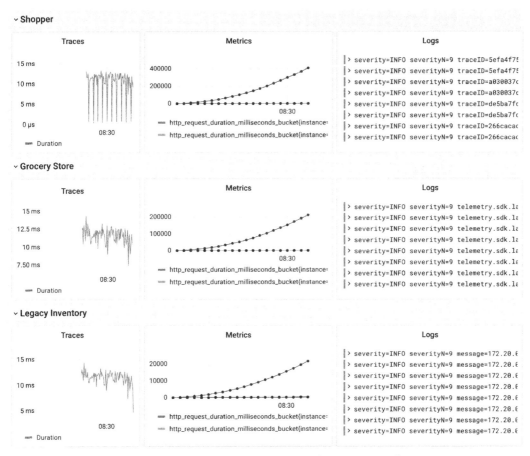

Figure 10.11 – Dashboard combining data across signals

There are many more capabilities to explore regarding each of the tools discussed in this chapter. A vast amount of information on all the features and configuration options is available on the website associated with each project. I strongly recommend spending some time familiarizing yourself with these tools.

Running in production

Using analysis tools in development is one thing; running them in production is another. Running a single container on one machine is not an acceptable strategy for operating a service that provides information that's critical to an organization. It's worth considering the challenges of scaling telemetry backends to meet the demands of the real world. The following subsections highlight areas that require further reading before you run any of the backends mentioned earlier in production.

High availability

The availability of telemetry backends is likely not as critical to end users as that of the applications they are used to monitor. However, having an outage and realizing that the data that's required to investigate is unavailable or missing during the outage causes problems. If an application promises an uptime of 99.99%, the telemetry backend must be available to account for those guarantees. Some aspects to consider when thinking of the high availability in the context of a telemetry backend are as follows:

- Ensuring the telemetry receivers are available to senders. This can be accomplished by placing a load balancer between the senders and the receivers.
- Considering how the backends will be upgraded and how to minimize the impact on the applications being observed.
- Understanding the expectations for being able to query the data.
- Deciding how much of the data needs to be replicated to mitigate the risks of catastrophic failure.

Additionally, geo-distributed environments must consider how the applications will behave if a backend is deployed in distant regions. Many of the backends we've discussed provide recommendations for deploying the backend in a mode that supports high availability.

Scalability

The telemetry backend must be able to grow alongside the applications they support. Whether that's by adding more instances or increasing the number of resources that are given to the backend, knowing what the tools support can help you decide which backend to use. Some questions that are worth asking are as follows:

- Can the components of the backend be scaled independently?
- Will scaling the backend require vertical scaling or horizontal scaling?
- How far will the solution scale? Is there a hard limit somewhere along the way?

When we think about scalability, it's essential to understand the limitations of the tools we're working with, even if we never come close to using them to their full extent.

Data retention

A key challenge in telemetry is the volume of data that's being produced. It's easy to lean toward storing every detail forever, as it is hard to predict when the data may become necessary. It's a bit like holding on to all those old cables and connectors for hardware that hasn't existed since the late 90s; you never know when it will come in handy!

The problem with storing all the data forever is that it becomes costly at scale. On the other hand, the cost tends to cause engineers to lean in the opposite direction too much, where we log or record so little that it becomes hard to find anything of value. Some options to think about are as follows:

- Identify an acceptable data retention period for the quantity of data that's being produced. This will likely change as teams become better at identifying issues within shorter periods.
- If long-term data storage is desirable, use lower-cost storage to reduce operational costs. This may result in longer query times, but the data will still be available.
- Tune a sensible sampling option for the different signals. More on this will be covered in *Chapter 12, Sampling*.

At a minimum, data retention should cover periods when engineers are expected to be away. For example, if no one is watching systems during a 2-day weekend, data should be retained for 3 or more days. Otherwise, events that occur during the weekend will be impossible to investigate.

Whatever you decide regarding the retention method, there are plenty of ways to fine-tune it over time. It's also critical for teams across the organization to be aware of what this data retention is.

Privacy regulations

Depending on the contents of the telemetry data that's produced by applications, the requirements for where and how the data can be stored vary. For example, regulations such as the **General Data Protection Regulation** (**GDPR**) recommend personally identifiable data to be pseudonymized to ensure nobody can be associated with the data without additional processing. Depending on the requirements in your environment and the telemetry data that's being produced, we have to take the following into account about the data:

- The data may need to remain within a specific country or region.
- The data may need to be processed further before being stored. This could mean many things, from the data being encrypted to scrubbing it of personally identifiable information or pseudonymization.
- The data may need access control and auditing capabilities.

Using the OpenTelemetry Collector as a receiver of telemetry data before sending the data to telemetry backends can alleviate concerns around data privacy. Various processors in the Collector can be configured to facilitate the scrubbing of sensitive information.

Summary

One of the many jobs of software engineers today includes evaluating the new technology and tools that are available to determine whether these tools would improve their ability to accomplish their goals. Leveraging auto-instrumentation, in-code configuration, and the OpenTelemetry Collector, we quickly sent data from one backend to another to help us compare these tools.

All the tools we've discussed in this chapter take much more than a few pages to become familiar with. Entire books have been written about running these in production, and the skills to do so well at scale require practice and experience. Understanding some areas that need additional thinking when those tools are deployed allows us to uncover some of the unknowns.

Looking through the different tools and starting to see how each one provides functionality to visualize the data gave us a sense of how telemetry data can be used to start answering questions about our systems. In the next chapter, we will focus on how these visualizations can identify specific problems.

11
Diagnosing Problems

Finally, after instrumenting application code, configuring a collector to transmit the data, and setting up a backend to receive the telemetry, we have all the pieces in place to observe a system. But what does that mean? How can we detect abnormalities in a system with all these tools? That's what this chapter is all about. This chapter aims to look through the lens of an analyst and see what the shape of the data looks like as events occur in a system. To do this, we'll look at the following areas:

- How leaning on chaos engineering can provide the framework for running experiments in a system
- Common scenarios of issues that can arise in distributed systems
- Tools that allow us to introduce failures into our system

As we go through each scenario, we'll describe the experiment, propose a hypothesis, and use telemetry to verify whether our expectations match what the data shows us. We will use the data and become more familiar with analysis tools to help us understand how we may answer questions about our systems in production. As always, let's start by setting up our environment first.

Technical requirements

The examples in this chapter will use the grocery store application we've used and revisited throughout the book. Since the chapter's goal is to analyze telemetry and not specifically look at how this telemetry is produced, the application code will not be the focus of the chapter. Instead of running the code as separate applications, we will use it as Docker (https://docs.docker.com/get-docker/) containers and run it via Compose. Ensure Docker is installed with the following command:

```
$ docker version
Client:
 Cloud integration: 1.0.14
 Version:           20.10.6
 API version:       1.41
 Go version:        go1.16.3 ...
```

The following command will ensure Docker Compose is also installed:

```
$ docker compose version
Docker Compose version 2.0.0-beta.1
```

The book's companion repository (https://github.com/PacktPublishing/Cloud-Native-Observability) contains the Docker Compose configuration file, as well as the configuration required to run the various containers. Download the companion repository via Git:

```
$ git clone https://github.com/PacktPublishing/Cloud-Native-Observability
$ cd Cloud-Native-Observability/chapter11
```

With the configuration in place, start the environment via the following:

```
$ docker compose up
```

Throughout the chapter, as we conduct experiments, know that it is always possible to reset the pristine Docker environment by removing the containers entirely with the following commands:

```
$ docker compose stop
$ docker compose rm
```

All the tools needed to run various experiments have already been installed inside the grocery store application containers, meaning there are no additional tools to install. The commands will be executed via `docker exec` and run within the container.

Introducing a little chaos

In normal circumstances, the real world is unpredictable enough that intentionally introducing problems may seem unnecessary. Accidental configuration changes, sharks chewing through undersea cables, and power outages affecting data centers are just a few events that have caused large-scale issues across the world. In distributed systems, in particular, dependencies can cause failures that may be difficult to account for during normal development.

Putting applications through various stress, load, functional, and integration tests before they are deployed to production can help predict their behavior to a large extent. However, some circumstances may be hard to reproduce outside of a production environment. A practice known as **chaos engineering** (`https://principlesofchaos.org`) allows engineers to learn and explore the behavior of a system. This is done by intentionally introducing new conditions into the system through experiments. The goal of these experiments is to ensure that systems are robust enough to withstand failures in production.

> **Important Note**
> Although chaos engineers run experiments in production, it's essential to understand that one of the principles of chaos engineering is **not to cause unnecessary pain** to users, meaning experiments must be controlled and limited in scope. In other words, despite its name, chaos engineering isn't just going around a data center and unplugging cables haphazardly.

The cycle for producing experiments goes as follows:

1. It begins with a system under a known good state or steady state.
2. A hypothesis is then proposed to explain the experiment's impact on the system's state.
3. The proposed experiment is run on the system.

4. Verification of the impact on the system takes place, validating that the prediction matches the hypothesis. The verification step provides an opportunity to identify unexpected side effects of the experiment. If something behaved precisely as expected, great! If it acted worse than expected, why? If it behaved better than expected, what happened? It's essential to understand what happened, especially if the results were better than expected. It's too easy to look at a favorable outcome and move right along without taking the time to understand why it happened.

5. Once verification is complete, improvements to the system are made, and the cycle begins anew. Ideally, running these experiments can be automated once the results on the system are satisfactory to guard against future regressions.

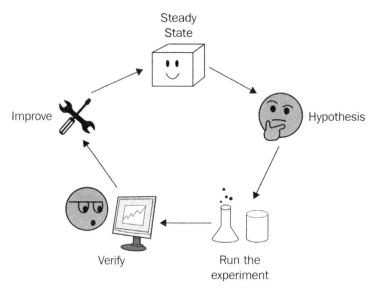

Figure 11.1 – Chaos engineering life cycle

The hypothesis step is crucial because if the proposed experiment will have disastrous repercussions on the system, it may be worth rethinking the experiment.

For example, a hypothesis that turning off all production servers simultaneously will cause a complete system failure doesn't need to be validated. Additionally, this would guarantee the creation of unnecessary pain for all users of the system. There isn't much to learn from running this in production, except seeing how quickly users send angry tweets.

An alternative experiment that may be worthwhile is to shut down an availability zone or a region of a system to ensure load balancing works. This would provide an opportunity to learn how production traffic would be handled in the case of such a failure, validating that those systems in place to manage such a failure are doing their jobs. Of course, if no such mechanisms are in place, it's not worth experimenting either, as this would have the same impact as shutting down all the servers for all users in that zone or region.

This chapter will take a page out of the chaos engineering book and introduce various failure modes into the grocery store system. We will propose a hypothesis and run experiments to validate the assumptions. Using the telemetry produced by the store, we will validate that the system behaved as expected. This will allow us to use the telemetry produced to understand how we can answer questions about our system via this information. Let's explore a problem that impacts all networked applications: latency.

Experiment #1 – increased latency

Latency is the delay introduced when a call is made and the response is returned to the originating caller. It can inject itself into many aspects of a system. This is especially true in a distributed system where latency can be found anywhere one service calls out to another. The following diagram shows an example of how latency can be calculated between two services. Service A calls a remote service (B), the request duration is 25 ms, but a large portion of that time is spent transferring data to and from service B, with only 5 ms spent executing code.

Figure 11.2 – Latency incurred by calling a remote service

314 Diagnosing Problems

If the services are collocated, the latency is usually negligible and can often be ignored. However, latency must be accounted for when services communicate over a network. This is something to think about at development time. It can be caused by factors such as the following:

- The physical distance between the servers hosting services. As even the speed of light requires time to travel distance, the greater the distance between services, the greater the latency.
- A busy network. If a network reaches the limits of how much data it can transfer, it may throttle the data transmitted.
- Problems in any applications or systems connecting the services. Load balancers and DNS services are just two examples of the services needed to connect two services.

Experiment

The first experiment we'll run is to increase the latency in the network interface of the grocery store. The experiment uses a Linux utility to manipulate the configuration on the network interface: Traffic Control (https://en.wikipedia.org/wiki/Tc_(Linux)). Traffic Control, or `tc`, is a powerful utility that can simulate a host of scenarios, including packet loss, increased latency, or throughput limits. In this experiment, `tc` will add a delay to inbound and outbound traffic, as shown in *Figure 11.3*:

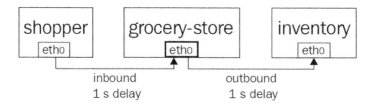

Figure 11.3 – Experiment #1 will add latency to the network interface

Hypothesis

Increasing the latency to the grocery store network interface will incur the following:

- A reduction in the total number of requests processed
- An increase in the request duration time

Use the following Docker command to introduce the latency. This uses the `tc` utility inside the grocery store container to add a `1s` delay to all traffic received and sent through interface `eth0`:

```
$ docker exec grocery-store tc qdisc add dev eth0 root netem
delay 1s
```

Verify

To observe the metrics and traces generated, access the **Application Metrics** dashboard in Grafana via the following URL: `http://localhost:3000/d/apps/application-metrics`. You'll immediately notice a drop in the **Request count** time series and an increase in **Request duration** time quantiles. As time passes, you'll also start seeing the **Request duration distribution** histogram change to show an increasing number of requests falling into buckets with longer durations that are as per the following screenshot:

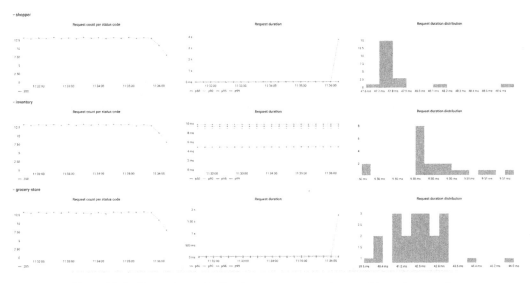

Figure 11.4 – Request metrics for shopper, grocery-store, and inventory services

Note that although the drop in request count is the same across the inventory and grocery store services, the duration of the request for the inventory service remains unchanged. This is a great starting point, but it would be ideal to identify precisely where this jump in the request duration occurred.

> **Important Note**
>
> As discussed earlier in this book, the correlation between metrics and traces provided by exemplars could help us drill down more quickly by giving us specific traces to investigate from the metrics. However, since the implementation of exemplar support in OpenTelemetry is still under development at the time of writing, the example in this chapter does not take advantage of it. I hope that by the time you're reading this, exemplar support is implemented across many languages in OpenTelemetry.

Let's look at the tracing data in Jaeger available at `http://localhost:16686`. From the metrics, we already know that the issue appears to be isolated to the grocery store service. Sure enough, searching for traces for that service yields the following chart:

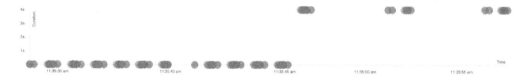

Figure 11.5 – Increased duration results in Jaeger

It's clear from this chart that something happened. The following screenshot shows us two traces; at the top is a trace from before we introduced the latency; at the bottom is a trace from after. Although the two look similar, looking at the duration of the spans named `web request` and `/products`, it's clear that those operations are taking far longer at the bottom than at the top.

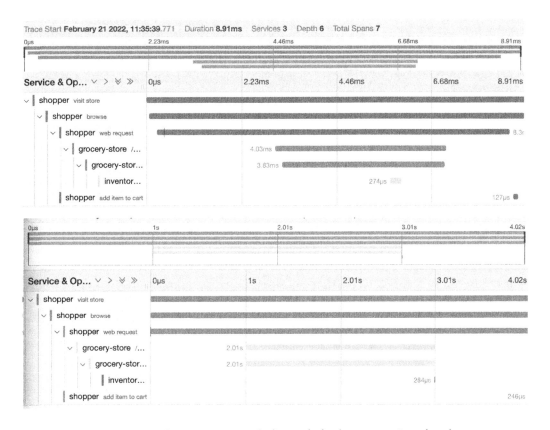

Figure 11.6 – Trace comparison before and after latency was introduced

As hypothesized, the total number of requests processed by the grocery store dropped due to the simulation. This, in turn, reduced the number of calls to the inventory service. The total duration of the request as observed by the shopper client increased significantly.

Remove the delay to see how the system recovers. The following command removes the delay introduced earlier:

```
$ docker exec grocery-store tc qdisc del dev eth0 root netem delay 1s
```

Latency is only one of the aspects of networks that can cause problems for applications. Traffic Control's network emulator (https://man7.org/linux/man-pages/man8/tc-netem.8.html) functionality can simulate many other symptoms, such as packet loss and rate-limiting, or even the re-ordering of packets. If you're keen on playing with networks, it can be a lot of fun to simulate different scenarios. However, the network isn't the only thing that can cause problems for systems.

Experiment #2 – resource pressure

Although cloud providers make provisioning new computing resources more accessible than ever before, even computing in the cloud is still bound by the physical constraints of hardware running applications. Memory, processors, hard drives, and networks all have their limits. Many factors can contribute to resource exhaustion:

- Misconfigured or misbehaving applications. Crashing and restarting in a fast loop, failing to free memory, or making requests over the network too aggressively can all contribute to a load on resources.

- An increase or spike in requests being processed by the service. This could be good news; the service is more popular than ever! Or it could be bad news, the result of a denial-of-service attack. Either way, more data to process means more resources are required.

- Shared resources cause resource starvation. This problem is sometimes referred to as the noisy neighbor problem, where resources are consumed by another tenant of the physical hardware where a service is running.

Autoscaling or dynamic resource allocation helps alleviate resource pressures to some degree by allowing users to configure thresholds at which new resources should be made available to the system. To know how these thresholds should be configured, it's valuable to experiment with how applications behave under limited resources.

Experiment

We'll investigate how telemetry can help identify resource pressures in the following scenario. The grocery store container is constrained to 50 M of memory via its Docker Compose configuration. Memory pressure will be applied to the container via stress.

The Unix stress utility (https://www.unix.com/man-page/debian/1/STRESS/) spins workers that produce loads on systems. It creates memory, CPU, and I/O pressures by calling system functions in a loop; `malloc`/`free`, `sqrt`, and `sync`, depending on which resource is being pressured.

Figure 11.7 – Experiment #2 will apply memory pressure to the container

Hypothesis

As resources are consumed by stress, we expect the following to happen:

- The grocery store processes fewer requests as it cannot obtain the resources to process requests.
- Latency increases across the system, as requests will take longer to process through the grocery store.
- Metrics collected from the grocery store container should quickly identify the increased resource pressure.

The following introduces memory pressure by adding workers that consume a total of 40 M of memory to the grocery store container via `stress` for 30 minutes:

```
$ docker exec grocery-store stress --vm 20 --vm-bytes 2M --timeout 30m
stress: info: [20] dispatching hogs: 0 cpu, 0 io, 10 vm, 0 hdd
```

Verify

With the pressure in place, let's see whether the telemetry matches what we expected. Looking at the application metrics, we can see an almost immediate increase in request duration as per the following screenshot. The request count is also slightly impacted simultaneously.

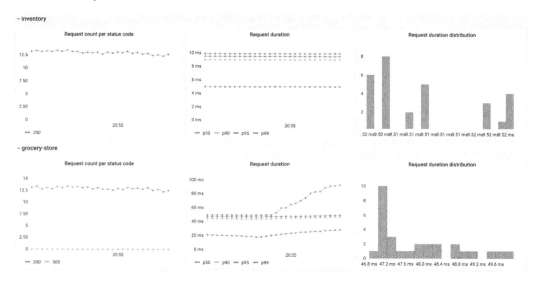

Figure 11.8 – Application metrics

What else can we learn about the event? Searching through traces, an increase in duration similar to what occurred during the first experiment is shown:

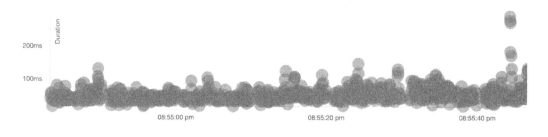

Figure 11.9 – Trace duration increased

Looking in more detail at individual traces, we can identify which paths through the code cause this increase. Not surprisingly, the `allocating memory` span, which locates an operation performing a memory allocation, is now significantly longer, with its time jumping from 2.48 ms to 49.76 ms:

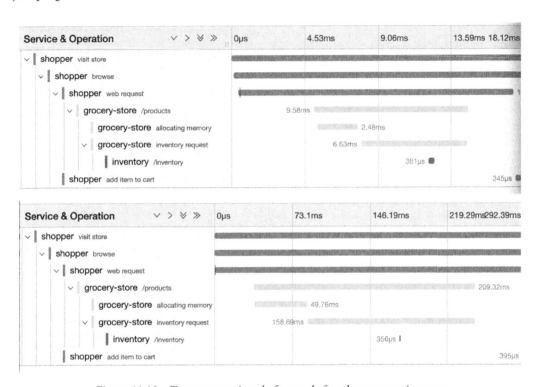

Figure 11.10 – Trace comparison before and after the memory increase

There is a second dashboard worth investigating at this time, the **Container metrics** dashboard (http://localhost:3000/d/containers/container-metrics). This dashboard shows the CPU, memory, and network metrics collected directly from Docker by the collector's Docker stats receiver (https://github.com/open-telemetry/opentelemetry-collector-contrib/tree/main/receiver/dockerstatsreceiver). Reviewing the following charts, it's evident that resource utilization increased significantly in one container:

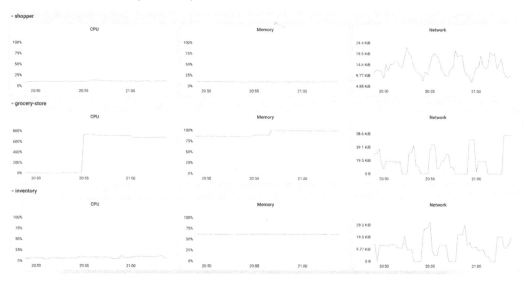

Figure 11.11 – Container metrics for CPU, memory, and network

From the data, it's evident that something happened to the container running the grocery store. The duration of requests through the system increased, as did the metrics showing memory and CPU utilization for the container. Identifying resource pressure in this testing environment isn't particularly interesting beyond this.

Recall that OpenTelemetry specifies resource attributes for all signals, meaning that if multiple services are running on the same resource, host, container, or node, it would be possible to correlate information about those services using this resource information, meaning that if we were running multiple applications on the same host, and one of them triggered memory pressure, it would be possible to verify its impact on other services within the same host by utilizing its resource attributes as an identifier when querying telemetry.

Resource information can help answer questions when, for example, a host has lost power, and there is a need to identify all services impacted by this event quickly. Another way to use this information is when two completely unrelated services are experiencing problems simultaneously. If those two services operate on the same node, resource information will help connect the dots.

Experiment #3 – unexpected shutdown

If a service exits in a forest of microservices and no one is around to observe it, does it make a sound? With the right telemetry and alert configuration in place, it certainly does. Philosophical questions aside, services shutting down happens all the time. Ensuring that services can manage this event gracefully is vital in dynamic environments where applications come and go as needed.

Expected and unexpected shutdowns or restarts can be caused by any number of reasons. Some common ones are as follows:

- An uncaught exception in the code causes the application to crash and exit.
- Resources consumed by a service pass a certain threshold, causing an application to be terminated by a resource manager.
- A job completes its task, exiting intentionally as it terminates.

Experiment

This last experiment will simulate a service exiting unexpectedly in our system to give us an idea of what to look for when identifying this type of failure. Using the `docker kill` command, the inventory service will be shut down unexpectedly, leaving the rest of the services to respond to this failure and report this issue.

Figure 11.12 – Experiment #3 will terminate the inventory service

In a production environment, issues arising from this scenario would be mitigated by having multiple instances of the inventory service running behind some load balancing, be it a load balancer or DNS load balancing. This would result in traffic being redirected away from the failed instance and over to the others still in operation. For our experiment, however, a single instance is running, causing a complete failure of the service.

Hypothesis

Shutting down the inventory service will result in the following:

- All metrics from the inventory container will stop reporting.
- Errors will be recorded by the grocery store; this should be visible through the request count per status code reporting status code 500.
- Logs should report errors from the shopper container.

Using the following command, send a signal to shut down the inventory service. Note that `docker kill` sends the container a `kill` signal, whereas `docker stop` would send a `term` signal. We use `kill` here to prevent the service from shutting down cleanly:

```
$ docker kill inventory
```

Verify

With the inventory service stopped, let's head over to the application metrics dashboard one last time to see what happened. The request count graph shows a rapid increase in requests whose response code is `500`, representing an internal server error.

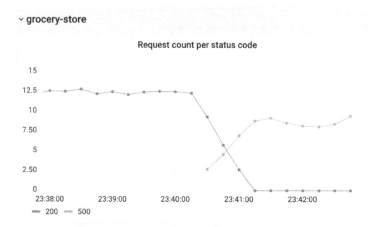

Figure 11.13 – The request counter shows an increase in errors

One signal we've yet to use in this chapter is logging. Look for the **Logs** panel at the bottom of the application metrics dashboard to find all the logs emitted by our system. Specifically, look for an entry reporting a failed request to the grocery store such as the following, which is produced by the shopper application:

Figure 11.14 – Log entry being recorded

Expanding the log entry shows details about the event that caused an error. Unfortunately, the message `request to grocery store failed` isn't particularly helpful here, although notice that there is a `TraceID` field in the data shown. This field is adjacent to a link. Clicking on the link will take us to the corresponding trace in Jaeger, which shows us the following:

Figure 11.15 – Trace confirms the grocery store is unable to contact the inventory

The trace provides more context as to what error caused it to fail, which is helpful. An exception with the message recorded in the span provides ample details about the **legacy-inventory** service appearing to be missing. Lastly, the container metrics dashboard will confirm the inventory container stopped reporting metrics as per the following screenshot:

Figure 11.16 – Inventory container stopped reporting metrics

Restore the stopped container via the `docker start` command and observe as the error rate drops and traffic is returned to normal:

```
$ docker start inventory
```

There are many more scenarios that we could investigate in this chapter. However, we only have limited time to cover these. From message queues filling up to caching problems, the world is full of problems just waiting to be uncovered.

Using telemetry first to answer questions

These experiments are a great way to gain familiarity with telemetry. Still, it feels like cheating to know what caused a change before referring to the telemetry to investigate a problem. A more common way to use telemetry is to look at it when a problem occurs without intentionally causing it. Usually, this happens when deploying new code in a system.

Code changes are deployed to many services in a distributed system several times a day. This makes it challenging to figure out which change is responsible for a regression. The complexity of identifying problematic code is compounded by the updates being deployed by different teams. Update the `image` configuration for the **shopper**, **grocery-store**, and **legacy-inventory** services in the Docker Compose configuration to use the following:

docker-compose.yml

```yaml
shopper:
  image: codeboten/shopper:chapter11-example1
...
grocery-store:
  image: codeboten/grocery-store:chapter11-example1
...
legacy-inventory:
  image: codeboten/legacy-inventory:chapter11-example1
```

Update the containers by running the following command in a separate terminal:

```
$ docker compose up -d legacy-inventory grocery-store shopper
```

Was the deployment of the new code a success? Did we make things better or worse? Let's look at what the data shows us. Starting with the application metrics dashboard, it doesn't look promising. Request duration has spiked upward, and requests per second dropped significantly.

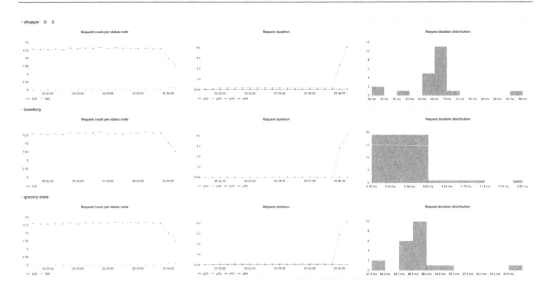

Figure 11.17 – Application metrics of the deployment

It appears to be impacting both the inventory service and grocery store service, which would indicate something may have gone wrong in the latest deployment of the inventory service. Looking at traces, searching for all traces shows the same increase in request duration as the graphs from the metrics. Selecting a trace and looking through the details points to a likely culprit:

Figure 11.18 – A suspicious span named sleepy service

It appears the addition of an operation called **sleepy service** is causing all sorts of problems in the latest deployment! With this information, we can revert the change and resolve the issue.

In addition to the previous scenario, four additional scenarios are available through published containers to practice your observation skills. They have unoriginal tags: `chapter11-example2`, `chapter11-example3`, `chapter11-example4`, and `chapter11-example5`. I recommend trying them all before looking through the `scenarios` folder in the companion repository to see whether you can identify the deployed problem!

Summary

Learning to navigate telemetry data produced by systems comfortably takes time. Even with years of experience, the most knowledgeable engineers can still be puzzled by unexpected changes in observability data. The more time spent getting comfortable with the tools, the quicker it will be to get to the bottom of just what caused changes in behavior.

The tools and techniques described in this chapter can be used repeatedly to better understand exactly what a system is doing. With chaos engineering practices, we can improve the resilience of our systems by identifying areas that can be improved upon under controlled circumstances. By methodically experimenting and observing the results from our hypotheses, we can measure the improvements as we're making them.

Many tools are available for experimenting and simulating failures; learning how to use these tools can be a powerful addition to any engineer's toolset. As we worked our way through the vast amount of data produced by our instrumented system, it's clear that having a way to correlate data across signals is critical in quickly moving through the data.

It's also clear that generating more data is not always a good thing, as it is possible to become overwhelmed quickly or overwhelm backends. The last chapter looks at how sampling can help reduce the volume of data.

12
Sampling

One of the challenges of telemetry, in general, is managing the quantity of data that can be produced by instrumentation. This can be problematic at the time of generation if the tools producing telemetry consume too many resources. It can also be costly to transfer the data across various points of the network. And, of course, the more data is produced, the more storage it consumes, and the more resources are required to sift through it at the time of analysis. The last topic we'll discuss in this book focuses on how we can reduce the amount of data produced by instrumentation while retaining the value and fidelity of the data. To achieve this, we will be looking at sampling. Although primarily a concern of tracing, sampling has an impact across metrics and logs as well, which we'll learn about throughout this chapter. We'll look at the following areas:

- Concepts of sampling, including sampling strategies, across the different signals of OpenTelemetry
- How to configure sampling at the application level via the OpenTelemetry **Software Development Kit (SDK)**
- Using the OpenTelemetry collector to sample data

Along the way, we'll look at some common pitfalls of sampling to learn how they can best be avoided. Let's start with the technical requirements for the chapter.

Technical requirements

All the code for the examples in the chapter is available in the companion repository, which can be downloaded using `git` with the following command. The examples are under the `chapter12` directory:

```
$ git clone https://github.com/PacktPublishing/Cloud-Native-Observability
$ cd Cloud-Native-Observability/chapter12
```

The first example in the chapter consists of an example application that uses the OpenTelemetry Python SDK to configure a sampler. To run the code, we'll need Python **3.6** or greater installed:

```
$ python --version
Python 3.8.9
$ python3 --version
Python 3.8.9
```

If Python is not installed on your system, or the installed version of Python is less than the supported version, follow the instructions from the Python website (https://www.python.org/downloads/) to install a compatible version.

Next, install the following OpenTelemetry packages via `pip`. Note that through dependency requirements, additional packages will automatically be installed:

```
$ pip install opentelemetry-distro \
              opentelemetry-exporter-otlp
$ pip freeze | grep opentelemetry
opentelemetry-api==1.8.0
opentelemetry-distro==0.27b0
opentelemetry-exporter-otlp==1.8.0
opentelemetry-exporter-otlp-proto-grpc==1.8.0
opentelemetry-exporter-otlp-proto-http==1.8.0
opentelemetry-instrumentation==0.27b0
opentelemetry-proto==1.8.0
opentelemetry-sdk==1.8.0
```

The second example will use the OpenTelemetry Collector, which can be downloaded from GitHub directly. The example will focus on the tail sampling processor, which currently resides in the `opentelemetry-collector-contrib` repository. The version used in this chapter can be found at the following location: `https://github.com/open-telemetry/opentelemetry-collector-releases/releases/tag/v0.43.0`. Download a binary that matches your current system from the available releases. For example, the following command downloads the macOS for AMD64-compatible binary. It also ensures the executable flag is set and runs the binary to check that things are working:

```
$ wget -O otelcol.tar.gz https://github.com/open-telemetry/opentelemetry-collector-releases/releases/download/v0.43.0/otelcol-contrib_0.43.0_darwin_amd64.tar.gz
$ tar -xzf otelcol.tar.gz otelcol-contrib
$ chmod +x ./otelcol-contrib
$ ./otelcol-contrib --version
otelcol-contrib version 0.43.0
```

If a package matching your environment isn't available, you can compile the collector manually. The source is available on GitHub: `https://github.com/open-telemetry/opentelemetry-collector-contrib`. With this in place, let's get started with sampling!

Concepts of sampling across signals

A method often used in the domain of research, the process of sampling selects a subset of data points across a larger dataset to reduce the amount of data to be analyzed. This can be done because either analyzing the entire dataset would be impossible, or unnecessary to achieve the research goal, or because it would be impractical to do so. For example, if we wanted to record how many doors on average each car in a store parking lot has, it may be possible to go through the entire parking lot and record the data in its entirety. However, if the parking lot contains 20,000 cars, it may be best to select a sample of those cars, say 2,000, and analyze that instead. There are many sampling methods used to ensure that a representational subset of the data is selected, to ensure the meaning of the data is not lost because of the sampling.

Methods for sampling can be grouped as either of the following:

- **Probabilistic** (https://en.wikipedia.org/wiki/Probability_sampling): The probability of sampling is a known quantity, and that quantity is applied across all the data points in the dataset. Returning to the parking lot example, a probabilistic strategy would be to sample 10% of all cars. To accomplish this, we could record the data for every tenth car parked. In small datasets, probabilistic sampling is less effective as the variability between data points is higher.

- **Non-probabilistic** (https://en.wikipedia.org/wiki/Nonprobability_sampling): The selection of data is based on specific characteristics of the data. An example of this may be to choose the 2,000 cars closest to the store out of convenience. This introduces bias into the selection process. The parking area located closest to the store may include designated spots or even spots reserved for smaller cars, therefore impacting the results.

Traces

Specifically, sampling in the context of OpenTelemetry really means deciding what to do with spans that form a particular trace. **Spans** in a **trace** are either processed or dropped, depending on the configuration of the sampler. Various components of OpenTelemetry are involved in carrying the decision throughout the system:

- A `Sampler` is the starting point, allowing users to select a sampling level. Several samplers are defined in the OpenTelemetry specification, more on this shortly.

- The `TracerProvider` class receives a sampler as a configuration parameter. This ensures that all traces produced by the `Tracer` provided by a specific TracerProvider are sampled consistently.

- Once a trace is created, a decision is made on whether to sample the trace. This decision is stored in the `SpanContext` associated with all spans in this trace. The sampling decision is propagated to all the services participating in the distributed trace via the `Propagator` configured.

- Finally, once a span has ended, the `SpanProcessor` applies the sampling decision. It passes the spans for all sampled traces to the `SpanExporter`. Traces that are not sampled are not exported.

Metrics

For certain types of data, sampling just doesn't work. Sampling in the case of metrics may severely alter the data, rendering it effectively useless. For example, imagine recording data for each incoming request to a service, incrementing a counter by one with each request. Sampling this data would mean that any increment that is not sampled would result in unaccounted requests. Values recorded as a result would lose the meaning of the original data.

A single metric data point is smaller than a single trace. This means that typically, managing metrics data creates less overhead to process and store. I say *typically* here because this depends on many factors, such as the dimensions of the data and the frequency at which data points are collected.

Reducing the amount of data produced by the metrics signal focuses on aggregating the data, which reduces the number of data points transmitted. It does this by combining data points rather than selecting specific points and discarding others. There is, however, one aspect of metrics where sampling comes into play: exemplars. If you recall from *Chapter 2*, *OpenTelemetry Signals – Traces, Metrics, and Logs*, exemplars are data points that allow metrics to be correlated with traces. There is no need to produce exemplars that reference unsampled traces. The details of how exemplars and their sampling should be configured are still being discussed in the OpenTelemetry specification as of December 2021. It is good to be aware that this will be a feature of OpenTelemetry in the near future.

Logs

At the time of writing, there is no specification in OpenTelemetry around if or how the logging signal should be sampled. The following shows a couple of ways that are currently being considered:

- OpenTelemetry provides the ability for logs to be correlated with traces. As such, it may make sense to provide a configuration option to only emit log records that are correlated with sampled traces.

- Log records could be sampled in the same way that traces can be configured via a sampler, to only emit a fraction of the total logs (`https://github.com/open-telemetry/opentelemetry-specification/issues/2237`).

An alternative to sampling for logging is aggregation. Log records that contain the same message could be aggregated and transmitted as a single record, which could include a counter of repeated events. As these options are purely speculative, we won't focus any additional efforts on sampling and logging in this chapter.

Before diving into the code and what samplers are available, let's get familiar with some of the sampling strategies available.

Sampling strategies

When deciding on how to best configure sampling for a distributed system, the strategy selected often depends on the environment. Depending on the strategy chosen, the sampling decision is made at different points in the system, as shown in the following diagram:

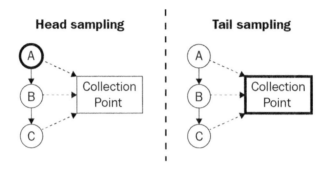

Figure 12.1 – Different points at which sampling decisions can take place

The previous diagram shows where the decisions to sample are made, but before choosing a strategy, we must understand what they are and when they are appropriate.

Head sampling

The quickest way to decide about a trace is to decide at the very beginning whether to drop it or not; this is known as **head sampling**. The application that creates the first span in a trace, the root span, decides whether to sample the trace or not, and propagates that decision via the context to every subsequent service called. This signals to all other participants in the trace whether they should be sending this span to a backend.

Head sampling reduces the overhead for the entire system, as each application can discard unnecessary spans without computing a sampling decision. It also reduces the amount of data transmitted, which can have a significant impact on network costs.

Although it is the most efficient way to sample data, deciding at the beginning of the trace whether it should be sampled or not doesn't always work. As we'll see shortly, when exploring the different samplers available, it's possible for applications to configure sampling differently from one another. This could cause applications to not respect the decision made by the root span, causing broken traces to be received by the backend. *Figure 12.2* shows five applications interacting and combining into a distributed system producing spans. It highlights what would happen if two applications, *B* and *C*, were configured to sample a trace, but the other applications in the system were not:

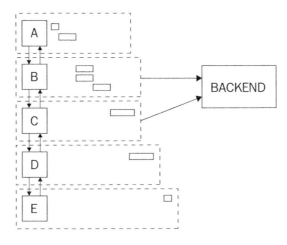

Figure 12.2 – Inconsistent sampling configuration

The backend would receive four spans and some context about the system but would be missing four additional spans and quite a bit of information.

> **Important Note**
> Inconsistent sampler configuration is a problem that affects all sampling strategies. Configuring multiple applications in a distributed system introduces the possibility of inconsistencies. Using a consistent sampling configuration across applications is critical.

Making a sampling decision at the very beginning of a trace can also cause valuable information to be missed. Continuing with the example from the previous diagram, if an error occurs in application *D*, but the sampling decision made by application *A* discards the trace, that error would not be reported to the backend. An inherent problem with head sampling is that the decision is made before all the information is available.

Tail sampling

If making the decision at the beginning of a trace is problematic because of a lack of information, what about making the decision at the end of a trace? **Tail sampling** is another common strategy that waits until a trace is complete before making a sampling decision. This allows the sampler to perform some analysis on the trace to detect potentially anomalous or interesting occurrences.

With tail sampling, all the applications in a distributed system must produce and transmit the telemetry to a destination that decides to sample the data or not. This can become costly for large distributed systems. Depending on where the tail sampling is performed, this option may cause significant amounts of data to be produced and transferred over the network, which could have little value.

Additionally, to make sampling decisions, the sampler must buffer in memory or store the data for the entire trace until it is ready to decide. This will inevitably lead to an increase in memory and storage consumed, depending on the size and duration of traces. As mitigation around memory concerns, a maximum trace duration can be configured in tail sampling. However, this leads to data gaps for any traces that never finish within that set time. This is problematic as those traces can help identify problems within a system.

Probability sampling

As discussed earlier in the chapter, **probability sampling** ensures that data is selected randomly, removing bias from the data sampled. Probability sampling is somewhat different from head and tail sampling, as it is both a configuration that can be applied to those other strategies and a strategy in itself. The sampling decision can be made by each component in the system individually, so long as the components share the same algorithm for applying the probability. In OpenTelemetry, the `TraceIdRatioBased` sampler (https://github.com/open-telemetry/opentelemetry-specification/blob/main/specification/trace/sdk.md#traceidratiobased) combined with the standard random trace ID generator provides a mechanism for probability sampling. The decision to sample is calculated by applying a configurable ratio to a hash of the trace ID. Since the trace ID is propagated across the system, all components configured with the same ratio and the `TraceIdRatioBased` sampler can apply the same logic at decision time independently:

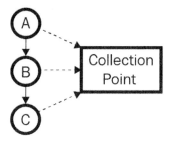

Figure 12.3 – Probabilistic sampling decisions can be applied at every step of the system

There are other sampling strategies available, but these are the ones we'll concern ourselves with for the remainder of this chapter.

Samplers available

There are a few different options when choosing a sampler. The following options are defined in the OpenTelemetry specification and are available in all implementations:

- **Always on**: As the name suggests, the `always_on` sampler samples all traces.
- **Always off**: This sampler does not sample any traces.
- **Trace ID ratio**: The trace ID ratio sampler, as discussed earlier, is a type of probability sampler available in OpenTelemetry.
- **Parent-based**: The parent-based sampler is a sampler that supports the head sampling strategy. The parent-based sampler can be configured with always on, `always_off`, or with a trace ID ratio decision as a fallback, when a sampling decision has not already been made for a trace.

Using the OpenTelemetry Python SDK will give us a chance to put these samplers to use.

Sampling at the application level via the SDK

Allowing applications to decide what to sample, provides a great amount of flexibility to application developers and operators, as these applications are the source of the tracing data. Samplers can be configured in OpenTelemetry as a property of the tracer provider. In the following code, a `configure_tracer` method configures the OpenTelemetry tracing pipeline and receives `Sampler` as a method argument. This method is used to obtain three different tracers, each with its own sampling configuration:

- `ALWAYS_ON`: A sampler that always samples.
- `ALWAYS_OFF`: A sampler that never samples.
- `TraceIdRatioBased`: A probability sampler, which in the example is configured to sample traces 50% of the time.

The code then produces a separate trace using each tracer to demonstrate how sampling impacts the output generated by `ConsoleSpanExporter`:

sample.py

```python
from opentelemetry.sdk.trace import TracerProvider
from opentelemetry.sdk.trace.export import BatchSpanProcessor, ConsoleSpanExporter
from opentelemetry.sdk.trace.sampling import ALWAYS_OFF, ALWAYS_ON, TraceIdRatioBased

def configure_tracer(sampler):
    provider = TracerProvider(sampler=sampler)
    provider.add_span_processor(BatchSpanProcessor(ConsoleSpanExporter()))
    return provider.get_tracer(__name__)

always_on_tracer = configure_tracer(ALWAYS_ON)
always_off_tracer = configure_tracer(ALWAYS_OFF)
ratio_tracer = configure_tracer(TraceIdRatioBased(0.5))

with always_on_tracer.start_as_current_span("always-on") as span:
    span.set_attribute("sample", "always sampled")
```

```
with always_off_tracer.start_as_current_span("always-off") as
span:
    span.set_attribute("sample", "never sampled")

with ratio_tracer.start_as_current_span("ratio") as span:
    span.set_attribute("sample", "sometimes sampled")
```

Run the code using the following command:

`$ python sample.py`

The output should do one of the following:

- Contain a trace with a span named `always-on`.
- Not contain a trace with a span named `always-off`.
- Maybe contain a trace with a span named `ratio`. You may need to run the code a few times to get this trace to produce output.

The following sample output is abbreviated to only show the name of the span and significant attributes:

output

```
{
    "name": "ratio",
    "attributes": {
        "sample": "sometimes sampled"
    },
}
{
    "name": "always-on",
    "attributes": {
        "sample": "always sampled"
    },
}
```

Note that although the example configures three different samplers, a real-world application would only ever use one sampler. An exception to this is a single application containing multiple services with separate sampling requirements.

> **Note**
>
> In addition to configuring a sampler via code, it's also possible to configure it via the `OTEL_TRACES_SAMPLER` and `OTEL_TRACES_SAMPLER_ARG` environment variables.

Using application configuration allows us to use head sampling, but individual applications don't have the information needed to make tail sampling decisions. For that, we need to go further down the pipeline.

Using the OpenTelemetry Collector to sample data

Configuring the application to sample traces is great, but what if we wanted to use tail sampling instead? The OpenTelemetry Collector provides a natural point where sampling can be performed. Today, it supports both tail sampling and probabilistic sampling via processors. As we've already discussed the probabilistic sampling processor in *Chapter 8, The OpenTelemetry Collector*, we'll focus this section on the tail sampling processor.

Tail sampling processor

In addition to supporting the configuration of sampling via specifying a probabilistic sampling percentage, the tail sampling processor can make sampling decisions based on a variety of characteristics of a trace. It can choose to sample based on one of the following:

- Overall trace duration
- Span attributes' values
- Status code of a span

To accomplish this, the tail sampling processor supports the configuration of policies to sample traces. To better understand how tail sampling can impact the tracing data produced by configuring a variety of policies in the collector, let's look at the following code snippet, which configures a collector with the following:

- The OpenTelemetry protocol listener, which will receive the telemetry from an example application
- A logging exporter to allow us to see the tracing data in the terminal
- The tail sampling processor with a policy to always sample all traces

The following code snippet contains the elements of the previous list:

config/collector/config.yml

```yaml
receivers:
  otlp:
    protocols:
      grpc:

exporters:
  logging:
    loglevel: debug

processors:
  tail_sampling:
    decision_wait: 5s
    policies: [{ name: always, type: always_sample }]

service:
  pipelines:
    traces:
      receivers: [otlp]
      processors: [tail_sampling]
      exporters: [logging]
```

Start the collector using the following command, which includes the configuration previously shown:

```
$ ./otelcol-contrib --config ./config/collector/config.yml
```

Next, the ensuing code is an application that will send multiple traces to the collector to demonstrate some of the capabilities of the tail sampling processor:

multiple_traces.py

```python
import time
from opentelemetry import trace
```

```
tracer = trace.get_tracer_provider().get_tracer(__name__)
with tracer.start_as_current_span("slow-span"):
    time.sleep(1)

for i in range(0, 20):
    with tracer.start_as_current_span("fast-span"):
        pass
```

Open a new terminal and start the program using OpenTelemetry auto-instrumentation, as per the following command:

```
$ opentelemetry-instrument python multiple_traces.py
```

Looking through the output in the collector terminal, you should see a total of 21 traces being emitted. Let's now update the collector configuration to only sample 10% of all traces. This can be configured via a policy, as per the following:

config/collector/config.yml

```
processors:
  tail_sampling:
    decision_wait: 5s
    policies:
      [
        {
          name: probability,
          type: probabilistic,
          probabilistic: { sampling_percentage: 10 },
        },
      ]
```

Restart the collector and run `multiple_traces.py` once more to see the effects of applying the new policy. The results should show roughly 10% of traces, which in this case would be about two traces. I say *roughly* here because the configuration relies on probabilistic sampling using the trace identifier. Since the trace ID is randomly generated, there is some variance in the results with such a small sample set. Run the command a few times if needed to see the sampling policy in action:

output

```
Span #0
    Trace ID        : 9581c95ae58bc8368050728f50c32f73
    Parent ID       :
    ID              : b9c3fb8838eb0f33
    Name            : fast-span
    Kind            : SPAN_KIND_INTERNAL
    Start time      : 2021-12-28 21:29:01.144907 +0000 UTC
    End time        : 2021-12-28 21:29:01.144922 +0000 UTC
    Status code     : STATUS_CODE_UNSET
    Status message  :
Span #0
    Trace ID        : 2a8950f2365e515324c62dfdc23735ba
    Parent ID       :
    ID              : c5217fb16c4d90ff
    Name            : fast-span
    Kind            : SPAN_KIND_INTERNAL
    Start time      : 2021-12-28 21:29:01.14498 +0000 UTC
    End time        : 2021-12-28 21:29:01.144996 +0000 UTC
    Status code     : STATUS_CODE_UNSET
    Status message  :
```

Note that in the previous output, only the spans named `fast-span` were emitted. It's unfortunate, because the information about `slow-span` may be more useful to us. It's additionally possible to configure the tail sampling processor to combine policies to create more complex sampling decisions.

For example, you may want to continue capturing only 10% of all traces but always capture traces representing operations that took longer than 1 second to complete. In this case, the following combination of a latency-based policy with a probabilistic policy would make this possible:

config/collector/config.yml

```
processors:
  tail_sampling:
    decision_wait: 5s
    policies:
      [
        {
          name: probability,
          type: probabilistic,
          probabilistic: { sampling_percentage: 10 },
        },
        { name: slow, type: latency, latency: { threshold_ms: 1000 } },
      ]
```

Restart the collector one last time and run the example code. You'll notice that both a percentage of traces and the trace containing `slow-span` are visible in the output from the collector. There are other characteristics that can be configured, but this gives you an idea of how the tail sampling processor works. Another example is to base the sampling decision on the status code, which is a convenient way to capture errors in a system. Another yet is to sample custom attributes, which could be used to scope the sampling to specific systems.

> **Important Note**
> Choosing to sample traces on known characteristics introduces bias in the selection of spans that could inadvertently hide useful telemetry. Tread carefully when configuring sampling to use non-probabilistic data as it may exclude more information than you'd like. Combining probabilistic and non-probabilistic sampling, as in the previous example, allows us to work around this limitation.

Summary

Understanding the different options for sampling provides us with the ability to manage the amount of data produced by our applications. Knowing the trade-offs of different sampling strategies and some of the methods available helps decrease the level of noise in a busy environment.

The OpenTelemetry configuration and samplers available to configure sampling at the application level can help reduce the load and cost upfront in systems via head sampling. Configuring tail sampling at collection time provides the added benefit of making a more informed decision on what to keep or discard. This benefit comes at the added cost of having to run a collection point with sufficient resources to buffer the data until a decision can be reached.

Ultimately, the decisions made when configuring sampling will impact what data is available to observe what is happening in a system. Sample too little and you may miss important events. Sample too much and the cost of producing telemetry for a system may be too high or the data too noisy to search through. Sample only for known issues and you may miss the opportunity to find abnormalities you didn't even know about.

During development, sampling 100% of the data makes sense as the volume is low. In production, a much smaller percentage of data, under 10%, is often representative of the data as a whole.

The information in this chapter has given us an understanding of the concepts of sampling. It has also given us an idea of the trade-offs in choosing different sampling strategies. In the end, choosing the right strategy requires experimenting and tweaking as we learn more about our systems.

Index

A

agent 62
agent deployment 267
aggregation
  about 14, 155, 156
  methods 155
always off sampler 337
always on sampler 337
Amazon Elastic Kubernetes Service
  URL 266
analysis 13
Apache Flume
  URL 8
application level sampling
  configuring, via OpenTelemetry
    SDK 338-340
application metrics
  reference link 315
application telemetry
  collecting 267, 268
  sidecar, deploying 269-271
asynchronous counter 140, 141
asynchronous gauge 147, 148
asynchronous instruments 137
asynchronous up/down counter 143-145

attributes 37
attributes processor
  about 241
  delete operation 241
  extract operation 241
  hash operation 241
  insert operation 241
  update operation 241
  upsert operation 241
auto-instrumentation
  about 60
  command-line options 204
  components 61, 62
  configuring 198-201
  environment variables 203
  limitations 62, 63
  OpenTelemetry configurator 202, 203
  OpenTelemetry distribution 201, 202
  reference link 226
auto-instrumentation, in Java
  monkey patching 66
  runtime hooks 66
auto-instrumentation, in Python
  Instrumentor interface 67, 68
  libraries, instrumenting 66, 67
  wrapper script 68, 71

automatic configuration
    about 211
    logs, configuring 216, 217
    metrics, configuring 215
    propagation, configuring 217, 218
    resource attributes, configuring 211, 212
    traces, configuring 213-215
Azure Kubernetes Service
    URL 266

B

ballast extension 246, 248
BaseDistro interface
    about 201
    reference link 202
basicConfig method, of logging module
    reference link 184
batch processor 245
BatchSpanProcessor 214
Byte Buddy
    URL 65

C

cardinality 47
cardinality explosion 47
centralized logging 8
chaos engineering
    about 311-313
    latency 313
    URL 311
cloud-based providers 5

cloud-native applications 4
Cloud Native Computing
    Foundation (CNCF) 295
cloud-native software
    observability 15
cloud providers 4
collector
    deploying, benefits 234, 235
command-line options 204
composite propagator 110-115
ConfigMap 274
configuration options
    excluded_urls 206
    name_callback 206
    span_callback 206
conflicting instruments
    handling 148
Context API
    about 82-90
    attach 83
    detach 83
    get_value 83
    set_value 83
context propagation
    about 23, 24, 106-109
    formats 109
ContextVar module 23
counter 138, 139
create, read, update, and delete (CRUD)
    reference link 221
cumulative aggregation 43
cumulative sum 43

D

DaemonSet 267, 273
Dapper
  reference link 9
dashboards
  using 9
data
  enriching 92-94
data point type
  histogram 44, 45
  sum 43
  summary 45, 46
data sampling
  with OpenTelemetry Collector 340
decorator 89
delta aggregation 43
DevOps 6
dimension 152-154
distributed tracing 33, 187, 189
Docker Compose
  about 28
  reference link 28
double instrumentation 210

E

entry points
  reference link 201
environment variables 203
event
  about 117
  recording 116
exception
  about 118-122
  recording 116

exemplars 47
exporters 21, 247, 248
extensions
  about 248
  ballast 248
  Health_check 248
  pprof 248
  zpages 248

F

filter processor 242
Flask
  about 49
  OpenTelemetry logging 189, 190
Flask documentation
  reference link 103
Flask library instrumentor
  about 225
  configuration options 225
Fluentd
  URL 8

G

gauge 44
GDB
  reference link 9
General Data Protection
        Regulation (GDPR) 308
golden signals
  reference link 158
Google Cloud Platform (GCP)
        resource detector 22
Google Kubernetes Engine
  URL 266

Grafana
    about 31, 303-305
    reference link 303
Graphite
    URL 9
grocery store application
    about 157, 158, 219-221
    concurrent number of requests
        metric 167, 168
    legacy inventory service 218, 219
    number of requests metric 161
    number of requests metrics 158-161
    request duration metric 162-166
    resource consumption metric 169-171
    revisiting 218
    shopper application 221-225

H

head sampling 334, 335
Health_check extension 248
Helm Charts
    reference link 272
Helm website
    URL 266
histogram 145, 146
HorizontalPodAutocaling 282
host metrics receiver 238

I

instrumentation libraries
    finding 226
    opentelemetry-bootstrap 227
    OpenTelemetry registry 226

J

Jaeger
    about 30, 295-299
    agent 295
    Collector 295
    ingester 295
    query 295
    reference link 295
Java archive (JAR) file 64
Java Instrumentation API
    reference link 63

K

Kubernetes
    URL 264

L

latency
    about 313, 314
    experiment 314
    hypothesis 315
    verifying 315-318
legacy inventory service 218, 219
LogEmitter
    about 176
    using 177-180
LogEmitterProvider 176
log files 48
logging pipeline
    components 175, 176
logging signal
    about 175
    working 185, 186

Index   351

LogProcessor 176
LogRecord
  fields 177, 178
logs
  about 48, 187, 302
  anatomy 48-50
  configuring 216, 217
  considerations 52
  correlating 50-52
  Grafana 303-305
  Loki 302, 303
  producing 177
  semantic conventions 52
Logstash
  URL 8
Loki 31, 302, 303
Loki, components
  distributor 302
  ingester 302
  querier 302
  query frontend 302
  ruler 302

M

manual instrumentation
  challenges 60, 61
manual invocation 206-210
measure 13
measurement 13
memory limiter processor 246
message 49
meter
  about 129
  obtaining 132-134

MeterProvider 129
MetricExporter 130
metric outputs, customizing with views
  aggregation 155, 156
  dimension 152-154
  filtering 149-152
MetricReader 130
metrics
  about 39
  anatomy 40, 42
  collecting, from applications 14
  configuring 215
  considerations 47, 48
  data point type 42, 43
  exemplars 47
  using 8, 9
metrics pipeline
  configuring 129-132
  meter, obtaining 132-134
  MeterProvider 129
  MetricExporter 130
  MetricReader 130
  pull-based exporting 134-136
  push-based exporting 134-136
  Views 129
metrics signal
  about 299
  Prometheus 300, 301
monkey patching
  reference link 66
monolith architecture
  versus microservice architecture 5, 6
monoliths, deploying to cloud provider
  challenges 5

N

Node 267
none values 97
non-probabilistic sampling
  about 332
  reference link 332
null values 97

O

observability
  about 3, 7
  history, reviewing 7
OpenCensus
  about 10, 13
  collector data flow 13
  URL 10, 13
OpenCensus Service
  URL 235
OpenMetrics
  reference link 46
Open-source telemetry backends
  exploring 288
  logs, analyzing 302
  metrics, analyzing 299
  traces, analyzing 289
OpenTelemetry
  components 216
  history 10
  log severity levels 179
opentelemetry-bootstrap 227

OpenTelemetry Collector
  collector, configuring 254-258
  exporter, configuring 253
  metrics, filtering 259-262
  need for 234
  spans, modifying 258, 259
  used, for sampling data 340
  using 252
OpenTelemetry Collector, components
  about 235, 236
  additional components 249
  exporters 247, 248
  extensions 248, 249
  processors 239-241
  receivers 236-238
opentelemetry-collector-
    contrib repository
  reference link 249
OpenTelemetry, concepts
  about 16
  context propagation 23, 24
  pipelines 20
  resources 22
  signals 16
OpenTelemetry configurator 202, 203
OpenTelemetry distribution 201, 202
OpenTelemetry Enhancement
    Proposal (OTEP) 17, 60
OpenTelemetry instrument
  asynchronous counter 140, 141
  asynchronous gauge 147, 148

asynchronous up/down
   counter 143, 145
counter 138, 139
duplicate instrument 148
histogram 145, 146
listing 137
selecting 137
up/down counter 142, 143
OpenTelemetry Java Agent 64-66
OpenTelemetry logging
   configuring 175-177
   with Flask 189, 190
OpenTelemetry Protocol (OTLP)
   design considerations 251
   encodings 251
   protocols 251
   telemetry, transporting via 249, 251
opentelemetry-python-contrib repository
   reference link 205
OpenTelemetry registry
   about 226
   reference link 226
OpenTelemetry SDK
   used, for configuring application
      level sampling 338-340
OpenTracing
   about 10-12
   URL 9

P

parent-based sampler 337
parent identifier 34
PDB
   reference link 9

percentile 45
Personally Identifiable Information
      (PII) 100, 242
pipelines 20
Pod 267
pprof extension 248
probabilistic sampling processor 243
probability sampling
   about 332, 336
   reference link 332
processors
   about 21, 239-241
   attributes processor 241
   batch processor 245
   filter processor 242
   memory limiter processor 246
   probabilistic sampling processor 243
   resource processor 244
   span processor 244
Prometheus
   about 31, 300, 301
   reference link 134
Prometheus Query Language
      (PromQL) 300
Prometheus server 300
Prometheus web UI 300
propagation
   configuring 217, 218
Propagators API 107
protobufs
   about 250
   reference link 249
provider 21
psutil
   reference link 169

pull-based exporting 134-136
push-based exporting 134-136
Python 3.7+ 23
Python docs
  reference link 180

Q

quantile 45

R

receivers
  about 236-238
  host metrics receiver 238
requests library
  reference link 101
Requests library instrumentor
  about 205
  additional configurable options 206
  configuration options 206
  double instrumentation 210
  manual invocation 206-210
resident set size
  reference link 147
resource attributes
  configuring 211, 212
resource correlation 192, 193
ResourceDetector 94, 95, 96
resource pressure
  about 318
  experiment 319
  hypothesis 319
  verifying 320, 322
resource processor 244

resources 22
resource usage information
  reference link 169
root span 35
runner 62

S

sampler
  options 337
sampling
  about 331
  concepts 331
  methods 332
sampling, across signals of OpenTelemetry
  logging 333
  metrics 333
  traces 332
sampling methods
  non-probabilistic 332
  probabilistic 332
sampling strategies
  about 334
  head sampling 334, 335
  probability sampling 336
  tail sampling 336
schema URL 54, 55, 133
semantic conventions
  about 52, 53
  adopting 53
  schema URL 54, 55
service level agreements (SLAs) 39
service level indicators (SLIs)
  about 39
  reference link 39

service level objectives (SLOs)
  about 39
  reference link 39
shopper application 221-225
Sidecar 267
sidecar deployment 267
signals
  about 16
  API 17
  data model 17
  instrumentation libraries 19, 20
  SDK 18
  semantic conventions 18, 19
  specification 17
site reliability engineering (SRE)
  about 39, 158
  reference link 39
software development kit (SDK) 13, 129
span 34
span attributes 96-100
span_context
  key information 106
SpanContext 34
SpanContext, trace element
  span ID 34
  trace flags 34
  trace ID 34
SpanKind
  about 100-105
  CLIENT 100
  CONSUMER 101
  INTERNAL 100
  PRODUCER 100
  SERVER 100
span processor 90, 91, 244

spans 137
span status codes
  ERROR 123
  OK 123
  UNSET 123
special interest groups (SIGs) 15
SQLite
  reference link 289
standalone service
  about 279-281
  autoscaling 282
standard logging library 180-184
StatsD
  about 134
  URL 9
status
  about 122-124
  recording 116
synchronous instruments 137
System Architecture diagram 299
system-level telemetry
  about 272
  agent, connecting 274-276
  agent, deploying 272, 273
  resource attributes, adding 277-279
  sidecar, connecting 274-276
system properties 64

T

tags 37
tail sampling 336
tail sampling processor 340-344
telemetry
  transporting, via OTLP 249, 251
  using 326-328

telemetry backends, in production
  data retention 307
  high availability 306
  privacy regulations 308
  running, considerations 306
  scalability 306
telemetry generators 21
telemetry pipeline
  provider 21
time-series database (TSDB) 300
timestamp 48
Trace Context
  reference link 34
trace-flags
  reference link 106
trace ID ratio sampler 337
Tracer 12, 79, 80, 137
TracerProvider interface
  defining 79
traces
  about 33, 34
  anatomy 34-37
  components 213
  configuring 213-215
  considerations 38
  span 37, 38
Trace state field 34
tracestate header
  reference link 106
tracing application
  applying 9, 10
tracing data
  Context API 82-90
  generating 80-82
  span processor 90, 91

tracing pipeline
  configuring 77, 78
tracing signal
  about 289, 290
  Jaeger 295-299
  Zipkin 291-294
traditional monolithic systems
  challenges 6
traffic control
  URL 314

U

unexpected shutdown
  about 323
  experiment 323
  hypothesis 323
  verifying 324, 325
Unix utility stress
  reference link 319
up/down counter 142, 143

V

views
  about 14
  used, for customizing
    metric outputs 149

W

W3C Trace Context 109
World Wide Web Consortium (W3C) 34
WSGI middleware
  using, for logging 191

Y

YAML 277

Z

Zipkin
  about 291-294
  reference link 291
Zipkin, core components
  collector 291
  query service or API 291
  storage 291
  web UI 291
zpages extension 248

Packt.com

Subscribe to our online digital library for full access to over 7,000 books and videos, as well as industry leading tools to help you plan your personal development and advance your career. For more information, please visit our website.

Why subscribe?

- Spend less time learning and more time coding with practical eBooks and Videos from over 4,000 industry professionals
- Improve your learning with Skill Plans built especially for you
- Get a free eBook or video every month
- Fully searchable for easy access to vital information
- Copy and paste, print, and bookmark content

Did you know that Packt offers eBook versions of every book published, with PDF and ePub files available? You can upgrade to the eBook version at packt.com and as a print book customer, you are entitled to a discount on the eBook copy. Get in touch with us at customercare@packtpub.com for more details.

At www.packt.com, you can also read a collection of free technical articles, sign up for a range of free newsletters, and receive exclusive discounts and offers on Packt books and eBooks.

Other Books You May Enjoy

If you enjoyed this book, you may be interested in these other books by Packt:

Cloud Native with Kubernetes

Alexander Raul

ISBN: 9781838823078

- Set up Kubernetes and configure its authentication
- Deploy your applications to Kubernetes
- Configure and provide storage to Kubernetes applications
- Expose Kubernetes applications outside the cluster
- Control where and how applications are run on Kubernetes
- Set up observability for Kubernetes
- Build a continuous integration and continuous deployment (CI/CD) pipeline for Kubernetes
- Extend Kubernetes with service meshes, serverless, and more

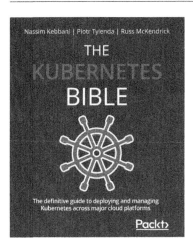

The Kubernetes Bible

Nassim Kebbani, Piotr Tylenda, Russ McKendrick

ISBN: 9781838827694

- Manage containerized applications with Kubernetes
- Understand Kubernetes architecture and the responsibilities of each component
- Set up Kubernetes on Amazon Elastic Kubernetes Service, Google Kubernetes Engine, and Microsoft Azure Kubernetes Service
- Deploy cloud applications such as Prometheus and Elasticsearch using Helm charts
- Discover advanced techniques for Pod scheduling and auto-scaling the cluster
- Understand possible approaches to traffic routing in Kubernetes

Packt is searching for authors like you

If you're interested in becoming an author for Packt, please visit `authors.packtpub.com` and apply today. We have worked with thousands of developers and tech professionals, just like you, to help them share their insight with the global tech community. You can make a general application, apply for a specific hot topic that we are recruiting an author for, or submit your own idea.

Share Your Thoughts

Now you've finished *Cloud-Native Observability with OpenTelemetry*, we'd love to hear your thoughts! Scan the QR code below to go straight to the Amazon review page for this book and share your feedback or leave a review on the site that you purchased it from.

`https://packt.link/r/1801077703`

Your review is important to us and the tech community and will help us make sure we're delivering excellent quality content.

método 3
DE ESPAÑOL

B1

método 3
DE ESPAÑOL

B1

Libro del profesor
ESPAÑOL LENGUA EXTRANJERA

Coordinadores
Sara Robles Ávila y Salvador Peláez Santamaría

Autores
Francisca Cárdenas Bernal
Antonio Hierro Montosa
Sara Robles Ávila

Coordinadores
Sara Robles Ávila, profesora titular del Departamento de Filología Española I de la Universidad de Málaga
Salvador Peláez Santamaría, profesor del Área de Lingüística General y coordinador académico del Curso de Español para Extranjeros de la Universidad de Málaga

Autores
Francisca Cárdenas Bernal, profesora y subcoordinadora académica del Curso de Español para Extranjeros de la Universidad de Málaga
Antonio Hierro Montosa, profesor del Curso de Español para Extranjeros de la Universidad de Málaga
Sara Robles Ávila, profesora titular del Departamento de Filología Española I de la Universidad de Málaga

4.ª reimpresión: 2015

Equipo editorial
Edición y coordinación: Milagros Bodas y Sonia de Pedro
Ilustración: Ximena Maier, Jesús Escudero
Cubierta: Proyectos gráficos/PGA
Diseño y maquetación: Mar Garrido
Corrección: Ana Morcillo
Edición gráfica: Nuria González y Mar Morales
Estudio de grabación: Texto-Directo

Fotografías
Agencia EFE; AGE Fotostock; Archivo Anaya (Bossavy, K.; Canto, M.; Cosano, P.; Jove, V.; Leyva, Á.de; Lezama, D.; Lucas, J.; Martín, J.A.; Moya, B.H.; Ortega, Á.; Padura, S.; Redondo, M.; Sánchez, J.; Steel, M.; Valls R.); Photo 12/Contacto; 123RF/Quick Images.

© de la autoría: Francisca Cárdenas Bernal, Antonio Hierro Montosa y Sara Robles Ávila
© de la coordinación: Sara Robles Ávila y Salvador Peláez Santamaría
© de los dibujos y gráficos: Grupo Anaya, S. A.
© de esta edición: Grupo Anaya, S. A. 2013

Depósito Legal: M-21545-2013
ISBN: 978-84-678-3056-9
Printed in Spain

Las normas ortográficas seguidas en este libro son las establecidas por la Real Academia Española en su última edición de la *Ortografía*.

Reservados todos los derechos. El contenido de esta obra está protegido por la Ley, que establece penas de prisión y/o multas, además de las correspondientes indemnizaciones por daños y perjuicios, para quienes reprodujeren, plagiaren, distribuyeren o comunicaren públicamente, en todo o en parte, una obra literaria, artística o científica, o su transformación, interpretación o ejecución artística fijada en cualquier tipo de soporte o comunicada a través de cualquier medio, sin la preceptiva autorización.

PRESENTACIÓN

El Libro del Profesor del MÉTODO Anaya Ele se presenta como una **herramienta muy útil** para el docente que le permite abordar el proceso de enseñanza-aprendizaje de una manera exhaustiva por varias razones:

1. **Muestra la concepción metodológica** que subyace en el manual de forma práctica y operativa en el proceder didáctico.

2. **Ofrece explicaciones y pautas** para tratar la secuencia didáctica del Libro del Alumno ejercicio por ejercicio.

3. **Recoge sugerencias y alternativas de trabajo** de las diferentes actividades que van más allá de los enunciados propuestos y que permiten una mayor explotación de los ejercicios que se proponen.

4. **Reproduce las páginas del Libro del Alumno** y mantiene el orden de las actividades, lo que permite al docente el fácil seguimiento de la secuencia.

5. **Presenta las soluciones** a los ejercicios del Libro del Alumno.

COMPETENCIA COMUNICATIVA

MÉTODO Anaya Ele parte de la consideración de que la lengua es un vehículo de comunicación, el más importante, y, por ello, el proceso de enseñanza-aprendizaje debe ir dirigido a cumplir el objetivo principal: **promover la competencia comunicativa** de nuestros alumnos. Para alcanzar este fin, en el manual hemos plasmado una propuesta integradora en la que se recogen los planteamientos que consideramos más acertados de distintas corrientes metodológicas, de diferentes enfoques y de los procedimientos que mejores frutos han dado en la enseñanza de lenguas extranjeras.

PRAGMÁTICA

Apostamos por una actuación aglutinadora en la que primarán la comunicación y la exposición de los alumnos a las producciones reales, sin olvidar la complejidad del sistema lingüístico. Por ello, en MÉTODO Anaya Ele se van a desarrollar acciones orientadas a un aprendizaje comunicativo, de manera que las funciones, las nociones, las estructuras lingüísticas y todo el componente pragmático, indispensable en cualquier intercambio humano, conduzcan a desarrollar **procesos y tareas de comunicación en el aula.** Y es precisamente en el **componente pragmático** en el que hemos puesto un especial interés en este método porque en muchos casos no ha sido considerado en toda su extensión y profundidad y, por ello, frecuentemente olvidado o tratado muy parcialmente en los manuales de español para extranjeros.

APRENDIZAJE GRADUADO

Así pues, con este manual hemos tratado de alcanzar un equilibro en la selección de los constituyentes puesto que se recoge tanto la **sistematización de la lengua** como su **utilidad instrumental**, de manera que el alumno podrá encontrar los contenidos lingüísticos y el funcionamiento de estos en contextos de uso reales con el objetivo de promover el desarrollo de las habilidades comunicativas. Entendemos que resulta clave para alcanzar la competencia comunicativa desarrollar un **aprendizaje bien graduado** en el que exista un equilibrio en la secuencia *input-output,* de manera que el proceso de enseñanza-aprendizaje fluya natural; a partir de textos y de contenidos aportados se obtienen productos generados por el alumno gracias a la construcción de una estructura de actividades que van desde las más dirigidas –en las que al estudiante se le facilitan recursos y estrategias para su ejecución– hasta las más libres, con las que el alumno ya goza de una mayor autonomía para su producción.

APRENDIZAJE INFERENCIAL

En esta concepción metodológica **la gramática** recibe un tratamiento especial ya que el acceso a ella la realiza el propio alumno –ayudado por el material– de una manera **inferencial, pedagógica y en uso:** a partir de la observación de los hechos lingüísticos, del funcionamiento de la lengua en contextos de comunicación, se promueven la reflexión metalingüística y la sistematización hasta llegar a la formulación de reglas gramaticales por parte del estudiante.

Índice

ÍNDICE

	Funciones comunicativas	Contenidos gramaticales
Unidad 1 **De viajes, historias y cuentos** pág. 12 Situación comunicativa: **Hablando de viajes; contando cuentos e historias**	• Hablar del momento presente y de temas cotidianos • Pedir y dar información general • Relatar experiencias pasadas • Expresar acciones previstas cumplidas o no • Narrar hechos del pasado • Hablar sobre los cambios y transformaciones que tienen lugar en nuestras vidas • Hablar de acciones habituales en el pasado • Expresar futuro	• Revisión del presente de indicativo • Revisión del futuro imperfecto de indicativo y de otras formas de expresar futuro • Revisión de los tiempos del pasado (I): pretérito perfecto, pretérito indefinido, pretérito imperfecto
Unidad 2 **¿Te acuerdas de...?** pág. 29 Situación comunicativa: **Recordando el pasado**	• Expresar anterioridad respecto a una acción pasada • Hablar del pasado	• Pretérito pluscuamperfecto • Revisión de los tiempos del pasado (II): pretérito perfecto, pretérito indefinido, pretérito imperfecto y pretérito pluscuamperfecto
Unidad 3 **Deberías hacerlo una vez en la vida** pág. 44 Situación comunicativa: **Hablando de deseos / haciendo suposiciones**	• Expresar deseos • Dar consejos y hacer sugerencias • Expresar cortesía • Expresar probabilidad en el presente y en el pasado	• El condicional simple: morfología y usos • Revisión del futuro • Pronombres personales (I)
Unidad 4 **Saber vivir** pág. 59 Situación comunicativa: **Recomendaciones para una vida saludable**	• Dar órdenes • Dar instrucciones • Expresar consejos y recomendaciones • Pedir algo a alguien • Permitir o prohibir algo	• El imperativo afirmativo y negativo: morfología y usos • Imperativos lexicalizados: *Venga; Vamos; Mira; Vaya; Anda* • El uso del imperativo en el español de América • Pronombres personales con el imperativo (II)
Unidad 5 **Y en el trabajo, ¿qué tal?** pág. 77 Situación comunicativa: **Debate sobre el trabajo**	• Expresar deseos • Expresar necesidad • Valorar situaciones y hechos	• Presente de subjuntivo • Estructuras con verbos que expresan deseo y necesidad • *Ser / Estar / Parecer* + adjetivo / adverbio + *que* + subjuntivo (I) • Repaso del presente de indicativo

Contenidos léxico-semánticos	Contenidos socioculturales	Contenidos pragmáticos	Contenidos fonéticos y ortográficos
• Recursos para describir • Léxico relacionado con los viajes • Léxico relacionado con los cuentos tradicionales	• Los cuentos tradicionales • Los viajes • Turistas y viajeros • Los viajes de los españoles	• Posición del hablante respecto al tiempo pasado (I) • La cortesía en las peticiones	
• Léxico usado para contar una anécdota • Vocabulario para reaccionar ante una situación • Léxico relacionado con Internet y las redes sociales	• Internet y las redes sociales	• Conectores discursivos: *pero, al final, bueno, así que, por eso...* • Marcadores discursivos para reforzar: *además, encima, para colmo* • Posición del hablante respecto al tiempo pasado (II)	• Revisión de los fonemas: /g/ - /x/
• Lenguaje del ámbito educativo • Profesiones y ciencias	• Experiencias educativas • El sistema educativo español	• Fórmulas de cortesía para expresar sugerencias o recomendaciones	
• Revisión y ampliación del léxico de la comida y la bebida • Léxico relacionado con la salud y el cuerpo • Léxico relacionado con la medicina	• Vida saludable • Alimentos saludables • Comidas y bebidas en Colombia	• Fórmulas de cortesía para expresar peticiones y órdenes: *por favor...* • Fórmulas para justificar una orden o la petición de un favor: *es que...*	• Reglas generales de acentuación
• Léxico referido al ámbito laboral • Profesiones	• La familia española: la independencia tardía de los hijos	• Repetición para mostrar acuerdo o desacuerdo: *claro, claro; no, no*	• La tilde en los monosílabos: *tú, él, mí, sí, té, dé, sé* • Los adverbios en *-mente*

ÍNDICE

	Funciones comunicativas	Contenidos gramaticales
Unidad 6 **Los otros** pág. 94 Situación comunicativa: En sociedad: reivindicaciones. Costumbres y hábitos culturales	• Expresar gustos y sentimientos • Expresar opiniones, actitudes y conocimiento • Constatar hechos	• Presente de subjuntivo • Estructuras con verbos de sentimiento • Estructuras con verbos de pensamiento, sentido y comunicación • *Ser / Estar / Parecer* + adjetivo / adverbio + *que* + indicativo / subjuntivo (II)
Unidad 7 **Quizás vaya a la fiesta** pág. 111 Situación comunicativa: La comunicación en la sociedad actual	• Expresar deseos referidos al futuro • Expresar duda e inseguridad • Expresar posibilidad • Expresar advertencias	• Enunciados desiderativos: 1. *Ojalá (que)… / (deseo) Que…* + subjuntivo 2. *Soñar con…* + infinitivo / *Soñar con que…* + subjuntivo 3. *A ver si…* + indicativo • Enunciados dubitativos: 1. *Quizá(s), tal vez, probablemente, posiblemente, seguramente* + subjuntivo / indicativo 2. *Es probable que… / Es posible que… / Puede (ser) que…* + subjuntivo 3. *A lo mejor* + indicativo • Enunciados exhortativos: *Que* + subjuntivo • Preposiciones de lugar
Unidad 8 **Nuevas amistades** pág. 132 Situación comunicativa: Haciendo amigos	• Expresar influencia: Dar órdenes, hacer peticiones, sugerencias y consejos • Hablar de las características de un objeto o una persona	• Presente de subjuntivo en construcciones con verbos de influencia: orden, petición, sugerencia y consejo • Oraciones adjetivas explicativas y especificativas en indicativo y subjuntivo
Unidad 9 **Lugares Patrimonio de la Humanidad** pág. 150 Situación comunicativa: Conociendo lugares	• Expresar causa • Expresar consecuencia • Expresar relaciones temporales • Expresar la finalidad y el propósito de algo	• Construcciones causales: *como, porque* + indicativo, *por* + infinitivo • Construcciones consecutivas: *por lo tanto, por tanto, así (es) que* + indicativo • Construcciones temporales con *cuando, siempre que, tan pronto como, en cuanto* + indicativo / subjuntivo, *antes de / después de* + infinitivo y *antes de que, después de que* + subjuntivo • Construcciones finales con *para que* + subjuntivo y *para* + infinitivo
Unidad 10 **¿Qué te ha dicho?** pág. 167 Situación comunicativa: Transmitiendo información	• Relatar lo que otros nos han contado • Expresar el inicio, la reiteración, la continuación o el final de una acción	• El estilo indirecto en el modo indicativo (verbos de lengua y comunicación) • Perífrasis verbales que indican inicio, reiteración, continuación y el final de la acción • Revisión de los usos estudiados en este nivel de los modos indicativo y subjuntivo

Transcripciones pág. 187

Contenidos léxico-semánticos	Contenidos socioculturales	Contenidos pragmáticos	Contenidos fonéticos y ortográficos
• Léxico relacionado con las relaciones interpersonales y el comportamiento social • Léxico referido a algunas costumbres españolas e hispanoamericanas • Medioambiente y fauna	• Relaciones interpersonales: usos sociales del beso y el abrazo, el saludo, el silencio, la distancia personal… • Tradiciones, hábitos y costumbres españolas e hispanoamericanas • Participación ciudadana: ONG, asociaciones… • Personajes destacados del mundo hispano (I)	• Recursos para atenuar opiniones, creencias y afirmaciones: *Creo que no debemos…, Me parece que no es bueno…*	• Diptongos e hiatos
• Los medios de comunicación: prensa, radio, televisión, Internet…	• Los medios de comunicación • Las bibliotecas vivientes	• Modalizadores atenuantes de las aserciones (*quizás, puede que…*) • Expresiones de deseo en situaciones de comunicación estereotipadas • La expresión de advertencia con *que* + subjuntivo • La expresión de deseo con *A ver si…* y sus matices de curiosidad y expectación	
• Palabras y expresiones relacionadas con el amor y la amistad	• El concepto de la amistad en España.	• Tratamiento amoroso	• Puntuación (I): el uso de la coma (,)
• Lugares representativos del mundo hispano: la avenida Corrientes (Buenos Aires), El Malecón de la Habana (Cuba); • Ciudades declaradas Patrimonio de la Humanidad por la Unesco: Cáceres, Salamanca, Potosí… • Léxico sobre espacios urbanos	• Acontecimientos relevantes de los países hispanos: Festival de los Patios Cordobeses en mayo; Feria de Abril en Sevilla; Fiesta del Fuego en Santiago de Cuba; El día de los Muertos en México…	• Marcadores justificativos: *como, es que…* • Conectores aditivos: *sobre todo, además…* • Elementos discursivos causales: *pues, cómo es que, ¿Y eso?* • Conectores consecutivos: *así que, por lo tanto* • Interjecciones: *¡Ajá!, ¡Eh!, ¿Eh?*	• Puntuación (II): el punto (.) y el punto y coma (;)
• Expresiones con *ser* relacionadas con la personalidad	• Personajes famosos del mundo hispano (II)	• Expresiones exclamativas con carácter superlativo: *¡Vaya…!, ¡Menudo/a…!* • Los sufijos aumentativos *-on, -ona, -azo, -aza*	• Marcas del estilo directo: las comillas («») • Abreviaturas de uso frecuente

Unidad 1
De viajes, historias y cuentos

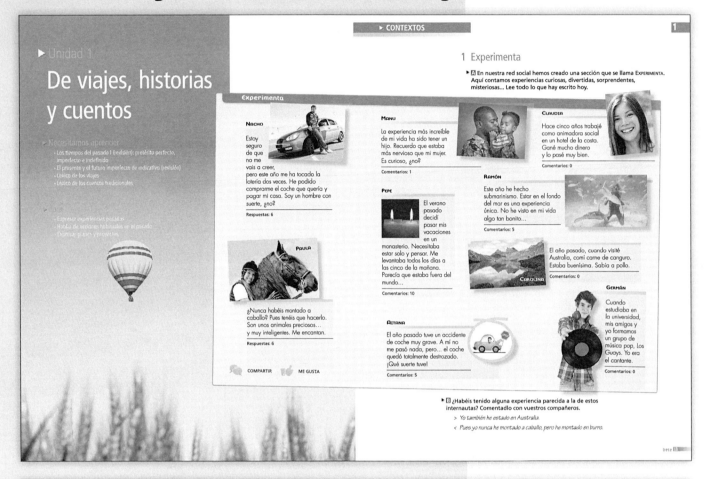

OBJETIVOS DE LA UNIDAD

En esta unidad repasamos contenidos ya estudiados en los niveles anteriores y que son esenciales para continuar el proceso de enseñanza-aprendizaje, ahora en un nivel más avanzado y con una perspectiva más amplia.

Las **funciones comunicativas** que abordaremos son: hablar de temas cotidianos, pedir y dar información general, expresar gustos y preferencias, expresar experiencias pasadas, narrar hechos del pasado, hablar de acciones habituales en el pasado y referirse al futuro.

Para ello, los alumnos deberán emplear unos **contenidos morfosintácticos** relacionados con los pasados de indicativo (revisión del uso y de la forma), con el contraste entre los tiempos de pasado y con la revisión del futuro simple.

En cuanto a los **contenidos léxico-semánticos**, repasamos y ampliamos los recursos para describir y narrar y, además, abordamos el léxico relacionado con los viajes y con los cuentos tradicionales.

Como **contenidos socioculturales** tratamos los referidos a los viajes; asimismo, reflexionaremos sobre los conceptos de *turista* y de *viajero*, aportando diferentes puntos de vista y estableciendo las semejanzas y diferencias con la propia experiencia de los alumnos. Por otro lado, abordaremos el tema de los cuentos tradicionales como manifestación de la identidad cultural en la que los alumnos están inmersos y como fórmula para procurar el conocimiento y el intercambio entre las culturas presentes en el aula.

Los **contenidos pragmáticos** en los que haremos hincapié son aquellos que tienen que ver con los organizadores del discurso para narrar hechos en el pasado.

CONTEXTOS

1 Experimenta

El objetivo de este bloque es la presentación de uno de los contenidos fundamentales de la unidad: el uso del pasado de indicativo, insistiendo en el contraste entre el pretérito imperfecto y el pretérito indefinido que, como es sabido, ofrece una especial dificultad para el alumno extranjero. Además, con la primera actividad, enfrentamos a los estudiantes a un formato que conocen y con el que, sin duda, están familiarizados: una red social.

A. En esta primera actividad haremos ver a nuestros alumnos que nos encontramos con una serie de comentarios o mensajes escritos por los miembros de una red social en la sección EXPERIMENTA. Antes de comenzar con la lectura, les preguntaremos cuál es la razón del nombre de la sección, por qué creen que se llama así. Después de oír sus opiniones, explicaremos que algunos de sus miembros acaban de escribir sobre experiencias muy distintas.

A continuación, pasaremos a la lectura de los mensajes y aclararemos las posibles dudas de vocabulario. Sería conveniente decirles que se presentan formas del pasado de indicativo que ya han estudiado en otros niveles. El objetivo es chequear o revisar la morfología y el uso de dichas formas verbales.

B. Proponemos, para que el alumno pierda la timidez inicial de los primeros días del curso, comenzar contando como ejemplo una experiencia propia.

Solución

Respuesta libre.

Sugerencia

La fase B de la actividad podría realizarse en parejas. Cada miembro toma nota de todas las experiencias del compañero que sean similares a las de la sección anterior y, a continuación, las comparte con el resto de los grupos. Si algún alumno no tiene ninguna coincidencia, se le pedirá que cuente, en plenaria y de forma oral, una experiencia divertida que vivió en su país antes de comenzar este curso.

Como actividad para revisar las tres formas del pasado de indicativo, proponemos que cada estudiante escriba sobre una experiencia divertida, buena, mala, interesante, curiosa…, que haya tenido. El profesor recogerá las composiciones, las repartirá de forma aleatoria y, por último, cada alumno leerá la que le ha correspondido. Voluntariamente se presentará el autor del escrito.

En cuanto al agrupamiento en parejas, una sugerencia importante es la siguiente: esta forma de trabajo no les gusta a todos los estudiantes, y una de las razones que exponen es que, aunque practican más la lengua, se quejan de que no son siempre corregidos por el profesor que, lógicamente, no puede atender a todos los grupos y estar presente en todos los momentos de la interacción. Por ello, después del trabajo en parejas, creemos necesario que se realice la misma práctica con el profesor.

2 La vivencias de…

Este bloque está concebido para contribuir a crear un clima de confianza y familiaridad que fomente las relaciones afectivas entre los miembros del grupo ya que acabamos de empezar el curso. Si conocen mejor a sus compañeros, los estudiantes superarán inhibiciones y posibles barreras en la interacción en clase.

A. Pediremos a los alumnos que se agrupen por parejas para realizar esta primera fase de la actividad y les explicaremos que se trata de anotar algunas experiencias vitales del compañero. Tendrán que utilizar los tiempos del pasado que ya conocen; así que les servirá para recordar sus formas y su uso. Si se cree conveniente, el profesor también podría interactuar con cada grupo, mientras los alumnos realizan esta parte, haciéndole preguntas: *¿Con quién fuiste? ¿Dónde has estado? ¿Cuándo lo compraste? ¿Habéis tenido experiencias similares?...*

B. Por último, solicitaremos que cada estudiantes intervenga hablando sobre una de las experiencias del compañero, la que prefiera o le parezca más interesante. Debemos animarlos a que expliquen las razones de su elección.

DE VIAJES, HISTORIAS Y CUENTOS

Sugerencia

Esta actividad nos puede servir para romper el hielo y que los alumnos vayan conociéndose y creando el clima de confianza y familiaridad necesario para un desarrollo adecuado del proceso de enseñanza-aprendizaje en grupo.

Para darle un carácter más lúdico sugerimos que, en plenaria, elijamos a las personas que tienen las experiencias más divertidas, afortunadas, inolvidables…

Solución

Respuesta libre.

OBSERVA, APRENDE Y RECUERDA

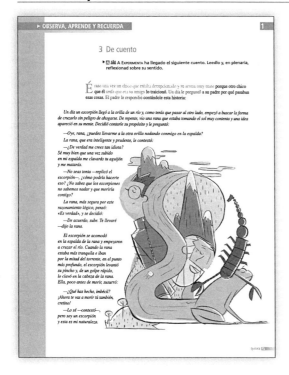

3 De cuento

En este bloque avanzaremos en el proceso de acercamiento del alumno a uno de los contenidos morfosintácticos fundamentales de la unidad: el uso y el contraste entre el pretérito indefinido y el pretérito imperfecto.

La aproximación y revisión de dichos contenidos las realiza el propio estudiante de una manera inferencial y en uso: a partir de la observación de estos hechos lingüísticos en contextos reales (los cuentos populares y la narración de un viaje).

A. En esta primera secuencia comenzamos explicando a los alumnos que vamos a leer un cuento tradicional que han enviado a la sección EXPERIMENTA. Antes de su lectura, podemos preguntar a los estudiantes si en sus países existen cuentos tradicionales, cuáles son los más populares y si conocen alguno de otro país.

Una vez superada esta fase de acercamiento a uno de los ámbitos temáticos que vertebran la unidad, los alumnos leerán el texto.

Finalmente, aclararemos las posibles dudas léxicas y llamaremos su atención para que reflexionen sobre la moraleja o la enseñanza que presenta el cuento. Se puede abrir una ronda de intervenciones para que cada alumno exponga su idea.

NOTAS

OBSERVA, APRENDE Y RECUERDA

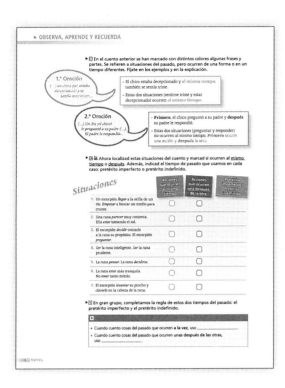

B. Comenzamos con el proceso inferencial de construcción del significado con la reflexión de los alumnos sobre los usos de los pretéritos indefinido e imperfecto en el texto previo. Animaremos a que se fijen en las partes del cuento que hemos marcado y en las explicaciones sobre el uso de uno u otro pasado.

Elegiremos a dos estudiantes para que cada uno lea el ejemplo y la explicación correspondiente.

A y B.

Solución

Respuesta libre.

C. Trabajamos en parejas. Continuando con la fijación de las reglas de uso, queremos que cada pareja localice en el cuento las situaciones propuestas en la tabla, que marque si se trata de acciones que ocurren al mismo tiempo o, por el contrario, una después de la otra y, a continuación, que identifique la forma de pasado que debe usarse en cada caso.

Solución

Acciones que ocurren una después de la otra: Pretérito indefinido: 1. 3. 5. y 7.

Acciones que ocurren al mismo tiempo. Pretérito imperfecto: 2. 4. y 6.

D. Ahora pediremos al grupo que complete la regla de uso de los dos tiempos del pasado analizados: pretérito indefinido y pretérito imperfecto. Se trata de que el estudiante llegue, mediante la reflexión metalingüística, a la sistematización y formulación de las reglas gramaticales.

Solución

Cuando cuento cosas del pasado que ocurren a la vez, uso el <u>pretérito imperfecto</u>.

Cuando cuento cosas del pasado que ocurren unas después de las otras, uso el <u>pretérito indefinido.</u>

OBSERVA, APRENDE Y RECUERDA

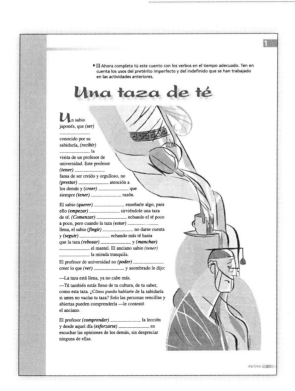

E. Para finalizar el bloque, proponemos un ejercicio de refuerzo de las formas verbales revisadas y presentadas en contexto. Los alumnos completarán el cuento popular *Una taza de té* con el tiempo adecuado. Recomendamos que el estudiante trabaje individualmente y, posteriormente, se realice una puesta en común. Debemos advertirlos de que han de prestar atención a los verbos irregulares.

Sugerencia

A propósito de esta práctica se podría hacer una revisión de los verbos irregulares en pretérito indefinido a partir de las propuestas de los alumnos. Hacemos hincapié en los irregulares en indefinido porque, sin duda, son el grupo más amplio y, además, presentan una mayor dificultad en su aprendizaje.

Solución

era - recibió - tenía - prestaba - creía - tenía - quiso - empezó - Comenzó - estaba - fingió - siguió - rebosó - manchó - tenía - podía - veía - comprendió - se esforzó.

DE VIAJES, HISTORIAS Y CUENTOS

OBSERVA, APRENDE Y RECUERDA

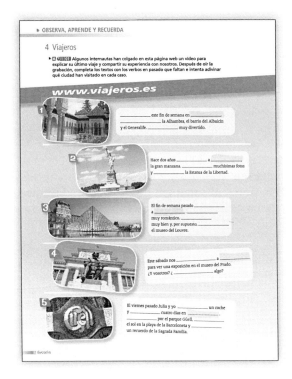

4 Viajeros

A. Esta actividad es la primera de las relacionadas con el ámbito temático de los viajes y con ella centraremos la atención de los alumnos, por un lado, en el contraste entre el pretérito perfecto y el indefinido y, por otro, en la revisión y ampliación de los usos del pretérito imperfecto de indicativo.

Comenzaremos por preguntar a los estudiantes qué les sugiere la palabra que da título al bloque temático. Después de que expongan en plenaria sus ideas y comentarios, iniciaremos el desarrollo de las distintas fases del ejercicio.

En primer lugar, les diremos a los estudiantes que hemos encontrado una página web donde algunos internautas han colgado un vídeo y han escrito sobre sus viajes.

A continuación, explicaremos que van a oír una grabación en la que cada viajero habla sobre su visita a una ciudad del mundo. Tendrán que completar los textos con los verbos en pasado que faltan y averiguar, según las pistas de la audición, el lugar que ha visitado cada persona.

Si fuera necesario, comentaremos que se trata de verbos en pretérito perfecto o en indefinido. Después de la audición, haremos una puesta en común.

Solución

1. Hemos estado - **Granada** - Hemos visto - Ha sido.
2. fuimos - **Nueva York** - Hicimos - vimos.
3. viajamos - **París** - Fue - Comimos - visitamos.
4. hemos marchado - **Madrid** - Habéis hecho.
5. alquilamos - pasamos - **Barcelona** - Paseamos - tomamos - compramos.

Sugerencia

Para provocar la interacción en el grupo, preguntaremos si han visitado las ciudades mencionadas, cuándo las han visitado, quién o quiénes no lo han hecho todavía, cuándo les gustaría ir...

Si hubiera estudiantes de diferentes nacionalidades, podrían comentar a qué ciudades de los países de sus compañeros han viajado, a cuáles no lo han hecho y cuáles querrían conocer.

NOTAS

OBSERVA, APRENDE Y RECUERDA

Resolveremos las posibles dudas referidas al léxico o al contenido morfosintáctico que practicamos.

Solución

1. has llegado.
2. Nací.
3. he perdido / perdí.
4. Estuve / He estado.
5. Has hecho.
6. Has visitado.

Sería recomendable mencionar que en algunas zonas de España e Hispanoamérica se usa de forma distinta el pretérito perfecto, o a veces incluso no se usa y en su lugar se prefiere el pretérito indefinido.

Sugerencia

A partir de las situaciones 1, 5 y 6, el profesor animará a los alumnos a que, en plenaria, respondan a las preguntas. De esta forma, contextualizaremos aún más los ejemplos de uso de estos dos pretéritos y afianzaremos este contenido.

NOTAS

B. Ahora los alumnos clasificarán los verbos en pasado de la actividad anterior en la columna correspondiente.

Solución

Pretérito perfecto: hemos estado - hemos visto - ha sido - habéis hecho.

Pretérito indefinido: fuimos - hicimos - vimos - viajamos - fue - comimos - visitamos - alquilamos - pasamos - paseamos - tomamos - compramos.

C. En esta parte se completa la regla de uso de los dos pasados que estamos trabajando.

Solución

Cuando el hecho del que hablo está relacionado con el tiempo en el que hablo, se utiliza el pretérito perfecto.

Cuando el hecho del que hablo NO está relacionado con el tiempo en el que hablo, se utiliza el pretérito indefinido.

D. Para asegurarnos de que han comprendido la diferencia entre estos dos tiempos del pasado de indicativo, proponemos una serie de situaciones en las que deberán marcar la posibilidad correcta.

Pediremos a los alumnos que, en primer lugar, resuelvan la actividad de forma individual y, finalmente, haremos una puesta en común.

DE VIAJES, HISTORIAS Y CUENTOS

OBSERVA, APRENDE Y RECUERDA

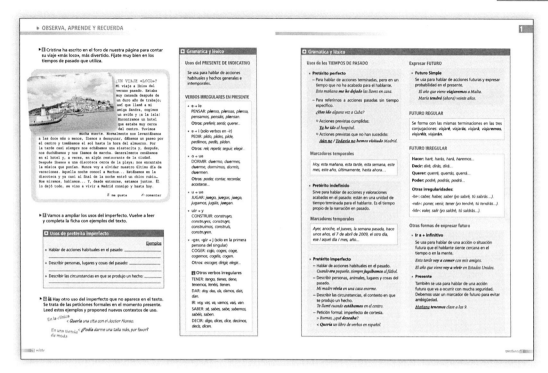

E. En esta fase pretendemos que los alumnos chequeen los usos del pretérito imperfecto de indicativo, ya estudiados en el nivel anterior, y el contraste con el pretérito indefinido sobre el que habíamos reflexionado en la actividad 3.

Hemos presentado estos contenidos en un contexto real y cercano al ámbito del estudiante, a través de un mensaje a un foro en el que la protagonista cuenta su viaje «más loco». Creemos que el hecho de narrar un viaje ameno y divertido incorpora un carácter lúdico necesario para el aprendizaje de los contenidos que estamos trabajando.

Para empezar, los estudiantes leerán la narración de Cristina y resolveremos las dudas de vocabulario que se les planteen. Antes de la lectura, insistiremos en que presten atención a los verbos en pasado que se utilizan.

Para finalizar, podríamos preguntar qué tiempos del pasado se han usado y con qué funciones; así promoveremos la revisión de los que ya conocen o debieran conocer, y la presentación de los que no recuerden o no hayan aprendido todavía.

F. Pediremos que, entre todos, recuerden la regla que habíamos visto en la actividad 3 sobre la diferencia de uso entre el indefinido y el imperfecto.

A continuación, explicaremos que en el texto del viaje «loco» de Cristina teníamos usos del pretérito imperfecto que habían aprendido en el nivel A2. Ahora, de forma individual, se concentrarán en completar la ficha con ejemplos del texto que ilustren estos usos.

Pasados unos minutos, el profesor hará una puesta en común para que compartan lo que han escrito.

Si se cree necesario, se pueden escribir las soluciones en la pizarra para aclarar las posibles dudas en torno a cuestiones como la morfología o el uso del imperfecto.

Solución

Hablar de acciones habituales en el pasado: *Nos levantábamos a las doce más o menos; íbamos a desayunar; dábamos un paseo por el centro; tomábamos el sol; nos echábamos una siestecita; nos duchábamos; nos íbamos de marcha; cenábamos en el hotel o en algún restaurante de la ciudad; bailábamos hasta las cuatro o las cinco de la madrugada.*

Describir personas, lugares y cosas del pasado: *Estaba muy cansada de un duro año de trabajo; (...) un hotel que estaba muy cerca del centro; nos encantaba la música...*

Describir las circunstancias en que se produjo un hecho: *Estábamos en la discoteca y...*

Sugerencia

Los alumnos podrían organizarse en parejas y escribir nuevos ejemplos para cada uno de los usos del pretérito imperfecto incluidos en la ficha.

Si logramos que partan de sus propias experiencias y les proponemos que incluyan en las frases a personas del grupo, intentando ser imaginativos, garantizaremos el desarrollo de la función lúdica en el proceso de aprendizaje y lograremos su implicación plena en la tarea.

G. Introducimos un nuevo uso del pretérito imperfecto que no aparece en el texto del ejercicio E: el imperfecto en las peticiones formales, también conocido como imperfecto de cortesía.

Partiremos de la lectura de las situaciones propuestas, haciendo que los alumnos reflexionen sobre la nueva función de este tiempo pasado. Posteriormente, dividiremos la clase en parejas y las animaremos a que escriban nuevas situaciones con este uso del tiempo verbal. Cuando todos los grupos hayan terminado, se realizará una lectura de los diálogos en la que el profesor corregirá los posibles errores. Si las características del grupo lo permitieran, realizaríamos la fase de elaboración de los ejemplos de forma oral. A continuación, proponemos una posible respuesta.

Solución

Posible respuesta

En un bar:
\> Buenos días, quería un café solo, por favor.
\< Ahora mismo.

En un hotel:
\> Necesitaba reservar una habitación doble para el próximo fin de semana. ¿Puede ser?
\< Sí, sí, por supuesto.

En una frutería:
\> ¿Qué quería?
\< Quería un kilo de tomates, de los maduros. Gracias.

PRACTICA

A. Presentaremos los perfiles en una red social de Ángel y Mirta, nuestros dos protagonistas.

Comentaremos a los alumnos que ambos forman pareja, aunque tienen intereses y personalidades muy diferentes.

A continuación, los animaremos a que lean los datos de cada perfil y aclararemos las dudas con respecto al léxico.

Con toda la información que saben, los estudiantes podrán comentar, usando el presente de indicativo, las semejanzas y diferencias entre ambos miembros de la pareja y, además, las cosas que tienen en común con ellos.

Se trata de orientar la actividad hacia la práctica oral del presente de indicativo, partiendo de una muestra de lengua escrita cercana a la realidad con la que está familiarizada el estudiante y con el objetivo de desarrollar sus habilidades comunicativas.

Solución

Respuesta libre.

5 Una historia de amor

La sección se abre con una actividad que plantea chequear la morfología y los usos fundamentales del presente de indicativo.

En un primer momento, podemos pedir a los alumnos que imaginen, según el título, de qué trata el ejercicio, de qué hablará…

DE VIAJES, HISTORIAS Y CUENTOS

PRÁCTICA

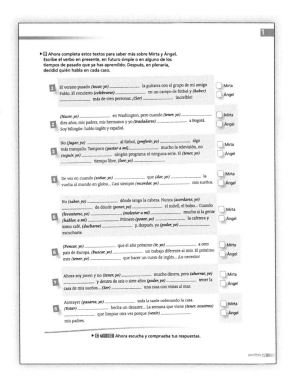

B. En esta fase volveremos sobre los tiempos del pasado ya practicados y el presente de indicativo, haciendo especial hincapié en las formas irregulares y pronominales. Añadiremos la revisión y refuerzo del futuro simple de indicativo.

Se trata de un ejercicio centrado en las formas lingüísticas y dirigido a afianzar la morfología y el uso de estos tiempos de indicativo.

Propondremos a los estudiantes que completen los textos para conocer más datos de la vida de Ángel y Mirta.

Aclararemos que se podrá usar el presente de indicativo, un tiempo del pasado (pretérito perfecto, indefinido e imperfecto) y el futuro simple de indicativo.

Pasado el tiempo que creamos necesario para la realización de esa parte individual y tras la puesta en común posterior, los alumnos decidirán a qué miembro de la pareja pertenece cada texto y justificarán sus razones de forma oral.

Solución

1. toqué - se celebró - había - Fue.

2. Nací - tenía - nos trasladamos.

3. juego - prefiero - me gusta - sigo - tengo - leo.

4. sueño - doy - recuerdo.

5. sé - me acuerdo - pongo - me levanto - me molesta - me habla - pongo - me ducho - puedo.

6. Pienso - iré / voy a ir - buscaré / voy a buscar - tendré / voy a tener.

7. tengo - ahorraré / voy a ahorrar - podré - Será.

8. pasé - estaba - tendremos - vendrán / van a venir.

¿Quién habla?

1. Habla Ángel porque una de sus pasiones es la música y es muy creativo.

2. Habla Mirta porque es de Colombia.

3. Habla Ángel porque es muy casero. Le gusta mucho hacer actividades en casa y leer.

4. Habla Ángel porque le encanta soñar y es muy idealista.

5. Habla Mirta porque es muy despistada. Habitualmente no recuerda dónde pone las cosas.

6. Habla Ángel porque dice que no le gusta mucho su trabajo. Además necesita un curso de inglés y no puede ser Mirta porque el inglés es su lengua materna.

7. Habla Mirta porque su sueño, su proyecto, es comprarse una casa maravillosa.

8. Hablan los dos. Mirta porque ella es más perfeccionista que Ángel y podemos suponer que es perfeccionista en todo, también en la limpieza y el orden de la casa, y Ángel porque es muy casero y le gustará tener la casa limpia.

C. Una vez presentadas sus opiniones en plenaria, escucharemos la grabación de Mirta y Ángel para que comprueben si han escrito los verbos de los textos en la forma adecuada y, por otra parte, si sabían la persona que hablaba en cada caso.

Posteriormente, podemos reflexionar en plenaria sobre los errores cometidos.

Sugerencia

Para darle un sentido más lúdico a esta última fase del ejercicio y, sobre todo, para hacer ver al alumno que el error debe ser entendido como un paso más en el proceso de aprendizaje, sugerimos que, una vez completados los textos, sean los alumnos los que corrijan entre ellos sus respectivas producciones de acuerdo con las soluciones de la grabación.

PRACTICA

7. Hablamos de…

Estamos ante una actividad orientada a reforzar la práctica del contraste entre el pretérito perfecto y el indefinido, en este caso de forma semidirigida.

Presentamos una serie de opiniones o reflexiones escritas en pasado y, en parejas, los alumnos deberán imaginar la situación con la que podrían relacionarse. Antes de empezar recomendamos que se lean todas las oraciones para solucionar los problemas de vocabulario.

A continuación, daremos algunos minutos para que cada pareja prepare las situaciones y las animaremos a que lo hagan con imaginación.

Finalmente, compartirán las experiencias que han escrito con los demás y se corregirán los errores.

Sugerencia

Si lo cree conveniente propondremos nuevos recuerdos para que los estudiantes los compartan en gran grupo.

Podemos hacer un turno final de preguntas de manera que los alumnos decidan qué pareja ha imaginado las mejores vacaciones, el verano más horrible, la noche menos divertida, etcétera.

Además, el profesor podría añadir nuevas cuestiones orientadas a la práctica y el refuerzo de otros contenidos morfosintácticos de la unidad: el presente de indicativo y el futuro simple.

Para ello, guiaremos nuestras preguntas para que los alumnos usen dichas formas verbales, por ejemplo, preguntando:

¿Qué harás el próximo verano?, ¿Qué hacéis tus amigos y tú por la noche?, ¿Qué haces normalmente para no pasar un día aburrido?, ¿Cómo es tu fin de semana aquí?, ¿Es muy diferente tu fin de semana en tu país?, ¿Qué harás el próximo fin de semana?, ¿Tienes plan para esta tarde?

6 Me acuerdo de…

Con este ejercicio presentamos una práctica de refuerzo de los usos de los tiempos del pasado, de forma oral y con una propuesta menos dirigida y, por lo tanto, más libre para que los alumnos hagan memoria y comenten sus recuerdos en torno a una comida de la infancia, un olor, una prenda de ropa, un regalo, un juguete…

Esta actividad se construye teniendo muy en cuenta el componente afectivo y su eficacia en el proceso de enseñanza-aprendizaje.

Sugerencia

Podría ser especialmente productivo, para el desarrollo de la competencia comunicativa, sugerirles que recordaran a alguna persona importante de su pasado: su primer profesor, su mejor amigo de la escuela, un profesor del instituto, alguien de la pandilla del barrio, su primer amor…, incluso recuerdos concretos: qué merendaban de pequeños, a qué jugaban…

NOTAS

▶ DE VIAJES, HISTORIAS Y CUENTOS

PRÁCTICA

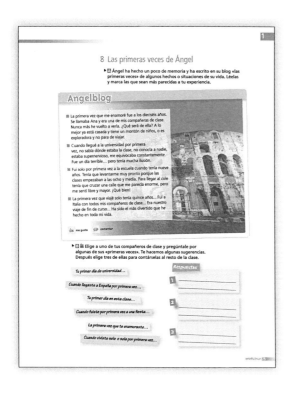

8 Las primeras veces de Ángel

Cerramos esta sección con dos actividades para practicar los tiempos del pasado integrando diversas destrezas.

Siguiendo con el ámbito temático de las experiencias pasadas, introducimos aquí el aspecto de la primera vez que se hace algo.

A. Explicaremos que Ángel ha publicado «las primeras veces» que ha hecho algo y algunas primeras experiencias de su vida. Después de leer el blog, los alumnos deberán marcar las experiencias que compartan con Ángel.

Sugerencia

Si hubiera algún estudiante que no coincidiera en nada con Ángel, le animaremos a que elija una de las situaciones, una de las «primeras veces», y le cuente su experiencia al resto de sus compañeros.

B. Ahora les pediremos que elijan a uno de sus compañeros para trabajar en parejas y conversar sobre las situaciones propuestas. Si se cree necesario, el profesor podrá interactuar con los grupos y hacerles algunas preguntas o comentarios. Los animaremos a que añadan otras primeras experiencias sobre las que les gustaría hablar. Por último, cada alumno elegirá tres para contárselas de forma oral al resto del grupo.

Sugerencia

Se han seleccionado en este ejercicio experiencias que nos parecen interesantes para comentar y que pueden resultar divertidas. Todavía estamos en la primera unidad del libro y, sin duda, este tipo de ejercicios ayuda a crear vínculos de familiaridad y afecto muy útiles en la práctica de las habilidades comunicativas. Fomentaremos la comunicación interpersonal que tan beneficiosa resulta en el proceso de aprendizaje del alumno.

EN COMUNICACIÓN

9 Ángel, amigos y familia

Abrimos esta sección con una primera actividad de expresión oral en la que se presentan los principales contenidos gramaticales de la unidad: el presente, los pasados y el futuro de indicativo.

A. Mostramos la cuenta de Facebook de Ángel, un personaje ya conocido por los alumnos. Explicaremos que ha colgado algunas «fotos» de su familia y amigos.

El objetivo de la actividad es que, fijándose detenidamente en las imágenes, los estudiantes completen los comentarios de Ángel.

Pueden hacer este ejercicio de forma oral o también, si el profesor lo cree oportuno, puede invitarlos a que pongan sus ideas primero por escrito para poder corregirlas luego en plenaria.

Solución

Posible respuesta

1. Este es mi amigo Pablo. Este verano en sus vacaciones ha estado en Londres. Ha visitado el Big Ben, Trafalgar Square, el museo Británico… También ha ido a la playa, ha estado en el pueblo de mis padres que está en la costa… Ha tomado el sol, ha ido a los bares de la playa…

2. Mirta, mi novia, no tiene una vida muy relajada… Todos los días se levanta muy temprano y coge el autobús para ir a la universidad. Tiene que estudiar mucho y, todas las tardes, va a la biblioteca y estudia durante dos o tres horas. Vuelve de la facultad a las seis más o menos y se acuesta a las doce y media porque, al día siguiente, tiene que madrugar.

3. Este es mi abuelo Paco. Murió el año pasado. Era granjero, así que tenía muchos animales. En su granja había gallinas, cerdos, etc. También tenía un huerto con árboles frutales donde cultivaba muchas verduras. Había tomates, lechugas, cebollas… Le encantaba el campo. Le gustaba mucho vivir allí porque la vida era más tranquila y relajada.

4. Laura es mi hermana favorita. El sábado que viene se marchará de España. Su avión sale o va a salir a las seis de la madrugada. En sus próximas vacaciones irá a trabajar a África. A mi hermana le encanta ayudar a los demás. Laura trabaja para Médicos Sin Fronteras y pasará sus vacaciones trabajando en un hospital infantil.

5. Estoy supercansado del trabajo. Esta noche no saldré / voy a salir de casa porque llueve. Estaré / Voy a estar tumbado en el sofá, dormiré / voy a dormir mucho, escucharé / voy a escuchar música, veré / voy a ver un rato la tele o alguna película en DVD.

6. A mi amiga Lola le encantan las exposiciones, el teatro, el cine, los conciertos… Con frecuencia va al cine, va al teatro, ve conciertos, asiste a exposiciones.

EN COMUNICACIÓN

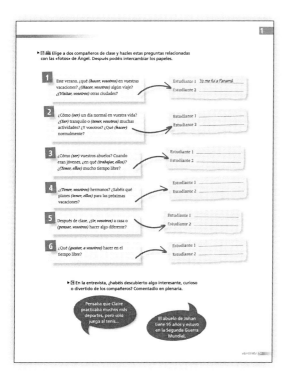

B. Después de organizar la clase en grupos de tres, invitaremos a los alumnos a mantener una conversación con los compañeros siguiendo las preguntas que se plantean.

Podemos pedir que anoten brevemente en el libro los resultados de su entrevista.

Solución

1. habéis hecho - Habéis hecho - habéis visitado.

2. es - es - tenéis - hacéis.

3. son - eran - trabajaban - tenían.

4. tenéis - tienen.

5. vais / vais a ir / iréis - pensáis.

6. os gusta.

C. Finalmente, los estudiantes presentarán en clase las conclusiones de sus entrevistas.

Cada alumno deberá elegir algunas de las informaciones que han averiguado de sus compañeros para explicárselas al resto del grupo.

Sugerencia

En plenaria, animaremos a los estudiantes a responder a esta serie de preguntas relacionadas con las entrevistas de la fase B para activar la práctica oral de los pasados, el presente y el futuro:

¿Qué persona de la clase ha pasado el mejor verano? ¿Quién tiene mejores planes para el próximo verano? ¿Qué persona de la clase organizará el mejor viaje para sus vacaciones? ¿Quién practica más deportes durante su tiempo libre? ¿Quién pasó las mejores vacaciones?

veintitrés

DE VIAJES, HISTORIAS Y CUENTOS

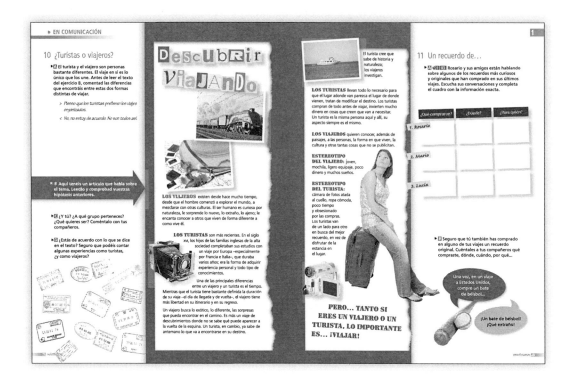

10 ¿Turistas o viajeros?

A. El bloque comienza con un intercambio de ideas en plenaria sobre los dos conceptos que dan título al mismo. Trataremos de conocer las opiniones de los alumnos y les instaremos a que comenten las diferencias que encuentran entre estas dos formas de viajar. Se puede hacer un listado en la pizarra de las ideas aportadas por los estudiantes.

B. Ahora invitaremos a los alumnos a que lean un artículo sobre el tema. A continuación, el profesor aclarará los problemas de vocabulario y, finalmente, en plenaria, cada alumno explicará si las ideas que había aportado en la fase anterior, en comparación con el texto, eran ciertas o no. En el artículo se han recuperado elementos léxicos relacionados con la temática de los viajes.

C. Proponemos una reflexión en plenaria sobre la forma de viajar preferida por el alumno. Los estudiantes podrían partir de la información que han leído y también de su propia experiencia.

D. Finalmente, podemos establecer un debate en torno al tema, teniendo en cuenta las reflexiones expuestas en el artículo y las opiniones de los alumnos a este respecto. Haremos hincapié en que justifiquen sus ideas. Para cerrar el bloque, comentarán en gran grupo algunas de sus experiencias como turistas o viajeros. Con ello trabajaremos los contenidos gramaticales de la unidad y el léxico relacionado con los viajes.

Solución

A. B. C. y **D.** Respuesta libre.

Sugerencia

Proponemos llevar a cabo una actividad que tenga como objetivo la reflexión de los estudiantes sobre los planes para sus futuras vacaciones. Cada alumno comentará en plenaria a qué país o a qué lugar viajará, con quién irá, qué cosas hará, qué visitará en ese destino escogido, etcétera.

11 Un recuerdo de…

A. Esta actividad de comprensión auditiva continúa con la línea temática que se abrió en el bloque anterior pero, en esta ocasión, nos centramos en los recuerdos que solemos comprar cuando visitamos alguna ciudad o algún nuevo destino.

Los alumnos escucharán la conversación de Rosario con sus amigos sobre los recuerdos que han comprado en sus últimos viajes y completarán el cuadro con la información que se solicita. Realizaremos dos escuchas para asegurar el éxito en la audición.

Solución

1. **Rosario:** Compró una botellita de vino dulce - En Málaga - Para su padre.
2. **Mario:** Compró una camiseta del Real Madrid - En Madrid - Para su hermano.
3. **Lucía:** Compró un sombrero mejicano - En Méjico - Para su marido.

Sugerencia

Siempre aconsejamos escuchar dos veces para hacer la actividad, pero una tercera audición con la transcripción delante para comprobar los resultados nos parece primordial. Es verdad que puede resultar repetitivo, pero son muchos los alumnos que demandan poder leer los textos al mismo tiempo que están oyendo la audición. Obviamente no es necesario llevarlo a cabo siempre, pero sí con regularidad.

B. Seguidamente, preguntaremos a los estudiantes si han comprado un recuerdo original en alguno de sus viajes y, si la respuesta es afirmativa, que comenten qué compraron, dónde, cuándo... Esta conversación relajada servirá de marco para contextualizar la audición.

Sugerencia

Si los alumnos son de diferentes nacionalidades, sugeriremos que expliquen a sus compañeros los recuerdos y los productos típicos que suele comprar la gente que visita su país. Si todos tuvieran la misma procedencia, podrían hablar de su región o de su ciudad. Los animaremos también a que, de forma distendida, comenten con sus compañeros si ya han comprado algún recuerdo típico del lugar donde estudian español.

¡extra! CONTEXTOS

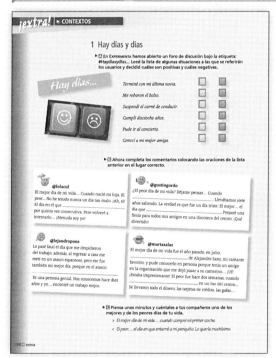

1 Hay días y días

A. y **B.** En esta secuencia retomamos el ámbito temático de las experiencias pasadas, el trabajo con los contenidos morfosintácticos fundamentales de la unidad y el formato textual con el que se abría: un foro.

Comenzaremos el bloque presentando el foro de opinión que se ha iniciado en EXPERIMENTA. Animaremos a los alumnos a que decidan si las situaciones propuestas por los internautas son positivas o negativas. Hemos incluido experiencias que, previsiblemente, son fácilmente clasificables. No obstante, si hubiera discrepancias, abriremos un debate al respecto.

Solución

A.
Posibles respuestas

Experiencias positivas: Cumplí dieciocho años - Pude ir al concierto - Conocí a mi mejor amiga.

Experiencias negativas: Terminé con mi última novia - Me robaron el bolso - Suspendí el carné de conducir.

B. @lolacul: suspendí el carné de conducir. **@lejandropons:** conocí a mi gran amiga. **@gustingordo:** terminé con mi última novia - cumplí dieciocho años. **@martasalas:** Pude ir al concierto - me robaron el bolso.

Sugerencia

Antes de empezar con la fase B de la secuencia, los estudiantes podrían compartir con sus compañeros alguna experiencia personal que fuera similar a las presentadas en la lista.

Después, de forma individual, los alumnos colocarán las oraciones del ejercicio en el comentario correcto. Seguimos la secuencia didáctica en torno a la práctica de los pasados, pero en este caso a través de la comprensión lectora. Sugerimos que, en primer lugar, compartan sus soluciones con alguno de sus compañeros, para fomentar el aprendizaje entre iguales y, posteriormente, en gran grupo.

C. Ahora se trata de que el alumno piense en su propia experiencia y recuerde el mejor y el peor día de su vida para contarlo en plenaria. Los animaremos a que, si fuera necesario, pregunten o pidan aclaraciones a sus compañeros sobre las historias que han contado.

Sugerencia

Si el profesor lo cree conveniente, puede proponer a los alumnos que presenten por escrito las dos experiencias.

DE VIAJES, HISTORIAS Y CUENTOS

¡extra! PRACTICA

2 Hans y sus problemas con el español

Tras las actividades de la sección PRACTICA, el alumno ya está suficientemente capacitado para llevar a cabo estos dos ejercicios que ponen fin a la revisión de los contenidos gramaticales de la unidad.

A. Para realizar este ejercicio correctamente, lo primero que se requiere es que los estudiantes lean el correo electrónico enviado por un alumno de español que tiene muchas dudas sobre el uso de los pasados de indicativo.

En un primer momento, cada alumno analizará de forma individual las situaciones propuestas y señalará la interpretación adecuada. Se corregirá en gran grupo y se aclararán las dudas que surjan.

Solución

1. A: cruzábamos.
   B: hemos cruzado.
2. A: sabía.
   B: he sabido.
3. A: llevamos.
   B: llevábamos.
4. A: volví.
   B: volvía.

3 Tú decides: ¿Por qué?

Esta actividad cierra el ciclo de chequeo y refuerzo de los contenidos gramaticales de la unidad con una práctica semidirigida de expresión e interacción orales.

Animaremos a que los alumnos respondan a una serie de preguntas usando la información que se aporta en los bocadillos y la forma verbal adecuada, advirtiéndolos de que puede haber más de una posibilidad.

Para ponerlo en práctica, se puede organizar al grupo por parejas: un alumno lee la situación y el otro responde. A continuación, se intercambiarán los papeles.

Si el profesor lo cree necesario, para revisar un determinado contenido, se pueden preparar nuevas situaciones.

Solución

Posibles respuestas

1. María aprendió chino y quiso empezar una nueva vida. En China tenía más posibilidades de trabajo / María ha aprendido chino y ha querido empezar una nueva vida. En China tenía más posibilidades de trabajo.

2. Nosotros éramos / somos muy diferentes. Paco siempre iba al fútbol con sus amigos. Terminamos el año pasado, discutíamos todo el tiempo y este año he empezado a salir con otro chico.

3. A Marcos no le gustaba estudiar, nunca aprobaba los exámenes y prefería trabajar.

4. No lo necesitaba. Vivía cerca del centro y el año pasado me compré una moto. Nunca me han gustado los coches.

NOTAS

¡extra! EN COMUNICACIÓN

4 Los viajes de los españoles

A. La actividad que abre esta última sección de la unidad se organiza en torno a un contenido sociocultural: los viajes de los españoles.

Explicaremos a los alumnos que los textos presentados ofrecen información sobre los españoles y sus preferencias a la hora de viajar.

Para comenzar, leerán en plenaria cada fragmento y aclararemos las posibles dudas léxicas.

A continuación, comentarán sus opiniones sobre las costumbres de los españoles y explicarán las similitudes y diferencias con las de sus países.

Sugerencia

Sugerimos completar la actividad con una práctica semidirigida de expresión escrita. Proponemos a cada alumno que elabore un pequeño informe sobre las costumbres de las personas de su país en torno a los viajes: destinos, motivación, preferencias... Si necesitaran datos para su realización, podrían consultar Internet.

B. Cerramos la actividad con un ejercicio de comprensión auditiva. Presentamos a cuatro españoles que explican sus experiencias negativas en algún viaje.

Antes de comenzar con la fase de escucha, animaremos a que los estudiantes cuenten, en plenaria, alguna mala experiencia en un viaje.

Seguidamente, oirán la audición y tomarán nota de todo lo que cuentan los cuatro protagonistas.

A continuación, pediremos que compartan con sus compañeros la información que han escrito para ver si están de acuerdo o no y, finalmente, el profesor dará la solución.

Sugerencia

Si se cree conveniente, volveríamos sobre las transcripciones para solventar todos los problemas léxicos. Asimismo, animaremos a los estudiantes con más dificultades a que realicen una lectura individualizada a fin de facilitarles la comprensión.

Solución

Posible respuesta

Lucas: Reservó una habitación en un hotel por Internet y cuando llegó al hotel no había ninguna reserva a su nombre.

Curra: Una noche en Londres salió sola porque sus amigos estaban muy cansados. Estuvo en un local de *jazz* y después se perdió en la ciudad.

Josefina: la compañía aérea le perdió las maletas y tuvo que comprarse todo lo que necesitaba. Todavía no ha recibido ninguna compensación económica de la compañía.

Ángel: Fue en un viaje de vuelta a España. Poco después de despegar el avión volvió a aterrizar porque no tenía combustible suficiente.

DE VIAJES, HISTORIAS Y CUENTOS

EXTRA COMUNICACIÓN

5 Un cuento diferente

A. Para finalizar la unidad, presentamos dos actividades que se relacionan con los cuentos tradicionales desde un planteamiento original. Están diseñadas teniendo en cuenta el aspecto lúdico y la participación activa del alumno. En esta ocasión queremos que, en parejas o en pequeños grupos, escriban un cuento en el que se incluyan todos los elementos que hemos propuesto. Para hacerlo, tienen los modelos del bloque 3.

Animaremos a que, si fuera posible, presenten la historia con ilustraciones. Terminado el proceso de escritura, pediremos a los estudiantes que pasen a la fase de lectura.

Aconsejaremos a los demás compañeros que interrumpan los relatos con las preguntas o aclaraciones necesarias.

Solución

Posible respuesta

Una vez el profesor de español tiró a la papelera un papel arrugado con anotaciones mientras explicaba los tiempos de pasado. Cuando terminó la clase y el profesor se fue, mi compañera y yo decidimos coger aquel papel arrugado.

Era el diario de su último viaje a Marruecos en verano en compañía de su hermana y su perro. Como visitó muchas ciudades, a mi compañera y a mí nos sirvió para nuestra redacción y puesta en práctica de los tiempos de pasado. Pero el profesor era más astuto que un zorro y pensó: «Seguro que algún estudiante lo recoge y lo utiliza».

Y así fue, pero todos los pasados estaban mal empleados y nosotros repetimos los mismos errores. Menuda vergüenza cuando nos tocó leer nuestra redacción. Cambiamos los nombres del país y de las ciudades pero no se nos ocurrió cambiar los pasados.

Nos hizo repetir la historia y nunca más olvidé cómo usar los tiempos de pasado.

B. Para llevar a cabo este segundo ejercicio, pedimos a los alumnos que hagan memoria y recuerden uno de los cuentos tradicionales de sus países.

Colocaremos a los estudiantes en círculo y les explicaremos que deben hacer de cuentacuentos y relatarnos el cuento. Así, promoveremos el intercambio y el conocimiento entre las culturas presentes en el aula.

Estamos seguros de que habrá coincidencias en el relato de todas esas historias tradicionales y, por tanto, sería interesante que las comentaran en gran grupo.

Sugerencia

Si el aula estuviera integrada por alumnos de diferente procedencia, la dividiremos por países y les pediremos que preparen una pequeña representación del cuento tradicional que hayan elegido.

En la primera sesión, escribirán los diálogos, decidirán quién encarnará a cada personaje, quién será el narrador, etcétera.

En la segunda sesión, cada grupo representará, como si se tratara de una obra de teatro, el cuento. Aprovecharemos para insistirles en la importancia de una correcta pronunciación, de la entonación, de los gestos...

Les sugeriremos a los estudiantes que introduzcan elementos originales en la creación de los diálogos y que intenten ser imaginativos.

Unidad 2
¿Te acuerdas de...?

OBJETIVOS DE LA UNIDAD

En esta segunda unidad revisamos los tiempos del pasado de indicativo (morfología y usos) ya trabajados previamente e introducimos el último de los tiempos del pasado de indicativo: el pretérito pluscuamperfecto.

Entre las **funciones comunicativas** que se abordarán en esta unidad están las referidas a la expresión del pasado y al relato de hechos ocurridos en ese marco temporal.

En cuanto a los **contenidos léxico-semánticos**, nos ocuparemos de los recursos que usamos para contar una anécdota y del campo léxico relacionado con Internet y las redes sociales, uno de los ámbitos temáticos sobre el que vertebramos la unidad.

Con relación a los **contenidos morfosintácticos**, partiremos de la presentación en contexto de una nueva forma verbal del pasado de indicativo: el pretérito pluscuamperfecto, para que el alumno, guiado por la secuencia didáctica, deduzca su morfología y sus usos, prestando especial atención a su relación con otros pasados, sobre todo con el pretérito indefinido. Asimismo, haremos hincapié en el contraste entre los cuatro tiempos pretéritos: perfecto, indefinido, imperfecto y pluscuamperfecto.

Como **contenido pragmático** incluimos los conectores discursivos para contar una anécdota, así como fórmulas para mostrar acuerdo o desacuerdo.

Por lo que respecta a los **contenidos socioculturales**, trataremos sobre la importancia de Internet y las redes sociales como nuevos recursos de comunicación.

Finalmente, los **contenidos fonéticos y ortográficos** se dedican a la revisión de los fonemas /g/ y /x/.

¿TE ACUERDAS DE...?

CONTEXTOS

1 Nuestra red social

Iniciamos una serie de actividades orientadas a la presentación en contexto de los contenidos lingüísticos de la unidad.

A. Presentamos al personaje de Malena, que se ha unido a *El libro de los amigos*. Aclararemos a los alumnos que, a través de esta red social, se ha reencontrado con una antigua amiga del instituto. Antes de empezar con la actividad propiamente dicha, podríamos preguntarles, en plenaria, si son miembros de alguna red social, de cuál se trata, para qué la usan y si se han encontrado alguna vez en una situación similar a la de nuestra protagonista: ¡contactar a través de una red social con un antiguo amigo!

A continuación, propondremos una lectura en plenaria de los mensajes de Malena y de su amiga, y aclararemos las dudas léxicas. Animaremos a los alumnos a que fijen su atención en que todos los mensajes están escritos en tiempos del pasado de indicativo que ya conocen, excepto el pretérito pluscuamperfecto en la penúltima intervención de Linda.

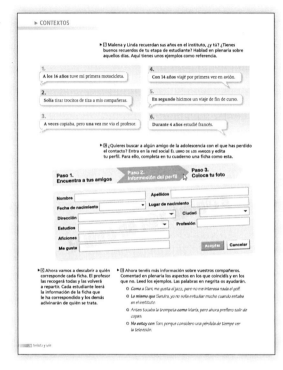

B. Para llevar a cabo esta segunda fase del ejercicio, queremos que los alumnos recuerden su adolescencia y su época de estudiante, como han hecho Malena y Linda. Se trata de una actividad de expresión oral para que, en plenaria, comenten sus recuerdos del pasado. Aunque hemos propuesto algunos ejemplos en las muestras de lengua, si el profesor lo cree conveniente, puede comenzar el ejercicio contando su propia experiencia. Estamos seguros de que esa iniciativa ayudará a los alumnos a superar cierta timidez al hablar de ellos mismos.

Sugerencia

En la actividad se han propuesto como ejemplos muestras de lengua relacionadas, sobre todo, con el ámbito académico; no obstante, si se cree conveniente, podrían añadirse nuevas que tengan que ver específicamente con el entorno personal (la familia o los amigos): *En el instituto conocí a mi mejor amigo / Con 14 años fui por primera vez de viaje con mis padres / Cuando estaba en el instituto, mi madre era muy estricta conmigo y no me dejaba salir por la noche...*

Solución

Respuesta libre.

C. La última fase se centra en un ejercicio de expresión e interacción escritas. Animaremos a los alumnos a que elaboren, en su cuaderno o en un folio aparte, una ficha como la del modelo propuesto en el libro, completándola con los datos indicados. Daremos unos minutos para que la rellenen y, a continuación, pediremos que la entreguen al profesor para comenzar con el punto D.

Solución

Respuesta libre.

D. Hacemos ahora una propuesta más lúdica: cada alumno leerá la información de la ficha que le ha correspondido, omitiendo el nombre, y los demás tendrán que adivinar de qué compañero se trata. Recomendamos que, cuando tengan claro de quién se trata, justifiquen sus hipótesis.

Solución

Respuesta libre.

E. Para terminar, ahora que los estudiantes ya tienen bastante información nueva sobre los compañeros de clase, haremos una puesta en común para que cada alumno exprese de forma oral sus coincidencias y diferencias con los demás. La ficha que habían completado en la fase C les permitirá hablar de aspectos relacionados con los ámbitos personal, profesional y educacional. Toda la actividad se organiza sobre la idea de que el conocimiento de los demás y las buenas relaciones ayudan a crear lazos afectivos en torno al nuevo idioma que se está aprendiendo y eso repercutirá en un mejor desarrollo del proceso de enseñanza-aprendizaje.

Sugerencia

Proponemos que todos los miembros de la clase, incluido el profesor, se inscriban en una de las múltiples redes sociales que existen en Internet y organicen un grupo para estar en contacto durante el curso o, si fuera posible, después de terminarlo. De esta forma, lograremos que los alumnos se comuniquen por escrito en un contexto cercano a su realidad. Los animaremos a que incluyan sus comentarios, escriban mensajes, hagan sugerencias sobre cualquier tema que les interese… De este modo, no limitan su práctica de la lengua únicamente a la dinámica del aula, sino que siguen mejorando su competencia comunicativa de una forma más libre, de acuerdo a sus motivaciones, gustos, preferencias… Con esta actividad complementaria trabajamos también la expresión escrita de una manera más dinámica y fluida, en un formato que manejan la mayoría de nuestros estudiantes y que les resulta especialmente atractivo.

Solución

Respuesta libre.

OBSERVA, APRENDE Y RECUERDA

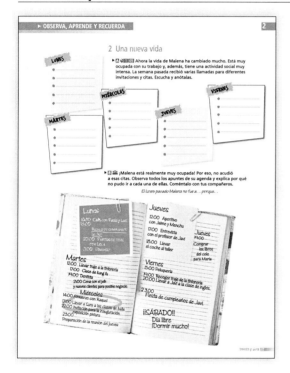

2 Una nueva vida

A. Para llevar a cabo esta actividad de comprensión auditiva, comentaremos a los estudiantes que vamos a oír varias llamadas con citas o invitaciones que recibió Malena, la protagonista de toda la sección. Debemos dejar claro que se trata de mensajes de la semana pasada. Haremos dos escuchas para que cada alumno, de forma individual, anote la información que haya oído. A continuación, tras la fase de audición, permitiremos que comparen sus datos con los de alguno de sus compañeros antes de realizar la puesta en común.

Solución

Lunes: fiesta de inauguración del bar de Pedro a las ocho.

Martes: cena con su padre a las nueve.

Miércoles: cine con Tomás a las diez.

Jueves: masaje de chocolate a las cinco.

Viernes: concierto de Marc Anthony a las once.

B. Como continuación del ejercicio anterior, los alumnos observarán los apuntes de la agenda de Malena y, de forma oral, explicarán por qué no acudió a las citas que le proponían. El profesor estará atento a las producciones y a corregir los errores que vayan surgiendo en el uso del pasado.

Sugerencia

Podemos presentar una actividad complementaria de expresión oral relacionada con la secuencia anterior: animaremos a los estudiantes a que hagan memoria y recuerden alguna cita importante a la que no acudieron; deberán explicar las razones por las que no lo hicieron. Les insistiremos para que usen las formas adecuadas del pasado y les pediremos que, cuando el compañero haya terminado, le hagan las preguntas o aclaraciones que consideren oportunas.

Si no recordaran ninguna historia, les ofreceremos algunas posibilidades: una cita romántica a la que no llegaron; la fiesta de cumpleaños de una persona importante en su vida a la que no acudieron; un examen importante que no hicieron; un avión, autobús, tren… que perdieron; una entrevista de trabajo a la que no fueron…

Solución

El lunes pasado Malena no fue a la fiesta de inauguración del bar de Pedro porque tenía partido de tenis con Lola.

El martes pasado Malena no fue a cenar con su padre porque tenía cena con su jefe y unos nuevos clientes.

El miércoles pasado Malena no fue al cine con Tomás porque estaba invitada a la inauguración de una exposición de pintura.

El jueves pasado Malena no se dio el masaje de chocolate porque tenía que hablar con el profesor de Javi.

El viernes pasado Malena no fue al concierto of Marc Anthony porque tenía la fiesta de cumpleaños de Javi.

¿TE ACUERDAS DE...?

OBSERVA, APRENDE Y RECUERDA

3 Miguel, «el experto»

Gran parte de esta sección va a desarrollarse en torno al trabajo inductivo de las formas y el uso del pretérito pluscuamperfecto de indicativo, que es el contenido gramatical nuevo de la unidad.

A. Comenzaremos con una actividad que continúa en la línea temática de los recuerdos de la adolescencia o la juventud: el viaje de fin de curso. Para iniciar esta secuencia didáctica, que nos llevará a la reflexión sobre la morfología del pretérito pluscuamperfecto, partimos de la lectura del texto. Como ejercicio previo, podemos preguntar a los alumnos si han realizado un viaje de este tipo, dónde fueron, qué hicieron... A continuación, leeremos el texto sobre Miguel y les pediremos que se fijen especialmente en las formas verbales que hemos marcado. Aclararemos las dudas léxicas.

B. En plenaria, los estudiantes tratarán de explicar cómo se forma el pretérito pluscuamperfecto de indicativo. Creemos que no resultará una tarea especialmente dificultosa, si tenemos en cuenta que ya tienen la referencia de la formación de otro tiempo compuesto, como es el pretérito perfecto de indicativo. Daremos algunos minutos para que expongan sus hipótesis.

Solución

El pretérito pluscuamperfecto se forma con el pretérito imperfecto del verbo *haber* + el participio.

C. A continuación, completarán la tabla según las conclusiones a las que han llegado en el ejercicio anterior. Aclararemos que hemos incluido algunos participios irregulares para revisarlos y reforzarlos. El profesor supervisará

OBSERVA, APRENDE Y RECUERDA

el trabajo y los ayudará durante el proceso, y, si es necesario, escribirá en la pizarra la morfología del verbo, insistiendo sobre todo en los participios irregulares.

Solución

Participio regular	Participio irregular
Yo había preparado	hecho - hacer
Tú habías estado	roto - romper
Usted había comido	abierto - abrir
Él / Ella había sido	muerto - morir
Nosotros / -as habíamos vivido	vuelto - volver
Vosotros / -as habíais salido	visto - ver
Ustedes habían querido	dicho - decir
Ellos / Ellas habían leído	puesto - poner

D. En esta fase trabajaremos con fragmentos de la muestra de lengua escrita del ejercicio 3A para ayudar a los alumnos a determinar, en contexto, el uso del nuevo tiempo de pasado que están aprendiendo. En un primer momento, de forma individual, el alumno leerá los ejemplos extraídos y marcará la respuesta correcta. Todas las situaciones y preguntas están orientadas a que el estudiante entienda el uso básico del pretérito pluscuamperfecto como expresión de una situación pasada anterior a otra también pasada.

Solución

1. Sí. **2.** Sí. **3.** Sí. **4.** No.

OBSERVA, APRENDE Y RECUERDA

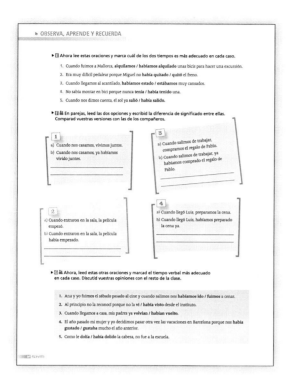

E. De nuevo chequeamos la comprensión del uso del pretérito pluscuamperfecto. Esta vez presentamos cinco situaciones referidas al texto del ejercicio 3A y los alumnos deberán elegir la forma verbal más adecuada en cada caso, discriminando distintos tiempos del pasado. Proponemos que, después del trabajo individual, se compartan los resultados en plenaria.

Solución

1. alquilamos; **2.** había quitado / quitó (en este caso *quitó* indica también una acción anterior a *era*); **3.** estábamos; **4.** había tenido; **5.** había salido.

F. Ahora trabajamos el mismo contenido, pero con nuevas situaciones. Así pues, esta actividad abre una fase de consolidación en el aprendizaje del uso del nuevo tiempo de pasado que los alumnos están aprendiendo, frente a otras formas que ya conocen. Animaremos a que, en parejas, analicen los cuatro pares de oraciones que hemos propuesto y determinen las diferencias de significado que encuentren. Finalmente, en gran grupo, comentaremos los resultados de cada pareja. Los ejemplos seleccionados ayudarán a que los alumnos entiendan la diferencia de significado que aporta el uso del pluscuamperfecto frente a otras formas pretéritas.

Solución

1. a) Primero se casaron y después vivieron juntos.
   b) Primero vivieron juntos y después se casaron.
2. a) Primero entraron a la sala y después empezó la película.
   b) Primero empezó la película y después entraron ellos.
3. a) Primero salieron de trabajar y después compraron el regalo.
   b) Primero compraron el regalo y luego salieron de trabajar.
4. a) Primero llegó Luis y luego prepararon la cena.
   b) Primero prepararon la cena y después llegó Luis.

G. Nueva práctica para consolidar el uso del pluscuamperfecto. En parejas deberán marcar el verbo adecuado en cada oración. Daremos un tiempo para terminar el ejercicio y, finalmente, los estudiantes expondrán las soluciones en plenaria. Insistiremos en que justifiquen cada una de sus elecciones.

Solución

1. fuimos (porque fueron a cenar después del cine).
2. había visto (porque entre el instituto y el encuentro no se vieron).
3. habían vuelto (la vuelta de los padres es anterior porque dice «ya»).
4. había gustado (porque dice «el año anterior»).
5. dolía (porque el hecho de doler la cabeza es simultáneo a la decisión de no ir a la escuela, no anterior). También sería correcto *había dolido* si se percibe como un hecho no simultáneo sino anterior a ir a la escuela.

NOTAS

¿TE ACUERDAS DE...?

H. Llegados a este punto, estamos seguros de que los alumnos habrán entendido plenamente los valores del pluscuamperfecto. No obstante, para chequear y reforzar dicho conocimiento, leeremos la ficha de uso de este tiempo verbal y los ejemplos correspondientes.

OBSERVA, APRENDE Y RECUERDA

4 Cuando cumplí los 18 años

El ejercicio está diseñado para que los alumnos observen las diferencias de uso entre el pretérito indefinido y el pretérito pluscuamperfecto en un contexto conversacional cercano a su realidad.

En primer lugar, antes de comenzar con la actividad propiamente dicha, sería necesario que aclarásemos que cumplir 18 años significa en muchos países, entre ellos España, pasar a la edad adulta; así que este se considera uno de los momentos importantes en la vida de una persona. Sería conveniente que los alumnos comentasen con cuántos años se alcanza la mayoría de edad en sus lugares de origen. Seguro que habrá diferencias culturales y sociales interesantes.

En segundo lugar, les pediremos que se fijen en los ejemplos y recordaremos que se ha usado el pretérito pluscuamperfecto para hablar de acciones anteriores a otras también pasadas. A continuación, los animaremos a que cuenten en clase todo lo que habían hecho, las experiencias que habían tenido, antes de cumplir los 18 años y, por otra parte, lo que hicieron después de cumplirlos. Esta fase de la actividad se desarrollará de forma oral. Si es necesario, dejaremos algunos minutos para que escriban las experiencias y, finalmente, las revisaremos en plenaria.

Sugerencia

Cada alumno compartirá con sus compañeros la experiencia de un cumpleaños que haya sido muy importante en su vida. Deberá explicar cómo lo celebró, qué hizo, quién asistió y, sobre todo, por qué lo recuerda como una fecha decisiva para su historia personal.

Solución

Respuesta libre.

OBSERVA, APRENDE Y RECUERDA

5 La fiesta del Vallesol

Cerramos la sección con una actividad que se relaciona, desde el punto de vista temático, con la que se abría la unidad. Se trata de antiguos alumnos de un colegio que celebran una fiesta para volver a encontrarse y saber de sus vidas.

A. En plenaria, leeremos la información sobre la vida de cuatro de esos antiguos estudiantes. Después, aclararemos las dudas de vocabulario y, posteriormente, propondremos que, en gran grupo, relacionen los textos con las personas del dibujo a las que creen que corresponden. Será necesario que justifiquen su elección. Si se considera conveniente, dejaremos algunos minutos para que los estudiantes piensen quién es quién y, pasado ese tiempo, permitiremos que comparen sus resultados con los de algún compañero antes de pasar a la puesta en común.

Solución

1. a; **2.** b; **3.** d; **4.** c.

34 treinta y cuatro

OBSERVA, APRENDE Y RECUERDA

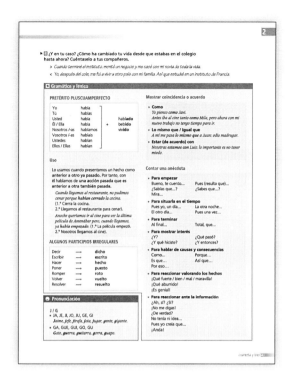

B. Para finalizar, cada alumno contará los cambios más interesantes de su vida desde que terminó el colegio hasta ahora. Insistiremos en que usen todas las formas del pasado que ya conocen y que hemos trabajado en niveles anteriores. Como estamos en la sección OBSERVA, APRENDE Y RECUERDA, el objetivo de esta actividad es recordar, chequear o revisar las formas y los usos de los pasados que han aprendido, aunque de una manera menos dirigida y a través de la práctica oral. Por ello, es recomendable que se aclaren las posibles dudas de uso y, sobre todo, que el profesor insista en la necesidad de utilizar correctamente todas las formas del pretérito.

Sugerencia

Dividiremos al grupo en parejas y les pediremos que hablen con una persona, fuera del ámbito de la clase, para conocer los cambios que se han producido en su vida desde que estaba en la escuela hasta ahora. Después de realizar la entrevista, presentarán sus conclusiones y comentarios al resto de los compañeros.

Solución

Respuesta libre.

PRACTICA

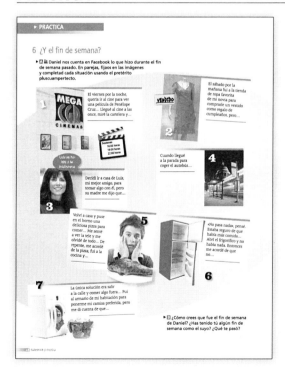

6 ¿Y el fin de semana?

A. Fijaremos la atención de los alumnos en las fotos que Daniel ha colgado en su cuenta de Facebook. Explicaremos que corresponden al fin de semana pasado. En parejas, teniendo en cuenta las imágenes, deberán completar los comentarios de Daniel con el verbo en el tiempo correcto (pretérito pluscuamperfecto). Recomendamos dejar unos minutos para el trabajo en grupo y, a posteriori, realizaremos la puesta en común.

A continuación, estableceremos un turno de palabra para que cada pareja compare sus respuestas con las del resto del grupo. El profesor corregirá los errores en la pizarra para que todos los alumnos los focalicen y los tengan en cuenta con el fin de evitarlos en el futuro.

Solución

1. … la película ya había empezado, porque era a las diez no a las once.
2. … el vestido ya se había vendido / ya habían vendido el vestido.
3. … se había ido a la biblioteca.
4. … ya había salido.
5. … la pizza se había quemado.
6. … había ido al súper a comprar comida.
7. … no había lavado la ropa.

B. Esta actividad de interacción oral tiene como objetivo que, en plenaria, los estudiantes vuelvan sobre la práctica de los contenidos gramaticales de forma más libre. Para ello tendrán que activar los contenidos que se muestran en la unidad, especialmente el pretérito pluscuamperfecto y el contraste entre los cuatro tiempos del pasado. Los alumnos intervendrán expresando su opinión sobre cómo fue el fin de semana de Daniel y comentando si, en alguna ocasión, les ha pasado algo similar.

¿TE ACUERDAS DE...?

Sugerencia

Si los alumnos son miembros de alguna red social, los animaremos a que comenten la historia de las últimas fotos o imágenes que han subido, hablando de dónde se las hicieron, quiénes aparecen en la foto, dónde estaban, con quién estaban, por qué han elegido esas y no otras...

Solución

Respuesta libre.

PRACTICA

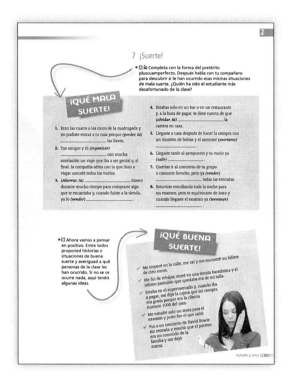

7 ¡Suerte!

A. En esta actividad se presentan situaciones consideradas de mala suerte y se propone una práctica formal sobre el pretérito pluscuamperfecto con una segunda parte de interacción oral.

Comenzaremos dividiendo la clase en parejas y explicando que hablaremos sobre experiencias en las que se reconoce haber tenido mala suerte. En un primer momento, los alumnos completarán las oraciones con la forma correcta del pretérito pluscuamperfecto y, en segundo lugar, hablarán con el compañero haciéndole preguntas para descubrir si ha vivido alguna situación similar.

A continuación, intercambiarán los papeles: uno pregunta y el otro responde. Después de esa fase de interacción oral, compartirán con el resto del grupo las experiencias desafortunadas que han descubierto del compañero.

En plenaria, elegiremos a los estudiantes con menos suerte. Tendrán que justificar su elección.

Solución

1. habías perdido.
2. habíais organizado.
3. habías ahorrado - habían vendido.
4. habías olvidado.
5. se había averiado.
6. había salido.
7. habían vendido.
8. había terminado.

B. Trabajamos en plenaria. Continuando con las experiencias personales, queremos que cada alumno piense en una situación de buena suerte que le ha ocurrido a él o a algún compañero y, a continuación, la cuente en plenaria. Los demás estudiantes podrán hacerle las preguntas o pedirle las aclaraciones que crean convenientes para, finalmente, decir quién creen que ha vivido esa situación. El objetivo lingüístico es la práctica de los pasados, pero no olvidemos que, al introducir un tema cercano, fomentamos también la interacción oral. En el caso de que los alumnos no recuerden ninguna experiencia, ofrecemos algunas sugerencias que seguramente provocarán el diálogo. El profesor puede aportar otras a la lista.

Sugerencia

Podemos animar a los alumnos a que redacten un texto escrito para explicar alguna de las experiencias de las que han hablado.

Solución

Respuesta libre.

NOTAS

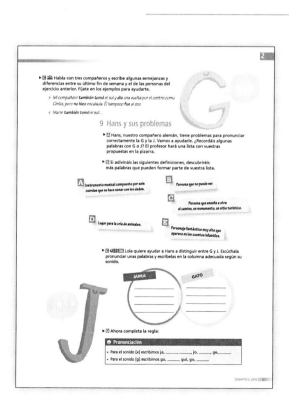

PRACTICA

8 El fin de semana de Martina

A. Como podemos observar, en la actividad se incluyen dibujos que explican cómo pasó Martina el fin de semana. Animaremos a los alumnos a que lo cuenten siguiendo la secuencia de las imágenes. A continuación, comentarán en gran grupo si les ha parecido divertido.

Solución

Posible respuesta

El fin de semana pasado Martina no salió de casa porque estaba lloviendo y había tormenta. Y además su gato estaba enfermo. Como estaba aburrida de leer, también escuchó música.

B. En la segunda fase, otras personas explican también cómo fue su fin de semana. Se trata de una actividad centrada en cómo los alumnos completan los huecos con la forma adecuada del pasado. Dejaremos algunos minutos para realizar esta primera parte de forma individual, antes de pasar a la corrección en plenaria. Es de gran utilidad que este bloque se haga en clase y que el profesor vaya observando la realización del ejercicio, resolviendo las dificultades que puedan surgir y aclarando las posibles dudas que se presenten.

Solución

Cintia: fuimos - habíamos estado - nos gustó - Tomamos - comimos - dimos.

Rocío: visitamos - Había - estaban - explicaron - era.

Iris: hicimos - nos quedamos - comimos.

Shanon: he probado - decidimos - había visto.

PRACTICA

C. Ejercicio de expresión e interacción oral y escrita que incide sobre el objetivo lingüístico de la práctica de los cuatro tiempos del pasado de indicativo. Animaremos a los alumnos a que hablen con tres compañeros para descubrir las semejanzas y diferencias entre su fin de semana y el de las personas de la actividad 8B. En un primer momento, deberán escribirlas y, posteriormente, presentarlas de forma oral en plenaria. Los instaremos a que relacionen ambas experiencias con las estructuras que hemos propuesto en el ejemplo: *también… / tampoco…*

Sugerencia

Propondremos a los alumnos que cuenten en gran grupo cómo ha sido su fin de semana para elegir el mejor y el peor de todos ellos. Podremos fomentar la imaginación de los estudiantes pidiéndoles que introduzcan en su historia algún hecho no real para que los demás compañeros tengan que adivinarlo.

Es importante que la actividad se haga en un ambiente relajado y distendido, ya que de esta forma conseguiremos un mejor aprovechamiento de esta y afianzaremos la seguridad del alumno en su producción oral.

¿TE ACUERDAS DE…?

9 Hans y sus problemas

En este ejercicio nos ocupamos de la fonética y la ortografía, y volvemos sobre la realización grafemática de los fonemas /x/ y /g/, que ya se habían trabajado en los niveles anteriores.

A. Pediremos a los alumnos que recuerden palabras que se escriben con *g* o *j*. El profesor hará una lista en la pizarra con todas sus propuestas.

Solución

Respuesta libre.

B. En esta fase los estudiantes deberán adivinar las palabras a las que corresponden cinco definiciones. Advertiremos que todas incluyen las letras *j* o *g*.

Solución

A. Guitarra. **B.** Ciega. **C.** Guía. **D.** Granja. **E.** Gigante.

C. En este ejercicio de audio los estudiantes tendrán que identificar sonidos y representarlos gráficamente. El alumno se enfrenta a las grafías *g* y *j*. La *g* para representar los sonidos [g] y [x] y la *j* para representar el sonido [x].

Solución

Jarra: ginebra, jamón, geranio, jefe, jirafa, rojo, genial, imaginación, gente, joven, girasol, jueves.

Gato: guerra, alguien, guapa, guitarra, algo, alguna, guantes.

D. Finalmente, completarán la regla de representación gráfica para los sonidos [x] y [g].

Solución

Para el sonido [x] escribimos **ja, je, ji, jo, ju, ge, gi.**

Para el sonido [g] escribimos **ga, gue, gui, go, gu.**

EN COMUNICACIÓN

10 Las redes sociales en Internet

Esta sección propone una reflexión en torno a las redes sociales y la revolución que suponen en el campo de la comunicación. Trataremos que los alumnos expresen su propio punto de vista sobre el tema y analicen posturas a favor y en contra.

A. La secuencia se abre con un ejercicio de comprensión lectora. Presentamos un texto que trata de la importancia de las redes sociales en la sociedad actual y de los aspectos positivos y negativos en el uso de esta nueva forma de comunicación. Antes de la lectura, podemos preguntar a los alumnos si han oído hablar de alguna red social importante en el mundo hispano.

Tras realizar la primera lectura en voz alta, es necesario que el profesor aclare las dudas que pueden haber surgido, o que pregunte a los estudiantes con el fin de conocer si han comprendido bien las ideas expuestas en el texto.

EN COMUNICACIÓN

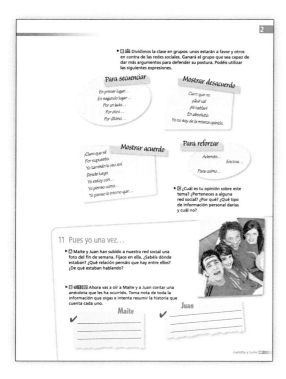

B. Una vez solventados todos los problemas léxicos y de comprensión, pasaremos a la siguiente fase del ejercicio. Dividiremos la clase en grupos para iniciar el debate sobre el tema: unos estarán a favor del uso de las redes sociales y otros en contra (también podemos formar dos grandes grupos y que cada uno defienda una postura). Elegiremos a los miembros de cada grupo de forma aleatoria. El profesor puede ejercer las labores de moderador para organizar y ordenar el debate. Cada equipo deberá defender su punto de vista con una argumentación bien fundamentada. Insistiremos en que usen las fórmulas para expresar acuerdo o desacuerdo, para secuenciar las ideas y para reforzar opiniones o contenidos.

C. La secuencia se cierra con un ejercicio de expresión oral en el que los estudiantes mostrarán su opinión sobre el tema. En plenaria, explicarán también si pertenecen a una red social y por qué. Además, si son miembros de alguna, comentarán qué tipo de información están dispuestos a dar y, desde su punto de vista, cuál no debería propiciarse. Perseguimos la práctica de los recursos para expresar opinión pero, en esta ocasión, de una manera más libre.

Sugerencia

Les propondremos a los alumnos, como actividad complementaria, la realización de una encuesta sobre el uso de las redes sociales en el lugar donde estudian español. En la primera sesión, dividiremos la clase en pequeños grupos y tendrán que preparar un cuestionario con unas 12 preguntas sobre el tema; pueden tratar aspectos como: la frecuencia de uso de las redes sociales, las razones para preferirlas a otro sistema de comunicación, ventajas e inconvenientes de su empleo, etc. Después de la recogida de datos, que se realizará fuera del aula, en la siguiente sesión pasaremos a la fase de la elaboración de conclusiones. Finalmente, en plenaria, los alumnos comentarán los datos más relevantes y significativos o los que más han llamado su atención.

11 Pues yo una vez…

Iniciamos una secuencia de actividades destinadas a fomentar la implicación del alumno en el tema de la unidad. Asimismo, para activar la práctica de las distintas destrezas comunicativas, trataremos de episodios anecdóticos que les hayan ocurrido a lo largo de su vida.

A. Pediremos a los alumnos que en plenaria describan la foto que han subido Maite y Juan a su red social favorita. Deberán comentar dónde creen que estaban, qué relación había entre ellos e imaginar de qué estarían hablando.

Solución

Respuesta libre.

B. Ejercicio de comprensión auditiva en el que Maite y Juan cuentan una anécdota. Haremos dos escuchas para que los alumnos entiendan bien lo que explica cada uno de los personajes y, después, puedan redactar un breve resumen. A continuación, expondrán sus resultados a los compañeros.

Solución

Posible respuesta

Maite: En el aeropuerto, saltó la alarma cuando pasó por el detector de metales.

Juan: En un bar, cuando fue a pagar, se dio cuenta de que no llevaba dinero.

NOTAS

¿TE ACUERDAS DE...?

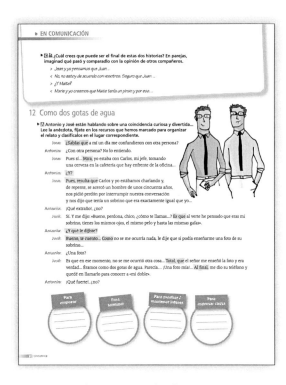

C. Después de organizar la clase en parejas, invitaremos a los estudiantes a que imaginen y escriban el final de las dos historias. Finalmente, cada grupo deberá leer su texto y establecer comparaciones con los finales de los demás.

Sugerencia

En plenaria podrían elegir qué grupo ha escrito el final más divertido.

12 Como dos gotas de agua

A. Actividad para la práctica de los recursos usados para contar una anécdota. En un primer momento, haremos que los estudiantes fijen su atención en la comparación que da título a la actividad. Les pediremos que especulen sobre su significado. Posteriormente, leeremos en plenaria la anécdota que José le cuenta a Antonio. Aclararemos las posibles dudas léxicas, y los alumnos tendrán que prestar atención a los recursos que hemos marcado en el texto. Explicaremos que sirven para contar una anécdota y, de forma individual, los clasificarán en su grupo correspondiente, según su función: para empezar, para terminar, para mostrar interés o para expresar causa... Después de esta fase individual, pasaremos a la puesta en común en gran grupo.

Solución

Para empezar: ¿Sabías qué...? - Mira... - Pues, resulta que... - Bueno, te cuento...

Para terminar: Total, que... - Al final...

Para mostrar / mantener interés: ¿Y? - ¿Y qué le dijiste?

Expresar causa: Es que... - Como...

B. Ahora, de forma individual, los alumnos deberán volver al texto para señalar las expresiones de sorpresa con las que Antonio reacciona a la historia de José. Comentaremos que este tipo de expresiones, además de sorpresa, pueden expresar sentimiento o incluso cierta valoración, como en el caso de *¡Qué casualidad!* A modo de conclusión, pueden comparar sus respuestas con las de algún compañero y, finalmente, las comentarán en plenaria y descubrirán la solución.

Sugerencia

Para concluir, sugerimos que, en gran grupo, los estudiantes cuenten si han tenido alguna experiencia parecida a la del texto, si alguien los ha confundido con otra persona, si creen que puede existir alguna persona físicamente idéntica a ellos...

Solución

¡Qué extraño! - ¡Qué fuerte!

C. En esta fase trataremos de que los estudiantes averigüen nuevos recursos para reaccionar ante una información y para expresar sentimientos. Agruparemos a los alumnos en parejas y les pediremos que vuelvan sobre el texto de la actividad 1A que abre la unidad. Les daremos tiempo para que escriban todos los recursos y, a continuación, compararán sus soluciones con las de los otros estudiantes.

Solución

Recursos para reaccionar ante una información: ¿Ah, sí? - ¡Anda! ¿De verdad?

Para expresar sentimientos: ¡Qué fuerte! - ¡Es genial! - ¡Qué bien! - ¡Qué gracioso! - ¡Madre mía ¡Cuánto tiempo! - ¡Fue increíble! - ¡Qué antipática era!

D. Actividad de expresión oral cuyo objetivo es que cada alumno narre una anécdota simpática, divertida, curiosa... que le haya ocurrido. Animaremos a los demás a que escuchen con atención y a que interrumpan a su compañero mostrando interés o reaccionando mientras cuentan la historia. Al final también podrán expresar sus sentimientos respecto a lo que se ha contado.

Sugerencia

Si se cree conveniente, pediremos a los estudiantes que, antes de contar la anécdota oralmente, la preparen por escrito. Luego cada alumno la presentará en plenaria.

¡extra! CONTEXTOS

Solución

María: la fiesta sorpresa para el cumpleaños.

Amelia: carnaval - disfrazamos.

Carla: excursión - era - bonita, muchísima gente guapa - comimos - pescadito.

Rodolfo: Nochevieja - salida - año - las uvas.

Raúl: musical - de miedo - bailar - espectáculo increíble.

B. Actividad de expresión e interacción orales en la que los estudiantes hablarán sobre recuerdos y momentos felices de su vida. Pediremos a cada alumno que charle con uno de sus compañeros y le pregunte acerca de ese momento de felicidad. Tras la conversación, compartirán el recuerdo con los demás.

Sugerencia

Para completar la actividad, podemos pedir a los alumnos que preparen por escrito sus experiencias para publicarlas en el blog de la escuela.

1 Una fiesta sorpresa

Este bloque se inicia con una actividad de comprensión auditiva para la revisión del uso de los tiempos del pasado.

A. En esta actividad los alumnos escucharán algunos recuerdos divertidos de los invitados a la fiesta que Maite y sus amigos le prepararon a Juan. Cada estudiante completará los huecos después de oír la grabación dos veces. Como en otras ocasiones, el profesor resolverá dudas y explicará ciertos significados que los alumnos no tengan claro, como puede ser el caso de *gente guapa* (personas famosas, de alta sociedad, *beautiful people*...). A continuación, cada alumno comparará sus resultados con los de sus compañeros y, finalmente, se comprobará que lo que han escrito es lo correcto.

NOTAS

¿TE ACUERDAS DE...?

¡extra! PRACTICA

2 Hans y sus problemas

De nuevo presentamos una actividad para el chequeo, el refuerzo y la revisión de los tiempos del pasado de indicativo. En este caso nos centramos en la morfología de las formas irregulares del pretérito indefinido. Los alumnos deberán corregir los errores que ha cometido Hans al escribir este tiempo del pasado. Daremos unos minutos para que cada alumno reescriba las formas correctamente y, a continuación, haremos una puesta en común.

Sugerencia

Antes de pasar a la fase de corrección, propondremos que comparen sus respuestas con las de algún compañero. Además, para la última parte, podrían intercambiarse el libro o el soporte en el que hayan escrito las soluciones para que otro alumno las corrija.

Solución

1. *conducí* – conduje.
2. *venió* – vino; *traió* – trajo.
3. *haciste* – hiciste; *podí* – pude.
4. *pedió* – pidió.
5. *sabí-* supe; *querí* – quise; *podí* – pude.
6. *dormieron* – durmieron.
7. *ponió* – puso; *hació* – hizo.
8. *tenimos* – tuvimos; *veímos* – vimos.
9. *andamos* – anduvimos.
10. *traducimos* – tradujimos.

¡EXTRA! PRACTICA

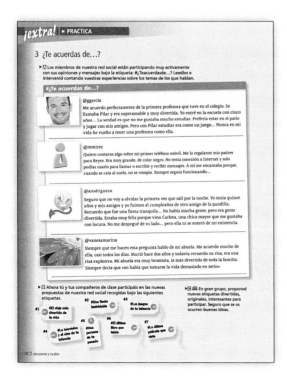

3 ¿Te acuerdas de...?

Con esta actividad abordaremos el contraste entre los cuatro tiempos del pasado del indicativo de forma más libre, menos dirigida. Además, siguiendo la idea de presentar la práctica comunicativa en contextos cercanos al alumno, hemos elegido el formato de la participación a través de las redes sociales.

A. Pediremos a los alumnos que lean los mensajes que han enviado los miembros de una red social. Tras aclarar las dudas sobre el léxico, los animaremos a que intervengan contando sus experiencias sobre los temas tratados.

B. Seguimos con la práctica de la expresión oral. Cada alumno contará sus vivencias en torno a nuevas propuestas de los miembros de una red social.

Sugerencia

Propondremos que cada estudiante elija una de esas situaciones (etiquetas) propuestas y exponga su experiencia por escrito, participando en la red social como si fuera un miembro más de esta.

C. En gran grupo, los alumnos deberán hacer nuevas propuestas para hablar sobre ellas. Animaremos a que sean ideas originales, divertidas e interesantes...

¡extra! EN COMUNICACIÓN

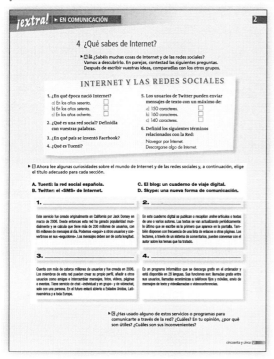

4 ¿Qué sabes de Internet?

Este bloque está pensado para trabajar sobre la relevancia de Internet y las redes sociales como nuevas formas de comunicación y de conocimiento del mundo y de los demás. Son temas próximos a la realidad de los alumnos que, sin duda, procurarán el diálogo intercultural y la implicación.

A. Pediremos que, en parejas, los alumnos respondan a las preguntas del test sobre Internet y las redes sociales. Los animaremos a que, aunque no sepan la respuesta, escriban sus hipótesis. A continuación, cada grupo comparará sus soluciones con las de los demás. Finalmente, el profesor aclarará las dudas que puedan surgir y resolverá el test.

Solución

1. c) En los años ochenta.
2. Grupos de personas relacionadas, conectadas por intereses comunes.
3. En Estados Unidos. Su creador fue Mark Zuckerberg, estudiante de la Universidad de Harvard.
4. Tuenti es una red social española, creada en 2006.
5. c) 140 caracteres.
6. **Navegar por Internet:** desplazarse por la red, mirar o consultar en diferentes lugares de Internet.

    Descargarse algo de Internet: es como copiar o coger algo de Internet para ponerlo en tu ordenador.

B. En plenaria, los alumnos leerán cuatro pequeños textos con algunas curiosidades de Internet y las redes sociales. Después de la lectura, resolveremos las dudas. Al final, los estudiantes elegirán el título adecuado para cada fragmento y comentarán sus opiniones con los demás para ver si están de acuerdo.

Solución

1. B. Twitter: el «SMS» de Internet.
2. C. El blog: un cuaderno de viaje digital.
3. A. Tuenti: la red social española.
4. D. Skype: una nueva forma de comunicación.

C. Para cerrar la sección, un ejercicio de expresión oral que tiene como objetivo que, en gran grupo, los estudiantes reflexionen sobre el tema y expliquen las utilidades y los inconvenientes de estas formas de comunicación.

Sugerencia

Proponemos una tarea final, para la práctica integrada de las destrezas, sobre el impacto de Internet en un país hispanohablante. Haremos que los alumnos se organicen en pequeños grupos, elijan el país y busquen información en la red para preparar una presentación oral del tema. Pueden tratar aspectos como: el número de usuarios, la frecuencia de uso y las razones para utilizar esta nueva forma de comunicación, su influencia en otros ámbitos de la sociedad, las redes sociales, la importancia económica, las ventajas y desventajas, los problemas relacionados con su uso…

Si se cuenta con un ordenador en el aula, podrán realizar la fase de recopilación de datos y elaboración del texto en clase; en cualquier caso, si no fuera posible, harán la tarea fuera del aula. Finalmente, cada grupo expondrá su presentación en clase. Los compañeros, al finalizar, podrán preguntarles o pedirles las aclaraciones que consideren oportunas.

En el caso de que a los alumnos les resultara especialmente dificultoso encontrar información sobre un país hispanohablante en concreto, cambiaríamos el tema por este otro, que posiblemente resultará más fácil de investigar: el impacto de Internet en la sociedad actual. En el trabajo podrán tratar los mismos aspectos que habíamos previsto para el primer asunto propuesto.

Solución

Respuesta libre.

Unidad 3
Deberías hacerlo una vez en la vida

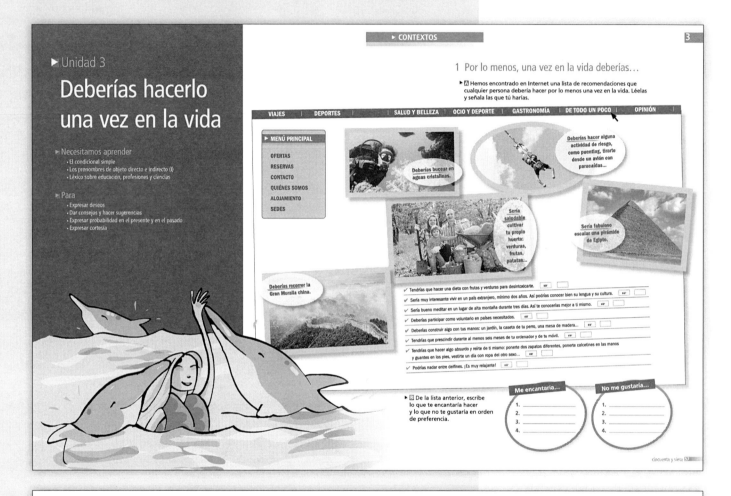

OBJETIVOS DE LA UNIDAD

En esta unidad nos adentramos en el ámbito de los consejos, las sugerencias y recomendaciones, para ello proponemos estudiar la morfología y los usos fundamentales del condicional simple, un tiempo verbal con el que el alumno entra ahora en contacto por primera vez.

Las **funciones comunicativas** que se presentan son: expresar deseos, ofrecer consejos y sugerencias, manifestar cortesía y expresar probabilidad en el presente y en el pasado. Así pues, en cuanto a **contenidos morfosintácticos**, tratamos el condicional simple (su morfología y sus usos) y los pronombres personales de objeto directo y de objeto indirecto (I).

Por lo que respecta a los **contenidos léxicos-semánticos**, al estudiante se le proporciona vocabulario del ámbito de las profesiones y las ciencias y se introduce el lenguaje del entorno formativo.

En relación con los **contenidos socioculturales** se hablará de experiencias educativas y del sistema de educación español.

Finalmente, los **contenidos pragmáticos** que se recogen son las fórmulas de cortesía para realizar sugerencias y recomendaciones.

CONTEXTOS

1 Por lo menos, una vez en la vida deberías…

Con esta secuencia de minitareas presentamos en contexto el contenido fundamental de la unidad: el condicional simple, con el objetivo de que el estudiante se vaya familiarizando con la forma y con las situaciones en las que se usa. El formato, una página web, puede resultarles atractivo a los alumnos y animarlos a la lectura.

A. Iniciaremos la secuencia con una lista que el estudiante tiene que leer donde se recoge una serie de recomendaciones de actividades para hacer alguna vez en la vida. Concluida la fase de lectura, el alumno tiene que elegir las que él haría. El objetivo es ponerlo en contacto con la forma del condicional simple.

Seguramente habrá dudas de vocabulario, por lo que sería conveniente que, después de una lectura individual por parte del estudiante, se haga una segunda en voz alta con todo el grupo, y así el profesor irá resolviendo cuantas dudas se presenten. Conforme vayan leyendo las recomendaciones, los alumnos irán comentado sus experiencias y preferencias, diciendo si están de acuerdo o no y por qué.

Solución

Respuesta libre.

B. El objetivo de esta actividad es que, aunque el estudiante no conoce aún de manera explícita la forma del condicional simple, se familiarice con ella aplicándola a los verbos *gustar* y *encantar*. Al mismo tiempo, tendrá que expresar su orden de preferencias respecto a las actividades del ejercicio A, siempre justificando su repuesta.

Sugerencia

Es recomendable hacer esta actividad en gran grupo, ya que, además de practicar las estructuras, permitirá que los estudiantes se conozcan más personalmente al compartir sus experiencias y hablar de sus preferencias.

Solución

Posible respuesta

Me encantaría…

Hacer algo absurdo y reírme de mí mismo, porque yo soy una persona un poco seria e introvertida.

Escalar una pirámide de Egipto, porque siempre me ha atraído el antiguo Egipto: los faraones, el Nilo…

No me gustaría…

Dejar mi teléfono móvil ni mi ordenador, porque necesito estar siempre comunicado.

Hacer ninguna actividad de riesgo porque me dan pánico las alturas y porque prefiero llevar una vida tranquila…

2 Lo que tú cambiarías

La idea del ejercicio es que el alumno, motivado por toda la información del ejercicio anterior y las opiniones que se expresan en él, sienta interés por el tema y se anime a manifestar su opinión.

A. En primer lugar, el estudiante tiene que leer las diferentes intervenciones en un foro en el que los participantes hablan de lo que cambiarían en su vida. Seguimos exponiendo al alumno al uso del condicional simple, pero ahora mediante los comentarios de otras personas que les pueden servir de estímulo para expresar lo que ellos piensan.

B. Es el momento de que el alumno exprese sus opiniones, que hable sobre lo que cambiaría en su vida y que conteste a otras preguntas. Lógicamente, cometerá errores al usar la forma del condicional, o simplemente no la usará; en este momento, eso no tiene importancia, ya que, si el estudiante utilizara espontáneamente alguna forma correcta, ya sería un gran logro.

Solución

Respuesta libre.

▶ DEBERÍAS HACERLO UNA VEZ EN LA VIDA

CONTEXTOS

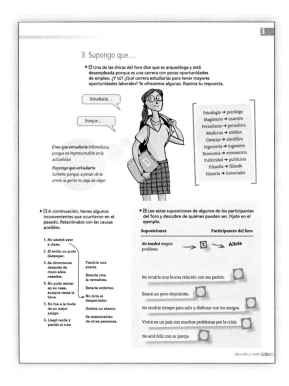

3 Supongo que…

Estamos ante una secuencia de actividades que presentan tanto el léxico que se trabaja en esta unidad como el uso del condicional con valor de la probabilidad en el pasado.

A. En esta actividad se introduce vocabulario referido a las profesiones y a las ciencias que el estudiante podrá utilizar al expresar su deseo de estudiar una carrera determinada.

Podemos empezar explicando las palabras nuevas para después aclarar qué significa la expresión *una carrera con salidas*.

A continuación, podemos preguntar a los alumnos cuáles son las carreras con más salidas en sus países y, por último, si ya han elegido o estudiado una carrera, nos podrán hablar de por qué la eligieron; y si todavía no lo han hecho, cuál elegirían de las que les proponemos para tener mejores ofertas laborales.

Solución

Respuesta libre.

B. El objetivo de este ejercicio es exponer al alumno a la expresión de la probabilidad en el pasado.

Para facilitar la comprensión, proporcionamos a los estudiantes una serie de hechos y sus posibles causas; el trabajo consistirá en relacionar cada hecho con su causa.

Lo que pretendemos es que el alumno capte, activando estrategias cognitivas, que el condicional simple se usa para expresar probabilidad en el pasado.

Solución

1. No oiría el despertador.
2. Tendría una avería.
3. Se enamorarían de otras personas.
4. Estaría rota la cerradura.
5. Estaría enfermo.
6. Habría un atasco.

C. Una vez que hemos introducido la probabilidad en el pasado con el condicional, queremos retomar otra idea ya estudiada, para contrastarlas, la probabilidad en el presente (con futuro simple).

De nuevo, el estudiante se encuentra con hechos y causas que podrá relacionar simplemente por el significado, pero percibirá que estos significados se expresan en futuro simple o condicional simple, según se refieran a hechos del presente o del pasado.

Solución

No tendría una buena relación con sus padres: 2 (Roberto).

Estará un poco deprimido: 10 (Diego).

No tendría tiempo para salir y disfrutar con los amigos: 7 (José).

Vivirá en un país con muchos problemas por la crisis: 9 (David).

No será feliz con su pareja: 6 (Belén).

NOTAS

OBSERVA, APRENDE Y RECUERDA

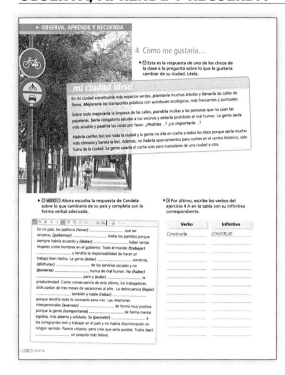

4 Cómo me gustaría…

Ejercicio de inferencia cuyo objetivo es que el estudiante identifique y aprenda la forma del condicional simple.

A. En primer lugar, nuestro objetivo es que el estudiante se fije en las formas verbales en condicional que aparecen en el texto y que, además, están resaltadas.

B. En segundo lugar, el alumno tiene que transcribir las formas verbales en condicional que escuche para completar el texto. Antes de proceder a la escucha leemos en grupo el texto y comentamos su contenido. Como trata de las cosas que cambiaría de su país, seguro que después de terminar el ejercicio de comprensión auditiva los estudiantes tienen algo que decir a este repecto.

Solución

tendrían - gobernarían - debería - trabajaría - estaría - disfrutaría - se pondría - habría - subiría - bajaría - robaría - avanzarían - se comportaría - permitiría - seríamos.

C. Por último, el estudiante tiene que recopilar todas las formas verbales en condicional que han aparecido en el ejercicio 4A y deducir el infinitivo correspondiente. Se supone que no tendrá mucha dificultad para realizar este ejercicio, solo puede que cometa algún error cuando se trate de los verbos irregulares *haber, poner* y *poder,* pero normalmente los estudiantes identifican estos verbos sin problemas.

Solución

Verbo	Infinitivo
Construiría	*CONSTRUIR*
Plantaría	PLANTAR
Llenaría	LLENAR
Mejoraría	MEJORAR
Pondría	PONER
Sería	SER
Estaría	ESTAR
Pediría	PEDIR
Podrías	PODER
Importaría	IMPORTAR
Habría	HABER
Iría	IR
Usaría	USAR

▶ DEBERÍAS HACERLO UNA VEZ EN LA VIDA

OBSERVA, APRENDE Y RECUERDA

D. Un paso más: queremos que el alumno relacione las terminaciones del tiempo verbal nuevo con las terminaciones de otra forma verbal que ya conoce: el pretérito imperfecto.

Solución

Se llama pretérito imperfecto.

E. En este punto, comparando las formas del imperfecto y del condicional del verbo *construir*, el estudiante se dará cuenta fácilmente de que la diferencia está en que en la formación del condicional las terminaciones se añaden directamente al infinitivo.

Solución

Se diferencian en que para formar el pretérito imperfecto quitamos la terminación del infinitivo (-ir) y añadimos la terminación propia de su tiempo: constru-ir → constru-ía; sin embargo, para conseguir la nueva forma verbal, añadimos la terminación directamente al infinitivo: contruir-ía.

F. Es el momento de decirle al estudiante el nombre de esta forma verbal y de confirmarle lo que él ya ha inferido tras realizar los ejercicios anteriores.

Su tarea, a continuación, es practicar la forma completando el paradigma del verbo *construir*.

Solución

construir**ía** - construir**ías** - construir**ía** - construir**íamos** - construir**íais** - constru**irían.**

G. Solo nos queda una última información: el paradigma es el mismo para las tres conjugaciones.

Para hacer que el alumno se de cuenta de este hecho, le pediremos que conjugue otros verbos de conjugaciones diferentes.

Sugerencia

Aconsejamos que, antes de pasar al siguiente apartado sobre los verbos irregulares, el profesor practique un poco más la forma con otros verbos regulares.

Una posibilidad es hacer preguntas a los estudiantes con el condicional y que ellos contesten:

¿Dónde te gustaría estar ahora?

¿Qué harías esta tarde?

¿A dónde irías de vacaciones?

¿Dónde vivirías?

¿Qué te apetecería hacer ahora mismo?...

Solución

SER	ESTAR
sería	estaría
serías	estarías
sería	estaría
seríamos	estaríamos
seríais	estaríais
serían	estarían

NOTAS

OBSERVA, APRENDE Y RECUERDA

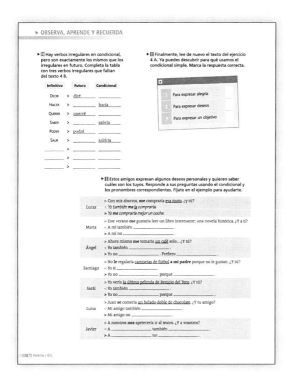

H. El objetivo de esta minitarea es el aprendizaje de los verbos irregulares.

En este estadio del proceso de enseñanza, es conveniente hacer ver al estudiante que las formas irregulares del condicional coinciden con las del futuro simple.

Solución

Infinitivo	Futuro	Condicional
Decir	dir**é**	dir**ía**
Hacer	har**é**	har**ía**
Querer	querr**é**	querr**ía**
Saber	sabr**é**	sabr**ía**
Poder	podr**é**	podr**ía**
Salir	saldr**é**	saldr**ía**
Tener	tendr**é**	tendr**ía**
Poner	pondr**é**	pondr**ía**
Haber	habr**é**	habr**ía**

I. Después de volver a leer el texto del ejercicio 4A, el estudiante inferirá sin ninguna dificultad que el condicional simple se usa para expresar deseos.

Llegados a este punto, es necesario hacer alguna practica más antes de continuar.

Para ello, podemos plantear a los alumnos alguna situación con el objetivo de que tengan que expresar sus deseos al respecto; por ejemplo: *Imagina que te toca la lotería; ¿qué harías?*

Es un caso que admite una gran variedad de posibles respuestas por lo que es ideal para practicar el condicional de verbos diferentes.

Solución

2. Para expresar deseos.

J. Ampliamos la expresión de deseos con el uso de los pronombres personales de objeto directo y objeto indirecto.

Sugerencia

No estaría de más continuar el ejercicio de una forma más libre; es decir, cada estudiante expresa un deseo, en el que puede incluir dos objetos, uno o ninguno. Después, pregunta a un compañero. Ejemplo:

> *Yo me tomaría un helado ahora. ¿Y tú?*

< *¡Claro que me **lo** tomaría! ¡Me encantan los helados!*

> *Tengo un amigo al que le gustaría viajar por el mundo en moto. Yo no **lo** haría, no me gustan las motos porque son peligrosas. ¿Y tú?*

< ...

Solución
Posibles respuestas

Marta: A mí también me gustaría. / A mí no me gustaría.

Ángel: Yo también me lo tomaría. / Yo no me lo tomaría. Prefiero un refresco.

Santiago: Yo sí se las regalaría. / Yo no se las regalaría porque tampoco le gustan.

Saraí: Yo también la vería. / Yo no la vería porque no me interesa el tema.

Luisa: Mi amigo también se lo comería. / Mi amigo no se lo comería porque no le gusta el chocolate.

Javier: A nosotros también nos apetecería. / A nosotros no nos apetecería porque estamos cansados.

▶ DEBERÍAS HACERLO UNA VEZ EN LA VIDA

OBSERVA, APRENDE Y RECUERDA

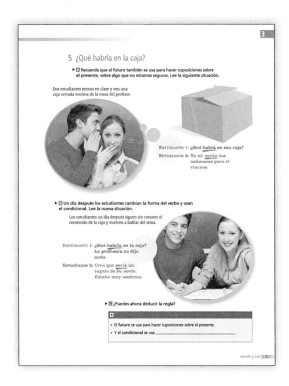

5 ¿Qué habría en la caja?

Con esta sección buscamos que el alumno descubra el valor de la probabilidad en el pasado, y lo haremos contrastando una misma situación en presente y en pasado. Para ello hemos planteado una circunstancia cercana a la realidad del alumno y, sobre todo, verosímil.

A y B. En esta primera fase el estudiante ha de leer dos diálogos que corresponden a dos situaciones diferentes.

Es importante que llamemos su atención sobre el hecho de que las situaciones ocurren en dos días distintos, de ahí el cambio en el tiempo verbal que utilizan: futuro para expresar probabilidad en el presente y condicional para expresar probabilidad en el pasado.

Es conveniente que el profesor se asegure de que los estudiantes notan ese cambio, pero procurando que lo deduzcan con su propia reflexión.

Solución

Respuesta libre.

C. Tras la reflexión, es el momento de que el estudiante tenga que deducir el segundo uso del condicional simple: hacer suposiciones en el pasado.

Como ayuda le recordaremos que el futuro se usa para hacer suposiciones en el presente.

Sugerencia

Proponemos que el profesor anime a los alumnos a practicar la probabilidad en el pasado antes de continuar con la observación y el aprendizaje de nuevos contenidos.

Una posibilidad es que un estudiante plantee una situación en el pasado y los demás hagan suposiciones sobre ese hecho pretérito: *No asistí al concierto del sábado (porque no tendrías entrada / no te gustaría el grupo / perderías la entrada…). El sábado por la noche me quedé en casa (porque tendrías invitados en casa / haría mal tiempo / no te apetecería salir…).*

Solución

El condicional se usa también para hacer suposiciones sobre el pasado.

NOTAS

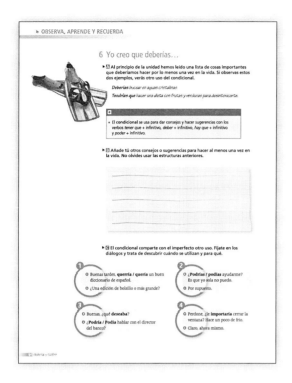

6 Yo creo que deberías…

En esta secuencia el objetivo es avanzar en los usos del condicional simple, en este caso, para ofrecer consejos y hacer sugerencias.

A. Empezamos leyendo dos frases pertenecientes a la lista del ejercicio 1A y, a continuación, damos la regla de uso.

En ella introducimos dos fórmulas más, aparte de las dos de los ejemplos, que se usan para expresar consejos y hacer sugerencias: *hay que* + infinitivo y *poder* + infinitivo.

Después podemos pedir a los estudiantes que se fijen en los verbos que se utilizan para expresar consejos en los dos ejemplos y que expliquen la diferencia entre *deber* + infinitivo y *tener que* + infinitivo: *deber* + infinitivo tiene un grado menor de obligación que *tener que* + infinitivo.

B. Usando las estructuras del ejercicio anterior, el estudiante debe dar consejos o plantear sugerencias sobre actividades para hacer al menos una vez en la vida, pero con el nuevo uso del condicional.

Solución

Posible respuesta

Deberías viajar una vez en helicóptero, es fabuloso.

Tendrías que tomarte un año sabático para pensar sobre tu vida y disfrutar del tiempo libre.

Podrías trabajar en algo totalmente diferente a lo que haces porque cambiar es bueno.

Habría que hacer algo de ejercicio todos los días para estar en forma.

C. En esta fase introducimos el valor de cortesía que desarrolla el condicional en determinados contextos discursivos y en ciertas situaciones de comunicación.

Aprovechamos para recordarles a los estudiantes que ya habían estudiado este uso con otro tiempo verbal: el imperfecto.

Pero aquí es importante que les digamos que no todos los verbos se usan con los dos tiempos, por ejemplo, el verbo *importar* se usa con el condicional (*¿Le importaría…*) y cuando preguntamos con el verbo *desear* usamos el imperfecto (*¿Qué deseaba?*) —no el condicional—; en cambio, en la respuesta sí podemos usar los dos tiempos (*Deseaba / Desearía…*). Con los verbos *querer* y *poder* se usan ambos tiempos verbales.

Sugerencia

En parejas, los estudiantes tienen que crear diferentes diálogos en situaciones en las que tengan que usar la cortesía, después escenificarán sus situaciones para el resto de sus compañeros.

Solución

Se utilizan para pedir algo de un modo más amable y formal a conocidos y desconocidos.

DEBERÍAS HACERLO UNA VEZ EN LA VIDA

PRACTICA

7 No lo sabemos

El objetivo de este bloque de actividades es que los estudiantes hagan suposiciones sobre el pasado.

Las imágenes desempeñan un papel importante al ilustrar las posibles situaciones.

A. Primero, los alumnos tienen que fijarse en las imágenes para usar el verbo que corresponda y expresar las posibles razones por las que Alberto no asistió a clase ayer.

Harán esta práctica individualmente y después, en grupo, compararán sus respuestas.

Sugerencia

Podemos ampliar el ejercicio pidiendo a los estudiantes que digan todas las razones posibles que se les ocurran para no ir a clase, animándolos a que lo hagan con sentido de humor.

A continuación, expresarán esas razones como probabilidades en el pasado.

Por ejemplo: otras posibles razones para no ir a clase pueden ser no tener ganas (*Alberto no tendría ganas de ir a clase*), haberse acostado tarde la noche anterior (*Alberto se acostaría tarde anoche*), haber apagado el despertador y haber seguido durmiendo (*Alberto apagaría el despertador y seguiría durmiendo*)…

Solución

No vino a clase porque…

1. No oiría el despertador. / Se estropearía el despertador.

2. Perdería el autobús.

3. Pensaría que era fiesta.

4. Anoche estaría de fiesta.

5. Se quedaría dormido.

6. Le dolería la cabeza.

B. En este caso, también podemos ampliar el ejercicio, si el profesor lo considera oportuno, pidiendo a los alumnos que, además de las suposiciones de los ejemplos, ellos aporten otras posibles. Normalmente, funciona bien decirles que no pueden repetir verbos o una misma idea; de esta manera los obligamos a esforzarse más. El éxito de la actividad también dependerá de si el grupo es más o menos numeroso. De este modo, a pesar de ser un ejercicio centrado en las formas, podemos ampliar el contexto para convertirlo en una práctica más real.

Solución

sería.

Conocería - invitaría.

Querría.

Estaría.

Se acostaría.

practicaría.

Se pondría.

Se divertiría.

NOTAS

PRACTICA

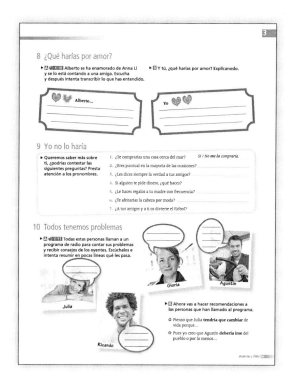

8 ¿Qué harías por amor?

Ejercicio de comprensión auditiva. Para entrar en situación, antes de proceder a la audición, los alumnos pueden ir comentando cosas que han oído acerca de lo que alguien ha hecho por amor. El profesor puede ir escribiendo los verbos en la pizarra; es posible que algunos coincidan con los que aparecen en la audición, así se facilitará la comprensión.

Solución

Posible respuesta

Alberto habla con una amiga, que le pregunta sobre su nueva relación. En realidad, hablan de lo que Alberto sería capaz de hacer por amor. Él dice que estaría dispuesto a irse a vivir en un país extranjero, piensa que se adaptaría bien, incluso le gustaría hacerlo para conocer una cultura diferente. Al final, Alberto le pregunta a su amiga qué estaría ella dispuesta a hacer por amor.

B. Ahora dejaremos unos minutos para que los alumnos escriban sobre lo que ellos harían por amor y después haremos una puesta en común. Seguro que habrá muchas coincidencias.

Además, si es un grupo de alumnos abiertos y hay empatía entre ellos, puede resultar una actividad bastante amena y divertida.

9 Yo no lo haría

Estamos ante un ejercicio para practicar el condicional y los pronombres. Hemos querido que las preguntas sean personales, algunas sobre aspectos que pueden crear debate y discusión en clase. Seguramente, en la pregunta número 2 se producirán errores en cuanto al pronombre, por lo que sería conveniente que recordáramos el uso en este caso: para el complemento de los verbos *ser*, *estar* y *parecer* usamos siempre *lo*.

Sugerencia

Para este contenido solemos hacer una práctica que realmente nos da resultados: consiste en hacer muchas preguntas simples y de forma dinámica a los estudiantes, para que las contesten lo más rápidamente posible. Les decimos que, como son preguntas con los verbos *ser*, *estar* y *parecer*, no tienen que pensar en el género, si es masculino, femenino, singular o plural, siempre usamos LO: ¿*Eres española?*/ *No lo soy*, *¿La puerta está abierta? / Sí/No lo está*, *¿Tu compañero es simpático? / Sí/No lo es*, *¿Los españoles son amables? / Sí/No lo son*, *¿Este ejercicio te parece práctico? / Sí/No me lo parece…*

Solución

1. Sí / No me **la** compraría.
2. Sí / No **lo** soy.
3. Sí / No se **la** digo.
4. Se **lo** doy / No se **lo** doy.
5. Sí / No se **los** hago.
6. Sí / No me **la** afeitaría.
7. Sí / No **nos** divierte.

10 Todos tenemos problemas

La finalidad de esta actividad es que los estudiantes sean capaces de dar consejos.

A. En primer lugar, los alumnos tienen que escuchar la audición y comprenderla, para, finalmente, sintetizar en una frase el problema de cada una de las personas que llaman al programa de radio. Lo importante es que entiendan cuál es el problema, aunque puede haber pequeñas diferencias en su descripción. La idea es que escriban de forma ordenada la información que han escuchado y que la recuerden, pero de forma muy resumida. Antes de corregir el ejercicio, propóngales que comenten sus escritos con algún compañero para ver si coinciden en la exposición.

Solución

Posibles respuestas

Julia: está cansada de la rutina diaria y quiere marcharse a otro país.

Gloria: está enamorada de un compañero de trabajo, pero no sabe si es correspondida.

Agustín: vive en un pueblo pequeño y le gustaría conocer gente nueva.

Ricardo: necesita mejorar su inglés conversacional para su trabajo.

▶ DEBERÍAS HACERLO UNA VEZ EN LA VIDA

B. Aunque los alumnos han de usar las estructuras para expresar consejos, tienen libertad para decir lo que quieran, comentar con sus compañeros y valorar entre todos las recomendaciones que crean que son más adecuadas en cada situación.

Sugerencia

Como siempre que sea posible, llevaremos la actividad al ámbito personal para implicar a los alumnos y que cada uno hable de sus experiencias personales, hasta donde quiera contar y compartir.

El profesor puede preguntar a los estudiantes si se sienten identificados con algunos de los problemas que han expuestos las personas que han llamado a la radio, y los animará a que cuenten cómo los solucionaron, qué hicieron y cómo fue su experiencia.

Para romper el hielo, el profesor puede comenzar exponiendo alguna experiencia similar.

Solución

Respuesta libre.

PRACTICA

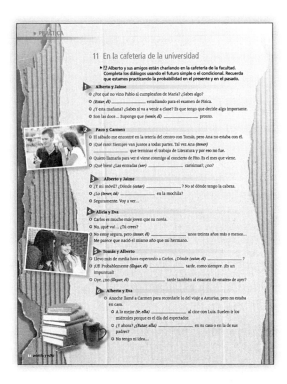

11 En la cafetería de la universidad

Se trata de una actividad para reforzar la expresión de la probabilidad en el presente y en el pasado.

A. En primer lugar tenemos seis diálogos que el estudiante ha de leer y completar usando la forma correcta en futuro o condicional, según se trate de probabilidad en el presente o en el pasado.

En algunos diálogos se usan adverbios de duda junto con el futuro o el condicional.

En estos casos conviene explicar a los estudiantes que realmente es una redundancia, que no es necesario usar el adverbio o locuciones adverbiales *(problamente, tal vez, a lo mejor...)*, que solo la forma de futuro o condicional ya expresa la suposición.

Solución

1. Estaría - vendrá.

2. tendría - serán.

3. estará - tendrás.

4. tendrá.

5. estará - llegará - llegaría.

6. iría / Estará.

PRACTICA

B. Recapitulamos todos los contenidos de la unidad.

Sugerencia

Si se han detectado frecuentes errores en el uso de los pronombres en los ejercicios anteriores, podemos seguir practicando de la siguiente forma: en parejas, cada estudiante tiene que preparar preguntas para su compañero usando el futuro o el condicional e incluyendo un objeto o dos; el compañero debe contestar usando los pronombres necesarios. Ejemplo: *¿Te pondrías un disfraz de pirata? Sí / No me lo pondría. ¿Le dirías a tu madre una mentira para conseguir algo? Sí / No se la diría. ¿Crees que el profesor nos pondrá ejercicios para mañana? Sí / No nos los pondrá.*

Solución

Posibles respuestas

Alberto: se acostaría.

Tú: se acostaría pronto.

Carmen: comprará.

Tú: No sé. La comprará en las tiendas del centro.

Eva: prepararía.

Tú: Ah, seguro que preparó su plato favorito: paella.

Tomás: Les escribirás a tus amigos.

Tú: Les escribiría, pero no sé su dirección.

Alicia: te gustaría.

Tú: Me encantaría el libro de Javier Marías *Los enamoramientos*.

Jaime: os disfrazaréis.

Tú: Sí, nos disfrazaremos de piratas.

Alberto: me podrás ayudar.

Tú: Claro que te ayudaré.

EN COMUNICACIÓN

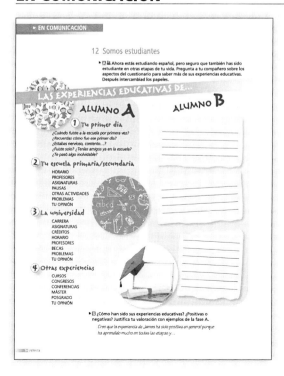

12 Somos estudiantes

En este bloque de actividades de expresión oral se pretende que el estudiante hable sobre sus experiencias educativas y que utilice un vocabulario específico de este ámbito temático.

A. Los alumnos, en parejas, tienen que realizar preguntas de un cuestionario y responderlas. Deben intercambiar los papeles para que la exposición sea más completa. Antes del trabajo en parejas el profesor debe explicar el vocabulario.

B. Con las notas sobre el compañero, ahora el estudiante tendrá que valorar si la experiencia ha sido positiva o negativa.

Si no disponemos de mucho tiempo en la clase o si queremos que elaboren más esta fase de la actividad, les podemos pedir que la preparen en casa y que al día siguiente hagan una minipresentación sobre las experiencias educativas de su compañero.

cincuenta y cinco

DEBERÍAS HACERLO UNA VEZ EN LA VIDA

Solución

A y **B.**

Posible respuesta

Creo que la experiencia de James ha sido positiva en general porque ha aprendido mucho en todas las etapas y… tiene muy buenos recuerdos de su época de estudiante. Nunca olvidará el primer día que fue al colegio, porque conoció a Marta, su mejor amiga. De la escuela primaria recuerda con cariño a los profesores, especialmente a uno de ellos, que le ayudó mucho con sus problemas de ortografía. En secundaria eligió las asignaturas de Dibujo Técnico e Historia del Arte. En la universidad, recuerda que le costó mucho decidirse entre dos carreras, Arquitectura y Bellas Artes, pero, finalmente, eligió la primera porque creía que tendría más salidas. Para completar sus estudios universitarios procura hacer cursos y asistir a congresos, por lo que viaja bastante.

EN COMUNICACIÓN

13 La educación a debate

A. El contexto sociocultural de esta actividad es el sistema educativo español.

En primer lugar, los estudiantes tienen que leer una serie de textos para, después, relacionarlos con el ámbito educativo al que se refieren. Trabajaremos en parejas para hacer más distendida y amena la actividad, al mismo tiempo buscamos la colaboración del compañero para intentar solucionar las dudas de léxico que seguro se van a plantear.

Solución

Marta Fernández: Educación primaria.

Luisa González: Educación secundaria.

Salvador Pérez: Guardería.

Alfonso Granados: Enseñanza privada.

B. Con esta propuesta queremos promover el autoaprendizaje. Los estudiantes tienen que buscar información en Internet para elaborar un informe que expondrán en clase.

Los alumnos no suelen tener problemas para manejarse en Internet, pero lo que se procura es que, además, sean capaces de sintetizar toda esa información que tienen a su alcance.

Sugerimos establecer un límite en la extensión del informe que tienen que presentar: un folio, dos…, dependiendo de las características del grupo.

Para realizar la actividad, la clase se dividirá en grupos en función de los tres temas propuestos: Becas y ayudas, Formación profesional y Bachillerato.

Para cada tema se ofrecen una serie de cuestiones que pueden servir a los alumnos como punto de partida en su búsqueda en Internet.

Lo primero que tendrán que hacer es definir bien el tema que elijan. Asimismo, el profesor les facilitará un listado de términos, que podrá dictar o escribir en la pizarra, para que los alumnos los incluyan en sus trabajos: colegio público / privado / concertado; instituto; universidad; carrera; créditos; máster; doctorado; asignatura, etcétera.

Sugerencia

Hasta aquí se han introducido, a grandes rasgos, características propias del sistema educativo español. En esta fase, el contexto sociocultural se puede ampliar con la intención de propiciar en clase un debate en el que cada estudiante hable de cómo es el sistema educativo en su país, comparándolo con el español.

Les preguntaremos a los alumnos qué semejanzas y qué diferencias encuentran entre este sistema y el de sus países respectivos, si tienen los mismos problemas, qué es lo que cambiarían etc., intentando que desarrollen una actitud crítica respecto a todo aquello que consideran que puede ser mejorable.

Si se cree conveniente, pueden trabajar en grupos y preparar una exposición.

Solución

Respuesta libre.

¡extra! CONTEXTOS

A. Iniciamos esta sección con un ejercicio de comprensión auditiva en el que los estudiantes tienen que ser capaces de discriminar cierta información y relacionarla con la imagen correspondiente.

Sugerencia

Como ampliación de esta actividad, sugerimos otra de expresión oral en la que se plantearía un debate sobre el tema de conocer o presentar nuestra pareja a nuestros padres. Podríamos hablar en clase de las diferencias entre las distintas culturas: cuándo se presenta la pareja a los padres, qué se suele hacer, si se lleva algún regalo, cuál es el papel de los suegros...

Solución

1. B; **2.** A; **3.** A; **4.** A; **5.** B.

B. Ahora realizaremos un trabajo en parejas para organizar una cena romántica y un fin de semana aventurero. Cuando se termine la actividad en parejas, haremos una puesta en común. Seguro que serán muchas las ideas que iremos comentando y valorando entre todos.

Sugerencia

Para terminar, podemos pedir a los alumnos que definan a una persona romántica y a una persona aventurera; pueden usar un adjetivo o una frase. Ejemplo: *detallista / que piensa en los detalles pequeños; valiente / que no tiene miedo*. Podemos organizar la clase en dos grupos y establecer una especie de concurso; ganará el que dé más definiciones.

Solución

Respuesta libre.

1 ¿Te gustaría conocer a mis padres?

Planteamos una situación concreta para que el estudiante fije el uso del condicional. Al mismo tiempo, el diálogo entre una pareja ampliará nuestro objetivo al abordar el tema de las relaciones pareja-familia: los alumnos conocerán otro aspecto de nuestra cultura.

¡extra! PRACTICA

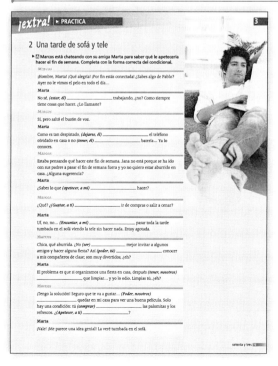

2 Una tarde de sofá y tele

A. Ejercicio centrado en las formas lingüísticas para reforzar el condicional simple y los diferentes usos estudiados en la unidad. Cuando hagamos este tipo de actividades, es interesante que insistamos en que los alumnos lean y comprendan la totalidad de los enunciados, que no se limiten a cambiar el verbo a la forma que se les pide. Una forma de asegurarnos de que efectivamente entienden todo es preguntar por el significado de aquellas palabras o expresiones que creamos que pueden desconocer. Además, podemos animarlos a que vayan diciendo por qué se usa el condicional en cada caso; así comprobaremos si realmente tienen claro cuándo lo tienen que utilizar.

Solución

estaría - se dejaría - tendría - me apetecería - Te gustaría - Me encantaría - sería - podrías - tendríamos - Podríamos - comprarías - ¿Te apetecería?

DEBERÍAS HACERLO UNA VEZ EN LA VIDA

¡EXTRA! PRACTICA

Me gustaría ver una comedia; tengo ganas de reírme un rato.

Te recomendaría un restaurante japonés que hay al lado de la catedral. Es buenísimo y no muy caro.

Deberíais salir, es carnaval y hay mucho ambiente en las calles.

Tendríais que ir a una discoteca nueva que han abierto en el centro.

3 ¿Sería un buen estudiante?

A. Estamos ante un ejercicio de expresión escrita en el que el estudiante tiene que hacer hipótesis sobre el pasado de la persona que elija. También les podemos proponer que escojan a una persona famosa y conocida por todos.

Sugerencia

Otra variante sobre esta actividad es la siguiente: en plenaria, cada estudiante elige a un compañero y expresa probabilidades sobre lo que este hizo ayer. Se trata de adivinar lo más posible sobre la vida del alumno elegido, usando correctamente el condicional: *Ayer te levantarías a las 8.30, desayunarías un café y tostadas con mantequilla, hablarías por teléfono con tu familia…*

Solución

Respuesta libre.

B. Completamos el ejercicio anterior: cada alumno leerá las frases que ha escrito, y los compañeros tendrán que adivinar de quién se trata.

B. Ejercicio libre en el que los estudiantes expresarán sus propios deseos y recomendaciones.

Solución

Posibles respuestas

Me apetecería viajar por Andalucía.

¡extra! EN COMUNICACIÓN

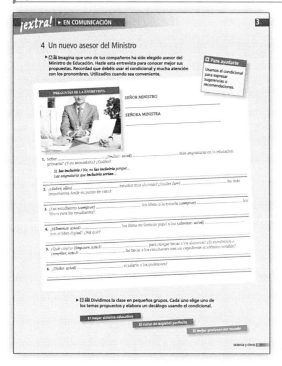

4 Un nuevo asesor del Ministro

A. En parejas, los estudiantes tienen que completar los verbos que faltan en una parrilla de preguntas y, después, contestarlas, utilizando el condicional y los pronombres adecuados. Les podemos pedir que amplíen la entrevista con otras preguntas que a ellos les gustaría hacer.

Solución

1. ministro / ministra - incluiría.
2. Deberían - serían.
3. comprarían - compraría.
4. Eliminaría - alternaría.
5. impondría - ampliaría.
6. Subiría.

B. Para terminar, han de elegir uno de los temas y elaborar un decálogo con el condicional. Esta es una actividad muy habitual, pero está justificada: el decálogo permite practicar una gran variedad de contenidos lingüísticos y al mismo tiempo da la posibilidad al estudiante de expresar su opinión.

Solución

Respuesta libre.

Unidad 4
Saber vivir

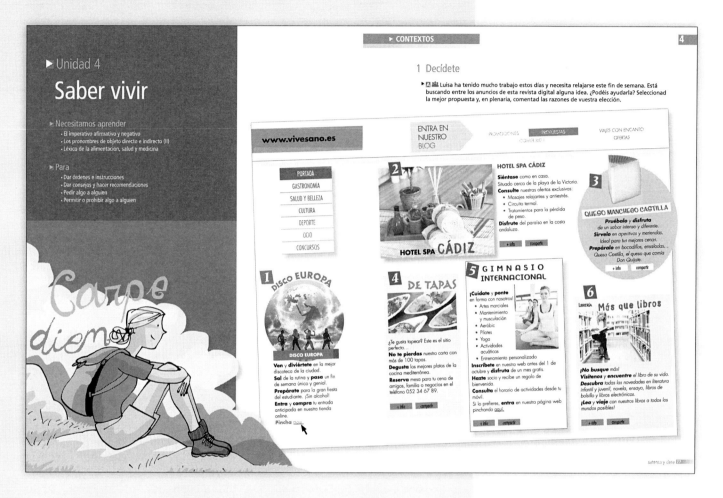

OBJETIVOS DE LA UNIDAD

En esta unidad nos introduciremos en el ámbito temático del bienestar personal y social, así como en el de la vida sana.

Las **funciones comunicativas** que se abordarán son: dar órdenes e instrucciones, expresar consejos y recomendaciones, pedir algo a alguien y permitir o prohibir algo.

Los **contenidos morfosintácticos** vinculados a las funciones anteriores son el imperativo afirmativo y el negativo —morfología y usos—, los imperativos lexicalizados *(Venga; Vamos; Mira; Vaya, Anda)* y el uso del imperativo en el español de América. Además, nos ocuparemos de la utilización de los pronombres personales cuando acompañan al imperativo (II).

Por lo que respecta a los **contenidos léxico-semánticos**, revisaremos y ampliaremos el léxico de la comida y la bebida; trataremos también el vocabulario relacionado con la salud y el cuerpo, la medicina, los medicamentos y los profesionales especialistas de este campo.

En lo que se refiere a **contenidos socioculturales**, haremos referencia a la vida y a los alimentos saludables, así como a las comidas y bebidas de Colombia.

Como **contenidos pragmáticos** presentaremos algunas fórmulas de cortesía para expresar peticiones y órdenes, y para justificar una orden o la petición de un favor.

Por último, por lo que respecta a los **contenidos fonéticos y ortográficos**, se presentan y practican las reglas generales de acentuación.

▶ SABER VIVIR

CONTEXTOS

1 Decídete

Iniciamos una serie de actividades orientadas a la presentación en contexto de los contenidos de la unidad.

A. En esta actividad, el alumno tiene que leer unos anuncios de una revista digital con el objetivo de elegir la mejor opción para pasar un fin de semana tranquilo y relajado. En grupos, tienen que escoger la mejor propuesta y después defenderla en plenaria. Creemos conveniente que, antes de que los estudiantes empiecen a presentar lo que han elegido, se haga una lectura en voz alta de todos los anuncios para resolver cualquier duda. En esta primera actividad, el alumno entra en contacto con el imperativo, en algunos casos acompañado de pronombre personal.

Solución

Posible respuesta

La mejor solución para Luisa podría ser el Hotel Spa Cádiz. Necesita relajarse y estar tranquila después de una dura semana de trabajo; por eso, este hotel es el lugar ideal. Allí tiene masajes antiestrés y circuitos termales.

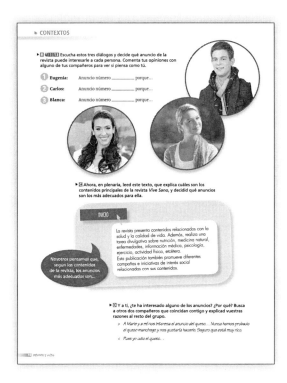

B. Ejercicio de comprensión auditiva en el que el estudiante, después de escuchar tres diálogos, tiene que relacionar cada persona con el anuncio que le puede interesar. Aunque es un ejercicio de respuesta única, si un estudiante diera otra solución diferente, siempre que justifique su respuesta, sería aceptable. En muchas ocasiones hay estudiantes con una gran imaginación que sorprenden con sus respuestas.

Solución

1. Eugenia: Anuncio número 1 porque le apetece bailar, tomar una copa y escuchar buena música, y puede hacerlo en la Disco Europa.

2. Carlos: Anuncio número 6 porque le gustaría comprar el libro que le ha recomendado Carmen, y en él se anuncia una librería.

3. Blanca: Anuncio número 5 porque ella tiene natación los sábados y el único lugar donde puede practicarla es en el Gimnasio Internacional; en su publicidad se anuncian actividades acuáticas.

C. Actividad de comprensión lectora: el alumno tiene que comprender perfectamente cuáles son los contenidos principales de la revista *Vive Sano* para decidir qué anuncios del ejercicio 1A son los más adecuados para publicitarse en ella.

Sugerencia

Podemos pedir a los alumnos que vayan recopilando algunos anuncios de periódicos o revistas, con el fin de tener más material real para trabajar en sucesivas clases y conforme se vayan consolidando los contenidos de la unidad. En los anuncios publicitarios es muy común el uso de los imperativos como reclamo.

Solución

Los anuncios más adecuados para la revista, si tenemos en cuenta sus contenidos, son el número 2 y el número 5. La revista publica artículos relacionados con el ejercicio y la actividad física, así que el anuncio número 5, el del gimnasio, es adecuado para dichos contenidos. El anuncio número 2 también puede ser apropiado porque se publicita un hotel spa que ofrece masajes o un circuito de aguas termales que ayudan a cuidar la salud y mejorar la calidad de vida.

D. Actividad de expresión oral: el alumno elige el anuncio que más le ha interesado y explica sus razones al resto del grupo. Puede ponerse de acuerdo con otros compañeros que coincidan con él para hacer una exposición común.

Como los asuntos son variados, esperamos que todos los estudiantes se identifiquen con alguno de los anuncios.

CONTEXTOS

2 ¡Venga! ¡Vamos a…!

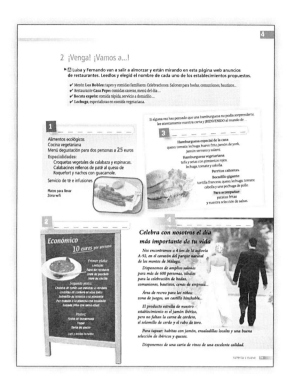

A. En este ejercicio de comprensión lectora el estudiante ha de escribir el nombre del establecimiento correspondiente en cada uno de los anuncios.

En primer lugar, deberíamos leer en plenaria todos los textos para resolver las dudas de vocabulario, que probablemente serán muchas.

El léxico es sobre comida y bebida.

> **Solución**
> 1. Lechuga.
> 2. Casa Pepe.
> 3. Bocata exprés.
> 4. Los Robles.

CONTEXTOS

B. Actividad de comprensión auditiva en la que el estudiante deberá entender el significado completo de la conversación para poder elegir el establecimiento al que la pareja va a ir a comer. Si se considera necesario, antes de poner la grabación, se puede hacer un resumen del contenido de cada anuncio, destacando lo fundamental y lo que lo diferencia del resto. De esta manera será más fácil identificar el restaurante elegido.

> **Solución**
>
> **Posible respuesta**
>
> Luisa y su pareja van a ir al restaurante Casa Pepe porque allí dan comidas caseras y tienen de menú del día pez espada a la plancha con ensalada, y a ella le apetece comer pescado a la plancha con algo de verdura. El restaurante vegetariano también tiene platos con verduras, pero a Luisa le parece una comida «demasiado sana» y, sobre todo, le apetece mucho comer pescado.

C. Uno de los anuncios es de comida vegetariana y con esta actividad de expresión oral queremos que los estudiantes den su opinión sobre este tipo de dieta.

No es necesario, en este momento, plantear un debate sobre el tema; bastará simplemente con que los alumnos contesten a las preguntas: si creen que la comida vegetariana es sana y por qué, y si suelen ir a esta clase de restaurantes.

El debate sobre este tema puede ser interesante y lo plantearemos más adelante.

D. El estudiante debe encontrar a tres compañeros que compartan sus gustos y quieran comer en el mismo lugar que él. Después, explicarán las razones de su elección.

sesenta y una 61

▶ SABER VIVIR

Sugerencia

Al final, cada grupo hablará del restaurante elegido y de las razones de su elección. Si el grupo es reducido, cuatro o cinco personas, cada una de ellas puede elegir a un compañero y preguntarle sobre sus preferencias; a continuación, se explicará al resto de la clase.

E. Terminamos la secuencia con este ejercicio en el que cada estudiante hablará sobre su restaurante, cafetería o bar favorito en la ciudad donde se encuentra.

Sugerencia

Podemos pedirles a los estudiantes que comenten si hay algo sobre la comida y la bebida en España que les ha llamado la atención. Los alumnos casi siempre nos refieren con sorpresa el hecho de que los españoles tomemos pan con aceite para desayunar, que se beba normalmente cerveza o vino con las comidas, que compartamos ciertos alimentos —por ejemplo, la ensalada— y que todos los comensales coman del mismo plato... La visión que cada alumno tenga dependerá de la cultura de su lugar de procedencia. En este punto, debemos promover el diálogo intercultural.

Solución

C, D y **E.** Respuesta libre.

OBSERVA, APRENDE Y RECUERDA

Toda la sección va a desarrollarse en torno al trabajo inductivo de las formas y el uso del imperativo en español.

3 ¿Una vida sana?

A. Estamos ante una actividad de comprensión auditiva con la que intentaremos que el alumno reflexione sobre el uso del imperativo afirmativo. En primer lugar, se leerá en plenaria el decálogo para una vida saludable. Tras comentar los diferentes puntos y resolver las dudas de vocabulario, pondremos la audición dos veces, si es necesario. El estudiante tendrá que comparar lo que se dice en el decálogo con lo que explica Alberto sobre su día a día. Obviamente tendrá que llegar a la conclusión de que no lleva una vida sana.

Solución

Posible respuesta

Alberto no lleva una vida saludable según el decálogo de la revista. Su vida es demasiado sedentaria; no hace ningún tipo de ejercicio físico. Tampoco suele practicar ningún deporte ni va al gimnasio. Además, a veces, come alimentos que no son muy saludables, como patatas fritas. Quizás trabaja demasiado y, seguramente, por eso tiene estrés.

B. Ahora queremos que sean los estudiantes los que amplíen el decálogo con sus propias recomendaciones para llevar una vida sana.

Intentaremos que usen la forma del imperativo afirmativo y, para ello, dirigiremos un poco la actividad.

Como no conocen aún la forma del imperativo, también pueden expresar la idea en infinitivo, pero seguro que muchos ensayarán esta nueva forma.

Solución

Posible respuesta

Pasa menos tiempo en el trabajo. Intenta hacer más ejercicio físico. Come menos patatas fritas. Bebe poca cerveza. Bebe más agua. Sal un poco cada día a pasear. Apúntate al gimnasio mañana mismo. Ve andando a casa al salir del trabajo. Relájate caminando.

NOTAS

OBSERVA, APRENDE Y RECUERDA

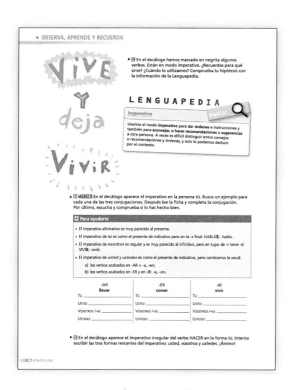

Ejemplo de verbos de la conjugación -IR en la segunda persona del imperativo regular: *vive* (vivir).

LLEVAR: tú lleva, usted lleve, vosotros /-as llevad, ustedes lleven.

COMER: tú come, usted coma, vosotros /-as comed, ustedes coman.

VIVIR: tú vive, usted viva, vosotros /-as vivid, ustedes vivan.

E. Es el momento de reflexionar sobre las formas irregulares y, para ello, partimos de una que aparece en el decálogo: *haz* (hacer, tú).

Sugerencia

En primer lugar, diremos a nuestros estudiantes que no se preocupen, porque no son muchos los verbos que tienen la forma del imperativo irregular en la persona *tú*; esto los tranquilizará bastante. Después, podemos dejarles unos minutos para que completen la conjugación del resto de las personas de este verbo.

A continuación, se escribirá la solución en la pizarra, explicando el porqué de cada forma:

(Usted) haga: como la 1.ª persona del presente de indicativo (*hago*) pero cambiando la vocal → *haga*.

(Ustedes) hagan: final + *-n*.

(Vosotros) haced: cambiamos la *-r* del infinitivo por la *-d*.

Finalmente, les daremos una nueva regla para el imperativo de las formas *usted* y *ustedes* con los verbos irregulares: en la primera persona del singular del presente de indicativo cambiamos la vocal; *hacer: hago → haga, hagan; poner: pongo → ponga, pongan; decir: digo → diga, digan; tener: tengo → tenga, tengan…*

Las irregularidades de verbos como *conducir (conduzco → conduzca, conduzcan)* o *coger (cojo → coja, cojan…)* las dejaremos para más adelante.

Solución

Usted haga, vosotros /-as haced, ustedes hagan.

C. En esta ocasión hemos preferido que el estudiante cuente con la regla de Lenguapedia sobre el imperativo, pero, después de leerla y volver a revisar el decálogo, tendrá que deducir que, en este caso, no se trata de órdenes, sino de consejos o recomendaciones.

Solución

Posible respuesta

En el decálogo se utiliza el imperativo para hacer recomendaciones o para aconsejar a otras personas.

D. En el decálogo hemos usado la segunda persona de singular *(tú)* y el objetivo de esta actividad es que el estudiante busque un ejemplo para cada una de las tres conjugaciones. La comprensión auditiva consiste en comprobar si se han conjugado bien los tres verbos que se proponen, con la ayuda de la ficha. Finalmente, debemos resaltar el hecho de que la forma de *vosotros/-as* siempre es regular; los estudiantes agradecen esta información.

Solución

Ejemplos de verbos de la conjugación -AR en la segunda persona del imperativo regular: *lleva* (llevar), *utiliza* (utilizar), *intenta* (intentar), *visita* (visitar), *olvida* (olvidar), *relájate* (relajarse).

Ejemplos de verbos de la conjugación -ER en la segunda persona del imperativo regular: *come* (comer), *bebe* (beber).

SABER VIVIR

OBSERVA, APRENDE Y RECUERDA

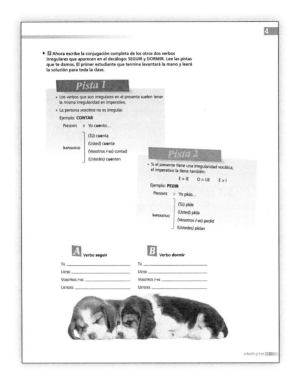

F. El estudiante ha de completar la conjugación del imperativo de dos verbos irregulares de forma individual. Después el profesor escribirá en la pizarra la solución. En este caso, se trata de verbos que tienen cambio vocálico. El alumno cuenta con la ayuda de las pistas 1 y 2.

Sugerencia

Como en el decálogo no aparece ningún verbo con el cambio vocálico *e → ie*, proponemos poner en la pizarra algún ejemplo (*cerrar, pensar…*) y conjugar en plenaria todas las personas en el imperativo afirmativo.

Solución

A. Seguir: tú sigue, usted siga, vosotros /-as seguid, ustedes sigan.

B. Dormir: tú duerme, usted duerma, vosotros /-as dormid, ustedes duerman.

OBSERVA, APRENDE Y RECUERDA

4 No escribas más notas, por favor…

A. Ahora es el momento de introducir el imperativo negativo y, para ello, propondremos a los estudiantes que se fijen en las notas que Luisa le ha dejado a Fernando y que reflexionen sobre la diferencia de estas formas con respecto a las anteriores.

Solo se espera que digan que son órdenes en forma negativa porque sí que interesa que se fijen por el contexto en que las notas recogen un tipo de órdenes en negativo.

Solución

La diferencia es que los verbos marcados en las notas están en imperativo negativo. Los verbos de las actividades anteriores estaban en imperativo afirmativo.

OBSERVA, APRENDE Y RECUERDA

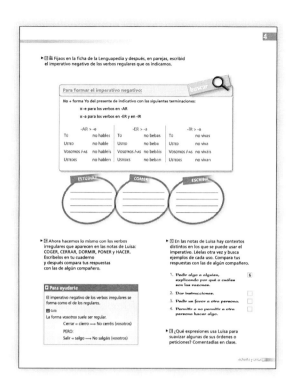

B. En esta actividad los alumnos tienen que escribir el imperativo negativo de tres verbos regulares propuestos con la ayuda de la ficha Lenguapedia.

Sugerencia

Es conveniente resaltar que para el imperativo negativo tenemos que cambiar la vocal en todas las personas.

Los alumnos se tendrán que fijar en que para las formas del imperativo negativo de *usted* y *ustedes* solo tenemos que añadir *no* al imperativo afirmativo, ya que para el imperativo afirmativo hicimos el cambio de vocal correspondiente.

Solución

ESTUDIAR: tú no estudies, usted no estudie, vosotros /-as no estudiéis, ustedes no estudien.

COMER: tú no comas, usted no coma, vosotros /-as no comáis, ustedes no coman.

ESCRIBIR: tú no escribas, usted no escriba, vosotros /-as no escribáis, ustedes no escriban.

C. Un segundo paso es conjugar el imperativo negativo de los verbos irregulares de las notas de Luisa.

Se trata de un trabajo individual para que el estudiante pueda reflexionar, comparar con los modelos anteriores y, finalmente, escribir la forma correcta.

Solución

COGER: tú no cojas, usted no coja, vosotros /-as no cojáis, ustedes no cojan.

CERRAR: tú no cierres, usted no cierre, vosotros /-as no cerréis, ustedes no cierren.

DORMIR: tú no duermas, usted no duerma, vosotras /-as no durmáis, ustedes no duerman.

PONER: tú no pongas, usted no ponga, vosotros /-as no pongáis, ustedes no pongan.

HACER: tú no hagas, usted no haga, vosotros /-as no hagáis, ustedes no hagan.

D. El objetivo de esta actividad es detectar los contextos de uso del modo imperativo. El estudiante debe leer de nuevo las notas de Laura y deducir los distintos valores según el contexto.

Trabajarán en parejas o individualmente y después compararán las respuestas con el resto de compañeros.

Sugerencia

Resulta necesario que después hablemos de otras situaciones posibles y que sean ellos los que creen sus propios ejemplos para cada situación.

Solución

2. (***No pongas*** *la lavadora…*). Nota 5.

3. (*¡**No cierres** la ventana, por favor!*). También podría ser la 4 (*Cariño, **no te duermas**…*). Nota 3.

4. (*¡**No comas** tantos dulces!*) También podría ser la 2 (*¡**No cojas** el ascensor!*), o la 4 (*…**no te duermas**…*).

E. Acabamos este apartado con algunas fórmulas de cortesía para expresar peticiones y órdenes que el alumno debe descubrir en las notas de Laura.

Sugerencia

Nuevamente sería recomendable que animáramos a los estudiantes a que piensen en otros contextos en los que podamos usar expresiones para minimizar la posible descortesía de una orden o petición. Para ello, podrían trabajar en grupos pequeños o en parejas.

Les proponemos estas otras: *¡Anda! Abre la ventana / **Si tienes tiempo**, plancha la ropa…*

Estas son expresiones pragmáticas que atenúan las peticiones.

Solución

Por favor… ¿Qué te parece? ¿Vale? Si no te importa…

SABER VIVIR

OBSERVA, APRENDE Y RECUERDA

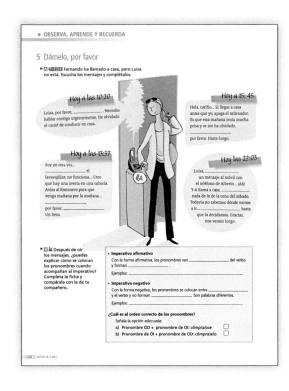

que escuchen la versión original. Es bueno que les indiquemos cuáles son las versiones personales que serían también posibles en estos contextos.

Solución

10:20: llámame.

13:37: No pongas / Avísalo / No lo olvides.

15:45: Apágalo.

22:03: mándame / no le digas / No se lo digas.

B. En este ejercicio introducimos un contenido nuevo: el uso de los pronombres personales de objeto directo y objeto indirecto con el imperativo.

El alumno suele ver rápidamente la diferencia de colocación según se trate del imperativo afirmativo (detrás, enclítico) o negativo (delante).

Además, deberá descubrir qué pronombre se usa en primer lugar cuando aparecen dos en la misma frase: OI siempre primero; después OD.

Sugerencia

Creemos conveniente aprovechar este momento para recordar a los estudiantes que, cuando se trata de un verbo pronominal, el pronombre también va delante del OD.

Ejemplo: ¡*Lávatelas*! (*Lavarse, tú, las manos*). Podemos conjugar este ejemplo en todas las personas para enlazar con el siguiente apartado.

Solución

Imperativo afirmativo: detrás – una sola palabra. Ejemplos: *avísalo; apágalo; mándame; llámame*.

Imperativo negativo: NO – dos palabras. Ejemplos: *no lo olvides; no le digas; no se lo digas*.

¿Cuál es el orden correcto de los pronombres? b)

5 Dámelo, por favor

Cerramos la sección con dos ejercicios diseñados para que los estudiantes observen la colocación de los pronombres personales cuando acompañan al imperativo.

A. Comprensión auditiva en la que los estudiantes tienen que completar los mensajes con los imperativos que faltan. Antes de iniciar la escucha les podemos pedir que intenten deducir los verbos correspondientes por el contexto, después veremos todas las versiones y, finalmente, pondremos la grabación para

NOTAS

OBSERVA, APRENDE Y RECUERDA

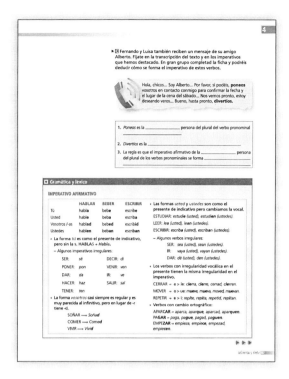

C. Con otro mensaje el alumno debe inferir que la forma del imperativo afirmativo de *vosotros,* cuando va con el pronombre, pierde la *-d*.

Completaremos este contenido aludiendo al caso del verbo *ir: idos*.

Solución

1. segunda – ponerse.
2. segunda persona del plural del verbo pronominal divertirse.
3. segunda – quitando la letra *d* del imperativo y añadiendo el pronombre *os*.

PRACTICA

6 ¡Apuntaos!

Abrimos esta sección con la información que aparece en el blog *Trotamundos,* que permitirá a los estudiantes completar los anuncios del ejercicio 6B con la forma del imperativo correcta y relacionar cada uno de ellos con las personas a las que les puede interesar.

A. Actividad de comprensión lectora en la que los estudiantes tienen que atender a las peticiones y consultas que han llegado al blog *Trotamundos*. Podemos hacer una lectura en plenaria para resolver cualquier duda.

Sugerencia

Tras la lectura, les indicaremos que comparen las peticiones del ejercicio: a qué actividades se refieren, que descubran quiénes utilizan en sus peticiones una forma ya estudiada en la unidad anterior. Es el caso de Ramón: *Necesitaría saber...,* o de Rosario: *Me gustaría hablar de...*

► SABER VIVIR

PRACTICA

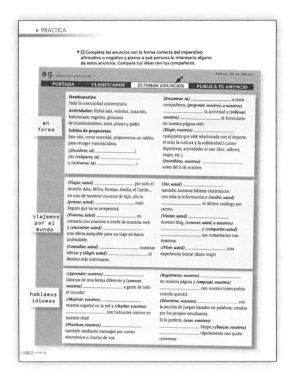

B. Ahora, el estudiante, individualmente, tiene que completar los anuncios con los imperativos adecuados. Podemos empezar explicando el significado de aquellas palabras o expresiones que creamos que pueden desconocer, animándolos a que pregunten otras dudas posibles según vayan leyendo los anuncios. Cuando estos se hayan completado y hayan sido corregidos, los alumnos tendrán que decidir a qué personas de las que escriben en el blog les pueden interesar estos anuncios.

Sugerencia

Colguemos un tablón de recomendaciones en la clase en el que cada estudiante semanalmente invite al resto de sus compañeros a conocer un lugar de la ciudad que ha visitado, a ver una película, a probar una comida…

Solución

En forma: Decídete - te relajes - actívate - Encuentra - proponednos - rellenad - Elegid - Inscribíos.

Este anuncio es perfecto para José porque busca un centro deportivo que esté cerca de su facultad.

Viajamos por el mundo: Viaje - piense - Póngase - encuentre - Consulte - elija - Vea - reciba - Visite - conózcanos - comparta - Viva.

Este anuncio es ideal para Ramón porque quiere un viaje especial para regalárselo a su mujer y un crucero de lujo sería perfecto.

Hablamos idiomas: Aprended - conoced - Mejorad - charlad - Practicad - Registraos - empezad - Divertíos - usad - buscad.

Este anuncio es ideal para Steve porque está buscando un lugar para hacer intercambio de idiomas de forma divertida.

PRACTICA

7 ¡Escúchame!, que soy tu abuela…

A. El objetivo de esta actividad es expresar consejos. Para ello, el alumno ha de completar los que le da a Laura su abuela. Son consejos muy propios de las abuelas.

Solución

1. no te pongas - ponte. **2.** andes. **3.** ayúdame. **4.** Hablad. **5.** veas. **6.** Escribe. **7.** desayuna. **8.** comáis. **9.** di - seas. **10.** pon. **11.** haz - dales. **12.** Sal - salgas.

B. Ahora los estudiantes descubrirán si los consejos que les dan sus abuelos o sus padres coinciden con los que la mayoría de los españoles reciben de los suyos.

Sugerencia

Podemos hacer un paréntesis en la práctica de los contenidos lingüísticos para que los estudiantes reflexionen sobre este aspecto cultural y hablen sobre el papel de los abuelos en la familia, su relación con ellos, etc. Por cierto, ¡es un momento ideal para explicarles una expresión nueva en español: *No tener abuela!*

Solución

Respuesta libre.

4. Baja la música si no te importa, por favor. Es que no puedo dormir. / Jaime, por favor, no pongas la música tan alta.

5. Carlos, perdona, es que no te oigo. Habla más alto si no te importa. / No hables en voz baja, por favor. / Háblame más alto, por favor. / Oye, por favor, habla más alto.

6. No compres el pan; ya lo he comprado yo esta mañana.

7. No vayáis a ver esa película. Es muy aburrida.

8. Señora, por favor, siéntese. / Señora, siéntese aquí, por favor.

9. Ven, ven, por favor. Será una fiesta genial. / Pablo, por favor, ven, ven… Será muy divertida. Lo pasaremos muy bien.

8 ¿Dónde está el acento?

En este grupo de ejercicios abordaremos los aspectos fonéticos y ortográficos de la unidad; revisaremos contenidos ya estudiados en niveles anteriores, la separación silábica y las reglas generales de acentuación en español.

A. Empezamos con una reflexión sobre el concepto de sílaba tónica, primordial para entender las reglas de acentuación.

Solución

b) Sílaba tónica.

B. Continuamos con un ejercicio de comprensión auditiva en el que los alumnos tienen que completar las reglas fundamentales de la acentuación en español.

Sugerencia

Para ayudar al alumno a recordar las reglas, les facilitaremos algunas palabras de ejemplo; aguda: *café;* llana: *libro;* esdrújula: *Málaga;* sobreesdrújula: *pregúntamelo*.

Solución

1. última sílaba.
2. penúltima.
3. antepenúltima.
4. anterior.

C. Aportamos diferentes situaciones para que el alumno pida un favor, aconseje, ordene o haga una invitación usando el imperativo. Los resultados serán más variados si primero hacen esta actividad individualmente y después van comparando las respuestas.

Solución

Posibles respuestas

1. Carlos, por favor, abre la ventana… Es que hace muchísimo calor.

2. Chicos, pedid una tapa de ensaladilla rusa ¡Esta riquísima! / Chicos, comeos una tapita de tortilla de patatas. Seguro que os gustará. Está para chuparse los dedos.

3. Cariño, no duermas tanto… Dormir tanto no es nada bueno para la salud. / Cariño, duerme menos, por favor. Es que quiero que por las mañanas me ayudes a preparar el desayuno.

NOTAS

▶ SABER VIVIR

PRACTICA

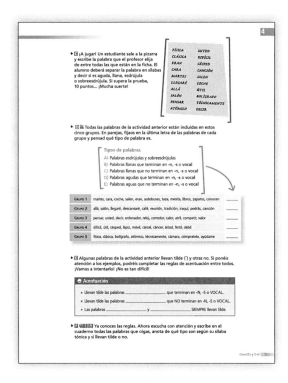

C. Esta es una actividad lúdica para separar las palabras silábicamente y posteriormente clasificarlas según su acentuación. Es importante llevarla a cabo de una forma muy distendida, ya que este contenido, aunque los estudiantes suelen demandarlo al principio, es habitual que se vuelva árido por su complejidad conforme van profundizando en él.

Solución

Fí- si-ca: esdrújula.
Clá-si-ca: esdrújula.
E-ran: llana.
Ca-ra: llana.
Mar-tes: llana.
Lle-ga-ré: aguda.
A-llá: aguda.
Sa-lón: aguda.
Pen-sar: aguda.
A-tó-mi-co: esdrújula.
Us-ted: aguda.
Di-fí-cil: llana.
Cés-ped: llana.
Can-ción: aguda.
Sa-len: llana.
Co-che: llana.
Ú-til: llana.
Bo-lí-gra-fo: esdrújula.
Téc-ni-ca-men-te: sobreesdrújula.
De-cir: aguda.

D. Una vez que dominan la separación silábica, animamos a los alumnos a que se fijen en las terminaciones de cada grupo para que descubran por qué, siendo el mismo tipo de palabras —agudas, por ejemplo—, unas llevan tilde y otras no.

Solución

Grupo 1: B.

Grupo 2: D.

Grupo 3: E.

Grupo 4: C.

Grupo 5: A.

E. Ahora los estudiantes podrán deducir y completar las reglas correspondientes.

Solución

Llevan tilde las palabras **agudas** que terminan en -N, -S o VOCAL.

Llevan tilde las palabras **llanas** que NO terminan en -N, -S o VOCAL.

Las palabras **esdrújulas** y **sobreesdrújulas** siempre llevan tilde.

F. Y para terminar, un ejercicio de audio en el que los estudiantes tendrán que poner en práctica todo lo deducido con anterioridad. Se trata de clasificar y acentuar, cuando sea necesario, las palabras que escuchen. Proponemos que se les dé un tiempo para contestar, e intentaremos buscar el componente lúdico para motivar e incitar a la participación.

Solución

Tómbola (esdrújula);

yogur (aguda);

látigo (esdrújula);

fútbol (llana);

helicóptero (esdrújula);

pídeselo (sobreesdrújula);

fajín (aguda);

alto (llana);

jabalí (aguda);

tempestad (aguda);

chófer (llana);

riñón (aguda);

ángel (llana);

alcánzamelo (sobreesdrújula);

pillar (aguda);

caramelo (llana);

balancín (aguda);

betún (aguda);

azúcar (llana);

regaliz (aguda);

reacción (aguda).

PRACTICA

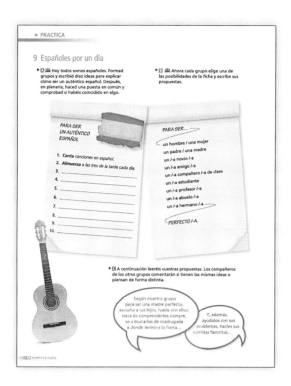

9 Españoles por un día

A. Volvemos con la práctica del imperativo, ahora con un trabajo en pequeños grupos que consiste en escribir frases en imperativo para explicar cómo ser un «auténtico español». Podemos animar a los alumnos a que lo hagan con sentido del humor. Después, en plenaria, se comentarán todas las propuestas. El profesor intentará romper tópicos y estereotipos.

B. En este ejercicio, completamos el anterior, pero, ahora, aplicando los supuestos que se plantean en el libro. Anime a los estudiantes a redactar enunciados originales.

C. El objetivo de esta actividad es generar debate para que se compartan en plenaria todos los puntos de vista. Es conveniente que se contrasten opiniones argumentando las causas del desacuerdo, en caso de que este se produzca.

Solución

A, B y **C.** Respuesta libre.

EN COMUNICACIÓN

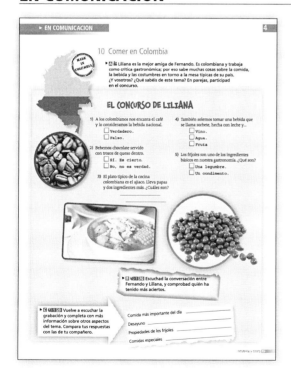

En esta sección, además de activar el empleo de los contenidos de la unidad, nos proponemos difundir algunos aspectos sobre ciertos países de Hispanoamérica para que el conocimiento de la cultura no quede reducido únicamente a la española.

10 Comer en Colombia

A. La secuencia arranca con una actividad que tiene como propósito dar a conocer aspectos de la comida, la bebida y algunas costumbres en torno a la mesa típicas de Colombia. Los alumnos tienen que responder a un test en el que se pondrán a prueba su experiencia y sus conocimientos anteriores. Podemos animarlos a que hablen sobre todo lo que saben acerca de este tema y no únicamente en relación con Colombia, sino también sobre cualquier otro país de Latinoamérica.

Solución

1. Verdadero.
2. Sí. Es cierto.
3. Maíz y pollo.
4. Fruta.
5. Una legumbre.

B. Actividad de comprensión auditiva que les sirve a los alumnos para verificar las respuestas que han dado en el test anterior.

C. Volvemos a escuchar la grabación con la idea de que los estudiantes se fijen en otros aspectos que se mencionan sobre el tema. Ahora el objetivo es que conozcan detalles culturales y que los contrasten con los suyos propios. Por ejemplo, se compararán las comidas familiares de Colombia con las típicas en España: Nochebuena, Navidad, Reyes —con el típico roscón—, los cumpleaños… Otro aspecto que se puede comentar es que los españoles asocian el chocolate a los churros, pero no al queso, por ejemplo.

▶ SABER VIVIR

Solución

La comida más importante del día para los colombianos es el almuerzo.

Los colombianos suelen desayunar dos veces: toman el desayuno y, después, las medias nueves, un segundo desayuno o un pequeño aperitivo de media mañana.

Propiedades de los fríjoles: son muy buenos para prevenir la diabetes.

Comidas especiales: en Colombia preparan un almuerzo especial para el Día de la Madre o del Padre y una torta para celebrar el cumpleaños.

Sugerencia

Para concluir esta serie de actividades, el profesor puede proponer a los alumnos que formen grupos por nacionalidades y preparen un trabajo en el que expongan las características de la gastronomía de sus respectivos países. Pueden hablar, por ejemplo, de cuestiones como las comidas del día, los ingredientes básicos, las bebidas más populares, la forma de preparar los alimentos, los platos típicos, las costumbres en torno a la mesa, las celebraciones familiares en torno a la mesa, entre otros aspectos que consideren interesantes.

En caso de que se trate de una clase con estudiantes de una misma nacionalidad, pediremos que cada uno prepare una exposición sobre la gastronomía de un país que le guste distinto al suyo.

Creemos que es necesario que los alumnos tengan suficiente tiempo para elaborar sus trabajos, así que lo mejor es plantearla como tarea para casa y que la exposición se realice en la siguiente sesión. Si en el aula tenemos alumnos a los que realmente les guste la cocina o sepan preparar algún plato de su país, les pediremos que den la receta al resto de la clase, indicándoles que deben utilizar la forma del imperativo para su redacción.

El profesor, por su parte, les podría dar una de algún plato típico español, como, por ejemplo, la tortilla de patatas, una comida muy típica que suele gustar mucho.

EN COMUNICACIÓN

11 ¡Vaya día!

A. Actividad de comprensión auditiva cuyo objetivo es que el alumno aprenda algunos imperativos lexicalizados. Para ello, tiene que completar las frases que dice Luisa con la expresión correspondiente.

Sugerencia

Es conveniente que informemos a los estudiantes de la importancia de la entonación en estos casos, pues tanto *¡Vaya!* como *¡Anda!* se pueden usar para indicar sorpresa positiva o negativa.

También les explicaremos que *Mira* se puede utilizar de dos formas distintas: *Mira, eres un poco mentiroso. ¡Mira **que** eres mentiroso!*

Solución

1. ¡Vaya!
2. ¡Anda!
3. Venga – vamos.
4. Mira.

EN COMUNICACIÓN

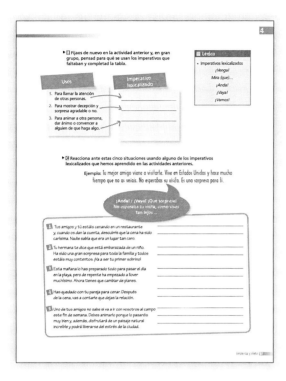

B. Ahora, con la ayuda de los ejemplos anteriores y los usos que se muestran, los alumnos tienen que deducir y relacionar cada uso con su imperativo correspondiente.

Solución

1. Mira…
2. ¡Vaya! ¡Anda!
3. ¡Venga! ¡Vamos!

C. Esta fase es fundamental y es la que nos va a decir si realmente los alumnos han comprendido el uso de los imperativos lexicalizados. En esta actividad planteamos una serie de situaciones y ellos deben reaccionar utilizando alguno de estos imperativos. En todos los casos son posibles varias opciones, excepto en el número 4.

Solución

Posible respuesta

1. **¡Vaya! / ¡Anda!** ¡Qué caro! No sabía que este restaurante era tan caro… ¡Qué barbaridad!
2. **¡Anda! / ¡Vaya!** ¡Qué alegría! Voy a ser tío por primera vez…
3. **¡Vaya! / ¡Anda!** Chicos, ¡qué mala suerte! Está lloviendo muchísimo. Creo que no podremos ir a la playa… Otro día será.
4. **Mira,** tengo que decirte algo importante: «Te dejo, ya no me gustas».
5. **Venga, vamos,** hombre… **Venga,** anímate… Seguro que lo pasaremos de miedo. Será un fin de semana para relajarte y muy divertido… **Vamos, venga…**

¡extra! CONTEXTOS

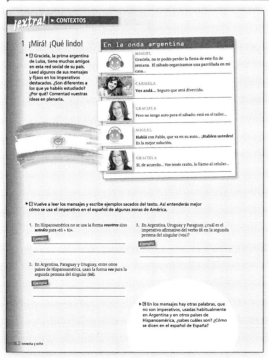

Este bloque se inicia con una actividad de comprensión lectora en la que el estudiante tiene que descubrir algunas características del español de América.

1 ¡Mirá! ¡Qué lindo!

A. En primer lugar, presentamos una muestra de imperativos en los mensajes que los alumnos tienen que leer. Después, les propondremos que comenten las diferencias con las formas que ellos han estudiado.

Solución

Posible respuesta

Estos imperativos se forman de manera distinta a los que ya hemos estudiado. También hay un uso diferente de la persona *ustedes;* no se emplea *vosotros,* en su lugar se utiliza *ustedes.* Además, se usa *vos* en vez de *tú.*

B. Ahora, presentamos las reglas y los alumnos tendrán que buscar los ejemplos correspondientes en los mensajes anteriores.

Sugerencia

Si los estudiantes muestran suficiente interés por el tema, podemos animarlos a que investiguen sobre el español de América y

setenta y tres **73**

SABER VIVIR

pedirles como tarea para casa que preparen una exposición sobre otras diferencias en relación con el español que se habla en la Península. Seguro que entre todos conseguiremos un compendio de rasgos característicos acorde a este nivel. Muchos estudiantes estarán interesados en el tema porque quizá quieran viajar a Latinoamérica, en muchos casos, para trabajar como voluntarios o porque se sienten atraídos por su cultura.

Solución

1. ¡Hablen ustedes!
2. Vos andá.
3. Andá.

C. Finalmente, los estudiantes deben descubrir otras palabras genuinas del español de América que aparecen en los mensajes.

Sugerencia

Abordaremos las diferencias entre el léxico de Hispanoamérica y el del español de España: *auto* por *coche*, *celular* por *teléfono móvil*, *computadora* por *ordenador*, *papas* por *patatas*... Podemos encargar a los alumnos la tarea de buscar diferencias léxicas entre el español de España y el de América. El objetivo no es que aprendan una lista inmensa de vocabulario localista de diferentes países de Latinoamérica, sino que conozcan algunas palabras de uso frecuente. De este modo, estaremos consiguiendo nuestro propósito de acercamiento a diferentes culturas.

Solución

Auto por coche; *celular* por teléfono móvil.

¡extra! PRACTICA

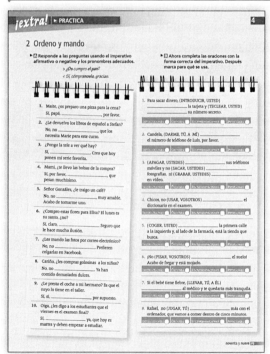

De nuevo presentamos una secuencia para chequear, reforzar y revisar el imperativo, así como practicar su uso con los pronombres personales.

2 Ordeno y mando

A. Primero el estudiante tiene que contestar a las preguntas con el imperativo y los pronombres adecuados.

Sugerencia

Normalmente, cuando el estudiante hace este tipo de ejercicios, se suele olvidar de poner las tildes correspondientes. Por eso, debemos recordárselo antes de empezar y ayudarlos explicándoles que si el verbo se compone de una sílaba y tenemos dos pronombres, el imperativo afirmativo lleva tilde (*dáselo, dímelo*), y que si la palabra es llana y tenemos dos pronombres, el imperativo afirmativo lleva tilde también (*préstaselo, devuélveselos, llévamelas...*). Recordaremos, asimismo, que se trata de palabras esdrújulas en el primer caso y de sobreesdrújulas en el segundo.

Solución

1. prepáranosla.
2. se los devuelvas.
3. ponla.
4. llévamelas.
5. me lo traiga.
6. cómpraselas.
7. se las mandes.
8. se las compro.
9. préstaselo.
10. dígaselo.

B. De nuevo revisamos la forma del imperativo. Además, los alumnos tendrán que señalar cuál es su uso en cada caso.

Sugerencia

Estamos terminando la unidad y ahora, en que los contenidos están consolidados, es buen momento para pedir a los estudiantes que analicen los anuncios que les habíamos pedido que recopilaran en el ejercicio 1C.

Solución

1. Introduzca - teclee. Instrucciones.
2. dame. Petición.
3. Apaguen - saquen - graben. Instrucciones.
4. uséis. Orden.
5. Coja. Instrucción.
6. piséis. Orden.
7. llévalo. Recomendación.
8. juegues. Orden / Petición.

¡extra! EN COMUNICACIÓN

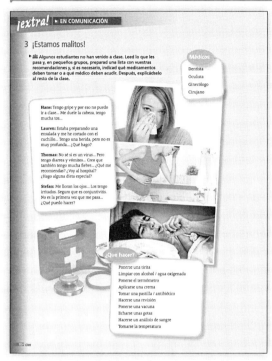

3 ¡Estamos malitos!

El objetivo fundamental de esta actividad es presentar el léxico relacionado con la salud, el cuerpo, la medicina, los medicamentos, los especialistas, los profesionales de la medicina... Se plantean algunos casos en los que los personajes explican sus problemas físicos, y los estudiantes, en grupos, deben hacer recomendaciones al respecto. Entre ellos mismos intentarán resolver las dudas de léxico; si no fuera posible, preguntarán a otro grupo y, en último caso, al profesor.

Solución

Posibles respuestas

Hans: Tómate una pastilla para el dolor de cabeza y para bajar la fiebre. Ponte el termómetro para comprobar si la fiebre es muy alta y, si no te encuentras mejor, ve al hospital. Allí te harán un análisis de sangre. / Acude al médico; a lo mejor te receta un antibiótico para la fiebre y el dolor.

Lauren: Limpia la herida con alcohol. / Límpiate la herida con agua oxigenada y ponte una tirita.

Thomas: Si tienes vómitos y diarrea, ve al hospital inmediatamente. Toma arroz cocido y alguna bebida isotónica. / No bebas vino, cerveza ni ningún otro tipo de alcohol. Haz una dieta blanda. Tómate la temperatura para ver si tienes fiebre. / Ponte el termómetro para ver si tienes fiebre alta.

Stefan: Ve al oculista. / Pregunta en la farmacia, compra algunas gotas para la conjuntivitis y échatelas.

NOTAS

SABER VIVIR

¡EXTRA! EN COMUNICACIÓN

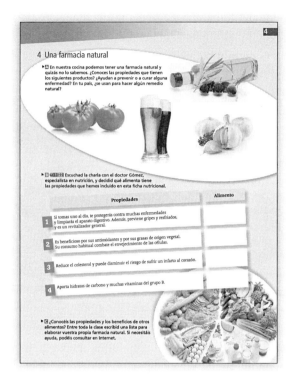

4 Una farmacia natural

A. Ejercicio de expresión oral en el que el estudiante tendrá que hablar de remedios caseros o naturales que conozca para prevenir o curar enfermedades.

El aceite de oliva en España es un producto casi milagroso para muchas personas, hasta el punto de que hay quienes lo utilizan para todo.

Seguro que otras culturas tienen también algún ingrediente curativo natural que se ha convertido en fetiche.

Solución

Respuesta libre.

B. Ejercicio de comprensión auditiva con el que el estudiante podrá conocer las propiedades de algunos ingredientes. En primer lugar y en plenaria, leeremos la ficha nutricional y resolveremos las dudas de léxico. Después escucharán la charla con el doctor especialista en nutrición.

Solución

1. El ajo.

2. El aceite de oliva.

3. El tomate.

4. La cerveza.

C. Cerramos la unidad tratando el tema de la alimentación, los beneficios y las propiedades de diferentes alimentos. En plenaria podemos animar a los estudiantes a que hablen sobre todos estas cuestiones.

Sugerencia

Como variante y ampliación de esta actividad, sugerimos dividir la clase en grupos y que cada uno de ellos se encargue de investigar en Internet sobre diferentes clases de alimentos; por ejemplo: frutas, verduras, carne, pescado, pan, chocolate... Otro debate que podemos plantear para terminar, y que habíamos dejado pendiente en una actividad anterior, es sobre la comida vegetariana. Dividiremos la clase en dos grupos, los que están a favor de este tipo de alimentación y los que no son partidarios. Ambos grupos tendrán que buscar argumentos para defender sus posturas. Pensamos que es un tema que requiere información y que es imprescindible que se prepare adecuadamente y con tiempo. Internet les servirá de gran ayuda para conseguir los datos que necesiten.

Solución

Respuesta libre.

Unidad 5
Y en el trabajo, ¿qué tal?

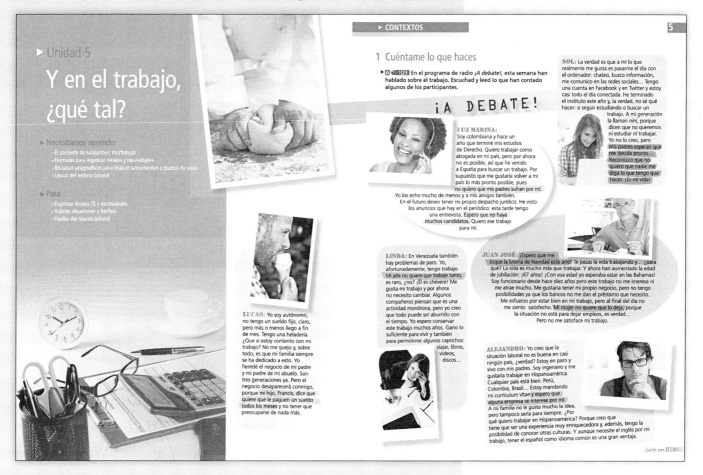

OBJETIVOS DE LA UNIDAD

En esta unidad se revisará, dentro de los **contenidos morfosintácticos**, la morfología del presente de indicativo para que, a través de esta forma verbal ya conocida por el alumno, se llegue a la sistematización de las formas correspondientes del presente de subjuntivo.

Introduciremos estructuras para las siguientes **funciones comunicativas:** expresar deseos y necesidades; valorar situaciones y hechos.

En cuanto a los **contenidos léxico-semánticos**, nos centraremos en el ámbito laboral y en el campo semántico referido a las profesiones.

Por lo que respecta a los **contenidos socioculturales**, hablaremos de la situación sociopolítica de España y otros países del entorno. Por otro lado, reflexionaremos sobre uno de los aspectos característicos de las familias españolas: la cada vez más demorada independencia de los hijos.

Los **contenidos pragmáticos** que se presentan son las enumeraciones para intensificar elementos del discurso y la repetición para mostrar acuerdo o desacuerdo (*claro, claro; no, no*).

Finalmente, en los **contenidos fonéticos y ortográficos** nos ocuparemos de la tilde diacrítica en los monosílabos (*tú, él, mí, sí, té, dé, sé, más*) y de la acentuación los adverbios acabados en *-mente*.

Y EN EL TRABAJO, ¿QUÉ TAL?

CONTEXTOS

1 Cuéntame lo que haces

Comienza la secuencia con una actividad de comprensión auditiva para introducir el uso del presente de subjuntivo en fórmulas que sirven para expresar necesidad y deseo, así como para valorar hechos o situaciones. Además, iniciamos una serie de ejercicios que giran en torno al ámbito temático del empleo.

A. Tenemos los testimonios de seis personas que han hablado para un programa de radio sobre diferentes aspectos relacionados con el mundo del trabajo. En un primer momento, comenzaremos con la escucha de la grabación. Sería conveniente que los estudiantes volvieran a leer los textos en voz alta para reforzar la comprensión, la vocalización y la entonación. La lectura en voz alta ayuda a desarrollar la comprensión auditiva y la producción oral. Finalmente, aclararemos las dudas léxicas que pudieran surgir. Esta fase final es muy importante porque en cada fragmento hemos incluido el vocabulario básico de este nivel relacionado con el ámbito temático del mundo laboral.

En el fragmento de Linda podríamos hacer ver a los alumnos la intensificación de los elementos de su discurso mediante las enumeraciones, por ejemplo, de algunos de los caprichos que puede permitirse.

Sugerencia

Como actividad previa a la lectura de los testimonios, podemos preguntar a los alumnos si están trabajando en ese momento, si les gusta su actual empleo, si preferirían cambiar de trabajo...

B. Los estudiantes responderán a una serie de cuestiones que tienen que ver con el tema del trabajo: tipo de actividad que les gustaría realizar, salario, satisfacción laboral, ambiente en su lugar de trabajo...

Sugerencia

Una variante sería realizar la actividad de manera individual por escrito y compartir los resultados con el resto del grupo.

Solución

Respuesta libre.

C. A continuación, los alumnos relacionarán las imágenes con las profesiones que aparecen en el recuadro. Una vez identificadas, deberán explicar las razones de su elección.

Solución

1. Bombero.
2. Veterinario.
3. Repartidor de pizzas.
4. Escritor.
5. Piloto de avión.
6. Diseñador.
7. Fontanero.

D. La siguiente actividad de comprensión e interacción orales está pensada para seguir trabajando el léxico relacionado con el ámbito laboral. Los alumnos escucharán la grabación. Seguidamente, resolveremos las dudas de vocabulario y, a continuación, los estudiantes escribirán las cuatro profesiones de las que se habla. A final, en plenaria, responderán a las preguntas que hemos planteado en el enunciado. De nuevo, la intención es desarrollar la práctica oral.

Sería interesante explicar a los alumnos uno de los contenidos pragmáticos que aparecen en los microdiálogos 2 y 4: la repetición para mostrar acuerdo o desacuerdo. En la segunda conversación se repite el adverbio *no* y en la cuarta advertiremos el uso de la interjección *claro* para dar por cierto o asegurar lo que se dice.

Solución

1. Repartidor de pizzas.
2. Fontanero.
3. Piloto de avión.
4. Veterinaria.

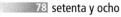

CONTEXTOS

2 Una empresa singular

A. Para continuar con la presentación en contexto de los contenidos léxicos y morfosintácticos de la unidad, presentaremos a los estudiantes el anuncio de una nueva empresa que necesita empleados y que ha sido publicado en una revista digital. Leerán los requisitos que piden a los solicitantes y, después de aclarar las dudas, les pediremos que, en plenaria, comenten de qué trabajo podría tratarse y si lo aceptarían o no. Cada alumno expondrá su punto de vista e insistiremos para que lo haga de forma razonada, justificando sus opiniones.

Solución

Posible respuesta

Es posible que sea un trabajo de vendedor o de comercial. Lo aceptaría porque soy una persona abierta y sociable, y podría vender cualquier cosa, porque me comprometo mucho con mi trabajo.

No lo aceptaría porque no quiero trabajar en exclusividad y quiero disponer de los fines de semana para mí.

B. Ahora cada estudiante deberá explicar, en gran grupo, para qué trabajo cree estar capacitado. Para hacerlo, previamente se fijará en las muestras de lengua presentadas y usará alguno de los adjetivos que hemos incluido en las cajas.

Solución

Respuesta libre.

OBSERVA, APRENDE Y RECUERDA

3 Hablemos claro

Comenzamos una serie de ejercicios en los que guiaremos al alumno en el aprendizaje de la morfología del presente de subjuntivo.

A. Presentamos el diálogo de una pareja, Marta y Luis, que han decidido hablar de todo lo que piensan el uno del otro, lo que desean, lo que necesitan... Pediremos a los alumnos que lean el diálogo y, a continuación, aclararemos las dudas léxicas surgidas, insistiendo en que presten atención a todas las formas verbales que hemos destacado en negrita.

B. En el círculo hemos escrito algunas de las nuevas formas verbales señaladas en el texto. Los alumnos deberán escribir el infinitivo correspondiente y, en plenaria, comentarán qué tienen de particular sus terminaciones. De esta forma, descubrirán que son muy similares a las del presente de indicativo que conocen.

Solución

Escuchar; regalar; leer; ver; escribir; pedir.

setenta y nueve 79

Y EN EL TRABAJO, ¿QUÉ TAL?

OBSERVA, APRENDE Y RECUERDA

E. Gracias al proceso de inferencia que han realizado, los alumnos llegarán a la conclusión de que las formas del presente de subjuntivo son como las del presente de indicativo, pero cambiando la vocal: si se trata de un verbo terminado en *-ar*, se cambiará por *-e* (*-ar* → *-e*; *amar* → *ame*); si es un verbo terminado en *-er* o en *-ir*, se cambiará por *-a* (*-er* o *-ir* → *-a*; *leer* → *lea*, *escribir* → *escriba*). La primera persona del singular siempre es como la tercera.

Sugerencia

Explicaremos a los alumnos que esta nueva forma, el presente de subjuntivo, es la misma que hemos utilizado en la unidad anterior para construir el imperativo negativo.

Solución

El presente de subjuntivo se forma con las mismas terminaciones que el presente de indicativo, pero cambiando la vocal: si es un verbo terminado en *-ar*, se cambiará por *-e*; si es un verbo terminado en *-er* o en *-ir*, se cambiará por *-a*. La primera persona del singular siempre es como la tercera.

C. Ahora queremos que los estudiantes escriban el infinitivo de los verbos que se presentan conjugados y que vuelvan a prestar atención a la flexión verbal.

Solución

Escuchar. Regalar.

D. Teniendo en cuenta los modelos anteriores, animaremos a los estudiantes a que completen la tabla con el paradigma completo de los verbos *leer* y *escribir*.

Solución

	Leer	**Escribir**
Yo	lea	escriba
Tú	leas	escribas
Él / Ella / Usted	lea	escriba
Nosotros /-as	leamos	escribamos
Vosotros /-as	leáis	escribáis
Ellos / Ellas / Ustedes	lean	escriban

NOTAS

OBSERVA, APRENDE Y RECUERDA

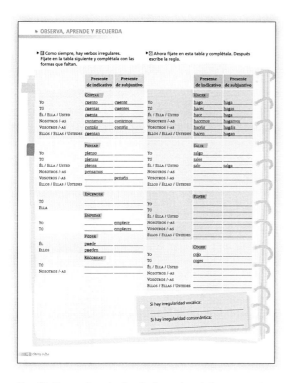

F y G. Tras el trabajo de los ejercicios anteriores, pediremos a los estudiantes que completen las formas que faltan de los verbos irregulares de las tablas.

A continuación, corregiremos la actividad en plenaria.

Finalmente, los alumnos tendrán que deducir la regla para la formación del presente de subjuntivo.

Sugerencia

Si se cree necesario, remitiremos a los alumnos al cuadro de GRAMÁTICA Y LÉXICO de la unidad.

Solución

F.

	Presente de indicativo	Presente de subjuntivo
	CONTAR	
Yo	c*ue*nto	c*ue*nte
Tú	c*ue*ntas	c*ue*ntes
Él / Ella / Usted	c*ue*nta	c*ue*nte
Nosotros /-as	contamos	contemos
Vosotros /-as	contáis	contéis
Ellos / Ellas / Ustedes	c*ue*ntan	c*ue*nten
	PENSAR	
Yo	p*ie*nso	p*ie*nse
Tú	p*ie*nsas	p*ie*nses
Él / Ella / Usted	p*ie*nsa	p*ie*nse
Nosotros /-as	pensamos	pensemos
Vosotros /-as	pensáis	penséis
Ellos / Ellas / Ustedes	p*ie*nsan	p*ie*nsen
	ENCENDER	
Tú	enc*ie*ndes	enc*ie*ndas
Ella	enc*ie*nde	enc*ie*nda
	EMPEZAR	
Yo	emp*ie*zo	*empiece*
Tú	emp*ie*zas	*empieces*
	PODER	
Él	p*ue*de	p*ue*da
Ellos	p*ue*den	p*ue*dan
	RECORDAR	
Tú	rec*ue*rdas	rec*ue*rdes
Nosotros /-as	recordamos	recordemos

G.

	Presente de indicativo	Presente de subjuntivo
	HACER	
Yo	ha*g*o	ha*g*a
Tú	haces	ha*g*as
Él / Ella / Usted	hace	ha*g*a
Nosotros /-as	hacemos	ha*g*amos
Vosotros /-as	hacéis	ha*g*áis
Ellos / Ellas / Ustedes	hacen	ha*g*an

Y EN EL TRABAJO, ¿QUÉ TAL?

	Presente de indicativo	Presente de subjuntivo
	Salir	
Yo	sal*go*	sal*g*a
Tú	sales	sal*g*as
Él/Ella/Usted	sale	sal*g*a
Nosotro /-as	salimos	sal*g*amos
Vosotros/-as	salís	sal*g*áis
Ellos/Ellas/Ustedes	salen	sal*g*an
	Poner	
Yo	pon*g*o	pon*g*a
Tú	pones	pon*g*as
Él / Ella / Usted	pone	pon*g*a
Nosotros /-as	ponemos	pon*g*amos
Vosotros /-as	ponéis	pon*g*áis
Ellos / Ellas / Ustedes	ponen	pon*g*an

	Presente de indicativo	Presente de subjuntivo
	Coger	
Yo	co*j*o	co*j*a
Tú	co*g*es	co*j*as
Él / Ella / Usted	co*g*e	co*j*a
Nosotros /-as	co*g*emos	co*j*amos
Vosotros /-as	co*g*éis	co*j*áis
Ellos / Ellas / Ustedes	co*g*en	co*j*an

Si hay irregularidad vocálica: Los verbos que diptongan en el presente de indicativo conservan la diptongación en las mismas personas del presente de subjuntivo. Las personas *nosotros* y *vosotros* son siempre regulares.

Si hay irregularidad consonántica: Todos los verbos cuya primera persona singular del presente de indicativo es irregular presentan esa irregularidad en todas las personas del presente de subjuntivo.

OBSERVA, APRENDE Y RECUERDA

H e I. En un primer momento, los alumnos, individualmente, tendrán que descubrir los dos verbos irregulares de la actividad 3A que no cumplen las reglas presentadas en el ejercicio anterior. No obstante, si no averiguaran cuáles son, el profesor dará la solución. En segundo lugar, los estudiantes leerán el presente de subjuntivo de los verbos irregulares en -IR que presentamos en la ficha. Finalmente, añadirán a la lista más ejemplos.

Sugerencia

Al final de la actividad, una vez que se ha presentado la formación de los verbos irregulares en este tiempo y modo verbal, podemos organizar un concurso para chequear y reforzar, de forma lúdica, el aprendizaje de la morfología del presente de subjuntivo.

Organización del juego: un alumno saldrá a la pizarra y escribirá la conjugación completa del presente de subjuntivo del verbo irregular que elija otro estudiante. Si lo hace correctamente, recibirá 10 puntos. Se descontará 1 punto por cada error. Otra posibilidad es que el profesor escriba el verbo en la pizarra, y el primer estudiante que levante la mano comenzará con el juego.

Solución

H. *Seamos* (ser) y *vayamos* (ir).

I. *Sentir, mentir, repetir,* medir, teñir, elegir, reír, servir, despedir, freír, seguir, vestirse, hervir, divertirse, impedir…

4 Lo que necesitan Marta y Luis

Iniciamos una serie de actividades con el objetivo de que los alumnos reflexionen sobre el uso del subjuntivo en oraciones sustantivas de deseo y necesidad.

A. Explicaremos que vamos a retomar algunos de los deseos y necesidades que surgieron en la conversación de Marta y Luis, la pareja del bloque anterior. Deberán prestar atención a los ejemplos que se presentan y, en plenaria, determinar por qué en unos casos se usa el infinitivo, y en otros, el subjuntivo. Llegarán a la conclusión de que el infinitivo se utiliza cuando los dos verbos tienen el mismo sujeto y el subjuntivo cuando tienen dos sujetos diferentes.

Solución

Ejemplos de la izquierda (Marta): En la primera parte de los dos ejemplos se utiliza el infinitivo porque ambos verbos tienen el mismo sujeto: *A veces (yo) necesito hablar (yo) de mi trabajo… Quiero (yo) sentirme (yo) libre…*. En la segunda parte de ambas oraciones se utiliza el subjuntivo porque los dos verbos presentan sujetos diferentes: *… y necesito (yo) que (tú) me escuches. … no quiero (yo) que (tú) me controles.*

Ejemplos de la derecha (Luis): Ocurre lo mismo que en el caso anterior. En la primera parte de los ejemplos se utiliza el infinitivo porque el sujeto es el mismo: *Necesito (yo) estar (yo) contigo… No me importa (yo) cocinar (yo)…* Y en la segunda parte cada verbo tiene un sujeto distinto: *… pero necesito (yo) que confíes (tú) en mí. … pero quiero (yo) que (tú) pongas la mesa y (tú) friegues los platos.*

B. Después de que los alumnos deduzcan la regla de uso del presente de subjuntivo en este tipo de oraciones compuestas, pediremos que marquen cuál es el esquema correcto.

Solución

Verbo + *que* + verbo.

C. Con la ayuda de los ejemplos que se incluyen, volveremos a aclarar, por si todavía quedaran dudas, la diferencia entre el uso del infinitivo y el subjuntivo en las oraciones sustantivas de deseo o necesidad y, a continuación, animaremos a los alumnos a que escriban dos ejemplos personales para cada caso. Los estudiantes leerán sus frases y, finalmente, las corregiremos en plenaria.

Solución

Posible respuesta

Necesito aprender español.

Necesito que me enseñe español.

Quiero probar el gazpacho.

Quiero que me des la receta del gazpacho.

No me importa practicar el subjuntivo.

No me importa que me obligue a practicar el subjuntivo.

NOTAS

Y EN EL TRABAJO, ¿QUÉ TAL?

OBSERVA, APRENDE Y RECUERDA

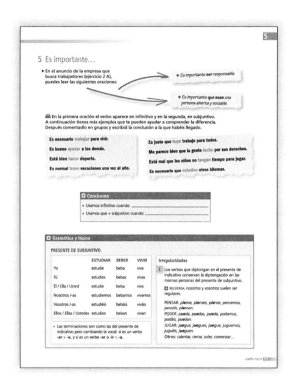
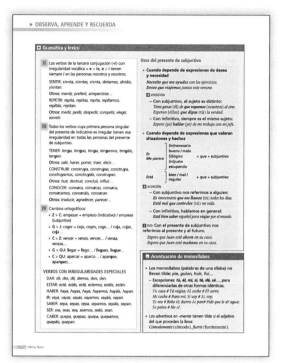

5 Es importante…

Con este ejercicio nos proponemos que los alumnos reflexionen sobre el uso del presente de subjuntivo para valorar situaciones y hechos.

Les explicaremos que, en primer lugar, vamos a analizar dos frases extraídas del anuncio de la empresa que presentamos en la actividad 2A y les pediremos que las lean, prestando atención a los verbos que se destacan.

A continuación, leerán los demás ejemplos incluidos en el ejercicio. Los animaremos a descubrir la diferencia de uso de las estructuras y los verbos destacados: infinitivo o subjuntivo. Dejaremos algunos minutos para que escriban, después de la lectura, sus propias conclusiones de forma individual. Después, formarán grupos para comentarlas y, a continuación, compartirán sus deducciones con el resto de la clase. El objetivo es que los estudiantes comprendan que utilizaremos el infinitivo cuando hablamos en general y el subjuntivo si nos referimos a una persona determinada. Finalmente, los alumnos completarán las reglas de uso.

Solución

Usamos infinitivo cuando hablamos en general.

Usamos *que* + subjuntivo cuando nos referimos a una persona determinada.

PRACTICA

6 Lo que necesita nuestro barrio

A. Gran parte de esta secuencia gira en torno al uso del subjuntivo en estructuras oracionales que sirven para expresar necesidad.

Antes de empezar con la actividad propiamente dicha, preguntaremos a los alumnos en qué barrio viven y les propondremos que expliquen a los demás cómo es, qué establecimientos y servicios públicos tiene, qué le falta, qué reformas necesita, etcétera.

A continuación, comentaremos que el barrio de Marta y Luis, los personajes de los ejercicios anteriores, necesita una serie de mejoras.

Deberán poner atención a las imágenes que representan dichas reformas y explicarlas completando la estructura que ofrecemos: *Nuestro barrio necesita que el ayuntamiento…*

Comenzará uno de los estudiantes y, cuando haya completado la frase correspondiente a la primera imagen, continuará el siguiente; así hasta que acaben la serie. Lo importante es que fijen la estructura, por eso pueden seguir practicando con imágenes nuevas.

Sugerencia

Esta fase de la actividad se desarrollará de forma oral; no obstante, si se cree conveniente, podemos dejar unos minutos para que los alumnos la realicen individualmente de forma escrita y, posteriormente, pasaremos a corregir las oraciones en plenaria.

Solución

Posibles respuestas

… organice más actividades para los jóvenes.

… ponga más farolas para iluminar las calles por la noche.

… construya más zonas verdes, parques, polideportivos, etcétera.

… cambie el mobiliario de la ciudad: papeleras, bancos, etcétera.

… limpie las calles con más frecuencia.

… pinte las fachadas de algunos edificios.

… construya más aparcamientos.

… ponga autobuses que pasen con más frecuencia.

B. Ahora queremos que cada alumno explique las necesidades de su ciudad usando las estructuras propuestas: *Necesita que* + subjuntivo; *Es necesario que* + subjuntivo; *Conviene que* + subjuntivo.

Dejaremos algunos minutos para que escriban sus opiniones y, después, las comenten con el resto del grupo.

Sugerencia

Para finalizar, es recomendable promover una reflexión escrita individual sobre las necesidades de la ciudad donde estudian español y que, a continuación, la comenten en plenaria.

Solución

Respuesta libre.

▶ Y EN EL TRABAJO, ¿QUÉ TAL?

7 Quejas y deseos

A. Comenzamos una serie de actividades destinadas a practicar y consolidar el presente de subjuntivo en oraciones sustantivas. Comentaremos a los alumnos que comenzaremos presentando las quejas o los deseos de una serie de personas. Posteriormente, les sugeriremos que completen los espacios con los verbos en infinitivo o con *que* + presente de subjuntivo, según corresponda. Al final, haremos una puesta en común para aclarar las dudas y, si fuera necesario, revisaremos los usos que puedan crear dificultades.

Solución

1. que la gente me envíe.
2. que el ayuntamiento solucione.
3. que los políticos escuchen - (que) hagan.
4. que las personas sean - (que) colaboren.
5. que mi jefe me respete.
6. vivir.
7. que haga.
8. que todos protestemos.
9. tener.
10. que mi hija hable - que me cuente.
11. trabajar - encontrar.
12. tener.
13. cambiar - que no sea.
14. que haya.

B. Seguidamente, pediremos a cada estudiante que, individualmente y de forma escrita, complete las notas con sus necesidades, deseos o quejas personales, de forma general. Dejaremos algunos minutos para que las escriban y, a continuación, las comentarán con el resto de los compañeros.

Sugerencia

Después de la puesta en común, animaremos a los estudiantes a comentar qué deseos de todos los que han presentado creen que se cumplirán y cuáles no. Tendrán que justificar sus opiniones de forma razonada.

Solución

Posible respuesta

Me parece mal que no haya zonas deportivas en mi barrio porque hay gente muy joven.

No es normal que el autobús solo pase cada 20 minutos.

Está bien construir pisos de protección oficial.

PRACTICA

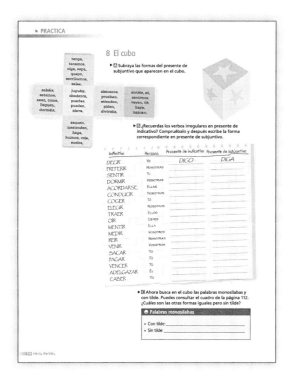

Solución

Estemos, sean, coma, lleguen, durmáis, tenga, oiga, sepa, escribamos, juguéis, obedezca, puedas, saquen, merienden, haga, coja, almuerce, divirtáis, sintáis, vayan, dé, haya, nazcan.

B. Continuamos con una actividad de carácter inferencial. Animaremos a los alumnos a que completen la tabla individualmente con las formas correctas del presente de indicativo y del presente de subjuntivo. Es de gran utilidad que se haga en clase y que el profesor vaya observando si el estudiante sigue los pasos de manera ordenada para evitar que llegue a conclusiones erróneas.

Solución

Digo-diga; elegimos-elijamos; venís-vengáis;
preferimos-prefiramos; traen-traigan; saco-saque;
sientes-sientas; oye-oiga; pagas-pagues;
dormís-durmáis; miente-mienta; venzo-venza;
se acuerdan-se acuerden; medís-midáis; adelgaza-adelgace;
conducimos-conduzcamos; reímos-riamos; quepo-quepa.
coges-cojas;

C. Actividad cuyo objetivo es que el alumno consiga, a través de la reflexión y la autonomía en su aprendizaje, a extraer las reglas de acentuación de los monosílabos.

En primer lugar, llamaremos la atención de los estudiantes sobre las palabras del cubo del apartado **A**. Les pediremos que, entre todos, seleccionen las que son monosílabas y llevan tilde.

A continuación, elegiremos a uno de los alumnos para que lea la regla de acentuación de monosílabos del cuadro de la página 112.

Solucionaremos las dudas que se pudieran plantear y, por último, pediremos a los alumnos que completen la ficha escribiendo las otras formas monosílabas que se escriben igual pero sin tilde.

Nos detendremos unos minutos para que reparen en la diferencia de significado entre la forma con acento gráfico y la que no lo lleva. De esta forma entenderán que la tilde se usa para diferenciar dos palabras que se escriben igual pero que no significan lo mismo.

Solución

Con tilde: sé (verbo saber/ser), dé (verbo dar).

Sin tilde: se (pronombre personal), de (preposición).

8 El cubo

Las actividades A y B revisan y refuerzan la morfología del presente de subjuntivo regular e irregular.

A. Explicaremos a los alumnos que en el cubo aparecen muchas formas verbales. Deberán señalar solo las que correspondan al presente de subjuntivo.

Si fuera necesario, dejaremos algunos minutos para que resuelvan la actividad de forma individual y, finalmente, pasaremos a la fase de corrección en plenaria.

Sugerencia

Podríamos plantear esta actividad de forma más lúdica, como si se tratara de un concurso. Dejaremos algunos minutos para que los estudiantes marquen los verbos y ganará el primero que logre decir todas las formas correctamente.

ochenta y siete 87

Y EN EL TRABAJO, ¿QUÉ TAL?

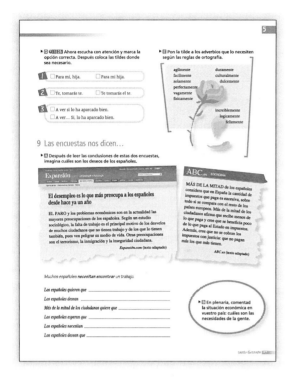

D. Ejercicio de comprensión auditiva para revisar la regla de acentuación de los monosílabos. Escucharemos tres parejas de frases y pediremos a los alumnos que marquen la opción que oigan y, a continuación, coloquen la tilde en su lugar correspondiente. Después de la fase de escucha, compartirán sus soluciones con las del resto del grupo.

Solución

1. Para mi hija.
2. T**é**, tomarás t**é**.
3. A ver… S**í**, lo ha aparcado bien.

E. Ahora nos ocupamos del uso del acento gráfico en los adverbios terminados en *-mente*. Antes de comenzar con el ejercicio propiamente dicho, y como actividad previa, podríamos hacer un breve repaso en la pizarra de las reglas generales que los estudiantes habían aprendido en la lección anterior. En segundo lugar, pediremos a un alumno que lea la regla de acentuación de los adverbios en *-mente* del cuadro de la página 112 y, por último, colocarán la tilde en aquellos que la necesitan. Corregiremos sus propuestas en plenaria.

Sugerencia

Si se cree conveniente, se propondrán nuevos adverbios que no están en la lista para que los alumnos practiquen esta regla de acentuación.

Por otro lado, la fase de revisión de las reglas generales de acentuación podría realizarse por grupos. Para ello, dividiremos la clase en tres grupos y pediremos que cada uno se encargue de recordar la regla correspondiente a cada una de las tres clases de palabras que existen según su acento (agudas, llanas y esdrújulas), y que busque ejemplos. Cuando hayan terminado el trabajo, lo presentarán al resto de la clase.

Solución

Ágilmente, fácilmente, físicamente, increíblemente, lógicamente.

9 Las encuestas nos dicen…

Actividad de comprensión lectora y práctica gramatical semidirigida que revisa el uso del presente de subjuntivo en oraciones sustantivas para expresar necesidad.

Antes de comenzar con el ejercicio, preguntaremos a los estudiantes si saben cuáles son los principales problemas o preocupaciones de los españoles. Después del intercambio de opiniones, pasaremos a las distintas fases de desarrollo de la actividad.

A. Presentamos las conclusiones de dos encuestas aparecidas en revistas digitales en las que se abordan los principales problemas y preocupaciones de los españoles en la actualidad.

Les pediremos a los alumnos que lean individualmente y que pregunten luego las dudas en torno al vocabulario que desconozcan. Comentaremos si los problemas a los que se habían referido en el coloquio que se planteó antes de empezar la actividad están presentes en estos textos. Les pediremos que justifiquen sus respuestas.

A continuación, los animaremos a imaginar cuáles son los deseos de mejora o las necesidades de los españoles completando las estructuras sustantivas propuestas. Daremos algunos minutos para que realicen esta fase escrita y, finalmente, compartirán sus ideas con el resto del grupo.

Dejaremos que comparen sus suposiciones con las de sus compañeros y expliquen las coincidencias.

Si fuera conveniente, resolveremos en la pizarra las dudas que pudieran surgir en torno al uso del subjuntivo frente al infinitivo en este tipo de construcciones complejas.

Solución

Respuesta libre.

B. Animaremos a los estudiantes a que, en plenaria, presenten las necesidades de la gente de su país de origen usando las estructuras anteriores. Si se cree conveniente, daremos algunos minutos para que escriban sus ideas antes de compartirlas con los demás. Conviene preguntarles si en su país existen preocupaciones similares a las que se presentaban en los textos sobre España.

Solución

Respuesta libre.

EN COMUNICACIÓN

10 Vivir con los hijos… de 29

A. Como actividad previa a la lectura del texto, fijaremos la atención de los estudiantes en su título y les pediremos que reflexionen en torno a su significado con preguntas del tipo: *¿Qué os sugiere el título del artículo? ¿De qué tema creéis que tratará? ¿Con qué asunto tiene que ver?…*

Después de la fase de lectura del artículo, aclararemos las dudas en torno al léxico.

B. Propondremos a los alumnos que, de forma individual, escriban las tres ideas principales del artículo, desde su punto de vista. Pasados algunos minutos, pediremos que las compartan con el resto de compañeros.

Puede resultar conveniente tomar nota en la pizarra de las opiniones coincidentes. Recordaremos a los estudiantes que deben justificar su elección de forma razonada.

Solución

Posible respuesta

Me parece interesante que los jóvenes españoles, en general, tengan tan buenas relaciones con sus padres.

Está bien que en época de crisis la familia ayude a los jóvenes.

Me parece normal querer independizarse con esa edad.

C. Abriremos un debate para que los alumnos expresen su opinión sobre las reflexiones relacionadas con el artículo y expliquen cuál es la situación en su país respecto a la edad de independencia de los jóvenes.

Los invitaremos a hacerlo usando las estructuras para valorar que han aprendido en la unidad, como en los ejemplos propuestos. Finalmente, conversarán libremente sobre los datos y las experiencias que han comentado sus compañeros destacando los que más les han llamado la atención o los que les han resultado más interesantes, sorprendentes, curiosos, etcétera.

Solución

Respuesta libre.

▶ Y EN EL TRABAJO, ¿QUÉ TAL?

EN COMUNICACIÓN

D. Esta es una actividad de comprensión auditiva cuyo objetivo es la práctica de contenidos léxicos relacionados con el ámbito laboral. En primer lugar, pediremos a los estudiantes que se fijen en los dos cuadros de vocabulario relacionado con el mundo del trabajo que se presentan en el ejercicio. Entre todos, explicaremos el significado de cada una de esas palabras o expresiones, pero antes dejaremos algunos minutos para que, en parejas, intenten escribir una definición breve de cada una de ellas. Una vez aclarados todos los significados, pasaremos a la fase de audición.

Diremos a los alumnos que van a escuchar a tres jóvenes españoles que hablan sobre su situación personal y laboral. Tendrán que tomar nota de los datos más importantes de cada uno de ellos. Les recordaremos que en la audición se usa el léxico de los cuadros que hemos explicado previamente. Cuando hayan terminado, compararán sus ideas con las del resto de sus compañeros. Si fuera necesario, antes de ponerlas en común en plenaria, comentarán en parejas lo que han escrito.

Sugerencia

Cuando termine la fase de audición, podemos plantear un coloquio en el que los estudiantes comenten si conocen a alguien con una situación similar a la de alguno de estos tres jóvenes. Podemos preguntarles si en sus respectivos países es habitual que se den situaciones laborales como estas. Si el grupo está formado por alumnos del mismo país, podemos hacer la misma pregunta pero referida a las diferentes regiones de procedencia.

Solución

Posible respuesta

Mateo: tiene veinticuatro años, no tiene un puesto de trabajo, ha presentado muchos currículum, no tiene experiencia, vive con sus padres.

Sonia: no tiene contrato, su sueldo no es fijo, vive con sus padres, tiene trabajos temporales, el año pasado estuvo de canguro, quiere trabajar en el extranjero.

Alicia: tiene un sueldo bajo porque su empresa está en crisis, le gustaría ser independiente y tener su propia casa, tiene veintiséis años, espera que la situación cambie pronto.

E. Estamos ante una nueva actividad de comprensión auditiva. Antes de comenzar el ejercicio, conviene que presentemos a su protagonista, Francis, que es el hijo de Lucas, una de las personas que contaban su experiencia en el ejercicio 1A. Diremos a los estudiantes que vamos a oír a Francis hablar sobre sus deseos de futuro y sus aspiraciones, y ellos deberán responder a algunas cuestiones al respecto. Les preguntaremos si recuerdan lo que significa la palabra *negocio,* que aparece en el enunciado de la actividad y estaba en uno de los cuadros de vocabulario del ejercicio anterior. Posteriormente, leeremos las preguntas para aclarar las dudas léxicas que pudieran presentarse.

Aclararemos a los alumnos que van a escuchar la audición una vez y que tendrán que contestar a las cuestiones planteadas en la ficha. Después, les pediremos que comparen lo que han escrito con las respuestas de un compañero. Si es necesario, haremos una segunda audición para terminar de completar la tarea. Finalmente, pasaremos a una puesta en común que servirá para corregir la actividad.

Sugerencia

Sería conveniente invitar a los alumnos a que reflexionasen sobre las palabras de Francis. Los animaremos a que comenten si están de acuerdo con su visión sobre el trabajo de autónomo, sobre el salario, etc. También podrían hablar acerca de sus experiencias personales: los pasos que han dado para conseguir un empleo, cuál sería su trabajo ideal, en qué han trabajado, si esas experiencias les han gustado o no, si les importaría ser autónomos, etcétera.

Solución

1. Le gustaría tener una estabilidad laboral, un contrato fijo y un horario flexible.
2. Tú eres tu propio jefe.
3. Tienes más preocupaciones, nunca sabes cuánto vas a ganar, trabajas cuando la gente tiene vacaciones y para ti nunca llega el momento de descansar.
4. Un sueldo fijo; no es necesario que sea muy alto, solo suficiente para vivir cómodamente.
5. Ha presentado varios currículum vítae.

¡extra! CONTEXTOS

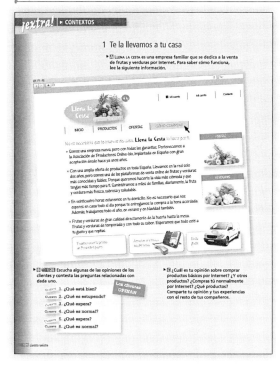

1 Te la llevamos a tu casa

En este bloque presentamos, en un contexto de comunicación cercano a la realidad, algunas de las estructuras que los alumnos han estudiado en la unidad —las estructuras oracionales con infinitivo o subjuntivo para expresar deseos o necesidades y valorar hechos o situaciones—, incluidas en un texto publicitario para la práctica de la comprensión lectora.

A. Llamaremos la atención de los alumnos sobre el texto del ejercicio, que publicita una empresa de venta de frutas y verduras por Internet. Antes de empezar con la fase de lectura, podemos preguntarles si conocen alguna empresa de este tipo y si, en alguna ocasión, han comprado esta clase de productos a través de la red.

A continuación, leeremos las características de la empresa, confirmaremos que han comprendido el contenido y solucionaremos las dudas sobre léxico.

Sería interesante que los estudiantes se fijaran en las estructuras oracionales que se presentan y que ya han aprendido a lo largo de la unidad. Les pediremos que marquen dichas construcciones, y las escribiremos en la pizarra para recordar sus usos.

B. Presentamos un ejercicio de comprensión auditiva en el que animaremos a los alumnos a escuchar las opiniones de varios clientes de esta empresa de venta por Internet.

Su objetivo es repasar el uso de las construcciones para valorar hechos o situaciones y para expresar deseos o necesidades.

Les diremos a los alumnos que, después de escuchar la audición, tendrán que contestar las preguntas que se plantean; primero lo harán individualmente y, luego, comentarán y contrastarán sus respuestas con las de sus compañeros.

Solución

1. Está bien que siempre haya en casa frutas y verduras.
2. Es estupendo no tener que cargar con las bolsas del supermercado.
3. Espera que la relación calidad-precio sea buena porque algunos productos son más caros que en las tiendas tradicionales.
4. Es normal que tengan tantos clientes.
5. Espera que no vuelva a ocurrir lo del último pedido: ¡no llegó nunca!
6. Es normal que la fruta dure más porque es ecológica.

C. Para terminar, proponemos una actividad de expresión e interacción orales. Presentaremos a los alumnos las preguntas del enunciado y los animaremos a que las respondan con sus propias opiniones y experiencias.

Les sugeriremos también la posibilidad de que ellos mismos planteen otras cuestiones relacionadas con el tema.

Solución

Respuesta libre.

Y EN EL TRABAJO, ¿QUÉ TAL?

¡extra! PRACTICA

2 Ideas

Este ejercicio está orientado a la práctica semidirigida de las estructuras sustantivas para valorar hechos o situaciones. Para ello, pediremos a los alumnos que valoren las sugerencias propuestas para ayudar a Alejandro mientras encuentra un empleo.

Les recordaremos que deberán usar las construcciones que han aprendido a lo largo de la unidad con *es bueno, es malo, es necesario, es importante, me parece bien, es normal, me parece estupendo…*

En primer lugar, escribirán las opiniones individualmente; a continuación, les pediremos que comparen sus valoraciones con las de otro compañero, y, finalmente, se corregirán en plenaria.

Solución

Posibles respuestas

2. Es horrible que tenga que esperar más y que no pueda independizarse.

3. Es necesario que vea todos los días los anuncios de la prensa.

4. Está bien que se matricule en un curso de inglés. Seguro que le será útil.

5. Me parece normal que haga un máster en Económicas. Así estará más preparado.

6. No me parece necesario que estudie otra carrera.

7. Es ilógico que se case en estos momentos.

8. Es estupendo que abra un negocio en Internet.

3. Es ideal…

Con esta actividad reforzamos la estructura de las oraciones subordinadas sustantivas para expresar deseo con infinitivo o *que* + presente de subjuntivo.

Para ello, los alumnos han de completar los deseos de Alejandro sobre su empleo ideal para el futuro con la forma correcta del presente de subjuntivo.

Harán esta fase de forma individual y, a continuación, corregiremos las oraciones en plenaria.

Finalmente, los animaremos a que aporten sus ideas personales sobre el tema. De esta manera, facilitaremos un mejor aprovechamiento de la actividad.

Solución

Posible respuesta

Deseo que el contrato **sea** fijo.

Quiero que **esté** bien pagado.

Necesito que el horario **sea** flexible.

Es importante que no **tenga** que conducir, que **pueda** ir andando.

Es estupendo que el jefe no **sea** muy estricto.

Es importante que **haya** buen ambiente entre los compañeros.

Es necesario que **sepa** cuáles son mis funciones perfectamente.

Es bueno que **pueda** dedicar tiempo a mi familia también.

Es estupendo que no **haya** mucha competitividad entre los compañeros.

Es ideal que **pueda** trabajar también desde casa.

NOTAS

EXTRA PRATICA

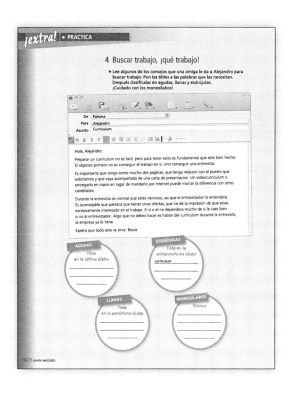

4 Buscar trabajo, ¡qué trabajo!

Actividad de chequeo y revisión de las reglas generales de acentuación y de las referidas a los monosílabos. Pediremos a los alumnos que lean el correo en el que una amiga de Alejandro le hace algunas recomendaciones para buscar empleo. Les pediremos que pongan tilde a todas las palabras que la necesiten. Finalmente, clasificarán las palabras acentuadas en su grupo correspondiente (agudas, llanas, esdrújulas, monosílabos).

Sugerencia

La actividad podría desarrollarse cambiando el procedimiento: la primera fase se haría en parejas, y la última, en gran grupo. Para completar la revisión de este contenido, pediremos a los estudiantes que incluyan cinco ejemplos más en cada uno de los grupos.

Solución

Currículum - fácil - éxito - esté - sí - páginas - relación - presentación - videocurrículum - estés - así - entenderá - dé - impresión - estás - sí - dependerá - currículum.

Agudas: esté - relación - presentación - estés - así - entenderá - impresión - estás - dependerá.

Llanas: fácil.

Esdrújulas: currículum - éxito - páginas - videocurrículum.

Monosílabos tónicos: sí - dé.

¡extra! EN COMUNICACIÓN

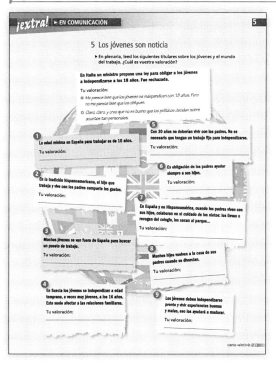

5 Los jóvenes son noticia

Comentaremos a los estudiantes que hemos seleccionado algunos titulares aparecidos en diferentes medios de comunicación sobre este tema. Los leeremos en plenaria y explicaremos los posibles problemas de comprensión. A continuación, los alumnos valorarán estos datos usando las estructuras que hemos aprendido en la lección. Para que no tengan dificultades, haremos que se fijen en las valoraciones del ejemplo. Esta fase del ejercicio podría realizarse de forma oral; no obstante, si fuera necesario, daremos algunos minutos para que escriban su valoración y después pasaremos a la fase de intercambio de opiniones con los compañeros.

Sugerencia

Podríamos proponer a los alumnos que, en pequeños grupos, hagan un trabajo de investigación sobre los problemas de los jóvenes del país de Hispanoamérica que elijan. Si se dispone de acceso a Internet en el centro de estudios, los estudiantes pueden llevarla a cabo durante el tiempo de clase. Si no es así, les propondremos realizarla fuera del aula y llevar los resultados a clase en la siguiente sesión. Asimismo, sugerimos que los alumnos elaboren un texto sobre los problemas de los jóvenes de su país en el ámbito laboral. Esta tarea es muy adecuada para practicar de una forma más significativa los contenidos léxicos y gramaticales aprendidos en la unidad.

Solución

Respuesta libre.

Unidad 6
Los otros

OBJETIVOS DE LA UNIDAD

En esta unidad avanzamos explorando nuevos usos del modo subjuntivo.

Las **funciones comunicativas** que abordaremos serán: expresar gustos y sentimientos; mostrar opiniones, actitudes y conocimiento, y constatar hechos.

Los **contenidos morfosintácticos** vinculados a las funciones anteriores serán las oraciones subordinadas sustantivas dependientes de verbos de sentimiento y de verbos de pensamiento, sentido y comunicación. Además, trataremos las estructuras de *Ser / Estar / Parecer +* adjetivo / adverbio *que + indicativo / subjuntivo*.

En los **contenidos léxico-semánticos,** nos ocuparemos del léxico relacionado con las relaciones interpersonales y el comportamiento social. También abordaremos el vocabulario sobre medioambiente y fauna.

En los **contenidos socioculturales,** haremos referencia a las relaciones sociales, a los comportamientos relacionados con las muestras de afecto en público y con los miembros de la familia, a las relaciones con los desconocidos —fórmulas y comportamientos sociales—, a las tradiciones, costumbres y hábitos españoles e hispanoamericanos, y por último a la participación ciudadana y al pluralismo. También presentaremos a personajes destacados del mundo hispano.

Los **contenidos pragmáticos** que trataremos son algunos recursos para atenuar opiniones y creencias: *Creo que no debemos…, Me parece que no es bueno…*

Por último, en cuanto a los **contenidos fonéticos y ortográficos,** continuamos con las reglas de acentuación, ocupándonos de los diptongos y los hiatos.

6

CONTEXTOS

1 Gran marcha en defensa del medioambiente

Con esta serie de actividades tratamos de poner en contacto al estudiante con nuevos usos del modo subjuntivo en el contexto del ámbito temático del medioambiente.

A. En esta primera fase trabajaremos en parejas o, si se prefiere, en plenaria. En primer lugar, leeremos las reivindicaciones sobre la naturaleza y los animales, y las opiniones de los internautas Alberto y Sandra. A continuación, los estudiantes tendrán que expresar su opinión sobre el tema utilizando las expresiones que aportamos. Con todas estas estructuras se usa indicativo, excepto con las dos formas negativas *(No creo que..., No es cierto que...)*; por ello, probablemente, los alumnos las usen mal, pero no sería este el momento de corregirlos. Les dejaremos que den su opinión sin tener en cuenta la forma.

Solución

Posible respuesta

Yo creo que, si todos ponemos de nuestra parte, se puede conseguir un verdadero ahorro energético.

Me parece que el calentamiento global es uno de los peligros más graves para el planeta por los deshielos.

No creo que talar árboles sea la solución para generar espacios donde construir viviendas.

Está claro que los animales tienen sus derechos.

No es cierto que los animales no tengan sentimientos y que no sufran.

He oído que algunas personas tienen animales exóticos en sus casas en jaulas muy pequeñas y en muy malas condiciones.

CONTEXTOS

B. Ejercicio de comprensión auditiva en el que los alumnos tienen que relacionar lo que dice cada persona con la imagen correspondiente.

Sugerencia

Antes de poner la grabación, sugerimos hacer una lluvia de ideas sobre el medioambiente: los estudiantes van diciendo sus opiniones y todo lo que se les ocurra sobre este tema, y el profesor lo va escribiendo en la pizarra. De esta manera, activaremos el vocabulario que ya sabían y lo ampliaremos con palabras nuevas.

Solución

1. Ahorro de energía. **2.** Bolsas de plástico. **3.** Parques naturales. **4.** Selva amazónica. **5.** Agujero de la capa de ozono. **6.** Centrales nucleares. **7.** Contenedores. **8.** Reciclaje.

C. Ahora dividimos la clase en grupos. Los estudiantes deben pensar en lo que hacen para cuidar el medioambiente y la razón por la que lo hacen. En nuestra experiencia con adultos de todas las edades, pero especialmente con jóvenes, hemos observado que este tema suele interesar a la mayoría porque les resulta muy cercano. Los jóvenes están muy concienciados con este asunto, por lo que generalmente colaboran de alguna manera en la protección y el cuidado del medioambiente. Luego haremos una puesta en común en la que cada estudiante dará su opinión y sus razones al resto de los compañeros.

Sugerencia

Creemos que en este caso estaría bien que el profesor se implicara y explicara cómo colabora él con el medioambiente. A los estudiantes les interesa saber lo que su profesor piensa sobre los temas que se discuten en clase. Es verdad que hay asuntos sobre los que es mejor no tomar partido y, en estos casos, basta con decirles que son ellos los que deben expresarse en español, y ellos lo suelen aceptar sin problema; pero escuchar la opinión del profesor los anima a manifestarse.

Solución

Respuesta libre.

noventa y cinco **95**

► LOS OTROS

CONTEXTOS

2 Refugios de animales

A. Actividad de comprensión lectora sobre el tema del abandono de animales, en este caso, de caballos. Puede plantearse como una actividad para hacer en casa; si fuera así, el estudiante tendría más tiempo para leer el texto con atención y pensar sobre las preguntas. Si hacemos en clase el ejercicio, podemos leerlo en plenaria y entre todos resolver las dudas que se planteen.

Sugerencia

Podríamos ampliar la lista con otras posibles preguntas si la participación y el ánimo de la clase así lo demandan. Podríamos hablar sobre la conveniencia de adoptar animales, por ejemplo, perros, en lugar de comprarlos, sobre tener mascotas o no, sobre la legitimidad de llevar a cabo ciertas actividades con animales, sobre las fiestas populares donde intervienen animales…

Solución

Posible respuesta

Yo pienso que es una práctica horrible, pues la mayoría de los animales que son abandonados mueren. Me parece que sí es una cuestión de educación social, pues nadie educado para amar y respetar a los seres vivos puede abandonar a un animal.

Imagino que, además de la falta de recursos, otra razón para abandonar a un animal es el trabajo que da.

Sí, porque está claro que los refugios de animales son necesarios para poder acoger a los que son abandonados.

Sí, suelo colaborar con un refugio de perros y sé que muchos de mis amigos colaboran con distintas asociaciones que protegen a animales.

B. Con este ejercicio ponemos a prueba la creatividad del alumno y le animamos a que se convierta por unos momentos en publicista. Para escribir el eslogan puede usar cualquier estructura y, obviamente, ha de tener en cuenta que se trata de tocar la sensibilidad de la gente con el objeto de concienciarla para que no abandone a los animales. Como hemos dicho anteriormente, este es un tema sobre el que la mayoría de los jóvenes están sensibilizados, por lo que en general participan con interés.

Solución

Posible respuesta

Piénsalo bien antes de comprarme; piénsalo bien antes de abandonarme.

NOTAS

OBSERVA, APRENDE Y RECUERDA

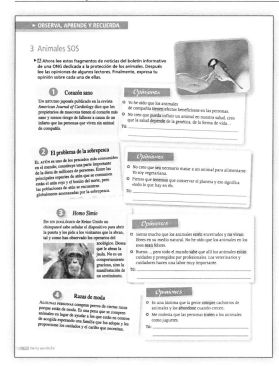

3 Animales SOS

Comenzamos una serie de ejercicios de inferencia de contenidos lingüísticos cuyo objetivo es, en esta ocasión, que el estudiante deduzca el uso de indicativo o subjuntivo con los verbos de pensamiento, sentido o comunicación en la forma afirmativa o negativa.

A. Primero les presentamos a los alumnos unos fragmentos de diferentes noticias del boletín informativo de una ONG dedicada a la protección de los animales junto con las opiniones de algunos lectores. Después de leerlas, ellos tendrán que dar su opinión. Pensamos que es mejor dirigir un poco el ejercicio; no queremos que el estudiante haga una exposición completa sobre el tema, sino que realice un comentario breve con las estructuras que usan los lectores. Más adelante habrá ocasión de hablar más libremente de estos asuntos.

Solución

Posible respuesta

1. Yo sé que un perro o un gato puede ser una gran compañía para las personas mayores que viven solas.

2. Me parece que la vida de nuestra fauna sí importa.

3. Es una lástima que los niños vean a los animales en zoos y no en la naturaleza.

4. Me pone triste que se abandonen tantos animales.

OBSERVA, APRENDE Y RECUERDA

B. Ahora el alumno tiene que volver a leer algunas de las opiniones del ejercicio 3A para intentar deducir por qué se usa indicativo o subjuntivo en cada una de ellas. Tras llegar a una conclusión individualmente, en plenaria se discutirán todas las propuestas. Finalmente, se escribirá la regla de uso. Lógicamente, si los alumnos no son capaces de llegar a la solución, el profesor tendrá que dar pistas o, en último caso, explicar la regla. Pero antes dejémosles el tiempo necesario para que sean ellos los que la descubran; de esta manera el aprendizaje será mucho más efectivo.

Solución

Usamos indicativo en el verbo subordinado si los verbos que expresan opiniones, actitudes y conocimiento van en forma afirmativa.

Usamos subjuntivo en el verbo subordinado si dichos verbos van en forma negativa.

C. En esta ocasión, empezamos dando a los estudiantes la regla: cuando hablamos de gustos y sentimientos usamos subjuntivo. Esto se debe a que ahora nuestro objetivo no es que descubran el modo que corresponde a este tipo de oraciones, sino que se fijen en que para usar subjuntivo tiene que haber dos sujetos diferentes. Eso lo descubrirán leyendo los tres ejemplos que se presentan. Además, deberán deducir que, si hay un único sujeto, se usa infinitivo. En plenaria se leerán los tres ejemplos y la *Ayuda*, y se les dará todo el tiempo necesario para

noventa y siete **97**

▶ LOS OTROS

que indiquen la respuesta. En teoría, no deberían tener mucha dificultad en encontrar la diferencia, ya que en la unidad 5, con los verbos de deseo y necesidad, estudiaron un caso similar.

Sugerencia

Cuando se tenga la solución, sugerimos volver a leer las opiniones 3 y 4 del ejercicio 3A para corroborar la conclusión a la que se ha llegado. A continuación, aconsejamos llamar la atención de los estudiantes sobre la expresión *Es una lástima que...*, para añadir otra: *Es una pena que...* Explicaremos que ambas se usan para expresar un sentimiento y, por tanto, siempre van seguidas de subjuntivo. Como esfuerzo, los alumnos podrían hablar, en plenaria, de situaciones que les causan este sentimiento. El profesor empezará escribiendo una oración en la pizarra; por ejemplo: *Es una lástima que este curso **tenga** que terminar...*

Solución

Usamos siempre subjuntivo con los verbos que expresan gustos y sentimientos cuando hay dos sujetos diferentes. Este es el esquema de oración: (Sujeto 1) + V1 + *que* + (Sujeto 2) + V2 en subjuntivo.

Con estos mismos verbos usamos siempre el infinitivo (sin *que*) cuando tenemos el mismo sujeto para los dos verbos.

OBSERVA, APRENDE Y RECUERDA

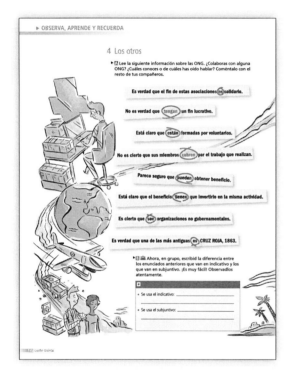

penden de expresiones que constatan y aseguran se usa indicativo, a no ser que vayan con negación, en cuyo caso se utiliza el subjuntivo. Esto es lo que los estudiantes, en grupo, deberán descubrir.

Sugerencia

Cuando se redacte la regla, sugerimos llamar la atención de los estudiantes sobre las palabras *verdad*, *claro*, *cierto* y *seguro*, y pedirles que piensen en otras palabras que indican seguridad (*evidente*, *obvio*, *real*, *demostrado*...) con el fin de ampliar el léxico de este ámbito semántico.

Solución

Se usa el indicativo en el verbo subordinado cuando el verbo principal (que constata y asegura) va en forma afirmativa.

Se usa el subjuntivo en el verbo subordinado cuando el verbo principal va en forma negativa.

NOTAS

4 Los otros

A. En esta primera secuencia empezamos explicando a los alumnos que vamos a leer una serie de enunciados sobre las ONG, pero que antes queremos que nos digan lo que ellos saben sobre este tema, si conocen alguna de estas organizaciones, de cuáles han oído hablar, etcétera. A continuación, leeremos en plenaria los enunciados y aclararemos las posibles dudas de vocabulario.

B. Empezamos el proceso inferencial con la reflexión de los alumnos sobre los enunciados del apartado A. Solo dos se expresan con el verbo subordinado en subjuntivo, cuando el V1 va en forma negativa. Han de ver que la clave está en que en los enunciados que de-

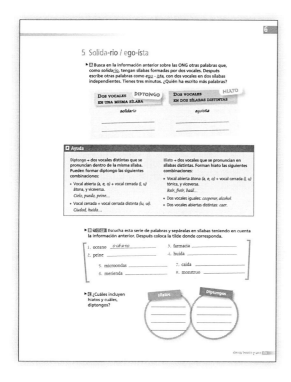
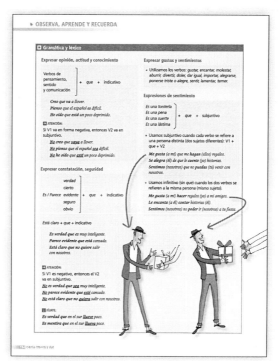

5 Solida-rio / ego-ísta

Nos centramos ahora en los contenidos fonéticos y ortográficos de la unidad: diptongos e hiatos.

A, B y **C.** Cambiamos radicalmente de objetivo, aunque vamos a trabajar con el texto sobre las ONG del ejercicio anterior. En primer lugar, los estudiantes deberán buscar en los enunciados palabras que tengan diptongos o hiatos. Pero antes debemos leer en plenaria la explicación que se incluye en la A*yuda* e intentaremos que quede perfectamente clara con la ayuda de los ejemplos que aparecen en el cuadro y de otros, si fueran necesarios. A continuación, realizaremos un ejercicio de comprensión auditiva para trabajar la separación silábica y la acentuación de una serie de palabras que contienen hiatos y diptongos. Finalmente, clasificaremos dichas palabras en dos grupos.

Sugerencia

Recomendamos que el trabajo se haga de manera individual con la idea de que los alumnos se concentren en la tarea. Aconsejamos realizar más ejercicios de práctica si han tenido dificultades en la realización de este. En la pizarra, por turnos, los estudiantes identificarán diptongos e hiatos, separarán en sílabas y acentuarán, si corresponde, la palabra que dicte el profesor.

Solución

A. Diptongos: so-li-da-rio; a-so-cia-cio-nes; vo-lun-ta-rios; cier-to; miem-bros; pue-den; be-ne-fi-cio; tie-nen; or-ga-ni-za-cio-nes; an-ti-guas.

Hiatos: e-go-ís-ta; re-a-li-zan.

B. 1. o-cé-a-no; **2.** pei-ne; **3.** far-ma-cia; **4.** hui-da; **5.** mi-cro-on-das; **6.** me-rien-da; **7.** ca-í-da; **8.** mons-truo.

C. Hiatos: océano, microondas y caída.

Diptongos: peine, farmacia, huida, merienda y monstruo.

NOTAS

LOS OTROS

PRACTICA

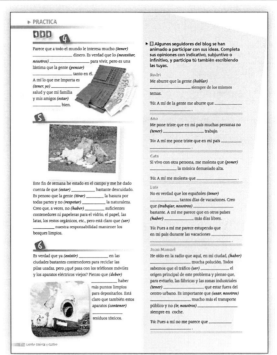

Iniciamos una serie de actividades de refuerzo de los usos del indicativo y del subjuntivo estudiados en la unidad. Además, repasaremos los otros contenidos de la unidad.

6 Alberto lo sabe todo

El estudiante debe leer con atención cada oración y elegir entre indicativo o subjuntivo. Aconsejamos que se haga individualmente y que en la corrección cada alumno vaya explicando por qué ha elegido un modo u otro.

Solución

1. sea – es.
2. está.
3. podamos.
4. no vendrá.
5. pueda – está.
6. se ha enamorado.
7. lloverá – no iremos
8. irán a montar.

7 Ideas ecologistas

A. En esta actividad el estudiante tiene que usar indicativo, subjuntivo e infinitivo. Las fotos ilustran el tema, y los alumnos, antes de completar las oraciones con la forma correcta, podrían hablar sobre lo que estas les sugieren y expresar su opinión sobre lo que ven.

Solución

1. haya.
2. usemos – perjudica – ahorramos – vaya.
3. tenga – sean – quedar.
4. tener – necesitamos – piense – tener – estén.
5. está – tire – respete – hay – es.
6. existen – debería – contienen.

B. Continuamos en el blog de Alberto; ahora los alumnos tienen que dar su opinión sobre diferentes temas, expresar sus sentimientos y hacer valoraciones.

Sugerencia

Si contamos con acceso a Internet en clase, podríamos crear un blog para el grupo de estudiantes en el que cada uno pudiera escribir sobre lo que quisiera; podría ser como un diario personal.

Solución

Rodri: hable.

Ana: tengan.

Cata: ponga.

Luis: tengan – trabajamos – hay.

Juan Manuel: hay – es – tienen – usemos – ir / vayamos.

Tú: Respuesta libre.

PRACTICA

C. Como ya hemos dicho, el tema del medioambiente suele interesar a la mayoría de los estudiantes. En primer lugar, preguntaremos a los alumnos si conocen lo que significa cada término y explicaremos los que no conozcan.

En segundo lugar, leeremos en plenaria las opiniones sobre tres de estos conceptos: capa de ozono, cambio climático y reciclaje. Por último, les pediremos que individualmente escriban su opinión sobre cada uno de estos conceptos.

Sugerencia

Aconsejamos que esta actividad se plantee como actividad para hacer en casa, ya que el alumno deberá contar con tiempo suficiente. Después de haber pensado y escrito sobre los diferentes temas, el estudiante tendrá las ideas más claras y podrá expresar su opinión con mayor conocimiento y un grado más alto de corrección.

Solución

Respuesta libre.

PRACTICA

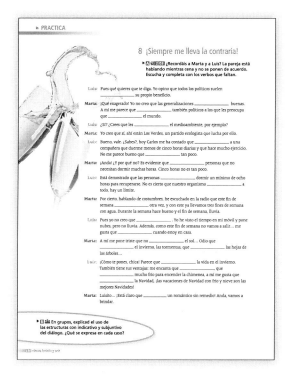

8 ¡Siempre me lleva la contraria!

A. Actividad de comprensión auditiva para reforzar el uso del indicativo y el subjuntivo. Cambiamos de tema recuperando a la pareja formada por Marta y Luis, protagonistas de la unidad anterior.

Una vez resueltas las dudas de léxico que les surjan a los alumnos, procedemos a oír la grabación.

Sugerencia

Cuando se trata de actividades de este tipo, en las que al estudiante no se le proporciona el verbo en infinitivo, somos partidarios de que, antes de poner la grabación, el alumno lea individualmente el texto e intente adivinar el verbo que falta. No va a acertar en todos los casos, pero probablemente elija verbos que podrían ser posibles, aunque no coincidan con los de la grabación. Con esa primera lectura, además de pensar en el verbo adecuado, intentamos que la comprensión del texto sea lo más completa posible.

Solución

Luis: querer.

Marta: sean – hay – mejore.

Luis: preocupa.

Luis: conoce – duerma.

Marta: hay.

Luis: necesitan – se acostumbre.

Marta: llueve.

Luis: llueva – llueva.

Marta: salga – llegue – se caigan.

Luis: se acaba – nieve – haga – llegue.

Marta: eres.

► LOS OTROS

B. Después de chequear los verbos que se han escrito, el alumno debe indicar la razón por la que se usa indicativo o subjuntivo.

Sugerencia

Conforme se va realizando la corrección, el profesor puede ir haciendo un esquema en la pizarra de todos los usos que aparecen. El esquema será lo más simple posible, con reglas concisas: un ejemplo puede ser suficiente para recordar un uso.

Solución

Luis: *Opino que* + indicativo: verbos de opinión en forma afirmativa.

Marta: *No creo* + subjuntivo: expresar parecer en forma negativa. *A mí me parece que* + indicativo: expresar parecer en forma afirmativa. *Les preocupa que* + subjuntivo: verbo de sentimiento.

Luis: *Crees que* + indicativo: pregunta sobre pensamiento.

Luis: *Contar que* + indicativo: verbo de comunicación en afirmativo. *No me parece bueno que* + subjuntivo: expresar parecer u opinión en forma negativa.

Marta: *Es evidente que* + indicativo: expresión de certeza.

Luis: *Está demostrado que* + indicativo: expresa certeza. *No es cierto que* + subjuntivo: expresa constatación o seguridad en forma negativa.

Marta: *He escuchado que* + indicativo: verbos de sentido en afirmativo.

Luis: *No creo que* + subjuntivo: expresa pensamiento en forma negativa. *Me gusta que* + subjuntivo: expresa gusto en forma afirmativa.

Marta: *A mí me pone triste que no* + subjuntivo: expresa sentimiento. *Odio que* + subjuntivo: expresa sentimiento.

Luis: *Parece que* + indicativo: expresa constatación en forma afirmativa. *Me encanta / me gusta que* + subjuntivo: expresa gusto en forma afirmativa.

Marta: *Está claro que* + indicativo: expresa certeza en forma afirmativa.

PRÁCTICA

9 ¿Blanco o negro?

Actividad de comprensión auditiva para que el estudiante discrimine los diptongos o los hiatos que hay en cada oración. En la corrección, que puede hacerse en la pizarra, los alumnos separarán en sílabas toda la oración y después señalarán los diptongos y los hiatos.

Sugerencia

Para hacerlo más fácil, en lugar de poner la grabación completa, podemos ir parando después de cada oración y repetirla. También puede ser interesante pedir a algunos alumnos que lean las oraciones en voz alta para que muestren la distinción entre diptongos e hiatos.

Solución

Diptongos

2. es-tu-dia.

3. rey.

4. bue-no.

6. sien-to; es-téis.

8. cie-rra; puer-ta; ai-re.

9. vien-to.

Hiatos

1. Ra-úl.

2. Fi-lo-so-fí-a.

3. le-ón.

4. Re-ír.

5. o-ír.

7. grú-a.

9. dí-as.

EN COMUNICACIÓN

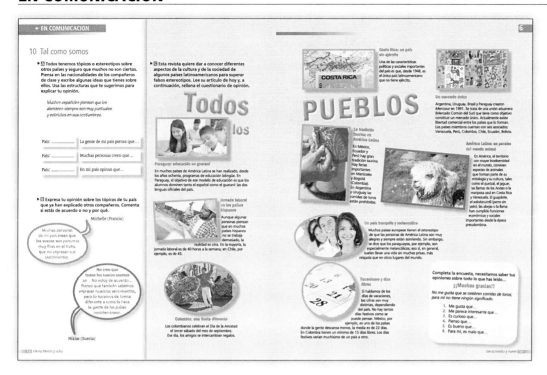

10 Tal como somos

Nos disponemos a iniciar una serie de actividades de tipo cultural en las que los estudiantes tendrán que comparar diferentes aspectos de su cultura con los de España y Latinoamérica.

A. Actividad de expresión escrita sobre los estereotipos de los diferentes países. Antes de que los alumnos realicen el ejercicio de forma individual, podemos empezar hablando, en plenaria, sobre los tópicos que existen en otros países sobre España, tratando aspectos positivos pero también otros que no lo son tanto. Nuestra actitud como profesor debe ser abierta, para que los estudiantes vean que los tópicos no nos afectan, aunque sean negativos. Así crearemos un ambiente distendido en la clase y evitaremos que alguien se sienta molesto si se dice algo no muy bueno sobre la gente de su país. Se trata de hablar de lo que otras personas piensan sobre nuestro país, y eso no quiere decir que todo sea cierto. Puede ocurrir que algunos alumnos no se sientan cómodos; en ese caso, tenemos que ser suficientemente hábiles para que no se cree mal ambiente en la clase, evitando incluso preguntar a ese alumno en particular y dejando que sea él quien diga lo que quiera.

Solución

Respuesta libre.

B. En este ejercicio, el estudiante puede manifestar su acuerdo o desacuerdo con todo lo que se ha dicho sobre su país. Es el momento de intentar romper esos estereotipos contrastándolos con la realidad.

Sugerencia

Si el profesor es español, hará lo mismo con los estereotipos que se han dicho sobre España para que los estudiantes no piensen, por ejemplo, que muchos hombres españoles son toreros, que todas las mujeres saben bailar flamenco, que todos los españoles duermen la siesta al mediodía, que son vagos porque hacen una pausa a mediodía para comer...

Si se cree conveniente, puede extender el ejercicio preguntando a los alumnos si conocen algunos estereotipos o tópicos de los países latinoamericanos, enlazando de este modo con el siguiente ejercicio.

Solución

Respuesta libre.

C. Es el turno de Latinoamérica. En general, en España se dice que los argentinos solo comen carne, que los brasileños están todo el día bailando... Hablar sobre estos temas suele ser divertido, y los estudiantes participarán sin problemas; pero muchas veces tendremos que recordarles que para expresar su opinión deben usar las expresiones que hemos estudiado, fijándose también en si tienen que usar indicativo o subjuntivo.

El objetivo de este ejercicio es fundamentalmente cultural: que el estudiante conozca diferentes aspectos sobre Latinoamérica. Después rellenará la encuesta para dar su opinión y la comparará con la idea que tenía anteriormente sobre estos países. Probablemente en muchos casos será información nueva para ellos.

► LOS OTROS

Sugerencia

Para completar esta actividad, podemos proponer a los alumnos que cada uno de ellos elija un país de Latinoamérica y, en casa, busque información sobre él. Después la compartirá con el resto de sus compañeros. Así contribuiremos al conocimiento y la difusión de la cultura de Latinoamérica.

Por otro lado, sugerimos hacer especial hincapié en uno de los temas que se tratan: las corridas de toros, que son muy populares en algunos países de Latinoamérica y en otros están prohibidas. Como en España existe un debate sobre este espectáculo, podemos plantear una conversación en clase sobre el tema. En realidad, los estudiantes suelen demandar hablar sobre las corridas de toros, ya que es un asunto que les suele parecer interesante y polémico.

Solución

Posibles respuestas

1. Me gusta que en Colombia haya una fiesta de la amistad porque me encanta estar con mis amigos y hacer amigos nuevos.
2. Me parece interesante que algunos países se hayan puesto de acuerdo para crear una unión aduanera.
3. Es curioso que no tengan ejército en Costa Rica, no lo sabía... Creo que en mi país sí hay ejército.
4. Pienso que muchos países de América Latina tienen pocos días de vacaciones y trabajan muchas más horas que en mi país.
5. Es bueno que exista una educación bilingüe. Creo que saber varios idiomas es fundamental hoy día.
6. Para mí, es malo que todavía haya corridas de toros en algunos países. No me gusta esta tradición.

EN COMUNICACIÓN

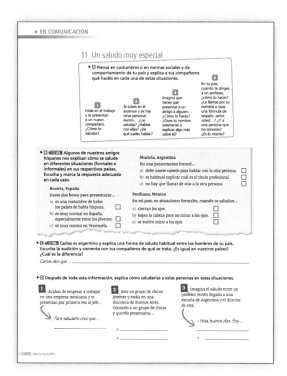

11 Un saludo muy especial

A. Seguimos con los contenidos socioculturales y ahora es el turno de las costumbres y normas sociales y de comportamiento de un país. El tema es el saludo en diferentes situaciones. Primero, debemos dejar que los estudiantes comenten cuál es la forma habitual de actuar en su país en las situaciones que les proponemos, después les preguntaremos si han observado cómo es en España. Por último, les diremos cuál es realmente en cada caso.

Solución

Respuesta libre.

B. Ejercicio de comprensión auditiva sobre el saludo en Argentina, España y México. Antes de oír la grabación les pediremos a los alumnos que lean las situaciones y elijan la opción que les parezca correcta. Después podrán comprobar si su intuición ha sido acertada.

Solución

Beatriz, España: b.

Mariela, Argentina: b.

Emiliano, México: c.

C. Ahora escucharán otra información sobre el saludo en Argentina y deberán comentarla en plenaria y compararla con lo que ocurre en su país en las mismas situaciones.

Solución

Respuesta libre.

D. Después de toda la información recibida, se les plantean a los alumnos diferentes situaciones para que expliquen cómo sería el saludo adecuado en cada una de ellas.

Solución

Posible respuesta

1. Para saludarlo creo que lo haría dándole la mano y, como es costumbre en su país, lo miraría a los ojos.
2. Me presentaría diciendo mi nombre y saludando a cada una de las chicas con un solo beso en la mejilla. Como estamos en Argentina, les daría un beso y no dos.
3. > Hola, buenos días. Soy el licenciado Rodríguez de las Casas. ¿Cómo está, señor director?

   < Muy bien, encantado. Yo soy el doctor González, es un placer conocerle... Bienvenido, señor Rodríguez, y me alegro de que empiece a trabajar con nosotros.

EN COMUNICACIÓN

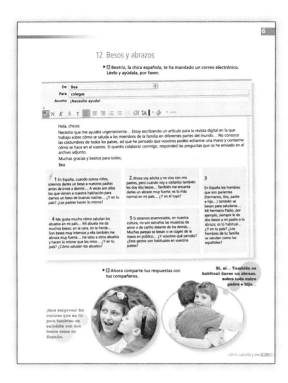

12 Besos y abrazos

A. Actividad de comprensión lectora sobre el saludo entre los miembros de la familia: hermanos, padres, abuelos...

Después de leer el texto y el archivo adjunto, y una vez resueltas las dudas de vocabulario, el estudiante tiene que responder explicando cómo es la forma de actuar en cada situación en su país.

La costumbre de los besos es muy diferente en los países asiáticos, como China o Japón. A muchos de los alumnos de estos países les suele gustar esta costumbre y terminan adoptándola como propia, aunque los primeros días en España se sorprendan mucho e incluso se sientan algo intimidados.

El hecho de que no se suelan besar los hijos y los padres, por ejemplo, no significa, obviamente, que no tengan los mismos sentimientos que en otras culturas que sí se besan; es simplemente que en estos países tienen otras formas de mostrar el cariño y el respeto.

B. Actividad de expresión oral en la que cada estudiante explicará a sus compañeros cómo es la forma de actuar en su cultura, compartiéndola y comparándola con el resto. De este modo, se plantean buenas prácticas de interculturalidad. Además, el alumno tiene la oportunidad de comentar lo que le ha sorprendido, lo que le parece bien aunque no lo comparta, lo que había oído y ahora comprende de forma diferente...

En definitiva, el estudiante se dará cuenta de que hay muchas formas de comportarse y que ninguna es mejor o peor que la otra, solo diferente.

Solución

A y **B.** Respuesta libre.

NOTAS

LOS OTROS

¡extra! CONTEXTOS

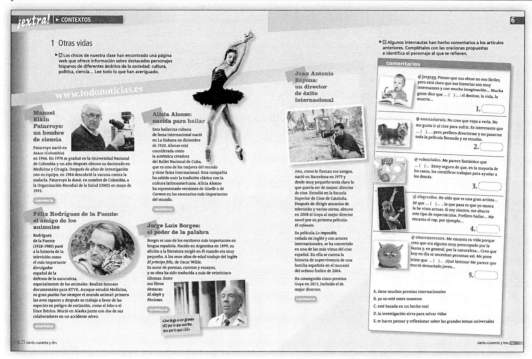

1 Otras vidas

El objetivo de esta serie de actividades también es cultural, en este caso, que los alumnos conozcan a destacados personajes del mundo hispano.

A. De nuevo recurrimos a un formato que resulta atractivo y familiar a los estudiantes: una página web. Presentamos a personajes importantes en diferentes ámbitos de la sociedad. Después de leer sobre cada uno de ellos podrán hacer algún comentario.

Sugerencia

Si tenemos la posibilidad de ponerles un documental sobre alguna de estas personas, sería una buena actividad de ampliación; en Internet seguro que encontraremos material. También podemos animar a los alumnos a que cada uno de ellos hable sobre un personaje de su país, alguien a quien admire por alguna razón o por el que tenga una simpatía especial.

B. A continuación, realizaremos otra actividad de comprensión lectora. Los alumnos leerán los comentarios que algunos internautas han escrito sobre los personajes del ejercicio 1A. Les diremos que tienen que completarlos con las oraciones propuestas e identificar a qué personaje se refiere cada una de ellas. Pensamos que es mejor que cada estudiante trabaje individualmente, subrayando y preguntando lo que no comprenda.

Solución

1-E: se refiere a Jorge Luis Borges.

2-C: se refiere a la película de Juan Antonio Bayona *Lo imposible*.

3-D: se refiere a Manuel Elkin Patarroyo.

4-A: se refiere a Alicia Alonso.

5-B: se refiere a Félix Rodríguez de la Fuente.

Sugerencia

Por último, en plenaria, cada estudiante puede señalar los aspectos más interesantes o que más le hayan llamado la atención sobre la vida de estos personajes famosos del mundo hispano.

Para hacer los comentarios les pediremos que se fijen en las expresiones que usan los internautas y en las de los ejemplos del ejercicio, para que intenten utilizarlas.

A continuación, podemos animarlos a que elijan al personaje con el que más se identifican, el que más les ha interesado…, y que expliquen por qué, empleando el mismo tipo de expresiones: *Me parece muy interesante la vida de Rodríguez de la Fuente. Admiro a la gente que ama tanto la naturaleza.*

¡extra! PRACTICA

2 ¡Es fantástico que seamos diferentes!

Con estos ejercicios ampliaremos el tema cultural a otros aspectos: comida, deportes, educación... Al mismo tiempo, practicaremos los contenidos morfosintácticos de la unidad, ya que los alumnos tienen que expresar sentimientos, mostrar opinión o valorar un hecho.

A. Los estudiantes deben completar una serie de fichas sobre temas diferentes. Después de corregirlas y de hablar sobre las cuestiones que se tratan, les pediremos que individualmente piensen en otro asunto que les interese, les preocupe o les guste, y que escriban algún comentario al respecto. Después leerán lo que han escrito a sus compañeros y hablarán sobre el asunto.

Sugerencia

Cuando un estudiante lea, podemos pedir a los demás que pongan atención y se fijen en si el uso que ha hecho del indicativo o el subjuntivo es correcto, identificando los posibles errores.

Solución

Posibles respuestas

1. muy sana – sea picante porque me encanta ese sabor – no hablemos de cosas tristes y charlemos sobre lo que hemos hecho durante el día – hablemos por el móvil o contestemos a mensajes y no está bien que comamos con la boca abierta.

2. ver el fútbol en televisión y practicarlo – el fútbol femenino no es muy popular – atletismo – practicar baloncesto e ir al gimnasio.

3. es muy buena, de muy buena calidad y que el sistema educativo no es muy caro – se estudien otros idiomas: inglés, francés, chino... – privadas los alumnos lleven uniforme – haya muchas asignaturas teóricas; prefiero que sean prácticas – no se pueda usar el diccionario en los exámenes de inglés – solo tengamos dos horas de Educación Física a la semana.

4. la economía vaya mal – es la falta de trabajo, el paro – cuidemos y protejamos el medioambiente – mucha gente no cuide las playas y los bosques y que no recicle – otras personas fumen en los espacios públicos – en el futuro no encuentre un buen trabajo.

5. navegar por Internet y usar las redes sociales – ir a conciertos y salir por la noche – quedar con sus amigos e ir a fiestas – ir al cine y leer – ir a las discotecas porque tengo que hablar a gritos.

6. son los perros y los gatos – el hámster – los loros – los maltraten o los abandonen – mucha gente compre un animal doméstico y, cuando se cansa o no puede cuidarlo, lo abandone.

B. Para completar el ejercicio anterior los estudiantes intercambiarán sus fichas y hablarán sobre aspectos del país de su compañero; de esta forma, tendrán que usar la tercera persona.

Solución

Respuesta libre.

NOTAS

LOS OTROS

3 ¿Qué animal serías?

A. Actividad de comprensión auditiva cuya finalidad es conocer el simbolismo de algunos animales. Posiblemente haya estudiantes que se identifiquen con otros diferentes a los que les proporcionamos; les pediremos que los mencionen y expliquen sus razones.

Solución

El gato: b. El perro: a. El caballo: b. La mariposa: a.

B. Se trata de otra actividad de comprensión auditiva en la que se habla sobre el simbolismo de otros animales distintos a los anteriores. En plenaria, cada estudiante expresará su opinión, sobre estos animales y los que han aparecido en el ejercicio 3A.

Solución

Posible respuesta

Me encanta que los perros sean fieles. A veces son mejores amigos que las personas.

Es una tontería que el caballo simbolice la inteligencia; no creo que sea más inteligente que otros animales.

Es fantástico que el león represente la fuerza porque es mi animal favorito.

Es increíble que las mariposas cambien por completo su estructura genética; parece mágico.

Pienso que la tortuga es símbolo de la paciencia; me gustaría ser como ella.

No pienso que la tortuga simbolice nuevas oportunidades por llevar la casa consigo.

Es verdad que, para mí, el oso simboliza la independencia; me encanta.

No es verdad que los gatos tengan siete vidas; es solo una leyenda.

C. El objetivo de esta actividad es doble: que los estudiantes amplíen su léxico sobre animales y que practiquen una vez más el uso del indicativo o del subjuntivo en los contextos estudiados en esta unidad. Para ello han de elegir a tres personas de la clase y relacionar a cada una de ellas con uno de los animales que les proponemos o con otros que ellos elijan. También pueden comentar el animal que nunca serían, explicando las razones.

Sugerencia

Para practicar un poco más el vocabulario de los animales, podemos hacer la siguiente práctica: describiremos de una forma imaginativa a distintos animales para que el resto de la clase adivine de cuál se trata. Gana el que más aciertos tenga. Ejemplos: *De flor en flor, así es su trabajo y así encuentra su comida (abeja). Cuando una persona no es muy inteligente se dice que lo es (burro). Cuando amanece, canta (gallo). De niño era el más feo, pero cuando creció cambió (cisne)...*

Solución

Posible respuesta

En mi opinión, está claro que mi compañera es una hormiga. Pienso que es ese animal porque es muy trabajadora. No creo que sea un grillo porque no le gusta mucho cantar.

Opino que mi compañero es un tigre. Creo que es este animal porque veo que es muy fuerte y sé que no se rinde ante los problemas. No creo que sea un mono porque no le gusta hacer bromas.

Parece evidente que mi compañera es una libélula ya que es elegante y sensible. Es este animal porque le gustan el arte y la danza. No pienso que sea un mosquito porque nunca molesta a los demás.

D. Por último, las personas que han sido comparadas con animales pueden decir si están de acuerdo o no con su identificación. Tras comentar con ellas el animal seleccionado y comprobar sus respuestas, cada estudiante explicará al resto de la clase los resultados.

Solución

Respuesta libre.

NOTAS

¡extra! EN COMUNICACIÓN

4 ¿Qué hacemos cuando…?

A. En esta actividad planteamos a los alumnos diferentes situaciones sociales para que expliquen cómo actuarían. Tenemos que decirles que aprender una lengua no es solo saber expresarse en ella, sino conocer cómo se relaciona la gente que habla esa lengua, ya que saber comportarse en todas las circunstancias posibles forma parte del aprendizaje. Las situaciones que les planteamos son muy cotidianas: la forma de pagar, dejar o no propina, qué llevar si te invitan a comer en una casa… Normalmente, los estudiantes responden a estas situaciones como lo harían en su país, así que se trata de ver esas diferencias que pueden ser tan importantes en una circunstancia determinada y cuyo incumplimiento puede tener como resultado, en ocasiones, que la persona sea considerada descortés e incluso maleducada.

Solución

1. Normalmente, en España, si vamos con un grupo de amigos a comer o a cenar, se paga la cuenta entre todos; todos ponemos la misma cantidad de dinero, dividimos el total en partes iguales. Eso se llama: *pagar a escote*. Si una persona solo ha tomado un refresco, una bebida o ha comido mucho menos que el resto, no suele pagar y la invitan los demás. A veces invitamos a todos nuestros amigos o familiares si se trata de una ocasión especial: cumpleaños, celebración particular… Es común dejar un 5% de propina y, a veces, hasta un 10%, si se trata de un restaurante de lujo o de calidad superior. En la mayoría de las ocasiones, si solo tomamos un café o alguna bebida, no dejamos propina.

2. En España, cuando alguien está enfermo, solemos llevarle un pequeño obsequio: una caja de bombones, flores, un libro, algunas revistas… Últimamente también se ha puesto de moda regalar una tarjeta con mensajes de amigos y familiares para desearle que se mejore.

3. Cuando nos invitan a comer o cenar, solemos llevar una botella de vino o cava; sobre todo si se trata de una comida de cumpleaños, de algún aniversario o de algún acontecimiento especial. También es habitual llevar algún dulce de postre para compartir después de la comida.

4. Es una costumbre muy extendida entre los españoles enseñar la casa cuando alguien nos visita por primera vez. Se suelen enseñar todas las habitaciones, incluidos el cuarto de baño y los dormitorios.

5. No solemos ser puntuales en este tipo de reuniones informales; se trata de una fiesta entre amigos. Como no es un acontecimiento formal o de trabajo, se puede llegar un poco más tarde de la hora fijada: unos quince o veinte minutos después, por ejemplo. Si nos retrasáramos mucho más tiempo, llamaríamos por teléfono para comunicarlo.

6. En España no es extraño hablar con gente desconocida en la calle, en el ascensor, en la cola del cine, en una tienda, en el supermercado, en la consulta del dentista, en el autobús… A veces, en el transporte público, hablamos con otras personas que viajan con nosotros y que no conocemos de nada. En los viajes largos en avión, en tren o en cualquier otro medio de transporte, se suele charlar con el compañero de asiento. En muchas ocasiones, después de un viaje así puede que nos demos el correo electrónico o el teléfono para mantener el contacto con la persona que acabamos de conocer, aunque sepamos que es posible que no volvamos a verla nunca más.

NOTAS

► LOS OTROS

¡EXTRA! EN COMUNICACIÓN

B. Actividad de comprensión auditiva sobre otras convenciones y normas de comportamiento social de la cultura española.

Solución

1-A; 2-B; 3-B.

C. Por último, el estudiante ha de leer, comentar y comparar con su cultura otras normas o comportamientos sociales.

Sugerencia

Después de leer los comentarios de la red social y opinar sobre ellos, podemos invitar a los estudiantes a que libremente vayan explicando algunas costumbres de sus países que les gustan o no les gustan, alguna que les parece interesante que los demás conozcan, etc.

En caso de estudiar en España, otra tarea que les podemos proponer para profundizar en el conocimiento de la cultura española es que se fijen con atención en su entorno, en el comportamiento de la familia con la que viven, de los estudiantes españoles con los que comparten piso, de la gente de la cafetería o del bar al que suelen ir, de la gente que va por la calle…; en definitiva, que observen todo lo que los rodea y busquen esas normas o costumbres que comparte toda la comunidad. Señalaremos una sesión para debatir sobre este tema y todos hablarán sobre el resultado de sus observaciones.

Solución

Respuesta libre.

NOTAS

Unidad 7
Quizás vaya a la fiesta

OBJETIVOS DE LA UNIDAD

En esta unidad continuamos desgranando los valores del modo subjuntivo en enunciados desiderativos: *ojalá (que)… / (deseo) que…* + subjuntivo, *soñar con…* + infinitivo, *soñar con que…* + subjuntivo. Siguiendo con este **contenido gramatical**, presentaremos la estructura *a ver si* + indicativo y, además, trataremos los enunciados dubitativos introducidos por *quizá(s) / tal vez / probablemente / seguramente* + subjuntivo / indicativo; *es probable que… / puede (ser) que…* + subjuntivo, y, por último, la locución adverbial *a lo mejor* + indicativo. Asimismo, abordaremos los enunciados exhortativos con *que* + subjuntivo y las preposiciones de lugar o localización.

Entre las **funciones comunicativas** trataremos la expresión del deseo y la manifestación de la duda y la inseguridad. Finalmente, nos centraremos en la ubicación de personas o cosas y en la expresión de la posibilidad y las advertencias.

Los contenidos **léxico-semánticos** tienen que ver con los medios de comunicación: prensa, radio, televisión e Internet.

Como **contenidos socioculturales** se introducen aquellos que tienen que ver con los medios de comunicación en el mundo hispano. Además, hablaremos de las bibliotecas virtuales, una novedosa forma de relacionarse, conocer gente y comunicarse con ella.

Finalmente, los **contenidos pragmáticos** van dirigidos al estudio de los modalizadores atenuantes de las aserciones *(quizás, puede que…)*, las expresiones de deseo en situaciones de comunicación estereotipadas, la formalización de advertencias con *que* + subjuntivo y la expresión de deseo con *a ver si…* y sus matices de curiosidad y expectación.

QUIZÁS VAYA A LA FIESTA

CONTEXTOS

1 La fiesta de Sandra

Comenzamos la sección con una actividad para presentar en contexto los enunciados exhortativos y dubitativos, dos de los principales contenidos gramaticales que se recogen en la unidad.

A. La secuencia se abre con un ejercicio de comprensión auditiva. Fijaremos la atención de los estudiantes en tres imágenes y les diremos que una de ellas pertenece a la fiesta de Sandra. Después de la fase de escucha, los animaremos a elegir la fotografía correcta, justificando sus respuestas.

Sería conveniente que, como paso previo a la fase de audición, pidiéramos a los estudiantes que describieran de forma oral los tres dibujos: qué ven, qué personas aparecen, cómo van vestidos, qué estarán haciendo...

A continuación, pasaremos a oír la grabación. Será suficiente con una sola escucha; no obstante, si se cree conveniente, haremos una segunda audición para asegurar la comprensión.

Cada estudiante, de forma individual, marcará la foto que corresponde a la fiesta de Sandra y, finalmente, comparará su hipótesis con las de sus compañeros.

Les propondremos que expliquen sus ideas usando alguna de las estructuras dubitativas que hemos señalado en los ejemplos: *Quizás la imagen... / Puede que la imagen... / Es, tal vez...* Así, desde el principio de la unidad, comenzarán a familiarizarse con los contenidos que aprenderemos a lo largo de esta y, con su uso en un contexto real.

Cuando hayamos descubierto la imagen que Sandra ha colgado en su red social, leeremos en plenaria los comentarios de algunos de sus amigos.

Propondremos una lectura en voz alta de cada uno y aclararemos las posibles dudas que se planteen.

Después de esta fase, haremos hincapié en que los alumnos observen las estructuras que hemos marcado en los textos.

Explicaremos que serán el contenido gramatical que vamos a aprender a lo largo de la unidad. Con esta actividad de observación en contexto de dichos elementos lingüísticos, los estudiantes empezarán a darse cuenta de su función y su significado.

Sugerencia

Si se cree conveniente podemos empezar ya a preguntarles para qué creen que servirán las estructuras que hemos señalado en los comentarios, con qué función las usamos...

Solución

La imagen que corresponde a la fiesta de Sandra es la A. En la audición escuchamos a dos chicas y un chico, tal y como se muestra en la imagen. Además, se ven platos que se mencionan, como el sushi o el gazpacho. Las otras dos imágenes no representan la fiesta porque en una aparecen personas disfrazadas, por lo que se trata de una fiesta de carnaval o de disfraces, y en la otra, personas que bailan en una discoteca.

> *Quizás la imagen de la fiesta de Sandra es la* **A** *porque* en la grabación se habla de comida como el sushi y hay varias chicas y un chico, como en la audición.

> *Puede que la imagen sea la* **A** *porque en la grabación* están hablando sobre la comida que han llevado a la fiesta y en el dibujo hay platos de comida: sushi, gazpacho...

> *Es, tal vez, la imagen* **A** porque en la grabación no se habla de baile ni de disfraces.

NOTAS

CONTEXTOS

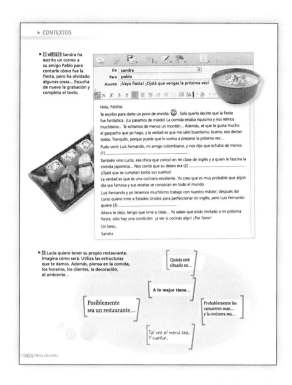

B. Continuamos con un nuevo ejercicio de compresión oral. Pediremos a los alumnos que escuchen de nuevo la grabación y completen el correo electrónico que Sandra ha enviado a uno de sus amigos con las palabras o las frases que faltan.

En esta muestra de lengua vuelven a aparecer los enunciados dubitativos y exhortativos que nos interesa presentar.

Antes de comenzar con la fase auditiva, leeremos el correo para solucionar las dudas léxicas.

A continuación, pasaremos a oír la grabación y a completar el texto con los datos que faltan. Esta primera parte puede realizarse de forma individual y, cuando hayan terminado, los alumnos compararán lo que han escrito.

Finalmente, corregiremos la actividad en plenaria.

De nuevo, fijaremos su atención sobre el tipo de oraciones que nos interesa trabajar, aquellas que expresan deseo, duda y posibilidad.

Solución

1. ... a su familia, a su esposa y a su bebito.
2. ... montar un restaurante japonés en España.
3. ... empezar con su beca de investigación en el departamento de genética.

C. Cerramos la serie de actividades con la práctica de la expresión y la interacción orales.

Animaremos a nuestros estudiantes a que piensen, de forma imaginativa, cómo será el restaurante que quiere abrir Lucía, una de las amigas de Sandra. Cada uno comentará sus ideas completando los enunciados dubitativos que ofrecemos en la ficha.

Si el grupo lo necesitara, dejaríamos algunos minutos para que escribieran sus propuestas y, a continuación, las explicaran en plenaria. No obstante, esta parte del ejercicio está concebida para que se realice de manera oral.

En los enunciados hemos incluido la forma verbal (subjuntivo o indicativo) para facilitar la tarea del estudiante porque todavía estamos en la fase de observación en contexto de los contenidos de la unidad, y aún no hemos pasado al proceso de conocimiento de la regla de uso. Insistiremos en que, al usar estos enunciados, estamos hablando de posibilidades, de hipótesis, de situaciones que no son seguras. Pueden referirse también a los horarios, la decoración, el ambiente...

En este caso, queremos que los alumnos hablen libremente, de forma menos dirigida, sin tener que usar necesariamente las estructuras anteriores.

Sugerencia

Aprovecharemos este ejercicio para que los alumnos realicen una presentación por escrito de su restaurante favorito. Pueden tratar los siguientes aspectos: descripción, localización, servicio, tipo de comida, ambiente, clientes, razones por las que lo recomiendan... También podemos hacer esta actividad de forma oral.

Solución
Posible respuesta

Posiblemente sea un restaurante tradicional de Japón porque su sueño es abrir un restaurante japonés.

Quizás esté situado en un barrio céntrico de la ciudad.

A lo mejor tiene sushi, porque es un plato que hace muy bien.

Tal vez el menú sea especial, diferente al de otros restaurantes... Tal vez sea un menú de degustación para probar un poco de todo... *y cueste* un poco caro; en general, los restaurantes japoneses son caros.

Probablemente los camareros sean muy amables y agradables con los clientes... *y la cocinera sea* Lucía. A ella le encanta cocinar y lo hace muy bien...

Horario: Tal vez abra a las doce y media o la una del mediodía y cierre a las doce o doce y media de la noche.

Clientes: A lo mejor tiene muchos clientes de Japón, pero creemos que también vendrán personas de otros países para probar sus platos.

Decoración: Puede que lo decore de forma tradicional, con cuadros y objetos de la cultura japonesa.

Ambiente: Seguramente el restaurante ofrecerá un ambiente muy agradable para comer y pasar un buen rato con los amigos o la familia.

ciento trece 113

QUIZÁS VAYA A LA FIESTA

CONTEXTOS

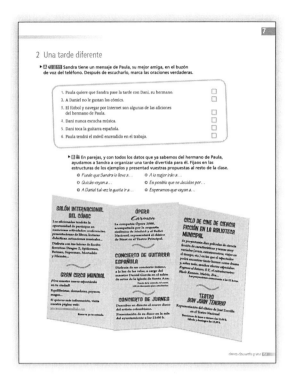

2 Una tarde diferente

Con este bloque practicaremos la comprensión auditiva y la expresión e interacción orales para seguir profundizando en el funcionamiento de los contenidos lingüísticos de la unidad en una situación comunicativa cotidiana: un mensaje telefónico.

A. Explicaremos a los alumnos que escucharán un mensaje de Paula, una de las mejores amigas de Sandra.

En primer lugar, tendrán que oírlo y, de entre todas las oraciones que hemos escrito en la ficha, marcar las que sean correctas, las que hayan escuchado en la grabación. Si es necesario, antes de comenzar con la fase de audición, haremos una lectura para aclarar las dudas de comprensión.

Finalmente, después de la fase de escucha, corregiremos la actividad en plenaria. Esta parte se realizará de forma individual; pero, antes de pasar a la corrección en gran grupo, cada estudiante podría comparar sus respuestas con las de algunos compañeros.

Solución

Las oraciones correctas son 1, 3 y 6.

B. Agruparemos a los estudiantes en parejas y aclararemos que el objetivo de este ejercicio es ayudar a Sandra para que el hermano de su amiga pase una tarde divertida.

Fijaremos su atención en todas las actividades de ocio que se presentan en la guía de la ciudad y, antes de empezar con la tarea, las leeremos en gran grupo para aclarar las dudas en torno al léxico. Recordamos que deberán hacer sus propuestas teniendo en cuenta las preferencias de Dani y toda la información que ya saben de él.

Pasados algunos minutos, presentarán sus ideas al resto de los grupos; haremos hincapié en que las expliquen con los enunciados de duda o posibilidad que tienen en las muestras de lengua.

Sugerencia

Para alcanzar un mayor grado de interacción entre el profesor y los alumnos y, al mismo tiempo, un desarrollo del componente afectivo, fundamental para un satisfactorio desarrollo del proceso enseñanza-aprendizaje, proponemos la siguiente variante de la actividad:

El profesor explicará a sus estudiantes sus preferencias de tiempo libre o alguna de sus aficiones y pedirá que, entre las propuestas de la guía cultural y de ocio de la ciudad, elijan las que podrían gustarle más, las que más se acerquen a sus gustos e intereses.

Tendrán que presentar sus ideas usando estructuras del tipo: *Al profesor quizás le interese… / El profesor tal vez quiera ir… / A lo mejor va a… / Puede que le guste…*

Solución

Posible respuesta

Puede que Sandra lo lleve al Salón Internacional del Cómic porque a Daniel le gusta leer cómics.

Quizás vayan al ciclo de cine de ciencia ficción de la biblioteca municipal porque al chico también le gustan este tipo de historias y, posiblemente, también le gusten este tipo de películas.

A Daniel tal vez le guste ir al concierto de guitarra española porque Paula, su hermana, dice que toca la guitarra eléctrica y, posiblemente, también le guste la guitarra española.

A lo mejor irán al concierto de Juanes. Es un chico adolescente y es posible que le guste este cantante porque su hermana nos ha contado que le gusta la música.

Es posible que se decidan por el Salón Internacional del Cómic y por el ciclo de cine de ciencia ficción. Seguro que le interesan a Dani porque le gustan los cómics y las películas de ese género.

Esperamos que vayan al ciclo de cine. Estoy seguro/a de que las películas que ponen le encantarán a Daniel.

OBSERVA, APRENDE Y RECUERDA

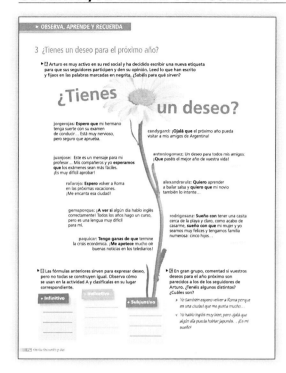

3 ¿Tienes un deseo para el próximo año?

Iniciamos una secuencia de actividades cuyo objetivo es la inferencia y la reflexión sobre los contenidos lingüísticos que vamos a ejercitar a lo largo de la lección.

A. A través de una situación comunicativa cercana a la realidad del estudiante y con la que se siente familiarizado, la participación en una red social, presentamos el uso del presente de subjuntivo, del infinitivo o del indicativo en los enunciados desiderativos.

Explicaremos a los estudiantes que Arturo ha pedido la colaboración de sus seguidores para que cuenten sus deseos para el año próximo.

Si es necesario, antes de continuar, aclararemos el significado de la palabra «etiqueta», relacionado con el campo léxico de las redes sociales.

A continuación, pasaremos a la lectura de los comentarios y resolveremos las dudas de comprensión.

Finalmente, fijaremos la atención de los estudiantes en las estructuras que hemos marcado y les preguntaremos cuándo se usan, para qué creen que sirven...

Pediremos que comenten sus ideas en plenaria. No les será difícil averiguar que se trata de expresiones de deseo. Si no llegaran a esta conclusión, el profesor dará la solución.

Solución

Las fórmulas que están en negrita se usan para expresar un deseo.

B. Ahora los estudiantes reflexionarán sobre la construcción de los enunciados desiderativos que aparecían en el ejercicio previo.

Se trata de que vuelvan a la actividad A y clasifiquen los ejemplos marcados escribiéndolos en la columna correspondiente, según se utilice infinitivo, indicativo o subjuntivo. De esta forma, inferirán las diferentes formas con las que se construyen estas estructuras desiderativas.

Solución

+ Infinitivo	+ Indicativo	+ Subjuntivo
Espero…	A ver si…	Espero que…
Quiero…		Ojalá (que)…
Sueño con…		Esperamos que…
Me apetece…		Que…
		Quiero que…
		Sueño con que…
		Tengo ganas de que…

C. Después de los procesos de inferencia y reflexión sobre el uso de los enunciados que se presentan en las fases anteriores, propondremos que cada alumno comente si sus deseos para el nuevo año coinciden con los de los seguidores de Arturo. Los animaremos a que los expliquen en gran grupo y de forma oral.

Sugerencia

Si se cree conveniente, para facilitar la interacción oral entre los alumnos del grupo, cambiaremos el procedimiento de la última fase de la actividad: cada estudiante elige a otro compañero y escribe sus deseos para el año nuevo; a continuación, los compartirá en plenaria.

Solución

Respuesta libre.

QUIZÁS VAYA A LA FIESTA

OBSERVA, APRENDE Y RECUERDA

4 ¿Alguna noticia interesante?

Este ejercicio está planteado para que los alumnos reflexionen sobre el uso del indicativo o del subjuntivo en los enunciados que expresan duda o posibilidad.

A. Comunicaremos a los estudiantes que vamos a leer algunas informaciones aparecidas en Internet y seleccionadas por Arturo, el protagonista del anterior bloque de actividades. Dividiremos al grupo por parejas y los animaremos a que conecten cada titular con la noticia a la que hace referencia. Antes de comenzar, si se cree necesario, explicaremos el significado de la palabra «titular», así como el de otros términos que desconozcan. Pasados algunos minutos, resolveremos la actividad en plenaria.

> **Solución**
>
> **1.** c;
>
> **2.** a;
>
> **3.** b;
>
> **4.** d;
>
> **5.** e.

OBSERVA, APRENDE Y RECUERDA

Queremos que reflexionen sobre las diferencias que existen con los enunciados desiderativos que ya conocen. En este caso, observarán que se trata de estructuras distintas que expresan duda o posibilidad.

> **Solución**
>
> Todas estas fórmulas expresan duda y probabilidad.

C. Ahora queremos que los estudiantes reflexionen sobre la diferencia en la construcción de los enunciados *Es probable que...* y *A lo mejor...*

Se trata de que infieran que el primero se construye con subjuntivo y el segundo, con indicativo. Además, pretendemos que observen que ambos sirven para la expresión de duda.

Esta parte se realizará de forma individual y, a continuación, procederemos a la corrección en plenaria.

Nos aseguraremos de no continuar con la actividad hasta que hayan entendido el sentido y la función de estas estructuras, así como la diferencia con las anteriores ya aprendidas.

> **Solución**
>
> **1.** b; **2.** a.

B. En esta segunda parte, los alumnos deberán prestar atención a las estructuras que hemos marcado en los artículos. Comentarán con sus compañeros, en gran grupo, cuál es su uso o, dicho de otra forma, qué función o funciones tienen.

D. Ponemos atención al uso del indicativo, del subjuntivo o de los dos modos verbales con los enunciados dubitativos. Animaremos a los estudiantes a que vuelvan a la sección A y completen la tabla señalando el modo que se utiliza para cada una de las estructuras. Con las muestras de lengua de las noticias, no tendrán dificultades para realizar la tarea. Completarán la actividad seleccionando un ejemplo extraído de los artículos para cada uno de los usos propuestos. Cuando hayan terminado, descubrirán que hay estructuras que solo se usan con indicativo, otras solo con subjuntivo y otras con las dos formas.

Sugerencia

Dividiremos la clase en parejas y propondremos que cada una escriba nuevos ejemplos para las estructuras dubitativas de la ficha. Pasado el tiempo estimado, corregiremos en plenaria sus soluciones.

Si queremos incorporar el componente afectivo, que garantizará una mayor implicación del alumno en la tarea, animaremos a que los protagonistas de las frases sean ellos mismos o los compañeros del grupo.

Solución

Es probable que...: Subjuntivo. Es probable que esta propuesta se haga realidad el año próximo.

A lo mejor: Indicativo. A lo mejor superamos las cifras del año pasado y recibimos a más de un millón de personas.

Es posible que...: Subjuntivo. Es posible que contemos con 105 kilómetros de pistas a disposición de nuestros visitantes este año.

Puede que...: Subjuntivo. Puede que visitar estos fantásticos lugares sea una de las principales razones por las que millones y millones de turistas vengan a nuestro país.

Quizás: Indicativo y subjuntivo. Quizás, en el futuro, ya no solo escriba y cante… Esta innovación –o «quizás es mejor llamarla revolución», como dice Drexler–, hace que…

Seguramente: Indicativo y subjuntivo. Seguramente estén entre los grandes atractivos culturales de España. Seguramente un grupo de delincuentes (…) planeó este robo.

OBSERVA, APRENDE Y RECUERDA

5 El test de las dudas

Presentamos una actividad lúdica para el chequeo y el refuerzo de los usos de las construcciones dubitativas presentados en las fases anteriores.

Los alumnos tendrán que completar de forma individual un test sobre el uso del indicativo o el subjuntivo en los enunciados que expresan duda o posibilidad.

Dejaremos algunos minutos para que lo hagan y, pasado este tiempo, intercambiarán su test con otro compañero, que lo corregirá y les dará los resultados. Solucionaremos las dificultades de comprensión que se presenten.

Solución

1. c;
2. a;
3. a;
4. a.

▶ QUIZÁS VAYA A LA FIESTA

OBSERVA, APRENDE Y RECUERDA

6 La noticia falsa

Secuencia de actividades cuyo objetivo es que los alumnos reflexionen sobre el uso de los adverbios de duda *(quizás, tal vez, posiblemente, probablemente* y *seguramente)* e infieran que se construyen con indicativo cuando van detrás del verbo.

A. Explicaremos a los estudiantes que van a leer tres noticias y tendrán que averiguar cuál es la falsa. En primer lugar, haremos una lectura en plenaria y aclararemos las dudas léxicas. A continuación, el alumno que crea saber la respuesta, contestará justificando su elección. Finalmente, el profesor dará la solución.

Sugerencia

Otra opción es realizar una votación para descubrir, según la mayoría, qué noticia es la falsa.

Solución

La noticia falsa es la número 3.

B y **C.** Los estudiantes volverán sobre los textos de las noticias y prestarán atención a los verbos y a las estructuras marcadas.

En plenaria, comentarán por qué aparecen solo con indicativo, cuál es la razón para este uso específico…

Si no lo han descubierto, en el ejercicio C proponemos dos nuevas muestras de lengua escrita que los ayudarán a reflexionar y así a avanzar en el descubrimiento de dicho uso, distinto a otros que ya habían aprendido anteriormente.

Por tanto, pretendemos que descubran que todos estos adverbios de duda se usan con indicativo cuando van en una posición concreta: detrás del verbo.

Cuando hayan llegado a esta conclusión, completarán la regla de uso.

Sugerencia

Aconsejamos no pasar a la siguiente sección hasta que no se resuelvan las dudas que pudieran surgirles a los alumnos. Si fuera necesario, propondremos nuevos ejemplos que garanticen la comprensión total de la regla.

Solución

Con las fórmulas de duda *quizá(s), tal vez, posiblemente, probablemente* y *seguramente* usamos indicativo solo cuando **van detrás del verbo** y podemos usar indicativo o subjuntivo si **van delante del verbo**.

OBSERVA, APRENDE Y RECUERDA

7 Última hora

Con esta actividad pretendemos que los alumnos accedan de manera inferencial al conocimiento del uso de las preposiciones de localización o lugar.

A. Agruparemos a los alumnos en parejas y los informaremos de que les vamos a mostrar una serie de fotografías que ha recibido Inés. Tendrán que ayudarla a conectar estas imágenes con los artículos a los que hacen referencia. Antes de empezar con la actividad propiamente dicha, sería conveniente que los estudiantes describieran en plenaria todas las fotos. A continuación, dejaremos algunos minutos para que cada pareja haga la selección. Durante este tiempo, el profesor puede ayudarlos aclarando el significado de las palabras que desconozcan. Finalmente, pasaremos a la comprobación de las respuestas.

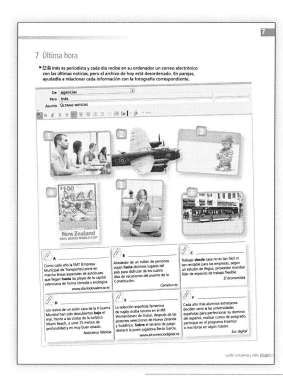

Solución

1. F; **2.** D; **3.** B; **4.** E; **5.** C; **6.** A.

OBSERVA, APRENDE Y RECUERDA

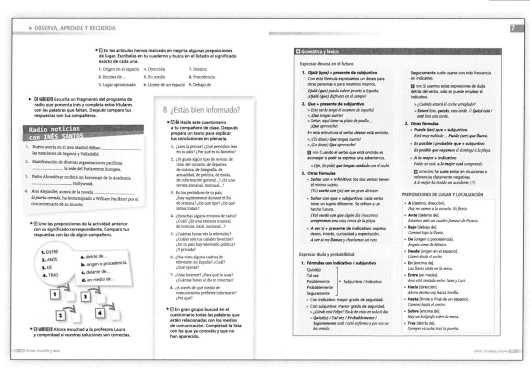

B. Pediremos a los estudiantes que vuelvan sobre los textos de la actividad anterior. Tendrán que fijarse en las palabras que hemos marcado; se trata de preposiciones que indican lugar o localización. Para comenzar, de forma individual, las escribirán y buscarán en el listado el significado adecuado para cada una. Cuando hayan terminado, compararán los resultados con algún compañero y, finalmente, corregiremos el ejercicio en gran grupo.

Solución

Hasta: 6. Límite de un espacio.

Hacia: 4. Dirección.

Desde: 1. Origen en el espacio.

Bajo: 9. Debajo de…

Sobre: 2. Encima de…

A: 7. Destino.

QUIZÁS VAYA A LA FIESTA

C. Continuamos con la reflexión sobre el uso de una nueva serie de preposiciones de lugar, esta vez, a través de un ejercicio de comprensión auditiva.

Animaremos a los alumnos a que escuchen el programa de radio de la periodista que habíamos presentado en la actividad anterior y a que completen las noticias con las preposiciones que faltan.

Haremos una primera escucha y, si fuera necesario, una segunda para facilitar la comprensión. Finalmente, pasaremos a la corrección en plenaria.

Solución

1. entre.
2. ante.
3. de.
4. Tras.

D y E. En la fase anterior los estudiantes solo habían inferido el uso de las preposiciones en contexto y, en esta nueva actividad, deberán conocer su significado teniendo en cuenta los ejemplos analizados en el ejercicio 7C.

Los alumnos relacionarán cada preposición con lo que significa y, a continuación, compararán sus hipótesis con las de algún compañero.

Al final, comprobarán sus respuestas atendiendo a una audición. Escucharán las soluciones que explica la profesora Laura y descubrirán sus posibles errores.

Sugerencia

En la última fase, durante la comprobación de respuestas con la comprensión oral, podríamos cambiar el procedimiento para activar el aspecto lúdico: los alumnos se intercambian el libro o el soporte en el que hayan escrito las soluciones para que otro compañero los corrija.

Solución

1. d;
2. c;
3. b;
4. a.

8 ¿Estás bien informado?

A. En este ejercicio trataremos de extraer el conocimiento previo que posee el alumno en relación con el campo léxico de los medios de comunicación y, además, trabajaremos para ampliarlo con nuevas palabras.

Presentaremos al grupo un cuestionario cuya intención es averiguar el uso que nuestros alumnos hacen de los medios de comunicación: prensa, radio, televisión e Internet. Cada estudiante elegirá a un compañero para que responda a las preguntas. Después, intercambiarán los papeles.

A continuación, elaborarán por escrito un breve informe en el que expongan sus conclusiones. Si se cree conveniente, antes de que comiencen con esta parte, aclararemos el significado de las palabras que desconozcan.

Finalmente, los animaremos a que compartan en plenaria la información o los datos más interesantes que hayan averiguado sobre su compañero.

Solución

Respuesta libre.

B. Propondremos a los alumnos que vuelvan a las preguntas del cuestionario y marquen todo el léxico relacionado con los medios de comunicación que encuentren.

Además, en gran grupo, completarán esta lista con nuevos términos. De esta forma, chequeamos su conocimiento de este ámbito léxico y, por otra parte, lo ampliamos.

Sugerencia

La fase de ampliación del campo léxico podría organizarse, antes de que pasaran a la presentación en plenaria, en pequeños grupos. Cada uno haría una lista con las palabras que conoce y que no aparecen en las preguntas del cuestionario. Finalmente, las compararían con las propuestas del resto de sus compañeros. Lo importante de este campo léxico es que se fijen en las colocaciones para denominar medios de comunicación.

Creemos oportuno que, al final de la sección, una vez que nuestros alumnos han inferido y reflexionado sobre los componentes gramaticales, hagamos referencia a dos de los contenidos pragmáticos fundamentales de la unidad: por un lado, los modalizadores atenuantes de la fuerza de las aserciones *(quizás, puede que...)* y, por otro, la expresión de deseo con *a ver si...* y sus matices de curiosidad y expectativa.

Solución

Posibles respuestas

Prensa, periódico, revista de cine, revista del corazón, revista de deportes, revista de música, revista de fotografía, revista de actualidad, revista de política, revista de moda, revista de información general, revista semanal, revista mensual, suplemento, emisora de radio, emisora musical, emisora de noticias, emisora local, emisora nacional, televisión, canal de televisión, televisión pública, televisión privada, cadena de televisión, Internet, medio de comunicación.

PRACTICA

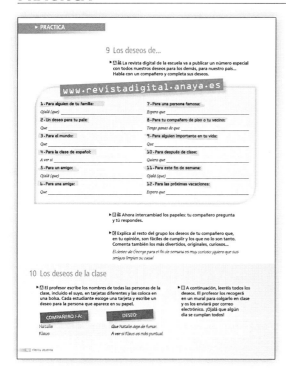

5. Ojalá (que) mi amigo Peter se mejore… Ahora está enfermo.

6. Que mi amiga Jessica venga con nosotros a visitar Londres.

7. Espero que Penélope Cruz haga más cine en España.

8. Tengo ganas de que Carlos prepare una tortilla de patatas para todos nosotros.

9. Que mi abuelo tenga buena salud.

10. Quiero que mis compañeros y yo tomemos unas tapas juntos.

11. Ojalá (que) haga buen tiempo y mis amigos y yo podamos ir a la playa.

12. Espero que viajemos a Roma.

C. Actividad de expresión e interacción orales. Estableceremos un turno de palabra para que cada estudiante comente en plenaria los deseos de su compañero; además, valorará cuáles son fácilmente realizables y, por otro lado, cuáles resultarán difíciles de llevar a cabo. El profesor controlará los posibles errores gramaticales y léxicos. Haremos especial hincapié en el uso correcto del indicativo o el subjuntivo en los enunciados desiderativos y les pediremos que se fijen en las muestras de lengua escrita que presentamos como ejemplos.

Sugerencia

Cada alumno elegirá a cinco personas que no estén en el grupo, fuera del aula, y les pedirá que cada una le cuente un deseo. Tras la fase de recopilación de datos, los presentarán al resto de los compañeros. Insistiremos en el uso de los enunciados desiderativos que ya conocen.

Solución

Respuesta libre.

9 Los deseos de…

En esta sección se ejercitan la expresión escrita y la oral para la práctica de las fórmulas y estructuras de deseo con indicativo y subjuntivo. Trabajamos también el carácter cooperativo y el aspecto lúdico del aprendizaje.

A y **B.** Organizaremos al grupo en parejas, o pequeños grupos si la clase fuera muy numerosa, para iniciar el desarrollo de la actividad. Presentaremos a los alumnos la revista digital de nuestra escuela y los animaremos a que escriban en su próximo número. Cada pareja completará los deseos para todas las situaciones y personas que proponemos. Sería conveniente que dejáramos el tiempo suficiente para que completaran las frases por escrito. Es importante que el profesor, durante ese proceso, ofrezca las explicaciones necesarias y esté atento para resolver dudas antes de pasar a la corrección en plenaria.

Solución

1. Ojalá (que) mi madre tenga mucha suerte con su nuevo trabajo.

2. Que mejore la situación económica.

3. Que seamos más felices y no haya guerras en ningún país del mundo.

4. A ver si aprendo el subjuntivo y lo uso como los españoles.

10 Los deseos de la clase

Este ejercicio vuelve a introducir la práctica, en esta ocasión de forma más libre, de las estructuras de deseo con indicativo y subjuntivo.

A y **B.** Animaremos a los alumnos a que escriban un deseo para algún miembro de la clase.

Cada uno elegirá una tarjeta, en la que aparecerá el nombre de alguien del grupo, y escribirá el deseo para esa persona.

Insistiremos en que pueden hacerlo usando cualquiera de las estructuras desiderativas que ya han aprendido, como en las muestras de lengua que incluimos en los ejemplos.

Finalmente, se podrían recoger todos los deseos en un mural para colocarlo en clase o, si hay posibilidades, se colgarían en la página web de la escuela o en alguna de las redes sociales usadas por los estudiantes.

Solución

Respuesta libre.

QUIZÁS VAYA A LA FIESTA

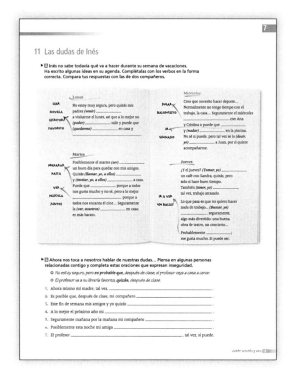

11 Las dudas de Inés

Este bloque está planteado para que los alumnos practiquen y consoliden el uso de los enunciados dubitativos construidos con indicativo o subjuntivo.

A. En primer lugar, nos detendremos en el título de la actividad. Les preguntaremos a los estudiantes de qué creen que tratará el ejercicio, qué contenido de la unidad piensan que practicaremos...

Posteriormente, les explicaremos que el objetivo es completar las posibilidades que tiene Inés para pasar su semana de vacaciones.

Aclararemos que nuestra protagonista ha escrito posibles actividades para llevar a cabo, pero ninguna con seguridad.

Les diremos que completen los espacios con los verbos en la forma correcta utilizando los elementos que hemos anotado al margen de la página de la agenda. Les pediremos que, una vez terminada la fase escrita, comparen sus respuestas con las de dos de sus compañeros.

Para fomentar la interrelación y dinamizar la clase, podemos pedir que se intercambien los libros o el soporte donde hayan hecho la actividad para corregirla.

Solución

Lunes: vengan / vienen; puedo; me quede; lea una novela de mi escritor favorito.

Martes: sea / es; los llame / los llamo / los llamaré / los voy a llamar; los invite / los invito / los invitaré / los voy a invitar; prepare / preparemos pasta; veremos / vamos a ver / veamos / vemos una película juntos; veremos / vamos a ver / veamos / vemos.

Miércoles: juegue / juego / voy a jugar / jugaré al baloncesto; vaya al gimnasio; nade; diga / digo / diré / voy a decir.

Jueves: Voy a tomar / Tomaré / Tomo; tendré / tengo / voy a tener; Buscaré / Voy a buscar / Busco; vaya a ver / iré a ver / voy a ver un ballet.

B. Proponemos un ejercicio semidirigido en el que se trabajan la expresión escrita y la expresión oral con el objetivo de reforzar y consolidar la práctica de las estructuras para expresar duda o posibilidad.

Presentamos una serie de oraciones que los alumnos deberán completar con sus opiniones usando el verbo en la forma correcta: indicativo o subjuntivo.

Les daremos tiempo para que preparen sus ideas y los animaremos a que sean divertidas, amenas y originales. Luego cada alumno las presentará a la clase.

Sugerencia

Si fuera necesario, con el objetivo de ampliar la práctica de los contenidos lingüísticos trabajados, incluiremos nuevas oraciones para que los alumnos las completen.

Solución

Posible respuesta

1. está / esté preparando una fiesta sorpresa para mi padre.
2. prepare el almuerzo / vaya a almorzar / coma en su restaurante favorito.
3. vayamos / vamos al Festival de Cine de Málaga.
4. hermano terminará sus estudios en la universidad después de 10 años.
5. vendrá a clase / venga a clase.
6. juegue / juega al fútbol con sus amigas.
7. se vendrá de tapas con nosotros, tal vez, si puede.

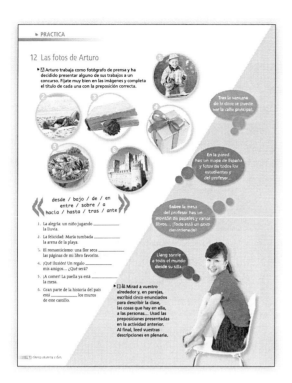

PRACTICA

12 Las fotos de Arturo

Comenzamos con una actividad para la práctica de las preposiciones de localización o de lugar.

A. Fijaremos la atención de los alumnos en una serie de fotografías que se han presentado a un concurso. Antes de empezar con el ejercicio, haremos una descripción de las imágenes en plenaria. A continuación, los estudiantes completarán, de forma individual, cada título con la preposición correcta. Deberán elegirla de entre las que les presentamos. Permitiremos que comparen sus respuestas con las de algún compañero y, finalmente, pasaremos a la corrección.

Solución

1. bajo; 2. sobre / en; 3. entre; 4. de; 5. en / sobre; 6. tras.

B. Esta segunda fase de la actividad se realizará en parejas. Cada una deberá escribir cinco oraciones, con las preposiciones que se incluían en el ejercicio 12A, para describir la situación de las personas de la clase, de las cosas que hay en ella, etcétera. Insistiremos en que se trata de que en las oraciones usen todas las preposiciones de localización que han aprendido.

Para finalizar, se hará una puesta en común de todas las descripciones, corregiremos los errores y solucionaremos las dudas de los alumnos si fuera necesario.

Solución

Respuesta libre.

PRACTICA

13 Noticias en imágenes

Con estas actividades seguimos profundizando en la práctica de los enunciados dubitativos con indicativo o subjuntivo y, además, en el léxico de los medios de comunicación, ahora con el que se refiere a las secciones de un periódico.

A. Los alumnos tendrán que imaginar la noticia que ilustra cada una de las fotografías. Los animaremos a que lo hagan de forma oral y usando alguna de las estructuras para expresar posibilidad que se les muestran. Esta fase la podríamos realizar en plenaria.

Solución

Posible respuesta

1. Tal vez el ministro de Economía decida subir los impuestos a los más ricos. / Es posible que esté dando una rueda de prensa para aclarar la última subida de impuestos.

2. Posiblemente sea una manifestación en protesta por los despidos. / A lo mejor no funcionan los medios de transporte y la gente va a pie.

3. Seguramente el equipo local ganará la liga. / Quizá el campeón de liga ha perdido otra vez en casa.

B. Esta segunda fase se realizará de forma individual. Cada estudiante escribirá un titular para cada una de las noticias.

▶ QUIZÁS VAYA A LA FIESTA

Si fuera necesario, remitiremos a los alumnos a los ejemplos que aparecían en la actividad 4A del apartado Observa, aprende y recuerda de esta unidad. Además, deberán pensar en qué sección del periódico incluirían las noticias.

A continuación, comentarán con sus compañeros los titulares y los apartados donde las han colocado. Finalmente, corregiremos los posibles errores.

Solución

Posible respuesta

1. El ministro de Economía y los impuestos a los ricos. Sección: Economía. La incluiría en la portada.
2. Nueva protesta por los despidos masivos en el sector industrial. Sección: Sociedad. La publicaría en la contraportada.
3. Nuevo partidazo del equipo local. Sección: Deportes. La publicaría en la contraportada.

C. Pediremos a los estudiantes que redacten por escrito una noticia para una de las secciones del periódico.

Antes de comenzar con la fase de escritura, en plenaria, tendrán que expresar, con *que* + subjuntivo, una serie de deseos o recomendaciones para conseguir una buena redacción.

Seguidamente, dejaremos el tiempo necesario para que escriban la noticia.

Sugerencia

Esta fase del ejercicio podría realizarse fuera del tiempo de clase. El profesor corregirá todas las noticias de los alumnos y, en la siguiente sesión, comentará los errores más comunes y resolverá las dudas que pudieran plantearse.

Solución

¡Que sea una noticia actual!

¡Que tenga una extensión máxima de un folio!

¡Que incluya alguna imagen!

¡Que no sea copia, que sea original!

14 Museos

En esta última actividad reforzamos y chequeamos el uso de las preposiciones de lugar con un ejercicio en el que los alumnos tienen que completar un texto.

Aprovecharemos la comprensión auditiva para poner en práctica el contenido gramatical.

En primer lugar, pediremos a los alumnos que elijan la preposición de lugar adecuada para completar cada espacio en blanco. Luego deberán confirmar su hipótesis con la audición.

Sería conveniente que volvieran a leer el texto de la descripción del cuadro para una mejor comprensión.

Sugerencia

En plenaria y, en una conversación relajada, pediremos a cada alumno que, siguiendo con la línea temática de la actividad, explique su última visita a un museo: *¿Cuál visitó? ¿Qué tipo de museo es? ¿Dónde está? ¿Cuándo lo visitó? ¿Es un lugar muy visitado?...*

Sugeriremos a los estudiantes que describan, siguiendo el modelo del texto que hemos propuesto en la actividad, su cuadro favorito, un cuadro que les guste mucho o, si el profesor lo prefiere, alguno que él mismo elija.

Lo concebimos como un ejercicio de expresión oral; aunque, si se cree conveniente, los alumnos pueden escribir el texto descriptivo en casa y, en la siguiente sesión, lo presentarán al resto del grupo.

Solución

ante – en – de – a – en – Tras – a – Delante del – En – bajo – En – desde – hasta – entre.

EN COMUNICACIÓN

15 Bibliotecas vivientes

A. Con esta actividad de comprensión lectora damos a conocer a los alumnos las denominadas «Bibliotecas Vivientes», una nueva manera de información y de comunicación.

Como actividad previa a la lectura, podemos preguntar a los estudiantes si han oído hablar de estas bibliotecas, si saben qué son, cómo funcionan, si suelen ir a las bibliotecas, si hay muchas bibliotecas en su ciudad, etcétera.

En primer lugar, haremos una lectura inicial del texto y solucionaremos los eventuales problemas de comprensión.

En plenaria, los alumnos podrán comentar qué les ha parecido el artículo, qué ha sido lo más interesante, qué les ha resultado más curioso… Por tanto, animaremos a los estudiantes a que comenten sus opiniones sobre el tema de forma ordenada.

Sugerencia

Después de la fase de lectura del texto, los alumnos, en parejas, podrían escribir cuatro ideas para resumirlo. Por último, compararán sus propuestas con las de las otras parejas.

B. Ejercicio de comprensión oral. Explicaremos a los estudiantes que vamos a escuchar las experiencias de dos integrantes de este tipo de bibliotecas. Antes de pasar a la fase auditiva, leeremos las preguntas y aclararemos las dudas de vocabulario. Después de oír la grabación, el alumno responderá a las preguntas. Sería conveniente, dada la dificultad del texto, una segunda escucha.

Para corregir, se podría proponer a los alumnos que se organizaran en parejas y, con la transcripción que incluimos al final del libro, se intercambiaran el trabajo, bajo la supervisión del profesor.

Solución

1. El libro viviente era María, una chica con una discapacidad física, era invidente.

2. La gente piensa que las personas con esta discapacidad no pueden hacer casi nada, que dependen de otras para realizar actividades tan cotidianas como el aseo personal: vestirse, lavarse…, y que no pueden desenvolverse solas en la ciudad para viajar en transporte público o cruzar una calle, por ejemplo.

3. Puedes conocer a personas de diferentes culturas y religiones, gente con la que normalmente no te relacionas en tu vida diaria.

4. Hablar con ella le hizo ponerse en su lugar. Le contó cómo era su vida y se dio cuenta de que no era muy diferente a la suya, que hacía las mismas cosas que las personas de su edad, que tenía problemas como todo el mundo, pero que se relacionaba y comunicaba con otras personas y hacía una vida normal.

5. Ella sueña con que algún día la gente vea a las personas con esta discapacidad como iguales, con que desaparezcan las barreras físicas en las ciudades.

6. Hablar con María le ha dado una visión diferente a la que tenía, y sobre todo ha aprendido que podemos parecer diferentes, pero en el fondo todos queremos lo mismo: ser felices.

C. Abriremos un turno de palabra para que los alumnos, en grupos, respondan a las preguntas que hemos planteado sobre el tema.

Propondremos, además, que, primero individualmente, hagan una lista con los libros que añadirían a la biblioteca y, después, en grupos, intercambien sus opiniones para crear un listado. Podríamos recoger en la pizarra sus propuestas.

Sugerencia

Podemos plantear un debate lanzando la siguiente pregunta: ¿Conocéis otras iniciativas o proyectos similares a las bibliotecas vivientes que luchen por acabar con los prejuicios y estereotipos de determinados grupos sociales?

Solución

Posible respuesta

Inmigrantes, padres adoptivos, budistas, religiosos, jubilados, parados…

QUIZÁS VAYA A LA FIESTA

EN COMUNICACIÓN

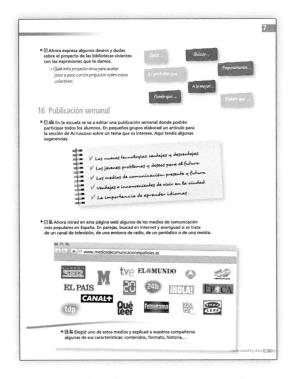

D. En esta fase chequeamos, a través de una actividad de expresión e interacción orales, los tipos de enunciados aprendidos a lo largo de la unidad. En gran grupo, los alumnos comentarán los deseos o dudas en torno a las bibliotecas vivientes. Los invitaremos a usar las estructuras que incluimos. Si es necesario, les daremos tiempo para que preparen sus ideas por escrito y, pasados algunos minutos, haremos la puesta en común.

Sugerencia

Finalmente, podemos sugerir a nuestros estudiantes que hablen sobre otros proyectos, programas o iniciativas que tengan el mismo objetivo que las «Bibliotecas Vivientes»: superar estereotipos o luchar contra los prejuicios. Proponemos el intercambio de experiencias e ideas de una forma menos dirigida, más libre que en las anteriores secciones de la serie.

Si los alumnos no conocieran ninguna experiencia de este tipo, les propondremos que, en parejas o pequeños grupos, busquen información en Internet. Prepararán una breve presentación para la clase con los proyectos o iniciativas que hayan encontrado. El resto de los compañeros podrá preguntarles o pedir aclaraciones si las necesitaran.

Solución

Respuesta libre.

16 Publicación semanal

Secuencia de actividades de expresión e interacción escritas que sigue con una de las líneas temáticas principales de la unidad: los medios de comunicación.

A. Antes de comenzar con el ejercicio, procederemos a organizar a los alumnos en pequeños grupos. Les explicaremos que deben escribir un artículo sobre un tema de actualidad que será publicado por la escuela. Hemos incluido algunas sugerencias, pero, si se cree oportuno, ellos pueden proponer otro tema de actualidad que consideren más atractivo o más adecuado a sus intereses.

Al final, invitaremos a los alumnos a presentar los artículos en clase.

Solución

Respuesta libre.

B y C. En primer lugar, animaremos a los estudiantes a que, en parejas, averigüen a qué tipo de medio de comunicación pertenecen los logotipos que se presentan. Necesitarán Internet para realizar esta primera fase del ejercicio.

En segundo lugar, cada pareja elegirá uno de esos medios y preparará un breve trabajo de investigación para presentarlo en clase.

Después de su exposición, los demás compañeros podrán hacerles preguntas o pedirles las aclaraciones oportunas. Si se dispone de Internet en clase, podemos visitar la página web del medio en cuestión.

Sugerencia

Abriremos un debate sobre el papel de los medios de comunicación y la importancia que tienen en la sociedad.

Agruparemos la clase por países de procedencia para que cada grupo prepare una pequeña presentación sobre los principales medios de comunicación: periódicos, revistas, radio, televisión, etcétera.

Si los alumnos son de una misma nacionalidad, cada grupo preparará un trabajo sobre un medio de comunicación concreto: prensa, radio, televisión…

Solución

B.
Canales de televisión: TVE, Antena 3, 24 Horas, Canal +, Teledeporte.
Emisoras de radio: Cadena SER, Onda Cero, 40 Principales.
Periódicos: *Marca, El País, El Mundo, 20 Minutos, informativos.net* (diario digital).
Revistas: *Qué Leer, Fotogramas, Hola, Época.*

C.
Respuesta libre.

¡extra! CONTEXTOS

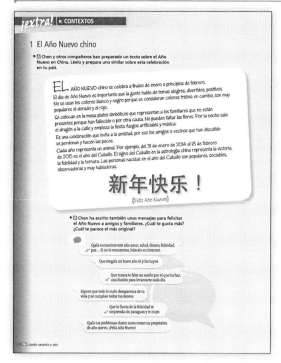

1 El Año Nuevo chino

Abrimos la sección extra con una actividad de compresión y expresión escritas que, además, presenta un contenido sociocultural que, sin duda, despertará la curiosidad de los alumnos.

A. Continuando con la línea temática de los deseos, explicaremos a los alumnos que van a leer un texto sobre la celebración del Año Nuevo en China. Haremos una primera lectura y aclararemos las dudas que surjan. El objetivo es que, con ese modelo, preparen, de forma individual, una breve presentación de cómo celebran el inicio del año en su país de origen. También podrían elaborar esa parte escrita en casa y, en la sesión siguiente, presentarla al resto del grupo. Cuando cada alumno realice la exposición, animaremos a los demás a que intervengan con preguntas o pidiendo aclaraciones, si las necesitan.

Sugerencia

En el caso de que los estudiantes tengan la misma nacionalidad, prepararán una presentación sobre la celebración de esta fiesta en su familia o, si hubiera costumbres diferentes, en la región de la que provienen.

Solución

Respuesta libre.

B. En esta segunda fase, de nuevo, fijamos la atención de los alumnos, en las fórmulas o estructuras analizadas en la unidad para la expresión del deseo. El objetivo será chequear su uso y reforzar su práctica en contexto. Los animaremos a que lean los mensajes de felicitación que ha recibido Chen y elijan los que les parezcan más originales o les gusten más. Dejaremos algunos minutos para que los seleccionen de forma individual y, a continuación, comentarán sus ideas con el resto de los compañeros.

Solución

Respuesta libre.

¡EXTRA! CONTEXTOS

C. En parejas, los estudiantes escribirán mensajes de felicitación para el año nuevo; tienen como modelo las muestras de lengua presentadas en el apartado 1B. Les diremos que intenten que los mensajes sean divertidos, originales, diferentes…

Sugerencia

Para que la actividad adquiera un matiz lúdico, si fuera posible, propondremos a los alumnos que envíen sus mensajes por móvil o a través de Internet. Seguro que les resultará más divertido.

Solución

Respuesta libre.

D. Propondremos a los estudiantes que lean los planes de futuro de Chen. Antes de la lectura, sería importante hacerles notar que nuestro protagonista tiene muchas dudas sobre lo que va a hacer. Una vez leído el texto, aclararemos los problemas de comprensión y les pediremos que marquen todos los enunciados dubitativos que encuentren; pueden comentar cuáles son y cómo se usan. Recordamos que todos han sido analizados y los han aprendido a lo largo de la unidad.

QUIZÁS VAYA A LA FIESTA

E. Nueva actividad de refuerzo y chequeo de las estructuras para expresar duda y deseo, esta vez, a través de la comprensión oral. Invitaremos a los alumnos a que escuchen el proyecto de Chen en España y completen los datos que les pedimos en la ficha. Llamaremos su atención sobre el hecho de que presentamos enunciados desiderativos y dubitativos en contexto. Realizaremos, si es necesario, dos escuchas y, finalmente, pasaremos a la fase de corrección. Insistiremos en que, cuando respondan o den sus soluciones, lo hagan usando las estructuras que se practican.

Sugerencia

Animaremos a los alumnos a que, de forma libre, hablen sobre uno de sus proyectos de futuro. Mostrarán sus deseos o sus dudas al resto de sus compañeros.

Solución

Su proyecto es escribir una novela.

Puede que sorprenda o parezca raro, pero quiere ser escritor.

Posiblemente, falte mucho para ver su novela publicada.

A lo mejor no se publica, ¡quién sabe!

Espera que sus amigos sean sinceros.

Chen sueña con que su novela sea un éxito y se imagina firmando autógrafos a miles de lectores.

Quizás no ocurra así, pero soñar es gratis.

¡extra! PRACTICA

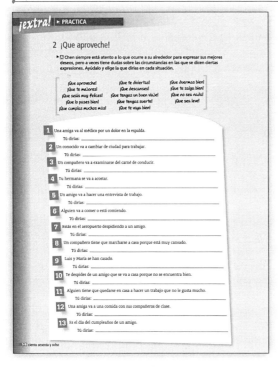

2 ¡Que aproveche!

En esta actividad de la sección EXTRA reforzamos la práctica de los enunciados desiderativos, haciendo hincapié en la estructura *que* + presente de subjuntivo.

A. Propondremos a los alumnos que ayuden a Chen a relacionar cada uno de los deseos incluidos en el recuadro con la situación en la que lo usarían. Harán esa primera fase de forma individual y, a continuación, pasaremos a la corrección en plenaria.

Sugerencia

Podemos ampliar la actividad con nuevas situaciones y deseos.

Solución

Posibles respuestas

1. ¡Que no sea nada!
2. ¡Que te vaya bien!
3. ¡Que te salga bien! / ¡Que tengas suerte!
4. ¡Que duermas bien! / ¡Que descanses!
5. ¡Que tengas suerte! / ¡Que te salga bien!
6. ¡Que aproveche!
7. ¡Que tengas (un) buen viaje!
8. ¡Que descanses!
9. ¡Que seáis muy felices!
10. ¡Que te mejores!
11. ¡Que sea leve!
12. ¡Que te diviertas! / ¡Que lo pases bien!
13. ¡Que cumplas muchos más!

¡EXTRA! PRÁCTICA

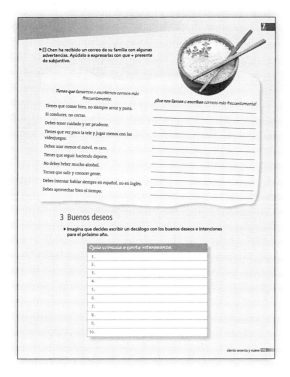

B. Ahora explicaremos que Chen ha recibido un correo electrónico de su familia con una serie de advertencias para que las tenga en cuenta durante su estancia en España. Antes de empezar con el ejercicio propiamente dicho, podemos preguntar a nuestros alumnos, si estuvieran estudiando fuera de su país de origen, si sus padres o amigos les han hecho algunas advertencias o recomendaciones antes de empezar el curso.

A continuación, de forma individual, tendrán que escribir las advertencias de la familia de Chen con la estructura *que* + subjuntivo. Pasados algunos minutos, intercambiarán sus respuestas con las de algún compañero y, finalmente, corregiremos la actividad en plenaria. Si fuera necesario, aclararemos las dudas en torno al uso de este tipo de enunciados. En principio, llegados a este punto de la unidad, no deberían tener especiales dificultades en la realización de la actividad.

Finalmente, podríamos hacer referencia a uno de los contenidos pragmáticos fundamentales de la unidad que aparece en la actividad A: las expresiones de deseo en situaciones de comunicación estereotipadas.

Solución

¡Que comas bien!

¡Que no corras si conduces!

¡Que tengas cuidado y seas prudente!

¡Que veas poco la tele y juegues menos con los videojuegos!

¡Que uses menos el móvil!

¡Que sigas haciendo deporte!

¡Que no bebas mucho alcohol!

¡Que salgas y conozcas gente!

¡Que intentes hablar siempre en español, no en inglés!

¡Que aproveches bien el tiempo!

3 Buenos deseos

Ejercicio para la revisión, esta vez de forma menos dirigida, de la estructura desiderativa *ojalá (que)* + presente de subjuntivo. Pediremos a los alumnos que escriban sus diez deseos para el próximo año.

Cuando hayan terminado de redactar su decálogo, lo compartirán con los demás compañeros. Finalmente, promoveremos una conversación relajada para comentar los distintos deseos en la que todos los alumnos intervengan con preguntas y comentarios.

Solución

Respuesta libre.

NOTAS

QUIZÁS VAYA A LA FIESTA

¡extra! EN COMUNICACIÓN

4 Comunicación por correo electrónico

La primera actividad de esta sección tiene que ver con una forma de comunicación con la que, sin duda, nuestros estudiantes están muy familiarizados y que, además, está muy presente en todo el manual: el correo electrónico.

En primer lugar, como actividad previa o de calentamiento, preguntaremos a los alumnos para qué utilizan el correo electrónico, a quién se lo envían, etcétera. En segundo lugar, fijaremos su atención en los cuadros con recomendaciones, consejos y advertencias para usar de manera adecuada este medio de comunicación interpersonal. Tendrán que leerlos y, después de aclarar los problemas de comprensión, completar la lista con sus propias ideas. Insistiremos en que usen la misma estructura (*que* + subjuntivo) que se ha utilizado en los ejemplos. Primero harán sus propuestas de forma oral; a continuación, daremos algunos minutos para que escriban las frases. Finalmente, las compartirán con el grupo.

Solución

Respuesta libre.

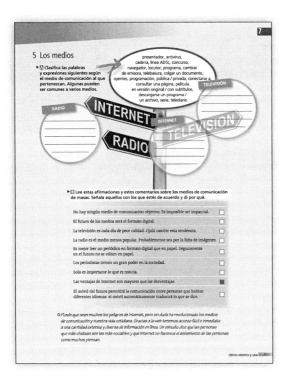

5 Los medios

La unidad se cierra con dos actividades para el chequeo y la ampliación del léxico relativo a los medios de comunicación.

A. Animaremos a los estudiantes a que clasifiquen las palabras y expresiones en el grupo del medio de comunicación al que pertenecen, advirtiéndolos de que algunos de esos términos pueden relacionarse con uno o más medios. Esta fase la podrán realizar individualmente y, a continuación, permitiremos que comparen sus soluciones con las de varios compañeros.

Sugerencia

Si se cree conveniente y para dinamizar más el ejercicio, propondremos a los estudiantes que se realice en gran grupo y de forma oral.

Solución

Radio	Internet	Televisión
• Cadena	• Antivirus	• Presentador
• Concurso	• Línea ADSL	• Cadena
• Locutor	• Navegador	• Concurso
• Programa	• Colgar un documento	• Programa
• Cambiar de emisora	• Conectarse (a)	• Telebasura
• Oyentes	• Consultar una página	• Programación
• Programación	• Descargarse un programa / un archivo	• Pública / privada
• Pública / privada		• Película en versión original / con subtítulos
		• Serie
		• Telediario

B. Fijaremos la atención de los alumnos en una serie de afirmaciones sobre diferentes medios de comunicación. Deberán marcar, individualmente, aquellas con las que estén de acuerdo. A continuación, abriremos un turno de palabra para que comenten con sus compañeros las ideas que compartan. Insistiremos en que den las razones que justifiquen sus opiniones.

Sugerencia

Podemos introducir nuevas afirmaciones sobre los medios de comunicación que permitan la discusión o el intercambio de opiniones de los estudiantes.

Solución

Respuesta libre.

NOTAS

Unidad 8
Nuevas amistades

OBJETIVOS DE LA UNIDAD

La unidad plantea como **contenidos morfosintácticos** el uso del modo indicativo o subjuntivo en las oraciones explicativas y especificativas. Además, seguiremos con el aprendizaje de un nuevo grupo de estructuras oracionales: las que van introducidas por verbos de influencia.

Con estas herramientas lingüísticas, y partiendo de su uso en contexto, los alumnos trabajarán las siguientes **funciones comunicativas:** hablar de las características de un objeto o de una persona y expresar influencia sobre alguien o sobre algo.

El hilo temático que vertebra la unidad conducirá a los estudiantes al siguiente **contenido léxico-semántico:** palabras y expresiones relacionadas con el amor y la amistad. Nos centramos, de nuevo, en el ámbito personal.

Muy vinculado con los anteriores exponentes lingüísticos se encuentra el **contenido sociocultural** que trataremos: el concepto de amistad en la cultura española.

En cuanto a los **contenidos pragmáticos**, hablaremos de los atenuantes en el tratamiento en las relaciones amorosas.

Finalmente, por lo que respecta a los **contenidos fonéticos y ortográficos**, trabajaremos los usos de la coma.

CONTEXTOS

1 Nuevos amigos

Abrimos la sección con la presentación en contexto de las herramientas lingüísticas que se practicarán en la unidad, mediante actividades de comprensión escrita y expresión oral. Es fácil que por el título del bloque los estudiantes concluyan el tema sobre el que va a tratar la secuencia. Estamos seguros de que sus hipótesis girarán en torno a ideas como la amistad, las relaciones con nuestros amigos, cómo hacer nuevas amistades… Antes de empezar con el ejercicio, haremos referencia a esta línea temática de la unidad.

A. Para presentar el ejercicio haremos ver a nuestros alumnos que, como en el caso de las personas de la actividad, mucha gente recurre a Internet para encontrar nuevas amistades. Antes de leer las experiencias de los seguidores del blog respecto al tema, podríamos preguntarles si ellos han hecho amigos a través de la red, si resultó ser una buena idea, si conocen a alguien que lo haya hecho, etcétera. A continuación, pasaremos a la fase siguiente: los alumnos se alternarán para leer, de modo que todos participen.

Sugerencia

Antes de pasar a la siguiente actividad, animaremos a los estudiantes a que expliquen a sus compañeros, en plenaria y de forma oral, un dato de la vida de cada uno de nuestros protagonistas que haya llamado su atención, que les haya parecido más interesante, curioso…

CONTEXTOS

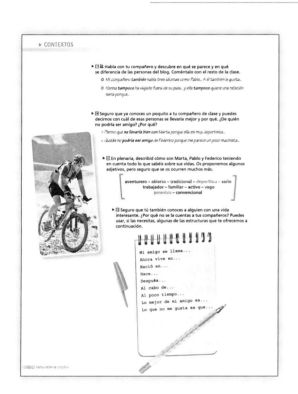

B. Organizaremos la clase en parejas y tendrán que hablar con su compañero, tomar nota de todo lo que tiene o no tiene este en común con los seguidores del blog y, finalmente, exponérselo al resto de la clase. Este diálogo y la posterior puesta en común ayudarán a que los estudiantes empiecen a familiarizarse con las estructuras oracionales de influencia.

Solución

Posible respuesta

A él / ella también le gustan las fiestas como a Pablo. También escucha todos los estilos de música.

A mi compañero/a también le gusta mucho dormir la siesta como a Federico, y no puede vivir sin su móvil. Tampoco se ha independizado; aún vive con sus padres.

C. Les propondremos que, teniendo en cuenta toda la información que conocen, decidan si su compañero podría tener amistad con alguno de los miembros del blog. Insistiremos en que, siempre que den su opinión, lo hagan de forma justificada, como en las muestras de lengua escrita de la actividad.

Solución

Respuesta libre.

D. Por último, les sugeriremos que, en gran grupo, describan a los tres protagonistas de los textos del ejercicio usando algunos de los adjetivos que les presentamos. No obstante, si lo creen oportuno, podrán utilizar otros, aunque no estén en la lista.

Sugerencia

Esta actividad puede servir para la revisión o el refuerzo de la práctica del léxico relacionado con el carácter y la personalidad. Hemos incluido algunos adjetivos que pertenecen a este campo; aunque, si fuera necesario, el profesor podría introducir nuevas palabras y expresiones, o revisar aquellas que el alumno debería conocer.

Solución

Posible respuesta

Marta López: Es una chica muy trabajadora / constante porque, después de mucho esfuerzo y diversas becas y prácticas de trabajo, tiene un buen empleo en una multinacional del diseño. Es seria y podemos pensar también que es responsable porque su trabajo en la empresa multinacional seguramente exigirá tener responsabilidades.

Pablo Callado: Es un chico activo porque el tipo de trabajo que desempeña le obliga a estar siempre viajando de un lugar para otro. También es trabajador; empezó desde muy pronto a experimentar en el mundo de la música, así que podemos pensar que ha tenido que hacer muchos esfuerzos para llegar a ser una persona importante en su trabajo.

ciento treinta y tres **133**

NUEVAS AMISTADES

Se puede decir que no es casero ya que su empleo exige estar siempre viajando. Podríamos decir que es abierto ya que, gracias a esos viajes, conocerá a mucha gente y tendrá contacto con gente de culturas muy diferentes. Pablo explica que, en este momento, no querría tener una relación seria, así que se puede decir que no es una persona demasiado tradicional. El tipo de vida que lleva, viajando siempre de un lado a otro, lo define también como un hombre aventurero.

Federico Plaza: No es un chico deportista porque no hace ninguna actividad física; prefiere actividades sedentarias, así que podríamos definirlo como un chico bastante sedentario. Quizás, como le encanta dormir la siesta, diríamos que es dormilón. Puede resultar que, si comparamos su forma o su estilo de vida con el de otras culturas u otros países, sea un chico raro ya que todavía vive con sus padres y tiene 27 años; aunque en España muchas personas de esa edad aún viven con su familia por la falta de trabajo, por comodidad, etc. Es un poco machista porque, si se casa, no quiere que su mujer trabaje.

E. Actividad de expresión e interacción orales cuyo objetivo es que el estudiante active sus habilidades comunicativas desde el ámbito de la relaciones interpersonales y, por tanto, desde su propio conocimiento. Estamos convencidos de que el alumno aprende mejor una lengua si partimos de su propia experiencia, de su universo personal, así como de sus intereses y preferencias.

Los estudiantes tendrán que hablar con sus compañeros sobre uno de sus amigos; podrán explicar datos de su vida y dar toda la información que les parezca oportuna. Hemos incluido en la ficha algunos elementos que los ayudarán en su exposición. Se trata de enunciados, palabras o estructuras que contribuirán a que el estudiante pueda usar formas verbales o tipos de oraciones que ya conoce.

Sugerencia

Podríamos cambiar el procedimiento de la actividad y dejar algún tiempo para que, antes de la fase oral, el alumno escribiera algunas notas con los datos que va a contar. Sigamos uno u otro procedimiento, sería conveniente que dejáramos unos minutos al final de las presentaciones para que los compañeros pregunten o pidan alguna aclaración.

Solución

Respuesta libre.

CONTEXTOS

Diremos a nuestros alumnos que vamos a conocer a Ana Mercado y a conocer datos de cómo es su vida en la actualidad. Antes de iniciar la fase de escucha, trataremos de hacerles ver que nuestra protagonista ha tomado una serie de decisiones importantes que han cambiado su forma de vivir y han sido determinantes para su futuro.

Como actividad previa a la audición, preguntaremos si alguno de ellos ha tomado una decisión importante que le ha hecho cambiar aspectos de su vida o, por lo menos, iniciar nuevos proyectos, proponerse nuevas metas u objetivos para el futuro, etcétera.

A continuación, pasaremos a la fase de escucha. En primer lugar, y de forma individual, tomarán nota de todo lo que oigan y, si el profesor lo cree conveniente, permitirá que comparen su información con la de algún compañero. Todavía no descubriremos si sus hipótesis se corresponden con las informaciones que han oído.

Solución

Posible respuesta

He oído que Ana estaba cansada de su vida y decidió cambiar de aires. Ella vivió durante mucho tiempo en una gran ciudad y tenía un buen trabajo porque era arquitecta. Decidió cambiar su forma de vida y se fue al campo, rodeada de naturaleza. También he oído que ahora ella está embarazada de gemelos y que volverá a la ciudad porque quiere que sus hijos vayan al colegio en Barcelona.

2 Una amiga más

A. Actividad de comprensión oral para la observación en contexto de los componentes gramaticales fundamentales de la unidad: oraciones de relativo y estructuras oracionales con verbos de influencia.

B. Volveremos a escuchar la grabación y los alumnos tendrán que ordenar los hechos o sucesos de la vida de Ana según el orden en que se mencionan en la audición (los avisaremos de que este no tiene que coincidir con el orden cronológico). Después, pasaremos a la corrección en plenaria. Si los estudiantes lo necesitan, los remitiremos a la transcripción de la grabación para garantizar que quedan resueltas todas las dudas de comprensión.

Solución

Tenía un buen trabajo, era arquitecta: 4.

Decidió cambiar su forma de vivir: 1.

Durante mucho tiempo vivió en una gran ciudad: 3.

Restauró una casa de campo: 2.

Va a tener hijos: 5.

C. En esta secuencia escucharán de nuevo la grabación para que, de forma individual, completen las cuatro oraciones que hemos incluido en el ejercicio. Después de esta fase, les sugeriremos que elijan a dos de sus compañeros para comparar sus respuestas. Seguramente será suficiente con una sola escucha; no obstante, si se cree conveniente, realizaremos otra más.

Solución

1. … un buen trabajo, una bonita casa en una zona residencial de la ciudad, una familia…

2. … cocinar, bailar, tomar el sol y disfrutar de toda la naturaleza que la rodea.

3. … ir de compras y cenar en un buen restaurante.

4. … vayan al colegio en Barcelona.

D. Continuamos con una actividad de expresión e interacción orales. Propondremos que los alumnos trabajen en grupos y que busquen entre ellos compañeros que piensen como Ana o que se encuentren en situaciones similares a las de ella. Les insistiremos en que justifiquen las razones para la elección de esos compañeros. Cuando hayan completado las oraciones, las comentarán en plenaria.

Solución

Respuesta libre.

E. Cerramos la actividad con una reflexión en plenaria sobre el nuevo tipo de vida que ha elegido nuestra protagonista. Animaremos a los alumnos a que compartan su opinión al respecto y expliquen, con experiencias propias o ajenas, los aspectos positivos y negativos de la decisión de Ana.

Sugerencia

Propondremos que, en gran grupo, comenten si conocen a alguna persona que tenga una vida poco convencional, muy distinta a la de la mayoría de la gente… Animaremos a los alumnos a que compartan con sus compañeros cómo sería, desde su punto de vista, una vida totalmente opuesta a la que llevan en este momento: qué harían, dónde vivirían, cómo sería su día a día, etcétera.

Solución

Respuesta libre.

NOTAS

NUEVAS AMISTADES

OBSERVA, APRENDE Y RECUERDA

3 Un chico que…

Iniciamos la secuencia de actividades destinadas a la inferencia y a la reflexión en torno a uno de los contenidos gramaticales principales de la unidad: las oraciones de relativo explicativas y especificativas en modo indicativo o subjuntivo.

A. Explicaremos a los alumnos que Marta, una de las seguidoras del blog del primer ejercicio de la unidad, quiere encontrar pareja a través de Internet. Tras la presentación y como actividad previa, preguntaremos en gran grupo si, en alguna ocasión, ellos mismos o alguien que conozcan han actuado como nuestra protagonista. Después de que expongan sus opiniones en plenaria, pasaremos al desarrollo de las distintas fases del ejercicio.

En primer lugar, los estudiantes leerán los anuncios y elegirán aquellos que puedan convenir a Marta. Daremos unos minutos para realizar esta tarea de forma individual y, posteriormente, corregiremos en gran grupo. Insistiremos en que justifiquen sus elecciones.

Solución
Los anuncios 1, 9, 10 y 11.

OBSERVA, APRENDE Y RECUERDA

al cuadro de Gramática y léxico de la unidad. Después de confeccionar la lista, tendrán que determinar a qué sustantivo hace referencia en cada caso el relativo *que*. De este modo, entenderán el concepto de *antecedente*, fundamental para comprender el uso de las estructuras de relativo. Tras este segundo paso, permitiremos que comparen sus resultados con los de algún compañero. Finalmente, corregiremos la actividad en plenaria. Si se cree conveniente, les propondremos que se intercambien con otro compañero la actividad para que la corrija. Con todo este procedimiento pretendemos que los alumnos reflexionen sobre las estructuras de relativo y sus valores contextuales; nuestro objetivo es que lleguen a la conclusión de que funcionan como un adjetivo.

Solución
1: el *que* se refiere a chica.
2: se refiere a alguien (a alguna persona).
5: a estudiantes.
6: a casa.
8: a canguro.
9: a chica.
10: a chica.
11: a novia.
12: a coche.
13: a apartamento.
14: a secretaria.
16: a cámara digital.

B. Ahora, también individualmente, los estudiantes volverán a los anuncios y les pediremos que escriban todas las oraciones de relativo que encuentren. Antes, uno de ellos leerá la ficha de gramática que explica dichas oraciones. Deberemos aclararles cualquier duda de comprensión antes de continuar con el proceso. Además, remitiremos a los alumnos

C, D y **E.** Seguimos con tres actividades que completan el proceso de inferencia de las oraciones adjetivas, esta vez, reflexionando sobre su uso con indicativo o con subjuntivo. En la fase C dividiremos al grupo en parejas y les pediremos que, de nuevo, fijen su atención en las oraciones de relativo de la actividad B y escriban el verbo en la casilla correcta. A continuación, presentamos dos ejemplos de este tipo de frases como muestras de lengua escrita y los alumnos tendrán que determinar, según su opinión, por qué se usan con modos diferentes: indicativo o subjuntivo. Escucharemos las distintas hipótesis, completarán la regla de uso y, finalmente, comprobarán sus respuestas consultando el cuadro de GRAMÁTICA Y LÉXICO de la unidad.

Solución

C. Indicativo: (6) está - (12) tiene - (13) está - (16) tiene.

Subjuntivo: (1) sea - (2) cuide; trate - (5) quieran - (8) pueda - (9) viva; guste - (10) hable - (11) tenga - (14) hable.

D. La diferencia es que usamos el indicativo cuando hablamos de algo o de alguien conocido. Cuando decimos *un coche que tiene...* sabemos a qué coche nos estamos refiriendo. Si usamos el subjuntivo, hablamos de algo o de alguien desconocido para nosotros. En el ejemplo *una chica que hable español...*, no conocemos a la chica, no sabemos quién será.

E. Usamos el indicativo cuando **hablamos de algo o de alguien conocido**.

Usamos el subjuntivo cuando **hablamos de algo o de alguien desconocido**.

OBSERVA, APRENDE Y RECUERDA

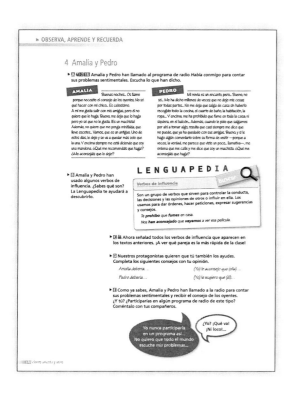
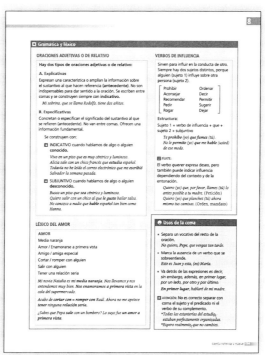

4 Amalia y Pedro

Cerramos la secuencia con una serie de actividades orientadas al aprendizaje significativo del uso del subjuntivo en las oraciones con verbos de influencia.

A. La primera fase se inicia con un ejercicio de comprensión y expresión orales. Diremos a nuestros alumnos que vamos a oír dos llamadas a un popular programa de radio en el que los oyentes hablan sobre sus problemas y preocupaciones. Antes de comenzar con la fase de audición, les preguntaremos si, en alguna ocasión, han escuchado un programa similar, si existen espacios como este en su país o si llamarían para contar lo que les preocupa, como han hecho Amalia y Pedro... Después de que expongan sus ideas al respecto de forma oral, pasaremos a la fase de escucha. Les aclararemos que, mientras oyen la grabación, podrán seguirla al mismo tiempo con la transcripción que hemos incluido en la actividad.

Sugerencia

Si fuera conveniente, se podrá cambiar el procedimiento: comenzaremos la primera fase con una lectura en voz alta de las transcripciones y, a continuación, los alumnos oirán la grabación.

En cualquier caso, aclararemos las dudas léxicas que pudieran presentarse.

ciento treinta y siete 137

NUEVAS AMISTADES

B. Explicaremos a nuestros alumnos que en las llamadas telefónicas de la actividad anterior se han usado verbos de influencia *(querer, prohibir, recomendar, aconsejar, decir, dejar, pedir, ordenar)*. Les preguntaremos si saben para qué sirven, cuándo se usan... Expondrán sus hipótesis en plenaria. Posteriormente, las comprobarán con la ficha de la Lenguapedia. Si fuera necesario, escribiremos en la pizarra las ideas de los estudiantes antes de que lean la definición. No pasaremos a la siguiente fase hasta que no se solucionen todas las dudas sobre el significado de este tipo de verbos; es fundamental que comprendan para qué y cuándo los utilizamos.

C. Dividiremos al grupo en parejas y les pediremos que marquen en los textos de la actividad A todos los verbos de influencia que descubran. Cuando hayan finalizado, compararán sus soluciones con las del resto de los grupos. Finalmente, corregiremos la actividad en plenaria.

Sugerencia

Esta fase del ejercicio podría plantearse de manera más lúdica, en forma de concurso: ganará la pareja que diga correctamente todos los verbos de influencia incluidos en las llamadas de Amalia y Pedro; pero por cada verbo incorrecto se descontará 1 punto.

Solución

Amalia: quiere - deja - está diciendo - recomendáis - aconsejáis.

Pedro: Me ha dicho - deja - ha prohibido - pido - ordena - aconsejáis.

D. Animaremos a los alumnos a que, en plenaria, den algunos consejos o hagan algunas recomendaciones para solucionar los conflictos de pareja que tienen Amalia y Pedro. Aún estamos en la fase de inferencia de los contenidos, así que no hemos de preocuparnos todavía por la corrección en el uso del modo con los verbos de influencia que aparecen en los ejemplos y que los alumnos deberán completar. Algunas de las muestras de lengua propuestas para aconsejar están en condicional; de esa forma revisaremos y chequearemos uno de sus usos básicos ya aprendidos en unidades anteriores.

Solución

Posible respuesta

Amalia debería ser más paciente con Pedro y compartir más las tareas del hogar. Debería salir también con él y no solo con sus amigas. Debería ponerse la ropa que más le guste a ella. No debería hacer tanto caso de su novio.

(Yo) le aconsejo que ella salga con sus amigas, pero que también dedique tiempo a su novio. Le aconsejo que se ponga la ropa que quiera. Le aconsejo que no haga caso a Pedro.

Pedro debería hablar con Amalia sobre el tema de la ropa. Pedro debería entender a su novia cuando quiere salir con sus amigas. Pedro debería ser más comprensivo con su novia. Pedro debería ayudar a su novia en casa. Pedro no debería fumar dentro de casa.

(Yo) le sugiero que le diga a su novia que le gustaría salir más con ella por ahí. Le sugiero que sea más comprensivo y que la ayude en las tareas de la casa. Le sugiero que no fume dentro de casa y que, si es posible, deje el tabaco.

E. Cerramos la actividad con un ejercicio de expresión oral más libre, no dirigido. Abriremos un turno de palabra para que nuestros estudiantes debatan sobre los programas de testimonios, como en el que participaron Amalia y Pedro. Hemos propuesto una pregunta para que comiencen a manifestar su opinión sobre el tema. No obstante, si se cree conveniente, añadiremos otras cuestiones que consideremos interesantes.

Sugerencia

Dividiremos al grupo en parejas y los animaremos a que escriban un diálogo que simule una llamada a un programa de radio parecido al de la secuencia anterior: uno será el oyente que cuente sus problemas y el otro el que le aconseje o le haga algún tipo de recomendación para solucionarlo. Cuando hayan terminado de escribir la situación, la representarán para todos sus compañeros. Insistiremos en que usen, sobre todo en los consejos, estructuras oracionales con verbos de influencia.

Solución

Posible respuesta

Yo tampoco participaré nunca en un programa de televisión. No me gusta que la gente conozca mi intimidad.

Pues a mí me gusta que la gente me aconseje y me ayude para arreglar mis problemas.

NOTAS

PRACTICA

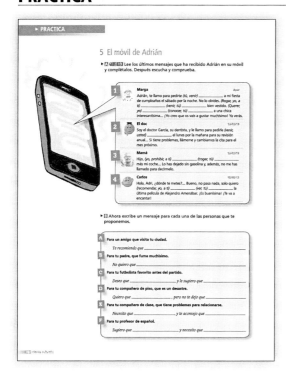

5 El móvil de adrián

Abrimos la sección con una actividad para la ejercitación dirigida y la práctica formal de las oraciones con verbos de influencia, y construidas con subjuntivo.

A. Fijaremos la atención de los alumnos en el título del ejercicio y les informaremos de que tenemos algunos mensajes o *whatsApps* del móvil de Adrián. Antes de comenzar con el desarrollo de la actividad, les preguntaremos si tienen móvil, de qué tipo, si lo usan mucho, para qué, si escriben muchos mensajes, etcétera.

A continuación, iniciaremos la primera parte del ejercicio y les pediremos que completen los mensajes utilizando la estructura *que* + subjuntivo. Esta fase la realizará cada alumno de forma individual y, cuando haya terminado, pasaremos a la última parte, la de comprobación y corrección de las oraciones, que se realizará mediante una actividad de comprensión auditiva.

Sugerencia

En la fase de corrección, los alumnos podrían intercambiar con algún compañero su ejercicio para que este lo corrija siguiendo las soluciones de la grabación.

Solución

1. que vengas - Te ruego que vengas - Quiero que conozcas.
2. que venga.
3. te prohíbo que cojas.
4. recomendarte que veas.

B. Continuamos con la ejercitación de estas estructuras, pero esta vez de forma menos dirigida. Proponemos una serie de mensajes construidos con verbos de influencia para que los estudiantes los completen con sus ideas o experiencias, libremente; además, los hemos contextualizado para que la tarea sea más fácil y no ofrezca excesivas dificultades.

Sugerencia

Proponemos una actividad complementaria de refuerzo para la práctica de los verbos de influencia seguidos de oraciones con subjuntivo. Si los alumnos disponen de móvil o de algún otro sistema de mensajes a través de la red, seguro que el ejercicio resultará más dinámico y lúdico, y nos garantizará su plena implicación. Tendrán que escribir un mensaje de texto para una persona de la clase (incluido el profesor) usando los verbos de influencia que aparecen en la actividad (*recomendar, querer, desear, sugerir, dejar, necesitar, aconsejar, permitir*). Durante la fase de escritura, estaremos atentos a sus producciones para corregir los errores gramaticales, de léxico… A continuación, cada alumno enviará su mensaje a través del móvil o, si no dispusieran de teléfono, a través de Internet.

Solución

Posible respuesta

A. *Te recomiendo que* vengas en verano porque el tiempo es mucho mejor. Te recomiendo que pruebes el plato típico de mi ciudad. Te recomiendo que visites el centro histórico. Te recomiendo que traigas ropa de abrigo; en invierno hace mucho frío…

B. *No quiero que* fumes tanto; es muy perjudicial para tu salud. No quiero que fumes en todas partes. No quiero que estés todo el día con el cigarrillo en la boca; es muy perjudicial para tu salud. No quiero que siempre estés fumando…

C. *Deseo que* marque muchos goles *y le sugiero que* esté concentrado en el partido. Deseo que consiga ganar el partido y le sugiero que controle bien el juego. Deseo que marque más goles que en el partido anterior y le sugiero que se defienda bien de los jugadores del equipo contrario…

D. *Quiero que* me ayudes con la limpieza del piso, *pero no te dejo que* planches porque lo haces fatal. Quiero que pongas la lavadora, pero no te dejo que limpies porque siempre dejas manchas por todas partes. Quiero que planches, pero no te dejo que laves los platos porque siempre rompes alguno.

E. *Necesito que* hables más español *y te aconsejo que* tengas amigos españoles y te relaciones con más gente. Necesito que me ayudes con los deberes y te aconsejo que salgas más con nosotros para relacionarte. Necesito que vengas con nosotros a mi fiesta del sábado y te aconsejo que hables con toda la gente; mis amigos son muy simpáticos.

F. *Sugiero que* hablemos más en clase *y necesito que* me ayude con los ejercicios de gramática. Sugiero que hagamos más audiciones y necesito que corrija mis composiciones. Sugiero que no escribamos tanto y necesito que hablemos más.

▶ NUEVAS AMISTADES

PRACTICA

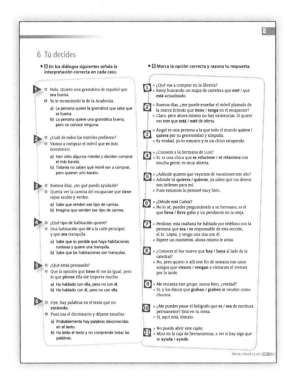

6 Tú decides

Reforzamos la práctica, el análisis y la reflexión sobre el uso de las oraciones adjetivas en contexto. En esta ocasión, no se trata de que nuestros alumnos completen un ejercicio con el verbo en la forma correcta, sino que buscamos chequear su conocimiento del valor de este tipo de estructuras en muestras de lengua escrita que nosotros les proporcionamos.

A. Presentamos una serie de microdiálogos en los que aparecen oraciones de relativo. En primer lugar, los estudiantes los leerán en gran grupo y, antes de pasar a la segunda parte, resolveremos las dudas sobre el vocabulario.

En segundo lugar, cada alumno marcará una de las dos posibilidades de interpretación que ofrecemos para cada situación. Insistiremos en que solo hay una opción correcta. Cuando hayan terminado, pasaremos a la corrección en plenaria. Si se cree conveniente, permitiremos que, antes de continuar, compartan sus soluciones con las de algún compañero.

Los diálogos ayudan a que el alumno reactive su conocimiento de lo aprendido sobre el uso del indicativo o del subjuntivo en las oraciones adjetivas.

Si fuera necesario, antes de seguir con la actividad, el profesor recordaría las reglas de uso de este tipo de estructuras en la pizarra.

Solución

1. b;

2. a;

3. a;

4. a;

5. b;

6. b.

B. Ahora los alumnos escogerán el verbo correcto para cada uno de los once diálogos. Dejaremos algunos minutos para que realicen esta primera parte y, a continuación, corregiremos en gran grupo.

Elegiremos a un estudiante para que comience con la actividad y resuelva la primera situación, y los demás continuarán con las siguientes.

Insistiremos en que, cuando digan cada una de las respuestas, las justifiquen de acuerdo a la regla de uso aprendida.

Sugerencia

Si el grupo lo necesitara, el profesor podría añadir algunos diálogos más que refuercen la práctica del contenido. Sería interesante que siguieran el objetivo que nos habíamos marcado, que ayudara al alumno a distinguir el uso del indicativo o el subjuntivo en las oraciones adjetivas.

Solución

1. **esté.** Subjuntivo porque no está pensando en un mapa en concreto sino en cualquier mapa actualizado.
2. **tiene - está.** Indicativo porque estamos hablando de un objeto que ambas personas conocen; los dos saben de su existencia. La persona que va a comprar quiere el móvil que ya ha visto y el dependiente le ofrece otro modelo que conoce.
3. **quiere.** Indicativo porque se refieren a una persona concreta y que conocen.
4. **se relaciona.** Indicativo porque saben que la hermana de Luis es una chica muy abierta; la conocen.
5. **quieras.** Subjuntivo porque no sabe dónde quiere ir de vacaciones; prefiere que sea la otra persona la que elija; no se está hablando de un lugar concreto.
6. **lleva.** Indicativo porque está describiendo a una persona concreta a la que conocen, a la que están viendo en ese mismo momento y saben cómo va vestido, qué lleva…
7. **es.** Indicativo porque ya ha hablado con este hombre y, por tanto, lo conoce, sabe quién es…
8. **hay - vienen.** Indicativo porque tiene conocimiento de la existencia de ese nuevo bar y porque se refiere a unos amigos concretos, conocidos.
9. **graban.** Indicativo porque se refiere a los discos actuales, que ya existen y son conocidos y concretos.
10. **es.** Indicativo porque se refiere a un bolígrafo concreto y que existe.
11. **ayude.** Subjuntivo porque la persona con la que habla no sabe exactamente qué tipo de herramienta necesita o le puede venir bien; no se refiere a una herramienta concreta.

7 Cuéntame los detalles

Esta actividad está relacionada con la ejercitación, de forma no dirigida, de una función comunicativa fundamental en la unidad: hablar de las características de un objeto. Además, está orientada a la revisión del léxico idóneo para las descripciones de objetos.

El ejercicio se vertebra sobre el desarrollo de la expresión en la interacción oral.

En primer lugar, para comenzar, animaremos a un estudiante a que escoja libremente un objeto cualquiera (un elemento de la clase, un objeto de uso cotidiano, algo que tenga en su habitación, algo que lleve en su mochila en ese momento…) y lo describa usando oraciones de relativo, como hemos presentado en el ejemplo. Los demás compañeros tendrán que adivinar de qué se trata; el estudiante que lo averigüe continuará con el juego.

Sugerencia

No hemos incluido ningún objeto concreto con la idea de que el alumno elija con total libertad el que quiera.

No obstante, si el profesor lo cree conveniente, podría añadir el campo o los campos léxicos que le interesen, tanto de este nivel como de los anteriores, con la idea de hacer una revisión o chequearlos: el vocabulario de los alimentos, la vivienda, la calle o la ciudad, los muebles y objetos de decoración de la casa, la ropa…

Solución

Respuesta libre.

8 Madre no hay más que una… ¡Por suerte!

A. Actividad de comprensión oral para la ejercitación de las oraciones completivas con verbos de influencia.

Antes de comenzar con el ejercicio, fijaremos la atención de nuestros alumnos en el enunciado del título y, seguidamente, les preguntaremos por su significado, su sentido, en qué situación se usaría… Les comentaremos que el texto de la actividad es la transcripción de una llamada telefónica de Marta, donde cuenta cómo es la relación con su madre.

Cada alumno tendrá que completar los huecos con la forma correcta del verbo; asimismo, les advertiremos de que, en algunas oraciones, falta el nexo *que* y ellos deberán incluirlo.

Dejaremos algún tiempo para que realicen esta parte y, a continuación, pasaremos a la fase de corrección, en este caso, a través de la comprensión auditiva. Creemos que será suficiente con una sola escucha; no obstante, si los alumnos lo necesitaran, se volvería a oír la grabación.

Sugerencia

La actividad está ideada para la práctica de uno de los contenidos fundamentales de la unidad, así es que sería importante que resolviésemos las dudas que los alumnos plantearan al respecto. Para ayudarlos en la comprensión y adquisición de este nuevo contenido, les propondremos que, según vayan completando, expliquen por qué han usado el subjuntivo o el infinitivo. El profesor podrá recordar los usos más difíciles o aclarar las oraciones más complicadas en la pizarra.

Por otro lado, después de esta primera parte de práctica gramatical, podríamos proponer a los estudiantes que, de forma oral y en plenaria, comenten con sus compañeros si sienten empatía por los problemas de Marta con su madre, si les ha ocurrido algo parecido, si alguna vez han tenido experiencias similares…

Hemos tratado el tema de las relaciones familiares, en este caso entre madre e hija, de una manera divetida, en tono humorístico y distentido, así que animaremos a nuestros alumnos a que, en ese mismo tono, comenten sus experiencias propias; no obstante, si el tema causara alguna susceptibilidad, nos quedaríamos únicamente en la fase de ejercitación formal.

Solución

lleve - me haga - me ponga - tenga - me relacione - fume - beba - que me deje - hable - se pongan - que no se preocupen - que me controlen - me dejen.

▶ NUEVAS AMISTADES

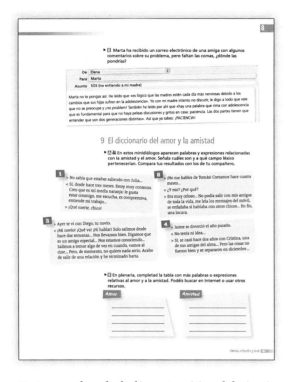

B. Aprovechando la línea temática del ejercicio anterior, ahora trabajaremos el contenido de puntuación de la unidad: el uso de la coma. Antes de presentar la actividad, informaremos a nuestros estudiantes de que una de las amigas de Marta le ha dado algunos consejos para resolver los problemas con su madre. Cada alumno leerá el correo y colocará las comas que faltan donde sea necesario. Dejaremos el tiempo necesario para que realicen esta fase y, finalmente, pasaremos a la corrección en gran grupo.

Sugerencia

Sería conveniente que, durante la fase de corrección, los alumnos comentaran las razones del uso de la coma en cada oración, justificándolas con las reglas que han aprendido y que hemos incluido en el cuadro de gramática de la unidad.

Solución

Marta, no te pongas así. He leído que «es lógico que las madres estén cada día más nerviosas debido a los cambios que sus hijas sufren en la adolescencia». Yo con mi madre intento no discutir, le digo a todo que vale, que no se preocupe y ¡no problem! También he leído por ahí que «hay una palabra que rima con adolescencia que es fundamental para que no haya peleas, discusiones y gritos en casa: paciencia. Las dos partes tienen que entender que son dos generaciones distintas». Así que ya sabes: ¡PACIENCIA!

PRÁCTICA

9 El diccionario del amor y la amistad

Bloque de actividades para la aprehensión y la práctica en contexto del léxico relacionado con el amor y la amistad. Así pues, trabajamos un vocabulario de gran importancia para desarrollar las habilidades comunicativas del alumno en el ámbito personal.

A. Para la realización de esta primera fase del ejercicio, dividiremos al grupo en parejas. Les informaremos de que en los cuatro minidiálogos aparecen una serie de palabras y expresiones relacionadas con el amor y la amistad; cada alumno tendrá que marcarlas y agruparlas en el ámbito temático adecuado. Cuando hayan terminado de hacer las dos listas, cada estudiante comparará sus resultados con el de su compañero. Posteriormente, se pondrán en común con el resto de la clase.

Solución

1. Salir con alguien: amor; ser (alguien) mi media naranja: amor.

2. Cortar con alguien: amor; ser (alguien) celoso: amor; amigos: amistad.

3. Novio: amor; salir con alguien: amor; llevarse bien: amor y amistad; ser (alguien) un amigo especial: amor; estarse conociendo: amor; relación: amor.

4. Divorciarse: amor; casarse con alguien: amor; amigo del alma: amistad; separarse de alguien: amor.

B. Ahora, en gran grupo, completaremos las dos listas con léxico, frases hechas, expresiones... En esta fase los alumnos podrán chequear vocabulario que ya conocen y, sobre todo, aprender términos nuevos y diferentes.

Cuando hayan incorporado todas las palabras y expresiones que recuerden, los animaremos a que usen distintos recursos (diccionario, Internet...) para buscar aportaciones nuevas con las que seguir ampliando las tablas.

Sugerencia

Podemos proponer a los alumnos que entre todos escriban un diccionario del amor y de la amistad. Para ello, los agruparemos en dos grandes grupos: el del amor y el de la amistad. Dejaremos que, libremente, cada estudiante se incorpore al que decida. Cada equipo tendrá que elegir palabras o expresiones relacionadas con su campo léxico. Lo primero que harán será definirlas; insistiremos en que tendrán que usar las oraciones de relativo que han aprendido. En segundo lugar, deberán incluirlas en un pequeño diálogo o ejemplo de uso. Si fuera necesario, podríamos proponer que trabajaran con un número concreto de términos; por ejemplo, cinco palabras o expresiones si fuera un grupo pequeño, y diez o más si lo formaran más miembros. Sería conveniente que durante la fase de preparación el profesor hiciera las correcciones necesarias o atendiera a las preguntas de los alumnos.

Por último, si se contara en el aula con los recursos necesarios, los alumnos podrían colgar en Internet el diccionario y, si esto no fuera posible, prepararían un mural para exponerlo en clase.

Solución

Posible respuesta

Amor: estar casados - comprometerse con - ser mi prometido/-a - estar prometido/-a - pareja - esposa = mujer / marido = esposo - tener una relación sentimental con alguien…

Amistad: tener una amistad con alguien - ser amigo del trabajo, de la oficina, de la escuela, de la universidad… - ser un buen amigo de… - ser el mejor amigo de… - ser (el) enemigo de… - ser uña y carne - ser un amigo del alma…

EN COMUNICACIÓN

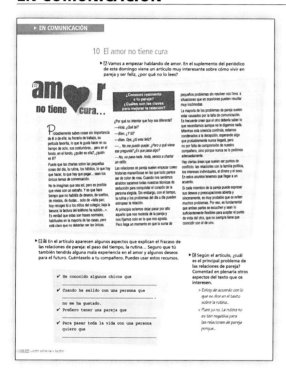

10 El amor no tiene cura

Iniciamos esta secuencia centrándonos en uno de los dos ejes temáticos de la unidad: el amor, esta vez a través de una actividad de comprensión escrita.

A. Antes de comenzar a leer el texto, fijaremos la atención de los estudiantes en el título de la actividad y los animaremos a que comenten lo que les sugiere, a qué puede hacer referencia, de qué tratará el artículo… A continuación, pasaremos a su lectura en voz alta. Posteriormente, aclararemos las dudas.

Sugerencia

Si se cree conveniente, antes de seguir, les pediremos a nuestros estudiantes que, de forma oral y en plenaria, expliquen, desde su punto de vista, las dos ideas fundamentales del artículo.

B. Partiendo del tema del fracaso en las relaciones de pareja al que se refiere el texto anterior, proponemos que los alumnos cuenten sus vivencias al respecto. Dividiremos al grupo en parejas y les pediremos que compartan con el compañero sus experiencias sobre este asunto; insistiremos en que lo hagan completando las estructuras que se proponen.

Así pues, se trata de presentarlas con los elementos lingüísticos que estamos aprendiendo en la unidad: las oraciones de relativo y las estructuras oracionales con verbos de influencia.

Solución

Posible respuesta

He conocido algunos chicos que eran demasiado celosos y eso no me gusta.

Cuando he salido con una persona que era muy posesiva o quería controlar toda mi vida: con quién iba, dónde estaba, etc., no me ha gustado.

Prefiero tener una pareja que me comprenda y me escuche. La comunicación es muy importante.

Para pasar toda la vida con una persona quiero que sea mi amigo y me entienda casi sin hablar.

C. Pediremos que, de forma oral y en plenaria, los alumnos expliquen la principal dificultad de la vida en pareja que se plantea en el artículo.

Además, expondrán libremente otras facetas del tema tratado que les resulten dignas de interés.

Sugerencia

También podríamos cambiar el procedimiento de esta fase de la actividad: les propondríamos que la realizaran por escrito y, a continuación, presentaran sus propuestas de forma oral y las compararan con las del resto de sus compañeros.

Solución

Posible respuesta

En el texto se apuntan diversas causas que podrían explicar los problemas de pareja: la rutina, la falta de comunicación y otros asuntos como las relaciones con la familia política, el dinero o el sexo.

También se habla de la falta de tolerancia en alguno de los miembros de la pareja para aceptar el diferente punto de vista del otro.

NUEVAS AMISTADES

11 Siete reglas de oro para ser feliz en pareja

Actividades de comprensión lectora y expresión oral que continúan en la línea temática de la anterior.

A. Animaremos a los alumnos a que lean las recomendaciones para tener éxito en las relaciones de pareja, y fijaremos su atención en cómo están escritas: de nuevo, las estructuras oracionales con verbos de influencia.

B. En la última fase nos proponemos desarrollar las habilidades comunicativas del estudiante pidiéndole que dé su opinión sobre los consejos anteriores. Además, los alumnos tendrán que hacer nuevas recomendaciones de acuerdo con sus ideas o vivencias. Lo harán de forma menos dirigida, más libre que en otras actividades de la sección.

Sugerencia

Si necesitamos reforzar la práctica de los contenidos gramaticales de la unidad, esta vez de forma semidirigida, propondremos a los alumnos que den sus ideas sobre las sugerencias de la doctora Amor usando estructuras que reactivan los contenidos aprendidos a lo largo de la lección: *Sugiero que… / Recomiendo a las parejas que… / Busco a una persona que… / He tenido un/a novio/-a que… y no me ha gustado / Quiero que mi pareja… / No estoy de acuerdo, yo a mi pareja solo le pido que… / No estoy de acuerdo, yo necesito que…*

Solución

Posible respuesta

Te recomiendo que dejéis un día a la semana para estar los dos solos.

Te prohíbo que habléis del trabajo.

Te recomiendo que le digas claramente lo que no te gusta de él o de ella.

Te prohíbo que discutáis sobre temas que no tienen importancia.

Te prohíbo que habléis mucho de dinero; seguro que traerá problemas.

Te recomiendo que hagáis, al menos una vez al mes, un pequeño viaje o una excursión juntos.

12 ¿Otro Día de los Enamorados?

A. Actividad que cierra la sección y completa el ámbito temático de las relaciones de pareja partiendo, como en otras ocasiones, de la experiencia del alumno y, en definitiva, de su realidad y sus conocimientos propios.

Pediremos a nuestros estudiantes que, en gran grupo, den su opinión sobre el tema de la actividad respondiendo a las diferentes preguntas que hemos propuesto en su enunciado. Facilitaremos un diálogo abierto y lo más espontáneo posible. Seguidamente, les diremos que van a descubrir cómo se celebra este día en España y, para eso, tendrán que señalar si las informaciones de la ficha les parecen verdaderas o no.

Esta primera fase se realizará de forma individual y, cuando hayan terminado, les permitiremos que comparen sus opiniones con las de sus compañeros, fomentando un coloquio en plenaria en el que compartan sus ideas.

Solución

1. no; **2.** no; **3.** no; **4.** sí; **5.** sí; **6.** sí; **7.** no.

B. En esta segunda fase, sugeriremos a nuestros estudiantes que comenten entre ellos cómo celebran en su país este día especial para las parejas. Con la idea de animar la conversación, hemos incluido datos de la celebración en Asia, Estados Unidos o Dinamarca, pero pretendemos que sean ellos los que expliquen las características de esta fiesta en su propia cultura.

Sugerencia

Si todos los estudiantes tuvieran el mismo origen, propondremos que comenten la forma de celebración en su región, en su ciudad..., o, si lo prefieren, los animaremos a hablar de lo que hacen personas de su entorno: sus padres, sus abuelos, sus amigos, sus tíos...

Solución

Respuesta libre.

EN COMUNICACIÓN

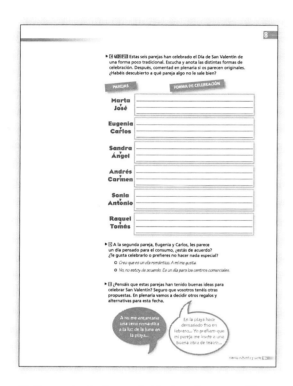

C. Después de las actividades de expresión e interacción orales, continuamos con un ejercicio de comprensión auditiva. Explicaremos a nuestros estudiantes que van a oír cómo organizaron el Día de los Enamorados diferentes parejas.

Procederemos de la forma habitual: escucharán dos veces la grabación y completarán los datos que pedimos. Después de la fase de escucha, pasaremos a la corrección en plenaria; cada alumno compartirá sus notas con el resto del grupo.

Finalmente, cuando hayamos aclarado todas las dudas de comprensión, abriremos un debate para que los estudiantes expresen su opinión sobre las distintas formas de celebración que han oído; les preguntaremos qué les parecen, si creen que son buenas ideas, si harían lo mismo... También tendrán que determinar cuál es la pareja que ha sufrido una mala experiencia con la preparación de su día de los enamorados.

Volveremos sobre la transcripción de los diálogos para explicar uno de los contenidos pragmáticos de la unidad: los atenuantes en el tratamiento para las relaciones de pareja. Explicaremos el uso de *cariño* en la primera conversación, la que mantienen Marta y José.

Solución

Marta y José: celebran el Día de los Enamorados con una barbacoa e invitan a todos sus amigos.

Eugenia y Carlos: van a quedarse en casa y van a pedir una pizza familiar.

Sandra y Ángel: Ángel le ha regalado una cesta de frutas a Sandra.

Andrés y Carmen: van a ir a un spa para relajarse.

Sonia y Antonio: Antonio le ha regalado una camiseta con mensaje a Sonia, pero se ha equivocado de nombre. Esta es la pareja a la que no le sale bien la celebración.

Raquel y Tomás: Tomás propone celebrarlo con una visita al zoo porque a Raquel le encantan los animales.

D. Aprovechando la consideración concreta sobre esta fiesta de la pareja formada por Eugenia y Carlos, pediremos que cada alumno exprese sus comentarios al respecto. Además, pediremos a los estudiantes que compartan con los demás cómo celebran ellos este día y digan si realmente les gusta hacerlo.

Solución

Respuesta libre.

E. Cerramos la actividad con una microtarea en la que los alumnos presentarán, en plenaria y de forma oral, sus propuestas, originales, diferentes, divertidas..., para el Día de San Valentín.

Sugerencia

El objetivo de esta última fase de la actividad es desarrollar la capacidad comunicativa de los estudiantes mediante las destrezas orales (expresión e interacción); no obstante, si se cree oportuno, podemos cambiar el procedimiento combinando la expresión escrita con la oral: dejaremos algunos minutos para que cada estudiante, de forma individual, escriba sus propuestas y, finalmente, las compartirán con los demás en plenaria.

Solución

Respuesta libre.

NUEVAS AMISTADES

¡extra! CONTEXTOS

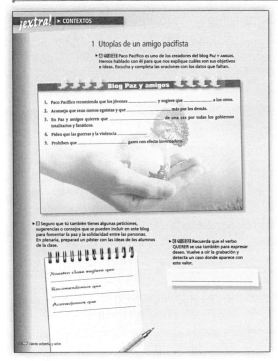

1 Utopías de un amigo pacifista

Abrimos la sección EXTRA con una actividad para chequear y revisar, en contexto, las oraciones con verbos de influencia.

A. Presentaremos el blog *Paz y amigos,* en el que uno de sus miembros explica algunas recomendaciones para mejorar el futuro de la humanidad y las relaciones con los demás. Animaremos a nuestros alumnos a que escuchen la grabación y completen las ideas con las palabras que faltan. Creemos que con una sola audición será suficiente; no obstante, si fuera necesario por las características del grupo, realizaremos dos escuchas.

Sugerencia

Para revisar los verbos de influencia que ya han aprendido a lo largo de la unidad, sugeriremos a los alumnos que, en plenaria, marquen todos los que aparecen en el texto.

Solución

1. sean más participativos - ayuden más.

2. se preocupen.

3. caigan.

4. desaparezcan.

5. se sigan emitiendo.

B. Incluimos una actividad de ejercitación de esta herramienta lingüística; esta vez de forma menos dirigida. Los alumnos completarán las frases (sugerencias, peticiones…) con sus ideas y los verbos en subjuntivo. La primera fase de la actividad se puede realizar de manera individual y como práctica escrita. A continuación, los estudiantes leerán sus producciones a sus compañeros. Finalmente, propondremos que preparen un mural con todas las ideas.

Solución

Posible respuesta

Nuestra clase sugiere que hagamos una fiesta el próximo sábado.

Recomendamos que la gente estudie otras lenguas y conozca otras culturas.

Aconsejamos que todos ayuden a una ONG.

C. Pediremos a los estudiantes que vuelvan a oír la grabación y descubran un uso del verbo *querer* como estructura desiderativa. Antes de volver a escuchar la audición para comprobarlo, preguntaremos si alguno de los estudiantes lo ha detectado.

Solución

¡Quiero irme a una isla desierta!

NOTAS

¡extra! PRACTICA

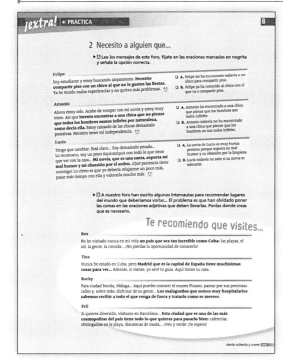

2 Necesito a alguien que…

Actividad para revisar y reactivar la práctica en contexto de las oraciones adjetivas explicativas y especificativas.

A. La primera fase de la actividad presenta una serie de opiniones de los miembros de un foro en las que hemos marcado las oraciones de relativo. Explicaremos a los estudiantes que el objetivo es que lean dichas frases en su contexto y señalen la interpretación, de acuerdo al sentido y al valor de la oración, que les parezca correcta. Dejaremos algunos minutos para que realicen individualmente la primera fase y, seguidamente, pasaremos a la corrección en plenaria.

Sugerencia

Si fuera necesario, de acuerdo con las características del grupo, recordaremos el uso del subjuntivo o el indicativo en las oraciones de relativo, que son las que hemos destacado en los mensajes del foro.

Solución

Felipe: A; **Antonio:** B; **Lucio:** A.

B. En esta fase trabajamos de nuevo las oraciones de relativo explicativas y especificativas. Pretendemos que la actividad sirva para reforzar la práctica de estas estructuras y, sobre todo, para que los alumnos recuerden las diferencias que podemos establecer entre ambas: mientras que las explicativas no son indispensables para dar sentido a la oración y van entre comas, las especificativas no las llevan y concretan el significado del antecedente. De ahí que el objetivo del ejercicio sea que nuestros estudiantes coloquen las comas en las oraciones que las necesiten. Dejaremos algunos minutos para que cada alumno realice la tarea y, finalmente, pasaremos a la corrección en gran grupo.

Sugerencia

Hemos incluido oraciones que, en principio, no ofrecen grandes dificultades para la realización del ejercicio; pero, no obstante, se podrían incluir más ejemplos de manera que los estudiantes continúen consolidando el uso de estos exponentes lingüísticos.

Solución

Rex: está bien como está.

Tina: … Madrid**,** que es la capital de España**,** tiene…

Rocky: Los malagueños**,** que somos muy hospitalarios**,** sabemos…

Feli: Esta ciudad**,** que es una de las más cosmopolitas del país**,** tiene…

NUEVAS AMISTADES

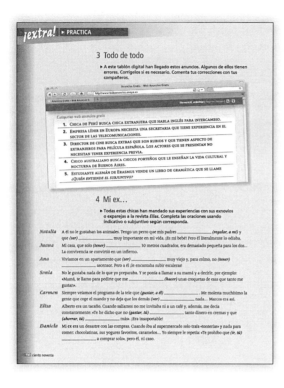

3 Todo de todo

Último ejercicio para repasar el uso del indicativo o del subjuntivo en las oraciones de relativo.

Antes de comenzar con el desarrollo de la actividad, y como ejercicio de calentamiento, fijaremos la atención de los alumnos en el título de esta y abriremos un turno de palabra para que cada uno explique lo que le sugiere… Seguidamente, como primera parte del ejercicio, leeremos las frases en plenaria y les explicaremos a los estudiantes que se trata de una serie de anuncios enviados a una página de Internet. Los animaremos a que los corrijan porque hay errores gramaticales que tienen que ver con el uso del indicativo o del subjuntivo en las oraciones de relativo.

Sugerencia

Como estamos en la sección Extra de la unidad y se trata de una revisión de contenidos, podremos cambiar el procedimiento de la actividad y realizarla en plenaria y de forma oral; además, las oraciones de relativo propuestas no presentan excesivas dificultades. Pediremos que un alumno, de manera voluntaria, comience con el primer anuncio y lo resuelva; cuando lo haya solucionado y el profesor haya aclarado las dudas de comprensión, continuaremos con la siguiente frase; así hasta el final.

Solución

1. … chica extranjera que **hable** inglés…
2. … una secretaria que **tenga** experiencia…
3. … extras que **sean** rubios y que **tengan** aspecto… Los actores que se **presenten** no necesitan…
4. … chicos porteños que le **enseñen** la vida…
5. … libro de gramática que se **llama**…

4 Mi ex…

Cierra el apartado una actividad de ejercitación formal para la consolidación de los dos contenidos gramaticales fundamentales de la unidad: las oraciones con verbos de influencia y las oraciones de relativo.

Diremos a los alumnos que hemos recogido una serie de testimonios de algunas chicas españolas sobre su vida con sus exparejas. Tendrán que completarlos usando el indicativo o el subjuntivo, según corresponda. Dejaremos algunos minutos para que completen las oraciones y, a continuación, pasaremos a la corrección en plenaria. Si se cree conveniente, les permitiremos que comparen sus respuestas con las de algún compañero. Procuraremos aclarar todas las dudas de comprensión que se puedan presentar porque se trata de la última actividad que trabaja de forma más dirigida los exponentes lingüísticos.

Sugerencia

Proponemos una actividad complementaria que gira en torno a la misma temática: las exparejas. Animaremos a los estudiantes a que escriban frases sobre exnovios, exnovias, exmaridos, exesposas…, usando estructuras sustantivas con verbos de influencia u oraciones adjetivas. Tienen como modelo las oraciones del propio ejercicio. Insistiremos en la idea de que no hace falta que reflejen experiencias reales; pueden ser totalmente inventadas y, preferiblemente, divertidas. Para lograr la mayor implicación de los alumnos, el profesor podría comenzar la actividad contando su experiencia con oraciones similares a las de estos ejemplos, que demuestran el matiz lúdico que se quiere dar a la actividad:

Mi exnovia tenía un coche que era muy estrecho y pequeño para mí… Nunca podía viajar con ella porque ¡no me cabían las piernas!

Mi exnovio era muy guapo, pero pasaba más de una hora arreglándose y eso no me gustaba nada…

Mi exnovio Pablo era un chico que siempre llegaba a tiempo a todas partes. Era superpuntual, y a mí me molesta que la gente sea tan puntual…

Solución

Natalia: me regalaron - es.

Juana: tiene.

Ana: era - tenía.

Sonia: hagas.

Carmen: le gustaba - vean.

Elisa: gastes - ahorres.

Daniela: vayas.

¡extra! EN COMUNICACIÓN

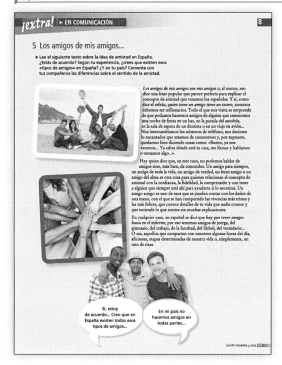

5 Los amigos de mis amigos…

Se cierra la sección Extra con una actividad de comprensión lectora que tiene que ver de nuevo con el ámbito temático de la amistad.

Antes de comenzar con las fases del ejercicio, proponemos la siguiente actividad de prelectura: realizaremos una lluvia de ideas sobre el tema. Recogeremos todas las palabras y expresiones que los estudiantes sepan relacionadas con este campo léxico. Con este trabajo previo conseguiremos que nuestros estudiantes chequeen todo el vocabulario que ya conocen y, sobre todo, aprendan términos nuevos, por lo que animamos al profesor a seguir mostrando más léxico sobre el tema.

A continuación, pasaremos a la fase de lectura del texto. Realizaremos este proceso en plenaria; elegiremos a uno de nuestros estudiantes para empezar a leer y seguiremos con otro de forma aleatoria. A continuación, aclararemos todas las dudas de vocabulario o de comprensión que pudieran presentarse. Finalmente, abriremos un debate en el que los estudiantes explicarán de forma oral su opinión sobre los tipos de amistad de los que se habla en el artículo y, además, compararán las conclusiones a las que llega el texto con su cultura de origen. Si nuestros alumnos estudian en España, comentarán también si tienen todas las clases de amigos que han sido mencionados. Además, los animaremos a que definan su concepto de la amistad.

Solución

Respuesta libre.

NOTAS

Unidad 9
Lugares Patrimonio de la Humanidad

OBJETIVOS DE LA UNIDAD

Esta unidad avanzamos en los usos del modo indicativo y del subjuntivo. Las **funciones comunicativas** que abordaremos serán expresar causa, consecuencia, relaciones temporales y, por último, finalidad y propósito.

Los **contenidos morfosintácticos** vinculados a las funciones anteriores serán las construcciones causales, las consecutivas, las temporales y las finales.

Por lo que respecta a los **contenidos léxico-semánticos**, nos ocuparemos del léxico sobre espacios urbanos, de lugares representativos del mundo hispano y de ciudades declaradas Patrimonio de la Humanidad.

En cuanto a los **contenidos socioculturales**, haremos referencia a acontecimientos relevantes de países hispanos: el Festival de los Patios Cordobeses en mayo; la Feria de Abril en Sevilla; la Fiesta del Fuego en Santiago de Cuba; el Día de los Muertos en México...

Los **contenidos pragmáticos** que trataremos son los marcadores justificativos, los conectores aditivos, los consecutivos y los temporales, además de los elementos discursivos causales y las interjecciones ¡Ajá!, ¡Eh! y ¿Eh?

En los **contenidos fonéticos y ortográficos** trataremos el punto (.) y el punto y coma (;).

CONTEXTOS

1 Lugares para no olvidar

En esta sección facilitamos a los estudiantes información sobre dos fiestas relevantes de España.

A. Empezamos la unidad con dos textos: uno sobre el Festival de los Patios Cordobeses y otro sobre la Feria de Abril de Sevilla. Antes de leerlos, instaremos a los alumnos a que comenten en plenaria lo que sepan sobre las dos ciudades en las que se celebran estos acontecimientos. A continuación, pasaremos a su lectura en plenaria y nos fijaremos especialmente en el léxico que se incluye al final de cada uno, fundamental para entenderlos.

Sugerencia

Para que los alumnos comprendan mejor estas dos celebraciones, nos parece primordial complementar esta actividad con material audiovisual en el que se aprecie cómo es el ambiente, cómo se mueve la gente, la ropa que lleva... Para ello, podemos recurrir a algún banco de imágenes o vídeos de Internet.

B. Después de que los alumnos expresen sus ideas y opiniones sobre las dos celebraciones que se han presentado, es el momento de que individualmente den a conocer a sus compañeros alguna fiesta o algún acontecimiento relevante de su país.

Sugerencia

Si hay varios estudiantes de una misma nacionalidad, cada uno puede encargarse de la fiesta de una región determinada o de una ciudad concreta... Lo que es aconsejable, como siempre en estos casos, es que los alumnos preparen la exposición previamente y, a la hora de redactarla, hagan una lista con todo el vocabulario que han tenido que consultar para presentárselo a sus compañeros antes de hacer la exposición. De esta manera, todos conocerán el léxico que se va a manejar. Además, como es habitual para buscar la interacción en las exposiciones orales, los estudiantes podrán hacer preguntas al compañero que está presentando su trabajo.

Solución

Respuesta libre.

CONTEXTOS

2 Callejeando

Nuestro objetivo con esta serie de ejercicios es dar a conocer a los estudiantes algunos lugares representativos de Latinoamérica.

A. En primer lugar, le toca a Argentina. Los alumnos tienen que escuchar una información sobre la avenida Corrientes de Buenos Aires para averiguar las razones por las que es famosa. Previamente, les pediremos que se fijen en el diálogo de los bocadillos, donde aparece una razón: *porque es una de las calles principales de Buenos Aires*. Pretendemos que al final de la actividad detecten de manera inferencial que, cuando se expresa la causa, después de *porque* siempre se usa indicativo.

Solución

Posible respuesta

La avenida Corrientes es famosa porque es una de las calles principales de Buenos Aires.

... porque es una calle muy larga.

... porque está muy asociada al tango.

... porque en ella abundan los lugares de entretenimiento.

... porque allí está el Obelisco, icono de la ciudad.

... porque hay locales públicos abiertos hasta altas horas de la noche.

ciento cincuenta y una 151

▶ LUGARES PATRIMONIO DE LA HUMANIDAD

B. A continuación, es el turno de Cuba, con una actividad de comprensión auditiva sobre el Malecón de La Habana. En esta ocasión, además de la información sobre el lugar, pediremos a los estudiantes que se fijen particularmente en el léxico referido a espacios urbanos y señalen en el cuadro las palabras que menciona Sabine en su intervención. Después, en parejas, comprobarán si conocen el significados de los demás términos del cuadro.

Sugerencia

Para practicar este tipo de léxico, podemos pedir a los alumnos que hagan una descripción de su ciudad y hablen sobre todo de los espacios más representativos. Como reto, podemos decirles que deben intentar utilizar todas las palabras del cuadro.

Solución

Malecón, avenida, carriles, paseo marítimo, ruinas y faro.

OBSERVA, APRENDE Y RECUERDA

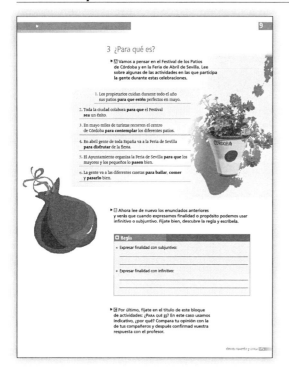

3. ¿Para qué es?

Empezamos una serie de ejercicios de inferencia cuyo objetivo es que el estudiante deduzca el uso del modo indicativo o el modo subjuntivo con diferentes construcciones.

A. En primer lugar, los alumnos tienen que leer unas oraciones referidas a los dos acontecimientos sobre los que se les ha informado en el ejercicio 1A. Todas indican finalidad, pero unas están construidas con infinitivo y otras, con subjuntivo. Les pediremos que se fijen en que en todas las oraciones se incluyen las expresiones *para* o *para que*, que aparecen destacadas.

Debemos intentar que sean ellos los que lleguen a la conclusión de que lo que tienen en común estas oraciones es que indican objetivo o finalidad.

B. Una vez que los estudiantes hayan reconocido el valor de finalidad en los enunciados de la fase A, les pediremos que los vuelvan a leer para descubrir por qué usamos subjuntivo con la expresión *para que* e infinitivo con *para*. Les daremos el tiempo que necesiten. Si se diera el caso de que nadie dedujera la regla, antes de dársela nosotros, los ayudaríamos con algunas pistas.

Por ejemplo, podemos escribir en la pizarra más ejemplos con infinitivo y subjuntivo, pidiéndoles que piensen en quién hace la acción del verbo principal y quién la del verbo subordinado (introducido por *para* o *para que*). Siempre hay quien lo descubre; si no es así, les preguntaríamos por el sujeto de cada verbo, hasta que se den cuenta de que se usa el infinitivo cuando el sujeto de los dos verbos es el mismo y se emplea el subjuntivo cuando existen diferentes sujetos.

Solución

Expresar finalidad con subjuntivo: *Para que* + subjuntivo si hay dos verbos con sujetos diferentes.

Expresar finalidad con infinitivo: *Para* + infinitivo si hay dos verbos con el mismo sujeto.

C. Por último, pediremos a los alumnos que se fijen en el título de este bloque de actividades, *¿Para qué es?*, con la intención de que se den cuenta de que, cuando planteamos una pregunta con *para qué*, usamos siempre el modo indicativo.

A continuación, los animaremos a que intenten deducir el motivo por el que ellos creen que se usa el indicativo en estos casos.

Sugerencia

Los estudiantes suelen tener problemas con el uso del modo correcto en las preguntas, ya que, aunque siempre les recordamos que las tildes en español son muy importantes y marcan diferencias fundamentales, lo suelen olvidar con frecuencia, lo que les hace confundirse, como, en este caso, entre *para que* y *para qué*. Este es el momento de volver a recordárselo e ir un poco más allá. En relación con el asunto que nos ocupa, los ayudaremos mucho si les decimos que con las partículas interrogativas *(qué, cuándo, quién, cuánto…)* nunca se usa subjuntivo.

Solución

Nunca se usa subjuntivo con las partículas interrogativas: *quién, cuándo, qué…*

OBSERVA, APRENDE Y RECUERDA

4 Porque hay mucha diversión

A. En esta actividad nos centraremos en las construcciones causales.

Para ello, en primer lugar, el estudiante tiene que leer un repertorio de oraciones con este tipo de estructuras, que hemos agrupado para intentar hacer lo más evidente posible su uso en cada caso: por un lado, las que llevan *porque* o *por*, y, por otro, las que incluyen *como*.

Podemos leer en plenaria todas las razones por las que es famosa la avenida Corrientes y resolver las dudas de vocabulario. Después, como en el ejercicio anterior, intentaremos que los estudiantes adviertan lo que tienen en común las tres palabras que hemos destacado en negrita: indican causa.

B. Una vez que los alumnos descubren lo que estas tres palabras (*porque*, *por* y *como*) tienen en común, deben darse cuenta de lo que las diferencia. Tras prestar atención de nuevo a los ejemplos, podrán deducir la regla fácilmente.

Sugerencia

Antes de pasar al ejercicio siguiente, sería conveniente hacer más prácticas. Proponemos que el profesor vaya preguntando a cada estudiante la causa de algún hecho: *¿Por qué decidiste estudiar español? ¿Por qué elegiste este lugar para estudiar? ¿Por qué vives con una familia española? ¿Por qué crees que tu profesor ha elegido el libro Método 3?*

Otra posibilidad es que el profesor o un estudiante diga una oración con *porque* y otro estudiante conteste cambiando el orden y utilizando *como*.

Ejemplo:

> Hans no vino a clase ayer **porque** perdió el autobús.

< Claro, **como** se acostó anoche tarde, esta mañana no podía levantarse.

Asimismo, aconsejamos que el profesor recuerde a los estudiantes que si después de una preposición hay un verbo este siempre es infinitivo; es algo que no solo ocurre con *para* y *por*.

Solución

POR

Lo usamos siempre con infinitivo. *La avenida Corrientes es famosa por ser una de las avenidas más largas del mundo.*

COMO

Lo usamos delante de la oración principal. *Como está el Obelisco, símbolo de la ciudad, todos los turistas pasan por aquí.*

PORQUE

Lo usamos después de la oración principal. *La Avenida Corrientes es famosa porque en ella puedes encontrar de todo.*

LUGARES PATRIMONIO DE LA HUMANIDAD

OBSERVA, APRENDE Y RECUERDA

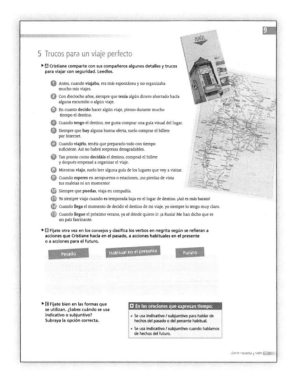

5 Trucos para un viaje perfecto

A. Ahora nos ocuparemos de las oraciones temporales. Los trucos para viajar de Cristiane son una muestra de las distintas posibilidades de uso de las construcciones temporales, según se refieran al pasado, al presente o al futuro.

Leeremos en plenaria todos los consejos y, al final, pediremos a los alumnos que observen lo que tienen en común las oraciones subordinadas: expresan tiempo. Cuando esté claro que se trata de oraciones temporales, les diremos que subrayen todas las palabras que se utilizan en cada caso para indicar tiempo: *antes, cuando, siempre que, siempre, en cuanto, tan pronto como, mientras*.

B y C. Es mejor que la clasificación de los verbos, según se refieran a acciones del pasado, habituales en el presente o el futuro, se haga individualmente. Después, cada estudiante observará en qué casos se usa indicativo y en cuáles subjuntivo, y, cuando todos tengan una respuesta, la compartirán con sus compañeros. Finalmente, se escribirá la regla.

Sugerencia

Para practicar el uso de las oraciones temporales con subjuntivo —que son las más problemáticas para los estudiantes—, podríamos hacer una actividad lúdica que consiste en lo siguiente: el profesor dice una oración que exprese tiempo; por ejemplo: *Cuando termine el curso, volveré a mi país*. A continuación, un estudiante retoma esta oración para continuar la secuencia temporal: *Cuando vuelva a mi país, me acordaré de mi profesora*. Otro continuará: *Cuando me acuerde de mi profesora, querré seguir estudiando español*. Y otro: *Cuando siga estudiando español, cada día hablaré mejor...* La serie seguirá hasta que cada estudiante haya dicho alguna oración. Suele ser divertido porque, a veces, se dicen cosas extrañas, pero el objetivo es practicar expresiones con *cuando* en futuro y comprobar que en estos casos siempre se usa el modo subjuntivo. Esta actividad ayuda al estudiante a mecanizar este valor.

Solución

B.
Pasado: viajaba, tenía.
Habitual en el presente: decido, tengo, hay, viajo, es, llega.
Futuro: viajéis, decidáis, esperes, puedas, llegue.

C.
Se usa <u>indicativo</u> para hablar de hechos del pasado o del presente habitual.
Se usa <u>subjuntivo</u> cuando hablamos de hechos del futuro.

NOTAS

OBSERVA, APRENDE Y RECUERDA

de. Dejaremos un tiempo y posteriormente se comentará en plenaria. Seguro que alguno encuentra la respuesta: se emplea *antes de que / después de que* si hay dos sujetos diferentes, y *antes de / después de* si hay un sujeto único.

Si se considera oportuno, podemos aludir a que en el lenguaje hablado podemos usar la estructura *antes de / después de* con infinitivo en casos en que hay dos sujetos distintos: *Antes de llamarle, apareció en casa*.

Sugerencia

El uso de *antes de que* o *después de que,* al ser menos habitual, resulta generalmente más complicado, por lo que es necesario practicar. Por ello, proponemos el siguiente ejercicio: el profesor dice una oración principal; por ejemplo, *Quiero ir esta noche al cine...*, y los alumnos tienen que continuarla, utilizando siempre un sujeto distinto: *... después de que terminemos la clase*. Otros ejemplos: *Siempre llego a clase... antes de que lleguéis vosotros. Seguimos este ejercicio... después de que termine la pausa*.

Solución

Usamos *antes de / después de* + **infinitivo** cuando **hay dos verbos con el mismo sujeto**.

Usamos *antes de que / después de que* + **subjuntivo** cuando **hay dos verbos con sujetos diferentes**.

NOTAS

6 ¿Antes de o después de?

A. Seguimos con las construcciones temporales tomando como referencia los trucos del ejercicio 5A. Primero, distinguiremos entre las cosas que Cristiane hace antes y después de viajar. Son acciones muy evidentes, por lo que el estudiante usará *antes de* o *después de* sin ninguna dificultad.

A continuación, pediremos a los alumnos que se fijen en los verbos que están destacados en negrita y les preguntaremos por qué creen que aparecen en infinitivo. Deberían ser capaces de decirnos que detrás de una preposición siempre se usa infinitivo (en el ejercicio 4B se trató este asunto).

Solución

Después de decidir el destino, compro una guía visual del lugar.

Antes de comprar el billete, miro las ofertas en Internet.

Antes de viajar, pienso bien en el destino.

Después de elegir el destino, saco el billete.

Antes de viajar, preparo todo para no tener sorpresas desagradables.

B. A continuación, pediremos a los estudiantes que lean las frases individualmente e intenten descubrir por qué en estas se usa *antes de que* o *después de que* y no *antes de* o *después*

ciento cincuenta y cinco 155

LUGARES PATRIMONIO DE LA HUMANIDAD

OBSERVA, APRENDE Y RECUERDA

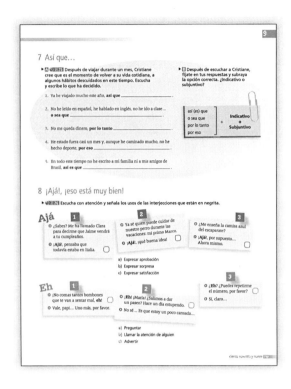

7. Así que...

A. Es el turno de las construcciones consecutivas. Empezamos con una actividad de comprensión auditiva en la que los estudiantes deben completar unas oraciones para explicar las decisiones de Cristiane, según lo que dice en la audición.

Sugerencia

Otra forma de plantear la actividad es pedir a los alumnos que, antes de escuchar la grabación, intenten completar los enunciados expresando la consecuencia y, después, comprueben con la audición si están en lo cierto o no. De esta forma, comprobaremos si usan indicativo o subjuntivo y, además, hacen el esfuerzo de construir unas oraciones con sentido.

Solución

1. ahora toca estudiar.

2. tengo que ponerme al día.

3. tengo que trabajar los fines de semana.

4. tengo que ir todos los días al gimnasio.

5. esta misma tarde les escribo a todos.

B. En esta segunda parte el estudiante tiene que fijarse en lo que ha transcrito en el ejercicio anterior para comprobar si se usa indicativo o subjuntivo después de las locuciones consecutivas.

Sugerencia

En este caso, también creemos que es necesario hacer aún alguna práctica más. Proponemos que el profesor o un estudiante comience diciendo una oración con una locución consecutiva para que otro la complete; por ejemplo: *No tengo dinero, así que... voy a trabajar este verano. He cogido unos kilos de más, por lo tanto... me voy a apuntar en un gimnasio...*

Solución

Indicativo.

8 ¡Ajá!, ¡eso está muy bien!

En este ejercicio nos ocupamos de las interjecciones *ajá* y *eh* a través de una actividad de comprensión auditiva. En este caso, el estudiante tiene el texto y ha de señalar el significado que tienen las interjecciones en cada caso. La entonación le ayudará a distinguir los diferentes usos.

Sugerencia

Después de escuchar la grabación y corregir la actividad, aconsejamos que, en parejas, los estudiantes vuelvan a leer los diálogos varias veces hasta que la pronunciación de las interjecciones sea la correcta.

Además, proponemos que, también en parejas, escriban varios diálogos con los distintos usos de las interjecciones *ajá* y *eh*, y los lean a los demás compañeros para que estos descubran lo que significan en cada caso.

Solución

Ajá: 1-b; 2-c; 3-a.

Eh: 1-c; 2-b; 3-a.

ciento cincuenta y seis

PRACTICA

Iniciamos una serie de actividades de refuerzo de los contenidos de la unidad.

9 Las preguntas de Cristiane

El estudiante ha de responder a las preguntas de Cristiane con oraciones en las que siempre tiene que expresar relaciones temporales. En plenaria podemos leer las preguntas y después dejar un tiempo para que cada alumno piense individualmente sus respuestas.

Sugerencia

Podemos organizar la clase en parejas de modo que los alumnos comparen sus respuestas entre ellos. Después, les pediremos que expliquen al resto de los compañeros las coincidencias que han encontrado. Como ayuda, les daremos algunos ejemplos: *Jasmine y yo nos enfadamos cuando nuestros compañeros de piso no nos ayudan a limpiar. A Markus y a mí nos cuesta mucho usar el subjuntivo siempre que tenemos que hablar. A nosotros nos molesta cuando los profesores hablan demasiado rápido porque no los entendemos bien.*

Solución

Posible respuesta

Cuando no estudio español, suelo trabajar de camarero en un bar del centro / hago una vida normal: me levanto, voy a la oficina, almuerzo, descanso…

Después de terminar las clases, vuelvo a casa y preparo la comida con mis amigos.

Cuando llegué el primer día, estaba un poco perdida, no hablaba muy bien español y no conocía a nadie.

Siempre que estoy en casa, escucho la radio. ¡Me encanta!

Me pongo nervioso/-a en cuanto tengo que hablar con los españoles porque pienso que todavía no lo hago muy bien y, a veces, hablan demasiado rápido para mí.

A mí, cuando salgo, me encanta ir a un karaoke y bailar en discotecas.

Yo haré un curso de alemán por Internet cuanto tenga tiempo.

A mí me gusta cuando la gente de mi país sale por la noche porque hacen cosas muy divertidas.

A mí me molesta cuando la gente fuma cerca de mí o en recintos cerrados, porque no me gusta nada el olor del tabaco.

Pues yo me compraré un ordenador cuando tenga un poco de dinero.

Cuando estudio español, me cuesta mucho utilizar las formas de pasado.

ciento cincuenta y siete

LUGARES PATRIMONIO DE LA HUMANIDAD

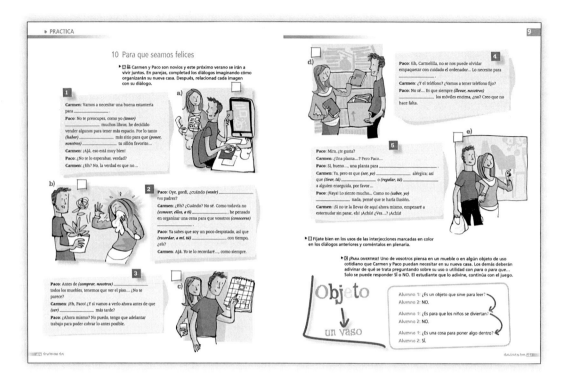

10. Para que seamos felices

A. En esta actividad pretendemos revisar varios de los contenidos estudiados en la unidad: el uso de indicativo / subjuntivo y la utilización de las interjecciones *ajá* y *eh*. Además, los alumnos han de comprender el texto en su totalidad para poder relacionar cada imagen con su diálogo. Aconsejamos hacer esta actividad en parejas; les podrá servir de ayuda si cada miembro elige un rol: Carmen o Paco.

Solución

1. colocar todos los libros - tengo - habrá - pongamos.
2. vienen - te conocen - os conozcáis - recuérdamelo.
3. comprarnos - sea.
4. trabajar / mi trabajo – llevamos.
5. decorar la casa - soy - tírala - regálasela - sabía.

Relación imágenes-diálogos:

d-1; **c**-2; **e**-3; **a**-4; **b**-5.

B. Ahora los alumnos han de fijarse en las interjecciones del diálogo anterior y comentar sus distintos usos.

Solución

1. *¡Ajá, eso está muy bien!:* expresa satisfacción.

¿Eh? No, la verdad es que no…: sirve para preguntar si algo no se ha entendido o como muletilla del discurso.

2. *¿Eh? ¿Cuándo? No sé:* se utiliza para preguntar.

… así que recuérdamelo con tiempo, ¿eh?: sirve para advertir.

Ajá. Yo te lo recordaré: para mostrar acuerdo.

3. *¡Eh, Paco!:* sirve para llamar la atención de alguien.

4. *¡Eh, Carmelilla!:* para llamar la atención de alguien.

5. *¡Si no te la llevas de aquí ahora mismo, empezaré a estornudar sin parar, eh!:* para advertir.

C. Cerramos este bloque con una actividad lúdica relacionada con el ejercicio anterior para seguir practicando las construcciones finales, al mismo tiempo que activamos el léxico sobre muebles y objetos de uso cotidiano. Así pues, planteamos un reto: que los estudiantes, mediante preguntas que expresen finalidad, lleguen a descubrir el objeto o el mueble en el que está pensando un alumno.

También se puede plantear el juego en grupos. En ese caso, será el profesor el que, en función de la clase, organice grupos de dos, tres, cuatro… alumnos. Hay que tener en cuenta que cuanto más pequeños sean más estudiantes podrán participar.

Sugerencia

Podemos hacer una actividad de ampliación de expresión oral sobre el tema que se trata en este bloque de ejercicios: las relaciones de pareja, vivir en pareja, encontrar una vivienda, el alquiler, los cambios de vivienda…

Solución

Respuesta libre.

PRACTICA

Solución

Lunes: a las siete de la tarde, ir a la presentación de la novela de Pedro.

Martes: a las cinco de la tarde, tomar un café en el centro con Eugenia y Rocío, y, por la noche, ir a ver la última película de Almodóvar.

Miércoles: a las seis y media, ir a la exposición de Goya en el Museo Central.

Jueves: a la una o una y media, salir de tapeo antes de comer.

B. Ejercicio relacionado con el anterior en el que el estudiante ha de comprender y explicar las razones por las que Carmen no puede quedar con sus amigos.

Solución

Lunes

< Es que el lunes a las dos voy a comer / almuerzo / tengo un almuerzo con Marina y José.

< A esa hora no es posible porque tengo que hacer / voy a hacer compras en el supermercado y tengo que ir a la tintorería.

Martes

< No puedo ir con vosotras porque tengo clases de inglés / voy a clases de inglés.

< Es que voy a picar algo y a salir con Pablo por el centro porque es su cumpleaños.

Miércoles

< Paco, ¡no es posible porque voy a jugar al pádel / he quedado para jugar al pádel con Julia!

Jueves

< Es que el jueves a esa hora voy a ir a la agencia para organizar el viaje a Londres / tengo que ir a la agencia para organizar el viaje a Londres.

11 No puedo porque…

A. Actividad de comprensión auditiva sobre la agenda de la semana de Carmen. Les podemos decir a los estudiantes que pueden usar el verbo en infinitivo si así está en la audición, pero que en la corrección del ejercicio tienen que decir las propuestas que tiene Carmen para cada día de la semana con el verbo conjugado.

NOTAS

LUGARES PATRIMONIO DE LA HUMANIDAD

PRACTICA

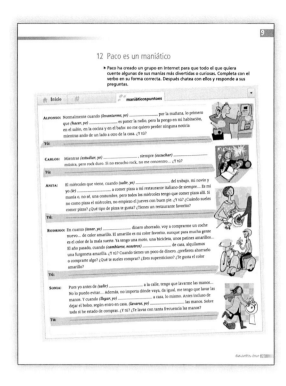

12 Paco es un maniático

Actividad de refuerzo sobre actividades cotidianas y relaciones temporales. El estudiante, después de completar los verbos individualmente, ha de chatear y ofrecer su experiencia personal. Todo el mundo tiene alguna manía, así que esperamos que puedan hablar sobre este tema, sobre sus costumbres y supersticiones, etc.

Sugerencia

Podemos pedirles a nuestros estudiantes que hablen no solo sobre supersticiones o creencias que ellos tengan, sino también sobre otras de las que hayan oído hablar. Ejemplo: *Algunas personas, cuando el pan cae bocabajo, lo ponen bocarriba porque piensan que significa que va a ocurrir algún desastre. Cuando un cuadro que estaba colgado en la pared se cae o simplemente está torcido, significa mala suerte. Otras personas ponen la escoba al revés detrás de la puerta porque piensan que trae buena suerte. Cuando tengo que pasar debajo de una escalera, no me importa, no soy supersticioso.*

Solución

Alfonso: me levanto - hago.

Carlos: estudio - escucho.

Anita: salga - iremos / vamos a ir / vamos.

Rodrigo: tenga - nos cambiamos.

Sonia: salir - llego - me lavo.

PRACTICA

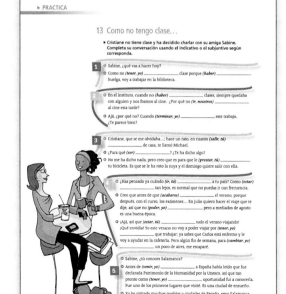

13 Como no tengo clase…

Terminamos los ejercicios de refuerzo con uno donde se recogen los usos del indicativo y del subjuntivo estudiados en la unidad. Individualmente, cada alumno completará el diálogo. Es importante que cuente con tiempo suficiente, que lo lea todo y no solo las oraciones de los verbos que tiene que cambiar, que pregunte todo el léxico que no conozca y que preste atención al tipo de construcción para deducir el modo adecuado.

Sugerencia

Podemos pedir a los alumnos que se fijen en las interjecciones del diálogo y que nos digan qué significan en cada caso.

Solución

1. tengo - hay.

2. había - vamos - termine.

3. saliste - será - prestes.

4. irás / vas a ir - está - se acabe - puedo / podré - vas a estar / estarás - tener - cambiar.

5. venir - tuve - vaya.

PRÁCTICA

14 Asunto: Salamanca

Nos fijamos ahora en los contenidos fonéticos y ortográficos. El estudiante debe separar el texto en párrafos y puntuar correctamente. Primero lo hará individualmente; después, en parejas, y finalmente en plenaria se verán las diferentes versiones.

Solución

Posible respuesta

La Plaza Mayor de Salamanca es el corazón de la ciudad y uno de los monumentos cumbres del barroco español. Fue construida entre los años 1729 y 1775 por Alberto Churriguera. Es una de las más bellas plazas porticadas españolas y de las más hermosas del mundo, con ochenta y ocho arcos y con forma de cuadrilátero irregular. El tono dorado de la piedra da a la plaza una maravillosa armonía. Es un punto de encuentro no solo para el ocio, sino también para el trabajo.

Es una plaza peatonal y tiene una magia especial a cualquier hora del día. Un lugar cosmopolita en el que se encuentran personas de todo el mundo, turistas y estudiantes, muchos de ellos de español. Vivir como estudiante en Salamanca es fácil y existen varias opciones: vivir en un piso con estudiantes; vivir con una familia; vivir en una residencia de estudiantes o alquilar un piso en solitario.

La catedral destaca desde cualquier rincón de la ciudad. Fue construida entre los siglos XVI y XVII básicamente en dos estilos: gótico tardío y barroco.

Salamanca tiene una importante tradición universitaria reconocida a nivel mundial. La causa principal es que su Universidad es la más antigua de España. Junto a la Plaza Mayor son muchos los lugares de interés que podemos visitar en esta ciudad maravillosa.

EN COMUNICACIÓN

En esta sección nos proponemos que los estudiantes conozcan diferentes ciudades y lugares representativos de España y de Latinoamérica.

15 Cuando visito una ciudad…

A y B. Para hablar de las ciudades que han visitado los alumnos y sus experiencias, primero han de hacer una actividad de expresión escrita que consiste en completar la ficha que se les presenta. Podemos animarlos a que añadan otros puntos que consideren importantes. Después se hará una puesta en común con todas sus experiencias y opiniones.

Sugerencia

El tema de los viajes le interesa a todo el mundo, así que también podemos proponer a los estudiantes que preparen una presentación sobre su mejor viaje, el más interesante, el más extraño… Si la clase es muy numerosa, para no cansar con el tema, recomendamos que sean los propios alumnos los que hagan una selección de los viajes que quieran conocer para que los presenten sus compañeros. Otra posibilidad es dedicar una sesión de la semana a hablar de viajes para que todos participen.

Solución

A y B. Respuesta libre.

LUGARES PATRIMONIO DE LA HUMANIDAD

EN COMUNICACIÓN

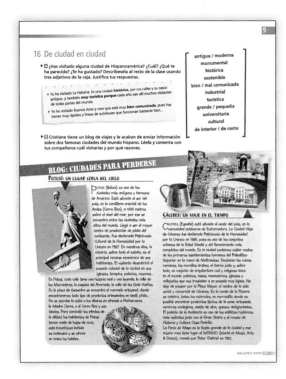

16 De ciudad en ciudad

A. En este ejercicio trabajaremos el léxico para definir distintos tipos de ciudades. En primer lugar, el profesor explicará el vocabulario que se presenta.

A continuación, los estudiantes describirán una ciudad hispanoamericana que hayan visitado. Si no conocen ninguna, les pediremos que busquen una localidad de su país que reúna algunas de las características recogidas en la caja, o bien, que describan su ciudad natal con algunos de los adjetivos que se proponen. Les diremos que en las descripciones intenten siempre justificar sus respuestas.

Solución

Respuesta libre.

B. Actividad de comprensión lectora sobre dos ciudades famosas del mundo hispano. Recomendamos que se haga una primera lectura de los textos individualmente y después otra en plenaria para resolver las dudas de vocabulario. Cuando el alumno no tenga ninguna duda, estará capacitado para dar su opinión sobre cuál de los dos lugares le gustaría visitar y por qué.

Sugerencia

Podemos pedir a los alumnos que elaboren un listado con las ciudades que han visitado y otro con las ciudades que desean conocer. Después, compararán los resultados; seguro que una amplia mayoría ha coincidido en sus gustos.

Solución

Respuesta libre.

NOTAS

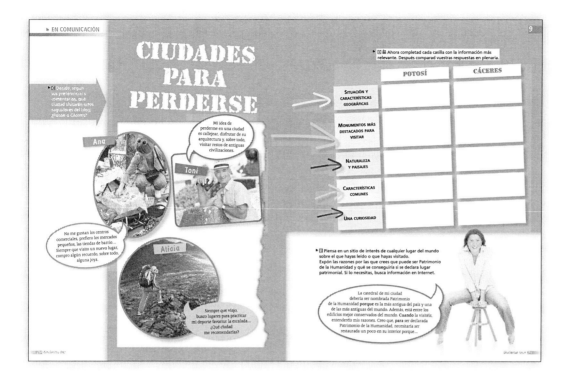

C. Atendiendo a los gustos y comentarios de los seguidores del blog, en esta actividad el alumno ha de decir cuál de las dos ciudades anteriores visitarán.

Solución

Posible respuesta

Ana va a visitar **Potosí** porque allí podrá ir a su mercado artesanal y comprar alguna joya. A ella le encantan, y en ese lugar las encontrará porque se venden, sobre todo, objetos hechos de plata. En el mercado artesanal de Cáceres no se venden objetos de plata ni joyas.

A Toni le gusta callejear y visitar restos de civilizaciones antiguas, así que visitará **Cáceres** porque hay restos de los primeros asentamientos humanos del Paleolítico Superior en la cueva de Maltravieso.

Alicia visitará **Potosí** porque así podrá practicar su deporte favorito: la escalada. Es ideal para esta actividad física porque la ciudad está situada en la cordillera oriental de los Andes (Cerro Rico), a 4100 metros sobre el nivel del mar; por eso se encuentra entre las ciudades más altas del mundo.

D. En parejas, realizaremos una nueva lectura detenida de los textos del ejercicio B para que puedan completar la información de cada casilla. A continuación, pediremos un voluntario para que hable de estos aspectos pero referidos a otro lugar, el que él quiera.

Solución

Posible respuesta

POTOSÍ

Situación y características geográficas: Potosí está en Bolivia, al sur del país, en la cordillera oriental de los Andes (Cerro Rico), a 4100 metros sobre el nivel del mar.

Monumentos más destacados para visitar: Iglesias, templos, palacios y casonas de arquitectura colonial. Calles con historia: la de los Mercaderes, la esquina del Ahorcado, la calle de las Siete Vueltas, la plaza de Saavedra. Además, tiene un mercado artesanal y los altares de Pachamama, la Madre Tierra.

Naturaleza y paisajes: El Cerro Rico y sus minas.

Características comunes: Ciudad Patrimonio de la Humanidad desde 1987.

Una curiosidad: Para combatir los efectos de la altitud, los habitantes de Potosí toman mate de hojas de coca.

CÁCERES

Situación y características geográficas: Cáceres está situada al oeste de España, en la comunidad autónoma de Extremadura.

Monumentos más destacados para visitar: Es uno de los conjuntos urbanos de la Edad Media y del Renacimiento más completos del mundo. Podemos visitar las ruinas romanas, las murallas árabes, el barrio judío, palacios, monasterios, iglesias, la Plaza Mayor, el palacio de la Audiencia, el Gran Teatro y el museo de Historia y Cultura Casa Pedrilla.

Naturaleza y paisajes: Allí se encuentran los primeros asentamientos humanos del Paleolítico Superior en la cueva de Maltravieso.

Características comunes: Ciudad Patrimonio de la Humanidad desde 1986.

Una curiosidad: En mayo tiene lugar el WOMAD (World Of Music, Arts & Dance) creado por Peter Gabriel en 1982.

LUGARES PATRIMONIO DE LA HUMANIDAD

E. Cada estudiante tiene que defender la candidatura de un lugar elegido por él para ser Patrimonio de la Humanidad y explicar sus razones.

Sugerencia

Para animar a los alumnos a que se expresen, les podemos decir que no tienen que elegir un lugar famoso, que puede ser cualquiera por pequeño que sea, un sitio importante para ellos por alguna razón…

Solución

Respuesta libre.

¡extra! CONTEXTOS

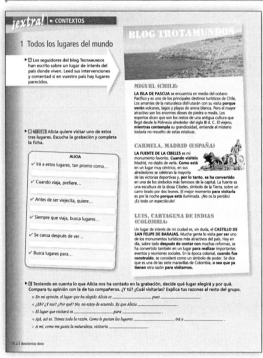

En esta sección seguimos trabajando en la difusión de la cultura hispana.

1 Todos los lugares del mundo

A. Los tres espacios que hemos elegido son muy representativos de los países a los que pertenecen y es posible que los alumnos hayan oído hablar de ellos. Por tanto, antes de leer la información del blog, dejaremos que los estudiantes cuenten lo que saben sobre ellos.

Sugerencia

Después de leer la información y comentarla en plenaria, les pediremos que se fijen en las frases destacadas y que digan a qué tipo de las que hemos estudiado en la unidad pertenecen (**expresan causa:** *porque verán volcanes…, como está en un lugar muy céntrico…, porque está iluminada…, por ser uno de los monumentos turísticos…;* **expresan consecuencia:** *por lo tanto, se ha convertido en uno de los símbolos…, o sea que ya tienen otra razón…;* **expresan tiempo:** *mientras contempla su grandiosidad…, cuando visitéis Madrid…, después de contar con muchas reformas…, cuando fue construido…;* **expresan finalidad:** *para visitarla, para realizar importantes eventos…, para visitarnos*).

Solución

Respuesta libre.

B. Actividad de comprensión auditiva en el que cada alumno, individualmente, tendrá que completar la información sobre Alicia. Después, comprobaremos las respuestas en plenaria.

Sugerencia

Tras la comprobación, propondremos a los alumnos que aporten los mismos datos sobre ellos mismos.

Solución

Irá a estos lugares, tan pronto como tenga tiempo y dinero.

Cuando viaja, prefiere irse lejos, a otro país del mundo… Le encanta conocer culturas muy diferentes a la suya.

Antes de ser viejecita, quiere dar, al menos una vez, la vuelta al mundo.

Siempre que viaja, busca lugares donde se mezclen la naturaleza y la cultura.

Se cansa después de ver monumentos, palacios, casas y museos.

Busca lugares para relajarse y descansar.

C. Finalmente, cada alumno tendrá que decidir cuál de los lugares del ejercicio A cree que elegirá Alicia, teniendo en cuenta lo que nos ha contado en la grabación. De este modo, comprobamos que la comprensión ha sido correcta. Concluida esta fase, ya solo nos queda que el estudiante se exprese, que él también elija; así daremos un paso más en el conocimiento de los miembros de la clase.

Sugerencia

Si el fin último de todo este proceso es que el estudiante se comunique en español, que utilice la lengua que está aprendiendo, permitámosle que se exprese en cualquier ocasión posible. Porque, además, será la forma de estrechar los lazos entre el grupo, conociéndose entre ellos a través de lo que cuentan y, aunque en ocasiones no lo hagan con toda la fluidez que nos gustaría, lo importante es que también compartan vivencias y se refuercen los vínculos afectivos.

Solución

Respuesta libre.

¡extra! PRACTICA

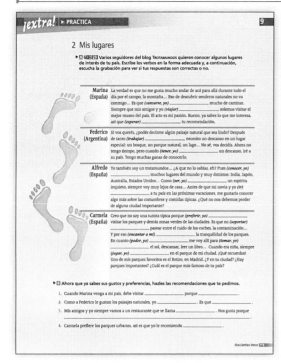

De nuevo presentamos una actividad para el chequeo, el refuerzo y la revisión de los usos del indicativo y del subjuntivo estudiados en la unidad.

2 Mis lugares

A. Antes de escuchar la grabación, cada estudiante tiene que completar los comentarios del blog usando la forma del verbo que crea correcta. Después, leeremos los textos en plenaria para comprobar si las diferentes versiones que los alumnos han escrito son acertadas y qué porcentaje de aciertos ha habido. Esto nos servirá para ver si los contenidos han sido asimilados y en qué medida. Finalmente, escucharemos la grabación para que los estudiantes corrijan lo que sea necesario y explicaremos de nuevo todos los casos en los que se haya producido algún error.

Solución

Marina: me canso - viajamos - espero.

Federico: trabajar - tenga.

Alfredo: conozco - soy - vayamos.

Carmela: prefiero - soporto - me encanta - puedo - tomar - jugaba.

B. Ahora el alumno tiene que hacer recomendaciones a los seguidores del blog, pero completando las oraciones que les proponemos. De este modo, expresará las ideas con los tipos de oraciones (de causa, consecuencia…) que son objeto de estudio de esta unidad.

Solución

Respuesta libre.

¡EXTRA! PRACTICA

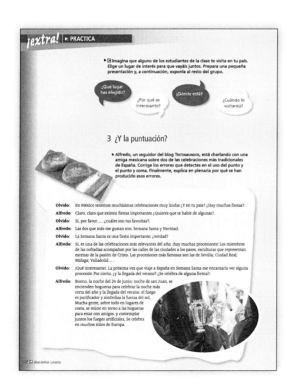

C. Para terminar, pediremos que cada estudiante se convierta en el guía turístico de un compañero que lo visita en su país. Para ello, elegirá un lugar y contestará a preguntas como las que se proponen.

Sugerencia

Una variante para que los estudiantes den a conocer su país de procedencia y para practicar uno de los contenidos de la unidad es que solo expresen las razones por las que aconsejan visitarlo. Por ejemplo: *porque se come bien, porque el tiempo invita a hacer actividades al aire libre, porque puedes hacer turismo de playa, pero también hay otras muchas opciones…* Al final, sus compañeros elegirán las razones que más les han interesado.

Solución

Respuesta libre.

3 ¿Y la puntuación?

Terminamos esta sección con una práctica sobre la puntuación. Se realizará individualmente o en parejas. Después se comentará en plenaria. Seguro que habrá versiones muy diferentes. La mayoría de los errores consisten en poner punto después de los signos de cierre de interrogación o exclamación, o después de puntos suspensivos. También se detecta la utilización incorrecta del punto y coma en una relación simple (Sevilla; Ciudad Real; Málaga; Valladolid…).

ciento sesenta y cinco 165

LUGARES PATRIMONIO DE LA HUMANIDAD

Sugerencia

Probablemente los estudiantes necesitarán hacer más prácticas. Para ello, podemos pedirles que escriban sobre algún tema de la unidad, que dividan el texto en párrafos y que usen comas, punto y coma, puntos y dos puntos. Después intercambiarán los textos y el que lo lea tendrá que ir explicando si la separación en párrafos y la puntuación son correctas.

Solución

Olvido: En México tenemos muchísimas celebraciones muy lindas. ¿Y en tu país? ¿Hay muchas fiestas?

Alfredo: Claro, claro que existen fiestas importantes. ¿Quieres que te hable de algunas?

Olvido: Sí, por favor…, ¿cuáles son tus favoritas?

Alfredo: Las dos que más me gustan son: Semana Santa y Navidad.

Olvido: La Semana Santa es una fiesta importante, ¿verdad?

Alfredo: Sí, es una de las celebraciones más relevantes del año; ¡hay muchas procesiones! Los miembros de las cofradías acompañan por las calles de las ciudades a los pasos, esculturas que representan escenas de la pasión de Cristo. Las procesiones más famosas son las de Sevilla, Ciudad Real, Málaga, Valladolid…

Olvido: ¡Qué interesante! La próxima vez que viaje a España en Semana Santa me encantaría ver alguna procesión. Por cierto, ¿y la llegada del verano? ¿Se celebra de alguna forma?

Alfredo: Bueno, la noche del 24 de junio, noche de san Juan, se encienden hogueras para celebrar la noche más corta del año y la llegada del verano; el fuego es purificador y simboliza la fuerza del sol. Mucha gente, sobre todo en lugares de costa, se reúne en torno a las hogueras para estar con amigos y contemplar juntos los fuegos artificiales. Se celebra en muchos sitios de Europa.

¡extra! EN COMUNICACIÓN

4 ¿Qué celebramos hoy?

Cerramos la unidad con la presentación de nuevas celebraciones del mundo hispano.

A. Primero queremos que, sabiendo solo los nombres de las celebraciones, los estudiantes, en grupos, imaginen en qué consisten. Por eso, el trabajo tendrá como resultado versiones diferentes.

Solución

Respuesta libre.

B. Después, con esta actividad de compresión lectora, los estudiantes descubrirán la información correcta, que se comparará con las distintas versiones presentadas y, así, se verá qué grupo se ha acercado más a la original. Los textos se pueden leer en grupos o en plenaria.

Solución

Respuesta libre.

C. Ahora los estudiantes, en grupos, deberán investigar sobre las fiestas que proponemos y redactarán textos semejantes a los que han leído anteriormente. Incluimos algunas indicaciones para organizar el escrito. Se puede proponer como tarea para casa. Entre ellos se organizarán para la búsqueda de información y para la elaboración del texto, así como para la exposición final de las redacciones.

Sugerencia

Los estudiantes ofrecerán su opinión sobre las celebraciones anteriores y hablarán de las más populares de sus países. Les pediremos que piensen a cuál de las mencionadas les gustaría asistir. Tendrán que exponer sus razones, sus propósitos y cuándo tienen intención de hacerlo. Ejemplo:

> A David y a mí nos gustaría ir a la fiesta del Día de los Muertos.

< ¿Y eso?

> **Es que** pensamos que es una fiesta rara y genuina… Además, se celebra en país increíble. Iríamos **para** disfrutar del ambiente y **para** disfrazarnos, claro.

Finalmente, el grupo se tiene que poner de acuerdo para elegir la celebración a la que les gustaría asistir a todos. El profesor puede ir anotando en la pizarra los puntos favorables de cada una con el fin de estructurar la puesta en común.

Solución

Respuesta libre.

Unidad 10

¿Qué te ha dicho?

OBJETIVOS DE LA UNIDAD

Como cierre del manual, en esta unidad nos ocuparemos de las siguientes **funciones comunicativas**: relatar lo que otros nos han contado y expresar el inicio, la reiteración, la continuación o el final de una acción.

Sobre los **contenidos morfosintácticos**, prestaremos especial atención al estilo indirecto en el modo indicativo (verbos de lengua y comunicación). Estudiaremos también las perífrasis verbales que indican inicio, reiteración, continuación o final de la acción. Por último, revisaremos los usos de los modos indicativo y subjuntivo que se han estudiado en este nivel.

Los **contenidos léxico-semánticos** que abordaremos están relacionados con algunas expresiones construidas con el verbo *ser* que tienen que ver con la personalidad.

En cuanto a los **contenidos socioculturales,** haremos referencia a algunos personajes famosos del mundo hispano de distintos ámbitos (deporte, política, cine, moda, flamenco...).

Los **contenidos pragmáticos** que abordaremos son algunas expresiones exclamativas con carácter superlativo *(¡Vaya...! ¡Menudo/a...!)* y los aumentativos.

Por último, en cuanto a los **contenidos fonéticos y ortográficos,** nos centraremos en el estudio de las marcas de estilo indirecto y en las abreviaturas de uso frecuente.

¿QUÉ TE HA DICHO?

CONTEXTOS

1 ¿Qué te ha dicho?

Comenzamos la sección con una actividad para presentar en contexto el estilo directo y el estilo indirecto, uno de los principales contenidos gramaticales que vertebran la unidad.

A. La secuencia se abre con un ejercicio de comprensión lectora: la conversación entre Linda y Javi. Pediremos a los estudiantes que se fijen en la viñeta porque los ayudará a comprender el diálogo.

B. Continuamos con un ejercicio de comprensión auditiva que tiene como finalidad la presentación del estilo indirecto. Siguiendo con la conversación entre Linda y Javi, ahora el estudiante tiene que completar un texto con la reproducción de las palabras de Sofía. Después de la fase de escucha y corrección, les pediremos a los alumnos que subrayen los verbos que introducen las palabras de otro interlocutor: *me ha dicho que…, dice que…, me dijo que…*

Sugerencia

Antes de seguir, proponemos hacer una sencilla práctica que consiste en que el profesor hace una pregunta a un estudiante y, después de escuchar su respuesta, le pregunta a otro alumno lo que ha dicho su compañero. Por ejemplo:

> Sandy, ¿a qué hora te has levantado?

< Me he levantado un poco tarde.

> Frank, ¿qué ha dicho Sandy?

< Ha dicho que se ha levantado un poco tarde.

Solución

está de cuatro meses – están muy enamorados – que se case con él – va a seguir estudiando – iban a alquilar un piso en Madrid – la lengua del amor es universal.

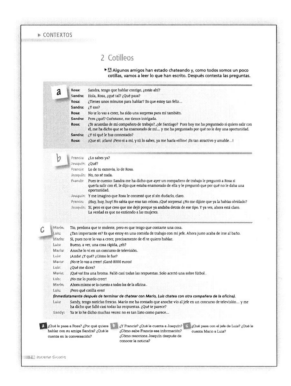

2 Cotilleos

A. Avanzamos un paso más en la presentación de estos contenidos en contexto. Primero elegiremos a dos estudiantes para leer el diálogo entre Rosa y Sandra. Posteriormente, de manera individual, los alumnos tendrán que subrayar los verbos que introducen las palabras de otro, cuando Rosa cuenta lo que ha hablado con su compañero de trabajo Santiago: *me ha preguntado si…, me ha dicho que…, me ha preguntado por qué…* Después les podemos preguntar qué verbo se utiliza por primera vez en este diálogo para introducir las palabras de otra persona, que no aparecía en el primer diálogo; ese verbo es *preguntar*.

Otros dos estudiantes leerán el diálogo entre Francis y Joaquín. Una vez resueltas las dudas de vocabulario, les diremos que hay un diferencia en los verbos que introducen las palabras de otros en este diálogo con respecto al anterior: están en pasado (*le preguntó…, le dijo que…, le contestó…*).

A continuación, los alumnos leerán los diálogos entre Mario y Luis y entre Luis y Sandy, en los que, de nuevo, presentamos el estilo directo e indirecto.

Por último, contestarán a las preguntas de comprensión sobre estos diálogos.

Sugerencia

Podemos plantear en la clase el tema del cotilleo, del interés por conocer aspectos de la vida ajena; preguntaremos a los alumnos si creen que todos somos realmente un poco cotillas, qué piensan sobre los programas del corazón que inundan todos los canales de televisión en España, si es así en su país también…

Será suficiente con dedicarle cinco o diez minutos para que los alumnos se relajen y entren en la siguiente sección con ánimo.

Solución

a) Rosa está muy feliz. Quiere contarle lo que le ha pasado. Le cuenta que su compañero de trabajo le ha preguntado si quiere salir con él, le ha dicho que está enamorado de ella y que le dé una oportunidad.

b) Francis le cuenta a Joaquín que un compañero de trabajo le ha pedido salir a su exnovia. Lo sabe porque se lo ha dicho Sandra, una amiga de ella. Cuando se entera, Joaquín se muestra algo celoso.

c) Mario le cuenta a Luis que vio a su jefe en un concurso de televisión y que falló casi todas las respuestas.

CONTEXTOS

B. Actividad sobre los contenidos léxico-semánticos de la unidad: expresiones con *ser* relacionadas con la personalidad. Esperamos que, por el contexto, los alumnos hayan podido deducir sin problema el significado de las expresiones *ser cotilla* y *ser celoso*. Nos aseguraremos de que es así; por ejemplo, podemos interpretar el papel de cotilla, preguntándoles algo personal, para que lo entiendan. Además, creemos que también podrán resolver las otras expresiones que se incluyen en este ejercicio con la ayuda de los dibujos. Después tendrán que relacionar cada expresión con el significado correspondiente.

Sugerencia

Saber lo que significa una expresión no quiere decir que se sepa utilizar correctamente, por eso debemos propiciar que los estudiantes las usen en un contexto adecuado y conveniente. Proponemos que, en pequeños grupos de tres o cuatro alumnos, creen un diálogo en el que incluyan una, dos… de las expresiones estudiadas. Podemos asignar a cada grupo diferentes expresiones para que haya más variedad en los diálogos. Finalmente, se escenificarán las conversaciones y entre todos se verá si se han usado bien las expresiones.

Solución

h. 1; **a.** 2; **i.** 3; **c.** 4; **g.** 5; **f.** 6; **e.** 7; **b.** 8; **d.** 9.

CONTEXTOS

3 ¡Nunca me casaré!

En esta secuencia los estudiantes tienen que leer los minidiálogos que proponemos con el fin de que vean otras muestras de estilo directo. En el diálogo 3 hemos querido exagerar la situación buscando el componente lúdico. En el minidiálogo 4 tendremos que explicarles lo que significa *no querer (ver) a alguien ni en pintura*; es recomendable ofrecerles otros ejemplos y que posteriormente ellos también usen esa expresión en contexto. Por ejemplo: *No quiero ver a ese político ni en pintura; ha subido los impuestos. Se peleó con su novio y no lo quiere ver ni en pintura*…

A continuación, el estudiante tiene que relacionar las dos partes de cada mensaje para transcribir las palabras de otro.

De nuevo, le podemos preguntar en qué tiempo está el verbo que introduce las palabras de la otra persona. Así iremos adelantando la reflexión que los alumnos tendrán que hacer en la siguiente sección.

Sugerencia

Como hicimos en el ejercicio 2A, podemos pedir que cada estudiante dé su opinión brevemente antes de continuar con el apar-

¿QUÉ TE HA DICHO?

tado siguiente. Una variante sería que contesten a la pregunta *¿Cuándo te casarás?* El profesor escribirá en la pizarra los siguientes ejemplos: *cuando me toque la lotería; cuando encuentre a alguien que me quiera; cuando las ranas críen pelo…*

OBSERVA, APRENDE Y RECUERDA

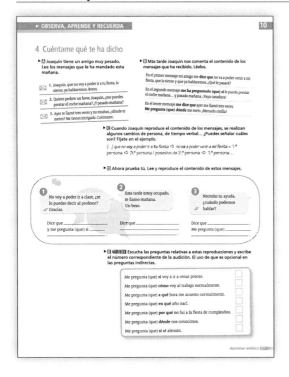

4 Cuéntame qué te ha dicho

Iniciamos una secuencia de actividades cuyo objetivo es la reflexión y la inferencia de los contenidos lingüísticos de esta unidad.

A. Empezamos con tres mensajes que ha recibido Joaquín y que los estudiantes tienen que leer. Probablemente desconozcan la expresión *¿dónde te metes?*, que aparece en el tercer mensaje. Tras resolver todas las dudas, pasamos al apartado B.

B. Ahora Joaquín le cuenta el contenido de los mensajes a su amigo Francis. Pediremos a los alumnos que se fijen en la parte destacada y que reflexionen sobre las diferencias que hay entre los tres mensajes: la primera es una frase afirmativa; la segunda es una pregunta cuya respuesta es *sí* o *no*, y la tercera es una pregunta también, pero con un adverbio interrogativo. Si se dan cuenta de esto, es suficiente para poder continuar.

C. Detallar todos los cambios que se producen al pasar de estilo directo a estilo indirecto es la siguiente tarea.

Además de crear un ambiente agradable en la clase, estaremos recordando un contenido de la unidad anterior: el empleo del subjuntivo en ciertas oraciones temporales.

Solución

1. *b;* **2.** f; **3.** c; **4.** e; **5.** a; **6.** d.

Solución

1. voy a poder → **va** a poder; **ir** a **tu** fiesta → **venir** a **mi** fiesta.

2. ¿me puedes prestar el coche mañana? → me ha preguntado (que) si **le puedo** prestar el coche mañana (pregunta directa, verbo en 2.ª persona → preguntar + si + verbo en 1.ª persona).

3. ¿Dónde **te metes**? → Me pregunta (que) dónde **me meto** (pregunta directa, verbo en 2.ª persona → preguntar + interrogativo *dónde* + verbo en 1.ª persona).

D. En esta fase el alumno tendrá que traspasar los mensajes de estilo directo a estilo indirecto. Se trata de fragmentos con las mismas características que los que le proporcionamos en los ejercicios A y B.

Solución

1. *Dice que* no va a poder ir a clase *y me pregunta (que) si* se lo puedo decir al profesor.

2. *Dice que* esta tarde está ocupado y (que) me llama / llamará mañana.

3. *Dice que* necesita mi ayuda. *Me pregunta (que)* cuándo podemos hablar.

E. Terminamos con un ejercicio de comprensión auditiva con el que pretendemos que los alumnos se fijen en las preguntas indirectas, que tendrán que numerar según el orden en el que aparezcan en la grabación.

Sugerencia

Si lo vemos necesario, podemos practicar las preguntas indirectas con la siguiente actividad. Ponemos en la pizarra: *Abuela, pregunta…* Después hacemos una pregunta, por ejemplo: *¿Cuántos años tienes?*, y un estudiante voluntario la transforma en indirecta, diciendo: *Abuela, pregunta que cuántos años tienes.* A continuación, será este alumno el que haga otra pregunta y contestará otro voluntario: *¿Has visto mi móvil? Abuela, pregunta que si has visto su móvil…*

Solución

Me pregunta (que) si voy a ir a cenar pronto: 1.

Me pregunta (que) cómo voy al trabajo normalmente: 7.

Me pregunta (que) a qué hora me acuesto normalmente: 3.

Me pregunta (que) en qué año nací: 4.

Me pregunta (que) por qué no fui a la fiesta de cumpleaños: 2.

Me pregunta (que) dónde nos conocimos: 5.

Me pregunta (que) si sé alemán: 6.

OBSERVA, APRENDE Y RECUERDA

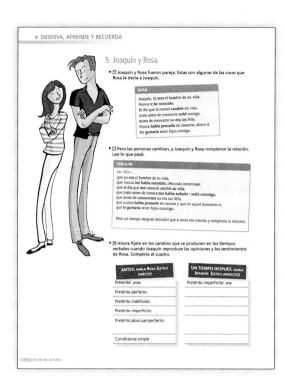

5 Joaquín y Rosa

A. En esta actividad, primero se transcriben las palabras que Rosa le dijo a Joaquín.

Destacamos el tiempo de los verbos porque el objetivo es concentrarse en el estilo indirecto en pasado y los cambios que se producen en los tiempos verbales.

Leeremos en plenaria las palabras de Rosa y les pediremos a los alumnos que digan cuál es el tiempo verbal de cada frase.

B. Un tiempo después Joaquín cuenta lo que le dijo Rosa. Los estudiantes tienen que leer lo que dice Joaquín y en este apartado solo pretendemos que se den cuenta por ellos mismos de algunos de los cambios que se producen cuando Joaquín reproduce las palabras de Rosa.

Tendrán que comparar los tiempos verbales del apartado A con los de este mismo apartado y también los pronombres personales y los posesivos, partículas todas ellas que varían al pasar de un a otro.

C. Individualmente el estudiante ha de registrar todos los cambios que afectan a los tiempos verbales provocados al pasar del estilo directo al estilo indirecto. Después se comenta la actividad y se corrige en plenaria.

Solución

ANTES: habla Rosa (estilo directo)	UN TIEMPO DESPUÉS: habla Joaquín (estilo indirecto)
Presente: eres	Pretérito imperfecto: era
Pretérito perfecto: he mentido	Pretérito pluscuamperfecto: había mentido
Pretérito indefinido: cambió; soñé	Pretérito indefinido: cambió
	Pretérito pluscuamperfecto: había soñado
	Pretérito indefinido: soñó
No cambian:	
Pretérito imperfecto: era	Pretérito imperfecto: era
Pretérito pluscuamperfecto: había pensado	Pretérito pluscuamperfecto: había pensado
Condicional simple: me gustaría	Condicional simple: le gustaría

¿QUÉ TE HA DICHO?

OBSERVA, APRENDE Y RECUERDA

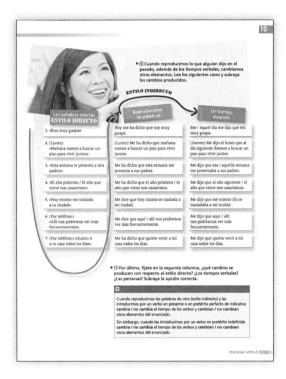

D. Para que el estudiante se fije en que, al pasar al estilo indirecto se producen otros cambios además de los tiempos verbales, tiene que leer una serie de oraciones.

De nuevo, nos parece conveniente que el alumno trabaje este apartado individualmente ya que necesita la máxima concentración para registrar todos los cambios.

Luego se leerán las frases en estilo directo e indirecto, y se comentarán las transformaciones.

Solución

1. Hoy me ha dicho que soy muy guapa. <u>Ese / Aquel</u> día me dijo que <u>era</u> muy guapa.

2. Me ha dicho que mañana vamos a buscar un piso para vivir juntos. <u>Me dijo</u> el lunes que <u>al día siguiente íbamos</u> a buscar un piso para vivir juntos.

3. Me ha dicho que esta semana me presenta a sus padres. <u>Me dijo</u> que <u>esa / aquella</u> semana <u>me presentaba</u> a sus padres.

4. Me ha dicho que el año próximo / el año que viene nos casaremos. <u>Me dijo</u> que <u>al año siguiente / el año que viene</u> nos <u>casaríamos</u>. (Importante: en este caso se podrá utilizar «al año siguiente» solo cuando ya haya pasado un año).

5. Dice que hoy mismo se traslada a mi ciudad. <u>Dijo</u> que <u>ese mismo día</u> se <u>trasladaba</u> a mi ciudad.

6. Dice que aquí / allí nos podremos ver más frecuentemente. <u>Dijo</u> que <u>aquí</u> / allí nos <u>podríamos</u> ver más frecuentemente.

7. Me ha dicho que quiere venir a mi casa todos los días. <u>Me dijo</u> que <u>quería venir</u> a <u>mi</u> casa todos los días.

E. Para terminar, el estudiante ha de percibir la diferencia entre el estilo indirecto en el mismo marco temporal en que ocurren los hechos y un tiempo después, en pasado.

Para comprobar que así ha sido, completará la regla subrayando lo que corresponda.

Sugerencia

Cada estudiante escribe en un papel una frase o una pregunta sobre el tema que quiera y pone su nombre al final. Cuando todos hayan terminado, intercambian los papeles y cada alumno reproducirá las palabras de la persona que le ha tocado: *Fran dice que... Fran pregunta si/dónde/cuándo...*

Al final, les diremos a los estudiantes que conserven los papeles porque, al día siguiente, los intercambiarán de nuevo y, después, cada estudiante reproducirá las palabras de la persona que le haya correspondido, pero ahora en pasado: *Fran dijo ayer que.... Fran preguntó si / dónde / cuándo...*

Solución

Cuando reproducimos las palabras de otro (estilo indirecto) y las introducimos con un verbo en presente o en pretérito perfecto de indicativo **no cambia** el tiempo de los verbos y **cambian** otros elementos del enunciado.

Sin embargo, cuando las introducimos con un verbo en pretérito indefinido **cambia** el tiempo de los verbos y **cambian** otros elementos del enunciado.

NOTAS

OBSERVA, APRENDE Y RECUERDA

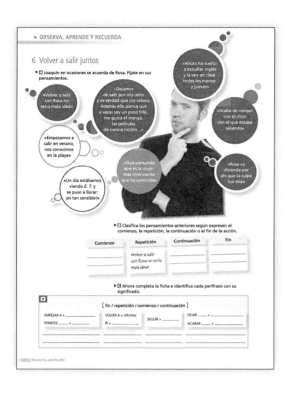

Fin: *Dejamos de salir* por mis celos y es verdad que soy celoso. Además ella piensa que a veces soy un poco friki… *Acaba de romper* con el chico con el que estaba saliendo.

C. Después de haber subrayado los verbos y de haber clasificado los pensamientos, el estudiante completará la ficha fácilmente.

De este modo, descubrirá la forma verbal que se usa en cada una de las perífrasis verbales, cómo se utiliza y cuál es su significado.

Sugerencia

Aunque en secciones posteriores vamos a practicar este contenido, nos parece necesario reforzarlo antes de seguir adelante. Para ello proponemos hacer la práctica que se explica a continuación.

El profesor escribe en la pizarra una frase que exprese comienzo, repetición, continuación o fin de la acción sin usar las perífrasis.

Ejemplo: *Hace un momento que he visto a tu amiga*. Sin decir qué idea expresa, pedirá a los estudiantes que la transformen con alguno de los verbos de la ficha. Solución: *Acabo de ver a tu amiga*.

El primero que diga la perífrasis correcta tendrá un punto.

Otro ejemplo: *Ya no estudia porque tiene que trabajar*. Solución: *Ha dejado de estudiar porque tiene que trabajar*.

Otra oración: *Va a cambiarse de casa, es la segunda vez este año*. Solución: *Vuelve a cambiarse de casa, es la segunda vez este año*.

Otra: *Todavía pienso que estudiaré otro curso de español*. Solución: *Sigo pensando que estudiaré otro curso de español*.

Otra: *Siempre que ve una película romántica, llora*. Solución: *Siempre que ve una película romántica se pone a llorar*.

Solución

Empezar a + infinitivo. Ponerse a + infinitivo. → Comienzo.

Volver a + infinitivo. Ir + gerundio. → Repetición.

Seguir + gerundio. → Continuación

Dejar de + infinitivo. Acabar de + infinitivo. → Fin.

6 Volver a salir juntos

Cambiamos de objetivo y ahora nos vamos a concentrar en las perífrasis verbales que hemos seleccionado para esta unidad.

A. Podemos hacer una primera lectura de los pensamientos de Joaquín en gran grupo.

En una segunda vuelta, ahora individualmente, sería conveniente que cada estudiante subrayara los verbos para después llamar su atención sobre el objeto de trabajo: las perífrasis verbales.

B. Por el sentido de los pensamientos, el alumno ha de clasificarlos según expresen el comienzo, la repetición, la continuación o el fin de la acción.

Solución

Comienzo: *Empezamos a salir* en verano, nos conocimos en la playa. Un día estábamos viendo *E.T.* y *se puso a llorar*: ¡es tan sensible!

Repetición: *Volver a salir* con Rosa no sería mala idea. Ahora *ha vuelto a estudiar* inglés y la veo en clase todos los martes y jueves. Rosa *va diciendo* por ahí que la culpa fue mía.

Continuación: *Sigo pensando* que es la mujer más interesante que he conocido.

¿QUÉ TE HA DICHO?

OBSERVA, APRENDE Y RECUERDA

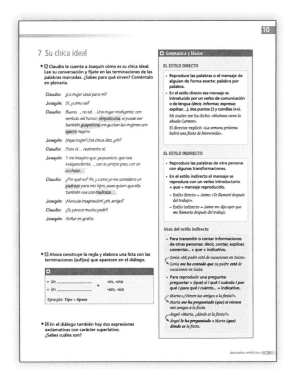

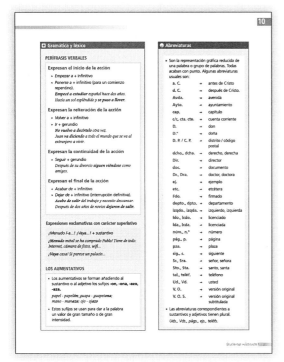

7 Su chica ideal

Con esta serie de actividades introducimos un nuevo contenido de la unidad: los aumentativos.

A. En primer lugar, los estudiantes tienen que leer cómo es la chica ideal de Claudio y explicar el significado de las palabras que están marcadas. Si vemos que están un poco despistados, los ayudaremos descomponiéndolas: *piso → pisazo; madre → madraza…*

B. Para construir la regla, si tienen dudas, podemos escribir en la pizarra más ejemplos hasta que den con la técnica. A continuación, los animaremos a que ensayen ellos con otros adjetivos y nombres.

Solución

Un **adjetivo** + -on, -ona.

Un **sustantivo** + -azo, -aza.

Simpática – simpaticona; guapa – guapetona; ojos – ojazos; coche – cochazo; padre – padrazo; madre – madraza.

C. Finalmente, han de descubrir las dos expresiones exclamativas con carácter superlativo del diálogo, lo que no debería tener mucha dificultad.

Sugerencia

El profesor puede preparar un archivo de imágenes variadas y especiales: una hamburguesa gigante, un árbol inmenso, un Ferrari, una casa maravillosa…, y pedirá a los estudiantes que vayan expresando exclamaciones con carácter superlativo conforme las vayan viendo: *¡Vaya hamburguesa! ¡Menudo árbol! ¡Qué cochazo!…*

Solución

¡Vaya mujer! ¡Menuda imaginación!

PRACTICA

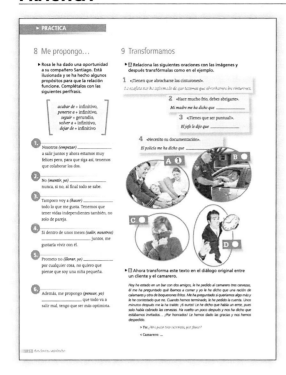

8 Me propongo…

Esta actividad está planteada para que los alumnos practiquen y consoliden el uso de las perífrasis verbales estudiadas en la unidad. En este caso, han de completar los textos con las perífrasis adecuadas.

El profesor debe insistir en que lean con atención las oraciones y que traten de comprender el significado para poder usar el verbo correcto. Así, antes de elegir una opción, deben preguntar las palabras que no comprendan.

Sugerencia

Se les puede proponer a los estudiantes que escriban algunas recomendaciones personales para la primera cita con una persona especial: puede ser una expareja, un compañero de la universidad que nos gustaba mucho, un vecino que nos enamoró… Deben intentar usar alguna perífrasis verbal de las ya estudiadas. Además, repasaremos el uso del subjuntivo estudiado en unidades anteriores. Si lo prefieren, los alumnos pueden trabajar en parejas. Les propondremos algunas entradillas, como: *Cuando quedes con alguien la primera vez… Te recomiendo que… Es bueno que… No es bueno que… No es necesario que… Está claro que… Creo que… Es importante que… Es lógico que… Me parece que… Está bien que…*

Solución

1. acabamos de empezar.

2. volveré a mentir.

3. dejar de hacer.

4. seguimos saliendo.

5. ponerme a llorar.

6. dejar de pensar.

9 Transformamos

A. En este apartado el estudiante tiene que cambiar unas oraciones a estilo indirecto pero, además, debe relacionar cada una con su imagen correspondiente, lo que nos asegura que comprende su significado. Damos solo las respuestas que completan las oraciones propuestas.

Solución

2-C. debo abrigarme.

3-D. tenía que ser puntual.

4-B. necesita mi documentación.

B. Para transformar el texto en diálogo aconsejamos guiar al estudiante de la siguiente manera: en primer lugar, que subraye los verbos y vaya haciendo los cambios correspondientes a los tiempos verbales; en segundo lugar, que se fije en los cambios posibles de otros elementos de la oración; después, que compare su versión con la de un compañero y hagan entre los dos una definitiva.

Finalmente, se leerán todos los diálogos y se elegirá el más fiel al texto.

Solución

Posible respuesta

Yo: ¿Nos puede traer tres cervezas, por favor?
Camarero: En seguida. ¿Qué van a comer?

Yo: Una ración de calamares y otra de boquerones fritos, por favor.
Camarero: ¿Quieren algo más?

Yo: De momento nada más, gracias.
(Un poco más tarde…)

Yo: ¿Me trae la cuenta, por favor?
Camarero: Aquí tiene. Son seis euros, por favor.
(Un poco más tarde…)

Yo: Perdone, hay un error, solo ha cobrado las cervezas.
(Un poco más tarde…)

Camarero: Están invitados, ¡por honrados!
Mis amigos y yo: ¡Muchas gracias! Hasta otro día.

▸ ¿QUÉ TE HA DICHO?

PRÁCTICA

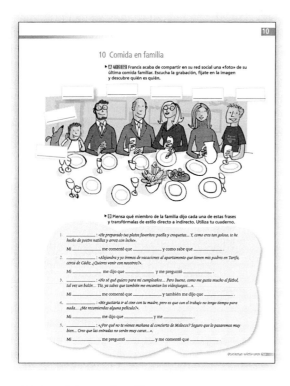

10 Comida en familia

A. Actividad de comprensión auditiva en la que, en primer lugar, el estudiante ha de identificar en la imagen a los miembros de la familia de Francis.

Solución

De izquierda a derecha: Galgo, Jorgito (mi sobrino), Jorge (mi cuñado), Juan (mi padre), Remedios (mi madre), Alejandra (mi hermana mediana) y Rafael (mi hermano pequeño).

B. Ahora ha de transformar a estilo indirecto las palabras de la familia de Francis.

Sugerencia

Podemos pedirles a los estudiantes que nos cuenten algunas de las cosas que siempre les dicen su madre, su padre, su abuela, su profesor, su jefe, su novia... Que nos hablen de su familia, de quién es el más goloso, el más pasota, el más friki, el más muermo... Que comenten sus comidas familiares: cuándo se reúnen para comer, si hay algún plato típico...

Solución

1. Remedios. Mi madre me comentó que había preparado mis platos favoritos y que, como sabe que soy tan goloso, me había hecho de postre natillas y arroz con leche.

2. Jorge. Mi cuñado me dijo que Alejandra y él irían de vacaciones al apartamento que tienen sus padres en Tarifa, en Cádiz, y me preguntó si quería ir con ellos.

3. Jorgito. Mi sobrino me comentó que no sabía qué quería para su cumpleaños, pero que, como le gustaba / gusta mucho el fútbol, tal vez un balón..., y también me dijo que ya sabía yo que le encantaban / encantan los videojuegos.

4. Juan. Mi padre me dijo que le gustaría ir al cine con mi madre, pero que con el trabajo no tenía tiempo para nada, y me preguntó si le recomendaba alguna película.

5. Alejandra. Mi hermana me preguntó (que) por qué no me iba al día siguiente al concierto de Melocos, que lo pasaríamos muy bien, y me comentó que creía que las entradas no serían muy caras.

NOTAS

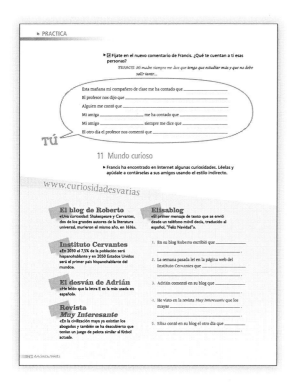

11 Mundo curioso

Con esta actividad, en la que presentamos algunas curiosidades de Internet, procuramos motivar al estudiante con un tema interesante, que les puede resultar atractivo. El objetivo último es la transformación a estilo indirecto. El trabajo se llevará a cabo de manera individual y, posteriormente, se corregirá en plenaria.

Sugerencia

Los estudiantes podrían buscar en Internet otras curiosidades y al día siguiente contarlas a sus compañeros. También les propondremos que elijan algún dato de la biografía de Cervantes que les llame la atención y lo comenten en clase. La idea es que aprendan algo más sobre el célebre escritor y no solo que es el autor de *El Quijote*. Por otra parte, también hay que tener en cuenta que son muchos los estudiantes que han oído hablar de Don Quijote, pero pocos saben quién es su autor.

Solución

1. Shakespeare y Cervantes habían muerto / murieron el mismo año, en 1616.

2. en 2030 el 7,5% de la población sería / será hispanohablante y en 2050 Estados Unidos sería / será el primer país hispanohablante del mundo.

3. la letra E es / era la más usada en español.

4. ya tenían abogados y que también se había descubierto que tenían un juego de pelota similar al fútbol moderno.

5. el primer mensaje de texto que se había enviado desde un teléfono móvil decía, traducido al español, «Feliz Navidad».

C. Para que los estudiantes completen sus comentarios, les diremos que se fijen atentamente en el tiempo en el que están escritos los verbos introductorios. Finalmente, se leerán y corregirán las diferentes versiones.

Solución

Respuesta libre.

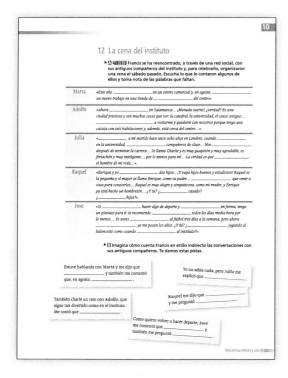

12 La cena del instituto

A. Actividad de comprensión auditiva en la que el alumno tiene que completar las palabras de los compañeros de instituto de Francis. Antes de escuchar la grabación, deberá leer las intervenciones, aunque estén incompletas. Después de la segunda escucha, se corregirán y se resolverán las dudas sobre el vocabulario. Prestaremos especial atención a todo lo que es contenido específico de esta unidad, como los aumentativos y las expresiones exclamativas con carácter superlativo.

Solución

Marta: he trabajado – empezaré – deportes.

Adolfo: vivo – Puedes venir.

Julia: Conocí – estábamos – éramos – casamos – es.

Raquel: tenemos – Tienes – Estás – Tienes.

José: quieres – mantenerte – correr – jugaba – no puedo – Sigues – íbamos.

B. Ahora el estudiante se tiene que poner en el papel de Francis y contar lo que dijeron sus compañeros durante la cena. Si es necesario,

¿QUÉ TE HA DICHO?

puede tener delante el cuadro de contenidos para hacer este ejercicio. Así podrá ir haciendo los cambios convenientes al pasar a estilo indirecto. Esperamos que más adelante pueda hacer estas transformaciones de forma más automática y autónoma.

Solución

Estuve hablando con Marta y me dijo que este año había trabajado en un centro comercial *y también me comentó que,* en agosto, empezaría un nuevo trabajo en una tienda de deportes del centro.

También charlé un rato con Adolfo, que sigue tan divertido como en el instituto. Me contó que en ese momento vivía en Salamanca, una ciudad preciosa y con muchas cosas que ver. Me dijo que podía ir a visitarlo y quedarme con ellos porque tenía una casaza con seis habitaciones y además estaba cerca del centro.

Yo no sabía nada, pero Julia me explicó que había conocido a su marido hace unos ocho años en Londres, cuando estaban en la universidad, eran compañeros de clase… Se casaron después de terminar la carrera… Me dijo que se llama Charlie, un tipo muy guapetón, muy agradable y fortachón, pero, ojo, también muy inteligente… Julia me dijo que era el hombre de su vida.

Raquel me dijo que Enrique y ella tenían dos hijos muy buenos y estudiosos. Raquel era / es la más pequeña y el mayor se llamaba / se llama Enrique, como su padre. Me dijo que tenía que ir a su casa para conocerlos. Me comentó también que Raquel era muy alegre y simpaticona, como su abuela / la madre de mi amiga Raquel, y que Enrique ya estaba hecho un hombretón, *y me preguntó* si yo estaba casado y si tenía hijos.

Como quiero volver a hacer deporte, José me comentó que, si quería mantenerme en forma, tenía un planazo para mí: me recomendaba correr todos los días media hora por lo menos… Me dijo que él antes jugaba al fútbol, pero que ya no podía porque ya le pesaban los años, *y también me preguntó* si yo seguía jugando al baloncesto como cuando íbamos al instituto…

PRACTICA

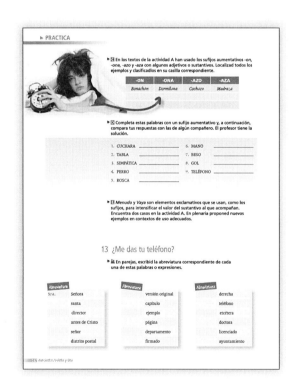

C. En esta fase de la secuencia, el alumno leerá de nuevo las intervenciones de los compañeros de Francis para localizar y clasificar los aumentativos, fijándose en los ejemplos y en si son adjetivos o sustantivos y masculinos o femeninos.

Solución

- **-on:** *bonachón,* guapetón, fortachón, hombretón.
- **-ona:** *dormilona,* simpaticona.
- **-azo:** *cochazo,* planazo.
- **-aza:** *madraza,* casaza.

D. Continuamos pidiéndole al estudiante que ensaye y construya los aumentativos de las palabras que le proponemos. Iremos aclarando los significados correspondientes, prestando especial atención a aquellos aumentativos que se han lexicalizado, como *telefonazo.*

Sugerencia

Tras la corrección, podemos dar a los estudiantes un tiempo, aproximadamente cinco minutos, para que piensen en otros aumentativos. Finalmente, comprobaremos quién es capaz de decir más palabras de este tipo.

Solución

1. cucharón; **2.** tablón; **3.** simpaticona; **4.** perrazo; **5.** roscón; **6.** manaza / manotazo; **7.** besazo; **8.** golazo; **9.** telefonazo.

E. Terminamos la serie fijándonos en las expresiones exclamativas del texto. Después serán los estudiantes los que propongan nuevos ejemplos en plenaria.

Sugerencia

Podríamos proponer a nuestros alumnos la siguiente tarea: tienen que imaginar que quieren vender algo que ya no necesitan o que no usan, pero que está en perfectas condiciones: una bicicleta, una raqueta de tenis… Para ofrecerlo a un posible comprador, deben usar algún aumentativo y alguna expresión exclamativa de las estudiadas. Otra variante sería pedirles que describan a una persona que admiren por alguna razón o a la que tengan especial cariño. Igualmente deben incluir un aumentativo o una expresión exclamativa.

Solución

¡Menuda suerte! ¡Y **vaya** hijos buenos y estudiosos!

Otros posibles ejemplos:

¡Menudo amigo! Muchas gracias por todo lo que haces por mí.

¡Vaya coche! Nunca había visto nada igual. Seguro que cuesta un ojo de la cara, ¿no?

¡Menuda película! Lo tiene todo: emoción, intriga, una buena historia, interpretaciones excelentes...

¡Vaya fiesta! Ha sido genial. Creo que todo el mundo se ha divertido muchísimo.

13 ¿Me das tu teléfono?

Acabamos esta sección con un trabajo en parejas en el que los estudiantes han de arriesgar en su elección de la abreviatura para cada una de las palabras o expresiones que les proponemos. En plenaria veremos las diferentes versiones y daremos la correcta.

Sugerencia

Cada alumno escribe un SMS o un *tuit* en el que incluya alguna abreviatura. Los demás tienen que descubrir a qué palabra o expresión corresponde.

Solución

Sta. – santa; Dir. – director; a. C. – antes de Cristo; Sr. – señor; D. P. – distrito postal; V. O. – versión original; cap. – capítulo; ej. – ejemplo; pág. / p. – página; depto. / dpto. – departamento; Fdo. – firmado; dcha. – derecha; teléf. / tel. – teléfono; etc. – etcétera; Dra. – doctora; lcdo. / ldo. – licenciado; ayto. – ayuntamiento.

EN COMUNICACIÓN

En esta sección proponemos que los estudiantes conozcan a algunos personajes famosos españoles y a otras personalidades importantes del mundo, que busquen información sobre ellos y que sean capaces de presentársela a sus compañeros.

14 He leído que son famosos por...

A. En primer lugar, el estudiante tiene que hablar sobre los personajes de las fotos. Esperamos que todos sean capaces de decir algo sobre la mayoría y que, de los que no conozcan, reciban información a través de otros compañeros.

Solución

Posible respuesta

Yo he leído que Rafael Nadal es considerado el mejor tenista del mundo en tierra batida.

Me han dicho que Estrella Morente es una cantante de flamenco muy buena.

Sé que J. K. Rowling es una escritora británica, creadora del personaje de Harry Potter.

Alguien me contó que Isabel Coixet es directora de cine y que había trabajado con Penélope Cruz.

Me han contado que Andrés Velencoso es modelo y que ha hecho campañas de publicidad para muchos diseñadores importantes.

He visto que Barack Obama ha viajado a Europa.

Me dijeron que el presidente Obama quiere impulsar el uso del español en Estados Unidos.

B. Como no tendrán muchos datos sobre estos personajes, tienen que elegir a uno de ellos y buscar en Internet más información. Creemos que es conveniente realizar esta fase en parejas para contrastar la información que anteriormente hayan buscado individualmente, si es que los alumnos no tienen la posibilidad de trabajar juntos en la clase.

Después, cada uno contará una parte al resto de sus compañeros.

Solución

Respuesta libre.

¿QUÉ TE HA DICHO?

EN COMUNICACIÓN

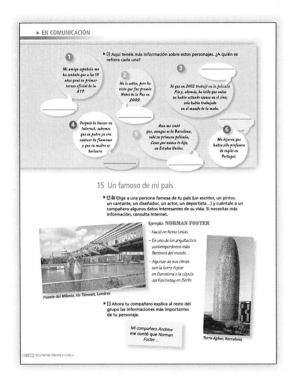

C. Termina esta serie con más información que el alumno tiene que relacionar con el personaje famoso correspondiente.

Sugerencia

Si los estudiantes están motivados con esta secuencia, les podemos plantear la posibilidad de dividir la clase en grupos y que cada uno se encargue de buscar información sobre otro personaje famoso español del ámbito que más les interese. Después cada grupo expondrá la información que ha encontrado y sus compañeros harán preguntas. El reto consiste en que el grupo sea capaz de contestarlas; por lo tanto, cuanta más información tenga sobre el personaje en cuestión, mejor.

Solución

1. Rafael Nadal.
2. Barack Obama.
3. Andrés Velencoso.
4. Estrella Morente.
5. Isabel Coixet.
6. J. K. Rowling.

15 Un famoso de mi país

A. Seguimos practicando los estilos directo e indirecto. En primer lugar, cada estudiante le habla a su pareja sobre un personaje de su país, y el compañero toma nota de toda la información. Podemos decir a los estudiantes que aporten datos no solo del presente, sino también del pasado de estos famosos para que la actividad resulte más completa.

B. Cada estudiante cuenta al resto de sus compañeros la información que tiene sobre el personaje conocido del país de su compañero.

Sugerencia

Si se eligen famosos que despierten el interés de la mayoría, los estudiantes estarán más motivados para escuchar la información.

Solución

A y B. Respuesta libre.

NOTAS

EN COMUNICACIÓN

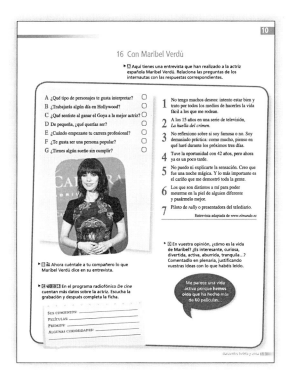

16 Con Maribel Verdú

A. El objetivo de esta actividad es dar a conocer a una de las mejores actrices del actual panorama cinematográfico español.

En primer lugar, el alumno ha de leer una entrevista, pero para ello ha de hacer el esfuerzo de relacionar cada pregunta con su respuesta correspondiente. Aconsejamos que los estudiantes lean primero todas las preguntas y, si hay algo que no entienden, lo pregunten.

A continuación, leerán todas las respuestas e, igualmente, el profesor les resolverá las dudas sobre el léxico.

Finalmente, se leerá la entrevista en plenaria.

> **Solución**
>
> A - 6; B - 4; C - 5; D - 7; E - 2; F - 3; G - 1.

B. En parejas, cada estudiante le cuenta a su compañero lo que dice Maribel Verdú en la entrevista. Para hacerlo más ameno, dividiremos el texto equitativamente, y los estudiantes intervendrán de forma alterna.

> **Solución**
>
> **Posible respuesta**
>
> Maribel Verdú dice que los personajes que le gusta interpretar son aquellos que le aportan cosas nuevas y los que son muy distintos a ella. Asegura que tuvo la oportunidad de ir a Hollywood con 42 años, pero cree que ahora ya es un poco tarde. Cuenta que la noche de los Goya fue mágica y que para ella lo más importante fue el cariño que le demostró toda la gente.
>
> También dice que de pequeña quería ser piloto de *rally* o presentadora del telediario y que comenzó su carrera profesional a los 15 años, en una serie de televisión.
>
> Sobre su popularidad, asegura que no reflexiona sobre si es famosa o no. Finalmente, confiesa que sus deseos son estar bien y hacer la vida fácil a los que la rodean.

C. Actividad de comprensión auditiva en la que el alumno ha de completar la información sobre la actriz.

> **Solución**
>
> **Sus comienzos:** Empezó como modelo de publicidad y a los quince años dejó los estudios para dedicarse por completo a la interpretación.
>
> **Películas:** Ha actuado en más de 60 películas, la mayoría de ellas españolas, así como en varias series de televisión.
>
> **Premios:** Entre ellos destacan el Premio Nacional de Cinematografía y la Medalla de Oro del Cine Español. En 2008 consiguió el Goya a la mejor actriz por *Siete mesas de billar francés*.
>
> **Algunas curiosidades:** Tiene dos hermanas gemelas y le encanta el arroz blanco con ajo. Entre sus aficiones están la lectura y escuchar música.

D. Actividad de expresión oral que consiste en que el estudiante dé su opinión sobre la vida de Maribel Verdú.

Además, con los datos que tiene, puede hacer suposiciones sobre otros aspectos de su vida: *Supongo que..., Me imagino que..., No creo que...*

> **Solución**
>
> Respuesta libre.

NOTAS

¿QUÉ TE HA DICHO?

¡extra! CONTEXTOS

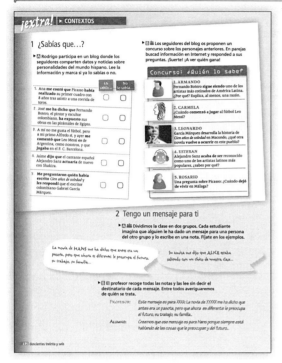

1 ¿Sabías que…?

Abrimos esta sección con información sobre otras personalidades del mundo hispano.

A. En primer lugar, los estudiantes deben leer los datos y las noticias que aparecen en un blog sobre algunos personajes famosos y decir si lo sabían o no.

Antes de empezar esta actividad, el profesor pondrá en la pizarra los nombres de las personas que aparecen en el blog y pedirá a los alumnos que hablen de lo que saben sobre ellos.

Solución

Respuesta libre.

B. En este apartado organizamos un concurso cuyo ganador será quien descubra algunos datos sobre los personajes del blog.

El objetivo de este ejercicio es que, además de practicar las perífrasis verbales y el estilo indirecto, el estudiante avance en el conocimiento de la cultura hispana.

Solución

Posible respuesta

1. Fernando Botero es uno de los artistas más cotizados de América Latina porque a lo largo de su carrera ha realizado más de 3000 pinturas y 300 esculturas, algunas de las cuales están instaladas en más de 60 museos del mundo. Sus trabajos artísticos han llevado a los críticos o especialistas a considerarlo como iconográfico; se habla del estilo de Botero o del «boterismo».

2. La familia de Messi dice que, desde muy pequeño, casi desde que dio sus primeros pasos, ya empezó su afición por el fútbol. Dejó Rosario (Argentina) cuando militaba en el Club Atlético Newell's Old Boys y se trasladó a Europa a los 13 años junto con su familia, donde el Fútbol Club Barcelona le ofreció pagar los gastos de su enfermedad hormonal y comenzar a prepararse en su escuela de fútbol.

3. *La hojarasca* también transcurre en Macondo.

4. Alejandro Sanz es reconocido como uno de los artistas latinos más populares porque ha vendido más de 22 millones de discos a lo largo de su carrera. Además es el cantante español con mayor número de premios Grammy hasta el momento.

5. A los 10 años, Picasso deja su Málaga natal y se traslada con su familia a La Coruña, donde continúa con sus estudios de arte.

2 Tengo un mensaje para ti

A. Con esta actividad sobre aspectos personales de los estudiantes, pretendemos motivar y aumentar su interés. En esta fase, cada estudiante ha de escribir un mensaje para un compañero.

El profesor se fijará en los ejemplos propuestos para **A** y para **B** puesto que son dos actividades complementarias divididas en dos fases.

Solución

Respuesta libre.

B. El profesor leerá los mensajes y los alumnos tendrán que averiguar a quién va dirigido cada uno.

Sugerencia

Una variante: los mensajes no tienen que ser totalmente ciertos, sino basados en una información concreta o simplemente en suposiciones. Así le daremos un sentido lúdico a la actividad.

Solución

Respuesta libre.

¡extra! PRACTICA

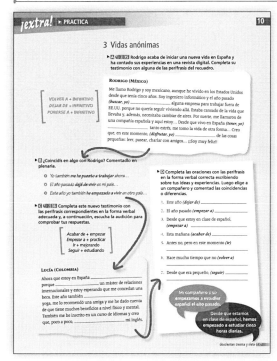

3 Vidas anónimas

En las actividades siguientes buscamos el chequeo, el refuerzo y la revisión de los contenidos fundamentales de la unidad.

A. Primero, el alumno completará el testimonio de Rodrigo con las perífrasis del cuadro. Además, le podemos pedir que imagine otros aspectos de la vida de Rodrigo en España.

Solución

me puse a buscar – he dejado de tener – vuelvo a disfrutar.

B. Ahora el estudiante ha de relacionar el testimonio de Rodrigo con su propia vida, mostrando las coincidencias y las divergencias.

Solución

Respuesta libre.

C. Actividad de comprensión auditiva para reforzar las perífrasis estudiadas.

Solución

sigo estudiando – acabo de empezar – he empezado a practicar – va mejorando.

D. Para terminar este bloque, los alumnos han de completar los enunciados con las perífrasis que les proponemos. Después comentarán los puntos en común que tengan con sus compañeros.

Sugerencia

El profesor puede escribir algunos buenos propósitos personales en la pizarra. A continuación, los estudiantes han de ir comentando si ellos también se han propuesto lo mismo en alguna ocasión de su vida. Ejemplo: *empezar a dar clases de baile, dejar de salir por la noche durante la semana, seguir practicando Pilates, no volver a mentir…* Otra variante: que cada estudiante hable sobre su vida en España comparándola con la vida que llevaba en su país. Tiene que comentar tanto los cambios como aquellos aspectos que siguen igual.

Solución

Respuesta libre.

¡EXTRA! PRACTICA

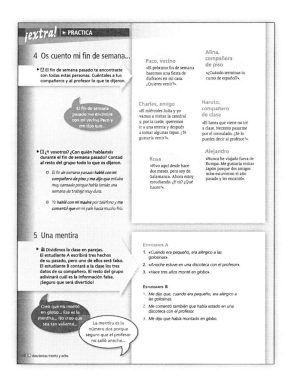

4 Os cuento mi fin de semana…

A. El estudiante tiene que reproducir las palabras de las personas con las que habló durante el fin de semana. Pensamos que en este momento de la unidad se podría hacer la actividad en gran grupo y directamente; pero, si los estudiantes todavía no se sienten muy seguros, les dejaremos unos minutos para que piensen en todos los cambios que han de hacer para pasar del estilo directo al estilo indirecto.

Solución

El fin de semana pasado me encontré con mi vecino Paco y me dijo que el fin de semana siguiente harían una fiesta de disfraces en su casa y me preguntó (que) si quería ir.

Alina, mi compañera de piso, me preguntó (que) cuándo terminaba mi curso de español.

Mi amigo Charles me comentó que el miércoles Julia y él irían a visitar la catedral y que, por la tarde, querían ir a una tetería y después a tomar algunas tapas. Me preguntó también (que) si me gustaría ir.

Haruto, mi compañero de clase, me dijo que el lunes no vendría a clase porque necesitaba ir al consulado y me preguntó (que) si se lo podía decir a nuestro profesor.

¿QUÉ TE HA DICHO?

Rosa me explicó que vivía ahí / allí desde hacía dos meses, pero que era de Salamanca y que en ese momento / ahora estaba estudiando en nuestra ciudad... También me preguntó (que) qué hacía yo.

Alejandro me contó que nunca había viajado fuera de Europa y que le gustaría visitar Japón porque dos amigos suyos habían estado allí el año anterior y les había encantado.

B. En este caso, el estudiante sí debe intentar contar lo que le dijeron las personas con las que habló durante el fin de semana directamente, sin preparación previa.

Solución

Respuesta libre.

5 Una mentira

Terminamos esta serie con una actividad lúdica en la que el grupo ha de descubrir la información falsa sobre cada estudiante. Debemos pedirles a los alumnos que la mentira que escriban sea sutil, no muy evidente, para que sus compañeros tengan cierta dificultad a la hora de descubrirla.

Solución

Respuesta libre.

¡extra! EN COMUNICACIÓN

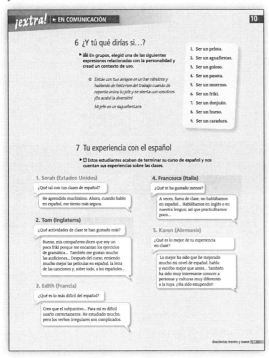

En esta sección nos ocuparemos principalmente de hacer una revisión de dos de los contenidos fundamentales de esta unidad: el uso de las perífrasis y el léxico de las descripciones.

6 ¿Y tú qué dirías si...?

El objetivo de esta actividad es repasar el léxico de las expresiones construidas con *ser* que están relacionadas con la personalidad. Los estudiantes tienen que explicar el significado de cada una de ellas en contextos de uso.

Sugerencia

El profesor puede ir presentando situaciones diferentes, y los estudiantes tienen que relacionarlas con las expresiones adecuadas. Gana el que primero la diga.

Ejemplo: *Elvira **dejó de salir** con Rodrigo porque no le gustaba el cine, no quería salir los fines de semana, prefería estar en casa viendo la televisión, pero solo quería ver documentales, el cine no le interesaba.* Solución: *Rodrigo era un **muermo**.*

Solución

Respuesta libre.

7 Tu experiencia con el español

Terminamos el curso y con esta actividad queremos que el estudiante valore cómo ha sido su proceso de enseñanza-aprendizaje del español.

A. Primero, tiene que leer las opiniones que han vertido distintos estudiantes sobre las clases de español: lo que les ha gustado más o les ha gustado menos, qué ha sido más difícil, qué les ha parecido más divertido, cómo ha mejorado su español...

Leeremos en plenaria estas opiniones y cada alumno irá haciendo sus propias consideraciones sobre los aspectos que se van planteando.

¡EXTRA! EN COMUNICACIÓN

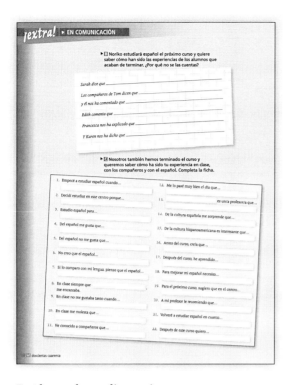

B. Ahora el estudiante tiene que contar a otra persona cómo fueron las experiencias de los estudiantes del ejercicio anterior.

Solución

Posible respuesta

Sarah dice que ha aprendido muchísimo y que ahora, cuando habla español, se siente más segura.

Los compañeros de Tom dicen que es un poco friki porque le encantan los ejercicios de gramática, *y él nos ha comentado que* le gustan mucho las audiciones y que, después del curso, entiende mucho mejor las películas en español, las letras de las canciones y, sobre todo, a los españoles.

Edith comenta que lo más difícil para ella es usar el subjuntivo correctamente. Nos explica que ha estudiado mucho, pero que los verbos irregulares son muy complicados.

Francesca nos ha explicado que lo que menos le ha gustado es que, a veces, fuera de clase hablaban en inglés o en su lengua, y así practicaban menos.

Y Karen nos ha dicho que su nivel de español ha mejorado mucho porque ahora habla y escribe mejor. Nos ha contado que ha sido muy interesante conocer a personas y culturas diferentes a la suya y que ha sido estupendo.

C. Actividad de repaso de los usos de los modos indicativo y subjuntivo estudiados en este nivel. El estudiante tendrá que expresar opiniones, valorar hechos, expresar sentimiento, finalidad, causa, deseo… Para completar la ficha sobre sus experiencias en clase, ha de activar una buena parte de los contenidos aprendidos en el curso.

El profesor podrá comprobar el grado de asimilación y de empleo en su comunicación cotidiana.

Solución

Respuesta libre.

¡EXTRA! EN COMUNICACIÓN

D. Por último, deseamos que el estudiante valore *Método 3*, esto ayudará al profesor a conocer mejor el material, desde la perspectiva del alumno, y a sacarle un mayor partido en los cursos sucesivos. Esperamos que la valoración general sea positiva, que el desarrollo de la clase haya sido ameno y distendido gracias a este manual y, por supuesto, que con *Método 3* el aprendizaje haya sido efectivo y eficaz para el alumno.

ciento ochenta y cinco 185

Transcripciones

TRANSCRIPCIONES

UNIDAD 1
Ejercicio 4 A

1. Hemos estado este fin de semana en _____ . Hemos visto la Alhambra, el barrio del Albaicín y el Generalife. Ha sido muy divertido.

2. Hace dos años fuimos a _____ , la gran manzana. Hicimos muchísimas fotos y vimos la Estatua de la libertad.

3. El fin de semana pasado viajamos a _____ . Fue muy romántico. Comimos muy bien y, por supuesto, visitamos el museo del Louvre.

4. Este sábado nos hemos marchado a _____ para ver una exposición en el museo del Prado. ¿Y vosotros? ¿Habéis hecho algo?

5. El viernes pasado Julia y yo alquilamos un coche y pasamos cuatro días en _____ . Paseamos por el parque Güell, tomamos el sol en la playa de la Barceloneta y compramos un recuerdo de la Sagrada Familia.

Ejercicio 5 C

1. **Ángel:** El verano pasado toqué la guitarra con el grupo de mi amigo Pablo. El concierto se celebró en un campo de fútbol y había más de cien personas. ¡Fue increíble!

2. **Mirta:** Nací en Washington, pero cuando tenía diez años, mis padres, mis hermanos y yo nos trasladamos a Bogotá. Soy bilingüe: hablo inglés y español.

3. **Ángel:** No juego al fútbol, prefiero algo más tranquilo. Tampoco me gusta mucho la televisión, no sigo ningún programa ni ninguna serie... Si tengo tiempo libre, leo.

4. **Ángel:** De vez en cuando sueño que doy la vuelta al mundo en globo...Casi siempre recuerdo mis sueños.

5. **Mirta:** No sé dónde tengo la cabeza. Nunca me acuerdo de dónde pongo el móvil, el bolso... Cuando me levanto, me molesta mucho si la gente me habla. Primero pongo la cafetera y tomo café, me ducho y, después, ya puedo escucharte.

6. **Ángel:** Pienso que el año próximo iré a otro país de Europa, voy a buscar un trabajo diferente al mío. El próximo mes voy a tener que hacer un curso de inglés... ¡Lo necesito!

7. **Mirta:** Ahora soy joven y no tengo mucho dinero, pero ahorraré y dentro de seis o siete años podré tener la casa de mis sueños... Será una casa con vistas al mar.

8. **Los dos:** Anteayer me pasé todo la tarde ordenando la casa. Estaba hecha un desastre... La semana que viene tendremos que limpiar otra vez porque van a venir mis padres.

Ejercicio 11 A

1. **Rosario:** Mi novio y yo estuvimos el año pasado en España, en Málaga... Compré una botellita de vino dulce para mi padre. Es una bebida muy típica de allá y a mi viejo le encanta. ¡Está riquísimo!

2. **Mario:** Hace tres años pasé el día de Navidad en Madrid... Fue una experiencia fantástica. Visité el museo del Prado y hasta tuve tiempo de comprar algo para mi hermano. Su cumpleaños es el día tres de enero así que le regalé una camiseta del Real Madrid... Es su equipo de fútbol favorito.

3. **Lucía:** Hemos ido de luna de miel a México. Solo hemos podido visitar la capital. Es un lugar muy distinto a todos los países que he conocido... La comida, la gente, la forma de vida... Estoy enamorada de ese país. ¡Ah! Y, por supuesto, le he comprado un gran sombrero mexicano a mi marido. Se lo puso y... bueno, ya os podéis imaginar... ¡Estaba monísimo!

¡Extra! En comunicación
Ejercicio 4 B

Curra: Estaba en Londres de vacaciones con unos amigos. Una noche salí sola porque mis amigos estaban muy cansados y se quedaron en el hotel. Cogí el metro para ir a una zona de mucho ambiente y estuve en un local de jazz. Cuando salí me apetecía pasear y recorrer el barrio. Después de un rato no encontraba ninguna estación de metro, era muy tarde y estaba perdida y sola. ¡Qué miedo pasé!

Josefina: Lo peor que te puede pasar es que la compañía te pierda las maletas. A mí me pasó una vez. Primero me dijeron: «Dentro de tres horas la tendrá en su hotel». Estuve esperando toda la tarde en mi habitación. No vino nadie, ni me llamaron por teléfono... ¡nada! ¿Qué hice? Tuve que ir a comprar todo lo que necesitaba. Todavía no he recibido ningún dinero de la compañía.

Ángel: Esta es la peor experiencia que he tenido en mi vida. Me ocurrió hace tres años, cuando volvía de las vacaciones de los Alpes a Madrid. Llevábamos unos diez minutos de vuelo más o menos y de pronto notamos que el avión se movía más de lo normal, entonces nos comunicaron que el avión tenía poco combustible y que íbamos a aterrizar de nuevo. Increíble, pero cierto.

Lucas: Quería un viaje económico y siempre es más barato por Internet: primero busqué el vuelo, lo pagué y me mandaron el billete electrónico por correo, ¡rápido y cómodo! Después, también por Internet y aprovechando una oferta, hice una reserva por diez días en un hotel bueno y céntrico. Llegué a las doce de la noche y cuando estaba en la recepción del hotel, ¡sorpresa! ¡No había ninguna reserva a mi nombre!... ¡Y ninguna habitación libre, claro!

UNIDAD 2
Ejercicio 2 A
Lunes

Malena, soy Pedro. Te llamo para invitarte a la fiesta de inauguración de mi bar Más Que Copas. Es a las ocho de la tarde en la Plaza del Teatro... No me faltes.

Martes

Malena, soy tu padre... Hija mía, siempre tienes el móvil apagado o fuera de cobertura. Bueno, ya sabes que hemos quedado para cenar el martes a las nueve.

Miércoles

Hola, guapa, soy Tomás. Te recuerdo que esta noche, a las diez, hemos quedado para ir al cine... Tú invitas, te acuerdas, ¿no?

Jueves

Malena, te llamaba para recordarte que esta tarde a las cinco tenemos cita para el masaje con chocolate que queríamos darnos en el salón de belleza Adonis.

Viernes

Malena, ya tengo las entradas para el concierto de Marc Anthony. Es esta noche a las once. No lo olvides.

Ejercicio 9 C

Ginebra, jamón, guerra, geranio, alguien, jefe, jirafa, rojo, genial, guapa, imaginación, guitarra, algo, alguna, gente, joven, girasol, jueves, guantes.

Ejercicio 11 B
Maite

Pues yo, el verano pasado, pasé una vergüenza tremenda... Llegamos al aeropuerto, facturamos las maletas... Todo perfecto... Pusimos el equipaje de mano en el escáner de la policía y cuando yo estaba pasando por el detector de metales empezó a sonar ese horrible piiiiiiiiiiiii... Así que me quité la chaqueta que tenía los botones metálicos y, nada, aquello seguía sonando... Después pensé que, a lo mejor, era el cinturón pero, nada... Total que...

Juan

Eso no es nada, Maite. Yo sí que pasé vergüenza la otra noche. Pues resulta que Rocío, Salva y yo estábamos tomando un cafelito en el bar de Jaime y decidí invitarlos porque era mi cumpleaños... Cuando fui a pagar, me di cuenta de que se me había olvidado la cartera en casa... No tenía ni un euro... Me puse rojo como un tomate y entonces...

¡Extra! Contextos
Ejercicio 1 A

MARÍA: Nunca voy a olvidar el día que preparamos la fiesta sorpresa para el cumpleaños de Roberto.

AMELIA: ¿Os acordáis del carnaval del año pasado? Nos disfrazamos de piratas. ¡Fue divertidísimo!

CARLA: Yo me reí mucho en la excursión que hicimos a Tarifa. La playa era muy bonita, había muchísima gente guapa y comimos un pescadito riquísimo.

RODOLFO: Yo siempre me acuerdo de la Nochevieja de hace cuatro años. Nos reunimos todos los amigos y celebramos la salida del año en la playa, nos tomamos las uvas y bailamos hasta la madrugada.

RAÚL: ¿Recordáis cuando fuimos al musical *Hoy no me puedo levantar*? Lo pasamos de miedo. Salimos con ganas de bailar, ¿verdad? Fue un espectáculo increíble.

UNIDAD 3
Ejercicio 4 B

En mi país, los políticos tendrían que ser sinceros, gobernarían todos los partidos porque siempre habría acuerdo y debería haber tantas mujeres como hombres en el gobierno. Todo el mundo trabajaría y tendría la responsabilidad de hacer un trabajo bien hecho. La gente estaría contenta, disfrutaría de los servicios sociales y no se pondría nunca de mal humor. No habría paro y subiría la productividad. Como consecuencia de esto último, los trabajadores disfrutarían de tres meses de vacaciones al año. La delincuencia bajaría también y nadie robaría porque tendría todo lo necesario para vivir. Las relaciones interpersonales avanzarían de forma muy positiva porque la gente se comportaría de forma menos egoísta, más abierta y solidaria. Se permitiría a los inmigrantes vivir y trabajar en el país y no habría discriminación en ningún sentido. Parece utópico, pero creo que sería posible. Todos seríamos un poquito más felices.

Ejercicio 8 A

Chica: Alberto, ¿te irías a vivir con ella?

Chico: Todavía es pronto para poder decirlo, no nos conocemos mucho.

Chica: Pero, por ejemplo, ¿tú te irías a un país extranjero a vivir con ella?

Chico: Claro, ¿por qué no?

Chica: Aquí tienes tu vida, ¿lo dejarías todo: a tu familia, a tus amigos...?

Chico: Vivir fuera no quiere decir no poder venir a España nunca más.

Chica: No, pero no es lo mismo. Sería una cultura diferente.

Chico: Sería interesante conocer otra cultura. La mía ya la tengo. Crecería como persona.

Chica: ¿Crees que te adaptarías bien?

Chico: Hombre... Al principio sería difícil, es normal, pero yo me adapto rápido a lo nuevo.

Chica: La verdad, a mí no me gustaría perderte como amigo.

Chico: No te preocupes, hombre, seguiríamos siendo amigos. Oye, y tú, ¿qué harías por amor?

Ejercicio 10 A

> Buenas noches a todos y bienvenidos a una nueva edición de su programa favorito de las madrugadas, *Problemas, problemas*... Como cada noche, estamos dispuestos a recibir sus llamadas y, si es posible, a ayudarles, darles consejos, recomendaciones, etcétera. Si ustedes quieren aconsejar o echar una mano a los oyentes, pueden hacerlo a través del teléfono y de nuestra página web: www.problemas-problemas.es. Me dicen mis compañeros que ya podemos recibir a un primer oyente... Buenas madrugadas, ¿con quién hablo?

< Hola, soy Julia...

> Dígame, Julia, ¿cuál es su problema?

< Bueno, no es un problema grave, pero es que... Es que estoy pensando en marcharme a otro país. Estoy un poco cansada de la misma rutina, de hacer siempre lo mismo y empiezo a aburrirme. Trabajo como conductora de autobús y, por un lado, me gusta lo que hago, pero, por otro lado, siempre veo las mismas caras, los mismos edificios, a los mismos compañeros... Necesito conocer a gente nueva, tener experiencias diferentes y, no sé, cambiar de aires... ¡¡¡Demasiado tiempo sentada al volante de un autobús!!! ¿Qué me aconsejan?

> Hola a todos, buenas noches... Mi nombre es Gloria y soy de Badajoz. Os llamaba porque quería ver si alguien ha pasado por alguna situación parecida a la mía. Desde hace algunos meses, me he dado cuenta de que me estoy enamorando de un compañero de trabajo, Paco. Llevo unos quince años trabajando con él y, hasta ahora, solo éramos compañeros de oficina y nada más. A veces íbamos a una fiesta con los demás, a tomar una copa después del trabajo y ya está... Pero, últimamente, intento hablar más con él, vamos a desayunar juntos, quedamos después del trabajo... Todavía no le he dicho nada porque no sé muy bien qué hacer... y no querría meter la pata.

> Buenas noches, me llamo Agustín, soy agricultor y vivo en un pequeño pueblo de Lugo, en Galicia. Me encanta la vida tranquila de aquí, pero no tengo muchas oportunidades para conocer a gente nueva. Aquí todos nos conocemos y somos como una gran familia... Bueno, como una pequeña familia porque solo somos veinte vecinos... ¿Qué puedo hacer para tener más amigos, para conocer a otras personas...? Me gustaría hablar con gente de otros lugares, otras culturas... Así no me sentiría tan solo.

> Me llamo Ricardo y tengo treinta años... Quería pedir consejo a todos los oyentes para ver si alguien puede echarme una mano con mi problema... Necesito mejorar mi nivel de inglés urgentemente, sobre todo para mi trabajo... He estudiado durante mucho tiempo, y creo que no tengo muchos problemas con la gramática; pero hablar es otra cosa... Cuan-

...do tengo que hablar en inglés, empiezo a ponerme rojo como un tomate, sudo y no tengo confianza en mí mismo... ¿Qué hago?

¡Extra! Contextos
Ejercicio 1 A

1. > Buenos días, ¿qué les apetecería tomar de primero?
   < Yo tomaría una ensalada... ¿Y tú, Jana?
   > No sé... ¿Podría esperar unos minutitos, por favor? Así lo pienso un poquito más.

2. > Mis padres han venido a verme. Mi madre hace una paella riquísima. ¿Querrías venir conmigo el domingo que viene a comer con mis padres?
   < ¿Con tus padres? Es que creo que todavía es muy pronto para conocerlos..., ¿no te parece?

3. > Tengo un dolor de cabeza terrible... Además, creo que tengo fiebre.
   < Quizás solo es un resfriado, pero puede ser también una gripe... Deberías ir al médico.

4. > ¿Y Pablo? ¿Por qué no vino ayer con nosotros? Yo lo llamé, pero no me cogió el teléfono...
   < No tengo ni idea, pero seguramente tendría mucho trabajo en la oficina o estaría en alguna reunión importante y por eso no contestó.

5. > Cariño, ¿qué hacemos para celebrar nuestro aniversario? ¿Se te ocurre algo? Yo tengo la idea perfecta: un viaje romántico a París...
   < ¿Un viaje romántico? Eso es lo que hace todo el mundo... Tendría que ser algo distinto, una experiencia emocionante. A mí me encantaría volar en globo y pasar un fin de semana en una casa rural.

UNIDAD 4
Ejercicio 1 B

1. **Eugenia:** No sé qué hacer este sábado... No me apetece mucho ir a casa de Tomás; ya sé que es su cumpleaños... Pero es que va a ir Marta y no nos llevamos muy bien...
   José: ¿Y si vamos al cine?
   Eugenia: ¿Al cine? ¿Qué ponen?
   José: La última peli del agente 007. Javier Bardem interpreta al malo.
   Eugenia: Ya, pero no me gusta ese tipo de películas. Es que siempre hacemos lo mismo, prefiero ir a bailar, tomar una copa y escuchar buena música. ¿Qué dices?

2. **Carmen:** Pues es una historia de misterio... Se desarrolla entre los años cuarenta y cincuenta y el protagonista es un chico joven que se llama Daniel y vive en Barcelona. Un día encuentra un libro maldito que cambia el destino de su vida... Bueno, no te cuento más. Tienes que comprártelo. Es una historia fantástica.
   Carlos: ¿Y cómo dices que se llama?
   Carmen: *La sombra del viento*.
   Carlos: Muchas gracias por tu recomendación. Mañana mismo, después del trabajo, iré a ver si lo tienen.

3. **Miguel:** ¿Y si vamos el sábado a jugar al tenis con María y Antonio?
   Blanca: El sábado no puedo... Ya te dije que tengo natación todos los sábados.
   Miguel: Es verdad... Qué cabeza tengo, no me acordaba. ¿Y el domingo?

Ejercicio 2 B
Fernando: Cariño, ¿qué te preparo hoy para almorzar? ¿Qué te apetece?
Luisa: Pues, déjame pensar... Algo ligerito... Un pescadito a la plancha con verduras...
Fernando: ¡Vaya! ¡Qué mala suerte! No he ido al mercado esta mañana y no tenemos pescado...
Luisa: ¿Y si salimos a comer fuera? Voy a buscar en Internet..., a ver si encuentro un restaurante de comida casera, con pescado bueno y... ¡baratito!
Fernando: También podemos ir a un vegetariano. Seguro que la comida es más sana y no tan pesada.
Luisa: No, no... Un vegetariano es demasiado... sano para mí.
Fernando: ¡Venga, mujer! ¡Vamos! Seguro que la comida es excelente.
Luisa: Ya, Fernando, pero no hay pescado... Y hoy me apetece pescado, anda, vamos a por el pescadito.

Ejercicio 3 A
Hola, chicos... ¿Qué tal? Yo creo que sí llevo una vida sana. Normalmente trabajo mucho, unas diez horas más o menos. El trabajo es salud. Eso dicen, ¿no? Soy programador informático y, casi todo el tiempo, estoy sentado delante del ordenador. ¡Es mi vida! Sí, una vida sedentaria, ya lo sé, pero ¡no puedo hacer nada! Eso sí, los deportes me encantan. Todos los domingos mis amigos y yo quedamos para ver el partido de fútbol en la tele. Hacemos mucho ejercicio porque tenemos que darnos prisa para preparar nuestra cervecita, patatitas fritas, aceitunas... La cerveza es mi bebida favorita, pero también bebo agua, si tengo sed. Casi todas las tardes juego a la videoconsola; es que, después del trabajo, estoy muy nervioso y necesito relajarme... Querría ir al gimnasio, lo que pasa es que es muy caro y, además, no tengo mucho tiempo libre. Le he prometido a mi novia que iré el mes que viene. Ahora viene el verano y quiero estar más delgadito...

Ejercicio 3 D
LLEVAR: Tú lleva, usted lleve, vosotros / vosotras llevad, ustedes lleven.
COMER: Tú come, usted coma, vosotros / vosotras comed, ustedes coman.
VIVIR: Tú vive, usted viva, vosotros / vosotras vivid, ustedes vivan.

Ejercicio 5 A

1. Luisa, por favor, llámame. Necesito hablar contigo urgentemente. He olvidado el carné de conducir en casa.

2. Soy yo otra vez. No pongas el lavavajillas; no funciona. Creo que hay una avería en una tubería. Avisa al fontanero para que venga mañana por la mañana. Avísalo, por favor. No lo olvides. Un beso.

3. Hola, cariño... Si llegas a casa antes que yo, apaga el ordenador. Es que esta mañana tenía mucha prisa y se me ha olvidado. Apágalo, por favor. Hasta luego.

4. Luisa, mándame un mensaje al móvil con el teléfono de Alberto... ¡Ah! Y si llama a casa, no le digas nada de lo de la cena del sábado. Todavía no sabemos dónde vamos a ir... No se lo digas hasta que lo decidamos. Gracias, nos vemos luego.

Ejercicio 8 B

1. Las palabras agudas son aquellas en las que el acento recae en la última sílaba. Ejemplo: *pared*.

2. En las palabras llanas el acento recae en la penúltima sílaba. Ejemplo: *maleta*.

3. En las esdrújulas el acento recae en la antepenúltima sílaba. Ejemplo: *pájaro*.
4. En las sobreesdrújulas el acento recae en cualquier sílaba anterior a la antepenúltima. Ejemplo: *explícaselo*.

Ejercicio 8 F

Tómbola, yogur, látigo, fútbol, helicóptero, pídeselo, fajín, alto, jabalí, tempestad, chófer, riñón, ángel, alcánzamelo, pillar, caramelo, balancín, betún, azúcar, regaliz, reacción.

Ejercicio 10 B

Fernando: El café de Colombia es el mejor del mundo, ¿no?

Liliana: Bueno, eso dicen… Es nuestra bebida nacional, especialmente, como decimos allá, en la forma del tinto… O sea, una tacita de cafesito fuerte.

Fernando: Mmm, ¡qué rico! ¿Y no tomáis chocolate?

Liliana: Sí, sí, claro, cómo no… En Bogotá se bebe el chocolate santafereño, servido con queso y pan. Normalmente, partimos el queso en trozos y lo introducimos en el chocolate. Seguro que les gusta cuando vengan a visitarme.

Fernando: ¿Cuál es el plato típico de la gastronomía colombiana?

Liliana: Se llama ajiaco y es una sopa de papas con maíz y pollo… Mmm. Ahora con tanto hablar de comida, estoy hambrienta…

Fernando: ¿Y el jugo? ¿Qué es?

Liliana: Es como su zumo. Está hecho con agua y fruta. También tenemos una bebida hecha con leche y fruta que se llama sorbete. En nuestra gastronomía también son ingredientes básicos la carne de ternera o de cerdo, las papas, o patatas como dicen acá, el arroz y los fríjoles.

Fernando: ¿Qué son los frijoles?

Liliana: Ustedes los llaman alubias o judías. En toda Latinoamérica son muy usados como plato principal, en sopas, en ensaladas… Si toman fríjoles, no tendrán problemas de diabetes. Estoy segura.

Fernando: ¿Y cuál es la comida del día más importante?

Liliana: El almuerzo, sí, sí, el almuerzo… Aunque en realidad, por la mañana desayunamos dos veces: el desayuno y las medias nueves; un segundo desayuno o un pequeño aperitivo a media mañana.

Fernando: Oye, Liliana, ¿en Colombia se celebran muchas comidas familiares?

Liliana: Sí, claro. Por ejemplo, preparamos un almuerzo especial con alimentos bien ricos para el Día del Padre o de la Madre… Hacemos una torta para los cumpleaños; bueno, claro que acostumbramos a reunirnos para comer, como ustedes en España.

Ejercicio 11 A

1. ¡Vaya! Otra vez llego tarde al trabajo… He perdido el autobús por los pelos…
2. ¡Anda! Mami, ¿qué haces aquí…? No te esperaba hasta el sábado.
3. Venga, Fernando, vamos… Es que no me apetece ir sola al dentista. Ya sabes que me da mucho miedo…
4. ¡Mira que eres desordenado…! ¿Qué has hecho esta tarde en el salón? ¡Qué desastre!

¡Extra! En comunicación
Ejercicio 4 B

Entrevistadora: Doctor Gómez, bienvenido a nuestro programa Saber Comer y, sobre todo, muchas gracias por estar aquí esta tarde.

Doctor Gómez: Muchas gracias… Es un placer estar con usted y con todos los oyentes del programa. Cuidar nuestra salud es fundamental para vivir más y mejor.

Entrevistadora: Doctor, ¿hay alimentos especialmente beneficiosos para la salud?

Doctor Gómez: Por supuesto que los hay. El ajo, por ejemplo, que es tan importante en las cocinas de España y América Latina, es un alimento casi mágico.

Entrevistadora: ¿Por qué lo dice usted…? ¿Por los vampiros?

Doctor Gómez: Jajajaja. No, no, mujer… Es que un diente de ajo al día le limpiará el aparato digestivo, le ayudará para la prevención de gripes y resfriados y, además, le dará mucha energía. Si usted come ajos habitualmente, combatirá la bajada de defensas.

Entrevistadora: Hay estudios que hablan también de los beneficios del aceite de oliva, ¿son fiables?

Doctor Gómez: Claro, claro… El aceite de oliva es un seguro de vida. Contiene antioxidantes y el llamado colesterol «bueno». También tiene grasas de origen vegetal que son sanas para nuestro organismo.

Entrevistadora: Entonces…, recomienda una tostadita de pan con aceite y ajo, ¿no?

Doctor Gómez: Sí y, no lo olvide, también tomate. El tomate previene los infartos al corazón porque reduce el colesterol. Hay que comérselo entero, con la piel, si es posible, o en zumo.

Entrevistadora: Algunos estudios científicos también recomiendan el consumo moderado de cerveza, ¿qué opina?

Doctor Gómez: El consumo moderado está bien… Es decir, una caña al día y, si es de cerveza sin alcohol, mejor. La cerveza contiene cebada y la cebada nos aporta muchas vitaminas. En concreto, la cerveza es muy rica en vitaminas del grupo B. También aporta hidratos de carbono y, sobre todo, ácido fólico, muy bueno para prevenir la anemia.

Entrevistadora: ¡Qué bien! ¡No lo sabía! Bueno, como ya hemos terminado, creo que ahora es el momento de tomarse una cañita… ¿Le apetece?

Doctor Gómez: Por supuesto… Y, si acepta mi invitación, yo pago.

UNIDAD 5
Ejercicio 1 A

Luz Marina: Soy colombiana y hace un año que terminé mis estudios de Derecho. Quiero trabajar como abogada en mi país, pero por ahora no es posible, así que he venido a España para buscar un trabajo.

Por supuesto que me gustaría volver a mi país lo más pronto posible, pues no quiero que mis padres sufran por mí. Yo los echo mucho de menos y a mis amigos también. En el futuro deseo tener mi propio despacho jurídico. He visto los anuncios que hay en el periódico: esta tarde tengo una entrevista. Espero que no haya muchos candidatos. Quiero ese trabajo para mí.

Sol: La verdad es que a mí lo que realmente me gusta es pasarme el día con el ordenador: chateo, busco información, me comunico en las redes sociales… Tengo una cuenta en Facebook y en Twitter y estoy casi todo el día conectada. He terminado el instituto este año y, la verdad, no sé qué hacer: si seguir estudiando o buscar un trabajo. A mi generación la llaman *nini*, porque dicen que no queremos *ni* estudiar *ni* trabajar. Yo no lo creo, pero mis padres esperan que me decida pronto… Reconozco que no quiero que nadie me diga lo que tengo que hacer. ¡Es mi vida!

Lucas: Yo soy autónomo, no tengo un sueldo fijo, claro, pero más o menos llego a fin de mes. Tengo una heladería. ¿Que si estoy contento con mi trabajo? No me quejo y, sobre todo, es que mi familia siempre se ha dedicado a esto. Yo heredé el negocio de mi padre y mi padre de mi abuelo. Son tres generaciones ya. Pero el negocio desaparecerá conmigo, porque mi hijo, Francis, dice que quiere que le paguen un sueldo todos los meses y no tener que preocuparse de nada más.

Linda: En Venezuela también hay problemas de paro. Yo, afortunadamente, tengo trabajo. Mi jefe no quiere que trabaje tanto, es raro, ¿no? ¡Él es *chévere!* Me gusta mi trabajo y por ahora no necesito cambiar. Algunos compañeros piensan que es una actividad monótona, pero yo creo que todo puede ser aburrido con el tiempo. Yo espero conservar este trabajo muchos años. Gano lo suficiente para vivir y también para permitirme algunos caprichos: viajar, libros, videos, discos…

Juan José: ¡Espero que me toque la lotería de Navidad este año! Te pasas la vida trabajando y… ¿para qué? La vida es mucho más que trabajar. Y ahora han aumentado la edad de jubilación: ¡67 años! ¡Con esa edad yo esperaba estar en las Bahamas! Soy funcionario desde hace diez años pero este trabajo no me interesa ni me atrae mucho. Me gustaría tener mi propio negocio, pero no tengo posibilidades ya que los bancos no me dan el préstamo que necesito. Me esfuerzo por estar bien en mi trabajo, pero al final del día no me siento satisfecho. Mi mujer no quiere que lo deje, porque la situación no está para dejar empleos, es verdad… Pero no me satisface mi trabajo.

Alejandro: Yo creo que la situación laboral no es buena en casi ningún país, ¿verdad? Estoy en paro y vivo con mis padres. Soy ingeniero y me gustaría trabajar en Hispanoamérica. Cualquier país está bien: Perú, Colombia, Brasil… Estoy mandando mi currículum vítae y espero que alguna empresa se interese por mí. A mi familia no le gusta mucho la idea, pero tampoco sería para siempre. ¿Por qué quiero trabajar en Hispanoamérica? Porque creo que tiene que ser una experiencia muy enriquecedora y, además, tengo la posibilidad de conocer otras culturas. Y aunque necesite el inglés por mi trabajo, tener el español como idioma común es una gran ventaja.

Ejercicio 1 D

1. > Y en tu trabajo, ¿qué tal?
   < Bueno, espero que sea temporal, gano muy poco, pero me da para mis gastos. Al menos estoy todo el día al aire libre y con mi moto.

2. > Oye, ¿tu padre a qué se dedica?
   < Es autónomo.
   > Pero eso no es una profesión, ¿no?
   < No, no, a ver si lo adivinas… se pasa el día arreglando tubos, grifos…

3. > Pues mi padre, por su profesión, para poco en casa.
   < ¿Ha tenido algún contratiempo alguna vez?
   > Solo una vez, por las condiciones meteorológicas, pero afortunadamente no pasó nada.

4. > Mi hermana desde pequeña tenía claro lo que quería ser de mayor.
   < Claro, claro, es que su pasión son los animales.

Ejercicio 8 D

1. Esto es para mi hija.
2. Té, tomarás té.
3. A ver… Sí, lo ha aparcado bien.

Ejercicio 10 D

Mateo

Yo tengo 24 años y todavía no sé lo que es tener un puesto de trabajo. Muchos anuncios…, algunas entrevistas… y he presentado el currículum vítae en más de cincuenta empresas y… ¡nada! Siempre me preguntan lo mismo: que si tengo experiencia. ¿Cómo voy a tener experiencia si no me dan trabajo? Espero firmar un contrato pronto, que me den alguna oportunidad laboral. No quiero estar con 29 años en casa de mis padres.

Sonia

Se puede decir que tengo un trabajo con un horario flexible, a veces trabajo y a veces no. ¡Es broma! No he firmado ningún contrato y mi sueldo depende del día: trabajo en un restaurante los fines de semana. Es lógico que viva con mis padres, ¿dónde voy a vivir? El año pasado estuve también de canguro y en verano viajé a Londres para aprender inglés. Compagino mi trabajo en el restaurante con mis estudios. Quiero probar en otro país; es posible que el próximo verano me vaya a Alemania.

Alicia

Con mi sueldo no puedo independizarme. Tengo 26 años. La empresa dice que hay crisis y que no puede pagarme más. En la casa de mis padres no estoy mal, pero a mí me gustaría ser independiente económicamente y tener mi propia casa. El último trabajo que tuve era mejor, pero al año me despidieron. La empresa cerró porque se jubiló el propietario. Espero que mi situación cambie antes de los 30.

Ejercicio 10 E

Yo no quiero dedicarme al negocio de mi familia, la heladería… Me gustaría más trabajar por cuenta ajena, tener una estabilidad laboral, un contrato fijo y un horario flexible. Ser autónomo como mi padre tiene sus ventajas, como que tú eres el jefe, estoy de acuerdo, pero también tiene muchos inconvenientes: tienes más preocupaciones, nunca sabes cuánto vas a ganar, trabajas más cuando los demás tienen vacaciones, en verano, y para ti nunca llega el momento de descansar.

Un sueldo fijo a final de mes está muy bien, te permite hacer planes en tu vida. No es necesario que sea un sueldo muy alto, solo suficiente para vivir cómodamente.

He estudiado Económicas, he presentado varios currículum vítae y me han llamado para hacer varias entrevistas, así que a ver si tengo suerte y firmo pronto un contrato.

¡Extra! Contextos

Ejercicio 1 B

1. El procedimiento de compra es muy cómodo, rápido y práctico. Está bien que siempre haya en casa frutas y verduras. Así siempre tienes lo que necesitas.

2. Excelentes productos, los melones son dulces y jugosos. ¡Es estupendo no tener que cargar con las bolsas del supermercado! Para mí es muy cómodo que te lo traigan todo a casa.

3. Espero que la relación calidad - precio sea buena, ya que algunos productos son más caros que en las tiendas tradicionales.

4. Tienen un sistema de envío perfecto y cumplen siempre: cuando estás en casa y a la hora elegida. ¡Es normal que tengan tantos clientes!

5. Llevamos mucho tiempo trabajando con ellos, pero el anterior pedido no llegó nunca; no sabemos qué pasó. Espero que no ocurra muchas veces.

6. Los precios en algunos productos son algo más caros que en la tienda, pero la fruta es riquísima y me dura fresca más tiempo que la que compraba en tiendas o supermercados. Es normal que dure más… porque es ecológica.

UNIDAD 6
Ejercicio 1 B

1. Pues... yo siempre compro bombillas de bajo consumo. Además, el uso adecuado del aire acondicionado y la calefacción, junto con algunos pequeños gestos en la vida cotidiana, pueden ayudar a bajar el consumo.
2. Se necesitan grandes cantidades de energía para su fabricación y, además, están compuestas de sustancias derivadas del petróleo que pueden tardar en descomponerse más de medio siglo. Contaminan los ecosistemas naturales. Muchos animales marinos, como ballenas, delfines y tortugas, mueren cuando las ingieren. Es importante que usemos otros materiales o reduzcamos su uso al máximo.
3. Es un espacio natural con características paisajísticas o biológicas especiales. El objetivo es la conservación y el mantenimiento de su flora y fauna. Los hay marítimos y terrestres. En Andalucía los hay en todas las provincias.
4. Allí existen innumerables especies de plantas todavía sin clasificar, miles de especies de aves y millones de insectos. La fauna y la flora son muy abundantes. Algunos de sus grandes problemas son, entre otros, la deforestación, la explotación de los recursos vegetales y animales, la contaminación del agua y los incendios provocados. ¡Los gobiernos deberían actuar ya para protegerla!
5. Es un potente filtro solar para evitar la radiación ultravioleta (UV), que puede producir daños muy graves en los seres vivos. Está demostrado que su deterioro es debido al uso indebido de los productos químicos que contienen, por ejemplo, los aerosoles y las pinturas. Hay que vigilar que el congelador de la nevera y el aire acondicionado de nuestras casas funcionen perfectamente y tendríamos que mentalizarnos para no comprar productos en espray con gases dañinos.
6. Un argumento a su favor es que su funcionamiento no depende de las condiciones climáticas, pueden funcionar 24 horas al día durante los 365 días del año, y esto supone una garantía de suministro. Un argumento en contra es el riesgo de posibles fugas de partículas radioactivas. ¿Vale la pena este riesgo? ¿No hay otras alternativas? Ese es el gran debate.
7. Una pila puede contaminar miles de litros de agua. No las tires, depósitalas en los lugares adecuados. Coloca el papel y el cartón en su lugar correspondiente; hazlo también con las botellas de vidrio y las latas y los plásticos. Si no hay en nuestra calle, seguro que hay en otra cercana, no es tan difícil dejar allí la basura bien clasificada.
8. El problema es la mentalidad de usar y tirar. Podemos transformar materiales usados en otros objetos muy valiosos. La separación de la basura: la recopilación de botellas de plásticos usadas, las latas, el papel, etcétera, es el primer paso para producir una gran cantidad de recursos beneficiosos para el medioambiente y la economía.

Ejercicio 5 B

1. océano
2. peine
3. farmacia
4. huida
5. microondas
6. merienda
7. caída
8. monstruo

Ejercicio 8 A

Luis: Pues qué quieres que te diga. Yo opino que todos los políticos suelen quieren su propio beneficio.

Marta: ¡Qué exagerado! Yo no creo que las generalizaciones sean buenas. A mí me parece que hay también políticos a los que les preocupa que mejore el mundo.

Luis: ¿Sí? ¿Crees que les preocupa el medioambiente, por ejemplo?

Marta: Yo creo que sí, ahí están los Verdes, un partido ecologista que lucha por ello.

Luis: Bueno, vale. ¿Sabes?, hoy Carlos me ha contado que conoce a una compañera que duerme menos de cinco horas diarias y que hace mucho ejercicio. No me parece bueno que duerma tan poco.

Marta: ¡Anda! ¿Y por qué no? Es evidente que hay personas que no necesitan dormir muchas horas. Cinco horas no es tan poco.

Luis: Está demostrado que las personas necesitan dormir un mínimo de ocho horas para recuperarse. No es cierto que nuestro organismo se acostumbre a todo, hay un límite.

Marta: Por cierto, hablando de costumbres, he escuchado en la radio que este fin de semana llueve otra vez, y con este ya llevamos tres fines de semana con agua. Durante la semana hace bueno y el fin de semana, lluvia.

Luis: Pues yo no creo que llueva. Yo he visto el tiempo en mi móvil y pone nubes, pero no lluvia. Además, como este fin de semana no vamos a salir... me gusta que llueva cuando estoy en casa.

Marta: A mí me pone triste que no salga el sol... Odio que llegue el invierno, las tormentas, que se caigan las hojas de los árboles...

Luis: ¡Cómo te pones, chica! Parece que se acaba la vida en el invierno. También tiene sus ventajas: me encanta que nieve, que haga mucho frío para encender la chimenea..., a mí gusta que llegue la Navidad, ¡las vacaciones de Navidad con frío y nieve son las mejores Navidades!

Marta: Luisito... ¡Está claro que eres un romántico sin remedio! Anda, vamos a brindar.

Ejercicio 9

1. Raúl no va a venir esta tarde.
2. Me parece que estudia Filosofía.
3. Se dice que el león es el rey de la selva.
4. Reír es bueno para la salud.
5. No es lo mismo escuchar que oír.
6. Siento que estéis enfadados conmigo.
7. Me parece que la grúa se ha llevado mi coche.
8. Cierra la puerta que hace mucho aire.
9. No me gustan los días de viento.

Ejercicio 11 B

Beatriz, España

Cuando un hombre y una mujer se conocen, pueden darse la mano, pero también es muy habitual darse dos besos, especialmente entre los jóvenes. Pienso que en muchos países de Latinoamérica solo se dan uno, por ejemplo, en Argentina, de donde es mi novio, o en Venezuela.

Mariela, Argentina

Creo que en América Latina, en general, la primera presentación es formal. Normalmente el tratamiento suele ser el de señora o señorita o señor, seguido del apellido. Es normal mencionar el título profesional de la persona (Arquitecto, Doctora, Licenciada, Profesor...) antes del apellido; si buscás un laburo o un trabajo como dicen ustedes, lo tenés que hacer así.

Emiliano, México

Ahorita, déjenme pensar y les digo algo... Bueno, es cierto que en situaciones formales, en el trabajo, por ejemplo, los hombres nos saludamos dándonos la mano; eso sí, bien fuerte... Es muy importante que se miren a los ojos cuando se den la mano; es lindo si lo hacen...Y si no lo hacen, ustedes serán maleducados. También es cierto que, cuando ganamos confianza o afecto, es más habitual saludarse con un abrazo o con palmadas en la espalda.

Ejercicio 11 C
Carlos, Argentina

¿Vos querés saber una curiosidad sobre la forma de saludo en mi país? Mirá, en algunas regiones de Argentina, sobre todo en ciudades grandes, los hombres se dan un beso en la mejilla, sin que haga falta mucha familiaridad para eso. En las ciudades pequeñas, se saludan con un apretón de manos; si son parientes, se dan un abrazo.

¡Extra! Practica
Ejercicio 3 A

Vamos a conocer más información sobre el significado psicológico, las características y la simbología de algunos de vuestros animales favoritos... ¿Con cuál os identificáis? A lo mejor tienen un carácter o una personalidad similar a la tuya, descúbrelo... Seguro que alguna vez habéis oído eso de que los animales acaban pareciéndose a su dueño... ¿Será verdad? ¿Habrá alguna razón para ello?

El gato:

Representa la independencia y, en muchas culturas, es símbolo de la fertilidad. Se considera como un animal de poder muy identificado con la magia, con lo oculto. Se le han atribuido cualidades de protección y también el poder de sobrevivir; solo tenemos que recordar el famoso dicho: Siete vidas tiene el gato.

El perro:

Simboliza el compañerismo, la lealtad, el amor y la protección. Si te identificas con este animal, quiere decir que en tu vida valoras a la familia y a los amigos. Te gusta ayudar a los demás y echar una mano a todo el mundo que lo necesite. Prefieres las cosas sencillas y cotidianas a los bienes materiales: un abrazo, una charla con amigos, un paseo, un beso...

El caballo:

Es un animal noble y poderoso. Simboliza la inteligencia, la libertad y la vitalidad. Si te identificas con él, seguramente te gustarán los viajes y te enfrentarás con fuerza a los problemas de la vida.

La mariposa:

Este insecto representa la transformación, el cambio, ya que es el único ser vivo que modifica por completo su estructura genética. Si es tu animal favorito, esto significa que estás listo en todo momento para los cambios que vengan en tu vida; normalmente tienes la necesidad de hacer cambios.

Ejercicio 3 B
La tortuga:

No necesita estar en un mismo lugar porque lleva su casa consigo. Así que simboliza la idea de encontrar nuevas oportunidades en cualquier sitio. Representa la capacidad de ser paciente y pensar las cosas dos veces, con mucha tranquilidad.

El oso:

Se le relaciona con los sueños. Las personas a las que les gusta este animal son autosuficientes, no quieren depender de nadie. También son considerados soñadores.

El león:

Como casi todo el mundo sabe, representa el poder y la fuerza; pero esa fuerza la usarán solo cuando sea necesaria; no son violentos sin motivo alguno.

¡Extra! En Comunicación
Ejercicio 4 B

1. Claro que es posible cenar hasta tarde en la mayoría de los restaurantes españoles... Sobre todo en los lugares turísticos. La cocina suele estar abierta hasta las diez y media o las once... No tendréis problemas para almorzar o cenar a la hora que queráis. Además, en muchas grandes ciudades también podrás comer algo incluso después de las once: hamburguesas, pizza, comida rápida...

2. ¿Que si se le puede preguntar la edad a las mujeres? No sé... Es un tema delicado... Pero, en general, no se suele preguntar a una mujer su edad. Y mucho menos si no es una chica; quiero decir si ya no es tan joven... Está claro que a una mujer madura no se le pregunta qué edad tiene. A algunas mujeres no les importa, pero es cierto que a muchas les molesta que les pregunten la edad; sobre todo si no tenéis con ella una relación de confianza.

3. Bueno, si una persona o un amigo me invita a tomar algo o a una fiesta y no puedo o no quiero aceptar su invitación, tengo que dar alguna explicación; debo decir la razón por la que no voy... No puedo decir solamente: No, muchas gracias... Lo normal es que digamos por qué no podemos ir: Es que no tengo tiempo... Es que tengo que trabajar... Hay que decir lo que sea... Muchas veces, si solo damos las gracias, y decimos que no, van a volver a insistir en invitarnos hasta que demos una explicación... Nos dirán eso de: Venga, vamos, vente... Tienes que venir...

UNIDAD 7
Ejercicio 1 A

Sandra: ¿Y tus clases qué tal?

Luis Fernando: Estoy muy contento... Quiero que todo salga bien con mi máster y espero que, cuando termine el curso, pueda empezar con mi beca de investigación en el departamento de genética...

Sandra: ¿Y echas de menos algo de Colombia? No sé... ¿La familia, los amigos... la comida?

Luis Fernando: Claro, claro... Echo de menos a mi familia. Ojalá que pronto puedan visitarme mi esposa y mi bebito... Tal vez, si tienen la chance, vengan en agosto. Tengo muchas ganas de verlos.... ¡Los extraño muchísimo!

Sandra: Bueno, no te pongas triste, seguro que muy pronto estaréis los tres juntos de nuevo... Por cierto, me encantan las papas con frijoles que has preparado. ¡Están para chuparse los dedos!

Luis Fernando: Muchísimas gracias, eres muy amable... A mí me ha gustado mucho tu gazpacho... Nunca había probado nada igual... Y el sushi de Lucía también está riquísimo.

Lucía: Pues es muy fácil de preparar... Solo tienes que hacerlo con cariño...

Sandra: Pero el cariño no es todo, ¿verdad? Probablemente yo lo preparo con el mismo cariño que tú y seguro que no me sale tan bien...

Lucía: Es que yo siempre estoy cocinando... y sobre todo platos japoneses. Puede que ese sea el secreto. Mi sueño es montar un restaurante japonés aquí, en España.

Luis Fernando: Ojalá que lo consigas... Además, quiero que hagas tu sueño realidad para comer gratis...

Lucía: ¿Comer gratis?

Luis Fernando: Claro, si tienes un restaurante, estoy seguro de que todos tus amigos comeremos gratis, ¿no es verdad?

Lucía: Bueno, a lo mejor… Ya veremos…

Ejercicio 2 A

Hola, Sandra, ¿cómo estás? Te llamaba porque necesito que esta tarde me hagas un favor… Es que hoy tengo trabajo y mi hermano pequeño ha venido a visitarme y quería pasar la tarde con él, pero, ya ves, no puedo… Se me ha ocurrido que tú podrías ayudarme y acompañarle a algún espectáculo, a hacer algo… No sé, algo divertido… Es que no conoce Valencia y solo tiene catorce años… Creo que todavía es demasiado joven para andar solo por una ciudad tan grande… A él le gusta hacer las cosas típicas de los chicos de su edad: leer cómics, las historias de ciencia ficción, el fútbol, la música, navegar por Internet… Además, toca la guitarra eléctrica y le encantan los ordenadores… Por favor, llámame si no puedes y ya buscaré yo a otra persona… Voy a tener el móvil encendido, pero seguramente no podré cogerlo; es mejor que me mandes un *whatsapp*… Muchísimas gracias, te debo una… ¡Ah! ¡Se me olvidaba! Se llama Dani, Daniel.

Ejercicio 7 C

Buenas noches, amigos y amigas radioyentes. Nueva cita con la información en su emisora de radio favorita, en la radio pública.

En las noticias nacionales: nueva avería en el tren Madrid-Bilbao entre las estaciones de Segovia y Valladolid.

En otro orden de cosas: manifestación de diversas organizaciones pacifistas ante la sede del Parlamento Europeo por el Día Internacional de los Derechos Humanos.

En las noticias culturales: Almodóvar vuelve a estar de enhorabuena. El director manchego recibirá un homenaje de la Academia de Hollywood con una retrospectiva de su carrera cinematográfica. Será el próximo día 13 en la Universidad de California.

También queremos citar a Ana Alejandre, autora de la novela *Tras la puerta cerrada*, por la publicación en su blog, titulado Bloc literario, de un excelente homenaje a William Faulkner por el cincuentenario de su muerte.

Es todo por hoy… Muchas gracias por su atención y mañana les espero, como siempre, a la misma hora con más información… Que descansen y hasta mañana.

Ejercicio 7 E

Todas estas palabras son preposiciones de lugar… Vamos a explicar qué significan…

«Entre» significa *en medio de*… Por ejemplo: *Juan está entre María y Clara*.

«Ante» es lo mismo que *delante de*… Por ejemplo: *Estamos ante un cuadro de Picasso*.

«Tras» significa *detrás de*… Por ejemplo: *Yo estoy tras la mesa del profesor*.

«De» la usamos para explicar *el origen, la procedencia*… Por ejemplo: *María viene de Colombia*.

Ejercicio 14

Estamos ante un cuadro en el que podemos diferenciar tres partes: tenemos un bosque inmenso de derecha a izquierda y en el fondo. Tras el bosque y a lo lejos se puede ver una montaña que parece nevada. Delante del bosque hay un río que lleva mucha agua. En las aguas del río se reflejan las nubes del cielo y bajo sus aguas transparentes hay piedras muy blancas. En primer plano se ve una casita solitaria; desde la casa hasta la orilla del río hay poca distancia, y entre la casa y el río vemos a un niño de unos cinco años que mira de frente, tranquilo y sonriente.

Ejercicio 15 B

María: el «libro»

Yo participé en una biblioteca viviente como «libro». Quería tener esta experiencia porque tengo una discapacidad física: soy invidente, y deseaba explicarles a otras personas cómo es mi vida. Mucha gente piensa que una persona ciega no puede hacer casi nada, que depende de otras para realizar actividades tan cotidianas como el aseo personal: vestirse, lavarse… y que no puede desenvolverse sola en la ciudad para viajar en transporte público o cruzar una calle, por ejemplo. Esto no es así. Es verdad que las ciudades y los lugares públicos en general no están pensados para las personas con alguna discapacidad física, pero tenemos otras alternativas para orientarnos. Mi vida es como la de otras personas videntes: me levanto por la mañana, me preparo, salgo de casa, voy a trabajar, hago la compra, cocino…

A veces tengo la sensación de que algunas personas sienten pena de mí y no me gusta. Yo estoy satisfecha con mi vida; tengo días mejores y días peores pero como todo el mundo. Lo único que no puede hacer una persona con discapacidad visual es conducir. Por otro lado, no tener el sentido de la vista nos hace ser más intuitivos y ver de otra forma, con la imaginación. El alfabeto braille nos permite leer y tener acceso al conocimiento, es una forma diferente de leer pero el resultado es el mismo.

Esto es lo que quería comunicar y compartir. Deseo que la gente abra su mente. Ojalá que este proyecto ayude a una mejor comunicación y comprensión de la gente con discapacidad visual.

Javier: el «lector»

Si eres de las personas que tienen curiosidad por conocer a otras, seguramente vas a disfrutar en este tipo de bibliotecas. Seguro que te sorprenderá lo que puedes aprender de los demás, también te da la posibilidad de hablar con personas de diferentes culturas y religiones, gente con la que normalmente no te relacionas en tu vida diaria. Yo conocí a María, una chica con una discapacidad física: es ciega desde niña. Hablar con ella me hizo ponerme en su lugar, me contó cómo era su vida y me di cuenta de que no era muy diferente a la mía, que hacía las mismas cosas que las personas de su edad, que tenía problemas como todo el mundo y que se relacionaba y comunicaba con otras personas y hacía una vida normal. Ella sueña con que algún día la gente vea a las personas con esta discapacidad como iguales, con que desaparezcan las barreras físicas en las ciudades. Ojalá sea así. Hablar con María me ha dado una visión diferente a la que tenía, y sobre todo he aprendido que podemos parecer diferentes, pero en el fondo todos queremos lo mismo: ser felices.

¡Extra! Contextos

Ejercicio 1 E

Tengo otro proyecto además de estudiar español: estoy escribiendo una novela. Puede que os sorprenda o que os parezca extraño, pero sí, quiero ser escritor. Posiblemente falte mucho para ver mi novela publicada, o a lo mejor no se publica, ¡quién sabe! Yo soy feliz construyendo una historia que cada día está más completa. Ya he escrito casi la mitad y puede que la termine antes de final de año. Les he leído el primer capítulo a varios amigos y me han dicho que es una buena historia: ¡espero que sean sinceros! ¿El tema de la novela?

Vampiros. Sueño con que sea un éxito y me imagino firmando autógrafos a miles de lectores. Quizás no ocurra así, pero… ¡soñar es gratis!

UNIDAD 8
Ejercicio 2 A

¡Algunos amigos pensaban que me había vuelto loca! Y todo porque, de pronto, le di un giro a mi existencia y me marché a vivir en plena naturaleza. Me lancé a la aventura de reconstruir una casa antigua y convertirla en un hotelito rural; mi profesión de arquitecta me permitió encontrar esa magnífica oportunidad. ¡Y es que estaba ya harta de vivir en Barcelona!, llevaba allí desde hacía más de quince años. Aparentemente tenía todo lo que cualquiera desearía para ser feliz: un buen trabajo, una bonita casa en una zona residencial de la ciudad, una familia… Pero ahora sí que me siento contenta. Está claro que no siento nostalgia de los malos humos de la gran ciudad. De vez en cuando, echo de menos ir de compras y cenar en un buen restaurante. Me encanta cocinar, bailar, tomar el sol y, sobre todo, disfrutar de toda la naturaleza que me rodea. Muy pronto mi vida volverá a cambiar… Estoy embarazada de gemelos y quiero que vayan al colegio en Barcelona… Por eso, tendremos que regresar el año que viene.

Ejercicio 4 A
Amalia

Buenas noches… Os llamo porque necesito el consejo de los oyentes. No sé qué hacer con mi chico… Es celosísimo. A mí me gusta salir con mis amigas, pero él no quiere que lo haga. Bueno, me deja que lo haga pero yo sé que no le gusta. ¡Es un machista! Además, no quiere que me ponga minifalda, que lleve escotes… Vamos, que es un antiguo. Uno de estos días, le dejo y se va a quedar más solo que la una. Y encima siempre me está diciendo que soy una mandona. ¿Qué me recomendáis que haga? ¿Me aconsejáis que lo deje?

Pedro

Mi novia es un encanto, pero… Bueno, no sé… Me ha dicho millones de veces que no deje mis cosas por todas partes… No me deja que salga de casa sin haberlo recogido todo: la cocina, el cuarto de baño, la habitación, la ropa…. Y encima, me ha prohibido que fume en toda la casa; ni siquiera, en el balcón… Además, cuando le pido que salgamos por ahí a tomar algo, resulta que casi siempre me dice que no puede, que ya ha quedado con sus amigas. Bueno, y si le hago algún comentario sobre su forma de vestir —porque a veces, la verdad, me parece que viste un poco… llamativa—, me ordena que me calle y me dice que soy un machista. ¿Qué me aconsejáis que haga?

Ejercicio 5 A

1. Adrián, te llamo para pedirte que vengas a mi fiesta de cumpleaños el sábado por la noche. No lo olvides. Te ruego que vengas bien vestido. Quiero que conozcas a una chica interesantísima… ¡Yo creo que os vais a gustar muchísimo! Ya verás.
2. Soy el doctor García, su dentista, y le llamo para pedirle que venga el lunes por la mañana para su revisión anual… Si tiene problemas, llámeme y cambiamos la cita para el mes próximo.
3. Hijo, te prohíbo que cojas más mi coche… Lo has dejado sin gasolina y, además, no me has llamado para decírmelo.
4. Hola, Adri, ¿dónde te metes?… Bueno, no pasa nada, solo quiero recomendarte que veas la última película de Alejandro Amenábar. ¡Es buenísima! ¡Te va a encantar!

Ejercicio 8 A

Mi madre es una neurótica, se pasa el día gritando. Estoy harta de la misma historia de siempre, cansada de soportarla. Se supone que tendría que ayudarme en vez de martirizarme, pero es que para ella nunca hago nada bien, ¡nuncaaaaaaaaa!, y no deja de gritar, me vuelve loca. Le molesta que lleve vaqueros muy estrechos y bajos de cintura, no me deja que me haga un tatuaje o que me ponga un pirsin en la nariz, dice que soy demasiado joven, que ya tendré tiempo para decidir si realmente eso es lo que quiero. De verdad, es que no sabes lo pesada que es, se pasa todo el día dándome consejos o, mejor dicho, órdenes: que tenga cuidado, que no me relacione con gente desconocida en Internet, que no fume ni beba. Bueno, lo típico.

Mi padre es más de lo mismo, pero la verdad es que no es tan pesado. Le he pedido que me deje ir a un concierto este viernes en la playa; es un concierto que dura toda la noche, y me ha dicho que hable con mi madre, que lo que diga ella. En fin, lo de siempre.

Yo sé que ellos quieren protegerme, pero les pido que, por favor, se pongan en mi lugar algunas veces e intenten comprenderme; y sobre todo, les digo a menudo que no se preocupen todo el tiempo por mí, que no me gusta que me controlen; en definitiva, deseo que me dejen tomar mis propias decisiones. ¡Jo, qué aguante hay que tener con los padres!

Ejercicio 12 C

1. **Marta:** Cariño, no quiero regalitos tontos para este san Valentín. Prefiero que hagamos una barbacoa e invitemos a todos nuestros amigos…
   José: ¿Y los niños?
   Marta: Los niños con nosotros. No hay problema.

2. **Eugenia:** Odio este día… Es el día de las compras. No me gusta tener que hacer un regalo porque sea el Día de los Enamorados.
   Carlos: ¿Y qué hacemos?
   Eugenia: Nada. Quedarnos en casa y pedirnos una pizza familiar.

3. **Sandra:** Mi novio ni se ha acordado de que hoy es san Valentín… Estoy supertriste. Yo quería un anillo de plata…
   Amigo: ¿No te ha regalado nada?
   Sandra: Al final me ha regalado una cesta de frutas porque dice que es muy sano…

4. **Andrés:** Este año se ha acabado salir a cenar como siempre… Vamos a pasar el día en un spa…
   Carmen: ¿En un spa? ¿Por qué?
   Andrés: Para hacer algo distinto. Seguro que después nos encontramos menos estresados…

5. **Sonia:** Mira, un regalo de mi marido por el Día de los Enamorados. ¿Qué será?
   Amiga: A ver, a ver, ábrelo.
   Sonia: Anda, parece una camiseta. ¡Qué original!
   Amiga: ¡Huy! Si tiene una foto y un mensaje. ¿Qué pone, Sonia?
   Sonia: Dice: «Marta, te quiero».
   Amiga: Huy, ¡por Dios!

6. **Tomás:** ¿Una visita al zoo?

   Raquel: ¿Tú crees que esoes una forma romántica de celebrar el Día de los Enamorados?

   Tomás: ¿Por qué no? A ti te encantan los animales…

¡Extra! Contextos
Ejercicio 1 A

> Pensamos que hablar de paz y solidaridad es, hoy día, más necesario que nunca… Recomendamos que los jóvenes sean más participativos y les sugerimos que ayuden más a los otros… Les aconsejamos que sean menos egoístas y que se preocupen más por los demás. Por eso, en nuestro blog, hemos incluido algunos consejos y sugerencias para ser mejores personas. ¿Los puedo leer?

< Claro que sí… Adelante, Paco.

> En *Paz y amigos* queremos que caigan de una vez por todas los gobiernos totalitarios y fanáticos. Pedimos que las guerras y la violencia desaparezcan. Prohibimos que se sigan emitiendo gases con efecto invernadero con el fin de cuidar y respetar el medioambiente…

< ¿No cree que ustedes son demasiado utópicos?

> No, no, por supuesto que no… Nosotros vamos a luchar por todas estas ideas y rogamos que todo el mundo lo haga… ¿Y usted? ¿No tiene ningún deseo?

< Sí, sí… Ahora sí. ¡Quiero irme a una isla desierta! Después de escucharlo, me he dado cuenta de que en esta sociedad solo hay problemas.

UNIDAD 9
Ejercicio 2 A

La avenida Corrientes es una de las principales calles de la Ciudad Autónoma de Buenos Aires (Argentina). Tiene una extensión de más de ocho kilómetros, setenta cruces y por debajo de ella circula la línea B del metro. Esta calle es el tema de muchos tangos por estar muy relacionada con este estilo musical: en sus bares y teatros nació el tango. Además, es el lugar principal de la vida nocturna y bohemia. Sus habitantes, los porteños, sienten esta calle muy ligada a su historia, y su Obelisco, icono de la ciudad, ha sido el punto de reunión de las mayores concentraciones políticas de la historia argentina. Fue construido en 1936 con motivo del cuarto centenario de la fundación de la ciudad. Su calle Florida, que es peatonal, representa un punto de diversión para los porteños y visitantes que la recorren a todas horas porque abundan los lugares de entretenimiento: espectáculos artísticos, culturales, librerías abiertas hasta altas horas de la madrugada, pizzerías, confiterías… Fue un periodista quien en los años cincuenta popularizó la frase «la calle que nunca duerme» para referirse a la avenida Corrientes.

Ejercicio 2 B

El malecón se encuentra en La Habana, la capital de la República de Cuba. Comprende una amplia avenida de seis carriles y un muro larguísimo que se extiende sobre toda la costa norte de la capital cubana a lo largo de ocho kilómetros. Es un paseo marítimo, punto de reunión predilecto de todo tipo de gente, con un ambiente especialmente intenso al atardecer. Un lugar donde toda la ciudad acude para relacionarse, pasear, hablar, jugar al dominó o tomarse algo. Es el espacio ideal para disfrutar de la hermosura del mar Caribe. El Malecón está rodeado de casas que pertenecieron a la clase alta habanera. Hoy día hay muchas de ellas que están en ruinas por el aire del mar y el abandono. Es muy recomendable subir al faro, desde donde se pueden contemplar unas vistas impresionantes.

Ejercicio 7 A

1. Ya he viajado mucho este año, así que ahora toca estudiar.
2. No he leído en español, he hablado en inglés, no he ido a clase… o sea que tengo que ponerme al día.
3. No me queda dinero, por lo tanto tengo que trabajar los fines de semana.
4. He estado fuera casi un mes y, aunque he caminado mucho, no he hecho deporte, por eso tengo que ir todos los días al gimnasio.
5. En todo este tiempo no he escrito a mi familia ni a mis amigos de Brasil, así es que esta misma tarde les escribo a todos.

Ejercicio 8
Ajá

1. > ¿Sabes? Me ha llamado Clara para decirme que Jaime vendrá a tu cumpleaños.

   < ¡Ajá!, pensaba que todavía estaba en Italia.

2. > Ya sé quién puede cuidar de nuestro perro durante las vacaciones: mi primo Marco.

   < ¡Ajá!, ¡qué buena idea!

3. > ¿Me enseña la camisa azul del escaparate?

   < ¡Ajá!, por supuesto… Ahora mismo.

Eh

1. > ¡No comas tantos bombones que te van a sentar mal, eh!

   < Vale, papi… Uno más, por favor.

2. > ¡Eh! ¡María! ¿Salimos a dar un paseo? Hace un día estupendo.

   < No sé… Es que estoy un poco cansada…

3. > ¿Eh? ¿Puedes repetirme el número, por favor?

   < Sí, claro…

Ejercicio 11 A

1. Carmen, mañana lunes, sobre las dos, queremos ir al hospital para visitar a Lola… No sé si lo sabías, pero ya es mami… ¿Te apuntas con nosotros o prefieres ir tú otro día? Espero tu llamada…

   (…)

   Carmen, soy Julio… Te llamo para recordarte que el lunes a las siete de la tarde es la presentación de la novela de Pedro. Vendrás, ¿no?

2. Te llamo porque hemos quedado el martes a las cinco con Eugenia y Rocío para tomar un cafelito en el centro… ¿Te apetece?

3. Soy yo otra vez… ¿Y por la noche? ¿Quieres venir al cine? Estrenan la última peli de Almodóvar y tenemos invitaciones… Llámame, por favor…

4. Cariño, ¿cómo es que no me has llamado? Bueno, no importa… Te llamaba para recordarte que el miércoles habíamos quedado sobre las seis y media para ir a la exposición de Goya en el Museo Central… Tú me llamas para confirmar la hora… ¿Vale? Hasta luego, besos…

5. Ay, hija, que soy yo otra vez. Estaba pensando en salir de tapeo el jueves con Pedro, para celebrar lo de su novela. ¿Qué dices? ¿Quedamos sobre la una o una y media, antes de comer? Dime algo, ¿eh? Un beso, hasta pronto.

TRANSCRIPCIONES

¡Extra! Contextos
Ejercicio 1 B

Me gustaría conocer estos tres lugares algún día, pero, claro, tan pronto como tenga tiempo y dinero… Yo soy de Toledo y cuando viajo prefiero irme lejos; así es que otro país del mundo no estaría mal… Es que me encanta conocer culturas muy diferentes a la mía. Antes de que sea viejecita quiero dar, al menos una vez, la vuelta al mundo. Solo una cosita más: siempre que viajo, busco lugares donde se mezclen la naturaleza y la cultura. Me canso después de ver muchos monumentos, palacios, casas y museos. Busco sitios que me ofrezcan posibilidades para relajarme y descansar más, con balnearios antiguos, para que todo el viaje no sea solo ver edificios y más edificios.

¡Extra! Practica
Ejercicio 2 A

Marina (España)

La verdad es que no me gusta mucho andar de acá para allá durante todo el día por el campo, la montaña… Eso de descubrir senderos naturales no va conmigo… Es que me canso mucho de caminar. Siempre que mis amigos y yo viajamos, solemos visitar el mejor museo del país. El arte es mi pasión. Bueno, ya sabes lo que me interesa, así que espero tu recomendación.

Federico (Argentina)

Si vos querés, ¿podés decirme algún paisaje natural que sea lindo? Después de tanto trabajar, necesito un descanso en un lugar especial: un bosque, un parque natural, un lago… No sé, vos decidís. Ahora no tengo tiempo, pero cuando tenga un descanso, iré a su país. Tengo muchas ganas de conocerlo.

Alfredo (España)

Yo también soy un trotamundos… ¿A que no lo sabías, eh? Pues conozco muchos lugares del mundo y muy distintos: India, Japón, Australia, Estados Unidos… Como soy un espíritu inquieto, siempre voy muy lejos de casa… Antes de que mi novia y yo vayamos a tu país en las próximas vacaciones, me gustaría conocer algo más sobre las costumbres y comidas típicas. ¿Qué no nos debemos perder de alguna ciudad importante?

Carmela (España)

Creo que no soy una turista típica porque prefiero visitar los parques y demás zonas verdes de las ciudades. Es que no soporto pasear entre el ruido de los coches, la contaminación… Y por eso me encanta la tranquilidad de los parques… En cuanto puedo me voy allí para tomar el sol, descansar, leer un libro… Cuando era niña, siempre jugaba en el parque de mi ciudad. ¡Qué recuerdos! Uno de mis parques favoritos es el Retiro, en Madrid. ¿Y en tu ciudad? ¿Hay parques importantes? ¿Cuál es el parque más famoso de tu país?

UNIDAD 10
Ejercicio 1 B

Linda: Pues sí, está embarazada de su nuevo novio. Me ha dicho que está de cuatro meses.

Javi: ¡Pero si se conocen desde hace menos de un año!

Linda: Ya ves… Dice que están muy enamorados y que le ha pedido que se case con él.

Javi: ¡Qué locura! ¿Y los estudios?

Linda: Me ha dicho que va a seguir estudiando.

Javi: ¿Y dónde van a vivir?

Linda: Pues me dijo que iban a alquilar un piso en Madrid. Él trabaja allí.

Javi: Tú conoces a su novio, ¿no? ¿Cómo es?

Linda: La verdad es que es una persona muy agradable; es alemán y vive en España desde hace mucho tiempo; habla español perfectamente.

Javi: ¿Y ella habla alemán?

Linda: Ella no, pero dice que la lengua del amor es universal, y como él habla español…

Javi: ¡Vaya! ¡Qué romántico!

Ejercicio 4 E

1. ¿Vas a venir a cenar pronto?
2. ¿Por qué no fuiste a la fiesta de cumpleaños?
3. ¿A qué hora te acuestas normalmente?
4. ¿En qué año naciste?
5. ¿Dónde os conocisteis?
6. ¿Sabes alemán?
7. ¿Cómo vas al trabajo normalmente?

Ejercicio 10 A

Hola, os quiero hablar un poquito sobre mi familia. Os presento a todas las personas que veis en la imagen: mi madre se llama Remedios, es la mujer rubia del pelo largo y la chaqueta negra. Mi padre está a su lado, el hombre de la corbata, se llama Juan. La chica del jersey rojo es Alejandra, mi hermana mediana, tiene 30 años y está casada con Jorge, el chico de las gafas. El otro chico, el que lleva una camiseta, es mi hermano Rafael; es el más pequeño y ya tiene 20 años. El niño de la casa es mi sobrino Jorgito; tiene 8 años y es muy divertido, me encanta estar con él. El último miembro de familia es nuestro perro, se llama Galgo y, aunque no te conozca, no te ladra; es superbueno.

Ejercicio 12 A

«Este año he trabajado en un centro comercial y, en agosto, empezaré un nuevo trabajo en una tienda de deportes del centro».

«Ahora vivo en Salamanca… ¡Menuda suerte!, ¿verdad? Es una ciudad preciosa y con muchas cosas que ver: la catedral, la universidad, el casco antiguo… Puedes venir a visitarme y quedarte con nosotros porque tengo una casaza con seis habitaciones y, además, está cerca del centro…».

«Conocí a mi marido hace unos ocho años en Londres, cuando estábamos en la universidad, éramos compañeros de clase… Nos casamos después de terminar la carrera… Se llama Charlie y es muy guapetón y muy agradable, es fortachón y muy inteligente…, por lo menos para mí… La verdad es que es el hombre de mi vida…».

«Enrique y yo tenemos dos hijos… ¡Y vaya hijos buenos y estudiosos! Raquel es la pequeña y el mayor se llama Enrique, como su padre… Tienes que venir a casa para conocerlos… Raquel es muy alegre y simpaticona, como mi madre, y Enrique ya está hecho un hombretón… ¿Y tú? ¿Estás casado? ¿Tienes hijos?…».

«Si quieres hacer algo de deporte y mantenerte en forma, tengo un planazo para ti: te recomiendo correr todos los días media hora por lo menos… Yo antes jugaba al fútbol tres días a la semana, pero ahora no puedo, ya me pesan los años… ¿Y tú? ¿Sigues jugando al baloncesto como cuando íbamos al instituto?».

Ejercicio 16 C

Hoy en el paseo de la fama de nuestro programa *De cine*, una de las grandes estrellas de nuestra cinematografía: Maribel Verdú.

La actriz madrileña se ha convertido en uno de los rostros más populares del cine español. Con una larga carrera que incluye